A Reference Grammar
of
Syrian Arabic

(Based on the Dialect of Damascus)

MARK W. COWELL

GEORGETOWN UNIVERSITY PRESS
Washington, D.C.

GEORGETOWN CLASSICS IN ARABIC
LANGUAGE AND LINGUISTICS
Karin C. Ryding and Margaret Nydell, series editors

For some time, Georgetown University Press has been interested in making available seminal publications in Arabic language and linguistics that have gone out of print. Some of the most meticulous and creative scholarship of the last century was devoted to the analysis of Arabic language and to producing detailed reference works and textbooks of the highest quality. Although some of the material is dated in terms of theoretical approaches, the content and methodology of the books considered for the reprint series is still valid and in some cases unsurpassed.

With global awareness now refocused on the Arab world, and with renewed interest in Arab culture, society, and political life, it is essential to provide easy access to classic reference materials such as dictionaries, reference grammars, and language teaching materials. The key components of this series of classic reprints have been chosen for quality of research and scholarship, and have been updated with new bibliographies and an introduction to provide readers with resources for further study.

Georgetown University Press hopes hereby to serve the growing national and international need for reference works on Arabic language and culture, as well as provide access to quality textbooks and audiovisual resources for teaching Arabic language in its written and spoken forms.

Books in the Georgetown Classics in Arabic Language
and Linguistic series:

Arabic Language Handbook
    Mary Catherine Bateson
A Basic Course in Moroccan Arabic with Audio MP3 Files
    Richard S. Harrell with Mohammed Abu-Talib and William S. Carroll
A Basic Course in Iraqi Arabic with Audio MP3 Files
    Erwin M. Wallace
A Dictionary of Iraqi Arabic: English–Arabic, Arabic–English
    B. E. Clarity, Karl Stowasser, Ronald G. Wolfe, D. R. Woodhead, and
    Wayne Beene, editors
A Dictionary of Moroccan Arabic: Moroccan–Arabic, Arabic–Moroccan
    Richard S. Harrell and Harvey Sobelman, editors
A Dictionary of Syrian Arabic: English–Arabic
    Karl Stowasser and Moukhtar Ani, editors
A Reference Grammar of Syrian Arabic
    Mark W. Cowell
A Short Reference Grammar of Iraqi Arabic
    Wallace M. Erwin

A Short Reference Grammar of Moroccan Arabic with Audio CD
    Richard S. Harrell
Eastern Arabic with MP3 Files
    Frank A. Rice and Majed F. Sa'id
Formal Spoken Arabic FAST Course with MP3 Files
    Karin C. Ryding and Abdelnour Zaiback
Modern Arabic: Structures, Functions, and Varieties, Revised Edition
    Clive Holes

Originally published in 1964.
Paperback with audio CD originally published in 2005.

The research reported herein was performed pursuant to a contract with the United States Office of Education, Department of Health, Education and Welfare.

Library of Congress Control Number: 2016931518

ISBN 978-1-62616-365-2 (pbk. : alk. paper)

♾ This book is printed on acid-free paper meeting the requirements of the American National Standard for Permanence in Paper for Printed Library Materials.

17 16   9 8 7 6 5 4 3 2   First printing

Printed in the United States of America

CONTENTS

Part I: Phonology

Consonants 2, Velarization 6, Vowels 9, Length 15,
Accentuation 17

Sound Combinations: Phrasing 21, Vowel Positions 22, Single
and Double Consonants 23, Two-Consonant Clusters 24,
Three-Consonant Clusters 25

General Sound Changes: Assimilations 26, Neutralizations 27,
Syncope 28, Anaptyxis 29

Introduction to Parts II and III

Inflectional Bases 35, Roots and Patterns 36, Pattern Alterations
40, Derivation 46

Part IIA: Base Forms

Simple Triradical Patterns 55, Augmented Triradical Patterns 77,
Pseudo-Quadriradical Patterns 109, True Quadriradical
Patterns 117

Part IIB: Inflectional Forms

Part IIIA: Derivational Categories

Part IIIB: Inflectional Categories

Part IV: Syntax

CONTENTS OF THE AUDIO FILES

Additional audio files accompany this book and are available at press
.georgetown.edu on the book's webpage. The files were remastered from
the original audiocassettes (containing the identical material), and the
sound quality reflects the early technology of the originals.

ARABIC RESEARCH AT GEORGETOWN UNIVERSITY

In the past forty years, the world of research in Arabic theoretical linguistics has expanded but the production of professional quality textbooks in colloquial Arabic has remained limited. Despite the passage of years, the Richard Slade Harrell Arabic Series has consistently been in demand from Georgetown University Press because of the quality of research that went into its composition, the solid theoretical foundations for its methodology, and the comprehensive coverage of regional Arabic speech communities.

The Department of Arabic Language, Literature, and Linguistics at Georgetown University (formerly Arabic Department) recognizes the need to sustain the tradition of research and publication in Arabic dialects and has continued dialectology field research and textbook production, most notably with Margaret (Omar) Nydell's *Syrian Arabic Video Course*, a three-year research project funded by Center for the Advancement of Language Learning from 1991 to 1994. Currently we are engaged in a four-year dialectology research project aimed at producing "conversion" courses to assist learners of Modern Standard Arabic in converting their knowledge and skills of written Arabic to proficiency in selected Arabic dialects. This project is part of a grant administered by the National Capital Language Resource Center under the directorship of Dr. James E. Alatis and Dr. Anna Chamot.

We pay tribute to the tradition initiated and led by Richard Harrell, the founder of this series, and of the original Arabic Research Program at Georgetown University. His scholarship and creative energy set a standard in the field and yielded an unprecedented and as yet unsurpassed series of, as he put it, "practical tools for the increasing number of Americans whose lives bring them into contact with the Arab world." We hope that this series of reprints, and our continuing efforts in applied Arabic dialectology research will yield a new crop of linguistic resources for Arabic language study.

Karin C. Ryding
Sultan Qaboos bin Said Professor of Arabic

THE HISTORY OF THE ARABIC RESEARCH PROGRAM
INSTITUTE OF LANGUAGES AND LINGUISTICS
GEORGETOWN UNIVERSITY

The Arabic Research Program was established in June of 1960 as a contract between Georgetown University and the United States Office of Education under the provisions of the Language Development Program of the National Defense Education Act.

The first two years of the research program, 1960–1962 (contract number SAE-8706), were devoted to the production of six books, a reference grammar, and a conversational English–Arabic dictionary in the cultivated spoken forms of Moroccan, Syrian, and Iraqi Arabic. The second two years of the research program, 1962–1964 (contract number OE-2-14-029), call for the further production of Arabic–English dictionaries in each of the three varieties of Arabic mentioned above, as well as comprehensive basic courses in the Moroccan and Iraqi varieties.

The eleven books of this series, of which the present volume is one, are designed to serve as practical tools for the increasing number of Americans whose lives bring them into contact with the Arab world. The dictionaries, the reference grammars, and the basic courses are oriented toward the educated American who is a layman in linguistic matters. Although it is hoped that the scientific linguist and the specialist in Arabic dialectology will find these books both of interest and of use, matters of purely scientific and theoretical importance have not been directly treated as such, and specialized scientific terminology has been avoided as much as possible.

As is usual, the authors or editors of the individual books bear final scholarly responsibility for the contents, but there has been a large amount of informal cooperation in our work. Criticism, consultation, and discussion have gone on constantly among the senior professional members of the staff. The contribution of more junior research assistants, both Arab and American, is also not to be underestimated. Their painstaking assembling and ordering of raw data, often in manners requiring considerable creative intelligence, has been the necessary prerequisite for further progress.

In most cases the books prepared by the Arabic Research Program are the first of their kind in English, and in some cases the first in any language. The preparation of them has been a rewarding experience. It is hoped that the public use of them will be equally so. The undersigned, on behalf of the entire staff, would like to ask the same indulgence of the reader as Samuel Johnson requested in his first English dictionary: To remember that although much has been left out, much has been included.

Richard S. Harrell
Professor of Linguistics
Georgetown University

Director,
Arabic Research Program

FOREWORD TO THE GEORGETOWN CLASSICS EDITION

In 1960 the late Richard S. Harrell, then director of the Georgetown University Arabic Research Program, initiated a series of basic courses, dictionaries, and reference grammars for the Moroccan, Syrian, and Iraqi Arabic dialects written by a number of outstanding Arabists. They have withstood the test of time and now are being reissued by Georgetown University Press, along with Mary Catherine Bateson's invaluable *Arabic Language Handbook*. The present volume, Mark W. Cowell's *A Reference Grammar of Syrian Arabic*, is one of the most outstanding descriptions of any Arabic dialect I have seen. It is comprehensive in its coverage—ranging from phonology, with hints on mastering nuances in pronunciation, to morphology and syntax—the analysis is insightful and original. His seminal analysis of the semantics of the verb and its active participle, with much attention to nuances of meaning in their various forms, is particularly noteworthy.

Based on the dialect of Damascus, the language covered in this book is part of what has variously been called "Syrian Arabic," "Eastern Arabic," and "Levantine Arabic," encompassing the dialects of Beirut, Amman, and Jerusalem, as well as that of Damascus. Occasional references are made to regional variants.

Georgetown University Press is to be thanked for making these basic tools for the learning of Arabic dialects available once again, especially at this time of critical national need.

Ernest N. McCarus
University of Michigan

INTRODUCTION

Syrian Arabic

The language described in this book is Arabic as it is used in everyday conversation by educated city-dwelling Syrians, and most particularly by natives of Damascus.

The spoken Arabic of Damascus is much like that of other cities in the western parts of Syria and in Palestine and Lebanon (for instance Beirut, Jerusalem, Aleppo). From a practical standpoint all the urban dialects of "the Syrian area" or "Greater Syria"—as we shall call this region—may be considered variants of one language which we call "Syrian Arabic." Any one of these dialects, well learned, is an adequate vehicle of spoken communication for the whole area.

There are, of course, a great many local speech variations of all sorts within this area. Some of the more obtrusive or systematic differences will be noted at the relevant points.

No attempt is made, however, to deal with the large variety of rural sedentary dialects of Greater Syria, some of which are quite unlike the urban speech represented in this book. Still farther beyond the range of our description is the speech of Bedouins.

As in all the Arab countries, everyday conversational language (Colloquial Arabic) in Syria differs radically in certain respects from the standard Arabic used in writing and formal speech, which we shall refer to—not quite accurately—as "Classical Arabic."[1]

The differences between Colloquial and "Classical" Arabic make it necessary, for present purposes at least, simply to treat them as different languages. The grammatical structure of Syrian Colloquial Arabic is autonomous, and must be described in its own right, without prejudice from Classical frames of reference.[2]

But while the two kinds of Arabic are indeed *different* languages, it cannot truly be said that they are *separate* languages. For most educated speakers, at least, there is and always has been an intimate association and mutual influence between them, with the influence of Classical upon Colloquial recently creating the more obvious—if not necessarily the deeper—currents of change.

Under modern conditions of mass communications and broadening literacy, it is therefore not surprising to hear many classicisms, pseudo-

---

[1] Arabists generally prefer to limit the application of the term 'Classical' to a certain (medieval) historical period, but we are using it in the loose nonhistorical sense, somewhat analogously to the term 'classical music' as distinct from 'popular music.'

[2] "Classical frames of reference" are, of course, perfectly adequate for our purposes to whatever extent Classical and Syrian Colloquial are alike—and to whatever extent these frames of reference are also adequate to their *original* purpose.

classicisms, neologisms, and journalese in almost everyone's conversation. By the same token, local or rustic styles of speech are constantly being suppressed or abandoned by some speakers in favor of something that sounds more cosmopolitan. These trends may be expected to continue as long as there is an increase in education and wide-range communication.

Aims and Methods

This reference grammar is intended, first of all, for students who have already acquired—or are in the process of acquiring—an elementary knowledge of Syrian Arabic, and who wish to enhance and confirm that knowledge. Second, it is intended to serve as a checklist of grammatical points for teachers; and third, as a source of information about this dialect for Arabists and linguists.[1]

Except in some of the footnotes, and in some of the phonetic descriptions in chapter 1, I have tried always to use ordinary English rather than modern linguistic jargon in the descriptive and explanatory passages. On the other hand, for concise reference to categories, constructions, etc.— many of which have often gone unnamed—I have not hesitated to use traditional Western or Arabistic grammatical terms where they seemed appropriate, or to coin terms where they did not.

About the methods of grammatical description there is little to be said except that they are eclectic. The presentation and most grammatical points was done in whichever way appeared to me the clearest in plain English or in familiar traditional terms. If some particular points are put in what seems a perversely novel or abstruse way, this may be in order to avoid a misleading ambiguity in the easier alternatives, or to highlight an important relationship which the traditional terms obscure.

Sources and Acknowledgments

The examples of Syrian Arabic speech used in illustrating this work come from a variety of native-spoken sources, including several previously published texts, responses to direct elicitation, and tape-recorded conversations (some spontaneous, others composed and read).[2]

---

[1]The coverage of grammatical points is by no means comprehensive. Knowledgeable readers will see at once that some parts of the book are much less detailed or less explicit than others, and that certain large areas of grammar are touched on superficially or not at all. I hope these faults (not to mention outright errors) will be glaring enough to stimulate more adequate treatment in later publications and teaching.

[2]In the syntactical parts, especially ad hoc elicitation was kept to a minimum; that is to say, particular grammatical points are illustrated insofar as possible either with previously recorded spontaneous utterances or else with sentences originally elicited for purposes other than the one at hand.

Perhaps more than to any other single body of data, I have had recourse to the work in progress on *A Dictionary of Syrian Arabic*, by Karl Stowasser and Moukhtar Ani (*English–Arabic*, number 5 of this series [reissued in 2004], and *Arabic–English*, forthcoming [never completed]). Most examples of usage in these works were produced by the same Syrian speakers whom I also consulted directly.

A particularly valuable unpublished source of material was lent me by Charles A. Ferguson, who, with the assistance of Moukhtar Ani and other speakers from Damascus, worked out some years ago a very thorough and accurate collation of Damascus Arabic verb forms.

Of previously published works, Ferguson and Ani's *Damascus Arabic* and Cantineau and Helbaoui's *Manuel élémentaire d'arabe orientale*[1] have been used intensively as sources of illustrative sentences, and Barthélemy's *Dictionnaire arabe–français* (subject to dialectal adaptations) as a source of word bases. A number of other works (see below) were similarly used to a lesser extent. Some examples come from non-Damascene sources, but in most cases these were *not* chosen to illustrate dialectal diversity; with minor adjustments they represent Damascene usage as well as that of their own locality. In all these examples, of course, the transcription has been altered to match our own.

Sentences taken from these previously published sources are identified as such; for instance the notation [DA-173] after a sentence means that it was taken from Ferguson and Ani's *Damascus Arabic*, page 173. Titles are coded as indicated in the list that follows. Examples taken from Stowasser and Ani's *Dictionary of Syrian Arabic*, however, are not identified, but remain unmarked like those originally produced for this grammar. (Single words and set phrases, of course, go unmarked in any case.)

My debt to coworkers in the Arabic Research Program at Georgetown University is greater than I can easily express. Special thanks go to Abdul Khalek Jallad and to Mary C. Chapple, both of whom did a great deal of valuable collation from texts and dictionairies.

As native-speaking consultants, Ziad H. Idilby and Abdul Khalek Jallad have given me expert assistance over a long period of time; for shorter but nonetheless fruitful periods I am indebted to Munir Jabban, Nazir Khaddam El-Jamie, and Sadalla Jouejati. The difficult job of typing most of the manuscript was expertly done by Alexandra Selim. I also owe thanks

---

[1]Many of the examples taken from this book are now thirdhand, having been Mr. Helbaoui's adaptation to his own speech of passages from other sources.

to Mahmoud Bagdash, Ali Bakri, Carolee Powers, Susan Luton, and Marie Roces.

I am especially grateful to Karl Stowasser and Moukhtar Ani, who have aided and encouraged me far beyond their call of duty as colleagues in the Arabic Research Program. Professor Ani has helped me with profound insight through many difficult problems, provided me with excellent examples, and read parts of the manuscript. Professor Stowasser has read and discussed many parts of the manuscript with me, at great length and with telling effect, and has helped me with innumerable other points as they came up.

Finally, I wish to thank Georgetown University, the Department of Health, Education, and Welfare, and the authors of the National Defense Department Act, for providing the opportunity and means to carry out this project.

M.W.C.

Washington, D.C.
September 1964

REFERENCES

The only works listed here are those from which examples have been taken. For bibliography, see "Syrian Arabic Studies," by Charles A. Ferguson, in *Arabic Dialect Studies*, Harvey Sobelman, editor (Center for Applied Linguistics of the Modern Language Association and The Middle East Institute, Washington, D.C., 1962).

Reference
Symbol

AO   J. Cantineau and Y. Helbaoui, *Manuel élémentaire d'arabe orientale (parler de Damas)*. Paris, 1953.

Bart.   A. Barthélemy, *Dictionnaire arabe-français (Dialectes de Syrie: Alep, Damas, Liban, Jérusalem)*. Paris, 1935–1954.

Bauer   L. Bauer, *Deutsch-arabisches Wörterbuch der Umgangssprache in Palästina und im Libanon*. Unter Mitwirkung von Anton Spitaler. 2. Auflage. Wiesbaden, 1957.

Bg.   G. Bergsträsser, *Zum arabischen Dialekt von Damaskus*. Hannover, 1921.

Cr.   A. J. M. Craig, *A Conversation Grammar of Colloquial Arabic*. Shemlan (Lebanon), 1956 (mimeographed).

DA   Charles A. Ferguson, with Moukhtar Ani and others, *Damascus Arabic* (available from the Center for Applied Linguistics, Washington, D.C.) 1961.

EA   Frank A. Rice and Majed F. Sa'id, *Eastern Arabic: An Introduction to the Spoken Arabic of Palestine, Syria and Lebanon*. Beirut, 1960. [Reissued by Georgetown University Press in 2005.]

PAT   Hassan El-Hajjé, *Le parler arabe de Tripoli (Liban)*. Paris, 1954.

PIPL   André d'Alvernys, *Petite introduction au parler libanais*. Bikfaya (Lebanon), 1950.

PVA   E. Lator, *Parlez-vous arabe? Arabe libano-syrien*. Beirut, 1953.

RN   Raphael Nakhla, *Grammaire du dialecte libano-syrien (phonétique, morphologie et syntaxe)*. Two volumes. Beirut, 1937–1938.

SAL   M Y. Van Wagoner, with Munah F. Dabaghi and Joseph T. Kiameh, *Introduction to Spoken Arabic of Lebanon*. Sidon (Lebanon), 1953. (Reproduced by The Institute of Languages and Linguistics, Georgetown University, Washington, D.C.)

SPA Michel Feghali, *Syntaxe des parlers arabes actuels du Liban.* Paris, 1928.

SVSA Haim Blanc, "Style Variations in Spoken Arabic: A Sample of Interdialectical Educated Conversation," in *Contributions to Arabic Linguistics,* C. A. Ferguson, editor. Cambridge, Mass., 1960.
Karl Stowasser and Moukhtar Ani, *A Dictionary of Syrian Arabic: English–Arabic.* Washington, D.C., 1964. [Reissued by Georgetown University Press in 2004.]

CHAPTER 1: SOUNDS

TRANSCRIPTION

The Arabic in this book is printed italically in a modified Roman alphabet as follows:

OUR SPELLING	ARABIC LETTER	PRONUNCIATION DESCRIBED ON page:	OUR SPELLING	ARABIC LETTER	PRONUNCIATION DESCRIBED ON page:
a	[fatḥa]	11	q	ق	4
b, (b̭)	ب	2, (6)	r, (ṛ)	ر	5, (6)
(č)		4	s	س	3
d	د	3	š	ش	3
ḍ	ض	6	ṣ	ص	6
e		10	t	ت	3
ə		10	ṭ	ط	6
f	ف	2	o	[ḍamma]	9
g		4	(v)		2
ġ	غ	4	w	و	9
(ǧ)	ج	3	x	خ	4
h	ه	5	y	ي	9
ḥ	ح	4	z	ز	3
i	[kasra]	9	ž	ج	3
k	ك	4	ẓ	ظ	6
l, (ḷ)	ل	5, (6)	ʕ	ع	4
m, (ṃ)	م	5, (6)	ʔ, (ʔ)	ء	5, (6)
n, (ṇ)	ن	5, (6)	(θ)	ث	3
o		10	(δ)	ذ	3
(p)		2	(δ̣)	ظ	6

Letters in parentheses represent sounds that are rare, or rarely distinctive, or characteristic of certain local dialects only.

Long vowels are written with a macron (¯): ā, ē, ī, ō, ū. Long consonants are indicated by doubling the letter: bb, ss, kk, etc.   [p.15].

The small raised letter ᵃ is pronounced the same as ə [p.30].

Accented syllables are sometimes indicated by an accent mark (´) over
vowels. [p.18].

Note to Learners

Since the Arabic in this book is exclusively <u>conversational</u> Arabic, mere
familiarity with the way it is transcribed in writing counts for nothing.
Familiarity with the live <u>sound</u> of the language is indispensable if practical
application is contemplated.

The terminology used in describing some of the sounds may not be completely intelligible to readers without phonetic training. These readers
are again reminded that actual exposure to the sounds is prerequisite or
co-requisite to the practical use of this book.

Parts of the Arabic sound system are rather difficult for most foreign
learners. For speakers of English the most serious difficulties involve
the contrast between plain and velarized sounds [p.6], the contrast between long and short sounds [15], the pharyngeal sounds [4] and their
contrast with laryngeals [5] on the one hand and with post-velars [4] on
the other. Intensive practice on these points is recommended.

LABIAL OBSTRUENTS: b, (p), f, (v).

b, **Bilabial Stop.** Similar to English b. Fully voiced before vowels and
voiced consonants, but tends to devoice — to sound like an unaspirated
English p — before voiceless obstruents (f, k, x, ḥ, q, s, š, ṣ, t, ṭ)
and sometimes at the end of a phrase. Examples (fully voiced): bāl,
byǝ̌ži, ʔabú, biḥǝ̌bbon, brūde, byǝ́bda, tǝ́bʔa, bbárṭel; (devoiced or partially devoiced): btǝ́bki, btǝ́šrab, bšīl.

p, **Voiceless Bilabial Stop.** Except as a contextual variant of b (see
above), p occurs very rarely in Syrian Arabic, in a few words of foreign
origin, for example paspṓr (or basbṓr) 'passport', ʔawrúppa (or ʔawrǝ́bba)
'Europe', pansyṓn 'boardinghouse'. This sound is written 'b' wherever it
may be treated as a contextual variant of b; and 'p' only otherwise.

f, **Labiodental Spirant.** Similar to English f. Generally voiceless, but
also sometimes voiced before g, ḍ, or other voiced oral obstruents.
Examples (voiceless) fáras, fīl, flā́ḥa, ftákar, ʔǝfʔl, ˍdáftar, xáffef,
sfǝnž, ʔalf; (voiced): ʔafḍal (pron. ʔávḍal), ḥǝfg (pron. ḥǝvg).

v, **Voiced Labiodental Spirant.** Besides being a contextual variant of f
(see above), this sound occurs in a number of words of foreign origin,
for example: krā́ve (or grā́fe) 'necktie', nárvaz (or nárfaz) 'to disturb,
make nervous', veránda 'balcony', brā́vo (or brā́bo) 'bravo'. This sound

is written '*f*' wherever it may be treated as a contextual variant of *f;* and '*v*' only otherwise.

PLAIN DENTAL OBSTRUENTS: *d, t, z, s, (δ, θ).*

d, **Voiced Dental Stop.**   Differs from English d in the somewhat more forward position of the tongue tip, which generally touches the upper teeth in Arabic but only the alveolar (gum) ridge in most kinds of English. Examples: *dār, diráse, drūs, džáwwaz, bádal, báddo, ?áddi, zdād, wáhᵊdna, bərd?án, ba?dúnes, dxūl, dmúɛa.*

t, **Voiceless Dental Stop.**   Differs from English t in the same respect as *d* from English d; generally somewhat less aspirated than English t in 'take'. Examples: *táxod, ttáfa?, ?atíl, tláte, ?áttat, stríh, bəthə́ll, mə́tᵊt, tmáne, tšáwer, btəštríha, žáməɛtna, smaɛt, t-tnēn, t?íl, txūt.*

z, **Voiced Alveolar Sibilant.**   Somewhat sharper (higher pitched) than most kinds of English z.   Examples: *zād, zdall, hazzét, ɛanze, zīd, ?ázzam, həzz, ?ázhar, z-zhūr, zríɛa, ɛazíz, hzērán.*

s, **Voiceless Aveolar Sibilant.**   Generally sharper and stronger than most kinds of English s as in 'sell', 'hiss'.   Examples: *sáyyed, siyáse, ?asás, ?ássas, həss, stáhsan, sfáržel, snáwla, žəns, žə́smi, s-sə́dᵊs, ?áslam.*

δ, **Voiced Interdental Spirant.**   Like English th in 'this'.   Not used in urban Syrian Arabic, but only in certain rural dialects, corresponding to Classical ﺝ and urban Syrian *d* or *z: háδa* 'this' (for *háda*), *?íδa* 'if' (for *?íza*).

θ, **Voiceless Interdental Spirant.**   Like English th in 'think'.   Rare in urban Syrian Arabic: *θáwra* (or *sáwra*) 'revolution', *θiqa* (or *síqa*) 'trust', *θaqáfa* (or *saqáfe*) 'culture', *hadíθ* (or *hadís*) '(Prophetic) tradition'. Used in classicisms, generally replaceable by s in less elegant style. Certain rural dialects, however, have this sound as a regular thing, corresponding to Classical ﺙ and urban Syrian *t: θáni* 'second' (for *táni*), etc.

PALATAL OBSTRUENTS: *ž, (ǧ), š, (č), g, k.*

ž, **Voiced Slit Spirant.**   Like the French j, or the English -si- in 'vision', but somewhat sharper and stronger.   Examples: *žāž, hə́žže, ž-žázar, hážar, žə́mᵊžme mžáwwaz, mə́ɛᵊže, hažž, mažbúr, džáwwaz, žnéne, žyūš, ždād, lāž?ín.*

ǧ, **Voiced Affricate.**   Like English j and dg in 'judge'.   Used in the Aleppo region, and in rural dialects in various parts of Greater Syria, instead of *ž.*

š, **Voiceless Slit Spirant.**   Somewhat sharper and stronger than English sh in 'shine', 'wash'.   Examples: *šāl, šēx, šə́rᵊš, wəšš, dáššer, šrít, štáǧal, šhūr, mášye, məšt, tšūf, š-šáraf, mšína, šɛēl.*

č, **Voiceless Affricate.** Like English ch in 'church'. Occurs in certain words in the Aleppo region, e.g. *čūx* 'cloth' (elsewhere *žūx*) *čálbane* 'elegance, chic' (elsewhere *šálbane*); and in certain rural dialects elsewhere, in place of *k* in certain positions: *čān* 'was' (for *kān*), *čalb* 'dog' (for *kalb*).

g, **Voiced Stop.** Like English g in 'give', 'good', its point of articulation varies between mediopalatal and velar, depending on neighboring sounds. This sound occurs mainly in words taken from foreign languages or other Arabic dialects: *sigára* 'cigarette', *ʔənglízi* 'English', *gádaƐ* 'brave fellow', *gdīš* 'horse, nag', *šángal* 'hook', *Ɛgāl* 'cord headband'.

k, **Voiceless Stop.** Like English k, its point of articulation varies between mediopalatal and velar, depending on neighboring sounds. It generally has somewhat less aspiration in release than English k, and is often unreleased finally. Examples: *kīf*, *kə́hᵊl*, *kūƐ*, *kámel*, *krēk*, *šákwak*, *máksab*, *hə́kme*, *mʔákked*, *kfūf*, *ktāb*, *rkōd*, *hkáye*, *byə́kšfu*, *bə́msko*.

POST-VELAR OBSTRUENTS: *x*, *ġ*, *q*.

x, **Voiceless Spirant.** Generally involves both uvular trill and velar "scrape". Like German ch in 'Bach'. Examples: *xōx*, *dáxxal*, *másxara*, *sə́xne*, *wə́şex*, *sīx*, *žaxxīx*, *xtáraƐ*, *txāf*, *şxūne*, *btə́xsel*, *xnáʔa*, *dəxt*, *xrās*.

ġ, **Voiced Spirant.** Generally a smooth spirant, involving neither trill nor scrape, but stronger than Spanish g in 'lago'. Examples: *ġáli*, *ġūl*, *šə́ġᵊl*, *šáġġal*, *šaġġíl*, *ġyāb*, *tġīb*, *baláġna*, *máblaġ*, *şāġ*, *ẓġīr*, *ġráybe*, *ʔáġniya*.

q, **Voiceless Uvular Stop.** Generally, though not always, unaspirated. In urban speech it occurs mainly in classicisms, and in some words is replaceable by *ʔ*. Certain rural dialects, however, have *q* generally corresponding to Classical ق and urban Syrian *ʔ*. Examples: *ʔəstəqlál* (or *ʔəstaʔlál*), *qánşol* (or *ʔánşol*), *huqúq* (or *hʔūʔ*), *qard*, *qrūd*, *l-qurʔán*.

PHARYNGEAL OBSTRUENTS: *ḥ*, *Ɛ*.

ḥ, **Voiceless Spirant.** Usually with strong friction but without scrape. (Must not be confused with *x* or with *h*). Examples: *ḥále*, *ḥíle*, *ḥōd*, *ḥəzb*, *báḥᵊr*, *wáḥed*, *baḥḥára*, *ḥsāb*, *ḥsēn*, *ḥkī-lna*, *ʔáḥla*, *tḥéwan*, *bḥə́bba*, *maḥbūb*, *şáleḥ*, *rūḥ*, *şaḥīḥ*, *şáḥḥəḥu*, *mə́lᵊḥ*, *mnāḥ*, *rəḥt*, *lḥə́ʔni*, *zə́lᵊḥfe*, *ḥzērán*.

The use of a subscript dot in transcribing the sound *ḥ* does **not** signify any relationship to the velarized sounds, also transcribed with the dot [p-6].

Ɛ, **Voiced Spirant.** A smooth but tense spirant, without the friction noise of *ḥ*. (Must not be confused with *ġ* or with *ʔ*.) Examples: *Ɛāl*, *Ɛanīd*, *Ɛōd*, *Ɛīd*, *Ɛēn*, *baƐīd*, *báƐes*, *šīƐi*, *bāƐ*, *bēƐ*, *šanīƐ*, *xáraƐ*, *mamnūƐ*, *bdƐƐad*, *báƐᵊd*, *saƐáde*, *Ɛyáde*, *Ɛtána*, *bəƐtə́ʔed*, *btə́Ɛni*, *btáƐti*, *btə́ʔeod*, *mƐáyade*, *muƐīn*, *šáƐƐlo*, *šƐāƐ*.

LARYNGEALS: *h, ?*.

h, **Glottal Continuant.** Much the same as English h, but generally with the larynx more open and more breath exhaled. Tends to be voiced when short between vowels or before voiced consonants, otherwise voiceless. Examples: *hōl, hắda, həzz, ḍắhᵊr, mᵊhᵊr, mahǘl, sắhhal, fahhᵊmni, mắhlak, mᵊhne, bahlǘl, hlᵊkt, mhəmm, muntázah, mnắbbeh, mašbǘh, zhūr, rắhbane, htáret, shǘle, ?ắšhor, dhān.*

?, **Glottal Catch.** Like the interruption in the middle of the English interjections 'oh-oh!' and 'unh-unh'. Examples: *?āl, ?ắhᵊl, ?īs, ra?ís, lắ?a, ra??ắṣ, rắ?be, btᵊ?mor, ?mōr, ?rūš, b?ūl, mắs?ale, sắba?, wa?t, s?íni, s?āl, btᵊ?ᵊdru, bắ??a, ra??sǘ, ḥtắra?, ?tōl, sū?, ?ṭắɛo, ṣ?ā?, ḥ?ǘ?.*

RESONANTS: *m, n, l, r.*

m, **Labial Nasal.** Labiodental before *f*, otherwise bilabial. Like English m. Avoid anticipatory denasalization before spirants — i.e. do not allow a 'p' glide to slip in after the *m* in words like *?ams* (not *"?amps"*), *?əmf* (not *"?əmpf"*). Examples: *māl, mūs, ?ắmal, ?ắmro, mrār, t?ắmmal, ɛambar, ?úmam, ?ām, ḥammām, mṭắblaž, mhūra, mžắdwwaze, mmắrrḍa, mmắssel, rmắdi, lmᵊsa, mbắla, mfắrnaž, ?ᵊmmhon.*

n, **Non-labial Nasal.** Similar to English n. Has the same point of articulation as a following dental or palatal obstruent (including *g, k*), otherwise alveolar. Avoid anticipatory denasalization before spirants: *bắnzel* (not *"bắndzel"*). Examples: *nāl, nūn, žəns, bənt, ngắsal, ?ənsān, nšūf, ntdha, bắnna, ?ᵊnnon, nnām, n?ắtal, bənž, nžāṣ, nhắra, nsāha;* (pronounced ng as in 'ink'): *sᵊnge, ?ənglízi, bᵊnkor, ṇkắsar.*

l, **Lateral.** Similar to "light" or "bright" English l as in 'link', 'let', not like "dark" or "heavy" l as in most kinds of English 'ball', hulk'. Tends to be nasalized in some positions, especially when long or after a long vowel; English speakers may sometimes mistake it for an n. Examples: *laff, lắzem, lōn, lífe, zāl, lēl, fūl, hōl, ?alíl, ?ắllel, dᵊllo, žallắd, mᵊắllef, l-lúга, llūm, ltắga, ?ᵊlt, ?ᵊtel, ?ắmᵊl, tlắte, l-yōm.*

r, **Apical Trill.** A single tap when short, a multiple trill when long *(rr)*. Tends to devoice before voiceless oral obstruents and sometimes finally; otherwise voiced. Examples: *rās, ríše, rᵊḥle, rūḥ, ɛắrab, žaraṣ, žarād, žaríde, žīrān, žardōn, bắrd, brūde, ṭrāb, zríɛa, šrāb, ?ắgrab, sᵊɛro, nār, nắhᵊr, zūr, dīr, rtắta, bərd?ān, rṣāṣ, rrūḥ, mắrra, barríd, ḥᵊrra, ḍắrar.*

VELARIZATION [1] *(at-tafxîm):* ṭ, ḍ, ṣ, ẓ, (ḍ), ḅ, ṃ, ṇ, ḷ, ṛ, (?).

The dot under these letters represents a "heavy" resonance which is
the effect of relatively low-pitched concentrations of acoustic energy —
in contrast to the "thin" or "light" quality of the sounds transcribed
without the dot. (Note that *ḥ* [p.4] is not one of the velarized sounds;
its dot is merely to distinguish it from *h.*)

In producing the plain sounds (i.e. those transcribed without the dot),
the tongue is usually arched upward and forward into a single hump (in
profile), leaving the pharyngeal and velar passages relatively open. For
the velarized sounds, on the other hand, the profile of the tongue usually
tends to be two-humped and low in the middle; the back hump narrows the
velar and pharyngeal passages.

The lips may also play a part in producing the
heavy resonance; velarization is sometimes accompanied
by protrusion and pursing of the lips, while retraction
and spreading of the lips help make the lighter, thinner
resonance.

Examples of the contrast between plain and velarized sounds:

	Plain		Velarized	
tīn	'figs'	....	*ṭīn*	'mud'[2]
dīm	'perpetuate'	....	*ḍīm*	'hurt'
sēf	'sword'	....	*ṣēf*	'summer'
būz	'muzzle'	....	*būẓ*	'ice'

---

[1] The term 'velarization' is not altogether satisfactory as a name for this
phonological component. Note that the post-velar sounds *x*, *ġ*, and *q* are
not inherently "velarized"; they may be either "plain" or "velarized",
depending on the neighboring sounds. The term 'pharyngealization', which
has sometimes been used instead of 'velarization', is even more misleading,
since the pharyngeal spirants *ḥ* and *ε* have still less in common with the
velarized sounds than the post-velars have.

Evidently the air-stream turbulence produced by primary velar or
pharyngeal stricture has sound effects quite unrelated — in Arabic, at
least — to the effect of so-called secondary stricture in these passages.
The secondary stricture does not produce audible turbulence, but serves to
modify the resonating chamber.

The traditional term 'emphatic' is also a bad name for the velarized
sounds, since it suggests (erroneously, it would seem) that these sounds
are more forcefully or tensely articulated than the plain sounds.

[2] Velarized *ṭ* is usually unaspirated while plain *t* is somewhat aspirated.

	Plain			Velarized
bába	'her door'	....	*ḅáḅa*	'papa'
wálla	'he appointed'	......	*wálḷa*	'by God' (mild oath)
máyyet	'dead'	....	*ṃayy*	'water'
náyem	'asleep'	....	*ṇáy*	'shepherd's flute'
žári	'flowing'	....	*žáṛi*	'my neighbor'
ʔáššaɾ	'he signalled'	......	*ʔáššaɾ*	'he peeled'

Speakers of English and many other languages are apt to be more sensitive to the effects of velarization on contiguous <u>vowels</u> than to the differences between plain and velarized consonants themselves. Compare *dall* 'to indicate' with *ḍaḷḷ* 'to remain', *sadd* 'close, block' with *ṣəḍḍ* 'repulse, refuse'. [pp. 10, 11]

Velarization is usually not limited to a single sound in a word, but commonly affects whole syllables and often whole words: *ḍaḷḷ, ṃaḅṣűṭ, ẓáḅeṭ.*

The dental obstruents *t/ṭ, d/ḍ, s/ṣ,* and *z/ẓ* are the only ones of these pairs that differentiate many words independently as illustrated above. With the others, the distinction between plain and velarized is usually a variation conditioned by the neighboring sounds, and is potentially significant only next to the vowel *a* and in the absence of dental obstruents.

Since velarization mainly affects sound sequences that involve dental obstruents, these obstruents are taken as the focal points of velarization wherever possible. Our transcription regularly shows velarization for these sounds, but not for other kinds of sounds affected in their neighborhood. Thus in the word *bóṭlaɛ*, for example, the dot under the 't' implies that the *b*, the *ə*, and the *l* are normally also velarized.

> This economical use of subscript dots is not unambiguous, since the scope of velarization — the "neighborhood" of a dotted letter — has not been defined, nor is there, apparently, any simple way to define it. In fact the scope of velarization varies considerably from word to word, speaker to speaker, and region to region. Furthermore, the velarization may vary in intensity; some parts of a word may be strongly velarized, other parts weakly.

Examples of velarized sounds:

ḍ	ṭ	ṣ	ẓ	Othᴇr
ḍaww	ṭāb	ṣāb	ẓā́lem	ʔállˌla
ḍēf	ṭēr	ṣēḍ	ẓənnā́r	báḷḷa
ḍā́ḍaḍ	ṭō̄ʔ	ṣōb	ẓuhú̆r	ɛ́ḍrab
ḍ-ḍuġú̆ṭ	ṭū̄l	ṣú̆ra	ẓġîr	ʔalˌmáni
bíḍ	žā̄ṭ	ṣîṣán	faẓîɛ	baṇk
márad̲	máṭtar	wə́ṣex	ʔaẓə́nn	verάnda
fáḍḍal	ṭaṭɛ̂îm	byə́ṣref	ʔáẓlam	ʔámaṛ
bə́drob	ṭhîn	nā́ṣer	byə́ghar	
ḍhū̄r	nə́ṭṭi	ʔaṣṣā́ṣ	mẓállaṭ	
ḍžîž	mə́šṭ	ḥṣān	bάwweẓ	

In some parts of Greater Syria, the plain/velarized distinction with
certain consonants is suppressed. In Damascus, for instance, there is no
contrast between r and ṛ in the same contexts; žā́ri 'flowing' and žā́ṛi 'my
neighbor' are pronounced alike [p.12]. In other regions the r/ṛ distinction — though not obliterated — is often subject to local and individual
variations to such an extent that its importance is very slight. Since
the Arabic in this book represents the Damascus variety, velarization of r
is ordinarily not marked.

In a large part of the central area, including Damascus and most of
Lebanon, the distinction between ʔ and ʔ̣ is likewise obliterated, and is
likewise subject to much vacillation elsewhere. Velarization of ʔ will
generally not be shown in this book.

Except for ʔ/ʔ̣ and a few other marginal cases[1], the
contrast between plain and velarized is limited entirely
to front sounds — labials and dentals. While the palatals
and back sounds may vary due to velarization, their variation
is virtually always conditioned by the neighboring sounds
and is not significant.

---

[1] There is a certain amount of regional and stylistic variation between x
and x̣, ġ and ġ̣, q and q̣.

VOWELS (AND SEMIVOWELS): *i* (and y), *u* (and *w*), *e*, *o*, *ə*, *a*.

i, High Front Vowel

Long *ī* is similar to the English i in 'machine', but not diphthongized or as lax as it commonly is in English. Examples: *brīd*, *kīf*, *fīʾ*, *šī*, *nīto*, *ʿīd*, *ʾīmān*, *žībī-li*, *nəsī*.

Short *i* is much the same in quality as long *ī*, though sometimes not so high and tense; less high and tense than the French i of 'vite', 'ici'. Examples: *binām*, *ʾiza*, *šífa*, *hánito*, *ṣábi*, *kə́li*, *rah-ikún*, *dirā́se*.

Next to a velarized consonant, *i* has a retracted sound [ɨ] similar to Russian ы: *biṣír*, *ḍīf*, *bīḍ*, *niẓā́m*, *ṣífa*. (Compare this with the sound of *ə* [p.10] in certain contexts: *ṣífa* vs. *naššə́fa*; the latter is lower, laxer, and more forward. The sound of *ə* in the velarized contexts, e.g. *byūṣə́fa*, is lower and farther back.)

The non-syllabic version of *i* — transcribed 'y'[1] — is substantially the same sound as an unaccented syllabic *i*, sometimes slightly shorter. It does not tend to develop palatal friction. Examples (short): *yōm*, *yatím*, *šāy*, *ṭáyfe*, *náyem*, *bayā́n*, *byára*, *híyal*, *hánye*, *yšīl*.

Non-syllabic and long *(yy)*, it is higher and tenser (but still does not have palatal friction): *sayyā́ra*, *ġayyúr*, *ṭáyyeb*, *ʾiyyā́m*, *hayy*.

u, High Back Rounded Vowel

Long *ū* is rounder and tenser than English u in 'rude', and is monophthongal. Examples: *šūf*, *brúde*, *būlā́d*, *byúṣal*, *mū*, *haṭṭú*.

Short *u* has much the same quality as long *ū*, but is sometimes less high and tense. Less high and tense than French ou in 'voulez', 'cou' Examples: *suʾā́l*, *fáruha*, *ʾúmam*, *dúwal*, *lúġa*, *hólu*, *muɛín*, *muttáhed*.

The non-syllabic version of *u* — transcribed 'w'[2] — is substantially the same sound as an unaccented syllabic *u*, though it may be slightly shorter and higher. Examples (short): *wādi*, *wə́ṣel*, *dáwle*, *wlād*, *háwal*, *žádwal*, *law*.

Non-syllabic and long *(ww)*, it is somewhat higher and tenser: *ʾáwwal*, *xawwíf*, *ɛadə́wwi*, *húwwe*, *w-wálado*.

---

[1] In many parts of Greater Syria *i* does not contrast with *ə* or with *e*, in which case the syllabic and non-syllabic sounds must be reckoned separate phonemes [p.13, footnote 2].

[2] In many parts of Greater Syria *u* does not contrast with *ə* or with *o*, in which case the syllabic and non-syllabic sounds must be reckoned separate phonemes [p.13, footnote 2]

e, Higher-Mid Front Vowel

Long ē is quite different from the English a in 'date', since it is monophthongal and higher than the first part of the English a. It is quite similar to French é as in 'zéro', but not as tense. Examples: *bēt, zēbaˀ, ˀēlŭl, trēn, šēx, ˀəžrē, žnēnə́tkon, bēbē.*

Short *e* has more or less the same quality as long ē — between the i of English 'sit' and the é of French 'été'. Examples: *málek, byə́lbes, ṭáyyeb, ḥále, bə́ke, ˀamerkānǐyye.* (Short *e* does not ordinarily occur accented [p. 28].)

Next to a velarized consonant, *e* has a somewhat retracted sound [ė]: *ẓä́beṭ, ṣēḍ, báwweẓ, ṭēr, wə́ṣex.*

Before a pharyngeal *(ḥ, ɛ)*, short *e* has a slightly lowered sound: *ṣä́leḥ, máryeḥ, bə́šeɛ, mənˀdṭeɛ.*

o, Higher-Mid Back Rounded Vowel

Long ō differs markedly from the English o in 'sole', being monophthongal, and higher and rounder than the first part of the English o. It is similar to the French ô in 'côte', only not so tense. Examples: *kōl, xōd, ktōb, bṓrad, žṓze, mōzä́t, bōrə́ma, māyṓ.*

Short *o* has about the same quality as long ō — between the oo of British English 'look' and the o of French 'zéro'. Examples: *byə́mlok, bə́ˀtol, bēto, ˀotēl, ˀašhor, mə́šmoš.* (Short *o* does not ordinarily occur accented [p. 28].)

ə, Higher-Mid Central Vowel

ə has a wide range of values, varying between the i of English 'pit', the u of English 'put', and the u of (American) English 'putt', depending on the neighboring sounds. (The raised letter *ᵊ* represents exactly the same sound as *ə;* see p. 19.)

The most forward pronunciation of *ə* — like the i in 'sit' (but always clipped short, never drawled or diphthongized) — occurs only next to plain dentals *(t, d, s, n, l)* or after *y*, when no back vowel *(o, u)* or velarized sound *(ṭ, ḍ, ṣ, ẓ, etc.)* is in its neighborhood. Examples: *sətt, də́llni, tə́nsa, byə́skar, təshádbha, tə́lᵊt, zə́n-li, ləzzēˀa, təlmǐz.*

The lowest pronunciation of *ə* — between the e in 'pet' and the u in 'putt' — occurs before pharyngeals *(ḥ, ɛ)*: *btə́hki, nə́hna, sə́ɛᵊr, žə́mᵊɛ, byəɛtə́ni, bilə́hh.* (This is very similar to the sound of *a* in certain contexts — but not in <u>these</u> contexts. The *a* in *rásme*, for example, is much like the *ə* in *rə́hle*, while the *a* before pharyngeals is considerably lower, e.g. *ráhme.*)

Several different factors tend to make ǝ sound more like the u in 'put' and less like the i in 'pit', especially when working in combination. These factors are velarization (caused by proximity of ṭ, ḍ, ṣ, ẓ, etc.), backing (caused by contiguity with a back consonant, especially x or ġ), rounding (caused by contiguity with labials or w). An o or u in the following syllable causes both backing and rounding. Contiguous r may also have a slight backing effect. Examples: ḍaḍḍ, ṣǝbb, ḥǝṭṭ, bṭǝ́ṣal, ʔǝ́ḍᵊwye, Ɛadǝ́ww, l-ᵊwrā́ʔ, rǝ́da, mǝrr, ʔǝ́xti, šǝ́gᵊl, rǝ́bᵊƐ, bǝ́ʔtol, ḥǝ́lu, ʔrǝ́mfol, wǝ́ššo, bẓǝnn, ʔǝ́mmi, Ɛǝ́ḍu, ẓǝbbā́ṭ.[1]

Unlike all other sounds in the language, ǝ never occurs long, or at the end of a word.

a, Low Vowel

a has a wide range of values, varying between sounds similar to those of English e in 'pet', a in 'pat', u in 'putt', and o in 'pot'.

What may be taken as the "standard" pronunciation of a is a slightly raised and retracted [æ], not quite so low and forward as the a in English 'bat', but lower than e in 'bet' and more to the front than u in (American) 'but'.

This standard a occurs mainly next to non-velarized front consonants — including k, g, and y, but excluding r. Examples (short): bass, laff, fazz, dall, madd, sabb, takk, žadd, šakk, kam, sǝ́naḍ, mǝ́salan, zǝ́lẓale, mǝ́lek, mažǝ́lle, dǝ́ššer, bǝ́ladi, sǝ́žžal, ḥíyal, kasǝ́l, mamnǝ́Ɛ, yasǝ́Ɛ, yatím, ballōr.

At the end of a word, short a tends to be slightly lower and farther back: sǝ́da, bǝ́dda, tǝ́nsa, šǝ́nta, ʔǝ́ša.

Long ā before and after plain front consonants varies regionally. In Damascus it tends to be a little lower and farther back than the "standard" a, while in certain coastal regions it is higher and more forward than the standard. Examples: kān, fās, zād, dāl, šāzz, š-šām, mǝ́lo, tyāb, ktāf, kǝ́tbe, nabāt, rǝžžāl, šǝbbāk, siyyās, žǝžā́t.

In the Damascus pronunciation ā at the end of a word has more or less the same sound as before a consonant, but in the coastal regions this sound is lower and farther back than the high front preconsonantal ā. Examples: mā, yā, mubālā, xabbā, ƐašǍ.

After back consonants and w and r, the pronunciation of a is more or less the same as after front consonants in Damascus and many other regions. In some of the coastal regions, however, long ā after a back consonant, especially ḥ or Ɛ, may be less high and front than it is after a front consonant.[2] Examples: Ɛāl, ḥāl, xāl, ġāḷ, ʔāl, rād; xadd,

---

[1] With a maximum of backing and rounding, ǝ tends to alternate with u: ʔebúwwe/ʔubúwwe, Ɛadúww/Ɛadúww, ʔawrǝ́bba/ʔawrúbba, etc. [See p.13.]

[2] This backing effect may sometimes be due to velarization: ʔāl (for ʔāl), xāl (for xāl), ṛās (for rās), maqāl (for maqǝ́l). In other instances, however, the backing may be too slight to attribute to velarization.

hazz, ġdnna, ʔdbᵊl, wálad, radd, staqdll, ḥdda.

Long *ā* after *q* is commonly pronounced farther back: *maqál, qānún.*[1]

Before a pharyngeal (*ḥ, Ɛ*), *a* has a low sound, generally more to the front than the usual American pronunciation of the *a* in 'father': *bāƐ, lāḥ, rāƐi, ydƐni, zdḥle.* In some of the coastal regions long *ā* in open syllables before *ḥ* or *Ɛ* is considerably higher, however, especially if there is an *i* or *e* in the following syllable: *sáƐa, wāḥed.*

Before *r* (in the Damascus pronunciation) *a* has a somewhat retracted and lowered sound similar to that of Middlewestern American a in 'far', 'part' (but without the retroflection): *fār, bárra, bár ᵊd, márto, dára, ʔárbƐa.* In many other parts of Greater Syria, however, plain *r* causes little or no retraction or lowering, while velarized *ṛ* causes considerably more than the Damascus *r* [p.8].

Before back consonants other than pharyngeals, especially in closed syllables, *a* commonly has a retracted and slightly lowered pronunciation: *ʔaxx, ʔáḥwe, law, ʔáwwal, ʔáġla, bdʔʔa, báxra, dāx, manáx.*

When *a* is followed by a single consonant plus *i* or *e* in the next syllable, the backing effect of back consonants or *r* or *w* is counteracted, and the *a* is more or less "standard": *báred, sáwi, dáxel, saxíf, báʔi.*

a next to front consonants only is also somewhat raised and fronted by a following *i* or *e*,, so that the *a* is slightly higher and more forward than standard: *máši, báli, máyyet.*

In the vicinity of a velarized consonant, *a* has a back sound between that of u in 'putt' and American o in 'pot'. (The "hollow" quality of velarization, however, is superimposed on the effect of this articulatory position.) Examples: *baṭṭ, faẓīƐ, ṣabb, ḥáṭab, ṃayy, ʔáḷḷa, ẓálem, bṣáṭ, ṣṭáḍ.*

When followed by a pharyngeal, velarized *a* is lower — in the approximate position of American o in 'pot': *ṣaḥḥ, máƐᵊt, ḍāƐ.* (This lowering is minimized, however, if *i* or *e* follows in the next syllable: *ḍáḥye, ṣáḥi.*)

---

[1]See Footnote 2, p. 11.

REGIONAL VARIATIONS IN THE VOWEL SYSTEM

Short Vowels

Many speakers, especially in Lebanon and Palestine but also in parts of Syria proper, have no vowel *ə* as a functionally distinct sound[1]; for them the front pronunciations corresponding to *ə* may be considered variants of *i*, and the back pronunciations, variants of *u*[2]; some of the more central *ə*-sounds are replaced by more *i*-like or *u*-like sounds, varying locally. For example:

nə́si	= *nísi*	*bəthə́tt*	= *bithútt*	
šə́ǧəl	= *šúǧul*	*byəktə́b-lak*	= *byiktíb-lak* or *b(y)uktúb-lak*	
bihə́bb	= *bihíbb*	*kəll*	= *kill* or *kull*	

In Lebanon, furthermore, many speakers generally do not differentiate between word-final *e* and *i* or between *o* and *u*. In their pronunciation *wárde* 'a rose' sounds just like *wárdi* 'rose-colored', and *tárako* 'he left it', like *táraku* 'they left'.

Before a word-final consonant, the difference between short *e* and *i* and between *o* and *u* is not significant in any case, and is subject to a great deal of regional and individual variation: *mə́šmoš* = *múšmuš*, *byə́hmel* = *byíhmil*.

The system of six short vowels represented in our transcription, then, is for some speakers reducible to five (eliminating *ə*), and for still others is perhaps reducible to three (eliminating also *e* and *o*). Note, however, that the actual differences in pronunciation implied by these reductions are slight, and — with the exception of word-final *o* vs. *u* and *e* vs. *i* — functionally insignificant.

There is one noteworthy variation in the occurrence (distribution) of the short vowel *a*. In central and northern Lebanon, and to some extent elsewhere, unaccented *a* before a single consonant disappears in many kinds of words: *mşári* (for *maşári*), *bárke* or *bárki* (for *bárake*), *mádərse* or *mádərsi* (for *madrase*), *l-hawn* (for *la-hón*), *Elayk* (for *Ealék*), *tEállmet* (for *tEállamet*), *zmēn* (for *zamān*).

---

[1] The functional autonomy of *ə* is marginal at best. (Its contrast with *i* can be heard in the phrase *ʔíza ʔə́ža* 'if he comes'.) Some speakers, however, usually pronounce *ʔə́za* instead of *ʔíza*; for them the difference is (if anything) stylistic, like that between *mə́mken* and *múmken* 'possible'. The use of *ə* in these words (for some speakers) is more informal or "folksy", while *i* and *u* are more elegant or Classical-sounding.

[2] Insofar as *i* and *u* merge with *ə*, they cannot be equated with *y* and *w*. This is because the sequences *-yí-* and *-wú-* (corresponding to *-yə́-* and *-wə́-*) remain distinct from *-í-* and *-ú-*, respectively. For example *l-wuld* 'the descendants' (= *l-wəld*) is not pronounced *"l-ūld"*. (If *i* = *y* and *u* = *w*, then *yi* = *ī*, *wu* = *ū*.)

Before two consonants (or a long consonant) in certain kinds of words, unaccented *a* is not lost but is changed to *ə* in these dialects (or to *i* before *y*, *u* before *w*): *bərṭált* (for *bartált*), *nəžžár* (for *nažžár*), *ẓəʕlə́n* (for *ẓaʕlán*), *siyyára* (for *sayyára*), *buwwáb* (for *bawwáb*).

Long Vowels

Five long vowels are found in most kinds of Syrian Arabic, but there are some notable divergences in the way these vowels are distributed in various kinds of words, as well as in their pronunciation.

In the more typical Lebanese dialects, the vowels *ē* and *ō* are replaced in most words[1] by the diphthongs *ay* and *aw*, respectively: *bayt* 'house' (for *bēt*), *hawn* 'here' (for *hōn*), *ʕ(a)láy* 'on it' (for *ʕalḗ*). In some words *ō* remains, however, notably in masculine/singular imperatives: *drōs* 'study', *kōl* 'eat'.

The vowel *ē* in these dialects (when not replaced by *ay*) is commonly replaced by *ɛ̄* — a sound slightly lower[2] than *ē*: *nzɛ́l* 'come down' (for *nzḗl*), *baɛdɛ́n* 'then, afterwards' (for *baɛdḗn*), *ʔamɛ́rka* 'America' (for *ʔamḗrka*). In still other words, it is replaced by *ī*: *līra* 'pound' (monetary) (for *lḗra*), *ʔī* 'yes' (for *ʔḗ*).

The vowel *ē*, then, is virtually eliminated from this type of Lebanese Arabic, but another vowel, *ɛ̄*, is very similar to it and more or less takes its place in the vowel system (though in individual words *ɛ̄* corresponds to *ā* more often than to *ē*; see below).

In a part of northern Lebanon (Tripoli and vicinity) the sound *ɛ̄* — instead of *ay* — also replaces *ē* in most closed syllables: *bɛ̄t* 'house' (for *bēt*), while *ay* is used in open syllables: *báyti* 'my house'. Similarly, the vowel *ā* — but with a low back pronunciation like that of the *a* in 'father' — replaces *ō* in most closed syllables: *māt* 'death' (for *mōt*), while *aw* replaces *ō* in open syllables: *máwtu* 'his death'. In some words, however, *ē*, as well as *ō*, is kept — notably in imperatives: *ḥmēl* 'carry', *ʔɛ̄ōd* 'sit'. This dialect, then, has six long vowels.

In these dialects *ɛ̄* replaces *ā*, almost everywhere the relatively high front pronunciation of *ā* is called for [p.11]: *tɛ̄ni* 'second' (for *tā́ni*), *mbɛ̄reḥ* 'yesterday' (for *mbā́reḥ*), *ktɛ̄b* 'book' (for *ktāb*).[3]

---

[1]Usually words whose Classical equivalents have *ay* or *aw*. (Note, however, *hawn* = Cl. *hunā*).

[2]Not as low as IPA [ɛ], however, which is in the *a*-territory of Arabic.

[3]*ā* and *ɛ̄* are almost — but not quite — in complementary distribution. Compare the disjunctive pronoun *yɛ̄* 'him, it' with the conjunction *yā* 'either, or'.

In the Aleppo region and to some extent elsewhere, the sound *ē* (rather than *ế*) replaces *ā* in various kinds of words, e.g. *fēteḥ* 'having opened', *ǧwếmeɛ* 'mosques' (for *ǧawắmeɛ*).

> This more extreme type of *ʔimāla* (raising of *a*) is much less general and automatic than the Lebanese raising of *ā* to *ế*. While the contrast between *ā* and *ế* is rarely signif- icant in the more typical[1] Lebanese dialects, that between *ā* and *ē* in Aleppo is quite often used to differentiate words that are otherwise alike. While the word *bắred*, for instance, meaning both 'cold' and 'stupid', is automatically converted to *bếred* in Lebanon, the Aleppo dialect distinguishes be- tween *bếred* 'cold' and *bắred* 'stupid'.

LENGTH *(al-madd wat-tašdīd)*

All the sounds have a long and a short version except *ǝ*, which is always short.

The main difference between long and short sounds is simply the rela-. tive length of time the articulation is held.[2] Long consonants, how- ever, are held not only longer but generally also "tighter" than short ones.[3]

> Modulations in volume, fundamental pitch, and tone quality interact with the actual time values in a complex way, to produce the overall rhythmic effect analyzed as "length". For practical purposes English-speaking learners should concentrate on the time element and let the other aspects of length "take care of themselves". Note, however, the somewhat different qualities of the long and short vowels *a*, *i*, and *u* [pp. 9, 11].

> English speakers should take pains not to drawl accented short vowels, which — in order not to sound long — must be clipped quite short, e.g. *ʔắwi* (not *"ʔāwi"*), *bard* (not *"bārd"*).

---

[1] Excluding the Tripoli-type dialect where *ā* may replace *ō:* *mết* 'he died' vs. *māt* [maːt] or [mɐːt] 'death'.

[2] The single tap of the tongue in a short *r*, however, cannot be "held"; long *rr* consists in repetions of the tap, i.e. in a multiple trill.

[3] The rare instances of triple consonants, as in *šakkkon* 'your (pl.) suspicion' (*šakk* + *kon*) can be pronounced still longer than double consonants (as in *šakko* 'his suspicion'), but they are normally reduced to the same length as double ones.

When reading from transcription, learners must be specially alert to the indications of length. Since doubled letters in English orthography (and the macron in English orthoepy) have nothing to do with length, English speakers sometimes forget to respond properly to these signs in Arabic transcription.

Contrastive examples:

Consonants:

Short		Long	
kátab	'to write'	káttab	'to have(s.o.)write'
ġáni	'rich'	ġánni	'sing'
mára	'a woman'	márra	'a time'
nṣśbo	'plant it'	nṣśbbo	'let's pour it'
saddáʔət	'you told the truth'	saddáʔət	'I believed (it)'
hamā́m	'pigeons'	hammā́m	'bath'
siyā́si	'political, politician'	siyyā́si	'my grooms'
būsha	'kiss her'	bbūsha	'I kiss her'
b-əžnḗne	'in a garden'	bəž-žnḗne	'in the garden'

Vowels:

Short		Long	
kátab	'to write'	kā́tab	'to write to(s.o.)'
málek	'king'	mā́lek	'owner'
Ɛáli	(a name)	Ɛā́li	'high'
sáƐa	'to endeavor'	sā́Ɛa	'hour', 'clock'
dawwára	'he wound it(f.)'	dawwā́ra	'gadabout(f.)'
sáwa	'together'	sā́wa	'to do, make'
wardát	'flowers'	wārdā́t	'imports'
ríʔa	'lung'	rī́ʔa	'her saliva'
l-kúra	'the globe, the ball'	l-kū́ra	(name of a village)

Short vowel + long consonant contrasted with long vowel + short consonant:

kammel	'continue, finish'	*kā̆mel*	'whole, complete'
náyyem	'put(s.o.)to sleep'	*nā̆yem*	'asleep'
mdáwwara	'round(f.)'	*mdā̆wara*	'evasion'
daḥḥakū̃	'they made him laugh'	*ḍāḥakū̃*	'they laughed with him'

On the neutralization of length contrasts in certain positions, see p. 27.

An accented long vowel — which is always the last long vowel in a word — is generally pronounced longer than an unaccented (pretonic) long vowel. In *ʕālā̆f*, for instance, the first *ā* is not as long as the second (but is longer than a short *a*).

Short vowels, on the other hand, are apt to be longer <u>after</u> the accent than they are when accented. In *sábab*, for instance, the second *a* is usually longer than the first if it comes at the end of a phrase, since the end of a phrase is often signalled by drawling out what comes <u>after</u> the accent, while an accented short vowel itself cannot be drawled.
With certain kinds of intonation — in questions, for instance — the phrase-end drawl is often exaggerated so that a post-tonic short vowel is as long as or longer than a true <u>long</u> vowel in other positions. In the question *kīf ḥā̆lak?* 'How are you?', the last *a* may actually be longer than the *ā* in the preceding syllable.

The vowel *ə*, however, is not only never long in the formal sense, but is also relatively insusceptible to phrase-end drawling. While the *e* in *fə́hmet?* 'Did she understand?' is drawled, the *ə* in *fhə́mᵊt?* 'Did you understand?' is not — at least not as much as other short vowels are.

ACCENTUATION

In words of two or more syllables, one of the syllables — the AC-CENTED syllable — usually sounds more stressed[1] or prominent than the others. With certain kinds of exceptions, the accentuation of a transcribed word may be deduced from its boundaries and its syllable structure.

---

[1] The term 'stress' is perhaps better avoided, since it is too suggestive of force, loudness, and emphasis. Not only is Arabic word-accent less "forceful" and "stressful" than that of English, but it also seems that accentual systems in general are more a matter of pitch and tempo modulation than of variations in loudness or "volume".

A syllable is considered LONG if its vowel is long or followed by a long consonant or by a group of more than one consonant.[1]

The general rule of accentuation is this: The last long syllable in a word is accented; if there is no long syllable, then the first syllable is accented. [But see also p. 20, (4).]

Examples:

Final Syllable Long	Penult Long	Antepenult or None Long
darastū́	darastū́ha	dárasu
darást	dardstu	dáraso
barrī́d	baráde	bə́rado
byəsmaɛū́k	byəsmáɛkon	byə́smaɛu
mawádd	madáres	mádrase
ftáḥ	fátḥet	fátaḥu
bətʔū́l	bətʔál-lha	bə́dalo
tɛallámt	tɛál lam	tɛál lamet
ʔamsā́l	mással	másalan

When accent marks are omitted, it will be understood that the word is accented according to this general rule. (In certain parts of this book, however, accent marks are used, redundantly, even when the general rule is followed.)

Proclitics

In this transcription certain particles are attached to the following word by a hyphen. These particles — PROCLITICS — are never accented; the accentuation of the word is reckoned as if the proclitic were not there: hal-wálad (not "hál-walad", which the general rule would yield if the hyphen were ignored), ka-wáṣi, ləl-ɛášа, raḥa-tə́ṣal, w-la-has-sábab.

Proclitics include the article l- [p. 493], the demonstrative particle hal- [556]; the conjunctions w-, fa- [391], n- [335], la- [358]; the prepositions b-, ka-, la-, ɛa- (apocopation of ɛala) [476]; the particle of antici-

---

[1]Every vowel marks the peak of a syllable. It is not necessary for present purposes to define syllable boundaries.

pation *raḥa–* and of actuality *ɛam–* [320].[1] (Certain combinations of particles are written as a single element:
ləṣ-ṣábi, bəl-ɛáks, ɛal-bálad, wən-šáfto. See pp.476,391 .)

The hyphenated suffixes *-l-* plus pronoun [480], unlike
the proclitics, count as part of the word (in respect to
accentuation, at least), and may themselves be accented in
some cases: *ʔəlt-állo, fatáḥ-lak, ḥaká-li, ʔaḥsál-lo.*

Length and Accent in Final Vowels

If a final vowel is accented, it is necessarily long, but if it is
unaccented, it varies between long and short depending on the phrasing and
intonation [pp.21,17]. Thus the *ī* in *xədī* is accented (i.e. *xədî*), while
the *i* in *xədi* is unaccented (i.e. *xədi*) but is sometimes actually long.

In the case of one-syllable words ending in a vowel, therefore, the
macron may be used to distinguish accented words from unaccented words[2]:
mā 'not' [383] vs. *ma* (subordinating conjunction [490]); *fī* 'in it, there
is' [415] vs. *fi* 'in'; *šū* 'what' [568] vs. *šu* 'well, why ...'. In all
these words the vowel is usually pronounced long.

If, on the other hand, a word such as these has a vowel
that is unaccented, short, and in close phrasing [21] with
the following word, then it is written as a proclitic:
fi-béti, ma-ʔátyabo.

The Helping Vowel ə

The vowel written 'ə' (which does not differ from ə in pronunciation,
but only in its morphological status [p.29]), is never accented, and is to
be ignored in reckoning the accentuation of a word. Thus *darasət* is accented on the second syllable (i.e. *darásət*), just as if the ə were not
there, as in *darást;* and *byəkətbu* is accented on the first syllable (i.e.
byə́kətbu), just as in *byə́ktbu.*

---

[1] Some proclitics are written as separate words: the prepositions *mən, ɛan,
ɛand,* and *ɛala;* the subordinating conjunction *ma* [490]. The policy has
been to hyphenate all proclitics which consist in a single consonant or
a consonant plus an actually <u>short</u> vowel, and all others except those
which are traditionally written separate in literary Arabic.

[2] This is actually a makeshift device, used in the absence of markings for
phrase-accent and intonation. A completely unambiguous transcription
would have to show length, accentuation, and intonation separately; but
since we do not mark phrase-accent (or junctures), the markings for length
(and word-accent) can be stretched a little beyond their proper function
to hint at the larger-scale prosodic features.

Further examples:

ləlᵖrki	(i.e. *tə́tərki*)	*ʔəbᵉnna*	(i.e. *ʔə́bənna*)
məšᵊmše	(i.e. *mə́šəmše*)	*fataḥ-ᵊlkon*	(i.e. *fatáḥ-əlkon*)
baƐᵊdkon	(i.e. *bə́Ɛədkon*)	*tƐallamᵊt*	(i.e. *tƐallámət*)
Ɛərᵊwto	(i.e. *Ɛə́rəwto*)	*māwarᵊd*	(i.e. *māwárəd*)

Exceptions to the General Rule of Accentuation

(1) A short syllable (as well as a long one) is accented before the pronoun suffixes *-a* 'her, it, its' and *-on* 'their, them' [p.541]: *darába* 'he hit her' (cf. *ḍárabo* 'he hit him'), *šáfə́ton* 'she saw them', *sakkə́ra* 'close it', *ḥālə́ton* 'their condition', *ʔabúwa* 'her father'.

> These suffixes may also be pronounced *-ha, -hon*, which makes the accentuation regular: *darábha, šáfə́thon, sakkə́rha, ḥālə́thon, ʔabúha.*

(2) With certain kinds of verb stem, the verbal subject-affix *-et* 'she, it' is accented (taking the form *-ə́t-*) before all the pronoun suffixes, including *-o* 'him, it', *-ak* 'you(m.)', and *-ek* 'you(f.)': *fahhamə́tak* 'she explained to you(m.)', *šāwarə́tek* 'she consulted you(f.)', *snāwalə́to* 'she caught it(m.)'. See p.181 for details.

(3) Words having certain base forms are accented on their short middle syllable instead of the first syllable: *byəštə́ǧel* 'he works', *bəftə́ker* 'I think', *byənḥə́ka* 'it is told', *məxtə́lef* 'different', *muttə́ḥed* 'united', *muʔtə́mar* 'conference', *mənʔə́ri* '(having been)read'.

These words are sound and defective verbs of Patterns VII [p.91] and VIII [95] in the imperfect without suffixes, and adjectives and nouns of the corresponding participial forms [135].

> Generally in Lebanon and Palestine, however, many words of this kind are accented regularly, on the first syllable (and generally without any middle vowel ə): *byə́štǧel, bə́ftker, mə́xtlef.* (With suffixes of any kind, however, the accentuation of these words with vowels ə and e is regular in any case: *byəštə́ǧlu, məftə́kro, məxtə́lfe* [p.31, bottom].)

(4) There are a few classicisms of four or more syllables whose last three syllables are all short. The accent, however, is not in any case farther front than third from the end (the antepenult): *muttáḥide* 'united (f.)' (cf. the pure colloquial form *məttə́ḥde*).

> The general rule of accentuation could be broadened to cover cases like this simply by adding a stipulation that no words are to be accented farther forward than the antepenult. Ordinary Syrian Arabic words have a syllabic

structure that makes this stipulation unnecessary: when
both of the last two syllables are short and unaccented,
the antepenult is either the first syllable or a long
syllable (or both).

These four kinds of exception to the general rule will always be
transcribed with an accent mark. The other exceptions — indicated by
hyphenization or by the raised letter ᵊ — will not usually carry an
accent mark, which for them is redundant.

SOUND COMBINATIONS

Phrasing

In CLOSE PHRASING, words are "run together", i.e. the last sound of
one word flows into the first sound of the next word as if they were in
the same word: *bəddna͜nzūro* 'We intend to visit him', *laḥm͜ᵊl-baʔar*
'beef' (lit. "meat of cattle"), *la-wēn͜bəddak͜ᵊtrūḥ?* 'Where do you want
to go?' [DA-143].

In OPEN PHRASING, words are slightly "separated" — not by any actual
pause, but by subtle modifications in the sounds at the word boundary.
The last part of the first word is often reduced in volume, while the
onset of the next word is relatively loud. The end of the first word is
sometimes drawled [p.17]. The last sound is never assimilated to the
first sound of the next word [24], nor are they ever linked by the help-
ing vowel [30]. For example: *bɡənn|baɛᵊrfo* 'I think I know him', *tfaḍḍal|
strīḥ* 'Please have a seat', *raḥa-nəbʔa|šī͜kam͜yōm* [DA-93] 'We're going to
stay a few days'.

Within any close phrase, one word is somewhat more strongly accented
than the others. In phrases, then, there are three degrees of accentuation, including the unaccented syllables. (The main accent of a phrase
may be marked ´, the subordinate accents, `): *bə̀ddna͜nzűro|báɛᵊd͜bə̀kra*
'We're going to see him the day after tomorrow'; *ʔiza͜mã́͜mənḥə̀bbo|mnã̄xod͜
ɡḗro* 'If we don't like it we'll get another' [DA-143].

In general, words are individually discriminable even in close phrasing, since each word (excepting certain particles) has one — and only one
— accent (main or subordinate).[1] Word boundaries, too, may sometimes be
"heard", even in close phrasing, because there are some sound combinations
which occur at word boundaries but not within words, and vice versa.

Phrasing is closely related to intonation, but not
wholly determined by intonation. Neither phrasing nor
intonation has been thoroughly or surely enough analyzed

---

[1] In actual running speech there are many stretches in which the accentuation — hence also the phonological autonomy of words — is indeterminate. The statement really applies only in certain (ideal) conditions.

for further treatment here. Nor are they ordinarily shown in our transcription, except when clearly essential in exemplifying certain grammatical constructions.

In the following sections of this chapter the term 'word' designates a sequence of sounds with only one accent (main or subordinate) and with no open phrasing between them. The term 'phrase' designates a sequence of words in close phrasing.

Vowel Positions

Vowels in general come only after consonants. That is to say, phrases do not begin with a vowel, but they may end with a vowel; and one vowel does not ordinarily come right after another.

Certain kinds of words, on the other hand, begin with a vowel when they follow certain words that end in a consonant: *tlǝtt ˌiyyām* 'three days', *xamst ˌǝšhor* 'five months' [p.171], *wlād ˌaxú* 'his brother's children'.

Exceptions.- Commonly in Lebanese pronunciation, and to some extent elsewhere, a short vowel *a*, *o*, or *u* (in the suffixes *-a* 'her, it', and *-on* or *-un* 'them, their' [p.541]) may follow a long accented vowel: *btǝˀrāon* (or *btǝˀrāun*) 'she reads them' (for *btǝˀrāhon*), *ɛalēa* (or *ɛaléya*) 'on it' (for *ɛalēha*).

In the case of *ū* and *ī*, we write *-uw-* and *-iy-*, respectively, before a vowel: *ˀabúwa* 'her father' (for *ˀabūha*), *nsíyon* 'forget(f.)them' (for *nsīhon*). This is merely a transcriptional convention, however; one might just as well write *ˀabūa, nsīon*.

By the same token we write *w* and *y* (the consonantal guise of the semivowels) at the beginning of a phrase before a consonant, or at the end of a phrase after a vowel; *wlādi mū ˌhōn* 'My children are not here', *šrāb ˌǝš-šāy* 'Drink the tea' — when in some instances the semivowels in these positions could just as well be considered syllabic: *ulādi, šāi*.

Particular Limitations. In the system of six short vowels, only *a* occurs in all types of vowel position.

1) *ǝ* does not occur at the end of a word.

2) *e* and *o* almost never occur accented, and rarely in open syllables except word-finally.

3) *i* and *u* (insofar as they are distinguished from *e* and *o* [p.13]) do not occur before a word-final consonant.

With regard to frequencies, it may be noted that *i*, *e*,
u, and *o* are rare within a word before two or more consonants (*ə* generally replacing all of them [pp.28,13]).
Classicisms, however, often have *u* before two consonants:
bukra 'tomorrow' (for *bəkra*), *mumken* 'possible' (for *məmken*), *mulḥaq* 'attaché'. (These considerations do not apply
to varieties of Arabic that have no distinctive vowel *ə*
[p.13].) Sometimes a long vowel before two consonants is
shortened: *ʔittēn* 'two hands' (for *ʔīdtēn*), *ʔamerkāniyye*
'American(f.)' (for *ʔamērkāniyye*).

The long vowels have no special positional limitations except those
implied in the general rule of accentuation: that a (distinctively) long
vowel does not occur post-tonically, since the last long syllable in a
word is accented.

Single and Double Consonants

Any single (i.e. short) consonant may occur initially, medially, or
finally, before or after any vowel.

This statement does not apply to the semivowels (*y*, *w*),
however; *y* and *w* almost never occur finally after *e* or *o*,
and *y* almost never occurs after *ə*.[1] The sequences *iy* and
uw are not distinguishable from the long vowels *ī* and *ū*,
respectively.

Any double (i.e. long) consonant may occur medially, between vowels.
Examples: *rabbi*, *ḥatta*, *bəddo*, *barrīd*, *šāzze*, *ražžāl*, *ḥazzo*, *səllom*,
ɛammi, *ʔūttēn*, *səkkīr*, *baʔʔa*, *faɛɛāl*, *fahhem*, *baḥḥāra*, *ʔaxxēn*, *šaġġīl*,
ṭayyeb, *wiyyāk*, *ɛaliyyi*, *ḥayyo*, *nawwamo*, *xawwīf*, *huwwe*.

In initial position, double consonants are limited to those formed by
the combination of a prefix or proclitic with the first stem consonant[2],
and since there happen to be no prefixes or proclitics that take the form
of the consonants *f*, *g*, *ġ*, *h*, *ḥ*, *k*, *q*, *x*, *ɛ*, or *ʔ* before another consonant, these do not occur doubled initially. Examples: *bbaxšeš*, *ttafaʔna*,
ddaḥraž, *mməll*, *nnām*, *ṭṭalaɛ*, *l-lōn*, *r-rabīɛ*, *z-zābeṭ*, *ṣ-ṣifāt*, *s-suʔāl*,
ḍ-ḍarb, *w-walado*.

In final position, any double consonant may occur after an accented
vowel. At the end of a phrase, however, long consonants (like long
vowels) do not actually contrast with short ones; writing them double
simply serves to show the position of the accent and their potential

---

[1] Exceptions are *ḥəyi* 'to be revived' and *ɛəyi* 'to weaken, get sick'.
Certain local dialects are more tolerant of combinations like *əy*. The
dialect of Zaḥle, for instance, has phrase-final forms like *nəsəy* 'to
forget' (instead of *nəsi*).

[2] Very few Arabic roots [p.37] have first and second consonants alike, and
the few that do, do not occur in base patterns [36] that juxtapose them.

significant length before vowels [p.27], Examples: *ʔaḥabb, xaff, mawādd, biḥəzz, səžəll, qšaɛarr, ḥaʔʔ*.

In many parts of Greater Syria (including Damascus) long consonants ,seldom occur before another consonant, except in sequences involving the article [p.493] or demonstrative [556] proclitics or the person suffix *-t* [175]: *z-zbūn* 'the customer', *har-ržāl* 'these men', *baɛattna* 'you sent us'.

Our transcription, however, shows other double consonants in this position, which are commonly pronounced short but which correspond to long consonants in other forms of the same word, before a vowel [p.28]: *waʔʔfi* 'stop(f.)', commonly pronounced *waʔfi;* cf. the masculine *waʔʔef* 'stop'. In some parts of Greater Syria these double consonants are pronounced long, optionally at least, in all positions. Examples: *bɛarrfak, fahhmūni, ṭawwlo, mḥayyrətni, ʔəl-lha, rabbkon, ṭaʔʔ ̮ḥanak, tlətt ̮marrāt.*

Two-Consonant Clusters

Across word boundaries, any sequence of two contiguous consonants may occur (though in close phrasing there is a tendency to eliminate certain ʺawkwardʺ clusters by assimilation: *rāɛ ̮ɛal-balad* for *rāḥ ̮ɛal-balad* 'he went to town').

Within a word, almost any sequence of two consonants may occur, with the following exceptions:

- (1) The back consonants *x, ġ, ḥ,* and *ɛ* do not ordinarily come next to one another, nor does *h* precede these sound, though it may follow them; and *k* and *g* do not precede *x* or *ġ*, though *k* may follow them.

(2) In a sequence of two dental obstruents (*d, ḍ, t, ṭ, s, ṣ, z, ẓ*), it is usually the case that both are velarized or both plain, and very seldom that one is velarized while the other is plain [p.26]. Examples (plain): *staxaff, bətsəbb, zdād, ʔaxadto;* (velarized): *ṣṭāḍ, bəṭṣəbb, məḍṭarr, ḥafaẓṭo.*

(3) A voiced consonant does not occur 'at the end of a phrase immediately after a voiceless one. (Note that in a sequence like *ḥəfẓ,* the *f* is voiced: *ḥəvẓ.*)

(4) The resonants (*l, m, n, r*) and the consonantal versions of the semivowels (*w, y*) are almost never heard immediately after another consonant at the end of a phrase, except that *m* and *n* sometimes occur after *l* or *r*: *ɛəlm, fərn* (or *ɛəlᵊm, fərᵊn*).

In final position, many other two-consonant clusters are less common than they are initially or medially, since potential clusters tend to be prevented by the ʺhelping vowelʺ *ᵊ*. See p.32.

Two-consonant final clusters are considerably more common in Palestine than farther north. In Syria and Lebanon one hears, for instance, either *bənt* or *bən³t* 'girl', while in most parts of Palestine the latter is seldom or never heard.

Three-Consonant Clusters

Sequences of three contiguous consonants virtually never occur finally. Initially, they are mainly limited to a few beginning with *st-*: *strîḥ, stfîd, stmanna.*

Otherwise three-consonant clusters are fairly common. The first two consonants may be any two than can occur together finally. The third — if it begins a new word in the phrase — may be any consonant at all: *bənt ‿ḥəlwe, ɛand‿tāžer, baṇk‿xāli, ḍarb‿ʔawi, sfənž‿ḡāli, kətf‿ɛarîd, ʔamḥ‿ʔarādîhon.* (But more usually *kət³f‿, ʔam³ḥ‿*, in Syria proper and Lebanon.)

Within a word, the third consonant of a cluster has to be compatible with the second as in a two-consonant cluster (e.g. *x* would not follow *ḥ*, etc.).

Many words with three-consonant clusters have optional variants with a helping vowel between the first two: *fatḥto* (or more usually *fat³ḥto*), *byəktbu* (or more usually *byək³tbu*), *təmski* (less usually *təm³ski*). Certain clusters, however, cannot be broken in this way. [See p. 33.]

Examples of three-consonant clusters within words: *ʔrəmfle, ɛandkon, ʔənglîzi, məstwiyye, bənd³iyye, bərd³ān, bəntkon, sānaɛtna, byəstrîḥ, məškle, byəštḡel* (Leb., Pal.), *byənkser* (Leb., Pal.), *ʔarbɛa.*

Three-consonant internal clusters are most common with a resonant or sibilant as the first consonant, and/or a dental stop as the second.

When a word or proclitic ending in one consonant is followed in close phrasing by a word beginning with two consonants, a helping vowel almost always keeps them apart, so that three-consonant clusters are not generally formed in this way. There are a few exceptions, however, e.g. *hal-blād* 'this country' (more usually *hal-³blād*).

There are no clusters of four or more consonants.[1]

---

[1] All these statements, of course, apply only within a close phrase [p. 21]. Sequences of consonants formed by words in open phrasing do not count as clusters; thus open phrases such as *tfaḍḍal|strîḥ* 'Please have a seat', *w-ʔəlt|xrās* 'And I said, "Be quiet!"' can have four or more consonants in a row, but the sequence is interrupted by a phrase boundary.

GENERAL SOUND CHANGES

The diverse concatenations of stem and affix, and of words within a phrase, require certain adaptive changes in form, in accordance with the allowable sound combinations of the language [p. 21].

Besides obligatory changes, there are also similar changes which are optional, whereby allowable but sometimes awkward combinations may be avoided.

Velarization

A plain dental obstruent (t, d, s, z), when brought into the neighborhood of a velarized dental obstruent in the same word, generally becomes velarized too (ṭ, ḍ, ṣ, ẓ). Thus the second-person affixes t- and -t [p. 175] become ṭ- and -ṭ, as in baṭṣəbb 'you pour' (cf. batsəbb 'you curse'), bṭəḍrob 'you hit' (cf. btədros 'you study'), ṣərṭ 'you became' (cf. zərt 'you visited'). Similarly the connective t [p. 163], as in ʔūḍṭo 'his room' (cf. ɛādto 'his habit'). The root consonant d of ṣayyād 'hunter' is changed to ḍ when it is closer to the initial ṣ, as in ṣēḍ 'hunting, game'.[1]

Since the scope of velarization tends to be rather vague [p. 7], a dental that is relatively far removed from the focus of velarization may not be affected, or may be very slightly affected. Thus ṣāret 'she became', with a plain t, or with the t slightly velarized; tfaḍḍal 'please'(invitational), with a plain t, or with velarization: ṭfaḍḍal.

As noted on p. 7, sounds other than dental obstruents are also velarized in assimilation to ṭ, ḍ, ṣ, or ẓ, but this assimilation is not indicated in our transcription.

Devoicing

A single dental or palatal voiced obstruent tends to be devoiced (d → t, ḍ → ṭ, z → s, ẓ → ṣ, ž → š) before voiceless obstruents. Devoicing is not obligatory, however; its incidence increases as speech becomes faster or more casually enunciated, and is more common in certain words and phrases than in others. It is less common in medial clusters than in final or initial clusters. Examples: štamaɛu (for žtamaɛu) 'they gathered' (intrans.), ʔūṭṭ ən-nōm (for ʔūḍṭ ən-nōm) 'the bedroom', ʔaxatto (for

---

[1]Most roots [p. 37] which theoretically contain both plain and velarized dentals (judging from Classical spelling or from historical or comparative data), in fact usually have only velarized dentals in Syrian pronunciation: b-ṣ-ṭ (as in baṣīṭ 'minor, simple'), which is theoretically b-s-ṭ; ḍ-ḍ-ḍ (as in ḍaḍḍ 'against'), theoretically ḍ-d-ḍ; ɛ-ṭ-ṣ (as in ɛaṭaṣ 'to sneeze'), theoretically ɛ-ṭ-s. Note, however, the form ɛaṭṣe 'a sneeze', alongside the expected form ɛaṭṣa [p. 138], which suggests that a plain s has sometimes been maintained after ṭ.

ʔ*axadto*) 'I took it', *l-ʔəts* (for *l-ʔəds*) 'Jerusalem'.

Assimilation of *n*

The sound *n* often becomes *m* before labials: *Čambar* 'storehouse' (cf. the plural *Čanāber* 'storehouses'), *məmmūt* (or *mənmūt*) 'we die', ʔ*əmf* (or ʔ*ənf*) 'nose', *məm bērūt* (or *mən bērūt*) 'from Beirut'.

n also commonly assimilates to the other resonants, *l* and *r:* ʔ*aḥsal-lak* (or ʔ*aḥsan-lak*) 'better for you', *r-rāḥ* (or *n-rāḥ*) 'if he goes'.

Neutralization of Length

A vowel that is long within a word or when accented loses its distinctive length when unaccented at the end of a word:

Non-Final		Final Accented		Final Unaccented	
nəsîha	'he forgot her'	*nəsî*	'he forgot him' ...	*nəsi*	'he forgot'
warāk	'behind you(m.)' ...	*warā*	'behind him'	*wara*	'behind'
Čašāhon	'their dinner'	*Čašā*	'his dinner'	*Čaša*	'dinner'
šāfūni	'they saw me'	*šāfū*	'they saw him'	*šāfu*	'they saw'
ḥkî-li	'tell me'	*ḥkî*	'tell it'	ʔ*əḥki*	'tell, speak'
ʔ*awiyye*[1]	'strong(f.)'			ʔ*awi*	'strong(m.)'

This kind of vowel alternation occurs mainly in connection with pronoun suffixes [p. 539], and the number and gender suffixes of nouns and adjectives [203, 211].

A consonant that is long before a vowel tends to lose its distinctive length before another consonant or at the end of a phrase. [See p. 24 for qualifications.] This loss of length is not shown in our transcription.

Long	Short (or Indistinctively Long)
biḥəbbo 'he likes it'	*biḥəbbna* 'he likes us'
bəthəbb ə̆š-šāy? 'Do you like tea?'	*bəthəbb təšrab šāy?* 'Would you like to have some tea?'
mət ʔassef 'sorry(m.)'	*mət ʔassfe* 'sorry(f.)'
naṭṭ ə̆ṣ-ṣabi 'the boy jumped'	*ṣ-ṣabi naṭṭ* (same translation)

---

[1] The spelling *-iy-* is equivalent to *-î-*.

Neutralization of Vowel Quality

Short *e* and *o* coming after the accented syllable before a word-final single consonant both become *ə* when accented. [p.22]

Unaccented			Accented	
tɛallamet	'she learned'	..... *tɛallamə́to*	'she learned it'	
byəlbes	'he wears'	.... *byəlbə́sa*	'he wears it(f.)'	
byəḍrob	'he hits'	.... *byəḍrə́bon*	'he hits them'	
ɛəmel	'he did'	.... *ɛmə́lt*	'you(or I) did'	
ʔənṣol	'consul'	.... *ʔənṣə́lna*	'our consul'	
səmeɛ	'he heard'	.... *səmə́ɛkon*	'he heard you(pl.)'	
btəktob	'you(m.)write'	.... *btəktə́b-ᵊlna*	'you write to us'	

In those varieties of Syrian Arabic which have no distinctive vowel *ə* [p.13], neutralization of the front and back vowels may nevertheless take place. For example (in a dialect of north central Lebanon): *btiktub* 'you write', but *btiktíba* 'you write it(f.)', with post-tonic *u* becoming tonic *i*. Other varieties, however, maintain the distinction under the accent. For example (in a Palestinian dialect): *btuktub* 'you write', and *btuktúbha* 'you write it' vs. *btimsik* 'you hold' and *btimsíkha* 'you hold it'.

Loss of *e* and *o*

Short *e* and *o* do not ordinarily occur before a single consonant + vowel within a word.[1] With a few exceptions, all words that have *e* or *o* before a final consonant lose this vowel when any suffix beginning with a vowel (except *-a* 'her', *-on* 'them' [p.541]) is added:

mɛallem	'teacher'	+ *-īn* (pl.)	→ *mɛallmín*	'teachers'	
xānom	'lady'	+ *-āt* (pl.)	→ *xānmāt*	'ladies'	
bāred	'cold(m.)'	+ *-e* (fem.)	→ *bārde*	'cold(f.)'	
ṭəleɛ	'he came out'	+ *-u* (pl.)	→ *ṭəlɛu*	'they came out'	
btəskon	'you(m.)dwell'	+ *-i* (fem.)	→ *btəskni*	'you(f.)dwell'	
šāyef	'seeing'	+ *-o* 'it(m.)'	→ *šāyfo*	'seeing it'	

---

[1] Certain foreign loan-words break this rule, e.g. *ʔotēl* 'hotel'.

šāfet 'she saw'	+ *-ek* 'you(f.)'	→ *šāftek*	'she saw you(f.)'
bāxod 'I'll take'	+ *-ak* 'you(m.)'	→ *bāxdak*	'I'll take you(m.)'
sāƐet 'watch of...'	+ *-i* 'me'	→ *sāƐti*	'my watch'

This rule does not apply to words in which the *e* or *o* comes between like consonants the first of which is double. In these cases *e* or *o* is changed to *ə*: *bisabbeb* 'it causes' + *-u* (pl.) → *bisabbəbu* 'they cause'; *taxaṣṣoṣ* 'specialization' + *-ak* 'you' · *taxaṣṣəṣak* 'your specialization'.

Any combination of dental stops (*t, d, ṭ, ḍ*) also counts as "like consonants": *fəḍḍeṭ* 'silver of...' + *-ek* 'your(f.)' → *fəḍḍəṭek* 'your silver'.

This rule also does not apply to certain nouns and adjectives — mainly classicisms — in which the *e* or *o* is usually changed to *i* or *u* (respectively): *muttáḥed* 'united (m.)' + *-e* (fem.) → *muttáḥide, malek* 'king' + *-e* (fem.) → *malike* 'queen', *taṣarrof* 'behavior' + *-āt* (pl.) → *taṣarrufāt* (but note *taṣarrfo* 'his behavior').

Anaptyxis

When there is a confrontation of consonants which cannot form a cluster, an **ANAPTYCTIC** or **HELPING VOWEL** *ə* is used as a transition between them.

To avoid a cluster of three or four consonants, the helping vowel is inserted before the last two:

l-	'the'	+ *ktāb* 'book'	→ *l-ᵊktāb*	'the book'
bənt	'girl'	+ *ẓġīre* 'little'	→ *bəntᵕᵊẓġīre*	'a little girl'
laḥm	'meat'	+ *baʔar* 'cattle'	→ *laḥᵊmᵕbaʔar*	'beef'
bəktob	'I'll write'	+ *-lkon* 'to you(pl.)'	→ *bəktᵊb-ᵊlkon*	'I'll write to you'
bəḥmel	'I'll carry'	+ *-o*	'it' (with loss of *e*)	→ *bᵊḥᵊmlo*	'I'll carry it'

At the end of a phrase, a <u>two</u>-consonant cluster is often avoided by inserting the helping vowel between them:

šū 'what'	+ *hal-* 'this' + *ʔakl* 'food'	→ *šū hal-ʔakᵊl*	'What is this food?'
ʔakl 'eating'	+ *l-* 'the' + *laḥm* 'meat'	→ *ʔaklᵕᵊl-laḥᵊm*	'eating the meat' (or 'the eating of meat')

In our transcription ə is printed smaller and raised
above the line (ᵊ) when it occurs as a helping vowel, to
distinguish it from the kind of ə that is an integral part
of the word. The pronunciation, however, is identical.

When ᵊ occurs between words, or between hyphenated
parts of a word, our convention is to write it always
<u>after</u> the space or hyphen.

Note that the helping vowel is never accented. Cf. the
affix-supporting vowel [p.31 (bottom), p.167].

Detailed rules for the use of the helping vowel:

(1) The Helping Vowel Between Words

Whenever a word ending in a consonant is followed in close phrasing by
a word beginning with two consonants (or a long consonant), a helping vowel
comes between them:

ržāl ᵊkbār	'big men'		sətt ᵊʔlām	'six pencils'
šāṭer ᵊktīr	'very clever'		ʔəbn ᵊt-tāžer	'the merchant's son'
rās ᵊž-žabal	'the top of the mountain'		kənt ᵊbbarṭel	'I would bribe'
mart ᵊl-ʔāḍi	'the judge's wife'		ʔām ᵊmmassel	'an actor got up'

(2) The Helping Vowel with Proclitics

With certain exceptions, the helping vowel is used between a proclitic
[p.18] ending in a consonant and the rest of the word beginning with two
consonants (or a double consonant):

l-ᵊblād	'the country'		hal-ᵊbḍāεa	'this merchandise'
l-ə ʔyās	'the measurement'		εam-ᵊnεallem	'we are teaching'
b-ᵊžbēl	'in Jubayl'		εam-ᵊttaržem	'she is translating'
n-ᵊštarā	'if he buys it'		bəl-ᵊmḥaṭṭa	'in the station'
ləl-ᵊwlād	'to the children'		raḥ-ᵊtkūn	'you're going to be'

A helping vowel is <u>not</u> used after the article [p.493] or the demonstrative [556] if the following consonant is one of those to which the l
of these proclitics is assimilated (t, d, ṭ, ḍ, s, z, ṣ, ẓ, š, ž, l, n, r):

z-zbūn	'the customer'	*haž-žsūra*	'these bridges'
r-rṣāṣa	'the bullet'	*ləz-zġîr*	'to the little one'
l-lḥāf	'the blanket'	*Ɛan-nsūra*	'about the vultures'[1]
hat-trēn	'this train'	*bəz-zmərrod*	'with the emeralds'

A helping vowel is also not used between the proclitic *Ɛam–* [p.320] and a following *b–* [176]: *Ɛam-bʔūl* 'I am saying', *Ɛam-byaʔder* 'he is able', *Ɛam-btəlƐab* 'you are playing'. (The *b–* in these forms is commonly elided: *Ɛam-ʔūl, Ɛam-yaʔder, Ɛam-təlƐab*.) [See also p.33]

(3) The Helping Vowel within Word Stems

If the stem vowel` e or o that is dropped when a suffix is added [p.28] is preceded by two (different) consonants, then its loss may cause a three-consonant cluster: *byəmsek + –u → byəmsku, bəndoʔ + –a → bəndʔa.*

More often, however, the three-consonant cluster is avoided by inserting a helping vowel before the last two consonants:

ʔatlet	'she killed'	+ –o	'him'	→	*ʔatəlto*	'she killed him'
raʔbe(t)	'neck(of)'	+ –o	'him'	→	*raʔəbto*	'his neck'
bədrob	'I'll hit'	+ –ak	'you'	→	*bəḍərbak*	'I'll hit you'
ġalṭet	'mistake of'	+ –i	'me'	→	*ġaləṭṭi*	'my mistake'
btəhmel	'you carry'	+ –u (pl.)		→	*btəhəmlu*	'you(pl.)carry'
kəlme(t)	'word'	+ –ēn (dual)		→	*kələmtēn*	'two words'
məslem	'Moslem'	+ –īn (pl.)		→	*məsəlmīn*	'Moslems'
məšmoš	'apricots'	+ –e (unit)		→	*məšəmše*	'an apricot'

In the examples above, the vowel that is dropped from the stem is preceded by a short vowel + two consonants.

If, on the other hand, the dropped vowel is preceded by a short vowel + three consonants, or by a long vowel + two consonants, then the potential cluster is broken by the vowel *ə*, but this is an accented vowel (unless the suffix itself is accented):

sənsle(t)	'chain(of)'	+ –o	'him'	→	*sənsə́lto*	'his chain'
səmble(t)	'sprig'	+ –ēn (dual)		→	*səmbəltə́n*	'two sprigs'
mtəržme(t)	'translator (f.)(of)'	+ –o	'it'	→	*mtəržə́mto*	'its translator(f.)'

[1]This is *Ɛala + n-nsūra*, not *Ɛan + n-nsūra*. The latter gives *Ɛan‿ən-nsūra*. Both might be translated 'about the vultures'. [Seep.476]

mɛallme(t) 'teacher(f.)   + -i 'me'   → mɛallə́mti 'my teacher(f.)'
             (of)'

žāmɛet   'university of'   + -ak 'you' → žāmə́ɛtak 'your university'

      The intrusive ə in this type of word formation is not
treated as a "helping vowel" strictly speaking, since it
takes the accent, in accordance with the general rule of
accentuation [p. 18].
      On the use of "connective t", which is involved in
many of these changes, see p. 163.

      Many words end in two consonants when followed in close phrasing by a
word that begins with two consonants, since a helping vowel comes between
the words: bənt əgg̣īre 'little girl', ɛašr əᵊrūš 'ten piastres'. But at
the end of a phrase, or before a word beginning with one consonant, a
helping vowel often breaks the word-final cluster: mīn hal-bənᵊt? 'Who is
that girl?', ɛašᵊr lērāt 'ten pounds'. Further examples:

Before ə + two consonants		Finally or before one consonant	
š-šahr ᵊl-māḍi	'last month'	haš-šahᵊr	'this month'
šəft ᵊl-bāxra?	'Did you see the ship?'	šəfᵊt bāxra?	'Did you see a ship?'
ḥasb ᵊt-takalīf	'calculating the expenditures'	ḥasᵊb takalīfna	'calculating our expenditures'
ʔabl ᵊḥrūb ᵊṣ-ṣalībiyye	'before the Crusaders' wars'	ʔabᵊl hal-ᵊḥrūb	'before those wars'

      Many such two-consonant clusters at the end of a word are tolerated,
however, especially if the first is a resonant, or if the second is t:
ʔalf lēra 'a thousand pounds', bənt ḥəlwe 'a pretty girl', taḥt ʔīdo
'available to him' (lit. "under his hand"), šəft bāxra? 'Did you see a
ship?' [See p. 25]
      Especially before a suffix beginning with one consonant, these
clusters are generally maintained and no helping vowel is used: šəftkon
'I saw you(pl.)', bəntna 'our daughter', šarraftna 'you have honored us',
baṣaṭṭni 'you have gladdened me', žənshon 'their kind'.

      The helping vowel is virtually always used, on the other hand, finally
or before a consonant, if the second of a word-final or stem-final cluster
is a resonant, or if the second is voiced and the first voiceless:

ʔəbn 'son'   + -kon   'you(pl.)' → ʔəbᵊnkon   'your son'

ḥabr 'ink'   + ʔaswad   'black'   → ḥabᵊr ʔaswad 'black ink'

ʔaṣl 'origin'   + hal-ʔəsm 'this name' → ʔaṣᵊl hal-ʔəsᵊm 'the origin of
                                                            this name'

ḥasb 'calculating'   + -ha 'it'   → ḥasᵃbha 'calculating it'

ʔaxd 'taking'   + -ni 'me'   → ʔaxᵃdni 'taking me'

There are two kinds of consonant clusters within words which are strictly immune to being split by the helping vowel:

(1) If the second consonant is the infix -t- [p.95], it must always adhere to the preceding consonant; or if the first two are a prefix st- [102], they must always cohere: mҙsthiyye 'embarrassed(f.)' (never -sᵃth-), mҙstfīd 'benefitting' (never -sᵃtf-), byҙštg̣el (or byҙštҙg̣el) 'he works' (never -šᵃtg̣-).

(2) If the first is m and the second b or f: žambna 'beside us, our side', sҙmble 'sprig, ear', ʔҙmf 'nose', byҙmbṣet (or byҙmbáṣet) 'he has a good time'.

> Most clusters of b with m or f are the result of assimi-
> lation of n to a following labial [p.27]. If the n remains
> unassimilated, a helping vowel may split the cluster: ʔanᵃf
> (or ʔҙnf) 'nose'.

> A combination of n with k or g (the n being pronounced
> in the velar position, as "ng") is generally also unsplit-
> table: baṇk 'bank' (never -ṇᵃk), ʔҙnglīzi 'English' (never
> -nᵃgl-).

CHAPTER 2: MORPHOLOGICAL PRINCIPLES[1]

In this chapter some basic terms and concepts used in dealing with Arabic word formation are explained for the novice
and sharpened (it is hoped) for the initiate.

INFLECTIONAL BASES

Syrian Arabic has three kinds of inflected words[2]:

<u>Nouns</u> are inflected for Number (Singular, Dual, Plural).

<u>Adjectives</u> are inflected for Number/Gender (Masculine, Feminine, Plural).

<u>Verbs</u> are inflected for: 1) Person (First, Second, Third)
                                 2) Number/Gender (Masculine, Feminine, Plural)
                                 3) Tense (Perfect, Imperfect)
                                 4) Mode (Indicative, Subjunctive, Imperative)

The inflectional categories are treated in detail in
Chapters 12, 13, and 14.

The inflections of an Arabic word are distinguished either by affixes
or by internal changes in form[3]. The plural of the adjective *taɛbān*
'tired', for instance, is produced by suffixing *-īn*: *taɛbānīn,* while the
plural of *ʔaṣīr* 'short' is formed by changing it internally to *ʔṣār.* (The
plural of the noun *raš²ḥ* 'a cold' is formed by internal change <u>plus</u> a
suffix: *ršūḥāt* 'colds'.)

Inflectional forms are treated in detail in Chapters

For each type of inflected Arabic word there is at least one inflection — the BASE INFLECTION — which is never formed with an affix. The
base inflection of nouns is the singular; of adjectives, the masculine/
singular; the base inflection of verbs is the third-person masculine/
singular perfect.[4]

---

[1] The term 'morphological' is used here in a broad sense, including both
grammatical and morphophonemic considerations.

[2] These statements are not to be construed as definitions. The parts of
speech are established syntactically.

[3] The term 'form', as used in this book, generally means 'phonological
expression', not 'grammatical structure'.

[4] Another base inflection in verbs is the masculine/singular imperative.
The third-person perfect, however, is the traditional citation form and
the one used in this book.

The base inflection is used as the CITATION FORM, i.e. its form is the one used for mentioning an inflected word as a whole rather than some particular inflection of it. The masculine/singular *taɛbān,* then, is used in referring to the adjective whose other inflections are *taɛbāne* (f.) and *taɛbānīn* (pl.). Likewise, the verbal citation form *katab* 'to write' subtends all twenty-seven inflections; *katab* as a particular inflection actually means 'he wrote', not 'to write'. (Arabic verbs have no infinitive, which is the usual citation form for verbs in modern European languages.)

A word conceived in abstraction from all its inflections is sometimes called a WORD BASE, or simply a BASE.

What follows in this chapter is exclusively concerned with word <u>bases</u>. As for their inflection, the terms and concepts dealing with it are familiar and easy enough not to require special treatment here.

ROOTS AND PATTERNS

Patterns *(aṣ-ṣīġa, al-wazn)*

Most Arabic word bases fit one or another significant PATTERN. That is to say, the <u>form</u> of a base usually implies something about its grammatical function, and perhaps also something about its meaning. Note, for instance, the pattern shared by these words:

žabne	'cheese'	*rakbe*	'knee'
ɛalbe	'box'	*nasbe*	'relationship'
xaṭbe	'marriage proposal'	*ʔabre*	'needle'
salfe	'sister-in-law'	*danye*	'world'
xadme	'service'	*barke*	'pool'

The pattern manifested in all these words consists in a sequence 'consonant + ə + two consonants + e'. This is one of the patterns characteristic of feminine nouns. This pattern, however, implies nothing about the words' meanings.

Note the pattern shared by these words:

ṭabbāx	'cook'	*ḥallāʔ*	'barber'
xayyāṭ	'tailor'	*fannān*	'artist'

žarrāḥ	'surgeon'	*xaddām*	'servant'
dahhān	'painter'	*sammān*	'grocer'
naššāl	'pickpocket'	*Ɛattāl*	'porter'

This pattern, 'consonant + a + double consonant + ā + consonant', is characteristic of masculine nouns which also have an element of meaning in common: they show the occupation or profession of the person referred to.

Another masculine noun pattern is shared by these words:

maṭbax	'kitchen'	*mathaf*	'museum'
masbaḥ	'swimming pool'	*maxzan*	'store'
malƐab	'playground'	*markaz*	'center'
matƐam	'restaurant'	*maktab*	'office'
maṣnaƐ	'factory'	*maṭraḥ*	'place'

This pattern, 'ma + two consonants + a + consonant', commonly occurs in words designating kinds of places.

There are numerous exceptions to the pattern implications, however. Note that *xazzān* 'reservoir' and *ṣabbāṭ* 'shoes' do not indicate people's occupations, nor does *maksab* 'profit' designate a kind of place. Some of the same patterns, too, are used in different parts of speech: *baṭṭāl* 'bad' and *ḥassās* 'sensitive', for instance, are not nouns, but adjectives.

Roots (*al-ʔaṣl, al-ǧiδr*)

If the pattern is analyzed out of a word, then the part left over — the part which differentiates that word from others of the same pattern — most typically consists of three particular consonants in a particular order. This set of consonants is called the ROOT of the word, and each separate consonant is called a RADICAL (*ḥarf ʔaṣlī*). Thus the root of *žabne* 'cheese' is *ž-b-n*, the root of *ṭabbāx* 'cook' is *ṭ-b-x*, and the root of *maṭbax* 'kitchen' is also *ṭ-b-x*.

Words with the same root commonly have related meanings:

ṭabbāx 'cook'	*maṭbax* 'kitchen'	(Root *ṭ-b-x*)
xaddām 'servant'	*xədme* 'service'	(Root *x-d-m*)
xaṭbe 'marriage proposal' ..	*xaṭīb* 'fiancé'	(Root *x-ṭ-b*)
maṣnaƐ 'factory'	*ṣināƐa* 'industry'	(Root *ṣ-n-Ɛ*)

There are countless exceptions, however. For instance:

   rəkbe 'knee' .... but   *markab* 'ship'   (Root *r-k-b*)

   bərke 'pool' .... but   *barake* 'blessing'   (Root *b-r-k*)

   ḥallāʔ 'barber' ..... but   *ḥalaʔa* 'link'   (Root *ḥ-l-ʔ*)

    Words having the same root and related meanings are PARONYMS; a set of paronyms constitutes a WORD FAMILY.

        It should be noted that the term 'root' is used in somewhat varied ways in various Arabic grammars and dictionaries. While in this book it designates a mere combination of radicals without regard to meaning, elsewhere it sometimes refers to a meaningful element — its meaning being that shared by all members of a word family. Quite often the concept of 'root' is used ambiguously, requiring interpretation now in one way, now in the other.

        In Arabic dictionaries, for instance, which are alphabetized by roots — not by bases as Western dictionaries are — "homonymous roots" are sometime entered separately, i.e. the mixing of different word-families in one main entry is sometimes avoided. This policy has never been consistently carried out, however; the more usual type of entry is the purely "formal" root, whose sub-entries may include words of various word-families, arranged without regard to meaning.

        It is often difficult, if not impossible, to decide without arbitrariness whether two words with the same (formal) root have "related meanings" or not. The use of etymology to resolve some of these difficulties only makes the concept of 'root' still more ambiguous.

Root and Pattern Symbols

    Roots, though unpronounceable in abstraction from words, may easily be represented by writing the radical letters in order, separated by hyphens; and orally, by simply naming the letters in quick succession.

    Handy reference to patterns, on the other hand, is a bit more difficult. In this book the traditional Arab technique is used: the pattern is applied to the sample root *f-ε-l*. Here we are not concerned with *f-ε-l* as a root of actual words (e.g. *faεal* 'to do, to act'), but only as a device for making abstract patterns pronounceable. (The *f* and the *l* of these pattern symbols will be capitalized.) Thus *FəεLe* is our formula for the pattern of *žəbne*, *εəlbe*, *xəṭbe*, etc.; *Faεεāl* represents the pattern of *ṭabbāx*, *xayyāṭ*, *žarrāḥ;* and *maFεaL* represents the pattern of *maṭbax*, *masbaḥ*, and *malεab*.

Number of Radicals

Most Arabic roots are TRILITERAL $(\theta u l \bar{a} \theta \bar{\iota})$: they have three radicals. There are, however, many four-radical or QUADRILITERAL $(rub\bar{a}\varepsilon\bar{\iota})$ roots, as in the following words:

(1) *žadwal* 'schedule'   (2) *zaxraf* 'to embellish'   (3) *ɛaṣfūr* 'bird'

    daftar 'notebook'   *taržam* 'to translate'   *sandū?* 'box'

    xanžar 'dagger'   *baxšaš* 'to tip'   *ṭarbūš* 'fez'

    (4) *taržame* 'translation'   (5) *mfarnaž* 'westernized'

      handase 'engineering'   *mlaxbaṭ* 'mixed up'

      falsafe 'philosophy'   *mšarṭaṭ* 'ragged'

Patterns for quadriliteral roots are symbolized on a dummy root $F-\varepsilon-L-L$; it is to be understood that the third and fourth radicals are usually different, though they are both represented by L in the formulas.

The pattern of the words in group 1 above (masculine nouns) is *FaɛLaL;* group 2 (verbs) also *FaɛLaL;* group 3 (masculine nouns) *FaɛLūL;* group 4 (abstract feminine nouns) *FaɛLaLe;* group 5 (passive participles) *mFaɛLaL*.

Roots of five or more radicals are found only in nouns (plus whatever adjectives may be derived from these nouns by suffixation): *banafsaž* 'violet(s)', *?əmbərāṭōr* 'emperor', *ṭrāblos* 'Tripoli', *ṭrāb^əlsi* 'Tripolitanian'.

    It is not worth while to symbolize these multiliteral roots or their patterns,[1] because the roots normally occur with one pattern only (plus or minus certain suffixes), and in many cases the pattern itself (if abstractable at all) occurs with only one root.

There are hardly any biliteral roots and no uniliteral roots in Syrian Arabic except in certain particles (e.g. *mən* 'from', *n–* 'if') and in the names of certain letters of the alphabet (e.g. *bē*, name of the letter ﺏ).

A small handful of miscellaneous simple nouns and derivative adjectives, however, also have biliteral roots:

    ri?a 'lung'   (Root *r–?*, Pattern *Fiɛa*)

    fi?a[2] 'class, bracket, rate'   (Root *f–?*, Pattern *Fiɛa*)

    səne 'year'   (Root *s–n*, Pattern *Fəɛe*)

---

[1] In Arabic dictionaries, however, it is necessary to extract these "roots" in order to alphabetize the words containing them.

[2] Also pronounced *fī?a*, implying a root *f–y–?* with Pattern *FəɛLe*.

mara 'woman'	(Root *m-r*, Pattern *Faɛa*)
yadawi 'manual, hand-'	(Root *y-d*, Pattern *Fatawi*)
damawi 'blood-, bloody'	(Root *d-m*, Pattern *Faɛawi*)

Note that the Classical words *yad* 'hand' and *dam* 'blood', from which *yadawi* and *damawi* are derived, correspond to three-radical words in Colloquial: *ʔīd* 'hand' (Root *ʔ-y-d*, Pattern *FəɛL* [p. 142]); *damm* 'blood' (Root *d-m-m*, Pattern *FaɛL*). A similar case is that of the dialectal form *riyye* 'lung' (Root *r-y-y*, Pattern *FəɛLe* [143]), which has been generally supplanted in educated urban speech by the classicism *riʔa*.

In the case of *mara* 'woman', the two-radical colloquial word corresponds to a three-radical word in Classical: *marʔa*. (The latter form is also sometimes used in Colloquial, however, when bookish or officialese style is called for.)

The terms 'biliteral', 'triliteral', 'quadriliteral', etc. in this book will only be applied to roots. To designate <u>words</u> whose roots have a certain number of radicals, or <u>patterns</u> applicable to roots of a certain number of radicals, the terms BIRADICAL, TRIRADICAL, QUADRIRADICAL, etc. will be used.

Compound words in Arabic (i.e. word bases including more than one root) are very rare. Note *raʔsmāliyye* 'capitalism', which includes the roots *r-ʔ-s* and *m-w-l* [p. 44]. The colloquial form of the word underlying this one, however, is pronounced *rəsmāl* ('capital'), which sounds like a simple word with four radicals (*r-s-m-l*) formed on Pattern *FəɛLāL*, rather than a compound of *rās* 'head' and *māl* 'property'.

Numerals from eleven to nineteen are compounds, consisting of a simple numeral plus 'ten' (*ɛ-š-r*). [See p. 170]

PATTERN ALTERATIONS

Root Types

Many patterns vary according to the type of root they are applied to. The verb pattern *FaɛaL*, for instance, when applied to a root like *ʔ-r-y*, does not yield a form "*ʔaray*". What happens is that the final radical semivowel disappears in this pattern: *ʔara* 'to read'.

This same verb pattern *(FaƐaL)*, applied to a root whose last two radicals are alike, such as *d-l-l*, loses its second vowel *a*, and the two like radicals cohere as a double consonant: *dall* 'to indicate' (not *"dalal"*).

Roots like *ʔ-r-y* and *d-l-l* are UNSTABLE: they have at least one radical that in certain patterns is subject to change, disappearance, or fusion. STABLE roots, on the other hand, keep all their radicals intact[1] and distinct in all patterns.

Unstable roots include GEMINATING roots (like *d-l-l*), whose last two radicals are alike and are sometimes fused together, and FLUCTUATING roots (like *ʔ-r-y*), which contain a radical that is sometimes changed, lost, or fused with some part of the pattern.

In fluctuating roots the unstable radicals are usually semivowels (*w* or *y*)[2], in some cases *ʔ*.

Some examples of radical fluctuation:

1) Change to another sound:

Pattern *FāƐeL* applied to Root *x-w-f* gives *xāyef* 'afraid' (not *"xāwef"*). (Rule: Medial radical *w* is changed to *y* in Pattern *FāƐeL*.)[3]

Pattern *FtaƐaL* applied to Root *w-f-ʔ* gives *ttafaʔ* 'to agree' (not *"wtafaʔ"*). (Rule: Initial radical *w* is changed to *t* in Pattern *FtaƐaL*.)

Pattern *FuƐāL* applied to Root *d-Ɛ-w* gives *duƐāʔ* 'supplication' (not *"duƐāw"*). (Rule: Final radical *w* is changed to *ʔ* in Pattern *FuƐāL*.)

Pattern *FaƐLe* applied to Root *ʔ-w-y* gives *ʔuwwe* 'power' (not *"ʔawye"*). (Rule: Final radical *y* is changed to *w* in Pattern *FaƐLe* after medial radical *w*.[4] Also: *ə* is changed to *u* in Pattern *FaƐLe* before medial radical *w*.)

---

[1] Intact, not counting the kinds of assimilation described as automatic sound changes [p. 26]. Thus the root *ž-m-Ɛ* is considered stable, even though the *ž* may be devoiced in Pattern *FtaƐaL*: *štamaƐ* 'to meet, get together'.

[2] The mere alternation of *w* with *u* and *y* with *i*, however, is automatic (subphonemic, in fact), and is not to be counted as radical fluctuation. Thus the radical *w* shows no fluctuation as between *ġazu* 'raiding' (Pattern *FaƐL*) and *ġazwe* 'a raid' (Pattern *FaƐLe*), but does show fluctuation in the verb *ġaza* 'to raid' (Pattern *FaƐaL*), where its disappearance is not a consequence of automatic sound changes.

[3] Except when the final radical is also a semivowel, in which case the medial *w* remains: *nāwi* 'intending' (Root *n-w-y*).

[4] Unless the medial *w* itself fluctuates, changing to *y*. See *niyye* 'intention', [p. 45]

2) Fusion with a part of the pattern:

Pattern *FəƐL* applied to Root *s-w-ʔ* gives *sū*ʔ 'market' (not *"səwʔ"*).
(Rule: Pattern vowel *ə* + medial radical *w → u.*)

Pattern *FaƐL* applied to Root *x-w-f* gives *xōf* 'fear' (not *xawf*[1]).
(Rule: Pattern vowel *a* + medial radical *w → ō.*)

Pattern *FaƐL* applied to Root *x-y-t* gives *xēṭ* 'thread' (not *xayṭ*[1]).
(Rule: Pattern vowel *a* + medial radical *y → ē.*)

Pattern *staFƐaL* applied to Root *ʔ-h-l* gives *stāhal* 'to deserve' (not
"staʔhal").
(Rule: Pattern vowel *a* + initial radical *ʔ* sometimes → *ā.*)

3) Loss without a trace:

Pattern *FaƐƐaL* applied to Root *x-f-y* gives *xaffa* 'to hide' (not
"xaffay").
(Rule: Final radical semivowels generally disappear from word-
final position after *a.*)

Pattern *FaƐaL* applied to Root *x-w-f* gives *xāf* 'to fear' (not *"xawaf"*).
(Rule: Medial radical semivowels generally disappear in Pattern
FaƐaL. xa- + -af = xāf.)

Pattern *staFƐaL* applied to Root *h-y-y* gives *staha* 'to be embarrassed'
(not *"stahyay"*).
(Rule: Medial radical *y* disappears in Pattern *staFƐaL* if the
final radical is also *y.*[2] The latter also disappears since it is
in word-final position after *a.*)

Pattern *FaƐLān* applied to Root *m-l-ʔ* gives *malān* 'full' (not *"malʔān"*).[3]
(Rule: Final radical *ʔ* sometimes disappears in Pattern *FaƐLān.*)[2]

Word Types

A word in which the radicals are all intact and distinct is called
SOUND (*sālim*).

A word in which two like radicals are fused together is called DOUBLED
or GEMINATE (*muḍāƐaf*): *šədde* 'intensity' (cf. sound *šadīd* 'intense'); *ḍarr*
'to damage' (cf. sound *ḍarar* 'damage'); *ḥaẓẓ* 'luck' (cf. sound *maḥẓūẓ*
'lucky').

---

[1] Forms like *xawf* and *xayṭ* generally occur in Lebanon, however. For the
typical Lebanese dialects, the fusion of *a* with *w* and *y* does not take place.

[2] This *"rule"* is not important since there are no other instances in which
it applies.

[3] Compare, however, the more common doublet of this root: *m-l-y*, whose final
radical does not disappear in Pattern *FaƐLān: malyān* 'full'.

Many patterns accomodate the fusion of like radicals without alteration. The double consonant occupies the same position in the pattern as two contiguous but distinct consonants: *ḥaẓẓ* (Pattern *FaƐL*); *šədde* (Pattern *FəƐLe*).

Some patterns, however, undergo a special alteration when applied to geminating roots, so that the like radicals are brought together while unlike radicals are kept apart by a vowel:

Pattern *staFƐaL* with Root *ḥ-ʔ-ʔ* gives geminate *staḥáʔʔ* 'to deserve' (not *"stáḥʔaʔ"*, which would be the sound form).

Pattern *maFƐaL* with Root *ḥ-l-l* gives geminate *maḥáll* 'place' (not *"máḥlal"*, which would be the sound form).

Pattern *ʔaFƐaL* with Root *x-ṣ-ṣ* gives geminate *ʔaxáṣṣ* 'most special' (not *"ʔáxṣaṣ"*, which would be the sound form).

A word is called WEAK *(muƐtall)* if in any of its forms a radical is changed, lost, or fused with some part of the pattern.

> While a stable root (by definition) produces only sound words, a fluctuating root may produce both sound and weak words. Thus the fluctuating root *š-w-f* with Pattern *FaƐaL* produces a weak verb *šāf* 'to see', but with Pattern *FaƐƐaL* it produces a sound verb *šawwaf* 'to show'.
> The root *z-w-r* with Pattern *FaƐaL* produces both a weak verb *zār* 'to visit' and a sound verb *zawar* 'to give (someone) a significant look'.
> The root *ʔ-k-l* with Pattern *FaƐaL* produces a base form in which all radicals are intact: *ʔakal* 'to eat'; but the initial radical *ʔ* is lost or fused in other inflections *(byākol* 'he eats', *kōl* 'eat!'), so the verb *ʔakal* is classified as weak.

In FINAL-WEAK or DEFECTIVE *(nāqiṣ)* words, it is the <u>last</u> radical that is changed, lost, or fused. Examples:

ʔara 'to read' (Root *ʔ-r-y*, Pattern *FaƐaL*)

> In the base form the final radical *y* is lost, while in certain other forms it is fused with parts of the pattern to give *ā* or *ē: ʔarāha* 'he read it', *ʔarēt* 'I(have)read'.

faršá 'to brush' (Root *f-r-š-y*, Pattern *FaƐLaL*)

> In other forms the radical *y* is not lost but fused: *faršēt* 'I brushed', *bfaršī* 'I brush it'.

ʔawi 'strong' (Root *ʔ-w-y*, Pattern *FaƐīL*)

The final *i* does not represent the radical *y*, but only the apocopated pattern vowel *ī*.

ʔuwwe 'strength' (Root *ʔ-w-y*, Pattern *FəƐLe*)

The final radical *y* is changed to *w* in this word.

nəsi 'to forget' (Root *n-s-y*, Pattern *FəƐeL*)

The final radical is fused with the pattern vowel (*e* + *y* → *ī* → final unaccented *i*) and is lost in the imperfect inflections: *byənsa* 'he forgets'.

muddƐi 'claimant' (Root *d-Ɛ-w*, Pattern *muFtaƐeL*)

The final radical is, strictly speaking, fused with the pattern (*e* + *w* → *ī* → final unaccented *i*) rather than lost.[1]

žaza or *žazāʔ* 'punishment' (Root *ž-z-y*, Pattern *FaƐāL*)

The form *žaza* shows total loss of the final radical *y* (with the pattern vowel shortened because it is unaccented finally), while in *žazāʔ* the radical is not lost but is changed to *ʔ*.

In MIDDLE-WEAK or HOLLOW (*ʔ aǧwaf*) words, a <u>middle</u> radical is changed, lost, or fused. Examples:

xāf 'to fear' (Root *x-w-f*, Pattern *FaƐaL*)

The radical *w* is totally lost in the perfect, while in the imperfect, strictly speaking, it fuses with the pattern vowel *a* to produce *ā:* *bixāf* 'he fears' (Pattern *byəFƐaL:* *w* + *a* → *ā*).

stafād 'to benefit' (Root *f-y-d*, Pattern *staFƐaL*)

The radical *y* fuses with the pattern vowel *a* to produce *ā*, while in the imperfect *byəstfīd* (Pattern *byəstaFƐeL*) it fuses with the pattern vowel *e* to produce *ī*.

šētān 'devil' (Root *š-y-ṭ-n*, Pattern *FaƐLāL*)

The pattern vowel *a* fuses with the radical *y* to produce *ē*. The radical remains intact in the plural: *šayaṭīn*.

---

[1]If it were lost, strictly speaking, the pattern vowel *e* would not be altered to *i*.

niyye 'intention' (Root *n-w-y*, Pattern *FəƐLe*)

The medial radical *w* is changed to *y*.[1]

šāyef 'looking at' (Root *š-w-f*, Pattern *FāƐeL*)

The medial radical *w* is changed to *y*.

mōt 'death' (Root *m-w-t*, Pattern *FaƐL*)

The pattern vowel *a* fuses with the medial radical to produce *ō*.

In INITIAL-WEAK words, the <u>first</u> radical is changed, lost, or fused. Examples:

ʔāman 'to believe' (Root *ʔ-m-n*, Pattern *ʔaFƐaL*)

The first pattern vowel *a* fuses with *ʔ* to produce *ā* in the perfect tense, but the initial radical remains intact in the imperfect: *byəʔmen* 'he believes'.[2]

ṭṭaṣal 'to get in touch' (Root *w-ṣ-l*, Pattern *FtaƐaL*)

The initial radical *w* is changed to *ṭ*, assimilated to the *-ṭ-* infix of the pattern.

yəbes 'to dry out' (Root *y-b-s*, Pattern *FəƐeL*)

The radical *y* is intact in the base form, but may be lost in the imperfect tense: *btəbas* 'it(f.)dries out'. (Alternatively, however, it may be fused with the prefix vowel: *btības*. *ī = iy ← ə + y*.)

wəled 'to be born' (Root *w-l-d*, Pattern *FəƐeL*)

The radical *w* is intact in the base form, but may be lost in the imperfect tense: *byəlad* 'he is born'. (Alternatively, however, it may be fused with the prefix vowel: *byūlad*. *ū = uw ← ə + w*.)

---

[1] The word *niyye* could just as well be spelled *nīye* [p. 22], in the light of which one could say that the medial *w* is fused with the pattern, rather than simply changed.

[2] *ʔāman* may also be construed as having Pattern *FāƐaL* rather *ʔaFƐaL*, in view of the imperfect *biʔāmen* 'he believes' in addition to *byəʔmen*. As a Pattern *FāƐaL* verb, it is sound, since the initial *ʔ* is then the radical rather than a pattern formative.

ṣifa 'attribute' (Root *w-ṣ-f*, Pattern *ɛiLa*)

> The initial radical is lost completely. (Pattern *ɛiLa* occurs only in initial-weak words, which is why it is shown without any *F.*)

mūḥeš 'desolate' (Root *w-ḥ-š*, Pattern *məFɛeL*)

> The Pattern vowel *ə* fuses with *w* to produce *ū*.

DERIVATION (*al-ištiqāq*)

Simple and Augmented Bases

An affix or a change of pattern that is used in forming a larger word base from a smaller one is called a BASE FORMATIVE. The prefix *m-* in *mɛallem* 'teacher', for instance, is a base formative (cf. *ɛallam* 'to teach'); likewise the suffix *-an* in *dāyman* 'always' (cf. *dāyem* 'lasting, permanent'), the infix *-t-* in *štamaɛ* 'to meet, get together' (cf. *žamaɛ* 'to bring together'), and the lengthening of the consonant and vowel in *ṭabbāx* 'cook' (cf. *ṭabax* 'to cook, prepare food').

Word bases that contain formatives (*ziyāda*) are called AUGMENTED (*mazīd fīhi*); those without formatives are SIMPLE (*muǧarrad*). *žamaɛ* and *ṭabax* are simple, while *štamaɛ* and *ṭabbāx* are singly augmented — they each contain one formative. *ɛallam* 'to teach' and *dāyem* 'lasting' are also singly augmented (cf. the simple words *ɛəlm* 'organized knowledge' and *dām* 'to last'). *mɛallem*, then, is doubly augmented — it contains both the *m-* and the lengthened *l*; *dāyman*, too, is doubly augmented — by the suffix *-an* and the active participial formative (consisting in a change from Pattern *FaɛaL* to Pattern *FāɛeL*)[1].

> Patterns, as well as word bases, may be spoken of as simple or augmented, since a word's formative are part of its pattern, not part of its root. Thus the pattern *FəɛL* (as in *ɛəlm*) is a simple pattern, as also the verb pattern *FaɛaL* (as in *žamaɛ*, *ṭabax*, and the hollow verb *dām*). Singly augmented patterns include *FtaɛaL* (as in *štamaɛ*), *FaɛɛaL* (as in *ɛallam*), *FaɛɛāL* (as in *ṭabbāx*), and *FāɛeL* (as in *dāyem*), while the patterns *mFaɛɛeL* (as in *mɛallem*) and *FāɛLan* (as in *dāyman*) are doubly augmented.

---

[1] The form *dāyman* is analyzed as *dāyem* + *-an;* the loss of *e* is not a change of pattern but merely an alteration in the pattern entailed by the addition of the suffix.

The Function of Base Formatives

Every formative has one or more regular functions. That is to say, there are certain regular differences in grammar or in meaning between words that contain a particular formative and words that lack it. A regular function of the formative *-t-*, for instance, is to convert active verbs like *žamaɛ* 'to bring together' into mediopassive verbs like *štamaɛ* 'to get together, to meet'.

If the only difference in structure between two paronyms is that one contains a base formative which the other lacks — <u>and</u> if the difference in their grammar or meanings can be accounted for as a regular function of that formative — then the word with the formative is said to be **DERIVED** (*muštaqq*) from the word without it. Thus *štamaɛ* is derived from *žamaɛ*, and *mɛallem* 'teacher' is derived from *ɛallam* 'to teach', and *dāyman* 'always' from *dāyem* 'lasting, permanent' — which, in its turn, is derived from the simple verb *dām* 'to last'.[1]

Not all derivatives are augmented. Any change in pattern may serve to distinguish a derivative from the word underlying it, provided that the same function is in some <u>other</u> cases regularly served by augmentation. For example the noun *šərb* 'drinking' — even though it lacks a formative — is considered a derivative of the verb *šəreb* 'to drink', since for countless other verbs this same kind of noun derivation (the gerund or *maṣdar* [284]) is regularly expressed with formatives: *ʔara* 'to read' → *ʔrāye* 'reading', *kātab* 'to write to' → *mkātabe* 'wr:ting, correspondence',

---

[1] It is quite usual in Arabic grammar to go on from here to say that *dām* is derived from the root *d-w-m*, and *žamaɛ* from *ž-m-ɛ*, and *ɛallam* from *ɛ-l-m*. To take this step implies that all patterns are formatives and all words derivatives.

But the relationship between a word base and its root (sometimes called 'primary derivation') should not be confused with the very different kind of relationship that holds between two paronymous word bases. It is gratuitous to say that *žamaɛ* is "derived from" *ž-m-ɛ*, when the same thing may be expressed simply by saying that the root of *žamaɛ* is *ž-m-ɛ*.

A more serious objection to saying that a base is "derived from" a certain root is this: Arabic roots (as usually conceived, and as presented in this book) enter into construction with augmented patterns as well as with simple patterns. Thus Root *ž-m-ɛ* + Pattern *FtaɛaL* → *štamaɛ*. No matter how convenient this kind of analysis may be in describing the <u>forms</u> (morphophonemics) of words, it is incompatible with the analysis of augmented word bases into underlying bases plus formatives: *žamaɛ* + *-t-* → *štamaɛ*. Therefore if we want to describe the hierarchical interrelationships of word bases, we cannot validly treat roots and patterns as grammatical entities at all.

The derivational system, then, is the system of interrelationships among members of a word family. A root, as conceived here, is neither parental nor ancestral to those members, but is merely their family resemblance.

Ɛallam 'to teach' → *taƐlīm* 'teaching, instruction'.[1]

Derivational Categories

There are approximately thirty regular ways in which Syrian Arabic words are produced by derivational formatives, including about fifteen kinds of verb derivation, ten kinds of noun derivation, four or five kinds of adjective derivation, and one kind of adverb derivation.

> Notwithstanding the fact that derivation is based on the regular correlation of formatives with functions, these correlations are in general not very neat. Some categories, e.g. abstract nouns [p 284], are expressed by a wide variety of formatives and other pattern changes, while many formatives, e.g. the *-e/-a* suffix [138], or the verb pattern *FaƐƐaL* [79],[2] serve regularly in a number of different functions.

> The derivational categories are treated in detail in Chapters

Unlike inflectional categories, the categories that are purely derivational have no unique syntactic or semantic properties. That is to say, there are always some simple underived words that have the same syntactic and semantic characteristics as the derivatives. Take for example causative verbs [p. 240] derived from simple transitive verbs: *fahham* 'to explain(to)', from *fəhem* 'to understand'. These causatives are doubly transitive and mean 'to cause(someone)to do(something)', thus *fahham* 'to cause(someone)to understand(something)'. But compare this with a simple verb like *Ɛaṭa* 'to give', which is likewise doubly transitive and might likewise be analyzed semantically as 'to cause(someone)to receive(something)'. The only relevant difference is that *Ɛaṭa* has no paronym meaning 'to receive'.

Or take for example occupational derivatives like *ṭabbāx* 'cook' (from *ṭabax* 'to cook, prepare food'), *fannān* 'artist' (from *fann* 'art'), *mƐallem* 'teacher' (from *Ɛallam* 'to teach'), *ʔāḍi* 'judge' (from *ʔaḍa* 'to pass judgement'). These derivatives are paralleled by simple words that likewise indicate occupations: *xūri* 'priest', *doktōr* 'doctor', *ʔəstāz* 'professor', *Ɛarṣa* 'pimp'.

[1] Since so many gerunds of simple verbs are formed on simple noun patterns, some scholars seem to have doubts about "which came first", the verb or the noun [284]. As a pseudo-historical question, this is perhaps an insoluble problem, but as a question of mere linguistic description it is no real problem at all. In actual practice everyone treats the gerund as a derivative of the verb — even those who would in theory maintain that the reverse is equally reasonable.

[2] Strictly speaking, patterns as such are not formatives; to call Pattern *FaƐƐaL* a formative means that the change from some other (usually simple) pattern to Pattern *FaƐƐaL* is a formative.

There are, however, several categories that are not purely derivational but rather QUASI-INFLECTIONAL, straddling the line between derivation and inflection. Active participles [p.265], elatives [313], true passive verbs [236], and transitive gerunds [440] have certain syntactic and/or semantic peculiarities that set them apart from any non-derivative words.[1]

Derivational Irregularities

While inflectional systems tend to be functionally regular and perfectly productive, derivational systems are normally riddled with gaps and irregularities.

First of all, no derivational categories (not even the quasi-inflectional ones) are as PRODUCTIVE as the inflectional categories. While the inflections of most words may be freely improvised as needed, derivational formatives on the other hand are not used so liberally. To improvise with a derivational formative is to produce a nonce word or to coin a word.

The derivational categories vary greatly in the extent to which they are exemplified in ready-made word bases, and in the precision with which a derivative's grammar or meaning may be deduced from that of the underlying word. These factors, in turn, have an effect on the frequency with which a given derivational formative is used in coinages or nonce formations.

The most common and productive derivational categories include causative, augmentative, applicative and (especially) passive verbs; participial and relative adjectives and nouns; and abstract, singulative, feminal, and elative nouns.

At the other end of the scale certain categories are so uncommon or so shot through with irregularities of one sort or another that their status as "regular" derivational functions is only marginal. This is the case, for instance, with descriptive verbs and diminutive nouns.

Beyond such marginal categories there lies an assortment of anomalous derivatives which do not fit any recognizable category at all.

Some words fit into a particular derivational category in form and meaning but have no underlying word. For example the instrumental noun *manžal* 'sickle' implies an underlying verb such as *"nažal"* (meaning, perhaps, 'to cut, mow'), but in fact no such verb exists. Similarly the reciprocative verb *ḍḍārab(u)* 'to fight(one another)' theoretically should be derived from a participative verb *ḍārab* 'to fight with' (which would be derived in turn from the simple verb *ḍarab* 'to hit'); in fact, however, no such verb as *ḍārab* is used in Syrian Arabic.

---

[1]The special features of these categories are dealt with, for convenience' sake, along with their more properly derivational functions, though strictly speaking those features belong in the chapters on inflectional categories.

Many augmented words seem to be derived from certain other words insofar as their form is concerned, but their meanings are wrong (i.e. cannot
be accounted for as a regular function of the formative). Thus *štarr* 'to
chew a cud, ruminate' is not to be counted as a derivative of *žarr* 'to
pull, drag'.[1]

Many words are IDIOMATICALLY derived. That is to say, the uses of two
paronyms may differ in such a way that the formative in one of them
accounts for some but not all of the semantic and syntactic difference
between them. The occupational noun *žarrāḥ* 'surgeon', for instance, is
mildly idiomatic with respect to its underlying verb *žaraḥ* 'to wound, to
cut or break (living flesh)', since there is nothing in the verb's meaning to hint that its occupational derivative would designate a kind of
therapist.

The verb *Ɛarraf* 'to present, introduce' is an idiomatic causative of
Ɛəref 'to know, get to know'. It is idiomatic mainly in its syntax:
instead of being doubly transitive — which is the normal thing for
causitives of transitive verbs — it takes only one object and a prepositional complement: *Ɛarraf (ḥada) Ɛala (ḥada)* 'to introduce (someone)
to (someone)'.

A more severe case of idiomatic derivation can be seen in the relationship between *ḥtaram* 'to respect' and *ḥaram* 'to deprive (someone) of (something)'. The regular mediopassive function of the *-t-* would theoretically
produce a derivative meaning 'to deprive one's self of, to hold aloof from'.
The actual meaning, however, is considerably altered, first by specialization in the sense 'to observe a taboo with respect to', thence by
generalization: 'to respect'.[2]

Strictly speaking, it is not words as wholes that are derived from
other words, but words as they are used in particular senses. The verb
ḥtaram means not only 'to respect', but also 'to miss, to be deprived of';
in this sense it is a fairly straightforward passive or *ḥaram*.

---

[1] Not a functional derivative, though it may be a historical derivative.
When in the course of history one or both paronyms undergo such drastic
changes in meaning that the connection between them is no longer apparent,
then the derivation has ceased to be functional.

[2] The derivation of *ḥtaram* from *ḥaram* is already well on the way to being
non-functional. While some native speakers may perceive the semantic
connection between the two words intuitively, others would have to "work
it out" or have it pointed out to them. Though the distinction between
functional and non-functional derivations is a real and useful one, it
is neither possible (by present criteria) nor desirable (for present
purposes) to draw a sharp line between them.

The verb *štaġal* 'to work', for instance, is the mediopassive of *šaġal* 'to occupy, make...busy', but this derivation applies only insofar as the subject-referent of *štaġal* is animate. When it is inanimate (say, a machine), then *štaġal* is not the mediopassive of *šaġal*, but rather of *šaġġal* 'to operate, put into operation'.[1]

---

[1]Or better, perhaps, *šaġġal* may be considered the causative of *štaġal*. Causative and mediopassive are the converse of each other [p. 238], and since both words are singly augmented, there is no basis for deciding which is derivative and which underlying.

Some scholars would object to calling either word a derivative of the other, on the grounds that both analyses imply etymologies that are very likely false. But it goes without saying, of any strictly synchronic method of analysis, that no etymologies — at least no particular etymologies — are implied, even though the analysis of the system as a whole may be so designed as to suggest good etymologies in most cases.

The present method does not imply that any given derivative necessarily "came from" (or "comes from") its underlying word, nor that it is necessarily more closely associated with its underlying word than with other paronyms. It merely implies that the category to which the derivative belongs is — on the whole — best described in terms of its underlying word's category.

The description of Arabic derivation in this book departs from more traditional descriptions, in that all derivational categories (except color and defect adjectives [p. 130]) are defined in terms of underlying word bases; none is treated as a primary category, i.e. none is defined in terms of roots.

One reason for stopping derivational analysis short of the root has been given in the footnote on p. 47. Another reason (or another aspect of the fundamental reason) has to do with the "meanings of roots".

The purported meaning of the root *k-t-b*, for instance, is sometimes formulated in English in the phrase 'having to do with writing'. Thus the locative noun *maktab* 'office' can be analyzed derivationally as meaning 'a place having to do with writing', and the occupational noun *kāteb* 'writer', 'clerk', as 'a person whose occupation has to do with writing'. (Note, however, that this type of analysis fails to reflect the more specific relationships such as that between *kāteb* 'clerk' and *maktab* 'office', or that between *ktāb* 'book' and the locative *maktabe* 'library'.)

But since the verb pattern *FaɛaL* cannot be associated with any specific kind of meaning, the simple verb *katab* 'to write' can only be analyzed as meaning 'to do something having to do with writing'. The tautology is obvious; the formula 'to write' and the formula 'having to do. with writing' differ only in that the latter is worded to sound vague and dissociated from any particular part of speech. The purported meaning of the root *k-t-b*, then, is seen to be merely the blurred and deverb-alized meaning of the verb *katab*.

So the functional head of this word family turns out after all to be a simple word base, while the root — in this light — appears as a sort

of family emblem or icon which has no intrinsic meaning but which is
invested with, and reflects, the meaning of the "head" word base.

A common objection to the foregoing argument is that there are many
word families in which certain derivatives have no underlying words, and
therefore if these orphan derivatives are to be analyzed at all, they
must be analyzed in terms of their roots and patterns.
This objection defeats itself, however. To observe that certain
derivatives have no underlying words is to point out missing members of
their word families; and to point out the missing members — to interpo-
late hypothetical underlying bases — validates and confirms the base-
hierarchy type of analysis while showing exactly how the root-pattern
analysis may be dispensed with.

Arabic roots could be utilized as derivational primes if the term
'root' were used to denote elements that enter into construction only
with primary patterns, i.e. patterns which specify no meanings but only
fix the parts of speech. In that case, however, the gaps left between
orphan derivatives and their roots would still have to be bridged by
hypothetical underlying bases.
For practical purposes it seems preferable to treat primary bases
(actual or hypothetical) as derivational primes, and not to tamper with
the traditional Arabistic concept of root, which is probably more useful, generally speaking, as it stands.

CHAPTER 3:   VERB PATTERNS (*ʔawzān l-fiɛl*)

WITH INFLECTIONAL PARADIGMS

Most of the Arabic verb patterns (commonly called "stems", "forms", or "measures") are traditionally designated in Western grammars and dictionaries by numerical labels. For instance "Pattern II" ("the second stem") is Pattern *FaɛɛaL*, "Pattern III" is *FāɛaL*, etc. The several simple patterns are designated collectively as "Pattern I".

The base inflection (3rd person masc./sing. perfect) is not sufficient as a citation form to differentiate the simple triradical patterns one from another, so these patterns (and the verbs instantiating them) are often cited with two "principle parts", the second of which is the 3rd p. masc./sing. imperfect indicative. Thus the verb *ḥamal, byəḥmel* 'to carry' is an example of Pattern *FaɛaL, byəFɛeL*. (Augmented verbs also are sometimes cited in this way, though their imperfect can be deduced from the perfect.) Pattern *FaɛaL, byəFɛeL* may also be cited as Pattern I(*a-e*) — with the first letter in the parenthesis showing the stem vowel of the perfect and the second letter showing the stem vowel of the imperfect.

Each pattern — and each alteration of it — is illustrated with at least one paradigm showing the complete inflection[1] of a verb. These inflectional paradigms constitute a sort of distributed appendix, serving not only this chapter, but also Chapter 6, in which the inflectional affixes and stem modifications are described.

It should not be supposed that each of the many paradigms in this chapter illustrates a different "conjugation" that has to be learned separately. The inflectional affixes are much the same for all patterns; the few variations they incur with different types of stem have relatively little to do with base patterns as such. Inflectional stem modifications, likewise, apply to verb classes each of which subsumes — or intersects — a number of different base patterns.

Index of Patterns

SIMPLE TRIRADICAL PATTERNS:

---

[1] Inflection does not include pronoun object suffixes.   See Ch. 21.

AUGMENTED TRIRADICAL PATTERNS:

PSEUDO-QUADRIRADICAL PATTERNS:

TRUE QUADRIRADICAL PATTERNS:

PATTERN I(a-o):   *FaɛaL, byəFɛoL*

Sound Verbs. Examples:

ʔamar, byəʔmor 'to command'	*xalaṣ, byəxloṣ* 'to finish'
daras, byədros 'to study'	*katab, byəktob* 'to write'
ṭabax, byəṭbox 'to cook'	*barad, byəbrod* 'to get cold'

INFLECTION OF *katab* 'to write'

	Perfect	Impf. Indic.	Impf. Subjn.	Impv.	
3m	*kátab*	*byə́ktob*	*yə́ktob*		'he'
f	*kátbet*	*btə́ktob*	*tə́ktob*		'she'
pl	*kátabu*	*byə́kᵊtbu*	*yə́kᵊtbu*		'they'
2m	*katáb(ᵊ)t*	*btə́ktob*	*tə́ktob*	*ktṓb*	'you'
f	*katábti*	*btə́kᵊtbi*	*təkᵊtbi*	*ktə́bi*	'you'
pl	*katábtu*	*btə́kᵊtbu*	*tə́kᵊtbu*	*ktə́bu*	'you'
1sg	*katáb(ᵊ)t*	*bə́ktob*	*ʔə́ktob*		'I'
pl	*katábna*	*mnə́ktob*	*nə́ktob*		'we'

Participles: Act. *kāteb*, Pass. *maktūb* (Gerunds: *ktābe, katᵊb*)

Initial-Weak Verbs: *ʔakal, byākol* 'to eat'; *ʔaxad, byāxod* 'to take'

The initial radical *ʔ* of these two verbs fuses with the prefix vowel of the imperfect to produce *ā*, and disappears entirely in the imperative. (In all other verbs on this pattern the initial radical *ʔ* is stable, e.g. *ʔamar, byəʔmor*.)

INFLECTION OF ʔaxad 'to take, get'

	Perfect	Impf. Indic.	Impf. Subjn.	Impv.	
3m	ʔáxad	byāxod	yāxod		'he'
f	ʔáxdet	btāxod	tāxod		'she'
pl	ʔáxadu	byāxdu	yāxdu		'they'
2m	ʔaxád(ᵃ)t[1]	btāxod	tāxod	xōd	'you'
f	ʔaxátti	btāxdi	tāxdi	xə́di	'you'
pl	ʔaxáttu	btāxdu	tāxdu	xə́du	'you'
1sg	ʔaxád(ᵃ)t[1]	bāxod	ʔāxod		'I'
pl	ʔaxádna	mnāxod	nāxod		'we'

Participles: Act. ʔāxed, Pass. maʔxūd (Gerund: ʔaxᵃd)

Hollow Verbs. Examples:

ʔāl, biʔūl 'to say'   kān, bikūn 'to be'

zār, bizūr 'to visit'   sāʔ, bisūʔ 'to drive'

māt, bimūt 'to die'   lām, bilūm 'to blame'

All these verbs have w as their middle radical. In the perfect the w disappears entirely, while in the imperfect it fuses with the pattern vowel o to produce ū.

---

[1]Or with assimilation of d to t [p. 26]: ʔaxátt.

INFLECTION OF $s\bar{a}^{\,?}$ 'to drive'

	Perfect	Impf. Indic.	Impf. Subjn.	Impv.	
3m	$s\bar{a}^{\,?}$	$bis\bar{u}^{\,?}$	$ys\bar{u}^{\,?}$		'he'
f	$s\bar{a}^{\,?}et$	$b\partial ts\bar{u}^{\,?}$	$ts\bar{u}^{\,?}$		'she'
pl	$s\bar{a}^{\,?}u$	$bis\bar{u}^{\,?}u$	$ys\bar{u}^{\,?}u$		'they'
2m	$s\acute{\partial}^{\,?}(^{\partial})t$	$b\partial ts\bar{u}^{\,?}$	$ts\bar{u}^{\,?}$	$s\bar{u}^{\,?}$	'you'
f	$s\acute{\partial}^{\,?}ti$	$b\partial ts\bar{u}^{\,?}i$	$ts\bar{u}^{\,?}i$	$s\bar{u}^{\,?}i$	'you'
pl	$s\acute{\partial}^{\,?}tu$	$b\partial ts\bar{u}^{\,?}u$	$ts\bar{u}^{\,?}u$	$s\bar{u}^{\,?}u$	'you'
1sg	$s\acute{\partial}^{\,?}(^{\partial})t$	$bs\bar{u}^{\,?}$	$s\bar{u}^{\,?}$		'I'
pl	$s\acute{\partial}^{\,?}na$	$m\partial ns\bar{u}^{\,?}$	$ns\bar{u}^{\,?}$		'we'

Participle: Act. $s\bar{a}ye^{\,?}$ (Gerund: $sy\bar{a}^{\,?}a.$)

There are no defective verbs [p. 43] with Pattern I(a-o) in Syrian Arabic (other than in classicisms such as $^{?}ar\check{z}\bar{u}k$ 'I beg of you'). All simple defective verbs have Pattern I (a-e) or (e-a).

In many parts of Greater Syria (including Damascus) geminate verbs [p. 42] have only ∂ as imperfect stem vowel, thus neutralizing the difference between Patterns I (a-o) and I (a-e). [See p. 13.] All simple geminates are classed here with Pattern I(a-o/e), p. 63.

PATTERN I (a-e): $Fa\mathcal{E}aL, by\partial F\mathcal{E}eL$

Sound Verbs. Examples:

$^{?}asam, by\partial^{?}sem$ 'to divide'	$\dot{g}asal, by\partial\dot{g}sel$ 'to wash'
$\hbar amal, by\partial\hbar mel$ 'to carry'	$\mathcal{E}a\check{z}ab, by\partial\mathcal{E}\check{z}eb$ 'to please'
$kama\check{s}, by\partial kme\check{s}$ 'to grasp'	$\mathcal{E}awa\check{z}, by\partial\mathcal{E}we\check{z}$ 'to bend'

INFLECTION OF *ḥamal* 'to carry'

	Perfect	Impf. Indic.	Impf. Subjn.	Impv.	
3m	ḥámal	byə́ḥmel	yə́ḥmel		'he'
f	ḥámlet	btə́ḥmel	tə́ḥmel		'she'
pl	ḥámalu	byə́ḥᵊmlu	yə́ḥᵊmlu		'they'
2m	ḥamál(ᵊ)t	btə́ḥmel	tə́ḥmel	ḥmēl	'you'
f	ḥamálti	btə́ḥᵊmli	tə́ḥᵊmli	ḥmə́li	'you'
pl	ḥamáltu	btə́ḥᵊmlu	tə́ḥᵊmlu	ḥmə́lu	'you'
1sg	ḥamál(ᵊ)t	bə́ḥmel	ʔə́ḥmel		'I'
pl	ḥamálna	mnə́ḥmel	nə́ḥmel		'we'

Participles: Act. *ḥāmel*, Pass. *maḥmūl*   (Gerund: *ḥamᵊl*)

There are a number of sound verbs on this pattern that have medial radical *w*. Most of them are correlative to defect-adjectives [p.130]: *ɛawar* 'to put out an eye' (cf. *ʔaɛwar* 'one-eyed'), *ɛawaž* 'to bend' (cf. *ʔaɛwaž* 'bent'), *ḥawal* 'to make cross-eyed' (cf. *ʔaḥwal* 'cross-eyed'). Also *zawar* 'to frown at, give a significant look'.

Otherwise, I(a-e) verbs with medial radical *w* (and stable final radical) are hollow [p.59].

INFLECTION OF *ɛawaž* 'to bend'

	Perfect	Impf. Indic.	Impf. Subjn.	Impv.	
3m	ɛáwaž	byə́ɛwež	yə́ɛwež		'he'
f	ɛáwžet	btə́ɛwež	tə́ɛwež		'she'
pl	ɛáwažu	byə́ɛᵊwžu	yə́ɛᵊwžu		'they'
2m	ɛawáž(ᵊ)t	btə́ɛwež	tə́ɛwež	ɛwēž	'you'
f	ɛawážti	btə́ɛᵊwži	tə́ɛᵊwži	ɛwə́ži	'you'
pl	ɛawážtu	btə́ɛᵊwžu	tə́ɛᵊwžu	ɛwə́žu	'you'
1sg	ɛawáž(ᵊ)t	bə́ɛwež	ʔə́ɛwež		'I'
pl	ɛawážna	mnə́ɛwež	nəɛwež		'we'

Participles: Act. *ɛāwež*, Pass. *maɛwūž*   (Gerund: *ɛawže*)

Initial-Weak Verbs.   Examples:

waɛad, byū́ɛed 'to promise'   waṣaf, byū́ṣef 'to describe'

wazan, byū́zen 'to weigh'   wažad, byū́žed 'to find'

    The prefix vowel ə merges with the initial radical w
to produce ū in the imperfect.

INFLECTION OF waṣaf 'to describe'

	Perfect	Impf. Indic.	Impf. Subjn.	Impv.	
3m	waṣaf	byū́ṣef	yū́ṣef		'he'
f	wáṣfet	btū́ṣef	tū́ṣef		'she'
pl	wáṣafu	byū́ṣfu	yū́ṣfu		'they'
2m	waṣáf(ə)t	btū́ṣef	tū́ṣef	wṣḗf	'you'
f	waṣáfti	btū́ṣfi	tū́ṣfi	wṣə́fi	'you'
pl	waṣáftu	btū́ṣfu	tū́ṣfu	wṣə́fu	'you'
1sg	waṣáf(ə)t	bū́ṣef	ʔū́ṣef		'I'
pl	waṣáfna	mnuṣef	nuṣef		'we'

Participles: Act. wā́ṣef, Pass. mawṣū́f   (Gerund: waṣəf)

Hollow Verbs.   Examples:

ʔām, biʔīm 'to remove'   ġāb, biġīb 'to be absent'

zād, bizīd 'to increase'   ɛāš, biɛīš 'to live'

bāɛ, bibīɛ 'to sell'   ṭār, biṭīr 'to fly'

    In the perfect the medial radical w or y disappears
entirely. In the imperfect, the semivowel fuses with
the pattern vowel e to produce ī. (n.b.: w + e → ī, as
well as y + e → ī.)

INFLECTION OF *faʔ* 'to wake up' (intrans.)

	Perfect	Impf.Indic.	Impf.Subjn.	Impv.	
3m	*fāʔ*	*bifīʔ*	*yfīʔ*		'he'
f	*fāʔet*	*bətfīʔ*	*tfīʔ*		'she'
pl	*fāʔu*	*bifīʔu*	*yfiʔu*		'they'
2m	*fə́ʔ(ə)t*	*bətfīʔ*	*tfīʔ*	*fīʔ*	'you'
f	*fə́ʔti*	*bətfīʔi*	*tfīʔi*	*fīʔi*	'you'
pl	*fə́ʔtu*	*bətfīʔu*	*tfīʔu*	*fīʔu*	'you'
1sg	*fə́ʔ(ə)t*	*bfīʔ*	*fīʔ*		'I'
pl	*fə́ʔna*	*mənfīʔ*	*nfīʔ*		'we'

Participle: *fāyeʔ*   (Gerund: *fēʔa*)

Defective Verbs.   Examples:

ḥaka, byəḥki 'to speak'	*ṭafa, byəṭfi* 'to extinguish'
bana, byəbni 'to build'	*tawa, byəṭwi* 'to fold'
ḥaya, byəḥyi 'to enliven'	*daƐa, byədƐi* 'to envoke'

In the base form (3rd p. pf.) the final radical *w* or *y* disappears; in the imperfect it fuses with the pattern vowel *e* to form *i*. (Note that *e* + *w* in these circumstances produces *i* just as *e* + *y* does: Root *d–Ɛ–w* with Pattern I (*a–e*) gives *daƐa*, *byədƐi*. (There are no defective verbs in Pattern I (*a–o*)).

INFLECTION OF *bana* 'to build'

	Perfect	Impf.Indic.	Impf.Subjn.	Impv.	
3m	bána	byə́bni	yə́bni		'he'
f	bánet	btə́bni	tə́bni		'she'
pl	bánu	byə́bnu	yə́bnu		'they'
2m	banēt	btə́bni	tə́bni	bnî, ꞓə́bni	'you'
f	banētí	btə́bni	tə́bni	bnî, ꞓə́bni	'you'
pl	banētu	btə́bnu	tə́bnu	bnū, ꞓə́bnu	'you'
1sg	banēt	bə́bni	ꞓə́bni		'I'
pl	banēna	mnə́bni	nə́bni		'we'

Participles: Act. *bāni*, Pass. *məbni*   (Gerund: *binā̆ꞓ*)

The verb *ɛaṭa* 'to give' has prefix-supporting vowel *a* in the imperfect:

3m	ɛáṭa	byáɛṭi	yáɛṭi		'he'
f	ɛáṭeṭ	bṭáɛṭi	ṭáɛṭi		'she'
pl	ɛáṭu	byáɛṭu	yáɛṭu		'they'
2m	ɛaṭēṭ	bṭáɛṭi	ṭáɛṭi	ɛáṭi[1]	'you'
f	ɛaṭēṭi	bṭáɛṭi	ṭáɛṭi	ɛáṭi	'you'
pl	ɛaṭēṭu	bṭáɛṭu	ṭaɛṭu	ɛáṭu	'you'
1sg	ɛaṭēṭ	báɛṭi	ꞓáɛṭi		'I'
pl	ɛaṭēna	mnáɛṭi	náɛṭi		'we'

Participle: Act. *ɛāṭi*   (Gerund: *ɛaṭā̆ꞓ*, *ɛaṭa*)

A medial radical *w* or *y* remains intact in defective verbs:

---

[1]Note the irregular imperative stem (instead of *ꞓaɛṭi*).

INFLECTION OF *ṭawa* 'to fold'

	Perfect	Impf. Indic.	Impf. Subjn.	Impv.	
3m	ṭáwa	byáṭwi	yáṭwi		'he'
f	ṭáwet	bṭáṭwi	ṭáṭwi		'she'
pl	ṭáwu	byáṭwu	yáṭwu		'they'
2m	ṭawēt	bṭáṭwi	ṭáṭwi	ṭwī, ᵓáṭwi	'you'
f	ṭawēti	bṭáṭwi	ṭáṭwi	ṭwī, ᵓáṭwi	'you'
pl	ṭawētu	bṭáṭwu	ṭáṭwu	ṭwū, ᵓáṭwu	'you'
1sg	ṭawēt	báṭwi	ᵓáṭwi		'I'
pl	ṭawēna	mnáṭwi	náṭwi		'we'

Participles: Act. *ṭāwi*, Pass. *məṭwi*   (Gerund: *ṭawye*)

Defective verbs with initial radical *w* are also initial-weak [see p. 187]:

INFLECTION OF *wafa* 'to fulfill'

	Perfect	Impf. Indic.	Impf. Subjn.	Impv.	
3m	wáfa	byūfi	yūfi		'he'
f	wáfet	btūfi	tūfi		'she'
pl	wáfu	byūfu	yūfu		'they'
2m	wafēt	btūfi	tūfi	wfī, ᵓūfi	'you'
f	wafēti	btūfi	tūfi	wfī, ᵓūfi	'you'
pl	wafētu	btūfu	tūfu	wfū, ᵓūfu	'you'
1sg	wafēt	būfi	ᵓūfi		'I'
pl	wafēna	mnūfi	nūfi		'we'

Participle: Act. *wāfi*   (Gerund: *wafi*)

Grammatical Characteristics of Pattern I(a-e). A large majority of the sound and defective verbs are transitive. Of the hollow verbs, however, there is no significant predominance of one syntactic type over others.

A few of the hollow verbs of this pattern[1] are derived as causatives [p. 240] from I *(a-o)* verbs:

dām, bidīm 'to make...last'	(← *dām, bidūm* 'to last')
ʔām, biʔīm 'to pick...up'	(← *ʔām, biʔūm* 'to get up')

MERGED PATTERNS I (a-o) and I (a-e)

The distinction between Pattern I *(a-o)* and Pattern I *(a-e)* is functional for hollow verbs only (*ʔām, biʔūm* 'to get up' v.s. *ʔām, biʔīm* 'to pick up, to remove').

No defective verbs have Pattern I *(a-o)*; as for sound verbs, some conform to one pattern and some to the other, but apparently no two verbs with the same root are distinguished only by the one's having imperfect vowel *o* while the other as *e*.

Many sound verbs belong to both patterns, the choice of imperfect vowel *o* or *e* being optional (or subject to unsystematic variation among individuals or regions):

ʔatal, byəʔtol/byəʔtel 'to kill' *ṣaraf, byəṣrof/byəṣref* 'to spend'

našar, byənšor/byənšer 'to saw' *lafat, byəlfot/byəlfet* 'to turn'

xabaz, byəxboz/byəxbez 'to bake' *tarak, byətrok/byətrek* 'to leave'

Note, furthermore, that when any kind of suffix is added to the imperfect stem of a Pattern I *(a-o)* or I *(a-e)* verb, the *e/o* distinction is obliterated [pp. 28, 197].

byəṭlob 'he asks for': *byəṭəlbu* 'they ask for'

byəḥmel 'he carries': *byəḥəmlu* 'they carry'

Geminate Verbs. Examples:

madd, bimədd 'to extend'	*ḥall, biḥəll* 'to solve'
ʔann, biʔənn 'to groan'	*daʔʔ, bidəʔʔ* 'to knock'
ṣabb, biṣəbb 'to pour'	*ḥass, biḥəss* 'to feel'

[1]Corresponding to Classical Pattern IV: *ʔadāma, yudīmu; ʔaqāma, yuqīmu.*

All these verbs have middle and final radicals alike.
(Note, however, that if the like radicals are semivowels
— as in the root *ḥ-y-y* — the verb will be defective, not
geminate: *ḥaya, byaḥyi* 'to revive'.)

The pattern vowel (perfect *a*, imperfect *o* or *e*) does
not appear between the two like radicals, which are fused
together as a double consonant in all inflections. Between
the first and middle radicals, the *a* of the perfect remains,
while *ə* is used in the imperfect.

Thus in many parts of the Syrian area (including the
Damascus standard used in this book) the distinction between
Patterns I *(a-o)* and I *(a-e)* is completely obliterated in
geminate verbs, since neither *o* nor *e* normally occurs before
two consonants — both being neutralized as *ə* [p.23]. In
parts of Lebanon and Palestine, on the other hand, one will
hear for example *ḥaṭṭ, biḥuṭṭ* 'to put' (with imperfect vowel
u) in contract to *ḥass, biḥiss* 'to feel' (with imperfect
vowel *i*). (Note, however, that *ə* before *ṭ* sounds very much
like *u*, and *ə* before *s* sounds very much like *i* [p.13].)

INFLECTION OF *ḥass* 'to feel'

	Perfect	Impf. Indic.	Impf. Subjn.	Impv.	
3m	*ḥáss*	*biḥə́ss*	*yḥə́ss*		'he'
f	*ḥásset*	*bətḥə́ss*	*tḥə́ss*		'she'
pl	*ḥássu*	*biḥə́ssu*	*yḥə́ssu*		'they'
2m	*hassēt*	*bətḥə́ss*	*tḥə́ss*	*ḥə́ss*	'you'
f	*ḥassēti*	*bətḥə́ssi*	*tḥə́ssi*	*ḥə́ssi*	'you'
pl	*ḥassētu*	*bətḥə́ssu*	*tḥə́ssu*	*ḥə́ssu*	'you'
1sg	*ḥassēt*	*bḥə́ss*	*ḥə́ss*		'I'
pl	*ḥassēna*	*mənḥə́ss*	*nḥə́ss*		'we'

Participles: Act. *ḥāses*, Pass. *maḥsūs*   (Gerund: *ḥəss*)

PATTERN I (a-a):   *FaɛaL, byəFɛaL*

Sound Verbs.   Examples:

saʔal, byəsʔal	'to ask'		*gahar, byəghar*	'to appear'	
fataḥ, byəftaḥ	'to open'		*baɛat, byəbɛat*	'to send'	
žamaɛ, byəžmaɛ	'to bring together'		*ḥafaẓ, byəḥfaẓ*	'to keep'	

The vast majority of these verbs have a back consonant (*x, ġ, q, ḥ, ɛ, h,* or *ʔ*) either as middle or last radical.

INFLECTION OF *saʔal* 'to ask'

	Perfect	Impf. Indic.	Impf. Subjn.	Impv.	
3m	*sáʔal*	*byə́sʔal*	*yə́sʔal*		'he'
f	*sáʔlet*	*btə́sʔal*	*tə́sʔal*		'she'
pl	*sáʔalu*	*byə́sʔalu*	*yə́sʔalu*		'they'
2m	*saʔál(ə)t*	*btə́sʔal*	*tə́sʔal*	*sʔāl*	'you'
f	*saʔálti*	*btə́sʔali*	*tə́sʔali*	*sʔáli*	'you'
pl	*saʔáltu*	*btə́sʔalu*	*tə́sʔalu*	*sʔálu*	'you'
1sg	*saʔál(ə)t*	*bə́sʔal*	*ʔə́sʔal*		'I'
pl	*saʔálna*	*mnə́sʔal*	*nə́sʔal*		'we'

Participles: Act. *sāʔel*   Pass. *masʔūl*.[1]

---

[1]Most commonly used idiomatically in the sense 'responsible, in charge'.

Initial-Weak Verbs: *waḍaɛ byūdaɛ* 'to place'; *wadaɛ, byūdaɛ* 'to entrust, deposit'.

These two verbs, like those of Pattern I *(a–e)*, have imperfect stems beginning with *-ū*, from the fusion of the prefix vowel with the initial radical *w*.

INFLECTION OF *waḍaɛ* 'to put, place'

	Perfect	Impf. Indic.	Impf. Subjn.	Impv.	
3m	*wáḍaɛ*	*byūḍaɛ*	*yūḍaɛ*		'he'
f	*wáḍɛet*	*bṭūḍaɛ*	*ṭūḍaɛ*		'she'
pl	*wáḍaɛu*	*byūḍaɛu*	*yūḍaɛu*		'they'
2m	*waḍáɛ(ᵊ)t*	*bṭūḍaɛ*	*ṭūḍaɛ*	*wḍāɛ*	'you'
f	*waḍáɛti*	*bṭūḍaɛi*	*ṭūḍaɛi*	*wḍáɛi*	'you'
pl	*waḍáɛtu*	*bṭūḍaɛu*	*ṭūḍaɛu*	*wḍáɛu*	'you'
1sg	*waḍáɛ(ᵊ)t*	*būḍaɛ*	*ʔūḍaɛ*		'I'
	waḍáɛna	*mnūḍaɛ*	*nūḍaɛ*		'we'

Participles: Act. *wāḍeɛ*, Pass. *mawḍūɛ*   (Gerund: *waḍᵊɛ*)

Hollow Verbs. Examples:

bān, bibān	'to appear'	*bāt, bibāt*	'to spend the night'
nāl, bināl	'to obtain'	*xāf, bixāf*	'to fear'
nām, binām	'to sleep'	*ġār, biġār*	'to be jealous'
hāb, bihāb	'to be awed'	*sāɛ, bisāɛ*	'to contain'

Hollow verbs of this pattern are rare; the above examples are the only ones found. The middle radical *w* or *y* disappears in the base form (3p. perf.) and the two *a*'s of the pattern run together as *ā;* in the imperfect, the radical semivowel fuses with the pattern vowel *a* to produce *ā*.

INFLECTION OF *nām* 'to sleep'

	Perfect	Impf.Indic.	Impf.Subjn.	Impv.	
3m	nām	binām	ynām		'he'
f	nāmet	bətnām	tnām		'she'
pl	nāmu	bināmu	ynāmu		'they'
2m	nə́m(ə)t	betnām	tnām	nām	'you'
f	nə́mti	bətnāmi	tnāmi	nāmi	'you'
pl	nə́mtu	bətnāmu	tnāmu	nāmu	'you'
1sg	nə́m(ə)t	bnām	nām		'I'
pl	nə́mna	mənnām	nnām		'we'

Participle: *nāyem*   (Gerund: *nōm*)

Defective Verbs. Only two defective verbs have Pattern I *(a-a)* consistently over the whole Syrian area:

ʔara, byəʔra   'to read'

raɛa, byərɛa   'to herd, tend'

Also commonly used are:

bada (or bədi), 'to begin'   saɛa (or səɛi), 'to make efforts'
    byəbda   byəsɛa

nama (or nəmi), 'to grow'   ḥawa (or ḥəwi), 'to contain'
    byənma   byəḥwa

ɛaṣa (or ɛəṣi), 'to disobey'
    byəɛṣa

All these verbs have a final radical *w* or *y*, which is lost or fused in all inflections.

INFLECTION OF ʔara 'to read'

	Perfect	Impf. Indic.	Impf. Subjn.	Impv.	
3m	ʔára	byáʔra	yáʔra		'he'
f	ʔáret	btáʔra	táʔra		'she'
pl	ʔáru	byáʔru	yáʔru		'they'
2m	ʔarḗt	btáʔra	táʔra	ʔrā, ʔáʔra	'you'
f	ʔarḗti	btáʔri	táʔri	ʔrī, ʔáʔri	'you'
pl	ʔarḗtu	btáʔru	táʔru	ʔrū, ʔáʔru	'you'
1sg	ʔarḗt	báʔra	ʔáʔra		'I'
pl	ʔarḗna	mnáʔra	náʔra		'we'

Participles: Act. ʔāri, Pass. məʔri   (Gerund: ʔrāye)

Geminate Verbs. Only two geminate verbs have Pattern I (a-a) consistently over the whole Syrian area:

> ḍaḷḷ, biḍaḷḷ   'to remain'
>
> tamm, bitamm   'to remain'

Also commonly used is ɛaḍḍ, biɛaḍḍ 'to bite' (but Palestinian also biɛəḍḍ); Palestinian ṣaḥḥ, biṣaḥḥ 'to be all right' (but elsewhere usually biṣəḥḥ).

INFLECTION OF tamm 'to remain'

3m	támm	bitámm	ytámm		'he'
f	támmet	bəttámm	ttámm		'she'
pl	támmu	bitámmu	ytámmu		'they'
2m	tammḗt	bəttámm	ttámm	támm	'you'
f	tammḗti	bəttámmi	ttámmi	támmi	'you'
pl	tammḗtu	bəttámmu	ttámmu	támmu	'you'
1sg	tammḗt	btámm	támm		'I'
pl	tammḗna	məntámm	ntámm		'we'

Participle: tāmem

PATTERN I (e-e):   *FəƐel, byəFƐeL*

Sound Verbs. Examples:

məsek, byəmsek 'to hold'	*nəzel, byənzel* 'to descend'
ləbes, byəlbes 'to dress'	*Ɛəmel, byəƐmel* 'to make'
ḥəsen, byəḥsen 'to be able'	*ʔəder, byəʔder* 'to be able'

This pattern is rare; the above examples are the only ones generally used. *Ɛəref, byaƐref* 'to know' conforms to this pattern except for the supporting vowel *a* with the subject prefixes [177] — also commonly used in *Ɛəmel, byaƐmel*. (*ġəder, byəġder* 'to be able' is a variant of *ʔəder, byəʔder*.) Regional variants include *byəʔdar* (Pal.), *byənzal* (Leb.), *byaƐmal* (Pal.), which put these verbs in Pattern I (*e-a*), and *məsak*, which puts this verb in Pattern I (*a-e*).

INFLECTION OF *nəzel* 'to descend'

	Perfect	Impf. Indic.	Impf. Subjn.	Impv.	
3m	*nə́zel*	*byə́nzel*	*yə́nzel*		'he'
f	*nə́zlet*	*btə́nzel*	*tə́nzel*		'she'
pl	*nə́zlu*	*byə́nzlu*	*yə́nzlu*		'they'
2m	*nzə́l(ə)t*	*btə́nzel*	*tə́nzel*	*nzḗl*	'you'
f	*nzə́lti*	*btə́nzli*	*tə́nzli*	*nzə́li*	'you'
pl	*nzə́ltu*	*btə́nzlu*	*tə́nzlu*	*nzə́lu*	'you'
1sg	*nzə́l(ə)t*	*bə́nzel*	*ʔə́nzel*		'I'
pl	*nzə́lna*	*mnə́nzel*	*nə́nzel*		'we'

Participle: Act. *nāzel*   (Gerund: *nzū̄l*)

The verb *Ɛəref* 'to know' (as usually also *Ɛəmel* 'to do') has *a* as prefix-supporting vowel in the imperfect:

	Perfect	Impf. Indic.	Impf. Subjn.	Impv.	
3m	Ɛə́ref	byáƐref	yáƐref		'he'
f	Ɛə́rfet	btáƐref	táƐref		'she'
pl	Ɛə́rfu	byáƐᵊrfu	yaƐᵊrfu		'they'
2m	Ɛrə́f(ᵊ)t	btáƐref	táƐref	Ɛréf	'you'
f	Ɛrə́fti	btáƐᵊrfi	táƐᵊrfi	Ɛrə́fi	'you'
pl	Ɛrə́ftu	btáƐᵊrfu	táƐᵊrfu	Ɛrə́fu	'you'
1sg	Ɛrə́f(ᵊ)t	bdƐref	ʔáƐref		'I'
pl	Ɛrə́fna	mnáƐref	náƐref		'we'

Participles: Act. *Ɛāref, Ɛarfān,* Pass. *maƐrūf*   (Gerund: *Ɛarafān*[1])

Defective Verbs. Only two verbs have this pattern consistently over the whole Syrian area:

> *bəki, byəbki*   'to cry'
>
> *məši, byəmši*   'to walk'

Commonly heard in Lebanon is *ḥəki* (for *ḥaka*), *byəḥki* 'to speak'.

INFLECTION OF *məši* 'to walk'

3m	mə́ši	byə́mši	yə́mši		'he'
f	mə́šyet	btə́mši	tə́mši		'she'
pl	mə́šyu	byə́mšu	yə́mšu		'they'
2m	mšīt	btə́mši	tə́mši	mšî, ʔə́mši	'you'
f	mšīti	btə́mši	tə́mši	mšî, ʔə́mši	'you'
pl	mšītu	btə́mšu	tə́mšu	mšū̂, ʔə́mšu	'you'
1sg	mšīt	bə́mši	ʔə́mši		'I'
pl	mšīna	mnə́mši	nə́mši		'we'

Participles: Act. *māši,* Pass. *məmši (Ɛalē)*   (Gerund: *maši)*

---

[1] In the sense 'acquaintance (with)', familiarity (with)', the hypostatic noun [p. 309] *maƐᵊrfe* is used.

PATTERN I (e-a): *FəƐel, byəFƐaL*

Sound Verbs. , Examples:

ʔəbel, byəʔbal 'to accept' *ləƐeb, byəlƐab* 'to play'

fəhem, byəfham 'to understand' *kəber, byəkbar* 'to grow up'

ʔətel, byəʔtal 'to be killed' *ṭuwel, byəṭwal* 'to grow tall'

The verb *ṭuwel* (or *ṭəwel*), with medial radical *w*, is an exception to the general rule that verbs with a semivocalic middle radical — and consonantal final radical — are hollow. (Cf. medial *w* sound verbs of Pattern I *(a-e)* [p.58].) (There is a hollow *(a-o)* verb with the same root: *ṭāl, biṭūl* 'to be a long time'.)

INFLECTION OF *ʔəbel* 'to accept'

	Perfect	Impf.Indic.	Impf.Subjn.	Impv.	
3m	*ʔə́bel*	*byə́ʔbal*	*yə́ʔbal*		'he'
f	*ʔə́blet*	*btə́ʔbal*	*tə́ʔbal*		'she'
pl	*ʔə́blu*	*byə́ʔbalu*	*yə́ʔbalu*		'they'
2m	*ʔbə́l(ə)t*	*btə́ʔbal*	*tə́ʔbal*	*ʔbāl*	'you'
f	*ʔbə́lii*	*btə́ʔbali*	*tə́ʔbali*	*ʔbə́li*	'you'
pl	*ʔbə́ltu*	*btə́ʔbalu*	*tə́ʔbalu*	*ʔbə́lu*	'you'
1sg	*ʔbə́l(ə)t*	*bə́ʔbal*	*ʔə́ʔbal*		'I'
pl	*ʔbə́lna*	*mnə́ʔbal*	*nə́ʔbal*		'we'

Participles: Act. *ʔābel*, Pass. *maʔbūl* (Gerund: *ʔəblān*)

INFLECTION OF *ṭəwel* or *ṭuwel* 'to grow tall'

	Perfect	Impf. Indic.	Impf. Subjn.	Impv.	
3m	*ṭə́wel (ṭúwel)*	*byə́ṭwal*	*yə́ṭwal*		'he'
f	*ṭə́wleṭ (ṭūleṭ)*	*btə́ṭwal*	*tə́ṭwal*		'she'
pl	*ṭə́wlu (ṭūlu)*	*byə́ṭwalu*	*yə́ṭwalu*		'they'
2m	*ṭwə́l(ə)t*	*btə́ṭwal*	*tə́ṭwal*	*ṭwāl*	'you'
f	*ṭwə́lṭi*	*btə́ṭwali*	*tə́ṭwali*	*ṭwáli*	'you'
pl	*ṭwə́lṭu*	*btə́ṭwalu*	*tə́ṭwalu*	*ṭwdlu*	'you'
1sg	*ṭwə́l(ə)t*	*bə́ṭwal*	*ʔə́ṭwal*		'I'
pl	*ṭwə́lna*	*mnə́ṭwal*	*nə́ṭwal*		'we'

Participle: *ṭawlān*   (Gerund: *ṭawalān*)

Defective Verbs: Examples:

bəʔi, byəbʔa 'to stay'	*nəsi, byənsa* 'to forget'
Ɛəṣi, byəƐṣa 'to get stuck'	*šəfi, byəšfa* 'to get well'
wəṭi, byūṭa 'to be low'	*ḥəyi, byəḥya* 'to be revived'

These verbs have a final radical *w* or *y* which fuses
with the perfect vowel *e* to form *i*, and which disappears
after the imperfect vowel *a*.

INFLECTION OF *bəʔi* 'to stay'

3m	*bə́ʔi*	*byə́bʔa*	*yə́bʔa*		'he'
f	*bə́ʔyet*	*btə́bʔa*	*tə́bʔa*		'she'
pl	*bə́ʔyu*	*byə́bʔu*	*yə́bʔu*		'they'
2m	*bʔīt*	*btə́bʔa*	*tə́bʔa*	*bʔā, ʔə́bʔa*	'you'
f	*bʔīti*	*btə́bʔi*	*tə́bʔi*	*bʔī, ʔə́bʔi*	'you'
pl	*bʔītu*	*btə́bʔu*	*tə́bʔu*	*bʔū, ʔə́bʔu*	'you'
1sg	*bʔīt*	*bə́bʔa*	*ʔə́bʔa*		'I'
pl	*bʔīna*	*mnə́bʔa*	*nə́bʔa*		'we'

Participle: *bāʔi, baʔyān* (Gerund: *baʔi*)

Medial radical semivowels remain intact in defective verbs:

INFLECTION OF ʔəwi 'to become strong'

	Perfect	Impf. Indic.	Impf. Subjn.	Impv.	
3m	ʔə́wi	byə́ʔwa	yə́ʔwa		'he'
f	ʔə́wyet	btə́ʔwa	tə́ʔwa		'she'
pl	ʔə́wyu	byəʔwu	yəʔwu		'they'
2m	ʔwī́t	btə́ʔwa	tə́ʔwa	ʔwā́, ʔə́ʔwa	'you'
f	ʔwī́ti	btə́ʔwi	tə́ʔwi	ʔwī́, ʔə́ʔwi	'you'
pl	ʔwī́tu	btə́ʔwu	tə́ʔwu	ʔwū́, ʔə́ʔwu	'you'
1sg	ʔwī́t	bə́ʔwa	ʔə́ʔwa		'I'
pl	ʔwī́na	mnə́ʔwa	nə́ʔwa		'we'

Participle: ʔāwi

INFLECTION OF ḥəyi 'to be revived'

	Perfect	Impf. Indic.	Impf. Subjn.	Impv.	
3m	ḥə́yi	byə́ḥya	yə́ḥya		'he'
f	ḥə́yyet	btə́ḥya	tə́ḥya		'she'
pl	ḥə́yyu	byə́ḥyu	yə́ḥyu		'they'
2m	ḥyī́t	btə́ḥya	tə́ḥya		'you'
f	ḥyī́ti	btə́ḥyi	tə́ḥyi		'you'
pl	ḥyī́tu	btəḥyu	tə́ḥyu		'you'
1sg	ḥyī́t	bə́ḥya	ʔə́ḥya		'I'
pl	ḥyī́na	mnə́ḥya	nə́ḥya		'we'

Defective verbs with initial radical *w* are also
initial-weak: imperfect prefix-vowel *ə* + *w* → *ū*.

INFLECTION OF *wəṭi* 'to be low'

	Perfect	Impf. Indic.	Impf. Subjn.	Impv.	
3m	*wə́ṭi*	*byūṭa*	*yūṭa*		'he'
f	*wə́ṭyeṭ*	*bṭūṭa*	*ṭuṭa*		'she'
pl	*wə́ṭyu*	*byūṭu*	*yūṭu*		'they'
2m	*wṭīṭ*	*bṭūṭa*	*ṭūṭa*	*wṭā, ʔūṭa*	'you'
f	*wṭīṭi*	*bṭūṭi*	*ṭūṭi*	*wṭī, ʔūṭi*	'you'
pl	*wṭīṭu*	*bṭūṭu*	*ṭūṭu*	*wṭū, ʔūṭu*	'you'
1 sg	*wṭīṭ*	*būṭa*	*ʔūṭa*		'I'
pl	*wṭīna*	*mnūṭa*	*nūṭa*		'we'

Participle: *wāṭi*   (Gerund: *wṭuww*)

Initial-Weak Verbs.   Examples:

  wəṣel, byəṣal   (or *byūṣal*)   'to arrive'

  wəʔeɛ, byəʔaɛ   (or *byūʔaɛ*)   'to fall'

  yəbes, byəbas   (or *byības*)   'to dry up'

The initial radical semivowel may either be lost
entirely in the imperfect or else fused with the prefix
vowel *ə* to form *ū* (or *ī*).   In some areas, especially in
Lebanon and Palestine, the forms with *ū* (or *ī*) are used
exclusively.
Some verbs are mainly limited in the imperfect to
forms with *ū* (or *ī*) in all Syrian areas: *wəret, byūrat*
'to inherit', *yəʔes, byīʔas* 'to despair'.   [187].

INFLECTION OF wə́ṣel 'to arrive'

	Perfect	Impf. Indic.	Impf. Subjn.	Impv.	
3m	wə́ṣel	byə́ṣal (byūṣal)	yə́ṣal (yūṣal)		'he'
f	wə́ṣlet	bṭə́ṣal (bṭūṣal)	ṭə́ṣal (ṭūṣal)		'she'
pl	wə́ṣlu	byə́ṣalu (byūṣalu)	yə́ṣalu (yūṣalu)		'they'
2m	wṣə́l(ᵊ)ṭ	bṭə́ṣal (bṭūṣal)	ṭə́ṣal (ṭūṣal)	wṣā́l	'you'
f	wṣə́lṭi	bṭə́ṣali (bṭūṣali)	ṭə́ṣali (ṭūṣali)	wṣáli	'you'
pl	wṣə́lṭu	bṭə́ṣalu (bṭūṣalu)	ṭə́ṣalu (ṭūṣalu)	wṣálu	'you'
1sg	wṣə́l(ᵊ)ṭ	bə́ṣal (būṣal)	ʔə́ṣal (ʔūṣal)		'I'
pl	wṣə́lna	mnə́ṣal (mnūṣal)	nə́ṣal (nūṣal)		'we'

Participle: wāṣel   (Gerund: wṣūl)

INFLECTION OF yəbes 'to dry up'

3m	yə́bes	byə́bas (byības)	yə́bas (yības)		'he'
f	yə́bset	bṭə́bas (bṭības)	ṭə́bas (ṭības)		'she'
pl	yə́bsu	byə́basu (byībasu)	yə́basu (yībasu)		'they'
2m	ybə́s(ᵊ)ṭ	bṭə́bas (bṭības)	ṭə́bas (ṭības)	ybās	'you'
f	ybə́sti	bṭə́basi (bṭībasi)	ṭə́basi (ṭībasi)	ybási	'you'
pl	ybə́stu	bṭə́basu (bṭībasu)	ṭə́basu (ṭībasu)	ybásu	'you'
1sg	ybə́s(ᵊ)ṭ	bə́bas (bības)	ʔə́bas (ʔības)		'I'
pl	ybə́sna	mnə́bas (mnības)	nə́bas (nības)		'we'

Participle: yābes   (Gerund: yabᵊs)

Derivational Types. Many Pattern I(*e-a*) verbs are passives [p. 234],
correlative to active verbs with *a-e* or *a-o* vowelling:

xəreb, byəxrab	'to be ruined'	(cf. *xarab, byəxrob* 'to ruin')
taɛeb, byətɛab	'to get tired'	(cf. *taɛab, byətɛeb* 'to tire')
ḥəyi, byəḥya	'to be revived'	(cf. *ḥaya, byəḥyi* 'to revive')

Some are inchoative or descriptive [p. 250], correlative to simple
adjectives:

kəber, byəkbar	'to grow up, become large'	(cf. *kbîr* 'large, adult')
ẓəġer, byəẓġar	'to become small'	(cf. *ẓġîr* 'small')
ṭuwel, byəṭwal	'to become long or tall'	(cf. *ṭawîl* 'long, tall')
səhel, byəshal	'to be easy'	(cf. *sahᵊl* 'easy')

ANOMALOUS VERB: ʔəža 'to come'

	Perfect	Impf. Indic.	Impf. Subjn.	Impv. (irregular)	
3m	*ʔə́ža*	*byə́ži*	*yə́ži*		'he'
f	*ʔə́žet*	*btə́ži*	*tə́ži*		'she'
pl	*ʔə́žu*	*byə́žu*	*yə́žu*		'they'
2m	*ʔžît*	*btə́ži*	*tə́ži*	*táɛa*	'you'
f	*ʔžîti*	*btə́ži*	*tə́ži*	*táɛi*	'you'
pl	*ʔžîtu*	*btə́žu*	*tə́žu*	*táɛu*	'you'
1sg	*ʔžît*	*bə́ži*	*ʔə́ži*		'I'
pl	*ʔžîna*	*mnə́ži*	*nə́ži*		'we'

Participle (irregular): *žāye*[1].

> Variant forms include *ʔaža, ʔažet, ʔažu* (Damascus and
> elsewhere; *b(y)îži, btîži,* etc. (in Palestine and parts of
> Lebanon); *žā, žāt, žū* (or *žaw), žît, žīna,* etc. (parts of
> Lebanon).

---

[1] With irregular suffixing forms: *žāyî-,* (f.) *žāyît-,* as in *žāyîni,*
žāyîtni 'having come to me'. In some regions the *-e* is lost in the
masculine absolute form: *žāy.*

PATTERN II: *FaɛɛaL, biFaɛɛeL*

Pattern II is augmented [p.46] with respect to Pattern I by a lengthening (or "doubling" [p.15]) of the middle radical. The pattern vowels are *a...a* in the perfect and *a...e* in the imperfect.

Sound Verbs. Examples:

sakkar, bisakker 'to close'	*ṣayyaf, biṣayyef* 'to spend the summer'
ḥammal, biḥammel 'to load'	*xawwaf, bixawwef* 'to frighten'
žarrab, bižarreb 'to try'	*saddaˀ, bisaddeˀ* 'to believe (to be true)'
sabbab, bisabbeb 'to cause'	*waṣṣal, biwaṣṣel* 'to deliver (to destination)'

INFLECTION OF *sakkar* 'to close'

	Perfect	Impf. Indic.	Impf. Subjn.	Impv.	
3m	*sákkar*	*bisákker*	*ysákker*		'he'
f	*sákkaret*	*bətsákker*	*tsákker*		'she'
pl	*sákkaru*	*bisákkru*	*ysákkru*		'they'
2m	*sakkár(ˀ)t*	*bətsákker*	*tsákker*	*sákker*	'you'
f	*sakkárti*	*bətsákkri*	*tsákkri*	*sákkri*	'you'
pl	*sakkártu*	*bətsákkru*	*tsákkru*	*sákkru*	'you'
1sg	*sakkár(ˀ)t*	*bsákker*	*sákker*		'I'
pl	*sakkárna*	*mənsákker*	*nsákker*		'we'

Participles: Act. *msakker* Pass. *msakkar;* Gerund: *taskír*

When the last two radicals are alike (as in *sabbab* 'to cause') the imperfect stem vowel *e* is not dropped when *-i* or *-u* is added, but is changed to *ə:*

	Perfect	Impf. Indic.	Impf. Subjn.	Impv.	
3m	sábbab	bisábbeb	ysábbeb		'he'
f	sábbabet	bətsábbeb	tsábbeb		'she'
pl	sábbabu	bisábbəbu	ysábbəbu		'they'
2m	sabbáb(ə)t	bətsábbeb	tsábbeb	sábbeb	'you'
f	sabbábti	bətsábbəbi	tsábbəbi	sábbəbi	'you'
pl	sabbábtu	bətsábbəbu	tsábbəbu	sábbəbu	'you'
1sg	sabbáb(ə)t	bsábbəb	sábbeb		'I'
pl	sabbábna	mənsábbeb	nsábbeb		'we'

Participles: Act. *msabbeb*, Pass. *msabbab;* Gerund: *tasbîb*

Defective Verbs. Examples:

malla, bimalli	'to fill'		*ɛawwa, biɛawwi*	'to bark'
faḍḍa, bifaḍḍi	'to empty'		*nažža, binažži*	'to save'
samma, bisammi	'to name'		*wadda, biwaddi*	'to lead'
ġanna, biġanni	'to sing'		*naʔʔa, binaʔʔi*	'to choose'

The final radical *w* or *y* disappears in the base form
(perfect); and in the imperfect, fuses with the pattern
vowel *e* to form *i*.

INFLECTION OF *samma* 'to name'

	Perfect	Impf. Indic.	Impf. Subjn.	Impv.	
3m	sámma	bisámmi	ysámmi		'he'
f	sámmet	bətsámmi	tsámmi		'she'
pl	sámmu	bisámmu	ysámmu		'they'
2m	sammēt	bətsámmi	tsámmi	sámmi	'you'
f	sammēti	bətsámmi	tsámmi	sámmi	'you'
pl	sammētu	bətsámmu	tsámmu	sámmu	'you'
1sg	sammēt	bsámmi	sámmi		'I'
pl	sammēna	mənsámmi	nsámmi		'we'

Participles: Act. *msammi*, Pass. *msamma;* Gerund: *təsmāye*

In Pattern II there are no unsound verbs other than defective: Fluctuating or geminating medial (or inital) radicals do not fluctuate or geminate in this pattern.

Pattern II is by far the most common of the augmented verb patterns.

Pattern II Derivational Types

Many are causatives [p. 240]:

faḍḍa	'to empty'	←	*fəḍi*	'to become empty'
ʔawwa	'to strenghten'	←	*ʔəwi*	'to become strong'
ḥammal	'to load'	←	*ḥamal*	'to carry'
šawwaf	'to show'	←	*šāf*	'to see'
fahham	'to explain(to)'	←	*fəhem*	'to understand'

Many are augmentatives [253]:

kassar	'to smash, break to pieces'	←	*kasar*	'to break'
žammaε	'to collect, assemble'	←	*žamaε*	'to bring together'
daffaš	'to push (several things or times)'	←	*dafaš*	'to push'

Some are ascriptive [243]:

sadda?	'to believe (to be true)'	←	*sada?*	'to be true'
xawwan	'to denounce as traitor'	←	*xān*	'to betray'
faḍḍal	'to prefer'	←	*ʔafḍal*	'favorite'

Many are applicative [256] (or denominatives of other kinds):

samma	'to name, call'	←	*ʔəsᵊm*	'name'
zayyat	'to oil'	←	*zēt*	'oil'
sabbab	'to cause'	←	*sabab*	'cause'

PATTERN III: *FāƐaL, biFāƐeL*

Pattern III is augmented with respect to Pattern I by a lengthening (or change) of the first pattern vowel to *ā*. The pattern vowels are *ā...a* in the perfect and *ā...e* in the imperfect.

Sound Verbs. Examples:

Ɛāmal, biƐāmel	'to deal with'	*kātab, bikāteb*	'to write to'
hāžam, bihāžem	'to attack'	*šāwar, bišāwer*	'to consult'
sāfar, bisāfer	'to travel'	*ʔāṣaṣ, biʔāṣeṣ*	'to punish'
bālaġ, bibāleġ	'to exaggerate'	*ḍāḍaḍ, biḍāḍeḍ*	'to oppose'

INFLECTION OF *sāƐad* 'to help'

	Perfect	Impf. Indic.	Impf. Subjn.	Impv.	
3m	*sāƐad*	*bisāƐed*	*ysāƐed*		'he'
f	*sāƐadet*	*bətsāƐed*	*tsāƐed*		'she'
pl	*sāƐadu*	*bisāƐdu*	*ysāƐdu*		'they'
2m	*sāƐád(ᵊ)t*[1]	*bətsāƐed*	*tsāƐed*	*sāƐed*	'you'
f	*sāƐádti*	*bətsāƐdi*	*tsāƐdi*	*sāƐdi*	'you'
pl	*sāƐádtu*	*bətsāƐdu*	*tsāƐdu*	*sāƐdu*	'you'
1sg	*sāƐád(ᵊ)t*[1]	*bsāƐed*	*sāƐed*		'I'
pl	*sāƐádna*	*mənsāƐed*	*nsāƐed*		'we'

Participles: Act. *msāƐed*, Pass. *msāƐad;* Gerund: *msāƐade*

If the last two radicals are alike (as in *hāžaž* 'to argue with') the imperfect stem vowel *e* is commonly dropped when *-i* or *-u* are suffixed: *bihāžžu;* or else *ə* may come between the like radicals as in Pattern II verbs [p. 72]: *bihāžəžu:*

---

[1]Or with assimilation of *d* to *t*: *sāƐátt, sāƐátti, sāƐáttu.*

	Perfect	Impf.Indic.	Impf.Subjn.	Impv.	
3m	ḥāžaž	biḥāžež	yḥāžež		'he'
f	ḥāžažet	bəthāžež	tḥāžež		'she'
pl	ḥāžažu	biḥāž(ə)žu	yḥāž(ə)žu		'they'
2m	ḥāždž(ə)t	bəthāžež	tḥāžež	ḥāžež	'you'
f	ḥāždžti	bəthāž(ə)ži	tḥāž(ə)ži	ḥāž(ə)ži	'you'
pl	ḥāždžtu	bəthāž(ə)žu	tḥāž(ə)žu	ḥāž(ə)žu	'you'
1sg	ḥāždž(ə)t	bḥāžež	ḥāžež		'I'
pl	ḥāždžna	manḥāžež	nḥāžež		'we'

Participles: Act. mḥāžež, Pass. mḥāžaž; Gerund: mḥāžaže

Defective Verbs.   Examples:

ḥāma, biḥāmi 'to protect'   sāwa, bisāwi 'to make'

ɛāda, biɛādi 'to treat as an enemy'   wāza, biwāzi 'to be parallel to'

ḥāka, biḥāki 'to talk to'   ɛāfa, biɛāfi 'to give strength and health to'

The final radical w or y disappears in the base form (perfect), and in the imperfect fuses with the pattern vowel e to form i.

INFLECTION OF ḥāka 'to talk to'

3m	ḥāka	biḥāki	yḥāki		'he'
f	ḥāket	bəthāki	tḥāki		'she'
pl	ḥāku	biḥāku	yḥāku		'they'
2m	ḥākēt	bəthāki	tḥāki	ḥāki	'you'
f	ḥākēti	bəthāki	tḥāki	ḥāki	'you'
pl	ḥākētu	bəthāku	tḥāku	ḥāku	'you'
1sg	ḥākēt	bḥāki	ḥāki		'I'
pl	ḥākēna	manḥāki	nḥāki		'we'

Participles: Act. mḥāki, Pass. mḥāka; Gerund: mḥakāt[1]

---

[1] Always used in construct [p.455]; absolute form would theoretically be "mḥakā".

In Pattern III there are no unsound verbs other than defective: unstable medial or initial radicals do not fluctuate or geminate in this pattern.

Pattern III Derivational Types

Many are participatives [p. 246]:

kātab	'to write to (someone)	←	katab	'to write (something)'
ḥāka	'to talk to (someone)'	←	haka	'to talk'
ḍāḥak	'to laugh with (s.o.)'	←	ḍaḥak	'to laugh'

Many are conatives [p. 245]:

sābaʔ	'to race' (trans.)	←	sabaʔ	'to get ahead of, pass'
lāḥaʔ	'to pursue'	←	ləḥeʔ	'to catch up with'
rāḍa	'to appease'	←	raḍa	'to gratify'

PATTERN IV: ʔaFɛaL, byəFɛeL

Pattern IV is augmented with respect to Pattern I by a prefix ʔa-, in the perfect tense only. There is no vowel between the first and middle radicals in either tense. The vowel between the middle and last radicals is *a* in the perfect and *e* in the imperfect.

Sound Verbs. Examples:

ʔakram, byəkrem	'to honor'	ʔaḍrab, byəḍreb	'to go on strike'
ʔarsal, byərsel	'to send'	ʔaɛlan, byəɛlen	'to advertise'
ʔazɛaž, byəzɛež	'to bother'	ʔaṣbaḥ, byəṣbeḥ	'to be...in the morning'

INFLECTION OF ʔaɛlan 'to announce'

	Perfect	Impf. Indic.	Impf. Subjn.	Impv.	
3m	ʔáɛlan	byáɛlen	yáɛlen		'he'
f	ʔáɛlanet	btáɛlen	táɛlen		'she'
pl	ʔáɛlanu	byáɛ(ə)lnu	yáɛ(ə)lnu		'they'
2m	ʔaɛlán(ə)t	btáɛlen	táɛlen	ɛlēn	'you'
f	ʔaɛlánti	btáɛ(ə)lni	táɛ(ə)lni	ɛláni	'you'
pl	ʔaɛlántu	btáɛ(ə)lnu	táɛ(ə)lnu	ɛlánu	'you'
1sg	ʔaɛlán(ə)t	báɛlen	ʔáɛlen		'I'
pl	ʔaɛlánna	mnáɛlen	náɛlen		'we'

Participles: Act. məɛlen (Pass. mʔaɛlan[1]); Gerund ʔəɛlān

Defective Verbs.   Examples:

ʔaġna, byəġni   'to make...rich'   ʔahda, byəhdi   'to present...a gift'

ʔasna, byəsni   'to commend'   ʔanha, byənhi   'to bring...to an end'

The final radical w or y disappears in the perfect, and in the imperfect fuses with the pattern vowel e to form i.

	Perfect	Impf. Indic.	Impf. Subjn.	Impv.		
3m	ʔáġna (ġána)	byáġni	yáġni			'he'
f	ʔáġnet (ġánet)	btáġni	táġni			'she'
pl	ʔáġnu (ġánu)	byáġnu	yáġnu			'they'
2m	ġanēt (ʔaġnēt)	btáġni	táġni	ġnî, ʔáġni		'you'
f	ġanēti (ʔaġnēti)	byáġni	táġni	ġni, ʔáġni		'you'
pl	ġanētu (ʔaġnētu)	btáġnu	táġnu	ġnū, ʔáġnu		'you'
1sg	ġanēt (ʔaġnēt)	báġni	ʔáġni			'I'
pl	ġanēna (ʔaġnēna)	mnáġni	náġni			'we'

Participles: Act. (and Pass.) məġni[1]; Gerund: ʔəġnāʔ

---

[1]The verb ʔaɛlan is commonly inflected as a pseudo-quadriradical [p. 116]; this passive participle is "borrowed" from the pseudo-quadriradical conjugation.

Many Pattern IV verbs have parallel Pattern I *(a–e)* forms that are synonymous to them: *ʔahda* or *hada* 'to give (as a gift)', *ʔazɛaž* or *zaɛaž* 'to annoy', *ʔaṣarr* or *ṣarr* 'to insist' In such cases the Pattern IV forms are used more in the third person than in the first or second persons.

Unsound verbs other than defective are rare in Pattern IV:

Geminate verbs:

ʔaṣarr 'to insist'

	Perfect		Impf.Indic.	Impf.Subjn.	Impv.	
3m	*ʔaṣárr*	*(ṣárr)*	*biṣə́rr*	*yṣə́rr*		'he'
f	*ʔaṣárret*	*(ṣárret)*	*bətṣə́rr*	*ṭṣə́rr*		'she'
pl	*ʔaṣdrru*	*(ṣárru)*	*biṣə́rru*	*yṣə́rru*		'they'
2m	*ṣarrēt*	*(ʔaṣarrēt)*	*bətṣə́rr*	*ṭṣə́rr*	*ṣərr*	'you'
f	*ṣarrēti*	*(ʔaṣarrēti)*	*bətṣə́rri*	*ṭṣə́rri*	*ṣə́rri*	'you'
pl	*ṣarrētu*	*(ʔaṣarrētu)*	*bətṣə́rru*	*ṭṣə́rru*	*ṣə́rru*	'you'
1sg	*ṣarrēt*	*(ʔaṣarrēt)*	*bṣə́rr*	*ṣə́rr*		'I'
pl	*ṣarrēna*	*(ʔaṣarrēna)*	*mənṣə́rr*	*nṣə́rr*		'we'

Participle: Act. *mṣərr;* Gerund *ʔəṣrār*

Hollow verbs:

ʔazāɛ 'to broadcast'

			Impf.Indic.	Impf.Subjn.	Impv.	
3m	*ʔazāɛ*	*(zāɛ)*	*bizîɛ*	*yzîɛ*		'he'
f	*ʔazāɛet*	*(zāɛet)*	*bədzîɛ*	*dzîɛ*		'she'
pl	*ʔazāɛu*	*(zāɛu)*	*bizîɛu*	*yzîɛu*		'they'
2m	*zə́ɛ(ə)t*	*(ʔazáɛt)*	*bədzîɛ*	*dzîɛ*	*zîɛ*	'you'
f	*zə́ɛti*	*(ʔazáɛti)*	*bədzîɛi*	*dzîɛi*	*zîɛi*	'you'
pl	*zə́ɛtu*	*(ʔazáɛtu)*	*bədzîɛu*	*dzîɛu*	*zîɛu*	'you'
1sg	*zə́ɛ(ə)t*	*(ʔazáɛt)*	*bzîɛ*	*zîɛ*		'I'
pl	*zə́ɛna*	*(ʔazáɛna)*	*mənzîɛ*	*nzîɛ*		'we'

Participles: Act: *m(u)zîɛ*, Pass. *m(u)zāɛ;* Gerund *ʔizāɛa*

Initial-weak verb:

ʔāman 'to believe'

	Perfect	Impf. Indic.	Impf. Subjn.	Impv.	
3m	ʔāman	byáʔmen	yáʔmen		'he'
f	ʔāmanet	btáʔmen	táʔmen		'she'
pl	ʔāmanu	byáʔ ᵊmnu	yáʔ ᵊnu		'they'
2m	ʔāmán(ᵊ)t	btáʔmen	táʔmen	(ʔāmen)	'you'
f	ʔāmánti	btáʔ ᵊmni	táʔ ᵊmni	(ʔāmni)	'you'
pl	ʔāmántu	btáʔ ᵊmnu	táʔ ᵊmnu	(ʔāmnu)	'you'
1sg	ʔāmán(ᵊ)t	báʔmen	ʔáʔmen		'I'
pl	ʔāmánna	mnáʔmen	náʔmen		'we'

Participles: Act. məʔmen, Pass. məʔman (fī); Gerund: ʔīmān

In ʔāman, the Pattern IV formative ʔa- combines with the first radical ʔ to produce ʔā-. The resulting form is like Pattern III (FāƐeL) [p.80], and in fact the verb is commonly converted enirely to Pattern III, with imperfect forms biʔāmen, bətʔāmen, etc. (Imperative forms are almost always Pattern III.)

Pattern IV verbs are comparatively rare in Colloquial Arabic, and many of those which do occur are sporadic classicisms. It is therefore difficult to discern any predominant derivational characteristics for this pattern except by reference to Classical Arabic itself, in which Pattern IV is common.

Some Pattern IV verbs are causative [p.240]: ʔaǵna 'to make...rich' ← ǵəni 'to become rich'; ʔaẓhar 'to reveal' ← ẓəher 'to appear'.

THE FORMATIVE t-

The base-formative prefix t- is used in various different patterns: tFaƐƐaL [p.86], tFāƐaL [88], tFaƐLaL [121], and pseudo-quadriradicals [109]. Its main derivational function is that of passive [p.234]; in Pattern tFāƐaL it also forms reciprocative [248] and simulative [249] verbs, and in Pattern tFaƐƐaL inchoatives [251].

t- is commonly voiced (changed to *d*) before voiced dental and palatal obstruents (*d, z, ž, ḍ, ẓ*): *džawwaz* 'to be married', *dzakkar* 'to remember', *ddōzan* 'to be in tune', *ddaεwas* 'to be trampled', *džāhal* 'to feign ignorance'.

This tendency to assimilate to a voiced radical is not equally strong in all words. Note that some speakers who normally voice the prefix in *džawwaz* 'to be married' normally do <u>not</u> voice it in *tžāwaz* 'to exceed' (or *tšāwaz* — with the radical *ž* devoiced rather than with *t* voiced).

t- is (automatically) velarized [p. 26], in the neighborhood of a velarized radical consonant: *ṭṣāfah(u)* 'to shake hands', *ṭʔāṣaṣ* 'to oe punished', *ḍẓannar* 'to gird one's self'.

The prefix *t-* is sometimes totally assimilated to a following sibilant (*s, ṣ, š, z, ẓ, ž*): *bazzakkar* 'I remember' (for *badzakkar*), *maṣṣaṭṭeh* (lying down' (for *maṭṣaṭṭeh*), *ẓẓannar* 'he girded himself' (for *ḍẓannar*).

PATTERN V: *tFaεεaL, byatFaεεaL*

Pattern V is augmented with respect to Pattern II, by prefixation of the formative *t* [   ]. It also differs from Pattern II in keeping the second pattern vowel *a* in the imperfect.

Sound Verbs.   Examples:

tεallam, byatεallam 'to learn'	*tġayyar, byatġayyar* 'to change, be changed'
tʔaxxar, byatʔaxxar 'to be late'	*tballal, byatballal* 'to get wet'
dzakkar, byadzakkar 'to remember'	*tfahham, byatfahham* 'to come to understand'

INFLECTION OF *tˀáxxar* 'to be late'

	Perfect	Impf. Indic.	Impf. Subjn.	Impv.	
3m	*tˀáxxar*	*byatˀáxxar*	*yatˀáxxar*		'he'
f	*tˀáxxaret*	*btatˀáxxar*	*tatˀáxxar*		'she'
pl	*tˀáxxaru*	*byatˀáxxaru*	*yatˀáxxaru*		'they'
2m	*tˀaxxár(ª)t*	*btatˀáxxar*	*tatˀáxxar*	*tˀáxxar*	'you'
f	*tˀaxxárti*	*btatˀáxxari*	*tatˀáxxari*	*tˀáxxari*	'you'
pl	*tˀaxxártu*	*btatˀáxxaru*	*tatˀáxxaru*	*tˀáxxaru*	'you'
1sg	*tˀaxxár(ª)t*	*batˀáxxar*	*ˀatˀáxxar*		'I'
pl	*tˀaxxárna*	*mnatˀáxxar*	*natˀáxxar*		'we'

Participles: *matˀaxxer, matˀaxxar*[1] ; Gerund: *taˀaxxor*

Defective Verbs. Examples:

tmanna, byatmanna 'to wish'   *tsamma, byatsamma* 'to be called, named'

ţġaţţa, byaţġaţţa 'to be covered'   *txabba, byatxabba* 'to hide, be hidden'

tražža, byatražža 'to implore'   *ţwaṣṣa, byaţwaṣṣa* 'to be recommended'

Final radical y or w disappears in all inflections.

INFLECTION OF *tmanna* 'to wish'

3m	*tmánna*	*byatmánna*	*yatmánna*		'he'
f	*tmánnet*	*btatmánna*	*tatmánna*		'she'
pl	*tmánnu*	*byatmánnu*	*yatmánnu*		'they'
2m	*tmannēt*	*btatmánna*	*tatmánna*	*tmánna*	'you'
f	*tmannēti*	*btatmánni*	*tatmánni*	*tmánni*	'you'
pl	*tmannētu*	*btatmánnu*	*tatmánnu*	*tmánnu*	'you'
1sg	*tmannēt*	*batmánna*	*ˀatmánna*		'I'
pl	*tmannēna*	*mnatmánna*	*natmánna*		'we'

Participles: Act. *matmanni*, Pass. *matmanna (ɛalē)*; Gerund: *tamanni*

---
[1] The passive form *matˀaxxar* is used in reference to inanimate objects while the "active" form applies to animate beings.

Derivational Types:

Most verbs of Pattern V are passives [235] of Pattern II verbs:

tƐallam	'to learn, be taught'	←	Ɛallam	'to teach'
tġayyar	'to change, be changed'	←	ġayyar	'to change' (trans.)
tšažžaƐ	'to take heart'	←	šažžaƐ	'to encourage'
tsamma	'to be called, named'	←	samma	'to call, name'

Some are inchoative [251]:

tfahham	'to come to understand better'	←	fəhem	'to understand'
tmallak	'to acquire'	←	byəmlok	'to own'
tḥassan	'to improve'	←	ʔaḥsan	'better'

Some are intransitive denominatives:

tsawwaʔ	'to go shopping'	←	sūʔ	'market'
džassas	'to spy'	←	žāsūs	'spy'

PATTERN VI: tFāƐaL, byətFāƐaL

Pattern VI is augmented with respect to Pattern III, by prefixation of the formative t [p. 85]. It also differs from Pattern III in keeping the second pattern vowel a in the imperfect.

Sound Verbs.   Examples:

tšāʔam, byətšāʔam	'to be pessimistic'	ttāwab, byəttāwab	'to yawn'
thāmal, byəthāmal	'to be negligent'	tḥādas(u), byətḥādas(u)	'to converse'
tʔāṣaṣ, byətʔāṣaṣ	'to be punished'	tṣāfaḥ(u), byətṣāfaḥ(u)	'to shake hands'

INFLECTION OF *tsāmaḥ* 'to be forgiven'

	Perfect	Impf. Indic.	Impf. Subjn.	Impv.	
3m	tsāmaḥ	byatsāmaḥ	yatsāmaḥ		'he'
f	tsāmaḥet	btatsāmaḥ	tatsāmaḥ		'she'
pl	tsāmaḥu	byatsāmaḥu	yatsāmaḥu		'they'
2m	tsāmáḥ(ᵊ)t	btatsāmaḥ	tatsāmaḥ		'you'
f	tsāmáḥti	btatsāmaḥi	tatsāmaḥi		'you'
pl	tsāmáḥtu	btatsāmaḥu	tatsāmaḥu		'you'
1sg	tsāmáḥ(ᵊ)t	batsāmaḥ	ʔatsāmaḥ		'I'
pl	tsāmáḥna	mnatsāmaḥ	natsāmaḥ		'we'

Participles: Act. *matsāmeḥ*, Pass. *matsāmaḥ (fī)*; Gerund: *tasāmoḥ*

Reciprocative verbs [p. 248] do not ordinarily occur in
the singular, hence the plural (-*u*) suffixes in some of
these examples.

Defective Verbs. Examples:

ṭḥāša, byaṭḥāša 'to avoid' *trāxa, byatrāxa* 'to be liberal, easygoing'

trāḍu, byatrāḍu 'to be concil- *tsāwa, byatsāwa* 'to be made'
iated'

ṭḥāku, byaṭḥāku 'to converse'

Final radical *y* or *w* disappears in all inflections.

INFLECTION OF *ṭḥāša* 'to avoid'

3m	ṭḥāša	byaṭḥāša	yaṭḥāša		'he'
f	ṭḥāšet	btaṭḥāša	taṭḥāša		'she'
pl	ṭḥāšu	byaṭḥāšu	yaṭḥāšu		'they'
2m	ṭḥāšēt	btaṭḥāša	taṭḥāša	ṭḥāša	'you'
f	ṭḥāšēti	btaṭḥāši	taṭḥāši	ṭḥāši	'you'
pl	ṭḥāšētu	btaṭḥāšu	taṭḥāšu	ṭḥāšu	'you'
1sg	ṭḥāšēt	baṭḥāša	ʔaṭḥāša		'I'
pl	ṭḥāšēna	mnaṭḥāša	naṭḥāša		'we'

Participles: Act. *maṭḥāši*, Pass. *maṭḥāša* (Gerund: *mḥāšā*)

Initial-Weak Verbs. The verbs *ttāxad* 'to be taken' and *ttākal* 'to be eaten, to be edible' [Cf. p. 235]:

INFLECTION OF *ttāxad* 'to be taken'

	Perfect	Impf. Indic.	Impf. Subjn.	Impv.	
3m	*ttāxad*	*byəttāxad*	*yəttāxad*		'he'
f	*ttāxadet*	*btəttāxad*	*təttāxad*		'she'
pl	*ttāxadu*	*byəttāxadu*	*yəttāxadu*		'they'
2m	*ttāxɜ́d(ə)t*	*btəttāxad*	*təttāxad*	*ttāxad*	'you'
f	*ttāxɜ́tti*	*btəttāxadi*	*təttāxadi*	*ttāxadi*	'you'
pl	*ttāxɜ́ttu*	*btəttāxadu*	*təttāxadu*	*ttāxadu*	'you'
1sg	*ttāxɜ́d(ə)t*	*btəttāxad*	*ʔəttāxad*		'I'
pl	*ttāxɜ́dna*	*mnəttāxad*	*nəttāxad*		'we'

Participle: *məttāxed*

  The initial radical *ʔ* is assimilated to the prefixed formative *t-*.

Derivational Types.

  Many Pattern VI verbs are passives of Pattern III verbs:

tbārak	'to be blessed'	←	*bārak*	'to bless'
tḥāfaẓ	'to be protected'	←	*ḥāfaẓ*	'to protect'
tsāmaḥ	'to be forgiven'	←	*sāmaḥ*	'to forgive'

Some are reciprocative [248]:

tḥāku	'to converse'	←	*ḥāka*	'to talk with'
trāḍu	'to be conciliated'	←	*rāḍa*	'to intgratiate one's self with'
tkātabu	'to write one another'	←	*kātab*	'to write to'

Some are simulatives [249]:

tġāšam	'to play dumb'	←	*ġašīm*	'naïve'
tẓāhar	'to feign'	←	*ẓəher*	'to appear'
tkāsal	'to loaf'	←	*kasūl*	'lazy'

PATTERN VII: *nFaɛaL, byənFǯɛəL*

Pattern VII is augmented with respect to Pattern I, by prefixation of the formative *n*.

Sound Verbs. Examples:

nkasar, byənkǎser 'to be broken'	*nžamaɛ, byənžǎmeɛ* 'to be brought together'
nṣaraf, byənṣǎref 'to be let out'	*mbaṣaṭ, byəmbǎṣeṭ* 'to have a good time'
nkatab, byənkǎteb 'to be written'	*nˀaṭaɛ, byənˀǎṭeɛ* 'to be cut off'

The formative *n* is generally assimilated to a first radical *b* (or *m*), producing *m*, as in *mbaṣaṭ* [p. 27].

In parts of Lebanon and Palestine, the first vowel of the stem is lost in the imperfect, and the accent shifted to the prefix syllable: *byǎnkser, byǎmbṣeṭ*. With suffixes *-i* or *-u*, however, the last stem vowel *e* is lost (as usual) and the first vowel *ə* restored: *btənkǎsri, byəmbǎṣṭu*.

INFLECTION OF *nsaḥab* 'to withdraw'

	Perfect	Impf. Indic.	Impf. Subjn.	Impv.	
3m	*nsáḥab*	*byənsǎḥeb*	*yənsǎḥeb*		'he'
f	*nsáḥbet*	*btensǎḥeb*	*tensǎḥeb*		'she'
pl	*nsáḥabu*	*byənsǎḥbu*	*yənsǎḥeb*		'they'
2m	*nsaḥáb(ə)t*	*btənsǎḥeb*	*tənsǎḥeb*	*nsǎḥeb*	'you'
f	*nsaḥábti*	*btənsǎḥbi*	*tənsǎḥbi*	*nsǎḥbi*	'you'
pl	*nsaḥábtu*	*btənsǎḥbu*	*tənsǎḥbu*	*nsǎḥbu*	'you'
1sg	*nsaḥáb(ə)t*	*bənsǎḥeb*	*ˀənsǎḥeb*		'I'
pl	*nsaḥábna*	*mnənsǎḥeb*	*nənsǎḥeb*		'we'

Participle: *mənsǎḥeb;* Gerund: *ˀənsiḥāb*

Defective Verbs (a-i).   Examples:

nt̲afa, byant̲áfi	(or *byant̲áfa*)	'to be extinguished'
nkawa, byənkə́wi	(or *byənkáwa*)	'to be ironed'
nʕad̲a, byənʕə́d̲i	(or *byənʕád̲a*)	'to be finished'

The imperf. voweling may be either *ə...i*[1] (corresponding to sound *ə...e*) or *a...a*.

INFLECTION OF *nkasa* 'to be clothed'

	Perfect	Impf. Indic.	Impf. Subjn.	Impv.	
3m	*nkása*	*byənkə́si* (*byənkása*)	*yənkə́si* (*yənkása*)		'he'
f	*nkáset*	*btənkə́si* (*btənkása*)	*tənkə́si* (*tənkása*)		'she'
pl	*nkásu*	*byənkə́su* (*btənkásu*)	*yənkə́su* (*yənkásu*)		'they'
2m	*nkasḗt*	*btənkə́si* (*btənkása*)	*tənkəsi* (*tənkása*)	*nkə́si* (*nkása*)	'you'
f	*nkasḗti*	*btənkə́si* (*btənkási*)	*tənkə́si* (*tənkási*)	*nkə́si* (*nkási*)	'you'
pl	*nkasḗtu*	*btənkə́su* (*btənkásu*)	*tənkə́su* (*tənkásu*)	*nkə́su* (*nkasu*)	'you'
1sg	*nkasḗt*	*bənkə́si* (*btənkásu*)	*ʕənkə́si* (*ʕənkása*)		'I'
pl	*nkasḗna*	*mnənkə́si* (*mnənkása*)	*nənkə́si* (*nənkása*)		'we'

Participle: *mənkə́si*   Gerund: *ʕənkisā́ʕ*

---

[1] As in sound verbs, the first stem vowel *ə* is lost — and the accent shifted to the first syllable — in parts of Lebanon and Palestine: *byə́nt̲fi, byə́nksi*, etc.

Defective Verbs (a-a).   Examples:

nḥaka, byənḥáka   'to be told'

nɛaṭa, byənɛáṭa   'to be given'

nˀara, byənˀára   'to be read'

The imperfect vowelling is *a...a*, just as in the perfect.   In some parts of the Syrian area, however, e.g. Lebanon, there is a tendency to use *ə...i* or *a...a* indiscriminately in the imperfect for all Pattern VII defectives.

INFLECTION OF *nɛada*   'to be infected'

	Perfect	Impf. Indic.	Impf. Subjn.	Impv.	
3m	*nɛáda*	*byənɛáda*	*yənɛáda*		'he'
f	*nɛádet*	*btənɛáda*	*tənɛáda*		'she'
pl	*nɛádu*	*byənɛádu*	*yənɛádu*		'they'
2m	*nɛadēt*	*btənɛáda*	*tənɛáda*	*nɛáda*	'you'
f	*nɛadēti*	*btənɛádi*	*tənɛádi*	*nɛádi*	'you'
pl	*nɛadētu*	*btənɛádu*	*tənɛádu*	*nɛádu*	'you'
1sg	*nɛadēt*	*bənɛáda*	*ˀənɛáda*		'I'
pl	*nɛadēna*	*mnənɛáda*	*nənɛáda*		'we'

Participle: *mənɛə́di*   Gerund: *ˀənɛidāˀ*

Hollow Verbs.   Examples:

nˀāl, byənˀāl 'to be said'	*nšāf, byənšāf* 'to be seen'
nžāb, byənžāb 'to be brought'	*mbāɛ, byəmbāɛ* 'to be bought'
nṣāb, byənṣāb 'to be hit'	*nˀām, byənˀām* 'to be removed'

Vowelling is the same in both tenses.

INFLECTION OF *nšāf* 'to be seen'

	Perfect	Impf.Indic.	Impf.Subjn.	Impv.	
3m	nšāf	byənšāf	yənšāf		'he'
f	nšā́fet	btənšāf	tənšāf		'she'
pl	nšāfu	byənšāfu	yənšāfu		'they'
2m	nšə́f(ə)t	btənšāf	tənšāf	nšāf	'you'
f	nšə́fti	btənšāfi	tənšāfi	nšāfi	'you'
pl	nšə́ftu	btənšāfu	tənšāfu	nšāfu	'you'
1sg	nšə́f(ə)t	bənšāf	ʔənšāf		'I'
pl	nšə́fna	mnənšāf	nənšāf		'we'

Participle: *mənšāf*

Geminate Verbs.   Examples:

nsadd, byənsadd	'to be stopped up'	*nmadd, byənmadd*	'to be stretched'
nʔaṣṣ, byənʔaṣṣ	'to be cut'	*nhazz, byənhazz*	'to be shaken'
nḥass, byənḥass	'to be felt'	*nḥaṭṭ, byənḥaṭṭ*	'to be put'

INFLECTION OF *nṣaff* 'to be lined up'

3m	nṣaff	byənṣáff	yənṣáff		'he'
f	nṣáffet	btənṣáff	tənṣáff		'she'
pl	nṣáffu	byənṣáffu	yənṣáffu		'they'
2m	nṣaffēt	btənṣáff	tənṣáff	nṣaff	'you'
f	nṣaffēti	btənṣáffi	tənṣáffi	nṣáffi	'you'
pl	nṣaffētu	btənṣáffu	tənṣáffu	nṣáffu	'you'
1sg	nṣaffēt	bənṣáff	ʔənṣáff		'I'
pl	nṣaffēna	mnənṣáff	nənṣáff		'we'

Participle: *mənṣaff*

Derivational Types: Almost all verbs of Pattern VII are passives [234] of Pattern I verbs:

nḥabas	'to be emprisoned'	←	ḥabas	'to emprison'
mbara	'to be sharpened'	←	bara	'to sharpen'
mbaṣaṭ	'to be pleased'	←	baṣaṭ	'to please'
nḥall	'to be solved'	←	ḥall	'to solve'
nnām	'to be slept (e.g....in)'	←	nām	'to sleep'

nzawa 'to withdraw, be by one's self' is an idiomatic denominative [256] of zāwye 'corner'.

PATTERN VIII: FtaƐaL, byəFtə́ƐeL

Pattern VIII is augmented with respect to Pattern I by infixation of the formative t [p.85] after the first radical.

Sound Verbs. Examples:

ftakar, byəftə́ker 'to think'	qtaṣad, byəqtə́ṣed 'to economize'
ntaʔal, byəntə́ʔel 'to be transferred'	rtakab, byərtə́keb 'to commit'
Ɛtaraf, byəƐtə́ref 'to admit'	ḥtaram, byəḥtə́rem 'to respect'

In parts of Lebanon and Palestine, the first imperfect stem vowel ə is lost and the accent shifted to the first syllable: byə́ftker, byə́štgel — except when the last stem vowel is lost before a suffix (requiring the restoration of the first vowel): btəftə́kri, byəštə́glo.

INFLECTION OF štagal 'to work'

	Perfect	Impf. Indic.	Impf. Subjn.	Impv.	
3m	štə́gal	byəštə́gel	yəštə́gel		'he'
f	štə́glet	btəštə́gel	təštə́gel		'she'
pl	štə́galu	byəštə́glu	yəštə́glu		'they'
2m	štagə́l(ə)t	btəštə́gel	təštə́gel	štə́gel	'you'
f	štagə́lti	btəštə́gli	təštə́gli	štə́gli	'you'
pl	štagə́ltu	btəštə́glu	təštə́glu	štə́glu	'you'
1sg	štagə́l(ə)t	bəštə́gel	ʔəštə́gel		'I'
pl	štagə́lna	mnəštə́gel	nəštə́gel		'we'

Participles: Act. məštə́gel, Pass. məštə́gal; Gerund: ʔəštigā̄l

Initial-Weak Verbs.   Examples:

ttafaʔ, byəlləfeʔ   'to agree'   *ṭṭaɒaf, byəṭṭə́ɒef*   'to be charac-
                                                          terized'

ṭṭaṣal, byəṭṭə́ṣel   'to be in   *ttaxaz, byəttə́xez*   'to undertake'
                     touch with'

ttásam, byəttə́sem   'to be   *ttakal, byəttə́kel*   'to depend, rely'
                     branded'

An initial radical *w* or *ʔ* is assimilated to the infix
t (or *ṭ*), producing *tt-* (or *ṭṭ-*): Pattern *FtaƐaL* with
Root *w-s-m* gives *ttasam;* Pattern *FtaƐaL* with Root *ʔ-x-z*
(*ʔ-x-d*) gives *ttaxaz.*

INFLECTION OF *ttafaʔ* 'to agree'

	Perfect	Impf. Indic.	Impf. Subjn.	Impv.	
3m	*ttáfaʔ*	*byəttə́feʔ*	*yəttə́feʔ*		'he'
f	*ttáfʔet*	*btəttə́feʔ*	*təttə́feʔ*		'she'
pl	*ttáfaʔu*	*byəttə́fʔu*	*yəttə́fʔu*		'they'
2m	*ttafáʔ(ə)t*	*btəttə́feʔ*	*təffə́feʔ*	*ttə́feʔ*	'you'
f	*ttafáʔti*	*btəttə́fʔi*	*təttə́fʔi*	*ttə́fʔi*	'you'
pl	*ttafáʔtu*	*btəttə́fʔu*	*təttə́fʔu*	*ttə́fʔu*	'you'
1sg	*ttafáʔ(ə)t*	*bəttə́feʔ*	*ʔəttə́feʔ*		'I'
pl	*ttafáʔna*	*mnəttə́feʔ*	*nəttə́feʔ*		'we'

Participles: Act. *məttə́feʔ*, Pass. *məttáfaʔ* (*Ɛalē*); Gerund *ʔəttifáʔ*

Defective Verbs.   Examples:

štara, byəštə́ri   'to buy'   *Ɛtana, byəƐtə́ni*   'to take care
                                                          of'

ktafa, byəktə́fi   'to be sat-   *ddaƐa, byəddə́Ɛi*   'to pretend'
                     isfied'

In parts of Lebanon and Palestine, the first stem
vowel *ə* in the imperfect is lost and the accent shifted
to the prefix: *byə́štri, byə́ktfi.*

INFLECTION OF *štaka* 'to complain'

	Perfect	Impf.Indic.	Impf.Subjn.	Impv.	
3m	*štáka*	*byəštə́ki*	*yəštə́ki*		'he'
f	*štáket*	*btəštə́ki*	*təštə́ki*		'she'
pl	*štáku*	*byəštə́k(y)u*	*yəštə́k(y)u*		'they'
2m	*štakḗt'*	*btəštə́ki*	*təštə́ki*	*štə́ki*	'you'
f	*štakḗti*	*btəštə́ki*	*təštə́ki*	*štə́ki*	'you'
pl	*štakḗtu*	*btəštə́k(y)u*	*təštə́k(y)u*	*štə́ku*	'you'
1sg	*štakḗt*	*bəštə́ki*	*ʔəštə́ki*		'I'
pl	*štakḗna*	*mnəštə́ki*	*nəštə́ki*		'we'

Participles: Act. *məštə́ki*. Pass. *məštáka* (*Ɛalḗ*); Gerund: *ʔəštikā́ʔ*

Defective Verbs (a-a). Only two Pattern VIII verbs have imperfect vowels *a:*

ltaʔa, byəltáʔa 'to be found'

ntala, byəntála 'to be filled'

In the sense 'to meet' (intr.), *ltaʔa* can also have the imperfect *byəltə́ʔi; ntala* likewise has an imperfect *byəntə́li* that is sometimes heard. Note, too, that *ntala* is irregular in having *n* instead of the expected radical *m* (cf. *málla* 'to fill'; it is therefore possible to interpret it as a Pattern VII verb with initial radical *t* (cf. Aleppo *talla* 'to fill').

INFLECTION OF *ntala* 'to be filled'

	Perfect	Impf. Indic.	Impf. Subjn.	Impv.	
3m	*ntála*	*byəntála* (*byəntə́li*)	*yəntála* (*yəntə́li*)		'he'
f	*ntálet*	*btəntála* (*btəntə́li*)	*təntála* (*təntə́li*)		'she'
pl	*ntálu*	*byəntálu* (*byəntə́lu*)	*yəntálu* (*yəntə́li*)		'they'
2m	*ntalēt*	*btəntála* (*btəntə́li*)	*təntála* (*təntə́li*)	*ntə́li*	'you'
f	*ntalēti*	*btəntáli* (*btəntə́li*)	*təntáli* (*təntə́li*)	*ntə́li*	'you'
pl	*ntalētu*	*btəntálu* (*btəntə́lu*)	*təntálu* (*təntə́lu*)	*ntə́lu*	'you'
1sg	*ntalēt*	*bəntála* (*bəntə́li*)	*ʔəntála* (*ʔəntə́li*)		'I'
pl	*ntalēna*	*mnəntála* (*mnəntə́li*)	*nəntála* (*nəntə́li*)		'we'

Participles: *məntə́li*[1]; Gerund: *ʔəntilāʔ*

Hollow Verbs.   Examples:

        ḥtāl, byəḥtāl 'to use deceit'

        ḥtāž, byəḥtāž 'to need'

        rtāḥ, byərtāḥ 'to rest, relax'

        zdād, byəzdād 'to increase' (intrans.)

---

[1] Some speakers distinguish between a mediopassive *məntə́li* '(having gotten) full' and true passive *məntála* '(having been) filled'.

INFLECTION OF *rtāḥ* 'to rest, relax'

	Perfect	Impf. Indic.	Impf. Subjn.	Impv.	
3m	rtāḥ	byertāḥ	yertāḥ		'he'
f	rtāḥet	btərtāḥ	tərtāḥ		'she'
pl	rtāḥu	byərtāḥu	yərtāḥu		'they'
2m	rtə́ḥ(ə)t	btərtāḥ	tərtāḥ	rtāḥ	'you'
f	rtə́ḥti	btərtāḥi	tərtāḥi	rtāḥi	'you'
pl	rtə́ḥtu	btərtāḥu	tərtāḥu	rtāḥu	'you'
1sg	rtə́ḥ(ə)t	bərtāḥ	ʔərtāḥ		'I'
pl	rtə́ḥna	mnərtāḥ	nərtāḥ		'we'

Participle: *mərtāḥ;* Gerund: *ʔərtiyāḥ*

Geminate Verbs.   Examples:

> *mtadd, byəmtadd* 'to extend' (intrans.)
>
> *ṭṭarr, byəṭṭarr* 'to be obliged, required'
>
> *štaʔʔ, byəštaʔʔ* 'to be derived'

INFLECTION OF *ḥtall* 'to occupy'

	Perfect	Impf. Indic.	Impf. Subjn.	Impv.	
3m	ḥtáll	byəḥtáll	yəḥtáll		'he'
f	ḥtállet	btəḥtáll	təḥtáll		'she'
pl	ḥtállu	byəḥtállu	yəḥtállu		'they'
2m	ḥtallēt	btəḥtáll	təḥtáll	ḥtáll	'you'
f	ḥtallēti	btəḥtálli	yəḥtálli	ḥtálli	'you'
pl	ḥtallētu	btəḥtállu	təḥtállu	ḥtállu	'you'
1sg	ḥtallēt	bəḥtáll	ʔəḥtáll		'I'
pl	ḥtallēna	mnəḥtáll	nəḥtáll		'we'

Participle: *məḥtall;* Gerund: *ʔəḥtilāl*

Derivational Types: Many Pattern VIII verbs are passives [234] of simple active verbs:

ntasa	'to be forgotten'	←	*nəsi*	'to forget'
ltaha	'to be distracted, entertained'	←	*laha*	'to distract, entertain'
xtana?	'to choke' (intrans.)	←	*xana?*	'to choke' (trans.)

In Pattern VIII mediopassives are much more common than true passives: *štaġal* 'to work' (cf. *šaġal* 'to occupy, to busy'); *mbaṣaṭ* 'to enjoy one's self' (cf. *baṣaṭ* 'to please'). See p. 234.

Some Pattern VIII verbs are abstractive [p. 252] with respect to simple concrete verbs:

ktašaf	'to discover'	←	*kašaf*	'to uncover, reveal'
ḥtawa (*ƐaLa*)	'to include, contain'	←	*ḥawa*	'to contain, keep'
mṭaṣṣ	'to absorb'	←	*maṣṣ*	'to suck'

Some are abstract denominatives:

Ɛtād	'to become habituated'	←	*Ɛāde*	'habit'
štarak	'to associate'	←	*šərke*	'association'
ḥtāl	'to be deceitful'	←	*ḥīle*	'trick, deceit'
ṭṭarr	'to be required, obliged'	←	*ḍarūra*	'necessity'

A fairly high proportion of Pattern VIII verbs are not functionally derivable from any underlying word (or are at least highly idiomatic in their derivation): *rtakab* 'to commit (e.g. a crime)', cf. *rakab* 'to ride'; *Ɛtaraḍ* 'to oppose, contradict', cf. *Ɛaraḍ* 'to show, display'; *žtarr* 'to chew a cud', cf. *žarr* 'to pull'.

Voicing of the −*t*− Formative

The infix −*t*− is changed to −*d*− after an initial radical *z* or *d*:

zdād	'to increase' (intrans.):	**Root** *z–w–d*	
zdara	'to scorn':	**Root** *z–r–y*	(Gerund *?əzdirā?*)
ddaƐa	'to claim, pretend':	**Root** *d–Ɛ–w*	(cf. participial noun *muddáƐi* 'claimant')

In the vicinity of a velarized root consonant, it is automatically velarized to *ṭ: ṣṭād* 'to hunt'. An initial radical voiced obstruent other than *z* or *d* is often devoiced before *-t-* [p. 26]: *štamaƐ* 'to meet': Root *š-m-Ɛ; ṭṭarr* 'to be required': Root *ḍ-r-r*.)

PATTERN IX: *FƐaLL, byəFƐaLL*

Pattern IX is augmented with respect to other patterns by lengthening of the final radical.

The only examples found are:

byaḍḍ, byəbyaḍḍ 'to become white'		*swadd, byəswadd* 'to become black'
ḥmarr, byəḥmarr 'to become red'		*xḍarr, byəxḍarr* 'to become green'
ṣfarr, byəṣfarr 'to become yellow'		*zraʔʔ, byəzraʔʔ* 'to become blue'
smarr, byəsmarr 'to tan, darken'		*šʔarr, byəšʔarr* 'to become blond'

Ɛwaž̌ž̌, byəƐwažž̌ 'to become bent'

INFLECTION OF *ḥmarr* 'to become red, blush'

	Perfect	Impf.Indic.	Impf.Subjn.	Impv.	
3m	*ḥmarr*	*byəḥmárr*	*yəḥmárr*		'he'
f	*ḥmárret*	*btəḥmárr*	*təḥmárr*		'she'
pl	*ḥmárru*	*byəḥmárru*	*təḥmárru*		'they'
2m	*ḥmarrēt*	*btəḥmárr*	*təḥmárr*	*ḥmarr*	'you'
f	*ḥmarrēti*	*btəḥmárri*	*təḥmárri*	*ḥmárri*	'you'
pl	*ḥmarrētu*	*btəḥmárru*	*təḥmárru*	*ḥmárru*	'you'
1sg	*ḥmarrēt*	*bəḥmárr*	*ʔəḥmárr*		'I'
pl	*ḥmarrēna*	*mnəḥmárr*	*nəḥmárr*		'we'

Participle: *məḥmarr;* Gerund *ʔəḥmirār*

Grammatical Characteristics. All Pattern IX's are inchoative [p. 250] derivatives of Pattern *ʔaFƐaL* adjectives [130]. All but one (*Ɛwažž̌*) are from color-adjectives.

byaḍḍ	'to become white'	←	*ʔabyaḍ* 'white'
zraʔʔ	'to become blue'	←	*ʔazraʔ* 'blue'
Ɛwažž̌	'to become bent'	←	*ʔaƐwaž̌* 'bent'

PATTERN X: *staFέaL, byəstaFέeL*

Pattern X is augmented with respect to Pattern I by prefixation of a formative *st(a)-*. The pattern vowels are *a...a* (pf.), *a...e* (impf.).

Sound Verbs. Examples:

stafham, *byəstafhem*	'to enquire'	*staḥsan,* *byəstaḥsen*	'to prefer'
stasmar, *byəstasmer*	'to exploit'	*stasέab,* *byəstasέeb*	'to find difficult'
stawrad, *byəstawred*	'to import	*statyab,* *byəstatyeb*	'to find tasty'

Sound verbs of this pattern include some with medial radical *w* and *y: stašwab* 'to question' (cf. hollow *stašāb* 'to grant'). Occasionally, one also hears a Pattern X verb with second and third radicals alike formed on the sound pattern (*stáxfaf* 'to treat lightly') instead of the usual geminate (*staxáff*) [p. 105]

INFLECTION OF *staʔbal* 'to welcome'

	Perfect	Impf. Indic.	Impf. Subjn.	Impv.	
3m	*stáʔbal*	*byəstáʔbel*	*yəstáʔbel*		'he'
f	*stáʔbalet*	*btəstáʔbel*	*təstáʔbel*		'she'
pl	*stáʔbalu*	*byəstáʔ(ə)blu*	*yəstáʔ(ə)blu*		'they'
2m	*staʔbál(ə)t*	*btəstáʔbel*	*təstáʔbel*	*stáʔbel*	'you'
f	*staʔbálti*	*btəstáʔ(ə)bli*	*təstáʔ(ə)bli*	*stáʔ(ə)bli*	'you'
pl	*staʔbáltu*	*btəstáʔ(ə)blu*	*təstáʔ(ə)blu*	*stáʔ(ə)blu*	'you'
1sg	*staʔbál(ə)t*	*bəstáʔbel*	*ʔəstáʔbel*		'I'
pl	*staʔbálna*	*mnəstáʔbel*	*nəstáʔbel*		'we'

Participles: Act. *məstaʔbel,* Pass. *məstaʔbal;* Gerund: *ʔəstəʔbāl*

Sound with medial radical *w:*   *stašwab* 'to question'

	Perfect	Impf. Indic.	Impf. Subjn.	Impv.	
3m	*stášwab*	*byəstášweb*	*yəstášweb*		'he'
f	*stášwabet*	*btəstášweb*	*təstášweb*		'she'
pl	*stášwab*	*byəstᾱš(ə)wbu*	*yəstᾱš(ə)wbu*		'they'
2m	*stašwᾱb(ə)t*	*btəstášweb*	*təstášweb*	*stášweb*	'you'
f	*stašwᾱbti*	*btəstᾱš(ə)wbi*	*təstᾱš(ə)wbi*	*stᾱš(ə)wbi*	'you'
pl	*stašwᾱbtu*	*btəstᾱš(ə)wbu*	*təstᾱš(ə)wbu*	*stᾱš(ə)wbu*	'you'
1sg	*stašwᾱb(ə)t*	*bəstášweb*	*ʔəstášweb*		'I'
pl	*stašwᾱbna*	*mnəstášweb*	*bəstášweb*		'we'

Participles: Act. *məstašweb,* Pass. *məstašwab;* Gerund: *ʔəstəšwᾱb*

Defective Verbs.   Examples:

     stahla, byəstahli 'to like'   *stakra, byəstakri*   'to rent, hire'

     stasna, byəstasni 'to exclude'   *stawla, byəstawli*   'to take over'

     staƐfa, byəstaƐfi 'to resign'   *starḍa, byəstarḍi*   'to make an apology'

     staʔwa, byəstaʔwi 'to take heart'   *staġla, byəstaġli*   'to consider expensive'

     Initial or medial radical *w* does not fluctuate in defective verbs of this pattern, but for medial *y,* see p.

INFLECTION OF *stahla* 'to like'

3m	*stáhla*	*byəstáhli*	*yəstáhli*		'he'
f	*stáhlet*	*btəstáhli*	*təstáhli*		'she'
pl	*stáhlu*	*byəstáhlu*	*yəstáhlu*		'they'
2m	*stahlēt*	*btəstáhli*	*təstáhli*	*stáhli*	'you'
f	*stahlēti*	*btəstáhli*	*təstáhli*	*stáhli*	'you'
pl	*stahlētu*	*btəstáhlu*	*təstáhlu*	*stáhlu*	'you'
1sg	*stahlēt*	*bəstáhli*	*ʔəstáhli*		'I'
pl	*stahlēna*	*mnəstáhli*	*nəstáhli*		'we'

Participle: Act. *məstáhli*

Hollow Verbs. Examples:

stašār, byəstašīr 'to consult'	staqāl, byəstaqīl 'to resign'
staṭāᴇ, byəstaṭīᴇ 'to be able'	stažāb, 'to grant'
	byəst(a)žīb
stafād, byəstfid 'to benefit'	starāḥ, byəstrīḥ 'to rest'
staᴇān, byəstᴇīn 'to ask for help'	staᴇād, byəstᴇīd to get back'

The occurrence of the formative vowel *a* in the imperfect
is partly a matter of style; it is more elegant to pronounce e.g. *byəstažīb*, while *byəstžīb* is more informal.
Therefore only words which are themselves elegant or
formal vocabulary items will be consistently pronounced
with the *a:* *byəstaṭīᴇ*.

Note that not all Pattern X verbs with medial radical
semivowel are hollow: compare *stažāb* 'to grant' with the
sound verb *stážwab* 'to question', both of which have the
root *ž-w-b*.

INFLECTION OF *starāḥ* 'to relax' (unstable *a*)

	Perfect	Impf.Indic.	Impf.Subjn.	Impv.	
3m	starāḥ	byəstrīḥ	yəstrīḥ		'he'
f	starāḥet	btəstrīḥ	təstrīḥ		'she'
pl	starāḥu	byəstrīḥu	yəstrīḥu		'they'
2m	stráḥ(ə)t	btəstrīḥ	təstrīḥ	strīḥ	'you'
f	stráḥti	btəstrīḥi	təstrīḥi	strīḥi	'you'
pl	stráḥtu	btəstrīḥu	təstrīḥu	strīḥu	'you'
1sg	stráḥ(ə)t	bəstrīḥ	ʔəstrīḥ		'I'
pl	stráḥna	mnəstrīḥ	nəstrīḥ		'we'

Participle: *məstrīḥ;* Gerund *ʔəstirāḥ*

INFLECTION OF *stašār* 'to consult' (stable *a*)

	Perfect	Impf. Indic.	Impf. Subjn.	Impv.	
3m	*stašār*	*byəstašīr*	*yəstašīr*		'he'
f	*stašāret*	*btəstašīr*	*təstašīr*		'she'
pl	*stašāru*	*byəstašīru*	*yəstašīru*		'they'
2m	*stašár(ə)t*	*btəstašīr*	*təstašīr*	*stašīr*	'you'
f	*stašárti*	*btəstašīri*	*təstašīri*	*stašīri*	'you'
pl	*stašártu*	*btəstašīru*	*təstašīru*	*stašīru*	'you'
1sg	*stašár(ə)t*	*bəstašīr*	*ʔəstašīr*		'I'
pl	*stašárna*	*mnəstašīr*	*nəstašīr*		'we'

Participles: Act. *məstašīr*, Pass. *məstašār;* Gerund *ʔəstišāra*

Note that in the first and second persons of the perfect, the last stem vowel remains *a* if the first stem vowel (*a*) is kept, but is usually changed to *ə* if the first stem vowel is dropped (see conjugation of *starāḥ,* above).

Geminate Verbs.   Examples:

staradd, byəst(a)rədd 'to get back' *staḥabb, byəst(a)ḥəbb* 'to like'

stamarr, byəst(a)mərr 'to continue'   *staḥaʔʔ, byəst(a)ḥəʔʔ* 'to deserve'

stagall, byəst(a)ġəll 'to exploit' *staxaff, byəst(a)xəff* 'to make light(of)'

INFLECTION OF *staradd* 'to take back'

3m	*starádd*	*byəstrádd*	*yəstrádd*		'he'
f	*staráddet*	*btəstrádd*	*təstrádd*		'she'
pl	*staráddu*	*byəstráddu*	*yəstráddu*		'they'
2m	*st(a)raddēt*	*btəstrádd*	*təstrádd*	*strádd*	'you'
f	*st(a)raddēti*	*btəstráddi*	*təstráddi*	*stráddi*	'you'
pl	*st(a)raddētu*	*btəstráddu*	*təstráddu*	*stráddu*	'you'
1sg	*st(a)raddēt*	*bəstrádd*	*ʔəstrádd*		'I'
pl	*st(a)raddēna*	*mnəstrádd*	*nəstrádd*		'we'

Participle: Act. *məstaradd;* Gerund *ʔəstərdād*

Initial-weak verb: *stāhal* 'to deserve'

	Perfect	Impf. Indic.	Impf. Subjn.	
3m	*stāhal*	*byəstāhel*	*yəstāhel*	'he'
f	*stāhalet*	*btəstāhel*	*təstāhel*	'she'
pl	*stāhalu*	*byəstāhlu*	*yəstāhlu*	'they'
2m	*stāhál(ə)t*	*btəstāhel*	*təstāhel*	'you'
f	*stāhálti*	*btəstāhli*	*təstāhli*	'you'
pl	*stāháltu*	*btəstāhlu*	*təstāhlu*	'you'
1sg	*stāhál(ə)t*	*bəstāhel*	*ʔəstāhel*	'I'
pl	*stāhálna*	*mnəstāhel*	*nəstāhel*	'we'

Participles: Act. *məstāhel*, Pass. *məstāhal*

stāhal is the only initial-weak Pattern X verb found.
The formative *sta–* combines with the first radical *ʔ* to
produce *stā–*. (Compare the sound verb *staʔzan, byəstaʔzen*
'to ask permission'.)

Hollow-defective verb: *staha, byəstə́hi* 'to be embarrassed'

3m	*stáha*	*byəstə́hi*	*yəstə́hi*	'he'
f	*stáhet*	*btəstə́hi*	*təstə́hi*	'she'
pl	*stáhu*	*byəstə́hu*	*yəstə́hu*	'they'
2m	*stahēt*	*btəstə́hi*	*təstə́hi*	'you'
f	*stahēti*	*btəstə́hi*	*təstə́hi*	'you'
pl	*stahētu*	*btəstə́hu*	*təstə́hu*	'you'
1sg	*stahēt*	*bəstə́hi*	*ʔəstə́hi*	'I'
pl	*stahēna*	*mnəstə́hi*	*nəstə́hi*	'we'

Participle: *məstə́hi;* Gerund: *ʔəstəhyāʔ*

stáha (Root *h–y–y*, cf. *hayy* 'bashful') is the only
Hollow-defective Pattern X verb found. Both radical
semivowels disappear in all inflections. The forms are
like those of Pattern VIII defective verbs, but *staha*
cannot be classified as Pattern VIII; that would imply
its root was *s–h–y*.

Another pseudo-Pattern VIII verb is *zdall* 'to conclude, gather' (Root *d-l-l*, cf. *dall* 'to indicate'). The formative is reduced from *sta-* to *st-*, but the combination *std-* cannot stand intact and is reduced to *zd-*. Compare the regularly formed doublet *stadall* 'to find the way'. (*zdall, byəzdall* is conjugated like Pattern VIII verbs [p. 99].)

Derivational Types: Many Pattern X verbs are estimative [p. 244]:

staġrab	'to be surprised at, to consider strange'	←	*ġarīb*	'strange'
stasɛab	'to find difficult'	←	*saɛb*	'difficult'
stáḥla	'to like, find nice'	←	*ḥə́lu*	'nice, pretty'

Many are eductive [244]:

staġfar	'to ask (God's) for-giveness'	←	*ġafar*	'to forgive'
staradd	'to get (something) back'	←	*radd*	'to give back'
stažwab	'to.question'	←	*žāwab*	'to answer'
staʔžar	'to rent, hire'	←	*ʔažžar*	'to rent, hire out'
staxbar	'to enquire, get information'	←	*xabar*	'news, information'

ANOMALOUS FORMS

Patterns V and X mixed: *stmanna* 'to wish'

	Perfect	Impf. Indic.	Impf. Subjn.	
3m	*stmánna*	*byəstmánna*	*yəstmánna*	'he'
f	*stmánnet*	*btəstmánna*	*təstmánna*	'she'
pl	*stmánnu*	*byəstmánnu*	*yəstmánnu*	'they'
2m	*stmannḗt*	*btəstmánna*	*təstmánna*	'you'
f	*stmannḗti*	*btəstmánni*	*təstmánni*	'you'
pl	*stmannḗtu*	*btəstmánnu*	*təstmánnu*	'you'
1sg	*stmannḗt*	*bəstmánna*	*ʔəstmánna*	'I'
pl	*stmannḗna*	*mnəstmánna*	*nəstmánna*	'we'

Participles: *məstmanni,* Pass. *məstmanna*

These forms are often replaced by the straight Pattern
V forms: *tmanna, byətmanna.*

Patterns V and X mixed, Initial-weak: *stanna* 'to wait'

	Perfect	Impf.Indic.	Impf.Subjn.	Impv.	
3m	*stánna*	*byəstánna*	*yəstánna*		'he'
f	*stánnet*	*btəstánna*	*təstánna*		'she'
pl	*stánnu*	*byəstánnu*	*yəstánnu*		'they'
2m	*stannēt*	*btəstánna*	*təstánna*	*stánna*	'you'
f	*stannēti*	*btəstánni*	*təstánni*	*stánni*	'you'
pl	*stannētu*	*btəstánnu*	*təstánnu*	*stánnu*	'you'
1sg	*stannēt*	*bəstánna*	*ʔəstánna*		'I'
pl	*stannēna*	*mnəstánna*	*nəstánna*		'we'

Participles: Act. *məstanni*, Pass. *məstanna*

A theoretical initial radical ʔ is lost in all inflections.

Patterns III and X mixed, with loss of *−t−:* *snāwal* 'to catch'

3m	*snāwal*	*byəsnāwel*	*yəsnāwel*		'he'
f	*snāwalet*	*btəsnāwel*	*təsnāwel*		'she'
pl	*snāwalu*	*byəsnāwlu*	*yəsnāwlu*		'they'
2m	*snāwál(ə)t*	*btəsnāwel*	*təsnāwel*	*snāwel*	'you'
f	*snāwálti*	*btəsnāwli*	*təsnāwli*	*snāwli*	'you'
pl	*snāwáltu*	*btəsnāwlu*	*təsnāwlu*	*snāwlu*	'you'
1sg	*snāwál(ə)t*	*bəsnāwel*	*ʔəsnāwel*		'I'
pl	*snāwálna*	*mnəsnāwel*	*nəsnāwel*		'we'

Participle: Act. *məsnāwel*

The form with *−t−* is also sometimes heard: *stnāwal,*
byəstnāwel.

PSEUDO-QUADRIRADICAL PATTERNS

Syrian Arabic has a number of triradical verb patterns that are used little or not at all in Classical Arabic and consequently have no traditional classification (or numerical labels). These patterns, described in the sections that follow, are *FaℰFaL, FaℰwaL, FōℰaL, FarℰaL, FaℰLan,* and *ʔaFℰaL* (with stable *ʔ* — not the same as Pattern IV [p. 82]). Each of these except *ʔaFℰaL* is paralleled by a pattern with the *t-* formative [85] *tFaℰFaL, tFaℰwaL,* etc.

> Besides these there are some very rare patterns, for example *FaℰLa* (as in *ṭaℰma, biṭaℰmi* 'to feed'), and some geographically limited patterns like the Lebanese *FayℰaL* (as in *ṭaylaℰ* 'to take up, out': elsewhere *tallaℰ* or *ṭālaℰ*).

Verbs with any of these patterns fall into the same form-types (and conjugational types) as quadriradical verbs. That is to say, their characteristic formatives are not distinguishable from an extra radical on the basis of form alone — hence they have sometimes been loosely classified with the true quadriradicals as examples of Pattern *FaℰLaL* (or *tFaℰLaL*) [p. 117].[1]

They differ from true quadriradicals in that they are derived (as regular functions of the given formatives [p. 47]) from triradical words. For instance the verb *madmad* 'to stretch, extend' is an augmentative [253] of the simple triradical verb *madd* (same translation); therefore it has the root *m-d-d* and the pattern *FaℰFaL* [111]. By way of contrast the verb *damdam* 'to mutter, grumble' is not related to any word with the

---

[1]Patterns are of course always defined relative to roots [p. 36]. None of the augmented verb patterns can <u>always</u> be identified on the basis of word-forms alone: for instance *ntaʔal* 'to move, be transferred' might be thought to have Pattern *nFaℰaL* and Root *t-ʔ-l;* only by knowing that its root is actually *n-ʔ-l* may one deduce that its pattern is definitely *FtaℰaL.*

The term 'quadriradical' (or 'quadriliteral'), however, has often been extended to encompass not only bases that have quadriliteral roots, but also many triliteral-root bases that are similar in form to the true quadriradicals. This classification is invalid, not only because it is a contradiction in terms to use 'quadriradical' (or 'quadriliteral') without reference to roots, but also because it is inconsistent to call all words formed on Pattern *FōℰaL,* for instance, "quadriradical" while classifying Pattern *FaℰaL* words as triradical. (The class of bases represented jointly by the formulae *CV̄CV(C)* and *CVCCV(C)* cannot exclude triradical patterns II and III except by ad hoc stipulations to that effect, which would covertly introduce derivational criteria into a supposedly formal base classification.)

root *d–m–m* and is therefore relegated to the quadriliteral root *d–m–d–m* and the pattern *FaƐLaL*.[1]

THE REDUPLICATIVE PATTERN

FaƐFaL, biFaƐFeL   *tFaƐFaL, byatFaƐFaL*

Reduplicative verbs are augmented with respect to simple verbs by a repetition of the first radical immediately after the second.

Sound Verbs, with Middle and Last Radicals Different.   Examples:

farfaḥ, bifarfeḥ 'to rejoice'   *ʔarʔaƐ, biʔarʔeƐ* 'to clatter'

ṭarṭaš, biṭarṭeš 'to splatter'   *ṣarṣaƐ, biṣarṣeƐ* 'to startle'

INFLECTION OF *farfaḥ* 'to rejoice'

	Perfect	Impf. Indic.	Impf. Subjn.	Impv.	
3m	*fárfaḥ*	*bifárfeḥ*	*yfárfeḥ*		'he'
f	*fárfaḥet*	*batfárfeḥ*	*tfárfeḥ*		'she'
pl	*fárfaḥu*	*bifár(ᵊ)fḥu*	*yfár(ᵊ)fḥu*		'they'
2m	*farfáḥ(ᵊ)t*	*batfárfeḥ*	*tfárfeḥ*	*fárfeḥ*	'you'
f	*farfáḥti*	*batfár(ᵊ)fḥi*	*tfár(ᵊ)fḥi*	*fár(ᵊ)fḥi*	'you'
pl	*farfáḥtu*	*batfár(ᵊ)fḥu*	*tfár(ᵊ)fḥu*	*fár(ᵊ)fḥu*	'you'
1sg	*farfáḥ(ᵊ)t*	*bfárfeḥ*	*fárfeḥ*		'I'
pl	*farfáḥna*	*manfárfeḥ*	*nfárfeḥ*		'we'

Participle: *mfarfeḥ;* Gerund: *farfaḥa*

---

[1]Pseudo-quadriradicals are also to be distinguished from SECONDARY QUADRIRADICALS like *thēwan* 'to blunder'. This verb, derived idiomatically as a simulative [p. 249] from *ḥēwan* 'animal', is analogous to *tšēṭan* 'to be naughty', similarly derived from *šēṭān* 'devil'. While *šēṭān* is a quadriradical word (Root *š–y–ṭ–n*), *ḥēwan* is actually triradical (Root *ḥ–y–y*) but *thēwan* is derived from it on Pattern *tFaƐLaL* [119] as if its root were *ḥ–y–w–n* — by analogy to formally comparable words like *šēṭān*.
        As distinct both from absolute quadriradicals like *tšēṭan* and secondary quadriradicals like *thēwan*, verbs such as *twaldan* 'to be child-ish' are genuinely <u>tri</u>radical: the final *n* cannot be traced back to the underlying word *walad* 'child', so it must be analyzed as a verb-formative affix — the characteristic formative of pseudo-quadriradical (i.e. triradical) Pattern (*t)FaƐLan* [115].

Sound Verbs, with Middle and Last Radicals Alike. Examples:

laflaf, bilaflef 'to wrap up'	*šamšam, bišamšem* 'to smell, sniff'
fatfat, bifatfet 'to crumble'	*madmad, bimadmed* 'to extend, stretch'
ʔaṣʔaṣ, biʔaṣʔeṣ 'to cut, snip'	*ḥalḥal, biḥalḥel* 'to untie, undo'

With geminating roots, the reduplicative infix comes between the like radicals, resulting in a repeated sequence of two consonants. Verbs of this form are quite common.

INFLECTION OF *laflaf* 'to wrap up'

	Perfect	Impf. Indic.	Impf. Subjn.	Impv.	
3m	*láflaf*	*biláflef*	*yláflef*		'he'
f	*láflafet*	*bətláflef*	*tláflef*		'she'
pl	*láflafu*	*biláfəlfu*	*yláfəlfu*		'they'
2m	*lafláf(ə)t*	*bətláflef*	*tláflef*	*láflef*	'you'
f	*láfláfti*	*bətláfəlfi*	*tláfəlfi*	*láfəlfi*	'you'
pl	*láfláftu*	*bətlafəlfu*	*tláfəlfu*	*lafəlfu*	'you'
1sg	*lafláf(ə)t*	*bláflef*	*láflef*		'I'
pl	*láfláfna*	*mənláflef* (*məll–*)	*nláflef* (*ll–*)		'we'

Participles: Act. *mlaflef*, Pass. *mlaflaf*; Gerund: *laflafe*

Hollow Verbs. Examples:

lōlaḥ, bilōleḥ	'to wave'
ṭōṭaḥ, biṭōṭeh	'to toss'
zōzaʔ, bizōzeʔ	'to decorate'

The first pattern vowel *a* fuses with the middle radical *w*, leaving *ō* between the initial radical and its duplicate. Verbs of this form are rare. (No hollow reduplicatives are found with medial radical *y*.)

INFLECTION OF *lōlaḥ* 'to wave'

	Perfect	Impf. Indic.	Impf. Subjn.	Impv.	
3m	lōlaḥ	bilōlaḥ	ylōleḥ		'he'
f	lōlaḥet	batlōleḥ	tlōleḥ		'she'
pl	lōlaḥu	bilōlḥu	ylōlḥu		'they'
2m	lōláḥ(ᵊ)t	batlōleḥ	tlōleḥ	lōleḥ	'you'
f	lōláḥti	batlōlḥi	tlōlḥi	lōlḥi	'you'
pl	lōláḥtu	batlōlḥu	tlōlḥu	lōlḥu	'you'
1sg	lōláḥ(ᵊ)t	blōleḥ	lōleḥ		'I'
pl	lōláḥna	manlōleḥ (mall-)	nlōleḥ (ll-)		'we'

Participles: Act. *mlōleḥ*, Pass. *mlōlaḥ;* Gerund: *lōlaḥa*

Reduplicative Verbs with *t* Formative. Examples:

tfarfad, byatfarfad   'to be set apart'

tlaflaf, byatlaflaf   'to be wrapped up'

ṭṭōṭaḥ, byaṭṭōṭaḥ   'to be tossed in the air'

Derivation. Almost all reduplicative verbs are augmentative [253]:

farfaḥ	'to rejoice'	←	fareḥ	(same translation)
laflaf	'to wrap up'	←	laff	'to turn; to wrap'
halḥal	'to untie, undo'	←	hall	'to untie; to solve'
lōlaḥ	'to wave'	←	lāḥ	(same translation)

The alliterative effect of reduplication seems to have a certain symbolic value, often connoting vividness, emphasis, or repetitiveness — hence the aptness of this pattern to express the augmentative derivation.

Some reduplicatives have no underlying simple verb, but may be correlated with a more or less synonymous Pattern II verb, or derived from a simple noun:

zōza⁹ 'to decorate': cf.   zawwa⁹ (same translation)

. cf.   zō⁹   'taste'

Verbs that are reduplicative in form but which are not functionally related to triliteral-root words are classified as true quadriradical [117].

OTHER INFIXING PATTERNS

FaƐwaL, biFaƐweL   *tFaƐwaL, byətFaƐwaL*

FōƐaL, biFōƐeL   *tFōƐaL, byətFōƐaL*

FarƐaL, biFarƐeL   *tFarƐaL, byətFarƐaL*

Verbs of these patterns are augmented with respect to simple verbs by an infix *w* immediately after the middle radical, or by *r* or *w* (*a + w → ō*) immediately <u>before</u> the middle radical. Examples:

Patterns *FaƐwal* and *tFaƐwaL:*

baxwaš,
  bibaxweš
	'to perforate'	*tbaxwaš,*
		  byətbaxwaš
			'to be perforated'

daƐwas,
  bidaƐwes
	'to trample'	*ddaƐwas,*
		  byəddaƐwas
			'to be trampled'

Ɛaṣwar,
  biƐaṣwer
	'to wring out '	*tƐaṣwar,*
		  byətƐaṣwar
			'to be wrung out '

	sadwad, bisadwed	'to stop up'	
	naṭwaṭ, binaṭweṭ	'to jump about '	
	šaxwaṭ, bišaxweṭ	'to scribble'	

Patterns *FōƐaL* and *tFōƐaL:*

bōram,
  bibōrem
	'to wind'..........	*tbōram,*
		  byətbōram
			'to be wound'

lō²aṭ,
  bilō²eṭ
	'to pick up'	*tlō²aṭ,*
		  byətlō²aṭ
			'to be picked up'

²ōṭar,
  bi²ōṭer
	'to tow,
	  pull' ....
		t²ōṭar,
		  byət²ōṭar
			'to be towed,
			  pulled'

	ḥōrak, biḥōrek	'to move around'	
	zōġal, bizōġel	'to cheat (in games)'	
	ḥōza², biḥōze²	'to have the hiccups'	

Patterns *FarɛaL* and *tFarɛaL:*

harbaš,
  biharbeš
	'to slash'	*tharbaš,*
		  byətharbaš
			'to be shashed'

šarbak,
  bišarbek
	'to complicate' ...	*tšarbak,*
		  byətšarbak
			'to be complicated'

xarmaš,
  bixarmeš
	'to scratch'	*txarmaš,*
		  byətxarmaš
			'to be scratched'

farʔaɛ,	*bifarʔeɛ*	'to set off (fireworks)'
karfat,	*bikarfet*	'to curse'
tɛarbaṭ,	*byətɛarbaṭ*	'to cling (in panic)'

Verbs of all these patterns are inflected like true quadriradicals [pp. 118-119].

Derivation.

Most of these verbs are augmentatives [p. 253]:

daɛwas	'to trample'	←	*daɛas*	'to tread on; run over'
naṭwaṭ	'to jump about'	←	*naṭṭ*	'to jump'
ḥōʒaʔ	'to have hiccups'	←	*ḥaʒaʔ*	'to hiccup.'
lōʔaṭ (frequentative)	'to pick up'	←	*laʔaṭ*	'to pick up'
karfat	'to curse' (freq. or intens.)	←	*kafat*	'to curse'
xarmaš	'to scratch'	←	*xamaš*	'to scratch'
tɛarbaṭ	'to cling (in panic)'	←	*ɛabaṭ*	'to grasp'

Some are more or less synonymous with Pattern II verbs, but have no underlying simple verbs:

xarṭaš	'to scribble'	(cf. *xaṭṭaš*)
fōxar	'to decay, rot'	(cf. *faxxar*)
ṣōfar	'to whistle'	(cf. *ṣaffar*)
šaḥwar	'to blacken, smoke'	(cf. *šaḥḥar*)

Some *w*-formative verbs are applicative [256] or similarly denominative:

sarwaž	'to saddle'	→	*sərž*	'saddle'
xōṭar	'to endanger'	→	*xaṭar*	'danger'
bōṭal ꞏᵥ	'to cheat'	→	*bəṭᵊl*	'cheating'
bōrad	'to cool off'	→	*barᵊd*	'cold' (abst. noun)
txašwan	'to rough it'	→	*xəšᵊn*	'rough'

Verbs which appear to have these patterns, but which are not derivable from some triliteral-root word by the addition of a verb-formative *w* or *r*, are classified as true quadriradical. [117]

THE *n* SUFFIX PATTERN

FaᶜLan, biFaᶜLen   *tFaᶜLan, byətFaᶜLan*

Verbs of this pattern are augmented with respect to other patterns by suffixation of a formative *n*. Examples:

ṣafran, *biṣafren*	'to make...faint'	*ṭṣafran,* *byəṭṣafran*	'to feel faint'
ḥalwan, *biḥalwen*	'to sweeten'	*twaldan,* *byətwaldan*	'to be childish'
tēsan, *bitēsen*	'to be stubborn'	*twaḥšan,* *byətwaḥšan*	'to get rough'
sōdan, *bisōden*	'to depress'	*tsōdan,* *byətsōdan*	'to be depressed'

For inflection, cf. True Quadriradicals [p. 118].

Derivation:

Verbs of Pattern *FaᶜLan* and *tFaᶜLan* are mainly derived from nouns or adjectives. Those without the *t* formative are usually causative [240] or ascriptive [243]:

ḥalwan	'to sweeten' (causative)	← *ḥəlu*	'sweet'
ṣafran	'to make...faint' (causative)	← *ʔaṣfar*	'yellow, pale'
sōdan	'to depress' (causative)	← *ʔaswad*	'black'
ḥamran	'to consider stupid' (ascriptive)	← *ḥmār*	'donkey, stupid'

Note, however, the verb *tēsan* 'to be stubborn', which is an idiomatic simulative from *tēs* 'billy-goat'. (One would expect a *t-* formative: *"ttēsạn"*.)

Those with the *t* formative are mainly simulatives [249], or passives of *FaɛLan* verbs:

twaldan	'to act childish' (simul.)	← *walad*	'child'
twaḥšan	'to act rough' (simul.)	← *waḥᵊš*	'wild beast'
tḥamran	'to act stupid' (simul.)	← *ḥmār*	'donkey, stupid'
tsōdan	'to be depressed' (pass.)	← *sōdan*	'to depress'

Miscellaneous derivations:

rōḥan	'to revive' (trans.)	← *rūḥ.*	'spirit'
tšahwan	'to crave'	← *šahwe*	'craving, desire'
tfakhan	'to eat fruit' (applicative)	← *fākha*	'fruit'
tšōfan	'to be "stuck up"'	← *šāyef ḥālo...*	'considering one's self (important)'

Verbs which appear to have these patterns, but which are not derivable from other words by the addition of a verb-formative *n*, are classified as true quadriradical [117].

THE ʔ PREFIX PATTERN

ʔaFɛaL, biʔaFɛeL

Verbs of this pattern are augmented with respect to other patterns by a formative prefix *ʔ*, which remains in all inflections. Examples:

ʔaslam, *biʔaslem*	'to become a Muslim'	*ʔazhar,* *biʔazher*	'to bloom'
ʔawraʔ, *biʔawreʔ*	'to leaf out'	*ʔaflas,* *biʔafles*	'to go bankrupt'
ʔaṣbaḥ, *biʔaṣbeḥ*	'to be...in the morning'	*ʔaɣlam,* *biʔaɣlem*	'to get dark'

Some verbs of this pattern are variants of Pattern IV verbs: cf. *ʔaṣbaḥ, byaṣbeḥ; ʔaɣlam, byaɣlem.* Pseudo-quadriradical Pattern *ʔaFɛaL* is rare.

INFLECTION OF *ʔaslam* 'to become a Muslim'

	Perfect	Impf. Indic.	Impf. Subjn.	Impv.	
3m	*ʔáslam*	*biʔáslem*	*yʔáslem*		'he'
f	*ʔáslamet*	*bətʔáslem*	*tʔáslem*		'she'
pl	*ʔáslamu*	*biʔásᵊlmu*	*yʔásᵊlmu*		'they'
2m	*ʔaslám(ᵊ)t*	*bətʔáslem*	*tʔáslem*	*ʔáslem*	'you'
f	*ʔaslámti*	*bətʔásᵊlmi*	*tʔásᵊlmi*	*ʔásᵊlmi*	'you'
pl	*ʔaslámtu*	*bətʔásᵊlmu*	*tʔásᵊlmu*	*ʔásᵊlmu*	'you'
1sg	*ʔaslám(ᵊ)t*	*bʔáslem*	*ʔáslem*		'I'
pl	*ʔaslámna*	*mənʔáslem*	*nʔáslem*		'we'

Participle: *mʔaslem*

Most of these verbs are inchoatives [250], derived from adjectives of the pattern *məFƐeL* [133]:

ʔaslam 'to become a Muslim'	←	*məslem* 'Muslim'
ʔawraʔ 'to leaf out'	←	*mūreʔ* 'in leaf, leafy'
ʔazhar 'to bloom'	←	*məzher* 'blooming, flowering'
ʔaglam 'to get dark'	←	*məglem* 'dark'
ʔaflas 'to go bankrupt'	←	*məfles* 'bankrupt'

Adjectives of the *məFƐeL* pattern are sometimes participles of Pattern IV verbs, but they cannot be considered participles of this pseudo-quadriradical pattern, since they contrast with the quadriradical-type participles: *mʔaslem* 'having become a Muslim', *mʔaglem* 'having become dark', etc.

THE SIMPLE QUADRIRADICAL PATTERN

FaƐLaL, biFaƐLeL[1]

True quadriradical verbs are those which actually have four radicals, as distinct from pseudo-quadriradicals [109], which have three radicals plus an affix that is indistinguishable from a radical in form.

---

[1] The traditional pattern formulas misleadingly use L (*lām*) for the fourth as well as the third radical, but it is to be understood that the last two radicals are usually different.

Sound Verbs. Examples:

taržam, bitaržem 'to translate'	*daḥraš, hidaḥreš* 'to roll' (trans.)
barṭal, bibarṭel 'to bribe'	*barhan, bibarhen* 'to prove'
damdam, bidamdem 'to mumble'	*harwal, biharwel* 'to hurry' (intrans.)
baxšaš, bibaxšeš 'to tip'	*xatyar, bixatyer* 'to age' (intrans.)

INFLECTION OF *taržam* 'to translate'

	Perfect	Impv. Indic.	Impf. Subjn.	Impv.	
3m	*táržam*	*bitáržem*	*ytáržem*		'he'
f	*tážamet*	*bəttáržem*	*ttáržem*		'she'
pl	*táržamu*	*bitáržmu*	*ytáržmu*		'they'
2m	*taržám(ə)t*	*bəttáržem*	*ttáržem*	*táržem*	'you'
f	*taržámti*	*bəttáržmi*	*ttáržmi*	*táržmi*	'you'
pl	*taržámtu*	*bəttaržmu*	*ttáržmu*	*táržmu*	'you'
1sg	*taržám(ə)t*	*btáržem*	*táržem*		'I'
pl	*taržámna*	*məntáržem*	*ntáržem*		'we'

Participles: Act. *mtaržem*, Pass. *mtaržam*; Gerund *taržame*

When the third and fourth radicals are alike, they do not geminate when *-i* or *-u* are suffixed in the imperfect, but are kept apart by *ə*:

INFLECTION OF *baxšaš* 'to tip'

3m	*báxšaš*	*bibáxšeš*	*ybáxšeš*		'he'
f	*báxšašet*	*bətbáxšeš*	*tbáxšeš*		'she'
pl	*báxšašu*	*bibáxšəšu*	*ybáxšəšu*		'they'
2m	*baxšáš(ə)t*	*bətbáxšeš*	*tbáxšeš*	*báxšeš*	'you'
f	*baxšášti*	*bətbáxšəši*	*tbáxšəši*	*báxšəši*	'you'
pl	*baxšáštu*	*bətbáxšəšu*	*tbáxšəšu*	*báxšəšu*	'you'
1sg	*baxšáš(ə)t*	*bbáxšeš*	*báxšeš*		'I'
pl	*baxšášna*	*mənbáxšeš*	*nbáxšeš*		'we'

Participles: Act. *mbaxšeš*, Pass. *mbaxšaš*; Gerund: *baxšaše*

Hollow Verbs.   Examples:

bōdar, bibōder 'to powder'	*ʔōnan, biʔōnen* 'to regulate (by rules)'
dōzan, bidōzen 'to tune'	*hēlam, bihēlem* 'to bluff'
sōgar, bisōger 'to insure'	*nēšan, binēšen* 'to aim at'

The first pattern vowel *a* fuses with the second radical *w* or *y* to produce *ō* or *ē* respectively. (This fusion does not take place in most Lebanese dialects, however, and the verbs remain sound: *dawzan* for *dōzan*, *nayšan* for *nēšan*, etc.)

INFLECTION OF *sōgar* 'to insure'

	Perfect	Impf. Indic.	Impf. Subjn.	Impv.	
3m	*sōgar*	*bisōger*	*ysōger*		'he'
f	*sōgaret*	*bətsōger*	*tsōger*		'she'
pl	*sōgaru*	*bisōgru*	*ysōgru*		'they'
2m	*sōgár(ə)t*	*bətsōger*	*tsōger*	*sōger*	'you'
f	*sōgárti*	*bətsōgri*	*tsōgri*	*sōgri*	'you'
pl	*sōgártu*	*bətsōgru*	*tsōgru*	*sōgru*	'you'
1sg	*sōgár(ə)t*	*bsōger*	*sōger*		'I'
pl	*sōgárna*	*mənsōger*	*nsōger*		'we'

Participles: Act. *msōger*, Pass. *msōgar;* Gerund: *sōgara*

INFLECTION OF *nēšan* 'to aim'

3m	*nēšan*	*binēšen*	*ynēšen*		'he'
f	*nēšanet*	*bətnēšen*	*tnēšen*		'she'
pl	*nēšanu*	*binēšnu*	*ynēšnu*		'they'
2m	*nēšán(ə)t*	*bətnēšen*	*tnēšen*	*nēšen*	'you'
f	*nēšánti*	*bətnēšni*	*tnēšni*	*nēšni*	'you'
pl	*nēšántu*	*bətnēšnu*	*tnēšnu*	*nēšnu*	'you'
1sg	*nēšán(ə)t*	*bnēšen*	*nēšen*		'I'
pl	*nēšánna*	*mənnēšen*	*nnēšen*		'we'

Participles: Act. *mnēšen*, Pass. *mnēšan;* Gerund: *nēšane*

Defective Verbs.   There are very few examples to be found:

farša, bifarši   'to brush'

ʔarža, biʔarži   'to show'

warža, biwarži   'to show'

Besides the forms *warža* and *ʔarža* 'to show', there is also *farža* (same meaning). The latter, however, is formed on the rare pseudo-quadriradical pattern *FaƐLa*: Compare *farraž* 'to show around' (and passive *tfarraž* 'to look around'); *ṭaƐma, biṭaƐmi* 'to feed' (Root *ṭ-Ɛ-m*).

INFLECTION OF *farša* 'to brush'

	Perfect	Impf. Indic.	Impf. Subjn.	Impv.	
3m	fárša	bifárši	yfárši		'he'
f	fáršet	bətfárši	tfárši		'she'
pl	fáršu	bifáršu	yfáršu		'they'
2m	faršēt	bətfárši	tfárši	fárši	'you'
f	faršēti	bətfárši	tfárši	fárši	'you'
pl	faršētu	bətfáršu	tfáršu	fáršu	'you'
1sg	faršēt	bfárši	fárši		'I'
pl	faršēna	mənfárši	nfárši		'we'

Participles: Act. *mfarši*, Pass. *mfarša*

Hollow-Defective Verbs.   The few examples found include:

bōya, bibōyi 'to polish'

ṣōṣa, biṣōṣi 'to squeak'

INFLECTION OF *bōya* 'to polish'

3m	bōya	bibōyi	ybōyi		'he'
f	bōyet	bətbōyi	tbōyi		'she'
pl	bōyu	bibōyu	ybōyu		'they'
2m	bōyēt	bətbōyi	tbōyi	bōyi	'you'
f	bōyēti	bətbōyi	tbōyi	bōyi	'you'
pl	bōyētu	bətbōyu	tbōyu	bōyu	'you'
1sg	bōyēt	bbōyi	bōyi		'I'
pl	bōyēna	mənbōyi	nbōyi		'we'

Participles: Act. *mbōyi*, Pass. *mbōya*

Derivational Types. Many simple quadriliteral verbs are applicative [256], derived from words of four or more radicals:

baxšaš	'to tip'	←	*baxšīš*	'tip, handout'
barhan	'to prove'	←	*bərhān*	'proof'
talfan	'to telephone'	←	*talifōn*	'telephone'
ʔōnan	'to regulate(by rules)'	←	*ʔānūn*	'rule, law'
basmal	'to say "bəsməllāh..."'	←	*b-ə sm-ə l lāh*	'In the name of God...'
bōya	'to polish'	←	*bōya*	'polish'

Some are denominatives of other sorts: *xatyar* 'to age, grow old' (inchoative [250]) from *ʔəxtyār* 'old man'

AUGMENTED QUADRIRADICAL PATTERN: *tFaɛLaL, byətFaɛLaL*

Sound Verbs. Examples:

tbarhan, byətbarhan	'to be proven'
tmarkaz, byətmarkaz[1]	'to take position'
ddaḥraž, byəddaḥraž	'to roll'(intrans.)
ttaržam, byəttaržam	'to be translated'

INFLECTION OF *tmarkaz* 'to consolidate one's position, settle'

		Perfect	Impf.Indic.	Impf.Subjn.	Impv.	
3m		*tmárkaz*	*byətmárkaz*	*yətmárkaz*		'he'
f		*tmárkazet*	*btətmárkaz*	*tətmárkaz*		'she'
pl		*tmárkazu*	*byətmárkazu*	*yətmárkazu*		'they'
2m		*tmarkáz(ə)t*	*btətmárkaz*	*tətmárkaz*	*tmárkaz*	'you'
f		*tmarkázti*	*btətmárkazi*	*tətmárkazi*	*tmárkazi*	'you'
pl		*tmarkáztu*	*btətmárkazu*	*tətmárkazu*	*tmárkazu*	'you'
1sg		*tmarkáz(ə)t*	*bətmárkaz*	*ʔətmárkaz*		'I'
pl		*tmarkázna*	*mnətmárkaz*	*nətmárkaz*		'we'

Participles: Act. *mətmarkez*, Pass. *mətmarkaz (fī)*; (Gerund: *markaze*)

---

[1] The *m* is a secondary radical: the original triliteral root is *r-k-z*, whence *markaz* 'position'.

Defective Verbs:

INFLECTION OF *tfarša* 'to be brushed'

	Perfect	Impf.Indic.	Impf.Subjn.	Impv.	
3m	tfárša	byətfárša	yətfárša		'he'
f	tfáršet	btətfárša	tətfárša		'she'
pl	tfáršu	byətfáršu	yətfáršu		'they'
2m	tfaršḗt	btətfárša	tətfárša	tfárša	'you'
f	tfaršḗti	btətfárši	tətfárši	tfárši	'you'
pl	tfaršḗtu	btətfáršu	tətfáršu	tfáršu	'you'
1sg	tfáršet	bətfárša	ʔətfárša		'I'
pl	tfaršḗna	mnətfárša	nətfárša		'we'

Participle: *mətfarši;* Gerund: *tfərši*

Hollow Verbs:

INFLECTION OF *tsōgar* 'to be insured'

	Perfect	Impf.Indic.	Impf.Subjn.	Impv.	
3m	tsōgar	byətsōgar	yətsōgar		'he'
f	tsōgaret	btətsōgar	tətsōgar		'she'
pl	tsōgaru	byətsōgaru	yətsōgaru		'they'
2m	tsōgár(ə)t	btətsōgar	tətsōgar	tsōgar	'you'
f	tsōgárti	btətsōgari	tətsōgari	tsōgari	'you'
pl	tsōgártu	btətsōgaru	tətsōgaru	tsōgaru	'you'
1sg	tsōgár(ə)t	bətsōgar	ʔətsōgar		'I'
pl	tsōgárna	mnətsōgar	nətsōgar		'we'

Participle: *mətsōgĕr*

INFLECTION OF *tšēṭan* 'to be naughty'

	Perfect	Impf. Indic.	Impf. Subjn.	Impv.	
3m	*tšēṭan*	*byətšēṭan*	*yətšēṭan*		'he'
f	*tšēṭanet*	*btətšēṭan*	*tətšēṭan*		'she'
pl	*tšēṭanu*	*byətšēṭanu*	*yətšēṭanu*		'they'
2m	*tšēṭán(ə)t*	*btətšēṭan*	*tətšēṭan*	*tšēṭan*	'you'
f	*tšēṭánti*	*btətšēṭani*	*tətšēṭani*	*tšēṭani*	'you'
pl	*tšēṭántu*	*btətšēṭanu*	*tətšēṭanu*	*tšēṭanu*	'you'
1sg	*tšēṭán(ə)t*	*bətšēṭan*	*ʔətšēṭan*		'I'
pl	*tšēṭánna*	*mnətšēṭan*	*nətšēṭan*		'we'

Participle: *mətšēṭen;* Gerund: *šēṭane*

Derivational Types. Most verbs of Pattern *tFaƐLaL* are passives of simple quadriradicals:

tbarhan	'to be proven'	←	*barhan*	'to prove'
ddōzan	'to be in tune'	←	*dōzan*	'to tune'
tsōgar	'to be insured'	←	*sōgar*	'to insure'

Some are simulative [**249**]:

tšeṭan	'to be naughty'	←	*šēṭān*	'devil, naughty'
tḥēwan[1]		←	*ḥēwān*	'animal'

Some are otherwise denominative: *tmarkaz* 'to take up a position' (from *markaz*[2] 'position').

PATTERN *FƐaLaLL*

Examples:

šmaʔazz, byəšmaʔəzz	'to be revolted, sickened'
ḍmaḥall, byəḍmaḥəll	'to fade away, die out'
ṭmaʔann, byəṭmaʔənn	'to be calm, feel secure'
qšaƐarr, byəqšaƐərr	'to shudder, have gooseflesh'

---

[1] the *n* is a secondary radical; the original triliteral root is *ḥ-y-y*, whence *ḥēwān.*

INFLECTION OF *šmaʕazz* 'to be revolted'

	Perfect	Impf. Indic.	Impf. Subjn.	
3m	*šmaʕázz*	*byəšmaʕə́zz*	*yəšmaʕə́zz*	'he'
f	*šmaʕázzet*	*btəšmaʕə́zz*	*təšmaʕə́zz*	'she'
pl	*šmaʕə́zzu*	*byəšmaʕə́zzu*	*yəšmaʕə́zzu*	'they'
2m	*šmaʕazzēt*	*btəšmaʕə́zz*	*təšmaʕə́zz*	'you'
f	*šmaʕazzēti*	*btəšmaʕə́zzi*	*təšmaʕə́zzi*	'you'
pl	*šmaʕazzētu*	*btəšmaʕə́zzu*	*təšmaʕə́zzu*	'you'
1 sg	*šmaʕazzēt*	*bəšmaʕə́zz*	*ʕəšmaʕə́zz*	'I'
pl	*šmaʕazzēna*	*mnəšmaʕə́zz*	*nəšmaʕə́zz*	'we'

Participles: Act. *məšmaʕəzz*, Pass. *məšmaʕazz (mənno)*; Gerund:
ʕəšməʕzāz

The verb *qšaɛarr* may also be pronounced *ʕšaɛarr*.

Verbs of Pattern *FɛaLaLL* are all intransitive, but are not derived or related in any regular way to other words. Note, however, that *ṭmaʕann* is related to the triliteral root *ṭ-m-n,* as in *ṭamman* 'to calm, assuage, assure'.

CHAPTER 4: ADJECTIVE PATTERNS

In this chapter the common base patterns [p. 36] for adjectives are exemplified, showing any alterations that are incurred with unstable roots [p. 41].

All adjectives are cited in the masculine/singular. The inflection of adjectives is described in Chapter 7.

Index of Patterns

PATTERN $Fa\mathcal{E}eL$

Sound:

bašeɛ	'ugly'	ɹašen	'rough, coarse'
xaṭer	'dangerous'	daleɛ	'bland'
raṭeb	'moist, humid'	wahes	'wild, savage'
šareh	'airy, healthful'	waṣex	'dirty'
ṣaleb	'hard, solid'	ɛaker	'turbid, troubled'
desem	'nourishing'	waɛer	'uneven, bumpt'

Geminate: harr   'free'   marr   'bitter'

Defective: halu   'sweet, pleasant, pretty'

The adjective *saxᵊn* 'hot' is exceptional in being formed on the pattern $Fa\mathcal{E}L$ [141]. For those who do not distinguish in pronunciation between *e* and *a* (or *i*) in this position [13], there is of course no difference between the two patterns.

Some adjective of this pattern are correlative to nouns of the $Fa\mathcal{E}L$ or $Fa\mathcal{E}aL$ patterns: *xaṭer* 'dangerous': *xaṭar* 'danger'; *waṣex* 'dirty': *waṣax* 'dirt, filth'; *wahes* 'wild': *wahᵊš* 'wild beast'.

PATTERN $Fa\mathcal{E}L$

Sound: ṣaɛᵊb   'difficult'   faxᵊm   'stately, elegant'

           sahᵊl   'easy'   daxᵊm   'heavy, big'

With last two radicals alike:

fašš	'unripe'	harr (or hārr)	'hot'
hayy	'alive'	hadd (or hādd)	'sharp'
nayy	'raw'		

With final radical semivowel: *raxu*   'loose, lax'

Adjectives with this typically nominal pattern [139] are not common.

PATTERN F€ĩL

nḍĩf	'clean'	txĩn	'thick, fat'
bxĩl	'stingy'	b€ĩd	'far, distant'
t⁹ĩl	'heavy'	ždĩd	'new'
rxĩṣ	'cheap'	ṣḥĩḥ	'whole, in one piece' (cf ṣaḥĩḥ, below)
ẓgĩr	'small, young'	ḍ€ĩf	'ill' (cf. ḍa€ĩf, below)
ktĩr	'much'	mnĩḥ	'good'

This pattern is not used with final (or medial?) radical semivowel, (for which see Pattern Fa€ĩL below).

Some adjectives of this pattern are correlative to descriptive verbs [251].

PATTERN Fa€ĩL

Sound:	⁹akĩd	'definite, certain'	badĩ€	'novel, original, exotic'
	baṣĩṭ	'easy, minor, simple'	barĩ⁹	'innocent' (cf. bari, below)
	sa€ĩd	'happy, fortunate'	žamĩl	'beautiful'
	žarĩḥ	'wounded'	xabĩr	'experienced'
	xafĩf	'light'	ḍa€ĩf	'weak'
	ṭawĩl	'long, tall'	ṣaḥĩḥ	'true'
	€atĩ⁹	'old'	€aẓĩm	'great, grand'
	faẓĩ€	'awful, marvelous'	⁹alĩl	'little, few'
	waḥĩd	'unique, only'	⁹adĩm	'ancient'

Defective: *zaki* 'intelligent, bright'   *bari* 'innocent' (or sound *barīʔ*)

         saxi 'generous'   *ġani* 'rich'

         ṭari 'fresh'   *šaʔi* 'hoodlum'

         ʔawi 'strong'   *wafi* 'dependable, true (to one's word)'

Some adjective of Pattern *FaƐīL* are correlative to descriptive verbs [251]. A few contrast, as qualitative adjectives, with stative adjectives: *fahīm* '(naturally) understanding': cf. *fahmān, fāhem* 'knowledgeable, having come to understand'; *ḥazīn* 'sad' (temperament): cf. *ḥaznān* 'sad' (mood); *ʔaxīr* 'last, final': cf. *ʔāxer* 'last, latest'.

PATTERN *FaƐƐeL* (Variant of Pattern *FaƐīL*)

žayyed 'good, excellent'   *ṭayyeb* 'good'

dayyeʔ 'narrow, tight'   *xayyer* 'charitable, benificent'

mayyet 'dead'   *hayyen* 'easy'

sayyeʔ 'bad, unfortunate'

This pattern is a modification of Pattern *FaƐīL* used with medical radical semivowels: –yye– in lieu of –yī–, and (sometimes) in lieu of –wī–.

PATTERN *FaƐūL*

žasūr 'daring'   *wadūd* 'devoted, fond'

naṣūḥ 'sincere, loyal'   *xadūm* 'solicitous, servile'

xadūƐ 'obedient'   *ṣabūḥ* 'radiant, bright, smiling'

ṭamūḥ 'ambitious'   *ʔanūƐ* 'contented, temperate'

This pattern is not used (?) with final radical semivowel. As medial semivowel, y is lengthened: *ġayyūr* 'jealous'.

Almost all adjectives of this pattern designate personal qualities or dispositions. Most of them are dispositional derivatives of simple verbs [277].

PATTERN *Faεεāl*

baṭṭāl 'bad'	*rannān* 'sonorous'
šaġġāl 'in operation, working'	*šaffāf* 'transparent, translucent'
naššāf 'blotting, drying, absorbent'	*ḥabbāb* 'lovable, amiable'
ṭawwāf 'floating, buoyant'	*ḥassās* 'sensitive'

Defective: *bakka* 'weeper, cry-baby'   *ḥakka* 'talkative'

Many adjectives of this pattern are dispositional [277]. Compare noun pattern *Faεεāl* [151].

PATTERN *Faεεīl*

lammīε 'shiny'	*šarrīb* 'heavy drinker'
žaxxīx 'show-off'	*rakkīb* 'good rider, horseman'
xawwīf 'timorous, cowardly'	*šarrīr* 'evil-doer, malicious'

This pattern is not used with final radical semivowel.

Some adjectives are formed on a slightly different pattern, *Fəεεīl: səkkīr* and *xəmmīr* 'drunkard, alcoholic', *šəllīf* (or *šallīf)* 'charging exorbitant prices'.

Pattern *Faεεīl* is used mainly in forming dispositional adjectives [277].

PATTERN ʔaFƐaL

ʔaṣfar 'yellow'   ʔabkam 'mute, dumb'

ʔaḥmar 'red'   ʔaṭraš 'deaf'

ʔazraʔ 'blue'   ʔaṣlaƐ 'bald'

ʔaxḍar 'green'   ʔaƐwar 'one-eyed'

ʔabyaḍ 'white'   ʔaƐraž 'lame'

ʔaswad 'black'   ʔaƐwaž 'bent, crooked'

ʔasmar 'dark-complexioned'   ʔažrad 'barren, bleak'

ʔašʔar 'blond'   ʔahbal 'dim-witted, feeble-minded'

ʔablaʔ 'piebald'   ʔabraṣ 'leprous'

ʔadham 'black' (horse)   ʔaḥmaʔ 'stupid, foolish'

ʔabraš 'grey; albino'   ʔazƐar 'crook, brigand'

ʔašhal 'having dark grey eyes'   ʔaƐzab 'unmarried'

Geminate: ʔaṣamm 'stone deaf'

Defective: ʔaƐma 'blind'

The ʔaFƐaL pattern is used 1.) for colors and 2.) for "defect" (mostly human lacks and imperfections).[1] The pattern is completely changed in the feminine (FaƐLa) and plural (FaƐL, FaƐLān) — See Adjective Inflection [208]. For elatives, see Noun Pattern ʔaFƐaL [310].

The adjective ʔarmal 'widowed' has the "defects" pattern in the masculine form, but the feminine ʔarmale and the plural ʔarāmel are formed as from a quadriradical noun of the FaƐLaL pattern [159].

---

[1]The color-adjectives and defect-adjectives, to judge from their augmented pattern and from their categories of meaning, would seem to be derivatives. In fact, however, there are no underlying words to derive them from — certainly not in the case of color-adjectives. Defect-adjectives, though they are generally paronymous to simple verbs (e.g. Ɛama 'to blind' and Ɛəmi 'to go blind'), are treated as underlying these verbs rather than as derivatives from them, since the verbs can be counted as inchoatives [250] and causatives [240], while the adjectives do not fit any otherwise established derivational category.

PATTERN *Fāɛ̌eL*

Sound:

bāred	'cold'	*šāṭer*	'clever, smart'
ṣārem	'strict, severe'	*ɛ̌ādel*	'just'
ɛ̌āṭel	'bad'	*wāseɛ̌*	'wide, broad'
ɛ̌āʔel	'wise, sensible'	*wāḍeḥ*	'clear'
nāšef	'dry'	*yābes*	'dry, hard'
ʔāxer	'last'	*šāreḥ*	'sharp, dangerous'
bāyet	'stale'	*xāyef*	'afraid'

Geminate:

xāṣṣ	'special, private'	*šāzz*	'odd, strange'
ɛ̌āmm	'general, public'	*ḥārr*	'hot'

Active participles of geminate verbs have the sound pattern in Colloquial, not the geminate: *ḥāṭeṭ* 'having put·' (not *ḥāṭṭ*). (In the feminine and plural, however, the sound becomes like the geminate: *ḥāṭṭe, ḥāṭṭīn* [p. 28].)

Some geminate adjectives belonging theoretically to this pattern are usually (if not always) pronounced with a short *a: ḥadd* 'sharp'. (See Pattern *Faɛ̌L* [126].)

Defective:

ɛ̌āli	'high'	*ġāli*	'expensive'
bāʔi	'remaining'	*wāṭi*	'low'
fāḍi	'empty, unoccupied'	*ɛ̌āṣi*	'stubborn' (inanim. 'stuck, jammed')
ṣāḥi	'wide awake'	*ʔāsi*	'hard, solid'

See adjective inflection [204].

In Pattern *Fāɛ̌eL*, medial radical *w* appears as *y* (*xāyef* 'afraid', Root *x-w-f*), unless the final radical is also a semivowel, as in *hāwi* 'windy' (Root *h-w-y*).

Many adjectives of Pattern *Fāɛ̌eL* are active participles of simple verbs. [p. 258].

PATTERN *FaɛLān*

baṭrān	'wasteful'	*raḍyan*	'pleased, satisfied'
ḥafyān	'barefoot'	*wartān*	'heir, having inherited'
naɛsān	'sleepy'	*talfān*	'worthless, ruined'
kaslān	'lazy, loafing'	*zaɛlān*	'displeased'
waɛyān	'conscious'	*yaʔsān*	'in despair'

With medial radical semivowel: *žūɛān* 'hungry' 'Root *ž–w–ɛ*)

With medial and final radical semivowels: *rayyān* 'swampy, irrigated' (Root *r–w–y*); *ɛayyān* 'sick' (Root *ɛ–y–y*).

Defective: *malān* 'full' (also sound: *malyān*) (Root *m–l–y* or *m–l–ʔ*)

With the exception of *malān*, adjectives on this pattern with final radical semivowel are sound, with *–y–* before the *–ān* ending.

Pattern *FaɛLān* is not used with geminating radicals [p. 41] other than semivowels.

Most adjectives formed on Pattern *FaɛLān* are participles of sound and defective simple intransitive verbs [259].

PATTERN *maFɛūL*

Sound:

maxlūṭ	'mixed'	*mamnūn*	'obliged'
mašhūr	'famous'	*mažnūn*	'insane'
masʔūl	'responsible'	*mawžūd*	'occurring, found, present'
madyūn	'indebted'	*mayʔus* (*mɐnno*)	'despaired (of)'
maɛwūž	'bent'	*maḥbūb*	'well-liked, beloved'
mablūl	'wet'	*maẓbūṭ*	'correct'

Hollow: *maḥūl* 'extraordinary' (Root *h–w–l*).

Defective: məʔli 'fried'   məhši 'stuffed'

                makwi 'ironed'   məbli 'afflicted'

                məlwi 'bent, curving'   mənsi 'forgotten'

In some areas (e.g. Palestine) these defectives are pronounced with *a* in the first syllable: *mahši, maʔli,* etc. Compare Pattern *maFɛeL* defective [below].

Most adjectives formed on Pattern *maFɛūL* are passive participles of simple verbs. [258].

PATTERN *məFɛeL* (*muFɛeL*)

Sound: məsmen 'fattening'   məfles 'bankrupt, broke'

             məfžeɛ 'frightful'   məslem 'Moslem'

             məglem 'dark, murky'   məmken (or *mumken*) 'possible'

             məžwez 'paired'   məxleṣ (or *muxleṣ*) 'faithful'

             məhyeb 'awesome'   məhrez 'worthwhile'

Initial Weak: mūžeɛ 'hurtful, inflicting pain'   mūheš 'desolate'

                    mūreʔ 'in leaf, leafy'

Geminate: mxəll 'immoral'   msəmm 'poisonous'

                mhəmm 'important'   mməll 'boring'

Hollow: mṭīɛ 'obedient'   mufīd 'useful, beneficial'

              mrīh 'comfortable, restful   muhīṭ (b-) 'surrounding'
              (also sound: *məryeh*)

Defective: məɛdi 'contagious'   mərḍi 'satisfactory'

                 məʔzi 'harmful'   məhwi 'draughty, airy'

In most parts of the Syrian area, defective participles of the pattern *maFɛūL* above have been assimilated to this pattern, so that there is no difference in form between the two kinds of defective pattern; see, however, pp. 203-204.

Many adjectives formed on Pattern *məFⱭⱭeL* are agentive [278] or characteristic [279] ; some are participles of Pattern IV verbs [82].

AUGMENTED PARTICIPIAL PATTERNS

Pattern *mFaⱭⱭeL:* *mrašše*ẖ 'having a cold', *mbayyen* 'apparent, seeming';
Defective: *mxalli* 'having left', *msawwi* 'having cooked'.

Used for Active Participles of Pattern II verbs [p.77].

Pattern *mFaⱭⱭaL:* *mtallaž* 'iced', *mžawwaz* 'married', *mhazzab* 'polite',
mⱭayyan 'definite, particular', *mwaffaʔ* 'fortunate'; Defective: *mrabba*
'brought up, educated', *msamma* 'named, called'.

Used for Passive Participles of Pattern II verbs.

Pattern *mFāⱭeL:* *msāfer* 'traveling', *mnāseb* 'suitable, convenient', *mžāweb*
'having answered, respondent'; Defective: *mlāʔi* 'having found', *msāwi*
'having made'

Used for Active Participles of Pattern III verbs [p.80].

Pattern *mFāⱭaL:* *mbārak* 'blessed', *mʔāṣaṣ* 'punished', *mžāwab* 'answered';
Defective: *mlāʔa* 'found', *msāwa* 'made'

Used for Passive Participles of Pattern III verbs.

Pattern *məFⱭeL:* (Rare as participle; see p.133 above): *məkrem* 'honoring'

Pattern *məFⱭaL:* *məkram* 'honored', *məⱭžab (b-)* 'admiring, impressed (by)';
Defective: *muġma (Ɛalē)* 'fainted'

Rare, as passive participle of Pattern IV verbs; see p.260.

Pattern *mətFaⱭⱭeL:* *mətʔaxxer* 'delaying, late', *mətkabber* 'haughty',
mədžawwez 'married', *mətradded* 'undecided', *məddayyen (mənno)* 'borrowed
(from)'; Defective: *mətrabbi* 'educated, well brought up'

Used for active participles of Pattern V verbs [p.86].

Pattern *mətFaⱭⱭaL:* *mətʔaxxar* 'delayed' (inanimate); Defective: *mətbanna*
'adopted'

Used for passive participles of Pattern V verbs.

Pattern *mətFāƐeL:* *mətwāḍeƐ* humble, modest', *mətšāmel* 'considerate
mətƐāmel 'dealt with'; Defective: *mətsāwi* 'equal, balanced', *mətnāhi*
'extreme'

Used for active participles of Pattern VI verbs [p.88].

Pattern *mətFāƐaL:* *mətbādal* 'mutual, reciprocal', *mətšāwaz* 'exceeded',
mətnāwal 'attainable, within reach'

Used for passive participles of Pattern VI verbs.

Pattern *mənFśƐeL, mənFáƐeL:* *mənkśser* 'defeated, broken', *mənṭśreb*
'enraptured' *mən⁹dṭeƐ* 'discontinued'; Geminate: *mənḥall* 'disbanded, dis-
charged'; Hollow: *mənšāf* 'seen'; Defective: *mən⁹śri* 'read'.

Used for "active" [267] participles of Pattern VII verbs [p.91].

Pattern *məFtśƐeL, məFtdƐeL:* *məƐtśdel* 'moderate, temperate, mild',
məxtślef 'different, differing', *məltśbes* 'ambiguous, obscure', *məntśxeb*
'having elected', *məzddḥem* 'crowded' [100]; Geminate: *məḥtall* 'occupy-
ing' Hollow: *mərtāḥ* 'comfortable, at ease', *məmtāz* 'excellent'; Defective:
məntśsi 'forgotten', *məstświ* 'cooked, done'; Initial weak: *məttśkel (Ɛala)*
'depending (on)', *muttdḥed* 'united', *məttśšeh (la-)* 'headed (for)'.

This pattern is used for active participles of Pattern VIII
verbs [p.95].

Pattern *məFtdƐaL:* *məḥtdram* 'respected, respectable', *məxṭdṣar* 'brief',
məntdxab 'elected'; Defective: *məḥtdwa (Ɛalē)* 'contained, included'
(Geminate and Hollow rare, same in form as Pattern *məFtśƐeL:)* *məḥtall*
'occupied'.

Used for passive participles of Pattern VIII verbs.

Pattern *məFƐaLL:* *məḥmarr* 'blushing, reddened', *məƐwašš* 'crooked, twisted'

Used for participles of Pattern IX verbs [101].

Pattern *məstaFƐeL;* *məstaḥsen* 'preferring', *məstaƐmel* 'using, having
used', *məstaƐžel* 'in a hurry', *məstašweb* 'having questioned'; Geminate:
məstƐədd 'ready, prepared'm *məst⁹əll* 'independent'; Hollow: *məstfīd*
'benefitting', *məstaṭīƐ* 'able'; Defective: *məstakri* 'renting'

Used for active participles of Pattern X verbs [102].

Pattern *məstaFɛaL:* *məstaɛmal* 'used', *məstaḥsan* 'preferred', *məstaɛžal* 'hurried, speeded'; Geminate: *məstaḥaʔʔ* '(one's) due'; Hollow *məstašār* 'consulted', *məstaɛān* 'called upon for help'

Used for passive participles of Pattern X verbs.

QUADRIRADICAL (AND PSEUDO-QUADRIRADICAL) PATTERNS

Pattern *FaɛLūL:* *farkūš* 'clumsy', *šaršūḥ* 'slovenly'

Pattern *FaɛLīL:* *zangīl* 'wealthy'

Pattern *mFaɛLeL:* *mfastek* 'depressed', *mbarǧel* 'grainy', *mbarṭel* 'having bribed, bribing', *mʔafles* 'having gone bankrupt'; Defective: *mfarži* 'having shown'

This pattern is used for active participles of simple quadriradical [117] and pseudo-quadriradical verbs [109].

Pattern *mFaɛLaL:* *mbarṭal* 'bribed', *mlaxbaṭ* 'mixed up', *mʔaɛlan* 'announced, advertized', *mṭablaž* 'plump', *mṭaḥbaš* 'wrecked', *mɛanṭaz* 'arrogant', *mšarṭaṭ* 'ragged'; Defective: *mfarža* 'shown'

This pattern is used for passive participles of simple quadriradical and pseudo-quadriradical verbs.

Pattern *mətFaɛLeL:* *məddaḥwer* 'decadent'

Used for "active" participles of augmented quadriradical and pseudo-quadriradical verbs [121].

Pattern *mətFaɛLal:* *məttaržam (mənno)* 'translated (from)'

Used for passive participles of augmented quadriradical and pseudo-quadriradical verbs.

Pattern *məFɛaLəLL:* *məšmaʔəzz* 'disgusted, nauseated' *mətmaʔənn* 'calm' secure'

Used for "active" participles of Pattern *FɛaLaLL* verbs [123]

Pattern *məFɛaLaLL:* *məšmaʔazz mənno* 'nauseating, revolting'

Used for passive participles of Pattern *FɛaLaLL* verbs. (Rare)

CHAPTER 5:   NOUN PATTERNS

In this chapter the more common base patterns [p. 36] for nouns are exemplified, showing any alterations that are incurred with unstable roots [p. 40].

Not included here, however, are several important kinds of noun patterns that are illustrated in other parts of the book: participial patterns (other than *Fāɛel*) [131, 258], augmented gerundial patterns [293], elative patterns [310], and patterns involving the relative suffix −*i* [280].

All nouns are cited in the absolute form of the singular. Dual and plural forms are shown in Chapter 8, and construct forms are treated at the end of the present chapter [162].

Index of Patterns

The Base-Formative Suffix *-e/-a*

Most noun patterns come in pairs — one with, and one without, the ending *-e*. (Compare the left and right columns in the index above.) This ending normally takes the form *-a* after velarized consonants (*ṭ, ṣ, ḍ, ẓ*) and back consonants (*x, ġ, q, ḥ, ɛ, h, ʔ*) and usually after *r* (but not usually after *-īr-*). Examples:

With *-e*		With *-a*	
raʔbe	'neck'	*žabha*	'front'
zīne	'decoration'	*ṣīġa*	'jewelry'
sakke	'track'	*ʔəṣṣa*	'story'
ɛāde	'custom'	*ḥāra*	'quarter'
ɛāṣfe	'storm'	*ṣānɛa*	'maid'
ʔasāwe	'harshness'	*safāra*	'embassy'
natīže	'result'	*ṭarīʔa*	'method'
ḍfīre	'braid'	*fḍīḥa*	'scandal'

There are exceptions to this rule, however, in which *-e* occurs after *r* (especially in Pattern *FəɛLe*): *ʔəbre* 'needle', *nəmre* 'number, class' (also *nəmra*), etc.; and sometimes after a velarized consonant: *ɛaṭṣe* 'a sneeze' (but more usually *εaṭṣa).* More common are cases in which the suffix appears as *-a* after plain front consonants: *ṣifa* 'attribute', *šōraba* 'soup', *ʔārma* 'sign, placard', *prōva* 'rehearsal', etc.[1]

The most notable formal features of the *-e/-a* suffix are its change to "connective *t*" in construct forms [163] and before the dual suffic *-ēn* [210], and its loss before the plural suffix *-āt* [214] and the relative suffix *-i* [280].

The *-e/-a* suffix has several derivational functions: singulative [p. 297], feminal [304], abstract [288]. In many (perhaps most) noun bases, however, it has no derivational significance, but merely indicates that the noun (if inanimate) is grammatically feminine [374].

This same suffix functions inflectionally in the fem- inine of adjectives [p. 202] and in the plurals of certain nouns [213].

PATTERN *FaεL*

Unaltered Pattern. Sound:

tax(ᵊ)t	'bed'	*ʔar(ᵊ)n*	'horn'
bar(ᵊ)d	'cold'	*ḍah(ᵊ)r*	'back'
ʔaṣ(ᵊ)l	'origin'	*kaε(ᵊ)b*	'heel'
waḥ(ᵊ)š	'wild beast'	*ʔalb*	'heart'
yaʔ(ᵊ)s	'despair'	*žamb*	'side'

The helping vowel *ᵊ* usually appears between the last two radicals at the end of a phrase or before a consonant. See p. 29 for details.

---

[1]Also *kahraba* 'electricity', *xawāža* 'gentleman', etc. Although the *-e/-a* suffix normally corresponds to ة in written Arabic, there are also cases in which it corresponds to ا or ى. The criterion for the *-e/-a* suffix is connective *t* in construct forms and duals: *kahrabet, kahrabt-* 'electric- ity of', *xawāžtēn* 'two gentlemen'.

Sound, with final radical semivowel:

Ɛažu	'pressed dates'	*ṣabi*	'boy'
faru	'fur'	*raʔi*	'opinion'
ʔabu	'basement'	*ḥaki*	'talk'

The radical semivowel appears as a consonant *w* or *y* before suffixes beginning with a vowel, otherwise usually as a vowel *u* or *i*: *raʔyak* 'your (m.) opinion', but *raʔikon* 'your (pl.) opinion'.

Geminate:

ḥaʔʔ	'right'	*wazz*	'geese'
xadd	'cheek'	*žaww*	'air, atmosphere'
samm	'poison'	*fayy*	'shade, shadow'

Altered Pattern. Hollow ($a + w \rightarrow \bar{o}$; $a + y \rightarrow \bar{e}$):

tōr	'bull'	*ṭēr*	'bird'
zōʔ	'taste'	*xēl*	'horses'
yōm	'day'	*sēf*	'sword'

Commonly in Lebanese speech, however, the radical semivowel does not fuse with the pattern vowel, the pattern remaining unaltered as with stable roots: *tawr* 'bull', *ṭayr* 'bird'. See p. 13.

Many nouns of Pattern *FaƐL* are gerunds of simple verbs [p. 289]: *ḍarb* 'striking, hitting' (cf. *ḍarab* 'to hit, strike'); *ḥaki* 'talk, talking' (cf. *ḥaka* 'to talk, speak'); *ʔaxᵃd* 'taking (cf. *ʔaxad* 'to take').

PATTERN *FaƐLe*

Unaltered Pattern. Sound:

raʔbe	'neck'	*žabha*	'front'
damƐa	'tear'	*ʔazme*	'crisis'
ḥafle	'party'	*baḥra*	'lake'
waṣfe	'prescription'	*farše*	'mattress'

Sound, with middle radical semivowel:

dawle	'nation'	*sawra*	'revolution'
Ɛawže	'bend'		

With final radical semivowel (Sound, or with exchange of *y* and *w*):

xaṭwe	'step, pace'	*ḥanye*	'bow; bend'
šarwe	'bargain'	*ṣafwe*	'ashes'

Before connective –*t*– plus suffixed vowel, the radical semivowel appears in its vocalic form; *xaṭutēn* 'two paces', *ḥanito* 'his bow'. See p. 166.

Geminate:

marra	'a time'	*salle*	'basket'
ḍaffe	'edge, bank'	*ḥayye*	'snake'

Altered Pattern. Hollow ($a + w \rightarrow \bar{o}$; $a + y \rightarrow \bar{e}$):

xēme	'tent'	*šōke*	'fork'
ḍēƐa	'village; estate'	*žōʔa*	'band'

Many nouns of Pattern *FaƐLe* are singulatives [p. 297], derived from Gerunds or collectives of Pattern *FaƐL: ġazwe* 'a raid' (cf. *ġazu* 'raiding'), *bēḍa* 'an egg' (cf. *bēḍ* 'eggs'). Others are gerunds [p. 292] and feminal derivatives [304].

PATTERN *FaƐL*

Unaltered Pattern. Sound:

ban(ᵊ)t	'girl, daughter'	*kab(ᵊ)š*	'ram'
ʔas(ᵊ)m	'name'	*žes(ᵊ)r*	'bridge'
Ɛam(ᵊ)r	'age'	*žans*	'kind'
bar(ᵊ)ž	'tower'	*malk*	'property'

On the use of the helping vowel (ᵊ), see p. 29.

Sound, with final radical semivowel:

    ʕaḍu 'member'   *ǯodi* 'kid'

On the alternation of *u* and *i* with *w* and *y,* see p.140.

Geminate:

    ʔəmm 'mother'   *ṭəbb* 'medicine'

    rəzz 'rice'   *wəǯǯ* 'face'

Altered Pattern. Hollow ($ə + w \rightarrow \bar{u};$ $ə + y \rightarrow \bar{\imath}$):

    ǯūx   'cloth'   *ʔīd*   'hand'

    būm   'owls' (coll.)   *bīr*   'well'

    sūʔ   'market'   *tīn*   'figs'

Anomalous hollow-defective: *ǯī* 'thing' (cf. classicism *ǯēʔ*)

> Commonly in Palestine this word is pronounced *ʔəǯi,*
> which is sound, with root *ʔ-ǯ-y.* (The initial *ʔ* also
> occurs in the plural *ʔaǯya* or *ʔəǯya,* which is used
> throughout Greater Syria.)

Some nouns of this pattern are abstract and gerundial derivatives
[p. 286]: *kəbᵊr* 'large size' (cf. *kbīr* 'large'); *ləʕb* 'play, game' (cf.
ləʕeb 'to play').

On plural Pattern *FəʕL,* see p.221.

PATTERN *FəʕLe*

Unaltered Pattern. Sound:

    ʔəǯra 'fee'   *tərbe* 'cemetery'

    rəhle 'trip, tour'   *fərṣa* 'opportunity'

    kəlme 'word'   *məʕze* 'goats' (coll.)

    ǯərke 'company'   *ʔəbre* 'needle'

Sound, with final radical semivowel:

ləhye	'beard'	*kəlwe*	'kidney'
dənye	'world'	*Ɛərwe*	'button-hole'

On the alternation of *u* and *i* with *w* and *y*, see p. 166.

Geminate:

šəffe	'lip'	*fəḍḍa*	'silver'
ʔeṣṣa	'story'	*səkke*	'track'

Altered Pattern. Semivowel-geminate, with assimilation of pattern vowel:

niyye 'aim, intention' (Root *n-w-y*)   *ʔuwwe* 'power' (Root *Ɛ-w-y*)

diyye 'blood money' (See p. 157)   *huwwe* 'precipice' (Root *h-w-y*)

See p. 166.

Hollow (*ə + y → ī; ə + w → ū*):

zīne	'decoration'	*ṣūra*	'picture'
ṣīğa	'jewelry'	*mūne*	'provision'
ḥīle	'trick'	*ʔūḍa*	'room'

Many nouns of this pattern are abstract or gerundial [287] or singulative [297]: *ʔəlle* 'scarcity' (cf. *ʔalīl* 'few, little'); *xədme* 'service' (cf. *xadam* 'to serve'); *fəkra* 'an idea' (cf. *fəkᵊr* 'thinking, thought').

PATTERN *FaƐaL*

Unaltered Pattern. Sound:

ʔamal	'hope'	*taman*	'price'
šaraf	'honor'	*ʔalaʔ*	'insomnia'
walad	'child'	*sabab*	'cause'
baʔar	'cattle'	*ḍarar*	'damage'

Altered Pattern. Hollow (Loss of middle radical):

šār	'neighbor'	*sāʔ*	'leg'
rās	'head'	*xāl*	'maternal uncle'
bāb	'door'	*ʔāƐ*	'bottom'

The word *šāy* 'tea' appears to belong to this pattern (though since it has no paronyms there is no basis for classifying it so), with final radical semivowel maintained. Otherwise, roots with final semivowel do not occur with this pattern. See pattern *FaƐāL* [146].

PATTERN *FaƐaLe*

Unaltered Pattern. Sound:

sakane	'barrack(s)'	*barake*	'blessing'
ṣalaṭa	'salad'	*ṭabaʔa*	'class'
daraše	'degree, step'	*ḥažara*	'a stone'

Altered Pattern. Hollow (Loss of Middle radical):

Ɛāde	'habit, custom'	*ḥāra*	'quarter, neighborhood'
ṭābe	'ball'	*rāye*	'banner'
wāƐa	'container'	*sāƐa*	'hour'

PATTERN *FāƐeL*

Sound:

bāƐes	'motive'	*žāmeƐ*	'mosque'
ḥāžeb	'eyebrow'	*wāžeb*	'duty'
ẓābeṭ	'officer'	*ḥādes*	'incident'

With middle radical semivowel:

$f\bar{a}ye\dot{z}$ 'usury' $z\bar{a}yer$ 'visitor'

A medial radical *w* is represented by *y* in this pattern; see Adjective Pattern *Fāƹel* [p. 131].

Defective (*e* + *y* or *w* → *ī*):

$r\bar{a}ƹi$ 'keeper, herdsman' $ʔ\bar{a}di$ 'judge'

Cf. Pattern *Fāƹel* adjectives.

Many nouns of this pattern are substantivized active participles of simple verbs: *kāteb* 'clerk', 'writer' (cf. *katab* 'to write'); *zāyer* 'visitor' (cf. *zār* 'to visit'); *māneƹ* 'inconvenience, obstacle, hindrance' (cf. *manaƹ* 'to prevent'); *nāʔeb* 'representative' (cf. *nāb* 'to represent'). See p. 276.

PATTERN *Fāƹļe*

ƹāṣfe	'storm'	*ṣānƹa*	'maid'
žāmƹa	'university'	*wāṣṭa*	'means'
ṭāwle	'table'	*ṭāyfe*	'sect'
zāwye	'corner'	*ḍāḥye*	'suburb'
mādde	'material'	*dābbe*	'beast of burden'

This pattern remains unaltered with all types of root, except that final or medial radical *w* commonly becomes *y*. [p. 44]. See also Construct Forms, p. 167.

PATTERN $Fa\mathcal{E}\bar{a}L$

Sound:

šamāl	'beauty	*ʔasās*	'foundation'
bayān	'statement'	*ħarām*	'taboo; shame'
šawāz	'permit'	*kalām*	'speech, words'
qarār	'decision'	*ġazāl*	'gazelle'

Defective (Loss of final radical semivowel):

ɛaša	'dinner, supper'	*sama*	'sky; heaven'
hawa	'air'	*masa*	'evening'
ġada	'lunch, dinner'	*dawa*	'medicine'
ħaya	'modesty'	*šaza*	'punishment, penalty'

The long $\bar{a}$ of the pattern is preserved in the suffixing forms of these words, see p. 27.

Defective, with final radical semivowel → ^{ʔ}: *šazāʔ* (= *šaza*).

PATTERN $Fa\mathcal{E}\bar{a}Le$

saɛāde	'happiness'	*wakāle*	'agency'
safāra	'embassy'	*šamāɛa*	'group of people'
rabābe	'rebab' (mus. instr.)	*baṭāṭa*	'potatoes'
ʔasāwe	'cruelty'	*ɛaṣāye*	'stick'

This pattern remains unaltered with all types of root.

Many nouns of this pattern are abstract derivatives of simple adjectives and nouns [285]: *saɛāde* 'happiness' (cf. *saɛīd* 'happy'); *safāra* 'embassy' (cf. *safīr* 'ambassador'); *ɛadāwe* 'enmity' (cf. *ɛaduww* 'enemy').

PATTERN *FƐāL*

Sound:

ḥṣān	'horse'	ḥmār	'donkey'
ʔmāš	'cloth'	blāš	'beach'
wžāʔ	'stove	ktāb	'book'
šƐāƐ	'ray, beam'	ʔyās	'measurement'
ṣʔāʔ	'street'	ġyāb	'absence'

Defective:

dəra	'corn, maise'	rəḍa	'contentment, satisfaction'
šəte	'winter; rain'	nəde	'dew'
ġəre	'glue'	ṣəde	'rust'

The long *a* of this defective pattern is preserved in the suffixing form [p. 27], while the absolute form has variants ending in *e* or *a*, as in the *–e/–a* suffix [p. 138]. The *ə* of the first syllable, which is lost in the sound version of this pattern, remains in all forms.

The anomalous noun *bəke* 'crying, weeping', is like these words in the absolute form, but has a suffixing form like Pattern *FəƐL* [142]: *bə́ki-hon* 'their crying' (cf. *šətā́–hon* 'their winter').

Many nouns of Pattern *FƐāL* are gerunds of simple verbs: *ġyāb* 'absence' (cf. *ġāb* 'to be absent'); *rəḍa* 'satisfaction' (cf. *rəḍi* 'to be satisfied').

For plural Pattern *FƐāL*, see p. 218.

PATTERN *FƐāLe*

xzāne	'closet'	bḍāƐa	'merchandise'
swāra	'bracelet'	rṣāṣa	'bullet'
zyāra	'visit'	mlāye	'veil'

This pattern remains unaltered with all types of root.

Many nouns of Pattern *FƐāLe* are gerunds of simple verbs: *Ɛbāde* 'worship' (cf. *Ɛabad* 'to worship'), *ʔrāye* 'reading' (cf. *ʔara* 'to read').

PATTERN *FiƐāL*

difāƐ	'defense'	*niẓām*	'system, order'
ʔilāh	'god'	*wisām*	'medal, badge'

Defective: *šifa* 'cure'

PATTERN *FiƐāLe*

ṣināƐa	'industry'	*nihāye*	'end'
zirāƐa	'agriculture'	*wilāye*	'state'
riwāye	'novel; play'	*siyāse*	'politics; policy'

Patterns *FiƐāL* and *FiƐāLe* are somewhat classicized variants of Patterns *FƐāL* and *FƐāLe* respectively.

Many nouns of Pattern *FiƐāLe* are gerunds of simple verbs: *dirāse* 'study' (cf. *daras* 'to study'); *zirāƐa* 'agriculture' (cf. *zaraƐ* 'to plant, cultivate').

PATTERN *FaƐīL*

ʔadīb	'man of letters'	*sabīl*	'way'
ʔamīs	'shirt'	*ṭabīb*	'physician'
raʔīs	'chief, head'	*yamīn*	'right (hand)'
ḥarīr	'silk'	*rabīƐ*	'spring(time)'

Defective: *waṣi* 'trustee, guardian'

Many nouns of Pattern *FaƐīL* that designate human beings are substantivized adjectives.   See p. 127.   Some are correlative to simple abstract nouns in the sense 'practitioner of' or 'versed in':   *ʔadīb* 'man of letters' (cf. *ʔadab* 'belles-lettres'); *ṭabīb* 'physician' (cf. *ṭəbb* 'medicine, physical therapy').

PATTERN *FaƐīLe*

natīǧe 'result'	*ǧarīme* 'crime'
ṭarīʔa 'method'	*madīne* 'city'
daʔīʔa 'minute'	*sarīƐa* 'Muslim law'

With final radical semivowel (*-iyy-* = *-īy-*):

xaṭiyye 'sin'	*ʔaḍiyye* 'case'
Ɛašiyye 'evening'	*waṣiyye* 'will, testament'

PATTERN *FƐīL*

žbīn 'forehead'	*rġīf* 'loaf'
rfīʔ 'companion'	*šrīṭ* 'string, wire'
šƐīr 'barley'	*gdīš* 'nag, horse'

This pattern is not used with middle or final radical semivowel.

Patterns *FaƐīL* and *FƐīL* are used in a number of gerunds, especially those designating noises: *ṣrīx* 'shouting', *šxīr* 'snoring', *ʔanīn* 'moaning', *ḍašīš* 'noise, tumult', *ranīn* 'tinkle', *bṣīṣ* 'glimmering, glimpse'.

PATTERN *FɛīLe*

ḏfīre	'braid'	*knīse*	'church'
fḏīẖa	'scandal'	*t̟hīne*	'sesame oil sauce'

With final radical semivowel (*y*) (*-iyy-* = *-īy-*):

hdiyye	'gift'	*wʕiyye*	'oka' (weight measure)

This pattern is not used with middle radical semivowel.

PATTERN *F(u)ɛūL*

zbūn	'customer'	*žnūb*	'south'
s(u)rūr	'joy, pleasure'	*f(u)t̟ūr*	'breakfast'
hžūm	'attack'	*t̟umūẖ*	'aspiration'

With final radical semivowel (*w*) (*-uww-* = *-ūw*):

ɛ(u)luww	'elevation, height'	*numuww*	'growth'

The pattern may also be altered (defective) in *ɛəlu* 'height' (suffixing form *ɛəlū-*).

Pattern *Fɛūl* is commonly used for gerunds of simple verbs [291]: *t̟lūɛ* 'coming out, going up' (cf. *t̟əleɛ* 'to come out, go up'); *šɛūr* 'feeling(s)' (cf. *šaɛar* 'to feel').

For plural Pattern *Fɛūl*, see p. 220.

PATTERN *FℰūLe*

rṭūbe	'humidity'	*ḥkūme*	'government'
xšūne	'roughness'	*ṣxūne*	'fever'
ṣℰūbe	'difficulty'	*ḥmūḍa*	'acidity'

With final radical semivowel (*-uww-* = *-ūw-*):

mruwwe	'mastery'	*ʔubuwwe*	'fatherhood'

This pattern is used mainly for abstract nouns derived from simple adjective and nouns [p. 286].

For plural Pattern *FℰūLe*, see p. 220.

PATTERNS *FāℰūL, FāℰūLe*

qānūn	'law'	*ṭāḥūn*	'mill'
xāzūʔ	'stake'	*xārūf*	'lamb'
ṣābūn	'soap'	*nāℰūra*	'water wheel'
qāmūs	'dictionary'	*māsūra*	'pipe, tube'

PATTERN *FaℰℰāL*

xabbāz	'baker'	*ḥaddād*	'blacksmith'
fallāḥ	'peasant'	*xayyāṭ*	'tailor'
ḥammām	'bath'	*ṣabbāṭ*	'(pair of) shoes'
tayyār	'current'	*dawwār*	'whirlpool'

Defective:

> *banna* 'builder, mason'   *hawwa* 'presser'

The long pattern vowel *ā* is retained in the suffixing form: *bannāhon* 'their mason'.

Pattern *FaɛɛāL* is commonly used for occupational nouns [305].   Cf. adjective pattern *FaɛɛāL* [129].

PATTERN *FaɛɛāLe*

kammāše	'pincers'	*sayyāra*	'automobile'
ʔallābe	'ferris-wheel'	*barrāde*	'refrigerator'
žabbāne	'cemetery'	*ṭarrāḥa*	'cushion'

With final radical semivowel *y*, unaltered:

maḥḥāye	'eraser'	*barrāye*	'pencil-sharpener'

Pattern *FaɛɛāLe* is commonly used for instrumental nouns [306]

PATTERNS *FəɛɛāL, FəɛɛāLe*

šəbbāk	'window'	*sənnāra*	'fish hook'
rəžžāl	'man'	*ɛəkkāze*	'crutch'
səžžād	'rugs' (collective)	*səžžāde*	'a rug'
təffāḥ	'apples (collective)	*təffāḥa*	'an apple'

Cf. plural pattern *fəɛɛāL* [223].

PATTERN *maFɛaL*

Unaltered Pattern. Sound:

madfaɛ	'cannon'	*manẓar*	'view'
maxbaz	'bakery'	*matɛam*	'restaurant'
mablaġ	'amount, sum'	*maʔzaq*	'bottleneck, strait'
maṣyaf	'summer resort'	*maytam*	'orphanage'

Altered Pattern. Geminate:

maḥall	'place'	*mafarr*	'escape, flight'
maṣabb	'mouth (of a river)'	*mamarr*	'aisle'

Hollow:

manām	'dream'	*maɛāš*	'salary'
maṭār	'airport'	*mažāl*	'space, scope'

Defective:

maɛna	'meaning'	*maʔwa*	'shelter'
maġza	'point, import'	*mawla*	'lord, master'

Most nouns of Pattern *maFɛaL* are locative [308], hypostatic [309], or instrumental [307].

PATTERN *maFɛaLe*

Unaltered Pattern Sound:

maḥrame	'handkerchief'	*marḥale*	'stage, step'
maɛlaʔa	'spoon'	*madxane*	'chimney'
masʔale	'matter, question'	*mawʔade*	'brazier, fireplace'
manfaḍa	'ashtray'	*maṣyade*	'trap, snare'

Altered Pattern. Geminate:

> *maḥabbe* 'love, affection'   *mawadde* 'love, friendship'
>
> *mažalle* 'magazine'

Hollow:

> *masāfe* 'distance'   *manāra* 'lighthouse'
>
> *maxāḍa* 'ford'   *maḍāfe* 'reception room'

Most nouns of Pattern *maFƐaLe* are locative [308], hypostatic [309] or instrumental [307].

PATTERN *maFƐeL*

Sound:

> *maržeƐ* 'source, reference'   *mawled* 'birth, birthday'
>
> *mažles* 'chamber, session room'   *mawḍeƐ* 'position'
>
> *mawʔef* 'stop, station'   *mawƐed* 'appointment'

Many nouns of this pattern have initial radical *w*.

Hollow: *maṣīr* 'course, destiny'

> Pattern *maFƐeL* is not used with geminating radicals or final radical semivowels.

Most nouns of Pattern *maFƐeL* are locative, hypostatic, or instrumental.

PATTERN *maFƐ(i)Le*

Sound:

> *manṭiʔa* 'district, zone'   *mawhibe* 'talent, gift'
>
> *maʔdira* 'ability, power'   *mawƐiža* 'lecture, reprimand'
>
> *maƐrife* or *maƐərfe* 'knowledge, acquaintance'

Hollow: *mašīʔa* 'will, wish'[1]

Initial Weak: *mādne* 'minaret' (Root *ʔ-d-n*)

Pattern *maFɛ(i)Le* is not used with geminating radicals or final radical semivowels.

Most nouns of this pattern are hypostatic or locative.

PATTERNS *maFɛaL* and *maFɛaLe*

For locative, projective, or instrumental nouns, these patterns are mainly used with geminating roots, and altered accordingly:

mʔaṣṣ	'scissors'	*mḥaṭṭa*	'station'
mfakk	'screwdriver'	*mʔašše*	'brown'
mḥaṭṭ	'object, point'	*mxadde*	'pillow'
		msabbe	'curse, invective'

Some nouns of Pattern *maFɛaL* (or more usually *muFɛaL*) are substantivized passive participles or hypostatic nouns corresponding to verb Pattern IV [p. 84]. These include sound: *mulḥaq* 'attaché', hollow: *murād* 'wish, desire', and initial weak: *mūžaz* 'outline, resumé'.

PATTERNS *maFɛeL* and *maFɛ(i)Le*

Sound:

maškel or *maškle*	'problem, difficulty'
maɛžize or *maɛʔžze*	'miracle'
makʔnse	'broom'

---

[1]This word is always used in construct, thus always in the construct forms *mašīʔet, mašīʔt-, mašīʔšt-*. E.g. *mašīʔet ʔabno* 'his son's wish', *mašīʔto* 'his wish'.

Hollow: *mṣība* 'misfortune, calamity'

Initial Weak: *mūsem* 'season'

Pattern *məFⱻeL* is more commonly used in substantivized personal adjectives [133, 382]: *məslem* 'Moslem', *məfti* 'mufti', *mudīr* 'director'.

PATTERNS *məFⱻāL and məFⱻāLe*

Sound:

mənšār	'saw'	*məšwār*	'walk, errand'
məzrāb	'gutter, drain'	*mənxār*	'nose'
məⱻyār	'balance, measure'	*məḥrāt*	'plow'

Initial Weak:

mīⱻād	'appointment'	*mīlād*	'birth, birthday, Nativity'
mīzān	'scale balance'	*mīsāq*	'pact, covenant'

The pattern vowel *ə* combines with initial radical *w* to produce *ī*.

With final radical semivowel (*y*), the suffix *-e* is used:

məkwāye	'(flat)iron	*məʔlāye* 'frying pan'
mədrāye	'winnowing fork'	*məṣlāye* 'trap'

Hollow: *mrāye* 'mirror' (Root *r-ʔ-y*)

In some parts of Greater Syria, final radical *y* produces defective nouns on Pattern *məFⱻāL*: *mədra* 'winnowing fork' (instead of *mədrāye*).

Most nouns of Pattern *məFⱻāL(e)* are instrumental or hypostatic.

MISCELLANEOUS TRIRADICAL PATTERNS

There are many nouns in Arabic whose patterns are rare or even unique. Some of these less common patterns are briefly exemplified here:

Pattern *ƐiLa:* *žiha* 'direction', *ṣifa* 'attribute, adjective', *siƐa* 'capacity' *θiqa* (or *siqa*) 'faith, trust'. (For construct forms, see p. 169)

> This pattern is applied exclusively to roots with initial *w*, which is lost. Thus *žiha* has Root *w-ž-h,* *ṣifa* has Root *w-ṣ-f,* etc. Nouns with this pattern are classicisms, with the marginal exception of *diyye* 'blood money', whose root, theoretically speaking, is *w-d-y,* but which has been altered colloquially to fit pattern *FəƐLe* as if its root were *d-y-y.* (It has no colloquial paronyms with either root.)

Patterns *F(u)ƐayyeL, F(u)ƐayLe, FwayƐeL:* *zġayyer* 'little one', *buḥayra* 'lake', *šwayye* 'a little'.

> These traditional diminutive patterns [p. 310] are quite unproductive in most kinds of Syrian Arabic.

Pattern *FƐēLe:* *žnēne* 'garden', *ḥmēra* 'measles', *žwēze* 'deuce'.

> This is an alteration of the diminutive pattern *F(u)ƐayLe.*

Pattern *FaƐeL:* *malek* 'king'

Pattern *FaƐoL:* *ražol* 'man' (classisism)

Pattern *FəƐeL:* *Ɛəneb* 'grapes'

Pattern *FəƐoL:* *təton* 'tobacco', *ʔəṭon* 'cotton' (Cf. plural pattern *FəƐoL* [p. 221].)

Pattern *FaƐūL:* *rasūl* 'apostle, messenger, prophet', *Ɛažūz* 'old person', *Ɛaduww* 'enemy'. (Cf. adjective pattern *FaƐūL* [p. 128].)

Pattern *FāƐaL:* *Ɛālam* 'world'

Pattern *FəƐƐoL:* *səllom* 'ladder', *ḥəmmoṣ* 'chick peas'

Pattern *FīƐāL:* *bīkār* 'compass' (for drawing), *dīnār* (monetary unit), *ʔīwān* 'sitting room', *nīsān* 'April'.

Pattern *FāƐōL:* *māƐōn* 'container', *bāṭōn* 'cement', *bālōn* 'balloon'.

Pattern *FūƐāL:* *būlād* 'steel'

Pattern *FəƐəLL:*   *səžəll* 'record'

Pattern *FuƐāL:*   *suʔāl* 'question', *buxār* 'steam', *duⱢāʔ* 'prayer of supplication' (defective; radical semivowel → ʔ).

Pattern *ʔəFƐūL:*   *ʔəṣṭūḥ* 'roof', *ʔəṣṭūl* 'fleet'

Pattern *FaƐaLān* (Hollow-defective):   *ḥēwān* 'animal' (Root *ḥ-y-y*)[Cf. p. 110]

Pattern *FaƐLūn:*   *zētūn* 'olives'

Pattern *FaƐlōn:*   *žardōn* 'rat' *ḥardōn* 'lizard'

Patterns *FəƐƐēL, FəƐƐēLe:*   *fəttēs* 'fireworks', *ləzzēʔa* 'adhesive tape',
duwwēxa 'merry-go-round'

Augmented Gerundial Patterns

All the patterns used for gerunds of augmented verbs, e.g. *taFƐīL*,
mFāƐaLe, *ʔəFƐāL*, *ʔənFiƐāL*, etc., are also used for ordinary nouns, i.e.
gerunds that have been concretized [p. 284] or otherwise altered from the
pure gerundial sense. These patterns are not separately illustrated here;
see p. 293.

Adjectival Patterns

Many adjectival patterns are used for nouns, insofar as adjectives
tend to be substantivized. Patterns *FāƐeL* and *FaƐƐāL* have been separately
illustrated for nouns and adjectives, but Patterns *FaƐƐīL* [p. 129] and
ʔaFƐaL [130] are shown only for adjectives, though many words with these
patterns are used substantivally.
Most important of all are the participial patterns [p. 258], e.g.
maFƐūL, mFaƐƐaL, məstaFƐeL, məFƐeL, etc. (only *FāƐeL* has been listed separately for nouns); a large number of nouns have these patterns, but are
not illustrated here.

For elative patterns, see p. 310.

QUADRIRADICAL (AND PSEUDO-QUADRIRADICAL)[1] PATTERNS

PATTERN $Fa\mathcal{E}LaL$

	ʔarnab 'rabbit'		baṭrak 'patriarch'
	xandaʔ 'ditch, trench'		šangal 'hook'
	žadwal 'schedule'		waṭwaṭ 'bat'
Hollow:	bēdar 'threshing floor'		zēbaʔ 'quicksilver'

PATTERN $Fa\mathcal{E}LaLe$

	taržame 'translation'		ṭanžara 'pot'
	ʔarwaše 'noise, disturbance'		damdame 'murmur, mumbling'
	maʔlase 'mockery'		
Hollow:	zōbaℰa 'storm'		šēṭane 'mischief'
	šōraba 'soup'		

ʔarmale 'widow' has a secondary radical ʔ, being related to the root r-m-l; tazkara 'ticket' has a secondary radical t, being related to the root z-k-r; waldane 'childishness', on the other hand, is a true triradical noun on the pattern FaℰLane, the n being a verb formative (twaldan 'to be childish'). [p. 110]

Pattern FaℰLaLe, and the pseudo-quadriradical patterns FaℰLane, FarℰaLe, FōℰaLe, and Faℰwale are used for gerunds of quadriradical and pseudo-quadriradical verbs [p. 295].

PATTERN $Fə\mathcal{E}LoL$

	mašmoš 'apricots'		bərġol 'wheat grits'
	bərnoṣ 'burnoose, bathrobe'		balbol 'oriental nightingale'
	ℰənṣor 'element'		ʔasʔof 'bishop'
	fəstoʔ 'pistachio'		xənfos 'beetles' (coll.)

---

[1] See p. 107.

PATTERN *Faε(ᵊ)LLe*

zalᵊᵛṭa	'wasp'	*xanᵊfse*	'beetle'
maščᵊmše	'apricot'	*žamᵊžme*	'crane'
mastke	'chewing gum'	*zalᵊhfe*	'tortoise'
sansle	'chain, series'	*ᵊamble*	'bomb'

On the use of the helping vowel ᵊ, see p. 31.

PATTERN *Faεlāl*

saεdān	'monkey'	*waṭwāṭ*	'bat' (also *waṭwaṭ*)
rafrāf	'fender'	*ᵊalmās*	'diamond(s)'

Hollow: *šēṭān*   'devil'

PATTERN *Faεlāl*

fanžān	'(coffee)cup'	*ᵊastāz*	'professor, teacher'
karbāž	'whip'	*barhān*	'proof'
bastān	'garden'	*εanwān*	'address'
ᵊabᵊāb	'clog, wooden sandal'	*resmāl*	'capital'[1]

With final radical semivowel (*y*), the suffix *-e/-a* is added:

faršāye	'brush'	*bardāye*	'(window) shade'

PATTERN *Faεlīl*

ᵊaṣḍīr	'tin'	*barmīl*	'barrel'
žanzīr	'chain'	*darwīš*	'dervish'
εafrīt	'demon'	*maskīn*	'poor thing, wretch'

PATTERN *FəƐLīL*

təlmīz	'student'	*məskīn* (or *maskīn*)	'poor wretch'
kəbrīt	'matches'	*Ɛəfrīt* (or *Ɛafrīt*)	'demon'
təšrīn	'October/November'		

Defective:

kərsi	'chair'	*bərġi*	'screw'

PATTERN *FaƐlūL(e)*

Ɛaṣfūr	'(passerine)bird'	*Ɛanʔūd*	'bunch of grapes'
raƐbūn	'(bank)deposit'	*ṭarbūš*	'tarboosh, fez'
sandūʔ	'box, chest'	*ġandūr*	'dandy, fop'

Hollow: *ʔēlūl* 'September'

With the *-e/-a* suffix: *šaxtūra* 'boat', *šarmūṭa* 'prostitute'

PATTERN *FəƐLēLe*

Ɛərtēle	'spider' (tarantulas and similar kinds)
bərnēṭa	'hat'
Ɛənzēʔa	'swing'
wəšwēše	'a whisper'

Miscellaneous Quadriradical

ḍəfḍaƐa	'frog'
təržmān	'interpreter, dragoman'
žəmhūr	'public, people, crowd' (also *žamhūr*)
zmərrod	'emeralds'
ṭarabēza	'table'
banadōra	'tomatoes' (coll.)

Miscellaneous Quinquiradical

sfaržel	'quince'	*ʔarnabīṭ*	'cauliflour'
ʔrənfol	'carnations'	*bardʔān*	'oranges'
banafsaž	'voilets'	*bētənžān*	'eggplant' (also *badanžān*)
baʔdūnes	'parsley'	*ʔaṭramīz*	'large glass jar'
bərnāmež	'program'	*žaɛžabōn*	'cobweb'
šaṭranž	'chess'	*banṭalōn*	'trousers'

Biradical Nouns

Very few nouns in Syrian Arabic qualify definitely as having a biliteral root; note, however: *fiʔa* 'class, group, bracket', *riʔa* 'lung', *səne* 'year', *mara* 'woman'.

> All these nouns have an *-e/-a* suffix. The noun *mara*, if compared to the classicism *marʔa*, might be analyzed as a defective triradical. Note the variant forms *riyye* (for *riʔa*) and *fīʔa* (for *fiʔa*), in which these words conform to triradical patterns. (Cf. *damm* 'blood', vis-à-vis Classical *dam*; *ʔīd* and *yadd* 'hand' vis-à-vis Classical *yad*.)

Inconformable Nouns

Unlike verbs and adjectives, Arabic nouns include many words which do not conform to any recognizable pattern, or whose root and pattern cannot be analyzed due to lack of paronyms. Most such nouns are modern foreign loan-words. For example:

kīlo	'kilogram'	*ʔotēl*	'hotel'
sbētro	'alcohol'	*vəranda*	'balcony, terrace'
prōva	'rehearsal'	*ṭrəmbe*	'pump'
žəġrāfiya	'geography'	*bēbē*	'baby'

CONSTRUCT FORMS

Certain kinds of nouns —mainly those ending in the *-e/-a* suffix [p. 138] —appear in a special form when standing IN CONSTRUCT with a following term. [See Annexion, p. 455 .]

The *-e/-a* suffix of a noun in construct takes the form *-et*, *-ét*, or *-t*, depending mainly on the form of the following term. Compare, for instance, the absolute form (i.e. non-construct form) of the noun ḥāle (as in ḥāle mnīḥa 'good condition') with the construct forms in ḥālet ᵊš-šərke 'the condition of the company', ḥālᵊtna 'our condition', ḥālto 'his condition'; similarly, absol. zyāra 'visit': constr. zyāret ᵓaxi 'my brother's visit', zyārᵊtkon 'your (pl.) visit', zyārtak 'your (m.) visit'.

The t in these construct forms is called CONNECTIVE t (tāᵓ marbūṭa).[1]

Connective t in Non-suffixing Forms

The connective t of a noun in construct with a separate word or phrase is in most cases preceded by the vowel e: ḥālet ᵓaxi 'my brother's condition'. The vowel is normally e even though the absolute form ends in a: absol. ḥāra 'neighborhood, quarter': constr. ḥāret ᵓahli 'my family's neighborhood'. Further examples:

Absolute Form		Construct Form (with Following Term)	
ḥafle	'party', 'show'........	ḥaflet mūsīqa	'concert'
ᵓəṣṣa	'story, account'.......	ᵓəṣṣet haz-zalame	'that fellow's story'
xzāne	'closet'..............	xzānet ᵓūḍti	'the closet of my room'
masᵓale	'matter, question'.....	masᵓalet šadd	'a matter of concern'
ᵓūḍa	'room'................	ᵓūḍet ᵊl-ᵓaɛde	'sitting room'

The suffix vowel e is often elided, however, when the following term begins with a vowel (which is usually the helping vowel ᵊ [p.30]): ᵓūḍt ᵊn-nōm 'the bedroom' (cf. ᵓūḍet nōm 'a bedroom'). The e is most apt to be dropped if the leading term is very commonly used in construct, or if the whole construct is a set phrase. Examples:

wazīft ᵊl-fīzya   'the physics assignment' (absol. wazīfe)

dōxt ᵊt-ṭayyāra   'airsickness' (absol. dōxa 'nausea')

ɛuqūbt ᵊl-ᵓəɛdām   'the death penalty' (absol. ɛuqūbe)

ḥāšt ᵊš-šəġᵊl   'the work requirements' (absol. ḥāše)

makīnt ᵊḥlāᵓa   'shaver' or 'clippers' (absol. makīne)

has-sallt ᵊl-ward 'this basket of flowers' (absol. salle) [SAL–193]

šarītt ᵊl-yōm   'today's paper' (absol. šarīde) [p. 26]

---

[1]The dropping of connective t from almost all absolute forms in Colloquial Arabic is, of course, a much broader and more consistent practice than the dropping of tāᵓ marbūṭa in the pronunciation of Classical "pause forms".

Note that the elision of *e* changes the accentuation in
nouns of certain patterns: *madrást ᵊl-walad* 'the boy's
school' (absol. *mádrase*). In the case of Pattern *FāᴱLe*
[145], a suffix-supporting vowel *ó* appears before the last
radical: *nāᵓólt ᵊz-zēt* 'the oil tanker' (absol. *nāᵓle*).
See Accentuation [p. 17]. Cf. Suffixing Forms [165].

The elision of *e* in nouns ending in *-iyye* results in
construct forms ending in *-īt: barrānīt ᵊl-bināye* 'the outside of the building' (absol. *barrāniyye*), *Ɛədwīt ᵊn-nādi*
'the membership of the club' (absol. *Ɛədwiyye*).

Sometimes *e* is elided even when the following term begins
with a consonant: *baᵓīt dēni* 'the remainder of my debt'
(absol. *baᵓiyye*), *mᵓaddámt l-ᵊktāb* 'the introduction of the
book' (absol. *mᵓáddame*), *b-wāṣóṭṭ ᵓaxi* 'through my brother
('s mediation)' (absol. *wāṣṭa*).

e is never elided in the non-suffixing construct forms
of sound words on Patterns *FaᴱLe* [140] or *FəᴱLe* [142]:
haflet ᵊl-mūsīqa 'the concert' (not *hafᵊlt...*); *šerket*
ᵊz-zēt 'the oil company' (not *šərᵊkt...*). Cf. Suffixing
Forms [166].

Nouns ending in *á* (which are mostly defective gerunds of Pattern
mFāᴱaLe [p. 293]) generally have construct forms in *āt: mlāᵓāt ᵊṭ-ṭarīᵓ*
'finding the way' (absol. *mlāᵓā*), *msāwāt ᵊl-fəxxār* 'the making of pottery'
(absol. *msāwā*).

The *-t* is sometimes kept in the absolute form of
mubārā(t) 'match, competition', and almost always in the
absolute forms of *hayāt* 'life' (Root *h-y-y*), *ṣalāt* (or
ṣala) 'prayer' (Root *ṣ-l-y*), *wafāt* 'death, demise' (Root
w-f-y).[1]

It should be noted that a number of plural patterns [p. 218] incorpo-
rate the *-e/-a* suffix and therefore have construct forms with *t* just as
singular nouns have. Pattern *FᴱūLe: šsūret ᵊl-madīne* 'the bridges of the
city' (abs. *šsūra*); Patterns *ᵓəFᵊᴱLe, ᵓaFᴱiLe: ᵓədᵊwyet ᵊl-bēt* 'the lights
of the house' (abs. *ᵓədᵊwye*), *ᵓasᵓilet l-ᵊmᴱallem* 'the teacher's questions'
(abs. *ᵓasᵓile*); Pattern *FᴱāLe: byār(e)t ᵊl-balad* 'the wells of the town'
(abs. *byāra*); *ᵓasātzet ᵊl-madrase* 'the teachers of the school' (abs. *ᵓasātze*),
malāyket ᵊs-sama 'the angels of heaven' (abs. *malāyke*); *haramiyyet ᵊl-madīne*
'thieves of the city' (abs. *haramiyye*).

There are many defective words [p. 43] ending in *a* and
a few ending in *e*; these endings are not to be confused with

---

[1] The words *bənt* 'daughter' and *ᵓəxt* 'sister' also theoretically have connective *t* in the absolute forms (cf. the diminutives *bnayye, xayye*).

the -e/-a suffix, and their construct forms do not have connective t^1: *ġaṭa ṭ-ṭāwle* 'the table cloth', *maɛna hal-kəlme* 'the meaning of this word', *ġəre samak* 'fish glue'.

There is also a formative suffix -a (which never takes the form -e) to be found in some words; this suffix does not develop a connective t in construct forms: *šakwa ž-žīrān* 'the neighbors' complaint', *mūsī?a r-rādyo* 'radio music'.[2]

Connective t before Suffixes -i, -o, -ak, and -ek

A short vowel e or o before a final consonant is dropped when any suffix beginning with a vowel is added (except -a 'her' and -on 'them, their' [p. 28]).[3] Thus with the pronoun suffixes -i 'me, my', -ak 'you, your(m.)', -ek 'you, your(f.)', -o 'him, his, it, its': *ṣāheb* 'friend' + -i → *ṣāḥbi* 'my friend', *mɛallem* 'teacher' + -o → *mɛallmo* 'his teacher', *taṣarrof* 'behavior' + -ak → *taṣarrfak* 'your(m.) behavior', etc.

In accordance with this rule, the -et of a construct form loses its vowel e when the following term is a pronoun suffix -i, -o, -ak, or -ek:

ṣūra : ṣūret 'picture(of)'	+ -i 'me'	→ *ṣūrti* 'my picture'
ɛāde(t) 'custom(of)'	+ -o 'him'	→ *ɛādto* 'his custom'
sayyāra : sayyāret 'automobile(of)'	+ -ak 'you(m.)	→ *sayyārtak* 'your car'
kənne(t) 'daughter-in-law(of)'	+ -ek 'you(f.)	→ *kənntek* 'your daughter-in-law'

Note the shift in accentuation caused by these suffixes with nouns that have short a between the last two radicals:

dáraže(t) 'degree(of)'	+ -i 'me'	→ *daróžti* 'my degree'
máḥrame(t) 'handkerchief(of)'	+ -ek 'you(f.)	→ *maḥrámtek* 'your handkerchief'
tázkara : tázkaret 'ticket(of)'	+ -o 'him'	→ *tazkárto* 'his ticket'
msáɛade(t) 'help(of)'	+ -ak 'you(m.)	→ *msáɛáttak* 'your help'

---

[1] Though there is a tendency on the part of native speakers themselves to reinterpret some of these words in terms of the -e/-a suffix, thus the construct form *maɛnet* 'meaning of...' is sometimes heard, as well as the suffixing form *maɛnāt-* [169].

[2] This formative generally corresponds to *ʔalif maqṣūra* in Classical Arabic.

[3] There are a few other exceptions. See pp. 29, 169.

When these suffixes are used with sound nouns of Patterns *FaɛLe* and *FəɛLe*, the helping vowel ᵊ [p. 31] is usually
inserted to break the potential three-consonant cluster resulting from loss of *e*: *FdɛᵊLt- FᵊɛᵊLt-*:

šaġle(t) 'job(of)'   + *-o* 'him'   → *šdġᵊlto* 'his job'

kəlme(t) 'word(of)'   + *-i* 'me'   → *kᵃlᵊmti* 'my word'

farše(t) 'bed(of)'   + *-ak* 'you(m.)' → *fdrᵊštak* (or *farštak*) 'your bed'

dawra:
dawret   'circulation(of)' + *-ek* 'you(f.)' → *ddwᵊrtek* (or *dawrtek*) 'your
                                                   circulation'

nəᵖṭa:
nəᵖṭeṭ   'point(of)'   + *-o* 'it(m.)' → *nᵃᵖᵊṭṭo* 'its point'

        If the last radical is *y*, however, it occurs in its
vocalic form *i* before connective *t* when these suffixes
are added:

ləhye(t) 'beard(of)'   + *-ak* 'you' → *lᵃḥitak* 'your beard'

ḥanye(t) 'bow, bending(of)' + *-o* 'him' → *ḥdnito* 'his bow'

        If the last radical is *w*, it may remain consonantal
with the helping vowel before it (*-ᵊw-*), but may also be
vocalized as *u*. (The distinction is subtle and non-
significant):

kəlwe(t) 'kidney(of)'   + *-i* 'me' → *kᵃlᵊwti* (or *kᵃluti*) 'my kidney'

xaṭwe(t) 'pace, step(of)'   + *-o* 'his' → *xdṭᵊwto* (or *xdṭuṭo*) 'his step'

        Nouns ending in *-iyye* or *-uwwe* have *-īt-* and *-ūt-*,
respectively, before these suffixes:

ᵖuwwe(t)   'strength(of)' + *-o* 'him' → *ᵖūto*   'his strength'

niyye(t)   'intention(of)' + *-ak* 'you' → *nītak*   'your intention'

ᵖaḍiyye(t)   'case(of)'   + *-ek* 'you' → *ᵖaḍītek*   'your case'

ɛamaliyye(t) 'operation(of)' + *-i* 'me' → *ɛamalīti* 'my operation'

        Nouns that have a double dental stop (*tt, dd, ṭṭ, ḍḍ*)
before the *-e/-a* suffix have *ə* before the connective *t*:

mxadde(t) 'pillow(of)'   + *-o* 'him' → *mxdddəto* 'his pillow'

ᵖaṭṭa : ᵖaṭṭet 'cat(of)'   + *-i* 'me' → *ᵖdṭṭəti* 'my cat'

fəḍḍa : fəḍḍeṭ 'silver(of)' + *-ak* 'you' → *fᵃḍḍəṭak* 'your silver'

Some nouns involve a sequence of three consonants (with or without ᵊ between the first two) before the ending *-e(t)*, as in *sənsle(t)* 'chain (of)'; or a sequence of a long and a short consonant, as in *mͼallme(t)* 'teacher (f.) (of)'; or a sequence of a long vowel plus two cosonants, as in *ṭāwle(t)* 'table(of)'. When the *e* in these nouns is dropped, then the last radical consonant stands immediately before the connective *t*, and is separated from the preceding consonant by the insertion of ə (which is accented, according to the general rule [p. 18]): *sənsə́lto* 'his chain', *mͼallə́mti* 'my teacher(f.)', *ṭāwə́ltak* 'your table'. Further examples:

ṣāḥbe(t) 'friend(f.)(of)'	+ *-ek* → *ṣāḥə́btek*	'your(f.)friend(f.)'
žāmͼa : žāmͼet 'university(of)'	+ *-ak* → *žāmə́ͼtak*	'your(m.)university'
fāyde(t) 'utility(of)'	+ *-o* → *fāyə́dto*	'its(m.)utility'
mtaržme(t) 'translator(f.)(of)'	+ *-o* → *mtaržə́mto*	'its(m.)translator(f.)'
məškle(t) 'problem(of)'	+ *-i* → *məškə́lti*	'my problem'
maͼᵊrfe(t) 'knowledge(of)'	+ *-ak* → *maͼrə́ftak*	'knowing you'
zmərrde(t) 'emerald(of)'	+ *-ek* → *zmərrə́dtek*	'your(f.)emerald'
ᵊaḥᵊṣne(t) 'horses(of)'	+ *-i* → *ᵊaḥṣə́nti*	'my horses'

If, however, the last consonant before *-e(t)* is *y*, then the suffixing form ends in *-ī́t-* (since *ə́* + *y* automatically → *-ī́-*):

ḥāšye(t)	'margin(of)'	+ *-o* → *ḥāšī́to*	'its margin'
zāwye(t)	'corner(of)'	+ *-ak* → *zāwī́tak*	'your corner'
nāḥye(t)	'environs(of)'	+ *-o* → *nāḥī́to*	'its environs'
ᵊaḏᵊwye(t)	'lights(of)'	+ *-o* → *ᵊaḏwī́to*	'its lights'

Note that while in their non-suffixing forms *mašye(t)* 'walk, walking' and *māšye(t)* 'livestock' differ only in the length of their first vowel, the suffixing forms differ also in the length of their second vowel and in accentuation: *mášito* 'his walk': *māšī́to* 'his livestock'.

Connective *t* before Suffixes *-na, -kon, -(h)a, -(h)on*

A short vowel *e* or *o* before a final consonant is changed to ə when accented [p. 28]. Thus with the pronoun suffixes *-na* 'us, our', *-kon* 'you, your(pl.)', *-(h)a* 'her, it, its', *-(h)on* 'them, their' [539]: *ṣāḥeb* 'friend' + *-na* → *ṣāḥə́bna* 'our friend', *ṭaṣarrof* 'behavior' + *-(h)a* → *ṭaṣarrə́f(h)a* 'her behavior', *mͼallem* 'teacher' + *-kon* → *mͼallə́mkon* 'your (pl.) teacher'.

In accordance with this rule, the -*et* of a construct form usually becomes -*ə́t*- when the following term is a pronoun suffix -*na*, -*kon*, -*(h)a*,
or -*(h)on*:

ṣūra : ṣūret 'picture(of)'   + -na → ṣūrə́tna   'our picture'

ɛ̄́ade(t) 'custom(of)'   + -on → ɛ̄́adə́ton   'their custom'

sayyāra : sayyāret 'car(of)'   + -kon → sayyārə́tkon 'your(pl.)car'

daraže(t) 'degree(of)'   + -a   → daražə́ta   'her degree'

msā́ɛade(t) 'help(of)'   + -na → msā́ɛadə́tna 'our help'

rəhle(t) 'trip(of)'   + -hon → rəhlə́thon   'their trip'

ġalṭa : ġalṭeṭ 'mistake(of)'   + -ha → ġalṭə́tha   'her mistake'

ʔəṣṣa : ʔəṣṣeṭ 'story(of)'   + -on → ʔəṣṣə́ṭon   'their story'

hanye(t) 'bow, bending(of)'   + -a   → hanyə́ta   'her bow'

ʔuwwe(t) 'strength(of)'   + -a   → ʔuwwə́ta   'her strength'

niyye(t) 'intention(of)'   + -on → niyyə́ton   'their intention'

ʔūḍa : ʔūḍeṭ 'room(of)'   + -kon → ʔūḍə́ṭkon   'your(pl.)room'

mḥaṭṭa : mḥaṭṭeṭ 'station(of)' + -na → mḥaṭṭə́ṭna   'our station'

In many cases, however, the construct form used with these suffixes is
the same as that used with -*i*, -*o*, -*ak* and -*ek*: *ɛarabītha* 'her car' (rather
than *ɛarabiyyə́tha*), *ṣānə́ɛtna* 'our maid' (rather than *ṣānɛə́tna*). These forms
are predominant among many nouns ending in -*iyye*, or of Pattern *Fā́ɛLe*, or
others of the type described on p. 167 above. (Compare the similar elision
of *e* in non-suffixing construct forms described on p. 163.) Further examples:

ʔaḍiyye(t) 'case(of)'   + -(h)on → ʔaḍīt(h)on 'their case'

ġənniyye(t) 'song(of)'   + -(h)a → ġənnīt(h)a 'her song'

bāxra : bāxret 'ship(of)'   + -na   → bāxərtna   'our ship'

ṭāyfe(t) 'sect; congregation(of)' + -kon → ṭāyəftkon 'your(pl.) congre-
                                                      gation'

ḍāhye(t) 'suburb(of)'   + -na   → ḍāhītna   'our suburb'

ʔəḍ²wye(t) 'lights(of)'   + -(h)a → ʔəḍwīt(h)a 'its lights'

Miscellaneous Irregularities with Connective *t*

The construct forms of *mara* 'woman, wife' and *səne*
'year' are always *mart* and *sənt*, respectively: *mart ʔaxi*
'my brother's wife', *sənt səttīn* 'the year (19)60'.

The classicism *θiqa* (or *siqa*) 'trust, faith' generally keeps the *a* in all construct forms: *θiqato* 'his faith', *θiqat ṣāḥbo* 'his friend's faith'. Similarly, *riʔa* 'lung' and *luġa* 'language' generally keep the *a* in suffixing forms: *riʔato* 'his lung', *luġati* 'my language'; but in non-suffixing forms *a* is usually changed to *e* in the regular way: *riʔet ᵊṣ-ṣabi* 'the boy's lung', *luġet ᵊš-šaɛb* 'the people's language'. The word *žiha* 'direction' has suffixing forms with long *ī*: *žīhto, žīhᵊta* 'its direction'.

A few nouns have connective *t* in construct forms but no *-e/-a* suffix in the absolute forms. *ɛarūs* 'bride' and *səkkīn* 'knife', for instance: *səkkīnet ʔəbni* 'my son's knife', *ɛarūset ʔəbni* 'my son's bride', *səkkīnto* 'his knife', *ɛarūsto* 'his bride'. *dəkkān* 'shop' and *madām* 'wife' must have *t* in the suffixing form: *dəkkānto* 'his shop', *madāmto* 'his wife', but it is optional in the non-suffixing form: *madām(et) ṣāḥbo* 'his friend's wife', *dəkkān(et) ʔaḥmad* 'Ahmed's shop'. With *faraṣ* 'mare', connective *t* is optional in the suffixing form also: *faraṣo* or *farᵊṣto* 'his mare'. (Note the loss of the last stem vowel *a* in the latter form.)

ḥamāye 'mother-in-law' has construct form *ḥamāt,* though the latter is sometimes also used as an absolute form (cf. *ḥayāt* 'life', *ṣalāṭ* 'prayer').

The plurals *rəfaʔa* 'companions' and *šəraka* 'partners' have suffixing forms ending in *-āt-*: *rəfaʔāti* 'my companions', *šərakātna* 'our partners', though the non-suffixing construct form is like the absolute: *rəfaʔa l-madrase* 'school companions', *šəraka ɛammi* 'my uncle's partners'. The word *maɛna* 'meaning' also has an optional suffixing form in *-āt-*: *maɛnāto* 'its meaning' (for *maɛnā*). *daɛwa* 'claim' (legal) has an optional suffixing form with *t*: *daɛᵊwto* 'his claim', *daɛwᵊta* 'her claim' (for *daɛwā* 'his claim', *daɛwāha* 'her claim').

Other Irregular Construct Forms

The nouns *ʔabb* 'father' and *ʔaxx* 'brother' have non-suffixing construct forms *ʔabu* and *ʔaxu* (though sometimes the forms *ʔabb* and *ʔaxx* are also used in construct): *ʔabu ṣ-ṣabi* 'the boy's father (or *ʔabb ᵊṣ-ṣabi*), *ʔaxu ɛali* 'Ali's brother' (or *ʔaxx ɛali*). The suffixing forms are *ʔabū-* and *ʔaxū-*: *ʔabūk* 'your(m.)father', *ʔaxūkon* 'your(pl.)brother', *ʔabūna* 'our father', *ʔaxū* 'his brother'. With the first-person singular *-i*, however, many speakers (e.g. in Damascus) use only the suffixing forms *ʔab-* and *ʔax-*: *ʔabi* 'my father', *ʔaxi* 'my brother'. Some speakers, on the other hand, also say *ʔabūyi* 'my father' and *ʔaxūyi* 'my brother'.[1]

---

[1] There are certain differences in the uses of the different construct forms; (*ya)ʔaxi*, for instance, is commonly used in addressing someone as 'my friend', while *ʔaxūyi* always means literally 'my brother'. (Note also the difference between *ʔaxx ɛali* 'Ali's brother' and *l-ʔaxx ɛali* "Brother Ali"; the latter is an appositive phrase, not a construct phrase [p. 506].) The form *ʔabu* is also used to mean 'owner of' or 'one who has': *ʔabu d-daʔᵊn* 'the one with the beard'; (also in names: *ʔabu nawwās* 'Abu Nawwas') while *ʔabb* as a construct form always means literally 'father of'.

The (pseudo-dual) plurals [p. 367] *ɛ̄nēn* 'eyes', *ʔīdēn* 'hands, arms', *ʔəžrēn* (or *rəžlēn*) 'feet, legs', and *ʔadanēn* 'ears' have suffixing forms without *n*: *ɛ̄nāhi* 'your(f.)eyes', *ʔīdōk* 'your(m.)hands'. *ʔadanē* 'his ears', *ʔəžrēna* 'our legs'. With the first-person singular *-i*, *ē* is changed to *-ayy-*: *ʔəžrayyi* 'my feet', *ʔīdayyi* 'my hands'.

Some speakers also have suffixing forms with *n*: *ʔīdēno* 'his hands', *ʔəžrēnak* 'your feet'.

NUMERAL CONSTRUCT FORMS

The cardinal numerals between three and nineteen have special kinds of construct forms. (On numeral constructs, see p.471.)

Absolute	Construct
tlāte 'three'	*tlətt* (Pal. and Leb.: *tlatt*)
ʔarbɛa 'four'	*ʔarbaɛ*
xamse 'five'	*xams*
sətte 'six'	*sətt*
sabɛa 'seven'	*sab(ə)ɛ*
tmānye or *tmāne* 'eight' (Pal. *tamānye*)	*tmənn* (Leb. *tmann*, Pal. *tam(ə)n*)
təsɛa 'nine'	*təs(ə)ɛ*
ɛašara 'ten'	*ɛaš(ə)r*
ʔidaɛ(ə)š or *hdaɛ(ə)š* 'eleven'	*ʔidaɛšar, hdaɛšar*
tnaɛ(ə)š 'twelve'	*tnaɛšar*
tləttaɛ(ə)š 'thirteen'	*tləttaɛšar*
ʔarba(ɛ)taɛ(ə)š 'fourteen'	*ʔarba(ɛ)taɛšar*
xamstaɛ(ə)š 'fifteen'	*xamstaɛšar*
səttaɛ(ə)š 'sixteen'	*səttaɛšar*
saba(ɛ)taɛ(ə)š 'seventeen'	*saba(ɛ)taɛšar*
tməntaɛ(ə)š 'eighteen'	*tməntaɛšar*
təsa(ɛ)taɛ(ə)š 'nineteen'	*təsa(ɛ)taɛšar*

Though the numerals from three through ten have the −*e*/−*a* suffix in their absolute forms, they drop the −*e* or −*a* in (non-suffixing) construct forms, instead of taking on a connective *t*[1].

The connective *t* is used, however, when a numeral (3-10) stands in construct with any one of a handful of noun plurals that begin with a vowel[2] after these numerals (but with ʔ otherwise): *ʔiyyām* 'days': *xamsᴜiyyām* 'five days'; *ʔəšhor* 'months': *ʔárbaɛtᴜə́šhor* 'four months'; *ʔālāf* 'thousands': *sabʔɛtᴜālāf* 'seven thousand'; *ʔənfos* 'persons, souls': *tməntᴜə́nfos* 'eight persons'; *ʔərʔġfe* 'loaves': *ɛašʔrtᴜə́rʔġfe* 'ten loaves'. (*tlətt* and *sətt* do not add another *t* since three *t*'s would in any case be reduced to two: *səttᴜiyyām* 'six days'; *tləttᴜālāf* 'three thousand'.) The connective *t* is also sometimes used with fractions: *ʔárbaɛtᴜə́xmās* 'four fifths'. See pp. 222, 223.

Another special construct form is used for *tlāte* and *tmāne* before *miyye* 'hundred': *tlāt miyye* 'three hundred', *tmān miyye* 'eight hundred'.

The construct form of *miyye* 'hundred' is always *mīt*: *mīt səne* 'a hundred years'.

The numerals from three through ten have suffixing forms used with the plural pronouns −*na* 'us', −*kon* 'you', and −*hon* 'them'. The suffixing forms are generally regular with respect to the absolute forms (changing −*e* or −*a* to −*ə́t*−): *tlātə́tna* 'the three of us', *xamsə́tkon* 'the five of you', *ɛašrə́ton* 'the ten of them'. The numeral *tnēn* 'two', however, has suffixing forms *tnēnə́t*− or *tnēnāt*−: *tnēnātkon* (or *tnēnə́tkon*) 'the two of you'. *ʔarbɛa* 'four' has the suffixing form *ʔarbɛát*−: *ʔarbɛátna* 'the four of us'.

---

[1]The second *t* in *tlətt* 'three...' might be considered "connective *t*", but note the similar doubling of *n* in *tmənn* 'eight...'. In some transcriptions these numerals are written '*tlət*', '*tmən*', at least before a single consonant; but before ə + two consonants they are clearly pronounced long: *tləttᴜə́wlād* 'three children', *tmənnᴜəʔrū́š* 'eight piastres'. (Note, however, *tmənᴜsnīn* 'eight years', more often heard than *tmənnᴜə́snīn*.)

[2]From the point of view of word-phonology, the *t* is better analyzed as a part of the following term: *xamsᴜtiyyām*, *ʔarbaɛᴜtəšhor*, etc. This analysis seems to go against the grain of many speakers' intuition, however.

CHAPTER 6: VERB INFLECTIONAL FORMS

Syrian Arabic verbs are inflected for:

Tense: Perfect, Imperfect [319]

Person: First, Second, Third [363]

Number/Gender: Masculine, Feminine, Plural [366, 420]

Mode: Indicative, Subjunctive, Imperative [343]

There is no mode inflection in the perfect tense, no person inflection in the imperative mode, and no gender inflection in the plural or in the first person singular. There are, in all, twenty-seven inflected forms.

Sample Conjugation: Inflections of the verb *ʔakal* **'to eat'**

This verb is chosen to illustrate the affixes (set off by hyphens), all of which appear in their basic forms. The stem, however, is exceptional: the initial radical ʔ appears only in the perfect tense. See p. 55.

PERFECT	3rd p.	Masc.	ʔákal	'he ate'
		Fem.	ʔákl-et	'she ate'
		Pl.	ʔákal-u	'they ate'
	2nd p.	Masc.	ʔakál-t	'you(m.) ate'
		Fem.	ʔakál-t-i	'you(f.) ate'
		Pl.	ʔakál-t-u	'you(pl.) ate'
	1st p.	Sing.	ʔakál-t	'I ate'
		Pl.	ʔakál-na	'we ate'

IMPERFECT
SUBJUNCTIVE

3rd p.	Masc.	*y-ākol*	'(that) he eat'
	Fem.	*t-ākol*	'(that) she eat'
	Pl.	*y-ākl-u*	'(that) they eat'
2nd p.	Masc.	*t-ākol*	'(that) you (m.) eat'
	Fem.	*t-ākl-i*	'(that) you (f.) eat'
	Pl.	*t-ākl-u*	'(that) you (pl.) eat'
1st p.	Sing.	*ʔ-ākol*	'(that) I eat'
	Pl.	*n-ākol*	'(that) we eat'

IMPERFECT
INDICATIVE

3rd p.	Masc.	*b-y-ākol*	'he eats'
	Fem.	*b-t-ākol*	'she eats'
	Pl.	*b-y-ākl-u*	'they eat'
2nd p.	Masc.	*b-t-ākol*	'you (m.) eat'
	Fem.	*b-t-ākl-i*	'you (f.) eat'
	Pl.	*b-t-ākl-u*	'you (pl.) eat'
1st p.	Sing.	*b-ākol*	'I eat'
	Pl.	*m-n-ākol*	'we eat'

IMPERATIVE

Masc.	*kōl*	'eat (m.)'
Fem.	*kśl-i*	'eat (f.)'
Pl.	*kśl-u*	'eat (pl.)'

All types of verb conjugation are illustrated in Ch. 3.

Expression of the Inflectional Categories

TENSE:

The perfect tense has person <u>suffixes</u>, while the imperfect has person <u>prefixes</u>: *ʔakal-t* 'you (m.) ate': <u>*t-ākol*</u> '(that) you (m.) eat'. The form of the stem is also different in most cases (pf. *ʔakal-:* impf. *-ākol*). (See p. 185.)

PERSON:

The **first person** is expressed in the perfect by the suffixes *-t* (sing.) and *-na* (pl.): *ʔakalt* 'I ate', *ʔakalna* 'we ate'; and in the imperfect by the prefixes *ʔ-* (sing.) and *n-* (pl.): *ʔākol* '(that) I eat', *nākol* '(that) we eat'. (*ʔ-* disappears after the indicative prefix *b-:* *bākol* 'I eat'.)

The **second person** is expressed by the suffix *-t* in the perfect and the prefix *t-* in the imperfect: *ʔakalt* 'you ate', *tākol* '(that) you eat'.

The **third person** is expressed by the prefix *y-* in the masculine and plural imperfect: *yākol* '(that) he eat', *yāklu* '(that) they eat', and by *t-* in the feminine: *tākol* '(that) she eat'. In the perfect, there is no third person affix: *ʔakal* 'he ate'; (but the feminine ending *-et* is used only in the third person: *ʔaklet* 'she ate'). For some verbs, the third person perfect also contrasts with the first and second persons in the form of the stem: *nām-et* 'she slept': *nəm-ti* 'you (f.) slept'. See p. 193.

> Note that in the imperfect the third person feminine form is the same as the second person masculine; thus the form *tākol* can mean either '(that) she eats' or '(that) you (m.) eat'.

> In the perfect, on the other hand, the second-person masculine form is the same as the first-person singular: *ʔakalt* 'you(m.) ate' or 'I ate'.

NUMBER/GENDER:

Feminine (/singular) is expressed by a suffix *-i* in the second person: *tākli* '(that) you (f.) eat', *kəli* 'eat (f.)!'; in the perfect, *-i* comes <u>after</u> the person suffix *-t:* *ʔakalti* 'you (f.) ate'. In the third person, feminine is expressed (simultaneously with the person) by *t-* (imperfect) and *-et* (perfect): *tākol* '(that) she eat', *ʔaklet* 'she ate'.

> Feminine and masculine are not distinguished in the first person: *ʔakalt* 'I(m. or f.) ate', *ʔākol* '(that) I(m. or f.) eat'.

Plural is expressed in the second and third persons by the suffix -u:
tāklu '(that) you (pl.) eat', *yāklu* '(that) they eat', *ʔakalu* 'they ate';
in the second person of the perfect, -u comes <u>after</u> the suffix t: *ʔahaltu*
'you (pl.) ate'. In the first person, the plural is expressed (simultaneously with the person) by the prefix n- in the imperfect and the suffix -na
in the perfect: *nākol* '(that) we eat', *ʔakalna* 'we ate'.

Masculine (/singular) is expressed by the lack of any feminine or plural
affix.

MODE:

The **indicative** mode is expressed by the prefix b- which precedes the
person prefixes: *byākol* 'he eats', *btākol* 'you (m.) eat', *bākol* 'I eat'
[p. 179].

> In the first person plural it is generally pronounced
> m-: *mnākol* 'we eat'. [p. 180]. The b- disappears, after
> the particle of anticipation *raḥa-* [322] and often also after
> the particle of actuality *ɛam-* [320], though verbs with
> these proclitics are counted as indicative rather than sub-
> junctive.

The **subjunctive** is expressed by the <u>lack</u> of the prefix b-: *yākol*
'(that) he eat', *tākol* '(that) you (m.) eat', *ʔākol* '(that) I eat' [p. 343].

> Note that there is no mode inflection in the perfect
> tense; all verbs in the perfect may be counted as indic-
> ative.

The **imperative** is expressed by lack of both b- <u>and</u> the person-prefix;
also, in many cases, by modification of the imperfect stem: *kōl* 'eat'
(m.). [p. 198].

> Formally speaking, the imperative belongs to the im-
> perfect tense and lacks person, while functionally speak-
> ing, it belongs to the second person and lacks tense.

VARIATIONS IN AFFIX FORM

The Prefixes with Supporting Vowel. Each inflectional prefix in its basic form consists of a single consonant (*b-; y-, t-, ʔ-, n-*). Since most imperfect stems (unlike *-ākol*, above) themselves begin with one or two consonants, prefixation of these basic forms would sometimes result in a pile-up of three of four consonants at the beginning of a word — an unallowable state of affairs in Syrian Arabic. See Sound Combinations [25].

Such consonant congestion is avoided by inserting a "supporting vowel", [Cf. p. 32] usually *ə*, before the last two consonants in the sequence:

$$b- \ + \ t- \ + \ -ktob \ \rightarrow \ bt\acute{ə}ktob \quad \text{'you (m.) write'}$$

$$b- \ + \ t- \ + \ -\check{s}\bar{u}f \ \rightarrow \ bət\check{s}\acute{\hat{u}}f \quad \text{'you (m.) see'}$$

$$ʔ- \ + \ -ftaḥ \ \rightarrow \ ʔ\acute{ə}ftaḥ \quad \text{'(that) I open'}$$

See, however, Vocalic Variant of the Prefix *y-*, below.

Using this rule, the supporting vowel's place in the sequence must be determined for the stem <u>without suffixes</u>, because when certain suffixes are added to stems like *-ktob* [p. 28], the stem vowel disappears, creating a longer consonant sequence: *byə́ktbu* (or *byə́kᵊtbu*) 'they write'. In such cases, the prefix-supporting vowel is inserted before the last <u>three</u> consonants, while a "helping vowel" (*ᵊ*) may also be heard before the last two.

The prefix-supporting vowel in verbs of Patterns I [p. 55] and IV [82] is accented,[1] except in hollow [p. 56] and geminate [p. 63] verbs (e.g. *bət\check{s}\acute{\hat{u}}f* 'you see', *batḥə́bb* 'you like'), (or unless the accent is shifted back by a pronoun suffix [539]: *byəftdḥ-lak* 'he opens...for you'). See Accentuation [19].

The supporting vowel is *a* (rather than *ə*) with the verbs *Ɛaṭa* 'to give', *Ɛaref* 'to know', and commonly also *Ɛəmel* 'to do': *bydƐṭi* 'he gives'; *btdƐref* 'you know', *bdƐref* 'I know', *ʔdƐref* '(ťhat) I know'; *bydƐmel* (or *byə́Ɛmel*) 'he does', etc.[2]

Vocalic Variant of the Prefix *y-*. After a consonant, with stems that begin with a single consonant, the third-person prefix appears as *i-*: *b-i-\check{s}\bar{u}f* 'he sees', *b-i-rīd i-\check{s}\bar{u}f* 'he'd like to see'.

---

[1] Also Pattern VII and VIII verbs in parts of Lebanon and Palestine: *byə́\check{s}tǵel* (instead of *byə\check{s}tə́gel* 'he works'), *byə́nkser* 'instead of *byənkə́ser* 'It gets broken'). [p. 20]

[2] With the verbs *ʔakal* 'to eat' and *ʔaxad* 'to take', the imperfect tense forms *byākol, byāxod*, etc. may be analyzed as consisting of the prefixes *b-, y-* etc. with a supporting vowel *a*, added to the stems *-akol, -axod* (initial-weak alterations of a theoretical *-ʔxod*). Thus *bya- + akol →* *byākol* (since *ā = aa*).

All these forms would seem to be remnants of a tendency to use supporting vowel *a* generally before *Ɛ* and *ʔ*, which has since been swamped by the tendency to use *ə* as supporting vowel before <u>any</u> consonant: *btə́Ɛni* 'you mean' *btə́ʔmor* 'you order'. (The form *ydƐni* 'that is to say' is a Classicism. Cf. *byə́Ɛni* 'it means'.)

The theoretical combination -ǝy- does not normally occur
in Syrian Arabic *("bǝyrīd ǝyšūf")* but is replaced by the
simple vowel *i.*
In the north and the south of the Syrian area (viz.
Aleppo, Jerusalem), the third-person prefix always appears
as -*i*- (or -*ǝ*- [13]) after *b*-, even when the stem begins
with two consonants: *bíktob* (or *bǝ́ktob*) 'he writes'. This
form is not confused with the first person because the latter has the vowel *a* in these areas: *bǽktob* 'I write'. [179].

The Suffix -*t* with Helping Vowel. With stems ending in a consonant, the
'you/I' suffix of the perfect has an optional variant -*ǝt* that is commonly
used at the end of a phrase or before a word beginning with a simple consonant: *šǝfǝt rǝžžāl* (or *šǝft rǝžžāl*) 'I saw a man'; *wēn kǝnǝt?* (or *wēn
kǝnt?)* 'Where were you?'; *ʔiza kān mǝtǝt* (or *mǝtt*) 'If I died...'.

The helping vowel is not used before -*t* if a following
word (in the same phrase) begins with two consonants, because in that case the four-consonant sequence is broken by
a helping vowel between the words: *šǝft ǝktāb* 'I saw a
book'. The helping vowel is also generally not used with
this suffix before a suffixed pronoun: *šǝ́ftna* 'you (m.)
saw us', *šǝ́ftkon* 'I saw you (pl.)'. See p. 32.

Velarization of Affixes. The suffixes -*t* and -*et* have velarized forms -*ṭ*
and -*eṭ*, respectively, with stems ending in a velarized sound [p. 26]:

xalǝ́ṣ-ṭ (or *xalǝ́ṣ-ǝṭ*)	'you finished'
xǝ́lṣ-eṭ	'she finished'

The prefix *t*- has a velarized form *ṭ*-, used with stems that <u>begin</u> with
a velarized sound, or with a sound that is conducive to velarization from
a subsequent sound:

bǝ-ṭ-ṣír	'it becomes'
b-ṭǝ́-ḍrob	'she hits'
bǝ-ṭ-ẓǝ́nn	'you suppose'
bǝ-ṭ-xǝ́ṣṣ	'it concerns'

Before stems beginning with a single consonant *ḍ*, however, the prefix has
the form *ḍ*- rather than *ṭ*-. (See below, Voicing...).

bǝ-ḍ-ḍǝ́ll	'She stays'

The affixes *b*-, *n*-, *ʔ*-, and -*na* are likewise velarized
in the neighborhood of velarized consonants, but this velarization is not separately indicated in our transcription [p. 7].

Voicing and Spirantization of the Prefix *t-*. The voiced form *d-* is used with stems that begin with a single consonant *d, z,* or *ž,* and the form *ḍ-* before a single consonant *ḍ:*

bə-d-zíd	'it increases'
bə-d-žîb	'you bring'
bə-d-dśll	'it indicates'
bə-ḍ-ḍáll	'it remains'

The prefix *t-* is sometimes totally assimilated to a following sibilant *z, ẓ, ž, s, ṣ, š*):

bə-z-zīd	'it increases'	(= *bədzīd*)
bə-ž-žîb	'you bring'	(= *bədžîb*)
bə-š-šūf	'you see'	(= *bətšūf*)
bə-ṣ-ṣəbb	'you pour'	(= *bətṣəbb*)

Assimilation of the Prefix *n-*. The first-person plural prefix has optional variants: *m-* before a single consonant *m* or *b, l-* before a single consonant *l,* and *r-* before a single consonant *r* [p. 27]:

mə-m-būs (or *mə-n-būs*)	'we kiss'
mə-m-mūt (or *mə-n-mūt*)	'we die'
mə-l-lūm (or *mə-n-lūm*)	'we blame'
mə-r-rūḥ (or *mə-n-rūḥ*)	'we go'

The First Person Singular Prefix. The prefix *ʔ-* disappears after the indicative prefix *b-*, and also in the subjunctive before any stem that begins with a single consonant:

Indicative	Subjunctive
bə́-ktob 'I write'	*ʔə́-ktob* '(that) I write'
bə-tɛ́dllam 'I learn'	*ʔə-tɛ́dllam* '(that) I learn'
bə-stdɛ́mel 'I use'	*ʔə-stdɛ́mel* '(that) I use'
b-šūf 'I see'	*šūf* '(that) I see'
b-ddbber 'I prepare'	*ddbber* '(that) I prepare'
b-ḥaṭṭ 'I put'	*ḥaṭṭ* '(that) I put'

In the north and the south of the Syrian area (viz. Aleppo, Jerusalem), the first singular affix is not *ʔ-*, but rather *ʔa-* (*-a-* after *b-*): *bdktob* 'I write', *ʔdktob* '(that) I write'; *bašūf* 'I see', *ʔašūf* '(that) I see'.

In certain classicisms, *ʔa-* is used instead of *b-* in the
first singular indicative: *ʔəškurak* 'I thank you' (instead
of *bəškrak*), *ʔəẓónn* 'I think...' (instead of *bẓonn*).

The Indicative Prefix. The prefix *b-* has an alternate form *m-* which is
used with the first-person plural prefix: *m-nə́-ktob* 'we write', *mə-n-šū́f*
'we see', *mə-m-bī́ɛ* 'we sell'.

In the Palestinian area, however, the form *b-* is generally used before all the prefixes, including *n-*: *bnə́ktob*
'we write', *bənšū́f* 'we see'.

b- also has an optional variant *f-* used before *f*:
f-fū́t 'I enter' (= *bfū́t*), *f-fakker* 'I think' (= *bfakker*).

Suffixes Ending in a Vowel. The vowels of the suffixes *-na* 'we', *-i* (fem.),
and *-u* (pl.) are lengthened and accented [p. 27] when they occur with suffix
pronouns [p. 539]:

šə́f-na	'we saw'	+ *-hon* 'them'	→	*šəf-nā́-hon*	'we saw them'
ʔdxad-u	'they took'	+ *-ha* 'her'	→	*ʔaxad-ū́-ha*	'they took her'
zā́r-u	'they visited'	+ *-k* 'you(m.)'	→	*zār-ū́-k*	'they visited you'
t-šū́f-i	'(that) you(f.) see'	+ *-na* 'us'	→	*t-šū́f-í-na*	'(that) you(f.) see us'
ftə́ḥ-u	'open (pl.)'	+ *-lna* 'for us'	→	*ftaḥ-ū́-lna*	'open...for us'
xə́d-i	'take(f.)'	+ *-o* 'it(m.)'	→	*xəd-í*	'take it' (*-o* disappears after vowels [p. 540].)

The Suffix *-et*. The basic form *-et* of the third-person feminine suffix
occurs always, and only, when no suffix pronoun follows. With following
pronouns, the alternants *-ə́t-*, *-ət-*, and *-t-* occur (with *ṭ* replacing *t*
after velarized sounds [p. 26]).

The factors that determine which alternate form is to be
used are rather complicated. These complications are less-
ened considerably for Palestinian Arabic, in which the forms
-at (and *-ə́t-*) are generally used throughout.
The differences among the various local dialects in the
forms of this suffix are also complicated; the forms described here are those of Damascus.

The form *-ə́t-* occurs:

1.) Before any suffix beginning with a consonant:

šā́f-et 'she saw' + *-ni* 'me' → *šāf-ə́t-ni* 'she saw me'

+ *-kon* 'you (pl.)' → *šāf-ə́t-kon* 'she saw you'

+ *-ha* 'her' → *šāf-ə́t-ha* 'she saw her'

+ *-lo* 'for him' → *šāf-ə́t-lo* 'she saw...for him'

Also before the suffixes *-a* 'her' and *-on* 'them' which are optional variants of *-ha* and *-hon* respectively [p.541]: *šāf-ə́t-a* 'she saw her' (= *šāf-ə́t-ha*), *šāf-ə́t-on* 'she saw them' (= *šāf-ə́t-hon*).

The change of *e* to *ə* is automatic, since short *e* does not normally occur accented [p.22]. For those varieties of Arabic speech in which there is no contrast between *e, ə,* and *i* in these positions [p.13], the form of the suffix here does not change except for the accentuation.

2.) The form *-ə́t-* also occurs before the suffix pronouns *-o* 'him', *-ak* 'you (m.)', and *-ek* 'you (f.)' with certain kinds of verb stems, namely: all sound augmented and quadriradical stems except those of Patterns VII, VIII, and IX. (See pp.182-183 below.) For example:

(II) *ɛ́allam-et* 'she taught' + *-ak* 'you (m.)' → *ɛallam-ə́t-ak* 'she taught you'

(III) *kā́tab-et* 'she wrote (to)' + *-ek* 'you (f.)' → *kātab-ə́t-ek* 'she wrote you'

(IV) *ʔákram-et* 'she favored' + *-ek* 'you (f.)' → *ʔakram-ə́t-ek* 'she favored you'

(V) *tɛ́allam-et* 'she learned' + *-o* 'it (m.)' → *tɛallam-ə́t-o* 'she learned it'

(VI) *tnā́wal-et* 'she obtained' + *-o* 'it (m.)' → *tnāwal-ə́t-o* 'she obtained it'

(X) *stɛ́mal-et* 'she used' + *-o* 'it (m.)' → *staɛmal-ə́t-o* 'she used it'

(Quad.) *táržam-et* 'she translated' + *-o* 'it (m.)' → *taržam-ə́t-o* 'she translated it'

Optionally, the accented form *-ə́t-* may also be used with geminate [p.42] and defective [43] augmented verbs whose last consonant is a dental stop (*d, ḍ, t, ṭ*): *staradd-ə́t-o* 'she got it back' (or *staráddd-ət-o*); *tḥadd-ə́t-o* 'she challenged him' (or *tḥáddd-ət-o*) (*tḥadda* 'to challenge, provoke'). See p.182, below.

The unaccented form -ət- is used before suffix pronouns -o, -ak, and -ek
with certain kinds of verb stems, namely:

1.) With simple defective a-stems [pp.60,67]:

ḥaka 'to tell':   ḥák-et 'she told' + -o   → ḥák-ət-o 'she told it'

ʔara 'to read':   ʔár-et 'she read' + -o   → ʔár-ət-o 'she read it'

kafa 'to suffice: káf-et 'it(f.)   + ak   → káf-ət-ak 'it sufficed
                              sufficed'   you(m.)'

ʔəǯa 'to come (to):   ʔəǯ-et 'she came' + -ek   → ʔə́ǯ-ət-ek 'she came to
                                                                   you(f.)'

      See p.

2.) With defective Pattern VIII stems [p.96]:

štara 'to buy':   štár-et 'she bought' + -o → štár-ət-o 'she bought it'

3.) with geminate stems [p.63] ending in dental stops (-dd, -ḍḍ, -tt,
-ṭṭ):

madd 'to stretch':   mádd-et 'she stretched' + -o → mádd-ət-o 'she stretched
                                                                it'

ɛaḍḍ 'to bite':   ɛáḍḍ-eṭ 'she bit' + -o → ɛáḍḍ-ət-o 'she bit it'

fatt 'to crumble: fáttet 'she crumbled' + -o → fáttəto 'she crumbled it'

haṭṭ 'to put':   háṭṭeṭ 'she put' + -o → háṭṭəto 'she put it'

staradd 'to get back': starádd-et 'she got...back' + -o → starádd-ət-o
                                                            'she got it
                                                            back'

      Augmented verbs, however, may also use the accented
   form -ə́t-: staradd-ə́t-o 'she got it back'.

   Optionally, defective augmented verbs with a dental stop as middle
radical may use the unaccented form: tḥadda 'to challenge, provoke':
tḥádd-et 'she provoked' + -o 'him' → tḥádd-ət-o).

      Except for those whose last stem consonant is a dental
   stop, geminate verbs and augmented defective verbs use the
   vowelless form -t- before these suffixes (see below). It
   would seem that the vowel is preserved before dd, etc., to
   avoid sequences like -ddt-, (usually reduced to -dt- or
   even -tt- [p. 26]), which might obscure the composition of
   the verb form.

The vowelless form *-t-* is used before *-o*, *-ak*, and *-ek* with all kinds of verb stems except those specified above in connection with the vowelled forms. Namely, *-t-* is used:

1.) With all simple triradical stems that are sound, geminate (other than dental stops), or hollow:

fatah 'to open': *fátḥ-et* 'she opened' + *-o* → *fát(ᵊ)ḥ-t-o* 'she opened it'

šəreb 'to drink': *šə́rb-et* 'she drank' + *-o* → *šə́r(ᵊ)b-t-o* 'she drank it'

xalaṣ 'to finish': *xál̦ṣ-et* 'she finished it' + *-o* → *xál(ᵊ)ṣ-ṭ-o* 'she finished it'

hazz 'to shake': *házz-et* 'she shook' + *-o* → *házz-t-o* 'she shook it'

šāf 'to see': *šā́f-et* 'she saw' + *-o* → *šā́f-t-o* 'she saw it'

2.) With sound Pattern VIII stems:

htamal 'to tolerate': *htáml-et* 'she tolerated' + *-o* → *htámᵊl-t-o* 'she tolerated it'

xtaraɛ 'to invent': *xtárɛ-et* 'she invented' + *-o* → *xtárᵊɛ-t-o* 'she invented
it'

> If there were any transitive verbs of Patterns VII and IX, they would presumably be like Pattern VIII, but only transitive verbs, of course, take pronoun suffixes.

3.) With simple defective *i*-stems [pp. 70, 72]: *nəsi* 'to forget':
nə́sy-et 'she forgot' + *-o* → *nəsi-t-o* 'she forgot it'.

> Defective *a*-stems [p. 60] sometimes have a variant stem with *-y-* before the third person suffixes, hence also *haky-et* 'she told' + *-o* → *hák̦i-t-o* 'she told it'. Some verbs only have this variant before *-t-* with a pronoun suf-fix: *ˀdri-t-o* (= *ˀdr-ət-o*) 'she read it' (but not *"ˀary-et"*, only *ˀar-et* 'she read').

4.) with all augmented verb stems that are geminate, hollow, or defec-tive — except Pattern VIII defectives, and geminates and defectives with stem-final dental stops [p. 182]:

xalla	'to allow':	*xál̦l-et*	+ *-ak* → *xál̦l-t-ak*	'she allowed you'
ḥāka	'to talk to':	*ḥā́k-et*	+ *-o* → *ḥā́k-t-o*	'she talked to him'
stanna	'to wait for':	*stánn-et*	+ *-ek* → *stánn-t-ek*	'she waited for you(f.)'
farša	'to brush':	*fárš-et*	+ *-o* → *fárš-t-o*	'she brushed it'

ḥtall	'to take over':	ḥtáll-et	+ -o → ḥtáll-t-o	'she took it over'
ḥtāž	'to need':	ḥtā́ž-et	+ -o → ḥtā́ž-t-o	'she needed it'
staḥaʔʔ	'to deserve':	staḥáʔʔ-et	+ -o → staḥáʔʔ-t-o	'she deserved it'
stašār	'to consult':	stašā́r-et	+ -ak → stašā́r-t-ak	'she consulted you'

The vowelless alternant -t- is a regular consequence of the general rule [p. 28] that a post-tonic e (or o) before a final consonant is dropped when any suffix beginning with a vowel (except -a, -on) is added. For example byə́ḥmel 'he carries' + -o → byə́ḥ(ə)mlo 'he carries it', ḥaflet 'party' (construct form) + -o → ḥáf(ə)lto 'his party'; by the same token ṣarfet 'she spent' + -o → ṣár(ə)fto 'she spent it'.

This vowelless form of the -et suffix, however, is used only with verbs that have a different stem form with the -t 'you/I' suffix; thus the two suffixes are not confused: šā́f-t-o 'she saw him' vs. šə́f-t-o 'you (or I) saw him'; ḥázz-t-o 'she shook him' vs. hazzé-t-o 'you (or I) shook him', xál(ə)ṣ-ṭ-o 'she finished it' vs. xaláṣ-ṭ-o 'you (or I) finished it'.

With verbs which have the same stem form (not counting the accent) before -et 'she' and -t 'you/I', the inflections are kept apart by using -ə́t- instead of -t- for 'she': taržam-ə́t-o 'she translated it' vs. taržám-t-o 'you (or I) translated it', ɛallam-ə́t-ek 'she taught you (f.)' vs. ɛallám-t-ek 'I taught you (f.)'.

INFLECTIONAL VARIATION IN STEMS

Most verbs undergo changes in the form of their stems depending on their inflection.

The most complex stem variation is that of tense. The section on tense variation is limited to a comparison of the 'he'-inflections (3rd p. masc./ sing.) of the perfect and imperfect.

The stem forms determined by person, number/gender, and mode variation are all deducible from one or the other of these 'he'-inflections.

Tense Variation in Simple Triradical Verb Stems

Sound Verbs. The base ('he') inflection of the perfect has two short vowels, *a-a* or *ə-e*, between the three radicals: *dáras* 'he studied', *ħámal* 'he carried', *ṣárax* 'he shouted'; *sámeƐ* 'he heard', *názel* 'he descended'.

In the imperfect there is only one stem vowel *o, e,* or *a,* which comes between the last two radicals: *byə́-dros* 'he studies', *byə́-ħmel* 'he carries', *byə́-ṣrax* 'he shouts', *byə́-smaƐ* 'he hears', *byə́-nzel* 'he descends'.

Verbs with *ə-e* in the perfect stem almost all have *a* in the imperfect [p. 71]:

> *kə́seb* 'he earned':   *byə́-ksab* 'he earns'
>
> *rə́keb* 'he mounted':   *byə́-rkab* 'he mounts'
>
> *fə́hem* 'he understood: *byə́-fham* 'he understands'

Several, however, have *ə-e* in the perfect and *e* in the imperfect [p.69]:

> *nə́zel* 'he descended': *byə́-nzel* 'he descends'
>
> *mə́sek* 'he took hold': *byə́-msek* 'he takes hold'

> (See p. 69 for others)

None with *ə-e* in the perfect has *o* in the imperfect.

Of verbs with *a-a* in the perfect, many have *o* in the imperfect [p. 55]:

> *dáras* 'he studied':   *byə́-dros* 'he studies'
>
> *ʔdƐad* 'he sat down':   *byə́-ʔƐod* 'he sits down'
>
> *bálaġ* 'he attained':   *byə́-bloġ* 'he attains'

Many have *e* in the imperfect [p. 57]:

ḥdmal	'he carried':	byə́-ḥmel	'he carries'
ġdsal	'he washed':	byə́-ġsel	'he washes'
ʔdsam	'he divided':	byə́ʔsem	'he divides'

Quite a few may have either *o* or *e* [p. 63]:

ʔátal	'he killed':	byə́-ʔtol or byə́-ʔtel	'he kills'
tárak	'he left':	byə́-trok or byə́-trek	'he leaves'
ldfat	'he turned':	byə́-lfot or byə́-lfet	'he turns'

Quite a few have *a* in the imperfect [p. 65]:

ṭdbaɛ	'he printed':	byə́-ṭbaɛ	'he prints'
sámaḥ	'he allowed':	byə́-smaḥ	'he allows'
bdɛat	'he sent':	byə́-bɛat	'he sends'

> Those with *a–a* in the perfect and *a* also in the imperfect almost all have a back consonant (*x, ġ, q, ḥ, ɛ, h,* or *ʔ*) as second or third radical. An exception: ḥáfaẓ 'he kept': byə́-ḥfaẓ 'he keeps'.

Defective Verbs. The vowelling of the perfect stem is *a–a* or *ə–e:* kə́fa 'it sufficed', ʔára 'he read'; bə́ʔi 'he stayed', mə́ši 'he walked'. The imperfect has *a* or *i*: byə́-kfi 'it suffices', byə́-ʔra 'he reads', byə́-bʔa 'he stays', byə́-mši 'he walks'.

Almost all which have *a–a* in the perfect have *i* in the imperfect [p. 60]:

bána	'he built':	byə́-bni	'he builds'
ṭáfa	'he extinguished':	byə́-ṭfi	'he extinguishes'
káwa	'he ironed':	byə́-kwi	'he irons'

A few, however, have *a–a* in the perfect and *a* also in the imperfect [p. 67]:

báda	'he began':	byə́-bda	'he begins'
ʔára	'he read':	byə́-ʔra	'he reads'

For others, see p. 67.

Almost all with *ə-i* in the perfect have *a* in the imperfect [p.72]:

nə́si	'he forgot':	*byə́-nsa*	'he forgets'
rə́ḍi	'he was satisfied':	*byə́-rḍa*	'he is satisfied'
bə́ʔi	'he remained':	*byə́-bʔa*	'he remains'

Only two have *ə-i* in the perfect and *i* also in the imperfect [p.70]:

bə́ki	'he cried':	*byə́-bki*	'he cries'
mə́ši	'he walked':	*byə́-mši*	'he walks'

Initial-Weak Verbs. Simple triliteral verbs whose first radical is *w* or *y* have imperfect stems beginning with *ū* or *ī,* respectively: *wáṣaf* 'he described': *by-úṣef* 'he describes', *wdfa* 'he fulfilled': *by-úfi* 'he fulfills'; *yə́ʔes* 'he despaired': *by-íʔas* 'he despairs'.

Two verbs with initial radical *ʔ* have imperfect stems beginning with *ā:* *ʔákal* 'he ate': *by-ákol* 'he eats'; *ʔáxad* 'he took': *by-áxod* 'he takes'.

All others with initial radical *ʔ* are sound: *ʔámar* 'he ordered': *byə́-ʔmor* 'he orders'.

Some verbs with imperfect stem vowel *a* may lose their initial radical *w* in the imperfect [p.74]:

wáṣel	'he arrived':	*byə́-ṣal* (or *by-úṣal*)	'he arrives'
wáʔeɛ	'he fell':	*byə́-ʔaɛ* (or *by-úʔaɛ*)	'he falls'
wáled	'he was born':	*byə́-lad* (or *by-úlad*)	'he is born'

In some parts of the Syrian area, however, notably in Lebanon and Palestine, these forms without -*ū*- are seldom or never used.

The initial radical *y* of *yə́bes* 'it dried up', may also be lost in the imperfect: *byə́-bas* (or *by-íbas*) 'it dries up'.

The inital radical *ʔ* or the anomalous verb *ʔə́ža* 'he came' is lost in the imperfect in many parts of the Syrian area (including Damascus): *byə́-ži* 'he comes'. In other parts (e.g. Palestine), the form *b(y)-íži* is generally used. [p.76].

All initial-weak verbs with stem vowels *ə-e* (or defective *ə-i*) in the perfect have *a* in the imperfect:

wáret	'he inherited':	*by-úrat*	'he inherits'
wážeɛ	'it was painful':	*by-úžaɛ* (or *byə́-žaɛ*)	'it is painful'
wáṭi	'it was low':	*by-úṭa*	'it is low'

Almost all initial-weak verbs with stem vowels *a–a* in the perfect have *e* (or *i* for defective) in the imperfect [p. 59]:

wd&ad   'he promised':   by-ǘ&ed   'he promises'

wdžaⳌ   'he hurt(someone)':   by-ǘžeⳌ   'he hurts...' (cf. *wəžeⳌ* above)

wdḥa   'he inspired':   by-ǘḥi   'he inspires'

Two exceptions, with imperfect vowel *a*, are *wdḍaⳌ* 'he placed': *by-ǘḍaⳌ* 'he places', and *wdḍaⳌ* 'he entrusted, deposited': *by-ǘḍaⳌ* 'he entrusts, deposits' [p. 66].

Hollow Verbs. The base ('he') inflection of the perfect has a long vowel *ā* between the first and last radicals: *lām* 'he blamed', *zād* it increased', *nām* 'he slept'; while the imperfect stem has *ū, ī,* or *ā* between the radicals: *bi-lǘm* 'he blames', *bi-zǐd* 'it increases*, *bi-nǎm* 'he sleeps'.

Examples with imperfect vowel *ū* [p. 56]:

rāḥ   'he went':   bi-rūḥ   'he goes'

šāf   'he saw':   bi-šǘf   'he sees'

māt   'he died':   bi-mǘt   'he dies'

With imperfect vowel *ī* [p. 59]:

fāʔ   'he woke up':   bi-fīʔ   'he wakes up'

šāl   'he picked up': bi-šīl   'he picks up'

žāb   'he brought':   bi-žīb   'he brings'

Only a few have imperfect vowel *ā* [p. 66]:

xāf   'he was afraid':   bi-xǎf   'he is afraid'

bāt   'he spent the night': bi-bǎt   'he spends the night'

(For others, see p. 66.)

Geminate Verbs. The base ('he') inflection of the perfect has a short vowel *a* between the first radical and the fused second and third radicals: *hǎzz* 'he shook', *Ⳍaḍḍ* 'he bit'; while the imperfect stem has *ə* or *a* in the same position: *bi-hǎzz* 'he shakes', *biⳌḍḍ* 'he bites'.

Almost all simple geminate verbs have *ə* in the imperfect [p.63]:

radd	'he gave back':	*bi-rə́dd*	'he gives back'
dall	'he showed':	*bi-də́ll*	'he shows'
ḥaṭṭ	'he put':	*bi-ḥə́ṭṭ*	'he puts'

Several, however, have *a* in the imperfect [p.68]:

ḍaḷḷ	'he remained':	*bi-ḍáḷḷ*	'he remains'
tamm	'he remained':	*bi-támm*	'he remains'

The verb *ɛaḍḍ* 'he bit', has imperfect *a* in much of the Syrian area, though in Palestine, for example, one hears *bi-ɛə́ḍḍ* 'he bites'; while on the other hand, the form *bi-ṣáḥḥ* 'it is all right' is heard in Palestine, while elsewhere it is usually *bi-ṣə́ḥḥ*.

Tense Variation in Augmented and Quadriradical Verb Stems

In the perfect ('he' inflection), the last vowel of the stem is always *a* (or *ā* for hollow triradicals): *ḥmarr* 'he blushed', *barṭal* 'he bribed' *stafād* 'he benefitted', *tɛállam* 'he learned', *ʔdhda* 'he gave' (a gift), *staḥább* 'he liked'.

In the imperfect, there are two kinds of vowelling, depending on the pattern and its alterations. For some types of verb, the imperfect stem is just like the perfect, its last vowel remaining *a*: *byə-ḥmárr* 'he blushes', *byə-tɛállam* 'he learns'.

For other types, the last vowel is changed in the imperfect to what may be called an i-type vowel, namely: *e* (for sound verbs), *i* (for defective), *ī* (for hollow) or *ə* (for geminate): *bi-bárṭel* 'he bribes', *byə́-hdi* 'he gives', *byə-stfīd* 'he benefits', *byə-stḥə́bb* 'he likes'.

Verbs with No Tense Variation in the Stem include:

All verbs with the stem-formative prefix *t-* [p.85]:

Pattern V:	*tǵáyyar*	'it changed':	*byə-tǵáyyar*	'it changes' [p.87]
	txábba	'it was hidden':	*byə-txábba*	'it is hidden' [87]
Pattern VI:	*tšāʔam*	'he was pessimis-tic':	*byə-tšāʔam*	'he is pessimistic' [89]
	trāxa	'he was easy-going':	*byə-trāxa*	'he is easygoing' [89]

Quadriradical (and Pseudo-quadriradical):

    tšárbak 'it became compli- *byə-tšárbak* 'it becomes compli-
             cated':   cated' [p. 121]

    tfárša 'it was brushed': *byə-tfárša* 'it is brushed' [122]

    Also the verbs of hybrid pattern V/X [107]: *stánna*
'he waited': *byə-stánna* 'he waits'; *stmánna* 'he wished':
byə-stmánna 'he wishes'.

    All unsound verbs of Pattern VII, geminate and hollow verbs of Pattern
VIII, and all verbs of Pattern IX:

Pattern VII Geminate: *nḥabb* 'he was loved': *byə-nḥább* 'he is loved' [p. 94]

    Hollow: *nʔāl* 'it was said': *byə-nʔāl* 'it is said' [94]

    Defective: *nʔára* 'it was read': *byə-nʔára* 'it is read' [93]

    Many defective verbs of this pattern, however, also
have the i-type imperfect vowelling: *nṭawa* 'it was folded':
byə-nṭáwi (or *byə-nṭáwa*) 'it is folded' [p. 92].

Pattern VIII Geminate: *štadd* 'it increased': *byə-štádd* 'it increases' [p. 99]

    Hollow: *ḥtāž* 'he needed': *byə-ḥtāž* 'he needs' [99]

    The defective verbs *ltáʔa* 'to be found' and *ntála* 'to
be filled' have a-type imperfect vowelling: *byə-ltáʔa,*
byə-ntála, but other defective Pattern VIII's have the
i-type [p. 97].

Pattern IX: *swadd* 'it turned black': *byə-swádd* 'it turns black'

                 ḥmarr 'he blushed':   *byə-ḥmárr* 'he blushes'[101]

Verbs with an i-Type Imperfect Vowel include all other types, namely:

    Patterns II, III, and simple quadriradicals (and pseudo-quadriradi-
cals)[1]:

    II. *fássar* 'he explained':   *bi-fásser* 'he explains' [p. 77]

        máyyaz 'he distinguished': *bi-máyyez* 'he distinguishes'

        xábba 'he hid' (trans.): *bi-xábbi* 'he hides' [78]

---

[1] In sum, all verbs whose stem consists of one consonant + short vowel + two
consonants + short vowel + (optional) one consonant: CVCCV(C), or one consonant + long vowel + one consonant + short vowel + (optional) one consonant: C͞VCV(C).

III: *sáfar* 'he travelled':   *bi-sáfer* 'he travels' [80]

   ʔáṣaṣ 'he punished':   *bi-ʔáṣeṣ* 'he punishes' [81]

   sáwa 'he made':   *bi-sáwi* 'he makes' [81]

Quadr.:   *táržam* 'he translated':   *bi-táržem* 'he translates' [118]

   báxwaš 'he drilled a hole':*bi-báxweš* 'he drills a hole' [118]

   bōdar 'he powdered':   *bi-bóder* 'he powders' [119]

   farža 'he showed':   *bi-fárži* 'he shows' [120]

Pattern IV verbs have a stem-formative prefix *ʔa-* in the perfect, and no vowel between the first and second radicals: *ʔáɛlan* 'he announced'. In the imperfect the formative *ʔa-* disappears,[1] and the vowel after the second radical is changed to an i-type [p. 189]: *byáɛlen* 'he announces'.

   Sound: *ʔáṣbaḥ* 'it became':   *byá-ṣbeḥ* 'it becomes [p.83]

   Defective: *ʔáhda* 'he gave':   *byá-hdi* 'he gives' [83]

   Geminate: *ʔaṣárr* 'he insisted':   *bi-ṣárr* 'he insists' [84]

   Hollow: *ʔaḥāl* 'he transformed':   *bi-ḥīl* 'he transforms' [84]

Sound verbs of Patterns VII and VIII have i-type imperfect stems, in which the next-to-last vowel is changed to *ə* (and the last vowel, to *e*):

Pattern VII: *nkásar* 'it was broken': *byə-nkáser* 'it is broken'

   nsáḥab 'he withdrew': *byə-nsáḥeb* 'he withdraws' [p.91]

   mbáṣaṭ 'he had a good time': *byə-mbáṣeṭ* 'he has a good time'

Pattern VIII: *ftákar* 'he thought': *byə-ftáker* 'he thinks'

   štáǧal 'he worked': *byə-štáǧel* 'he works' [95]

In some parts of the Syrian area, the next-to-last vowel is dropped, the accent falling on the inflectional prefix: *byá-nkser, byá-štǧel.*

---

[1]But cf.pseudo-quadriradical Pattern *ʔaFɛaL* [117]: *ʔaslam* 'he became a Muslim': *bi-ʔáslem* 'he becomes a Muslim'.

Some Pattern VII defective verbs (and in some areas, e.g. Lebanon, practically all of them) have i-type imperfect stems in addition to the a-type stems: *nṭáfa* 'it was extinguished': *byə-nṭə́fi* 'it is extinguished'; *nkára* 'it was rented': *byə-nkə́ri* 'it is rented' (also *byənṭáfa, byənkára*) [p. 97].

The Pattern VIII defective verb *ltáʔa* 'to be found', 'to meet', has an i-type (as well as a-type) imperfect *byəltə́ʔi* (or *byəltáʔa*) 'he meets', but in the sense 'he is found', only the form *byəltáʔa* is used.

The anomalous Pattern VIII (or VII) verb *ntála* 'it was filled' has an i-type imperfect *byəntə́li* 'it is filled', as well as the a-type *byəntála* [98].

Pattern X imperfect stems are all i-type:

Sound: *stáɛmal* 'he used':   *byə-stáɛmel*   'he uses'

            stáfham 'he inquired':   *byə-stáfhem*   'he inquires' [102]

            stášwab 'he questioned':   *byə-stášweb*   'he questions' [103]

Defective: *stáḥla* 'he liked':   *byə-stáḥli*   'he likes' [103]

Hollow: *stašār* 'he consulted':   *byə-stašír*   'he consults' [105]

Geminate: *stamárr* 'he continued':   *byə-stamárr*   'he continues' [105]

Initial-
  weak: *stáhal* 'he deserved':   *byə-stáhel*   'he deserves' [106]

The Hollow-defective verb *stáḥa* 'he was embarrassed' [p. 106] has the next-to-last imperfect vowel *ə*, just like Pattern VIII verbs (from which it is indistinguishable in form [97]): *byə-stáḥi* 'he gets embarrassed'.

On the other hand, the anomalous Pattern X verb *zdall* 'he concluded' [107] keeps *a* in the imperfect, like Pattern VIII geminates: *byə-zdáll* 'he concludes'.

The hybrid Pattern III/X verb *snáwal* (or *stnáwal*) 'he caught' has an i-type imperfect: *byə-snáwel* 'he catches' [p. 108].

Quadriradical Pattern *FɛaLaLL* verbs [p. 124] (like Pattern X geminates) have *ə* as the last stem vowel of the imperfect:

            šmaʔázz 'he was disgusted': *byə-šmaʔázz* 'he gets dis-
                                                           gusted'

            qšaɛárr 'he shuddered':   *byə-qšaɛárr* 'he shudders'

Person Variation in Verb Stems.

In the first and second persons of the perfect, i.e. before the suffixes
-*t* 'you/I' and -*na* 'we', the base ('he') form is altered as follows:

In simple sound verbs with vowels *ə-e*, the first vowel (*ə*) is dropped
and the last vowel (*e*) is changed to *ə*:

sə́meɛ	'he heard':	*smə́ɛ-t*	'you (m.)/I heard'
		smə́ɛ-t-i	'you (f.) heard'
		smə́ɛ-t-u	'you (pl.) heard'
		smə́ɛ-na	'we heard' [p.71]
ɛə́mel	'he did':	*ɛmə́l-t*	'you (m.)/I did'
		ɛmə́l-t-i	'you (f.) did'
		ɛmə́l-t-u	'you (pl.) did'
		ɛmə́l-na	'we did' [p.70]

The change from *e* to *ə* is an automatic consequence of
sound combination rules [p.28].

Stem vowels *a* remain unaltered except in accentuation:
kátab 'he wrote': *katáb-t* 'you/I wrote'; *tɛállam* 'he
learned'; *tɛallám-na* 'we learned'. See Accentuation [p.18].

In simple defective verbs with vowels *ə-i*, the first vowel (*ə*)
is dropped and the last vowel (*i*) is lengthened to *ī:*

nə́si	'he forgot':	*nsī-t*	'you (m.)/I forgot', etc.
		nsī-na	'we forgot' [p.72]
bə́ki	'he cried':	*bkī-t*	'you/I cried', etc.
		bkī-na	'we cried' [70]

See p.27 .

In defective verbs stem-final *a* is changed to *ē:*

⁷ᵈra	'he read':	⁷arḗ-t	'you/I read'
		⁷arḗ-na	'we read' [p.68]
ᵋᵈt̞a	'he gave':	ᵋat̞ḗ-t	'you/I gave'
		ᵋat̞ḗ-na	'we gave' [61]
sᵈmma	'he named':	sammḗ-t	'you/I named'
		sammḗ-na	'we named' [78]
stᵈnna	'he waited':	stannḗ-t	'you/I waited'
		stannḗ-na	'we waited' [108]
štᵈra	'he bought':	štarḗ-t	'you/I bought'
		štarḗ-na	'we bought' [97]
stᵈᵋfa	'he resigned':	staᵋfḗ-t	'you/I resigned'
		staᵋfḗ-na	'we resigned' [103]

Verb stems ending in a double consonant add *ē:*

sabb	'he cursed':	sabbḗ-t	'you/I cursed'
		sabbḗ-na	'we cursed' [p.64]
ḥat̞t̞	'he put':	ḥat̞t̞ḗ-t	'you/I put'
		ḥat̞t̞ḗ-na	'we put'
htamm	'he cared':	htammḗ-t	'you/I cared'
		htammḗ-na	'we cared' [99]
ḥmarr	'he blushed':	ḥmarrḗ-na	'you/I blushed'
		ḥmarrḗ-na	'we blushed' [101]
staḥᵈbb	'he liked':	staḥabbḗt	'you/I liked'
		staḥabbḗ-na	'we liked' [105]
t̞maᵛᵈnn	'he felt secure':	t̞maᵛannḗ-t	'you/I felt secure'
		t̞maᵛannḗ-na	'we felt secure [124]

In hollow triradical verbs (excepting some of those in Pattern X), the *ā* is changed to *ə:*

šāf	'he saw':	*šəf-t*	'you/I saw'
		šə́f-na	'we saw' [p. 57]
nām	'he slept':	*nəm-t*	'you/I slept'
		nə́m-na	'we slept' [67]
šāb	'he brought':	*šəb-t*	'you/I brought'
		šə́b-na	'we brought' [60]
ḥtāš	'he needed':	*ḥtəš-t*	'you/I needed'
		ḥtə́š-na	'we needed' [99]
nšāf	'he was seen':	*nšəf-t*	'you/I was seen'
		nšə́f-na	'we were seen' [94]
starāḥ	'he rested':	*strə́ḥ-t*	'you/I rested'
		strə́ḥ-na	'we rested' [104]

In hollow verbs of Pattern X the first stem vowel *a* tends to disappear both in the first and second persons of the perfect <u>and</u> in the imperfect stem: *byə-strī̆ḥ* 'he rests'. In some verbs, however, the first *a* tends to remain in all forms, and the last *a* does not change to *ə: stašár* 'he consulted': *stašár-t* 'you/I consulted', *byə-staši̊r* 'he consults' [p. 105].

On the assimilation of voiced obstruents to the suffix *-t* (e.g. *ʔáxad* 'he took': *ʔaxát-t* 'you/I took'), see p. 26.

Number/Gender Variation in Verb Stems

In the imperfect, the final vowel (*a* or *i*) of a defective stem is dropped before the feminine and plural suffixes *-i* and *-u:*

3rd person: *byə́nsa* + *-u* → *byə́ns-u* 'they forget'

2nd person: *btə́nsa* + *-u* → *btə́ns-u* 'you (pl.) forget'

btə́nsa + *-i* → *btə́ns-i* 'you (f.) forget' [p. 72]

3rd person: *bisámmi*   + *-u* → *bisámm-u*   'they name'

2nd person: *bətsámmi*   + *-u* → *bətsámm-u*   'you (pl.) name'

              bətsámmi   + *-i* → *bətsámm-i*   'you (f.) name' [p. 78]

    If the stem vowel is *i*, its replacement by the feminine suffix *-i* makes no distinction in form between masculine and feminine: *bətsámmi* 'you (m. or f.) name'.

    In the third-person perfect, the final *a* of a defective stem is dropped before the feminine and plural suffixes *-et* and *-u:*

        ʔára   + *-et* → *ʔár-et*   'she read'

        ʔára   + *-u* → *ʔár-u*   'they read' [p. 68]

        fárša   + *-et* → *fárš-et*   'she brushed'

        fárša   + *-u* → *fárš-u*   'they brushed' [120]

But stem-final *i* is generally retained as *y:*

        máši   + *-et* → *mášy-et*   'she walked'

        máši   + *-u* → *mášy-u*   'they walked' [70]

        nási   + *-et* → *násy-et*   'she forgot'

        nási   + *-u* → *násy-u*   'they forgot'

    Or again as *i*, before the feminine suffix (*-t-*) followed by a pronoun suffix *-o*, *-ak*, or *-ek* [p. 183]: *násy-et* 'she forgot' + *-o* 'him' → *nási-t-o* 'she forgot him', + *-ak* → *nási-t-ak* 'she's forgotten you'.

    See also p. 166.

    Before the suffix *-et* only, sound a-stems of Patterns I, VII, and VIII drop their second *a:*

Pattern I: *fátah*   + *-et* → *fáth-et*   'she opened' [p. 65]

           dáras   + *-et* → *dárs-et*   'she studied' [55]

Pattern VII: *nkásar* + *-et* → *nkásr-et*   'it (f.) was broken' [91]

Pattern VIII: *ftákar* + *-et* → *ftákr-et*   'she thought' [95]

In many parts of the Syrian area, however (e.g. Palestine, southern Lebanon), this *a* is not dropped: *fátaḥet* (or *fátaḥat*), *nkásaret* (or *nkásarat*), etc.

Certain other stem changes occur before *-i*, *-u*, and *-et* as before all suffixes beginning with a vowel (except *-a* 'her', *-on* 'them' [541]):

Stem vowels *e* and *o* are dropped [p. 28]:

btádros	+ *-i*	→ *btád(ə)rs-i*	'you (f.) study' [p.55]
byámsek	+ *-u*	→ *byámsk-u*	'they hold' [69]
másek	+ *-u*	→ *másk-u*	'they took hold'
másek	+ *-et*	→ *másk-et*	'she took hold'
bisákker	+ *-u*	→ *bisákkr-u*	'they close' [77]
btəstáɛmel	+ *-i*	→ *btəstáɛ(ə)ml-i*	'you (f.) use' [102]

Note, however, that Pattern II verbs with middle and last radicals alike do not generally lose the *e*, but rather change it to *ə*: *bisábbeb* + *-u* → *bisábbəb-u* 'they cause' If the *e* is lost in such cases, a theoretical triple-consonant sequence (*"bisábbbu"*) is normally reduced to a double consonant [p. 27]. These reduced forms may be heard in some parts of the Syrian area (with some verbs, at least,) but note that a Pattern II verb then takes on the form of a geminate Pattern I, and in some cases homophony would result (cf. *bisábbu* 'they curse'), which is avoided by retaining the stem vowel (*bisábbəbu* 'they cause').

As before all suffixes, *ā* in the imperative of simple sound triradical verbs is shortened to *a*, and *ē* and *ō* are both changed to *ə* [p. 198]:

ftāh	+	*-u*	→ *ftáḥ-u*	'open' (pl.)
msēk	+	*-i*	→ *msák-i*	'hold' (f.)
drōs	+	*-u*	→ *drás-u*	'study' (pl.)

Mode Variation in Verb Stems: Imperative Forms

The imperative may be formed by dropping the person prefix (shown here as 2nd p.) from the imperfect stem and modifying the stem in certain ways:

In simple sound triradical stems, the vowel is lengthened when no suffix follows:

(tə́)-ftaḥ:	ftāḥ	'open' (m.)	[p.65]
(tə́)-msek:	msēk	'hold' (m,)	[69]
(tə́)-ktob:	ktōb	'write' (m.)	[55]

But if there is a suffix of any kind, the stem vowel remains short:

(tə́)-ftaḥ-i:	ftáḥ-i	'open' (f.)
(tə́)-ftaḥ-o:	ftáḥ-o	'open (m.) it (m.)'
(tə)-msə́k-ọn:	msə́k-on	'hold (m.) them'
(tə)-ktə́b-a:	ktə́b-a	'write (m.) it (f.)'

And if the suffixing stem has no vowel between the last two radicals, ə is inserted there:

(tə́)-msk-i:	msə́k-i	'hold (f.)'
(tə́)-msk-o:	msə́k-o	'hold (m.) it (m.)'
(tə)-k(ə)tbū́:	ktəb-ū́	'write (pl.) it (m.)'

In non-defective verbs whose first radical is a semivowel (w, y), the initial vowel (ū, ī)[1] is shortened to w or y, respectively:

(t)-ū́ṣef:	wṣēf	'describe' (m.)	[p.59]
(t)-ū́ṣal:	wṣāl	'arrive' (m.)	[75]
(t)-íbas:	ybās	'dry up'[2] (m.)	[75]

The stem-initial ā in the imperfect of ʔakal 'to eat' and ʔaxad 'to take' is dropped in the imperative [p.56]:

(t)-ā́kol:	kōl	'eat' (m.);	(t)-ā́xod:	xōd	'take(m.)
(t)-ā́kli:	kə́li	'eat' (f.);	(t)-ā́xdu:	xə́du	'take(pl.)

---

[1] Imperatives in Syrian Colloquial are not formed from the imperfect stem in which the initial radical is lost (e.g. tə́-ṣal) [p.75].

[2] An unlikely command; the translation is not meant in the slang sense, but literally. Good examples with initial radical y are hard to find.

In simple defective verbs with no pronoun suffix, the imperative stem usually has *ʔə́-* before the first radical; and the final vowel is unaltered:

(tə́)-nsa: *ʔə́nsa*   'forget' (m.) [p.72]

(tə́)-nsi: *ʔə́nsi*   'forget' (f.)

(tə́)-nsu: *ʔə́nsu*   'forget' (pl.)

In the first radical is *w*, however, the imperative begins with *ʔű-:*

(t)-űfi: *ʔűfi*   'fulfill' (m. or f.) [p.62]

(t)-űfu: *ʔűfu*   'fulfill' (pl.)

But when the final vowel is lengthened and accented (viz. before a suffix pronoun), the first syllable is reduced as it is with non-defective verbs (see above):

(tə́)-nsä́-ha: *nsä́-ha*   'forget (m.) it (f.)'

(tə)-nsî́-ha: *nsî́-ha*   'forget (f.) it (f.)'

(t)-ūfî́-ha: *wfî́-ha*   'fulfill it'

> In the Palestinian area and to some extent elsewhere, the imperative with *ʔ-* is commonly used instead of the vowel lengthening, in sound verbs as well as defectives: *ʔə́ftaḥ* instead of *ftāḥ*, *ʔə́msek* instead of *msēk*, etc.
> In Lebanon and to some extent elsewhere, on the other hand, vowel lengthening is commonly used in defective verbs as well as sound: *nsā* instead of *ʔə́nsa*, *wfī* instead of *ʔūfi*, etc.

With all other types of verb — namely, with augmented verbs and with hollow, geminate, and quadriradical simple verbs — there are no mode variations in the stem at all:

(t)-sákker: *sákker*   'close' (m.) [p.77]

(t)-sákkri: *sákkri*   'close' (f.)

(t)-sákkru: *sákkru*   'close' (pl.)

(tə)-stáƐmel: *stáƐmel*   'use' (m.) [102]

(tə)-stáƐ(ə)mlo: *stáƐ(ə)mlo*   'use (m.) it (m.)'

(t)-taržmű-li: *taržmű-li*   'translate (pl.) for me' [118]

(t)-ḥəṭṭ: *ḥəṭṭ*   'put' (m.) [64]

(t)-šīl: *šīl*   'take away' (m.) [60]

(t)-nām: *nām*   'sleep' (m.) [67]

(tə)-tƐállam: *tƐállam*   'learn' (m.) [87]

(tə)-tƐallamî́:   *tƐallamî́*   'learn (f.) it (m.)'

Note that augmented and simple hollow verbs with stem
vowels a (or $\bar{a}$) in the imperfect have masculine and plural
imperatives with the same form as the third person perfect·
nām 'he slept' and 'sleep (m.)', nāmu 'they slept' and
'sleep (pl.)'; tɛ́dllam 'he learned' and 'learn (m.)',
tɛ́dllamu 'they learned' and 'learn (pl.)'.

Irregular Imperatives. The verb ʔəža 'to come' [p.76] has no imperative of
its own but is suppleted by the forms tɑ́ɛa 'come' (m.), tɑ́ɛi (f.), tɑ́ɛu
(pl.) (or sometimes taɛāl, taɛāli, taɛālu).

The verb ɛaṭa 'to give' (Impf. (ṭ)-dɛ́ṭi) has an imperative form ɛ́dṭi
(m., f.), ɛ́dṭu (pl.), commonly used instead of the regular forms ʔdɛ́ṭi,
etc. [p.61].

The imperative of the verb ʔaɛad 'to sit' (Impf. (tə́)-ʔɛod) [p.55] commonly loses its initial radical ʔ in the imperative: ɛōd 'sit down', ɛə́di
(f.), ɛə́du (pl.).

The exclamation ʔóɛa 'watch out!' is generally used instead of the regular imperative form ʔúɛa (of wəɛi, Impf. t-úɛa 'to be aware, wide awake'),
and the form ʔə́shak 'take care (lest...)', for ʔə́sha plus pronoun suffix -k
(the expected form would be "shāk") (imperative of ṣəhi, Impf. ṭ-ə́sha 'to
be wide awake').

The "demonstrative" [p.564] verb hāt 'give (it) here' (f. hāti, pl.
hātu) has imperative only, while the form xē 'here, take (it)', is <u>feminine</u>
imperative only.

CHAPTER 7: ADJECTIVE INFLECTIONAL FORMS

Adjectives have a three-way inflection for number/gender: masculine (/singular), feminine (/singular)[1], and plural. Masculine is the base inflection; the feminine is usually formed by suffixation of *-e/-a* [p. 138]; the plural is usually formed by suffixation of *-īn* or by a change in the base pattern.

It is the function of an adjectives's inflection to show agreement [p. 420] with the term to which it is predicate [403] or attribute [501], or, in some cases, to show the "natural" number/gender of its referent [427].

> While number and gender are separate categories with respect to nouns, they fall together in Syrian Arabic for verbs [p. 175], for pronouns [539], and — less completely — for adjectives. Masculine and feminine are distinguished only in the singular, and dual is not distinguished from plural.

> Adjectives, however, are not always clearly separable from nouns, especially in the case of personal adjectives that are often used substantivally. The word *maslem* 'Moslem', for instance, as a noun, has the plural *masᵊlmīn* and the feminal derivative *masᵊlme,* which in turn has a plural *masᵊlmāt* 'Moslems (f.)'. The feminine plural may sometimes be used attributively: *naswān masᵊlmāt* 'Moslem women' (more usual: *naswān masᵊlmīn*), thus inviting analysis as a feminine plural adjective (or alternatively, an appositive noun [506]).

> Some adjectives may be heard with the *-āt* ending even when there is no question of substantivization, when attributive to a plural in *-āt* of a feminine count noun [p. 425]: *banadōrayāt māwiyyāt* 'juicy tomatoes' (or, more usually, *banadōrayāt māwiyye*). Similarly, a <u>dual</u> adjective may sometimes be heard: *l-ɛanṣurēn ᵊl-kimyāʔiyyēn* 'The two chemical elements' (or, more colloquially, *l-ɛanṣrēn ᵊl-kimāwiyyīn*).

> Generally speaking, these usages are rare enough to be treated as exceptional. It should be kept in mind, however, that adjectives, which are noun-like in base form, are at least potentially also noun-like in inflection, to the extent of an occasional feminine plural *(-āt)* or, rarely, a dual.

> A few adjectives are uninflected. See Agreement [p. 428].

---

[1]Feminine "singular" only in the sense that it stands in contrast to the plural form. Functionally speaking, the feminine form is used as much in agreement with plurals as with singulars [p. 423].

Regular Inflection: Feminine $-e/-a$, **plural** $-\bar{\imath}n$.

At least some of the adjectives in every pattern except ${}^{\circ}a\bar{F}\mathcal{E}aL$ [p. 130] — and all of the adjectives in most patterns — are inflected only with the suffixes $-e/-a$ and $-\bar{\imath}n$.

On the alteration of $-e$ with $-a$, see p. 138.

Examples of regular adjective inflection:

Masculine	Feminine	Plural	Meaning
ṭamūḥ	*ṭamūḥa*	*ṭamūḥīn*	'ambitious'
našīṭ	*našīṭa*	*našīṭīn*	'active, energetic'
kazzāb	*kazzābe*	*kazzābīn*	'lying, liar'
səkkīr	*səkkīre*	*səkkīrīn*	'drunkard'
mərr	*mərra*	*mərrīn*	'bitter'
ḥəlu	*ḥəlwe*	*ḥəlwīn*	'sweet', 'pretty'
fāḍi	*fāḍye*	*fāḍyīn*	'empty, free'
fax°m	*faxme*	*faxmīn*	'stately, elegant'
lammī€	*lammī€a*	*lammī€īn*	'shiny'
malān	*malāne*	*malānīn*	'full'
za€lān	*za€lāne*	*za€lānīn*	'displeased'
mašġūl	*mašġūle*	*mašġūlīn*	'busy'
mhəmm	*mhəmme*	*mhəmmīn*	'important'
mṭī€	*mṭī€a*	*mṭī€īn*	'obedient'
mufīd	*mufīde*	*mufīdīn*	'useful'
mžawwaz	*mžawwaze*	*mžawwazīn*	'married'
mšarṭaṭ	*mšarṭaṭa*	*mšarṭaṭīn*	'ragged'
məṭmaˀənn ..	*məṭmaˀənne* ..	*məṭmaˀənnīn*	'calm, secure'

Stem Modifications with the Suffixes

Adjectives whose base (masculine) forms end in e + consonant generally drop their e when the feminine or plural suffix is added [p. 28]:

Masculine	Feminine	Plural	Meaning
rəṭeb	rəṭbe	rəṭbīn	'humid, moist'
dayyeʔ	dayyʔa	dayyʔīn	'narrow, cramped'
ṭayyeb	ṭayybe	ṭayybīn	'good'
ɛāṭel	ɛāṭle	ɛāṭlīn	'bad'
mnāseb	mnāsbe	mnāsbīn	'suitable'
mətʔaxxer .	mətʔaxxra ..	mətʔaxxrīn	'late'
məxtélef ..	məxtélfe ...	məxtəlfīn	'different'
mfastek ...	mfastke	mfastkīn	'depressed'

With anaptyxis [p.31] (cf. faxᵊm, above):

médhen	médᵊhne	mədᵊhnīn	'greasy, fat'
mə́zweʔ	mə́zᵊwʔa	məzᵊwʔīn	'having good taste'

With vocalization of y [p.166] (cf. ḥəlu, fāḍi, above):

mə́hyeb	mə́hibe	məhibīn	'awesome'

e is not dropped but is changed to ə, when it comes between a double and a single consonant which are alike [29, 77]:

mṣammem ...	mṣamməme ...	mṣamməmīn	'determined, intent (on)'

If the base form (masculine) ends in -i, then in some cases this ending is lengthened to -iyy- before the feminine and plural suffixes, while in other cases it is reduced to a non-syllabic -y-. In relative adjectives [p.280], for instance, -i is always lengthened:

ləbnā́ni ...	ləbnāníyye .	ləbnāniyyīn	'Lebanese'

It is also lengthened in defective adjectives of Pattern FaɛīL [128]:

sáxi	saxíyye	saxiyyīn	'generous'

And in the defective version (məFɛi) of Pattern maFɛūL [p.133]:

mánsi	mənsíyye ...	mənsiyyīn	'forgotten'
mə́kwi	məkwíyye ...	məkwiyyīn	'ironed'

Even when adjectives of the defective pattern məFɛi correspond to Pattern məFɛəL [p.133] rather than maFɛūL, their final i is still usually lengthened in the feminine or plural: məʔzi 'harmful': fem. məʔzíyye, pl. məʔziyyīn;

márḍi 'satisfactory': *marḍĭyye, marḍiyyīn*. There are a
few exceptions, however, in which the *i* is reduced and
the accentuation of the feminine is like that of the
masculine (as in sound Pattern *maFƐeL*): *mə́ġri* 'alluring,
enticing', fem. *mə́ġ^ərye,* pl. *maġ^əryīn; mə́hwi* 'airy,
draughty':   fem. *mə́huye* (with vocalization of the medial
w).

The final *–i* of defective Pattern *FāƐeL* adjectives [p. 131] is always
reduced to non-syllabic form (*y*) with the suffixes:

Masculine	Feminine	Plural	Meaning
Ɛāli	*Ɛālye*	*Ɛālyīn*	'high'
bā^ʔi	*bā^ʔye*	*bā^ʔyīn*	'remaining'

Note the difference in stem modifications, then,
between *Ɛāli: Ɛālye* 'high' and *Ɛādi: Ɛādĭyye* 'usual,
customary'. The latter is a relative adjective with the
suffix *–i* (from *Ɛāde* 'custom') and is not to be confused
with Pattern *FāƐeL* adjectives.

With some exceptions, defective adjectives of the augmented participial
patterns [p. 134] have *–y–* (rather than *–iyy–*) before the suffixes; before
–īn, furthermore, the *y* may disappear entirely:

mrabbi ...	*mrabbye*	*mrabb(y)īn*	'bringing up, having brought up'
msāwi	*msāwye*	*msāw(y)īn*	'making, having made'
mətxabbi .	*mətxabbye*	*mətxabb(y)īn*	'hiding, hidden'
mənṭə́fi ..	*mənṭəfye*	*mənṭəf(y)īn*	'extinguished'
məktə́fi ..	*məktəfye*	*məktəf(y)īn*	'contented'
məstakri..	*məstak^ərye*	*məstak(^ə)r(y)īn*	'renting, having rented'
məstanni .	*məstannye*	*məstannyīn*	'waiting'

On pronoun-suffixing forms of transitive feminine
participles in *–ye*, cf. p. 168. E.g. *mrabbīto* '(f.) bring-
ing him up', *msāwīto* '(f.) making it'.

There are some Pattern VIII participles, however, which usually (in
some cases always) have *–iyy–* before the suffixes. For example:

Masculine	Feminine	Plural	Meaning
məstə́wi ..	*məstwíyye*	*məstwiyyín*	'done, cooked, ripe'
məštə́hi ..	*məšthíyye*	*məšthiyyín*	'desirous, craving'
məɛtə́ni ..	*məɛtníyye* ..... or *məɛtə́nye* .	*məɛtniyyín* *məɛtən(y)ín*	'taking care'
məntə́si ..	*məntsíyye* ..... or *məntə́sye* .	*məntsiyyín* *məntəs(y)ín*	'forgotten'

Note also the comments on Pattern *məFɛeL,* above.

There is also vacilation between –y– and –iyy– in the rare defective quadriradicals [136]:

mfaršiyye ...	*mfaršiyye* ..... or *mfaršye* ..	*mfaršiyyín* *mfarš(y)ín*	'having brushed'

If the masculine form of an adjective (defective passive participle) ends in –a, then the feminine has –āye, and the plural, –āyín (or –ayín):

msamma ...	*msammāye*	*msammāyín*	'named'
msāwa	*msāwāye*	*msāwāyín*	'made'
mfarša ...	*mfaršāye*	*mfaršāyín*	'brushed'

Adjectives with Internal Plurals

Almost all adjectives of Pattern *FɛíL* [p. 127] and many non-defective ones of Pattern *FaɛíL* [127] form plurals on Pattern *FɛāL:*

nḍíf	*nḍífe*	*nḍāf*	'clean'
mníḥ	*mníḥa*	*mnāḥ*	'good'
ktír	*ktíre*	*ktār*	'much, many'
kbír	*kbíre*	*kbār*	'big, large'
ẓġír	*ẓġíre*	*ẓġār*	'little, small'
tʔíl	*tʔíle*	*tʔāl*	'heavy'
ṭawíl	*ṭawíle*	*ṭwāl*	'long, tall'
xafíf	*xafífe*	*xfāf* (also *xafifín*)	'light'
ʔaríb	*ʔaríbe*	*ʔrāb* (also *ʔaribín*)	'near'

The adjectives *ždīd* 'new' and *ɛatī⁹* 'old' form plurals
on the pattern *FəɛaL* as well as *FɛāL:* m. *ždīd*, f. *ždīde*, pl.
žədad or *ždād:* m. *ɛatī⁹*, f. *ɛatī⁹a,* pl. *ɛəta⁹* or *ɛtā⁹*.

Many non-defective adjectives of Pattern *FaɛīL* applied to human beings
have plurals formed on Pattern *FəɛaLa:*

Masculine	Feminine	Plural	Meaning
karīm	*karīme*	*kərama*	'generous'
fa⁹īr	*fa⁹īre* (or *fa⁹īra*)	*fə⁹ara*	'poor'
laṭīf	*laṭīfe*	*ləṭafa* (or *laṭīfīn*)	'nice, pleasant'
baxīl	*baxīle*	*bəxala* (or *baxīlīn*)	'stingy, miser'
saɛīd	*saɛīde*	*səɛada*	'happy'

Some adjectives applied to human beings, mainly of Pattern *FaɛīL*,
have plurals formed on pattern *FaɛāLa:*

⁹awi	*⁹awiyye*	*⁹awāya* (or *⁹awiyyīn*)	'strong'
dani	*daniyye*	*danāya*	'low, vile'
ḥazīn	*ḥazīne*	*ḥazāna*	'mournful, sad'
hani	*haniyye*	*hanāya* (or *haniyyīn*)	'happy'
baṭrān	*baṭrāne*	*baṭāra* (or *baṭranīn*)	'wasteful'
----	*ḥəble*	*ḥabāla*	'pregnant'
⁹atīl	*⁹atīle*	*⁹ətala*	'killed'
žarīḥ	*žarīḥa*	*žəraḥa*	'wounded'

Many defective adjectives of this same sort have plurals formed on
Pattern *⁹əFⁿɛLa* or *⁹aFɛiLa:*

ġani	*ġaniyye*	*⁹əġⁿnya* or *⁹aġniya*	'rich'
ta⁹i	*ta⁹iyye*	*⁹ət⁹⁹ya*	'God-fearing'
zaki	*zakiyye*	*⁹əzⁿkya*	'bright, intelligent'

A number of other plural patterns are used for adjectives applicable to human beings, though they are more typical of nouns. They are, in fact, generally used substantivally, while plurals of the same word with *-īn,* if any, are more purely adjectival.

Masculine	Feminine	Plural	Meaning
raᵹīl	*raᵹīle*	*ˀarᵹāl* (*raᵹilīn, rᵹāl*)	'vile, despicable'
mayyet	*mayyte*	*ˀamwāt, mawta* (*mayytīn*)	'dead'
ḥayy	*ḥayye*	*ˀaḥyāˀ*	'living, alive'
ḥərr	*ḥərra*	*ˀaḥrār* (*ḥərrīn*)	'free'
ġašīm	*ġašīme*	*ġəšᵊm* or *ġəšama*	'naive'
ˀadīm	*ˀadīme*	*ˀədᵊm* or *ˀədama* (inanimate *ˀdām*)	'ancient'
ˀāṣer	*ˀāṣra*	*ˀəṣṣar* (*ˀāṣrīn*)	'underage, minor'
žāhel	*žāhle*	*žəhhal* (*žāhlīn*)	'ignorant'
šužāʿ	*šužāʿa*	*šəžʿān*	'brave'
šāᵹᵹ	*šāᵹᵹe*	*šawāᵹᵹ* (*šāᵹᵹīn*)	'strange, odd'
mažnūn	*mažnūne*	*mažanīn*	'crazy'
zangīl	*zangīle*	*zanagīl* (*zangīlīn*)	'rich'
marīḍ	*marīḍa*	*marḍa* or *məraḍa*	'ill'
ḍaʿfān	*ḍaʿfāne*	*ḍaʿfa*	'ill'

Most noun/adjectives of the pattern *FaʿʿīL* [p.129] form feminine and plural both with the suffix *-e/-a:*

| *šarrīb* | *šarrībe* | *šarrībe* | 'heavy drinker' |
| *šaġġīl* | *šaġġīle* | *šaġġīle* | '(good) worker' |

Adjectives of Pattern *ʔaFƐaL* [p.130] form their feminine on Pattern
FaƐLa, and their plural on Pattern *FəƐL* or sometimes (animate only)
FəƐLān:

Masculine	Feminine	Plural	Meaning
ʔaṣfar	ṣafra	ṣəfᵊr	'yellow'
ʔazraʔ	zarʔa	zərᵊʔ	'blue'
ʔašʔar	šaʔra	šəʔᵊr	'blond'
ʔabyaḍ	bēda	bīḍ	'white'
ʔaswad	sōda	sūd	'black'
ʔaƐwar	Ɛōra	Ɛūr	'one-eyed'
ʔaʔraƐ	ʔarƐa	ʔərƐān	'bald'
ʔaḥdab	ḥadba	ḥədbān	'hump-backed'
ʔaƐma	Ɛamya	Ɛəmyān	'blind'
ʔaxras	xarsa	xərs, xərsān	'deaf-mute'
ʔazƐar	zaƐra	zəƐrān	'crooked, criminal, bandit'

The word *ʔaƐzab* 'unmarried' has the expected feminine
form *Ɛazba*, but no plural (except the suppletive form
Ɛazzābīn, which belongs more properly to the singular
Ɛazzābi 'bachelor'). The word *ʔarmal* 'widowed', however,
is inflected as a quadriradical: f. *ʔarmale*, pl. *ʔarāmel*.

CHAPTER 8: NOUN INFLECTIONAL FORMS

Many nouns have a three-way inflection for number: singular, dual, plural. Singular is the base inflection; the dual is formed by adding a suffix *-ēn*. The plural is formed in a variety of ways [211 ff], depending to some extent on the form of the singular, but to a large extent on the idiosyncracy of individual nouns. Examples:

Singular			Dual			Plural
kaff	'glove'......*kaffēn*		'two gloves'......*kfūf*			'gloves'
kəlme	'word'........*kəlᵊmtēn*		'two words'.........*kəlmāt*			'words'
ʔarnab	'rabbit'......*ʔarnabēn*		'two rabbits'......*ʔarāneb*			'rabbits'
ʔasᵊm	'name'........*ʔasmēn*		'two names'........*ʔasāmi*			'names'
daʔīʔa	'minute'......*daʔīʔtēn*		'two minutes'......*daʔāyeʔ*			'minutes'
mhandes	'engineer'....*mhandsēn*		'two engineers'....*mhandsīn*			'engineers'
sažara	'tree'........*sažartēn*		'two trees'........*sažarāt*			'trees'
ġalṭa	'mistake'.....*ġalᵊṭṭēn*		'two mistakes'.....*ġalṭāṭ*			'mistakes'
tərki	'Turk'........*tərkiyyēn*		'two Turks'........*ʔatrāk*			'Turks'
harāmi	'thief'.......*harāmiyyēn*		'two thieves'......*haramiyye*			'thieves'

The use of the number categories is treated in Chapter 14.

The Dual Suffix *-ēn:* Stem Modifications

As generally before suffixes beginning with a vowel [p. 28], *e* and *o* before a stem-final consonant are dropped when *-en* is added: *ṣāḥeb* 'friend' + *-ēn* → *ṣāḥbēn* 'two friends', *səllom* 'ladder' + *ēn* → *səllmēn* 'two ladders'.

In certain classicisms, however, *e* and *o* are not dropped but are changed to *i* and *u*, respectively: *malek* 'king' + *-ēn* → *malikēn*, *ʕənṣor* 'element' + *-ēn* → *ʕənṣurēn* (or, more colloquially, *ʕənṣrēn*).

The loss of *e* or *o* often involves compensatory anaptyxis [p. 31]: *mažles* 'chamber' + *-ēn* → *mažᵊlsēn*, *ʔasʔof* 'bishop' + *-ēn* → *ʔasᵊʔfēn*.

The base-formative suffix -e/-a [p.138] takes the form -t- before -ēn,
just as it does before the pronoun suffixes [p.165]:

sayyāra	'care'	+ -ēn →	sayyārtēn	'two cars'
madrase	'school'	+ -ēn →	madrastēn	'two schools'
marra	'(one)time'	+ -ēn →	marrtēn	'two times, twice'
sane	'year'	+ -ēn →	santēn	'two years'

With anaptyxis:

badle	'suit'	+ -ēn →	badᵊltēn	'two suits'
dawle	'nation, state'	+ -ēn →	dawᵊltēn	'two nations'
buḥayra	'lake'	+ -ēn →	buḥayᵊrtēn	'two lakes'

With other compensatory vocalizations [pp.31,166,167]:

ḥanye	'bow, bend'	+ -ēn →	ḥanitēn	'two bows, bends'
xaṭwe	'step, pace'	+ -ēn →	xaṭuṭēn	'two steps'
ḥāšye	'margin'	+ -ēn →	ḥāšītēn	'two margins'
zāwye	'corner'	+ -ēn →	zāwītēn	'two corners'
ṭāwle	'table'	+ -ēn →	ṭāwəltēn	'two tables'
məšᵊmše	'apricot'	+ -ēn →	məšməštēn	'two apricots'

With reduction of -iyye(t) to -īt- and -uwwe(t) to -ūt- [p.166]:

Ɛamaliyye	'operation'	+ -ēn →	Ɛamalītēn	'two operations'
hdiyye	'gift'	+ -ēn →	hdītēn	'two gifts'
ʔuwwe	'power'	+ -ēn →	ʔūtēn	'two powers'

Note also the following exceptional forms involving the
base-formative -e/-a: luġa 'language' + -ēn → luġatēn,
riʔa 'lung' + -ēn → riʔatēn 'two lungs', žiha 'direction'
+ -ēn → žihatēn or žīhtēn [cf.p.169]; mubārā 'match, competition' + -ēn → mubārāytēn, veranda 'balcony' + -ēn →
verandāytēn.

Nouns ending in the suffix -āt, e.g. ṣalāt 'prayer'
ʔadāt 'instrument', ḥayāt 'life', do not ordinarily have
duals.

Feminine nouns that have no -e/-a suffix in the absolute
(or non-suffixing) form but which have -t- in the suffixing
form [p.169] also have -t- in the dual: Ɛarūs 'bride' + -ēn
→ Ɛarūstēn, dəkkān 'shop' + -ēn → dəkkāntēn, Ɛēn 'eye' + -ēn
→ Ɛēntēn. (The forms Ɛēnēn 'eyes', ʔəžrēn 'feet', etc. are
used as plurals, not as duals [p.367].)

Stem-final *i* or *u* in nouns of Patterns *FaƐL* [p. 140] and *FəƐL* [142] become *y* or *w*, respectively, before *-ēn:*

Ɛədu	'member'	+ *-ēn* → *Ɛədwēn*	'two members'	
žaru	'pup, cub'	+ *-ēn* → *žarwēn*	'two cubs	
žədi	'kid' (goat)	+ *-ēn* → *žədyēn*	'two kids'	
raˀi	'opinion'	+ *-ēn* → *raˀyēn*	'two opinions'	
ṣabi	'boy'	+ *-ēn* → *ṣabyēn*[1]	'two boys'	

With most other nouns ending in a vowel, *-y-* is added before *-ēn;* and a vowel *a* or *i* is usually lengthened (giving *-āy-, -iyy-*):

kīlo	'kilogram'	+ *-ēn* → *kīloyēn*	'two kilograms'
məstašfa	'hospital'	+ *-ēn* → *məstašfāyēn*	'two hospitals'
šakwa	'complaint'	+ *-ēn* → *šakwāyēn*	'two complaints'
kərsi	'chair'	+ *-ēn* → *kərsiyyēn*	'two chairs'
wādi	'valley'	+ *-ēn* → *wādiyyēn*	'two valleys'
maƐna	'meaning'	+ *-ēn* → *maƐnāyēn*	'two meanings'
waṣi	'guardian'	+ *-ēn* → *waṣiyyēn*	'two guardians'
muddáƐi	'claimant'	+ *-ēn* → *muddaƐiyyēn*	'two claimants'

Some defective nouns of active participial patterns [258ff] tend to have only *-y-* (rather than *-iyy-*) before *-ēn: rāƐi* 'shepherd, keeper' + *-ēn* → *rāƐyēn* (or *rāƐiyyēn*, *muḥāmi* 'lawyer, defense attourney' + *-ēn* → *muḥāmyēn* (or *muḥāmiyyēn*). [Cf. p. 204 .]

PLURAL SUFFIXES (*al-žamƐ s-sālim*, Sound or External Plurals)

There are three suffixes used in forming noun plurals: *-īn, -e/-a*, and *-āt*.

Stem Modifications. Attachment of a plural suffix changes the form of certain kinds of noun base:

If the singular ends in the formative *-e/-a* [p. 138], this formative disappears when a plural suffix is added: *kəlme* 'word' + *-āt* → *kəlmāt*, *sāƐa* 'hour' + *-āt* → *sāƐāt*, *səne* 'year' + *-īn* → *snīn* [213].

---

[1]Note that *ṣabi* is in some respects treated as a defective noun on Pattern *FaƐīl* [p. 149]: the feminal derivative [304] is *ṣabiyye* 'girl' (not "*ṣabye*"). One may also sometimes hear *ṣabiyyēn* 'two boys', *ṣabīhon* 'their boy' (for *ṣabyēn, ṣabihon*).

If the singular of a defective [p.43] noun ends in $-a$, $-\bar{a}$, or $-\bar{a}t$, these endings are changed to $-aw-$ or $-ay-$ when a plural suffix is attached: *sama* 'sky' + $-\bar{a}t$ → *samawāt*, *banna* 'builder' + $-\bar{\imath}n$ → *bannayīn*, *mubārā* 'match, competition' + $-\bar{a}t$ → *mubārayāt*, *ṣalāṭ* 'prayer' + $-\bar{a}t$, → *ṣalawāt*. $-aw-$ is used if the noun's pattern is simple [46] and the final radical is w: *ʔadāt* 'device' + $-\bar{a}t$ → *ʔadawāt;* $-ay-$ is used otherwise: *wafāt* 'death, demise' + $-\bar{a}t$ → *wafayāt*, *muštašfa* + $-\bar{a}t$ → *mustašfayāt*.

If the singular ends in the formative $-i$ [p.281], this formative is lengthened to $-iyy-$ before a plural suffix: *ləbnāni* 'Lebanese' + $-\bar{\imath}n$ → *ləbnāniyyīn*, *ḥarāmi* 'thief' + $-e/-a$ → *ḥaramiyye*.
Miscellaneous other kinds of nouns ending in a vowel also generally add *y* before a plural suffix, in some cases with further modification of the base: *manṭo* 'coat' + $-\bar{a}t$ → *manṭoyāt*, *zəkra* 'remembrance' + $-\bar{a}t$ → *zəkriyāt*, *bəbbu* or *bēbē* 'baby' + $-\bar{a}t$ → *bəbbiyāt* or *bēbiyāt* (respectively). More rarely, *h* is used instead of *y* before the suffix: *māyō* 'bathing suit' + $-\bar{a}t$ → *māyohāt* (or *māyoyāt*).

Examples of irregular base modifications: *ɛazzābi* 'batchelor' + $-\bar{\imath}n$ → *ɛazzābīn;* *ɛarḍ* 'bid, offer' + $-\bar{a}t$ → *ɛrūḍāt;* *ʔəmm* 'mother' + $-\bar{a}t$ → *ʔəmmahāt* (but also regular *ʔəmmāt*); *rfīʔ* 'companion' + $-\bar{a}t$ → *rəfaʔāt* (but absolute form [p.455] also *rəfaʔa*); *ṭarīʔ* 'road, way' + $-\bar{a}t$ → *ṭərʔāt* (but also *ṭaroʔ*); *ʔaxx* 'brother' and *ʔəxt* 'sister' + $-\bar{a}t$ → *ʔəxwāt* 'brothers and/or sisters'.

As generally before suffixes beginning with a vowel [p.28], *e* or *o* before a stem-final consonant is dropped when a pluralizing suffix is added: *mɛallem* 'teacher' + $-\bar{\imath}n$ → *mɛallmīn*, *mnabbeh* 'alarm-clock' + $-\bar{a}t$ → *mnabbhāt*, *xānom* 'lady, miss' + $-\bar{a}t$ → *xānmāt*. There are certain classicisms, however, in which the vowel is not dropped, but is changed to *i* or *u* or *ə*: *kāʔen* 'being' + $-\bar{a}t$ → *kāʔināt*, *ṭaṣawwor* 'imagining, picturing' + $-\bar{a}t$ → *ṭaṣawwurāt* or *ṭaṣawwərāt*. (All Pattern *taFaɛɛoL* or *taFāɛoL* gerunds are like *ṭaṣawwor* in this respect.)
If *e* or *o* comes between like consonants the first of which is double, it is not dropped in any case, but is retained as *i* or *u*, or *ə* (or sometimes *a*): *mubarrer* 'justification, excuse' + $-\bar{a}t$ → *mubarrirāt* (or *mubarrarāt*) [p.29].

The Suffix $-\bar{\imath}n$ is used with certain kinds of augmented [p.46] nouns whose singular designates a male person. (The plural, however, may refer to a group including both sexes):

1.) With substantivized participles [p.276], excepting most of those on Pattern *FāɛeL* [131]:

Singular		Plural	Singular		Plural
mƐallem	'teacher'	.....*mƐallmīn*	*mulḥaq*	'attaché'	......*mulḥaqīn*
mwaẓẓaf	'employee'	....*mwaẓẓafīn*	*mhandes*	'engineer'	.....*mhandsīn*
mlākem	'boxer'	.......*mlākmīn*	*mtaržem*	'translator'	...*mtaržmīn*
məslem	'Moslem'	......*məsᵊlmīn*	*mandūb*	'delegate'	....*mandūbīn*

Most nouns of the simple active participial pattern
FāƐeL have internal plurals [p. 218]: *Ɛāmel* 'worker', pl.
Ɛəmmāl; ʔātel 'killer', pl. *ʔətala; ʔāḍi* 'judge', pl.
ʔəḍāt; ṣāḥeb 'friend', pl. *ṣḥāb*, etc. Some, however, have
plurals in *-īn*, either exclusively or in addition to an
external plural: *lāže ʔ* 'refugee', pl. *lāžʔīn;* in general,
the *-īn* plural with these bases is a sign of adjectival
[207] or "true participial" [265] use, as opposed to true
substantival use.

2.) With most occupational nouns of the pattern *FaƐƐāL* [p. 305] (but see
also *-e/-a*, (3), below):

nažžār	'carpenter'	...*nažžārīn*	*mallāk*	'proprietor'	...*mallākīn*
kazzāb	'liar'	........*kazzābīn*	*fallāḥ*	'peasant'	......*fallāḥīn*
ṭabbāx	'cook'	........*ṭabbāxīn*	*ṣayyād*	'hunter'	.......*ṣayyādīn*
xayyāṭ	'tailor'	......*xayyāṭīn*	*banna*	'builder'	......*bannāyīn*

The suffix *-īn* is also used with a few nouns of other
patterns: *səne* 'year', pl. *snīn; Ɛaduww* 'enemy', pl.
Ɛaduwwīn.

See also pseudo-dual *-ēn*, [p. 367].

The Suffix *-e/-a* is used for the plural:

1.) With nouns ending in the suffix *-ži* [p. 306]:

bōyaži	'bootblack'	...*bōyažiyye*	*ʔahwaži*	'coffeehouse keeper'. *ʔahwažiyye*
xəḍarži	'greengrocer'. *xəḍaržiyye*	*Ɛarbaži*	'carriage driver'	....*Ɛarbažiyye*
kəndarži	'cobbler'	.....*kəndaržiyye*	*ballorži*	'glass maker'	........*balloržiyye*

2.) With many nouns ending in the formative -*i* [p. 280], and a few ending in radical *i:*

ḥarāmi	'thief'.........*ḥaramiyye*	*ɛazzābi*	'batchelor'.....*ɛazzābiyye*
sankari	'tinsmith'......*sankariyye*	*frənsāwi*	'frenchman'.....*frənsawiyye*
bawāyki	'chandler'......*bawāykiyye*	*ləbnāni*	'Lebanese'......*ləbnāniyye*
taḥarri	'detective'.....*taḥarriyye*	*wāwi*	'jackal'........*wāwiyye*

Some of these may also have plural -*īn*: *frənsawiyyīn*, *ləbnāniyyīn*, *ɛazzābīn* [213], etc.

A few nouns have no -*i* in the singular, but have -*iyye* in the plural: .*əxtyār* 'old man', pl. *ʔəxtyāriyye*; *šofōr* 'chaffeur', pl. *šofōriyye*.

3.) With many occupational nouns of the pattern *FaƐƐāL* [p. 305]:

dahhāḥ	'painter'.......*dahhāne*	*ɛattāl*	'porter'........*ɛattāle*
sammān	'grocer'........*sammāne*	*baḥḥār*	'sailor'........*baḥḥāra*
farrāš	'bellboy'.......*farrāše*	*ṣarrāf*	'moneychanger'..*ṣarrāfe*

4.) With substantivized adjectives of the pattern *FaƐƐīL* [p. 129]:

šaġġīl	'(good) worker'..*šaġġīle*	*ballīf*	'bluffer'..........*ballīfe*
šarrīb	'heavy drinker'..*šarrībe*	*rakkīd*	'(good) runner'.....*rakkīde*

The Suffix -*āt* is the most common and productive of all noun pluralizers. It is regularly used with certain kinds of derivatives, and commonly also with other nouns of various patterns.

1.) With feminal derivatives [p. 304]:

Singular		Plural	(Derived from:)	
xāle	'(maternal)aunt'...........*xālāt*		*xāl*	'(maternal)uncle'
mɛallme	'(female) teacher'.........*mɛallmāt*		*mɛallem*	'(male)teacher'
ʔənglīziyye	'Englishwoman'............*ʔənglīziyyāt*		*ʔənglīzi*	'Englishman'
xayyāṭa	'seamstress, dressmaker'..*xayyāṭāt*		*xayyāṭ*	'tailor'
kalbe	'female dog, bitch'.......*kalbāt*		*kalb*	'dog'

The plural suffix -āt with human and animal designations
is by no means reserved for the female sex, however, Note
ʔabbāt 'fathers', xawāžāt 'gentlemen', ʔamiralāt 'admirals'
ʔəxwāt 'brothers and/or sisters', zbūnāt 'customers (male
and/or female)', etc. (The last example stands in spite of
the derivative zbūne '(female) customer' from zbūn '(male)
customer', and the alternative plural zabāyen.)

2.) With singulatives [p. 297]:

Singular		Plural	(Derived from:)	
təffāḥa	'an apple'.............	təffāḥāt	Collective təffāḥ	'apple(s)'
kūsāye	'a (zucchini) squash'..	kūsayāt	Collective kūsa	'squash'
žāže	'a chicken, a hen'.....	žāžāt	Collective žāž	'chicken(s)'
ḍarbe	'a blow, a stroke'.....	ḍarbāt	Gerund ḍarb	'hitting, striking'
ɛaṭṣa	'a sneeze'.............	ɛaṭṣāṭ	Gerund ɛaṭˀṣ	'sneezing'
maṭar	'a rain'..............	maṭarāt	Ger.(or Col.)maṭar	'rain'
nabāt	'a plant'.............	nabatāt	Ger.(or Col.)nabāt	'vegetation'
zyāra	'a visit'.............	zyārāt	Gerund zyāra	'visiting'

Some unit nouns also have internal plurals: warde 'a
flower', pl. wardāt or wrūd(e); ḥabbe 'a pill'; pl. ḥabbāt
or ḥbūb, etc. See p. 367.

3.) With concretized gerunds [p. 284] of Patterns III-X [293]:

		Singular	Plural	(Derived from:)	
Pat.	III	mġāmara	'venture, adventure'..mġāmarāt	tġāmar	'to venture'
	IV	ʔəɛlān	'announcement,notice'.ʔəɛlānāt	ʔaɛlan	'to announce'
	IV	ʔizāɛa	'broadcast'...........ʔizāɛāt	ʔazāɛ	'to broadcast'
	V	ṭaṣawwor	'visualization'.......ṭaṣawwarāt	ṭṣawwar	'to visualize'
	VI	tažāwoz	'passing, exceeding'..tažāwəzāt	tžāwaz	'to pass, exceed'
	VII	ʔansiḥāb	'retreat, withdrawal'.ʔansiḥābāt	nsaḥab	'to withdraw'
	VIII	ʔəxtirāɛ	'invention'...........ʔəxtirāɛāt	xtaraɛ	'to invent'
	X	ʔəstəsmār	'investment, profit'..ʔəstəsmārāt	stasmar	'to exploit, invest'

Plurals in -āt are also common with nouns of Gerundial Pattern II
(*taFƐīL*): *ţaşlīḥ* 'repair, correction', pl. *ţaşlīḥāt,* etc., but some have
internal plurals (Pattern *taFaƐīL* [p. 228]):   *tadbīr* 'preparation', pl.
tadabır.

4.) With inanimate nouns having any of the augmented participial
patterns [p. 134]:

Singular		Plural
mġallaf	'envelope'	.................*mġallafāt*
mnabbeh	'alarm clock'	.............*mnabbḥāt*
məşţálaḥ	'term, expression'	.........*məşţalaḥāt*
məntázah	'park'	...................*məntazahāt*
məstašfa	'hospital'	................*məstašfayāt*

5.) With hollow [p. 44] and geminate [p. 42] nouns having other patterns
with prefix *m* [pp. 153-156]:

Singular		Plural	Singular		Plural
mažāl	'space, room'	......*mažālāt*	*maţār*	'airport'	...........*maţārāţ*
mamarr	'passageway'	.......*mamarrāt*	*mḥaţţa*	'station'	...........*mḥaţţāţ*
mˀaşş	'scissors'	.........*mˀaşşāţ*	*mrāye*	'mirror'	............*mrāyāt*
maḍafe	'reception room'	...*maḍāfāţ*			

6.) With most nouns in a variety of other patterns, e.g. *FaƐaLe* [144],
FaƐāLe [146], *FaƐƐāLe* [152], *F(i)ƐāL(e)* [147], *F(u)ƐūLe* [151], *ƐiLa* [158],
etc.

wakāle	'agency'	..........*wakālāt*	*ˀyās*	'measurement'	.....*ˀyāsāt*
šahāde	'certificate'	.....*šahādāt*	*ḥsāb*	'account'	.........*ḥsābāt*
ḥkūme	'government'	......*ḥkūmāt*	*xzāne*	'closet, cupboard'	.*xzānāt*
sƐūbe	'difficulty'	......*sƐūbāt*	*wilāye*	'state'	...........*wilāyāt*
barake	'blessing'	........*barakāt*	*sayyāra*	'automobile'	......*sayyārāt*
ţabaˀa	'class, level'	....*ţabaˀāt*	*maḥḥāye*	'eraser'	.........*maḥḥāyāt*
sāƐa	'hour'	...........*sāƐāt*	*žiha*	'direction'	.......*žihāt*
ţābe	'ball'	...........*ţābāţ*	*şila*	'connection'	......*şilāt*

7.) With most nouns ending in -iyye:

Singular		Plural	Singular		Plural
Ɛamaliyye	'operation'	..*Ɛamaliyyāt*	*ḥanafiyye*	'faucet'	.......*ḥanafiyyāt*
žəmhuriyye	'republic'	...*žəmhuriyyāt*	*tamsiliyye*	'play, drama'	..*tamsiliyyāt*
kəlliyye	'college'	....*kəlliyyāt*	*niyye*	'aim, goal'	....*niyyāt*

Some nouns of the patterns *FaƐLiyye* and *FəƐLiyye*, however, have plurals of Pattern *FaƐāLi* [p.224], either exclusively or in addition to the external plural.

8.) With most modern foreign "loan-words" which do not fit the more
common noun patterns:

bābor	'steamship'	........*bāborāt*	*ʔotēl*	'hotel'	.......*ʔotēlāt*
ʔamirāl	'admiral'	..........*ʔamirālāt*	*xawāža*	'gentleman'	...*xawažāt*
ʔadrēs	'address'	..........*ʔadrēsāt*	*trēn*	'train'	.......*trēnāt*
bēbē	'baby'	.............*bēbiyāt*	*banṭalōn*	'trousers'	....*banṭalōnāt*
bəsʔklēt	'bicycle'	..........*bəsʔklētāt*	*bānyo*	'bathtub'	.....*bānyoyāt*

In addition to the types of nouns listed above, the plural suffix -āt
is used with many nouns of many other types. For example:

nahfe	'joke'	.............*nahfāt*	*ʔabb*	'father'	........*ʔabbāt*
marra	'a time'	...........*marrāt*	*ʔāgān*	'water heater'	..*ʔāganāt*
žāmƐa	'university'	........*žāmƐāt*	*bīkār*	'compass'	.......*bīkarāt*
buḥayra	'lake'	.............*buḥayrāt*	*təzkār*	'souvenir'	......*təzkārāt*
taržame	'translation'	.......*taržamāt*	*tayyār*	'current'	.......*tayyarāt*
kōme	'pile, heap'	........*kōmāt*	*ḥēwān*	'animal'	........*ḥēwānāt*
məƐžize	'miracle'	..........*məƐžizāt*	*sabaʔ*	'race'	.........*sabaʔāt*
ġāl	'lock'	.............*ġālāt*	*kāʔen*	'being'	........*kāʔināt*

INTERNAL PLURAL PATTERNS

(*al-ǧamɛ l-mukassar*, Broken or Internal Plurals)

A large proportions of Arabic nouns are pluralized by changing the base pattern, for example sg. *kalb* 'dog': pl. *klāb* 'dogs'; sg. *hdiyye* 'gift': pl. *hadāya* 'gifts'; sg. *ktāb* 'book': pl. *kətob* or *kətᵊb* 'books'.

There are many different pluralizing patterns. Some of them are used more or less exclusively for plurals (e.g. Patterns *FaɛoL*, as in *kətob*), while others are common also as singular patterns (e.g. Pattern *FɛāL*, as in pl. *klāb* 'dogs' and in sg. *ktāb* 'book').

In most cases it is not possible to deduce the plural pattern from the singular — or vice versa — with any high degree of certainty; the plurals of most nouns must be learned individually.

PATTERN *FɛāL*

Most nouns with this plural pattern have singular patterns *FaɛL*, *FəɛL*, or *FaɛaL*.

Singular		Plural	Singular		Plural
kaɛᵊb	'heel'	*kɛāb*	*kətᵊf*	'shoulder'	*ktāf*
ḍabᵊɛ	'hyena'	*ḍbāɛ*	*rəbᵊɛ*	'fourth, quarter'	*rbāɛ*
waʔᵊt	'time'	*wʔāt*	*kəbᵊš*	'ram'	*kbāš*
ṣōṭ	'voice, sound'	*ṣwāṭ*	*zərr*	'button'	*zrār*
tōr	'bull, ox'	*twār*	*sənn*	'tooth'	*snān*
raʔbe	'neck'	*rʔāb*	*kūɛ*	'elbow'	*kwāɛ*
ḍaffe	'bank, side'	*ḍfāf*	*kīs*	'bag'	*kyās*

Singular		Plural
walad	'children'	*wlād*
ʔalam	'pencil, pen'	*ʔlām*
ǧabal	'mountain'	*ǧbāl*
bāb	'door'	*bwāb*
waraʔ(a)	'paper, leaf' [p. 369]	*wrāʔ*
ṣāḥeb	'friend'	*ṣḥāb*
rəǧǧāl	'man'	*rǧāl*

Pattern *FɛāL* is not generally used for nouns with a final radical semivowel. Note, however, the modifications of this pattern in *ʔuḍāṭ* 'judges' (sg. *ʔāḍi*) and *ǵuzāt* 'conquerors' (sg. *ǵāzi*), and *ləḥe* (suf. form *ləḥā-*) 'beards' (sg. *ləḥye*). [Cf. p. 147.]

This pattern is not used for nouns with medial radical *y* whose singular is on Pattern *FaɛL* (e.g. *ṭēr* 'bird').

Colloquial plurals in *FɛāL* correspond to Classical Patterns *FiɛāL* and *ʔaFɛāL*. The latter, however, also occurs in Colloquial (see below).

PATTERN *ʔaFɛāL*

Almost all nouns with this plural have singular patterns *FaɛL*, *FəɛL*, or *FaɛaL*.

Singular		Plural	Singular		Plural
šaxṣ	'person'	*ʔašxāṣ*	*ḥəzb*	'(political) party'	*ʔaḥzāb*
waḍ³ɛ	'situation'	*ʔawḍāɛ*	*xabar*	'news'	*ʔaxbār*
səɛ³r	'price'	*ʔasɛār*	*sabab*	'cause'	*ʔasbāb*
žəz³ʔ	'part'	*ʔažzāʔ*	*ɛamal*	'work, deed'	*ʔaɛmāl*
māl	'wealth, property'	*ʔamwāl*	*ɛīd*	'holiday'	*ʔaɛyād*
ḥāl	'situation'	*ʔaḥwāl*	*žīl*	'generation'	*ʔažyāl*
lōn	'color'	*ʔalwān*	*nūr*	'light'	*ʔanwār*

Unlike Pattern *FɛāL* (above), Pattern *ʔaFɛāL* is used for some nouns that have a final radical semivowel, represented in this pattern by *ʔ*: *ʔaɛḍāʔ* members': sg. *ɛəḍu; ʔažwāʔ* 'atmosphere, air': sg. *žaww*. Note also *ʔasmāʔ* 'names': Root *s–m–y* but singular *ʔəs³m*. The plural of *šī* 'thing' is generally defective: *ʔašya* 'things' (but there is also the sound form *ʔašyāʔ* (and singular *šēʔ*).

Quite a few nouns have plurals that vacilate between *ʔaFɛāL* and *FɛāL*: *ʔawʔāt* or *wʔāt* 'times', *ʔaṣwāṭ* or *ṣwāṭ* 'voices, noises', etc. Pattern *ʔaFɛāL* in such cases sounds more "Classical", and *FɛāL*, more dialectal.

The word *yōm* 'day' has a classisizing plural *ʔayyām*, and the more colloquial *ʔiyyām* (which loses its *ʔ* after a numeral: *xamst iyyām* 'five days' [p. 171]).

The plural of *raʔi* 'opinion' is *ʔārāʔ*, and one plural of *bīr* 'well' is *ʔābār*. (The first *a* is lengthened, instead of there being *ʔ* or *y* before the second *ā*.)

PATTERN *FɛūL*

Most nouns of this pattern have singular patterns *FaɛL* or *Fəɛl.*

Singular	Plural	Singular	Plural
ʔaṣᵃl 'origin'....,...*ʔṣūl*		*kaff* 'glove'........*kfūf*	
žahᵃd 'effort'........*žhūd*		*xaṭṭ* 'line'.........*xṭūṭ*	
žəfᵃn 'eyelid'........*žfūn*		*xēṭ* 'thread'.......*xyūṭ*	
ʔərᵃš 'piastre'.......*ʔrūš*		*ɛēn* 'eye'.........*ɛyūn*	
damɛa 'tear'..........*dmūɛ*		*žēbe* 'pocket'.......*žyūb*	
malek 'king'..........*mlūk*			

This pattern is not used for nouns with final radical semivowels, nor with medial *w.* The noun *rās* 'head' has the hollow plural form *rūs* 'heads'. The singular of *wžūh* 'faces, surfaces', is generally pronounced *wəšš* in the sense 'face', though the classicising form *wažᵃh* is generally used for 'surface'.

The classicising Pattern *FuɛūL* is used for some nouns: *ḥuʔūʔ* 'rights' (sg. *ḥaʔʔ*), *žuyūš* 'armies' (sg. *žēš*), *ɛuṣūr* 'ages' (sg. *ɛaṣᵃr*).

PATTERN *FɛūLe*

Most nouns with this pattern have singular patterns *FaɛL* or *Fəɛl.* Most may also have the plural without *-e/-a: FɛūL.*

baṇk 'bank'.........*bnūk(e)*		*ward(e)* 'flower[ ].wrūd(e)*	
baḥᵃr 'sea'..........*bḥūr(a)*		*nəsᵃr* 'vulture'......*nsūr(a)*	
žəsᵃr 'bridge'.......*žsūr(a)*		*ḥall* 'solution'.....*ḥlūl(e)*	
ʔann 'chicken coop'.*ʔnūne*		*dīk* 'cock, rooster'.*dyūk(e)*	
məhᵃr 'colt'.........*mḥūra*		*tēs* 'billy goat'...*tyūs(e)*	

Like Pattern *FɛūL*, this pattern is not used with final radical semivowel or medial *w.*

On construct forms, see p. 164.

PATTERN $Fə\mathcal{E}L$

Nouns with this pattern have various singular patterns, especially Patterns $F(a)\mathcal{E}īL(e)$ and $F\mathcal{E}āL(e)$.

Singular		Plural	Singular		Plural
$ʔšāṭ$	'belt'	$ʔəšᵊt$	ḥaṣīre	'mat'	ḥəṣᵊr
lḥāf	'blanket'	ləḥᵊf	safīne	'ship'	səfᵊn
ktāb	'book'	kətᵊb	gdīš	'horse, nag'	gədᵊš
$\mathcal{E}aṣāye$	'stick, cane'	$\mathcal{E}əṣi$	zalame	'man'	zəlᵊm
$\mathcal{E}abāye$	'abaya'	$\mathcal{E}əbi$	walad	'children, descendant'	wəld

PATTERN $Fə\mathcal{E}oL$

Nouns with this pattern have various singular patterns, especially $F\mathcal{E}āL$ and $Fa\mathcal{E}īL(e)$:

bṣāṭ	'rug'	bəṣoṭ	ṭarīʔ	'road'	ṭaroʔ
ʔasās	'foundation'	ʔəsos	sabīl	'way'	səbol
niẓām	'system'	nəẓom	madīne	'city'	mədon
ktāb	'book'	kətob	rasūl	'apostle'	rəsol

Some nouns (e.g. ktāb 'book', safīne 'ship') vacilate between Patterns $Fə\mathcal{E}oL$ and $Fə\mathcal{E}L$ in the plural. With suffixes the difference between the two patterns disappears, since o is dropped or changed to ᵊ [p. 28].

PATTERN $Fə\mathcal{E}aL$

Most nouns with this pattern have singular pattern $Fə\mathcal{E}Le$:

nəʔṭa	'point'	nəʔaṭ	ḥīle	'trick'	ḥiyal
bərke	'pools'	bərak	līfe	'fiber brush'	liyaf
rətbe	'rank'	rətab	ṣūra	'picture'	ṣuwar
šəffe	'lip'	šəfaf	ʔūḍa	'room'	ʔuwaḍ

The first pattern vowel (ə) becomes i before y, and u before w and in certain classicisms: ʔumam 'nations' (sg. ʔumme).

This pattern is also used for some nouns (especially hollow ones) of singular pattern *FaƐLe:*

Singular		Plural	Singular		Plural
xēme	'tent'	*..........xiyam*	*šōke*	'fork'	*..........šuwak*
dawle	'nation, state'	*..duwal*	*šanta*	'bag, suitcase'	*..šənat*

PATTERN *FəƐaLa*

Nouns with this pattern designate human beings. Many are substantivized adjectives [Cf.p.206], and most have the singular pattern *F(a)ƐīL.*

šrīk	'partner'	*.......šəraka*	*faʔīr*	'poor, indigent'	*......fəʔara*
raʔīs	'chief, head'	*...rəʔasa*	*ʔadīb*	'literary scholar'	*....ʔədaba*
baxīl	'miser'	*.........bəxala*	*šāƐer*	'poet'	*...............šəƐara*
xabīr	'expert'	*........xəbara*	*Ɛālem*	'scholar, scientist'	*..Ɛəlama*
wazīr	'minister'	*......wəzara*			

Pattern *FəƐaLa* is not used with medial or final radical semivowel. Note, however, the form *mudara* 'directors' (sg. *mudīr,* root *d-w-r*).

PATTERNS *ʔəFƐoL, ʔaFƐoL*

Most nouns with these patterns have singular pattern *FaƐL.*

šah³r	'month'	*..........ʔəšhor, ʔašhor*	*saṭ³r*	'line'(of writing)	*...ʔəṣṭor*
sah³m	'share'(of stock)	*..ʔəshom, ʔashom*	*nafs*	'persons, selves'	*....ʔənfos*
nah³r	'river'	*..........ʔənhor, ʔanhor*	*drāƐ*	'cubits'	*.............ʔədroƐ*
ḥarf	'letter'	*..........ʔəḥrof, ʔaḥrof*	*lsān*	'tongue, talk'	*.......ʔəlson*
	(alphabet)				

The *ʔəFƐoL* forms (but not the *ʔaFƐoL* forms) commonly lose their initial *ʔ* after the numerals, and the numerals have connective *t: xamstᵤə́nhor* 'five rivers' (or *xams ʔənhor, xams ʔanhor*). The forms without *ʔ* (and with connective *t*) are obligatory after numerals for *ʔəšhor, ʔənfos,* and *ʔədroƐ.* See p.171.

PATTERNS *ʔəFᵊƐLe, ʔaFƐiLe*

Singular		Plural	Singular		Plural
rġīf	'loaf'..............	*ʔarᵊġfe*	*wisām*	'medal'.........	*ʔawsime*
ḥṣān	'horse'............	*ʔəhᵊṣne*	*niẓām*	'system'........	*ʔanẓime*
ṣahᵊr	'brother-in-law'...	*ʔaṣᵊhra*	*suʔāl*	'question'......	*ʔasʔile*
dawa	'medicine'.........	*ʔədᵊwye*	*dmāġ*	'brain'.........	*ʔadmiġa*
ḍaww	'light'............	*ʔəḍᵊwye*	*raṣīd*	'balance, re- mainder'......	*ʔarṣide*
ʔanāye	'irrigation ditch'.	*ʔəʔᵊnye*	*ʔimām*	'imam'..........	*ʔaʔimme*
hawa	'air, breeze'......	*ʔəhuye*	*šƐāƐ*	'ray'...........	*ʔašiƐƐa*

Note also: *ʔaṭəbba* or *ʔaṭabba* 'physicians' (sg. *ṭabīb*), *ʔadəlle* 'indications' (sg. *dalīl*).

Pattern *ʔaFƐiLe* is the classicising version of the more colloquial *ʔəFᵊƐLe*.

Some plurals of pattern *ʔəFᵊƐLe* lose their initial *ʔ* after numerals (with connective *t*) [p.171]; obligatorily in the case of *ʔarᵊġfe: xamstᵕᵊrᵊġfe* 'five loaves'; optionally for *ʔəhᵊṣne, ʔaṣᵊhra, ʔəžᵊhze* (pl. of *žihāz* 'set') *ʔəᵊṣfe* (pl. of *rṣīf* 'sidewalk').

On construct forms, see p.164.

PATTERN *FəƐƐāL*

Nouns with this pattern designate human beings; almost all have the singular pattern *FāƐeL*.

tāžer	'merchant'.........	*təžžār*	*zāyer*	'visitor'.........	*zuwwār*
Ɛāmel	'worker'...........	*Ɛəmmāl*	*nāʔeb*	'representative'..	*nuwwāb*
rākeb	'passenger'........	*rəkkāb*	*ḥāyek*	'weaver'..........	*ḥiyyāk*
ẓābeṭ	'officer'..........	*ẓəbbāṭ*	*sāyes*	'groom'...........	*siyyās*
ḥakam	'umpire'...........	*ḥəkkām*	*ḥažž,* *ḥažži*	'pilgrim'(Msl.)...	*ḥəžžāž*

The first pattern vowel (*ə*) becomes *u* before medial radical *w*, and *i* before *y*.

This pattern is not used with final radical semivowels.

PATTERN *FəɛLān*

Singular		Plural	Singular		Plural
?amīṣ	'shirt'	?əmṣān	gadaɛ	'brave fellow'	gədɛān
ṣabi	'boys'	ṣəbyān	žār	'neighbor'	žīrān
xalīž	'gulf'	xəlžān	fār(a)	'mouse'	fīrān
rāɛi	'shepherd'	rəɛyān	sāʸ	'leg'	sīʔān
rāheb	'monks'	rəhbān	ṣūṣ	'chick'	ṣīṣān
blād	'country'	bəldān	ġūl	'ghoul'	ġīlān, ġūlān
ġazāl	'gazelle'	ġəzlān	xēṭ	'thread'	xīṭān
wādi	'valley'	wədyān	hēṭ	'wall'	hīṭān

The first pattern vowel (*ə*) generally combines with a medial radical semivowel to produce *ī;* note, however, the form *ġūlān* (also *ġīlān*), and the shortened *i* in *hiṭān* (and optionally also in *xiṭān/xīṭān*).

The singular patterns of these nouns are various, but do not include sound patterns *Faɛl* and *Fəɛl*.

PATTERN *Faɛāli*

Most nouns with pattern have singular stem pattern *Faɛl* or *Fəɛl*, usually plus a suffix *-e/-a*, *-a*, *-āye*, or *-iyye*.

?arḍ	'land'	?arāḍi	šakwa	'complaint'	šakāwi
?ahᵊl	'family'	?ahāli	šanta	'suitcase'	šanāti
?əsᵊm	'name'	?asāmi	?əntāye	'female'	?anāti
lēl(e)	'night'	layāli	šamsiyye	'umbrella'	šamāsi
?ahwe	'cafe'	?ahāwi	barriyye	'desert, country'	barāri
?ərne	'corner, part'	?arāni	ṣədriyye	'vest'	ṣadāri
ɛərwe	'buttonhole'	ɛarāwi	ġənniyye	'song'	ġanāni
kəlwe	'kidney'	kalāwi			

Note also *maṣāri* 'money', whose singular *maṣriyye* is seldom used.

When the final radical is *y*, the last pattern vowel is *a* instead of *i*:

Singular		Plural	Singular		Plural
hdiyye	'gift'..........	*hadāyʌ*	*zāwye*	'corner'..........	*zawāya*
xaṭiyye	'sin'...........	*xaṭāyʌ*	*hayye*	'snake'..........	*hayāya*
ʔaḍiyye	'case'..........	*ʔaḍāya*	*žədi*	'kid'............	*žadāya*

The noun *ġənniyye* 'song', however, has the plural *ġanāni*, as if its root were *ġ-n-n* and its pattern *FaƐLiyye* (whereas its root is actually *ġ-n-y* and its pattern *FaƐƐīLe*.)

QUADRILITERAL-TYPE PLURAL PATTERNS

The true quadriradical patterns are *FaƐāLeL*, *FaƐāLLe*, and *FaƐaLīL*[1]. The pseudo-quadriradical patterns are *FaƐāyel*, *FawāƐeL*, *maFāƐeL*, *ʔaFāƐeL*, *FawaƐīL*, *FaƐaƐīL*, *maFaƐīL*, *taFaƐīL*, and *ʔaFaƐīL*.

All these patterns reduce to three (as represented by the true quadriradicals, or by the formulae $C_1 a C_2 \bar{a} C_3 e C_4$, $C_1 a C_2 \bar{a} C_3 C_4 e$, and $C_1 a C_2 a C_3 \bar{\imath} C_4$). In general, the pattern with *ī* in the last syllable is used for quadriradical or augmented triradical nouns which also have a long vowel before the last radical in the singular. The pattern with *e* in the last syllable is used for most other quadriradicals and other triradicals of several kinds.

PATTERN *FaƐāyeL*

Almost all nouns with this pattern have singulars with a long vowel before the last consonant and a short vowel or none at all before the middle consonant. The majority have the *-e/-a* suffix in the singular.

bḍāƐa	'merchandise'........	*baḍāyeƐ*	*Ɛ ažūz*	'old person'........	*Ɛažāyez*
xzāne	'closet'............	*xazāyen*	*fḍīḥa*	'scandal'..........	*faḍāyęh*
ḍfīre	'braid'.............	*ḍafāyer*	*natīže*	'result'...........	*natāyež*
knīse	'church'............	*kanāyes*	*sigāra*	'cigarette'.........	*sagāyer*
ḥaʔīʔa	'truth'.............	*ḥaʔāyeʔ*	*žnēne*	'garden'...........	*žanāyen*
xarīṭa	'map'...............	*xarāyeṭ*	*kənne*	'sister-in-law'......	*kanāyen*
zbūn	'customer'..........	*zabāyen*	*wāṣṭa*	'mediator'..........	*waṣāyeṭ*

This pattern is not used with medial or final radical semivowels.

---

[1]As in all the quadriradical formulae, the use of *L* to represent both the third and fourth radical does not mean they are the same.

PATTERN *Fawāƹeᴸ*

Most nouns with this pattern have singulars with a long vowel (usually *a*) after the first radical, and a short vowel or none at all after the second.

Singular		Plural	Singular		Plural
žāmeƹ	'mosque'	*žawāmeƹ*	*bāyke*	'sheepfold'	*bawāyek*
bāƹes	'motive'	*bawāƹes*	*žāyze*	'prize'	*žawāyez*
ḥāžeb	'eyebrow'	*ḥawāžeb*	*ṭāyfe*	'sect'	*ṭawāyef*
šāreƹ	'street'	*šawāreƹ*	*rīḥa*	'smell'	*rawāyeḥ*
bāxra	'steamship'	*bawāxer*	*ḥāšye*	'margin'	*ḥawāši*
ʔāƹde	'base'	*ʔawāƹed*	*xābye*	'jar'	*xawābi*
ḥādse	'accident'	*ḥawādes*	*ḍāḥye*	'outskirt, suburb'	*ḍawāḥi*
ʔādami	'nice person'	*ʔawādem*	*nādi*	'club'	*nawādi*
yāxūr	'stable'	*yawāxer*	*ʔamᵊr*	'order'	*ʔawāmer*

Geminate forms: *mawādd* 'materials' (sg. *mādde*), *ḥawāss* 'senses' (sg. *ḥāsse*), *dawābb* 'pack animals' (sg. *dābbe*), *ƹawāmm* 'masses' (sg. *ƹāmme*)

PATTERN *Fawaƹīᴸ* (and *Fawāƹīᴸ*)

Nouns with this pattern have singulars with long vowels after both the first and middle consonants.

xārūf	'lamb'	*xawarīf*	*bābōr*	'steamship'	*bawabīr*
šākūš	'hammer'	*šawakīš*	*māƹōn*	'container'	*mawāƹīn*
xāzūʔ	'stake, pole'	*xawazīʔ*	*tārīx*	'date'	*tawarīx*
ṭāḥūn	'mill'	*ṭawaḥīn*	*žākēt*	'jacket'	*žawākīt*
nāƹūra	'water-wheel'	*nawaƹīr*	*ḥēwān*	'animal'(fig.)[1]	*ḥawawīn*
ʔīwān	'sitting room'	*ʔawawīn*	*ṣārūx*	'rocket'	*ṣawārīx*

This pattern is not used with final radical semivowel.

---

[1] In the literal sense of 'animal', the plural *ḥēwānāt* is used; *ḥawawīn* is only used as a derrogatory term for people.

PATTERN *FaƐaƐīL* (and *FaƐāƐīL*)

Almost all nouns with this pattern have singulars with a long middle consonant followed by a long vowel.

Singular		Plural	Singular		Plural
tannūra	'skirt'	*tananīr*	*sənnāra*	'fish-hook'	*sananīr*
ḥammām	'bath'	*ḥamamīm*	*šəbbāk*	'window'	*šababīk*
dəkkān	'shop'	*dakakīn*	*ṣabbāṭ*	'pair of shoes'	*ṣababīṭ*
ẓənnār	'belt'	*ẓananīr*	*ṭarrāḥa*	'cushion'	*ṭararīḥ*
səkkīn	'knife'	*sakakīn*	*kabbūt*	'coat'	*kababīt*

This pattern is not used with final radical semivowel.

The plural *danānīr* 'dinars' is anomalous, since the singular *dīnār* has a long *ī*, not a long *n*.

The rare pattern *FaƐāƐeL* is found in *salālem* 'ladders', whose singular is *səllom* (also a rare pattern: *FəƐƐoL*).

PATTERN *maFāƐeL*

Most nouns with this pattern have singular pattern *maFƐaL(e)*.

mablaġ	'amount, sum'	*mabāleġ*	*madxane*	'chimney'	*madāxen*
maxbaz	'bakery'	*maxābez*	*mamša*	'corridor'	*mamāši*
madfaƐ	'cannon'	*madāfeƐ*	*maʔwa*	'shelter'	*maʔāwi*
maṭraḥ	'place'	*maṭāreḥ*	*mənxol*	'sifter, sieve'	*manāxel*
maƐlaʔa	'spoon'	*maƐāleʔ*	*mūsem*	'season'	*mawāsem*
maƐraka	'battle'	*maƐārek*	*mawhibe*	'talent'	*mawāheb*
masʔale	'matter'	*masāʔel*	*məkwāye*	'(flat) iron'	*makāwi*
maṣlaḥa	'interest'	*maṣāleḥ*	*məṣlāye*	'trap'	*maṣāli*

A number of nouns with this pattern have no singular: *malāmeḥ* '(facial) expression', *mašāhel* 'unknown regions', *maƐālem* 'salient features', *manāfeƐ* 'utilities', *maxāwef* 'fears', *maḥāsen* 'advantages', etc. Note also *mašāyex* 'sheikhs' (cf. sg. *šēx*, regular pl. *šuyūx*).

PATTERN *maFaɛīL* (and *maFāɛīL*)

Most nouns with this pattern have singular patterns *maFɛūL, moFɛāL.*

Singular	Plural	Singular	Plural
maktūb 'letter'	*makatīb*	*maftāh* 'key'	*mafatīh*
mašrūɛ 'project'	*mašarīɛ*	*məhrāt* 'plow'	*mašrūɛ*
maṣrūf 'expenditure'	*maṣarīf*	*məzrāb* 'gutter'	*mazarīb*
mawḍūɛ 'topic'	*mawaḍīɛ*	*məxtār* 'elder'	*maxatīr*

mīɛād 'appointment' .....*mawaɛīd*

mīzān 'scale balance'...*mawazīn* or *mayazīn*

PATTERN *taFaɛīL*

Nouns with this pattern have singulars of the patterns *taFɛīL* or *təFɛāL.*

Singular	Plural
tadbīr 'arrangement, preparation'	*tadabīr*
taṣrīh 'declaration'	*taṣarīh*
taqrīr 'report'	*taqarīr*
taṣmīm 'design'	*taṣamīm*
təmsāl 'statue'	*tamasīl*

PATTERNS *ʔaFāɛeL* and *ʔaFāɛīL*

ḍəfʔr	'(finger)nail'	*ʔaḍāfer*
swāra	'bracelet'	*ʔasāwer*
waɛa	'garment'	*ʔawāɛi* 'clothes'
brīʔ	'jug'	*ʔabarīʔ*
sbūɛ	'week'	*ʔasābīɛ*

Note, however, that *ʔabarīʔ* and *ʔasābīɛ* would be considered quadriliteral pattern *FaɛaLīL* if compared with the singular forms *ʔəsbūɛ, ʔəbrīʔ.*

PATTERN *FaƐāLeL*

Most nouns with this pattern have singular Patterns *FaƐLaL*, *FaƐLaLe*, *FəƐLoL*, or *FəƐ ᵊLLe*.

Singular		Plural	Singular		Plural
ʔarnab	'rabbit'...........	ʔarāneb	Ɛənṣor	'element'..........	Ɛanāṣer
xanžar	'daggar'...........	xanāžer	ʔənfod	'hedgehog'.........	ʔanāfed
daftar	'notebook'.........	dafāter	qanṣol	'consul'...........	qanāṣel
šaršaf	'sheet'............	šarāšef	falfol	'pepper' [p. 368]....	falāfel
tazkara	'ticket'...........	tazāker	dəfdaƐa	'frog'.............	dafādeƐ
ṭanžara	'pot'..............	ṭanāžer	zəlᵊḥfe	'tortoise'.........	zalāḥef
ʔarmal(e)	'widow(er)'........	ʔarāmel	žəmᵊžme	'skull'............	žamāžem
bēdar	'threshing floor'..	bayāder	kərsi	'chair'............	karāsi
fəršāye	'brush'............	farāši	ʔaṣbaƐa	'finger'...........	ʔaṣābeƐ

Note also *barāmež* 'programs', whose five-consonant singular *bərnāmež* loses its third radical in the plural.

PATTERN *FaƐāLLe*

(Pattern *FaƐāLLe* consists of *FaƐāLeL* plus the *-e/-a* suffix [p. 28]).

This pattern is used only with certain nouns designating human beings. The singular patterns are various.

Singular		Plural
doktōr	'doctor'.....................	dakātra
ʔəstāz	'professor, teacher'.........	ʔasātze
təržmān	'interpreter-guide'..........	tarāžme
ġandūr	'dandy'......................	ġanādra
bērūti	'Beiruti'....................	bayārte
dimašqi	'Damascene'..................	damāšqa
mārūni	'Maronite'...................	mawārne

Singular		Plural	
fōʔāni	'upper'...............	*fawāʔne*	'people living upstairs'
taḥtāni	'lower'......................	*taḥātne*	'people living downstairs'
xūri	'priest'....................	*xawārne*	
ʔasʔof	'bishop'....................	*ʔasāʔfe*	
baṭrak	'patriarch'.................	*baṭārke*	
maṭrān	'metropolitan, archbishop'....	*maṭārne*	

Note that *xūri* 'priest' takes on another consonant *(n)* in the plural, while *tərǧmān* 'dragoman' loses its ending *-ān*.

Note that the plural *malāyke* 'angels' (sg. *malak* or *malāk*) fits this pattern, but since its root (theoretically, at least) is *l-ʔ-k,* the plural pattern would have to be analyzed as *maFāƐLe*. (In any case the forms of this word are anomalous in one way or another).

On construct forms, see p. 164.

PATTERN *FaƐaLīL*

Almost all nouns with this pattern have a singular pattern with a long vowel before the last consonant.

Singular		Plural	Singular		Plural
ṣarṣūr	'cricket'..........	*ṣaraṣīr*	*bəstān*	'garden'.....	*basatīn*
barġūt	'flea'.............	*baraġīt*	*barmīl*	'barrel'.....	*baramīl*
dastūr	'constitution'.....	*dasatīr.*	*Ɛəfrīt, Ɛafrīt*	'demon'.......	*Ɛafarīt*
sandūʔ	'box, chest'.......	*sanadīʔ*	*təlmīz*	'student'....	*talamīz*
Ɛaṣfūr	'bird'.............	*Ɛaṣafīr*	*ǧardōn*	'rat'........	*ǧaradīn*
Ɛənwān	'address'..........	*Ɛanawīn*	*balkōn*	'balcony'....	*balakīn*
fənǧān	'cup'..............	*fanaǧīn*	*šēṭān*	'devil'.......	*šayaṭīn*
kərbāǧ	'whip'.............	*karabīǧ*	*bərnēṭa*	'hat'........	*baranīṭ*
rəsmāl	'capital'[ ]...	*rasamīl*	*nišān*	'medal'......	*nayašīn*

Some nouns have a long second *a* (usually optional): *basātīn* 'gardens', *fanāǧīn* 'cups', *šayāṭīn* 'devils'.

Note also the optional forms *ʔaṣābīᵉ (/ʔaṣābeᵉ)* 'fingers' (sg. *ʔəṣbaᵉ* or *ʔəṣbaᵉa), baranīṣ (/barāneṣ)* 'burnoose, bathrobe' (sg. *bərnoṣ*).

This pattern is not used with final radical semivowel (see Pattern *FaᵉāLeL*, above).

UNCOMMON PATTERNS

Pattern *FaᵉīL:* *ḥamīr* 'donkeys' (sg. *ḥmār*), *ᵉabīd* 'slaves' (sg. *ᵉabd*)

Pattern *FāᵉāL (F = ʔ):* *ʔādāb* 'culture, arts' (sg. *ʔadab*), *ʔāfāʔ* 'horizons' (sg. *ʔəfəʔ*), *ʔālāf* 'thousands' (sg. *ʔalf*), *ʔāmāl* 'hopes' (sg. *ʔamal*)

Pattern *FᵉāLe:* *fᵉāle* 'laborer' (sg. *fāᵉel*), *byāra* 'wells' (sg. *bīr*)

Pattern *FᵉuLāt:* *ršūḥāt* 'colds' (sg. *rašºḥ*), *wṣūlāt* 'receipts' (sg. *waṣºl*), *lḥūmāt* 'meat hors-d'oeuvres' (no sing.)

CHAPTER 9: VERB DERIVATION

Index of Categories[1]

    Not all of these categories are equally clear-cut. While some (e.g. causative) include many verbs showing a high degree of semantic and syntactic consistency among themselves, others (e.g. eductive) encompass relatively wide deviations from the norm. (See p. 49 ff.)

    There are, furthermore, many augmented verbs whose meanings do not allow for inclusion in any of the derivational categories.

---

[1] These categories are related to one another in several dimensions and degrees. The structure of this system is not made explicit here, but may be inferred from the way some of the categories are defined and described relative to others.

PASSIVE VERBS

In this book the term 'passive' is used to subsume both the true passive and the mediopassive. On the distinction between these two categories, see p. 238.

Formation

The passive of simple triradical verbs is most commonly formed on Pattern VII *(nFaɛaL)* [p. 91]:

Active			Passive	
ġalab	'to beat, win'	......	*nġalab*	'to be beaten, to lose'
səmeɛ	'to hear'	....	*nsamaɛ*	'to be heard'
šāf	'to see'	....	*nšāf*	'to be seen'
ɛaṣa	'to disobey'	....	*nɛaṣa*	'to be disobeyed'

Pattern VIII *(Ftaɛal)* [95] forms the passive of quite a few simple verbs.

rata	'to mend'	....	*rtata*	'to be mended'
naʔal	'to transfer'	....	*ntaʔal*	'to be transferred, to move'
nəsi	'to forget'	....	*ntₐasa*	'to be forgotten'

For true passives, Pattern VIII is most often used with initial radical *n* or *r;* for mediopassives, it is used regardless of the initial radical: *xtanaʔ* 'to choke' (intrans.), from *xanaʔ* 'to choke' (trans.).

Some active verbs of Patterns *Faɛal, byəFɛeL* [p. 57] or *Faɛal, byəFɛoL* [55] have passives on the pattern *Fəɛel, byəFɛaL* [71]:[1]

ʔatal, byəʔtol	'to kill'	....	*ʔətel, byəʔtal*	'to be killed'	
taɛab, byətɛeb	'to tire' (trans.)	....	*təɛeb, byətɛab*	'to get tired'	
raḍa, byərḍi	'to please, satisfy'	.....	*rəḍi, byərḍa*	'to be pleased, satisfied'	

---

[1] In the case of *ʔətel, byəʔtal* 'to be killed', this colloquial pattern corresponds to a true internal passive in Classical Arabic: *qutila, yuqtalu.* (Note also the "impersonal" passive *ġəmi ɛalē* 'he's fainted': Cl. *ġumiya ɛalayhi.*) Most of these colloquial passives, however, correspond to Classical verbs of Pattern *Faɛila, yaFɛaLu.*

The passives of Pattern II(*FaƐƐaL*), Pattern III(*FāƐaL*), quadriradical (*FaƐLaL*), and pseudo-quadriradical verbs is formed by prefixation of *t* [p. 85] resulting in verbs of Patterns V(*tFaƐƐaL*) [86], VI(*tFāƐaL*) [88], *tFaƐLaL* [121], etc.:

Active		Passive	
kannas	'to sweep'	*tkannas*	'to be swept'
ʔāṣaṣ	'to punish'	*tʔāṣaṣ*	'to be punished'
taržam	'to translate'	*ttaržam*	'to be translated'
sōdan	'to depress'	*tsōdan*	'to be depressed'

The irregular initial-weak verbs *ʔakal* 'to eat' and *ʔaxad* 'to take' [p. 56] have passives formed on Pattern VI: *ttākal* 'to be eaten', *ttāxad* 'to be taken' [90].[1] (Regular Pattern VII forms *nʔakal* and *nʔaxad* also exist.)

Generally speaking, active verbs that are formed on Patterns IV through X have no passives (except in their participles [p. 260]).

A few augmented verbs have passives formed on Pattern VII or VIII: *štara* 'to buy' → *nšara* 'to be bought'; *sawwa* 'to cook, do' → *stawa* 'to be cooked, done'.

The verb *ntala* 'to get full, be filled' is generally considered an irregular Pattern VIII passive of *malla* 'to fill', with *n* in place of the initial radical *m*. (But note that some speakers have an active verb *talla* 'to fill' [Bart. 92], in view of which *ntala* would belong to Pattern VII.)

Occasionally passives are improvised by changing the stem vowels as in the Classical passive inflection (perfect *a...a* → *u...ə*; impf. *ə...e/o* → *u...a*): *nuqəlt mən yōmēn* 'I was transferred two days ago' (Cf. the more colloquial *ntaʔalt...* 'I was transferred...' or 'I moved...'). *l-mara ʔəla ħaʔʔ ʔənn təntə́xeb u-tuntə́xab* [SAL-154] 'Women have the right to elect and to be elected.' The Classical internal passive is also used in certain set phrases, e.g. *Ɛala ma yurām* 'as (well as could possibly be) desired'.

---

[1] These verbs are sometimes said to be formed on Pattern VIII, or on a hybrid of Patterns VI and VIII. Note, however, that *ʔaxad* already has a (Classicizing) Pattern VIII derivative *ttaxaz* [p. 252]. (Cf. also the initial-weak Pattern VIII verb *ttakal* 'to rely', whose root, however, is *w-k-l* not *ʔ-k-l*.) The verb *ttākal* has a sound doublet *tʔākal* 'to be eaten away, corroded'.

The True Passive

The subject of a true passive verb corresponds to the object of its underlying active verb:

Active	Passive
n-nādi r-riyādi ǧalab farīʔna	*farīʔna nǧalab*
'The Athletic Club beat our team'	'Our team was beaten'
mā ḥada bisaddeʔ hal-ʔəṣṣa	*hal-ʔəṣṣa mā btətsaddaʔ*
'No one would believe that story'	'That story is unbelievable'
bətšūf ᵊl-balad ši mən rās *ᵊž-žabal?*	*l-balad btənšāf ši mən rās* *ᵊž-žabal?*
'Can you see the town from the top of the mountain?'	'Is the town visible from the top of the mountain?'

The true passive construction in Arabic does not — as a general rule — include an agentive phrase. If the agent is to be named at all, it should be as subject of the active verb. To achieve an effect similar to that of the English sentence 'Our team was beaten by the Athletic Club', the Arabic object may be extraposed [p. 431] and the verb and subject inverted [432]: *farīʔna ǧalabo n-nādi r-riyādi* "Our team, the Athletic Club beat it".

There are some exceptions, however, whereby an agentive phrase with *mən* [p. 239] is used with what seems to be a true passive: *l-ʔəttifāʔiyye lāzem tətsaddaʔ mən mažles* *ᵊš-šuyūx* 'The treaty has to be ratified by the senate'. These cases may perhaps be due to the extensive loss of contrast in modern Arabic between true passive and mediopassive (with which agentive phrases are often used), and perhaps in part due to the effect of journalistic translations from other languages. (Agentive phrases with *mən qəbal* or *mən ṭaraf* 'by' may be used more broadly than the simple preposition *mən*, but such usage is limited to a rather pedantic classicising style, and is not often heard in ordinary conversation.)

While an agentive phrase is not normally used in the true passive construction, nevertheless the true passive — unlike the mediopassive — implies that there ·is an external causative agent involved in the event referred to, though that agent may be unknown (*maǧhūl*).

The Impersonal Passive. In Arabic as in English, an intransitive verb, or a transitive verb with its object suppressed, is sometimes[1] converted to passive, provided it has a prepositional complement:

Active	Passive
mā ḥada nām b-hat-taxᵊt .... 'Nobody has slept in this bed'	*mā nnām b-hat-taxᵊt* 'This bed hasn't been slept in'
ṣəfi šī nⁱāmen fī? .... 'Is there anything left we can believe in?'	*ṣəfi šī yətⁱāman fī?* 'Is there anything left to be- lieve in? (i.e. '...to be be- lieved in?')
mā ḥada byəhrob mən has-səžᵊn .. 'Nobody escapes from that prison'	*ma byənhə́reb mən .has-səžᵊn* 'That prison cannot be escaped from'
dafaɛnā-lak 'We've paid you' ...	*ndafaɛ-lak* 'You've been paid' (lit. "There has been paid to you")

In Arabic, if the active verb has no object, then its passive has no subject, and remains always in the third-person masculine/singular. This subjectless, or **IMPERSONAL**, passive is quite unlike the English construction, in which the prepositional complement of an active verb corresponds to the subject of its passive.

One should not be misled by the impersonal passive with extraposed [p.433] prepositional complement. In the translation of 'These beds haven't been slept in' as *hat-txūt mā nnām fīha*, note that *txūt* is not the subject of *nnām*, but rather the antecedent of *-ha:* "These beds, there has not been slept in them". Further examples with extraposed complement:

hat-ṭanžara mā bəṭbox fīha ..... 'This pot I don't cook in'	*hat-ṭanžara mā byənṭə́bex fīha* 'This pot is not to cook in'
has-suⁱālāt mā žāwabt ɛalēha ... 'These questions, you haven't answered'	*has-suⁱālāt mā džāwab ɛalēha* 'These questions haven't been answered'
šū l-ⁱālāt yalli ɛam-idəⁱⁱu fīha? .... 'What are the instruments they are playing (on)?'	*šū l-ⁱālāt yalli ɛam-yənda?? fīha?* 'What are the instruments being played (on)?'

---

[1] As in English, some prepositionally complemented verbs are commonly converted to passive, while others are not. As with all derivational categories, the question whether or not a theoretically possible derivative is actually used is largely a matter of lexical idiosyncracy.

The Mediopassive

As distinct from the true passive, the mediopassive does not imply an external causative agent. If an active verb means '(X) does Y to (Z)', then its mediopassive derivative means '(Z) undergoes Y', but an external agent X is not implied (nor is it ruled out).

Active	Mediopassive
ṣəffhon 'Line them up!'	*ṣtaffu* (or *nṣaffu*) 'Line up!'
ḥammamti l-ᵊwlād wəlla ləssa? ... 'Have you bathed the children yet?'	*l-ᵊwlād thammamu wəlla ləssa?* 'Have the children had their baths yet?'
d-doktōr manaƐo Ɛan ʔakl ᵊl-laḥᵊm .... 'The doctor forbade his eating meat'	*Ɛam-yəmtə́neƐ Ɛan ʔakl ᵊl-laḥᵊm* 'He's abstaining from eating meat'

No grammatical distinction is made in Arabic verbs between "reflexive" acts and spontaneous developments — what one does to one's self and what simply happens to one are equally accomodated by the mediopassive: *tƐallam* 'to learn' (spontaneously or by self-instruction, or — as a true passive — 'to be taught'); *thammam* 'to have a bath' ('to bathe one's self' or as a true passive, 'to be bathed').

> The mediopassive derivation is the converse of the causative [p. 240]: an active verb is to its mediopassive as a causative is to the verb underlying it. In the case of correlative pairs like *sawwa* 'to cook, do' and *stawa* 'to be cooked, done' [p. 51], it is impossible to distinguish between the two types of relationship, since both verbs are singly augmented. Similarly, both of the pair *taƐab* 'to tire' (trans.) and *təƐeb* 'to get tired' are simple: if *taƐab* is counted as primary, then *təƐeb* is its mediopassive, but if *təƐeb* is primary, then *taƐab* is its causative.

The distinction between mediopassive and true passive is formally expressed — in relatively few cases — in the contrast between Pattern VIII (for mediopassive) and Pattern VII (for true passive):

Mediopassive		True Passive	
štamaƐ	'to meet, get together' ..	*nšamaƐ*	'to be brought together'
mtanaƐ	'to abstain' (from...) ...	*nmanaƐ*	'to be prevented' (from...)
mtadd	'to extend, stretch' ..... (intrans.)	*nmadd*	'to be extended, stretched'

rtafa£ 'to rise, be high up' .... *nrafa£* 'to be raised'

štaġal 'to work' .... *nšaġal* 'to be made busy'

Of the fairly numerous pairs of Pattern VII and VIII verbs, however, most do not actually contrast as true passive to mediopassive. Compare, for instance, *nkasa* and *ktasa*, both of which (for many speakers, at least) mean either 'to be clothed, outfitted' (by someone), or 'to clothe, outfit one's self'; or *nhara* and *htara*, both meaning either 'to be worn out' (by something), or 'to wear out' (by its own action).

Even some of the five pairs listed above are not always used in a clearcut contrastive way. *nmadd*, for instance, can be used in a mediopassive sense, and *rtafa£*, in a true passive sense; while *štaġal* in commonly construed as a primary active verb, and *nšaġal* as a mediopassive.

Unlike true passives, some mediopassive verbs are transitive, their underlying active verbs being doubly transitive:

Active	Mediopassive
mīn £allamak £arabi?	*mnēn t£allamt £arabi?*
'Who taught you Arabic?'	'How did you learn Arabic?'
žawwazū banthon	*džawwaz banthon*
'They gave him their daughter in marriage'	'He married their daughter'
nāwalni š-šanta	*tnāwalt ᵊš-šanta*
'He handed (or passed) me the bag'	'I took (or reached) the bag'

Likewise in contrast to true passives, many mediopassives take a prepositional complement with *man* [p.478] or *b-* [479], which may be construed as an agentive phrase, corresponding to the subject of the underlying active verb:

l-bank dayyanni maṣāri	*ddayyant maṣāri mn ᵊl-bank*
'The bank lent me money'	'I borrowed money from the bank'
laṭāfto ʔassaratni ktīr	*tʔassart ᵊktīr man laṭāfto*
'His kindness touched me deeply'	'I was deeply touched by his kindness'
ʔaxti £adatni bal-ᵊhmēra	*n£adēt bal-ᵊhmēra man ʔaxti*
'My sister infected me with the measles'	'I caught the measles from my sister'
hal-ᵊhsābāt £am-tašġalni ktīr ..	*£am-ʔanšáġel ᵊktīr b-hal-ᵊhsābāt*
'These accounts are keeping me quite busy'	'I'm being kept quite busy with these accounts'

Some mediopassive verbs, like *štaǵal* in *Ɛam-ʔəštǽǵel*
ᵊktīr b-hal-ᵊḥsābāt 'I'm working hard on these accounts',
are idiomatically specialized in a "reflexive" sense; i.e.
the causative agency is conceived always as inhering in
the subject-referent (in this case, the worker), while the
referent of the prepositional complement (the accounts)
enters the picture as a mere recipient of the "action".
Thus *štaǵal* is just as much an "active" verb as the English
verb 'to work', despite its derivational status as a mediopassive.

Most passive verbs can be interpreted either as mediopassive or as true
passive, depending on the context and circumstances in which the verb is
used: *tḥammam* 'to bathe one's self' (adult), or 'to be bathed' (baby);
nṣaraf 'to get out' (e.g. of school) or 'to be let out...'; *tʔaxxar* 'to
delay' (intrans.) or 'to be delayed'.

CAUSATIVE VERBS

The Causative derivation is usually expressed with Pattern II *(FaƐƐaL)*
[p. 77]; rarely (in Colloquial) with Pattern IV [82] or Pattern I*(a–e)*
[63] or others [243].

Most causatives are derived from simple verbs. If the simple verb
means 'X happens', then its causative means '(Y) makes X happen' (or
'...lets X happen', or '...has X happen'). Examples:

Underlying Verb		Causative	
nəzel	'to descend, go down' ..	*nazzal*	'to take down, bring down'
nām	'to go to sleep'	*nayyam*	'to put to sleep'
ʔaƐad	'to sit'	*ʔaƐƐad*	'to seat'
ẓəher	'to appear'	*ʔaẓhar*	'to reveal'
dār, bidūr	'to turn' (intrans.) ...	*dār, bidīr*	'to turn' (trans.)

The causative, it may be noted, is the converse of the
mediopassive derivation. See p. 238.

If a simple verb is transitive, then its causative is <u>doubly</u> transitive
— the first object [p. 438] corresponding to the subject of the simple verb:

Underlying	Causative
ʔabna katab maktūb .... 'Her son wrote a letter'	*l-ʔəmm kattabet ʔəbna maktūb.* 'The mother had her son write a letter'
rah-nəsmaɛ ᵊl-ʔaṣtwāne ž-ždīde 'We're going to hear the new recording'	*rah-isamməɛna l-ʔaṣtwāne ž-ždīde* · 'He's going to let us hear the new recording'
d-daktōr bəddo yšūf žərḥak ..... 'The doctor wants to see your wound'	*šawwef ᵊd-daktōr žərḥak* 'Let the doctor see your wound'
ʔabūk bəddo yəsmaɛ darsak ...... 'Your father wants to hear (you recite) your lesson'	*sammeɛ ʔabūk darsak.* 'Let your father hear (you recite) your lesson'

In some cases — as in the last two examples — the first object of the causative may be replaced by a *la-* phrase and put after the remaining object: *šawwef žərḥak ləd-daktōr* 'Show your wound to the doctor', *sammeɛ darsak la-ʔabūk* 'Recite your lesson for your father'. The use of a prepositional complement with a causative in lieu of a first object generally implies a certain idiomatic specialization with respect to the underlying simple verb: *sammaɛ* meaning 'to recite', *kattab* meaning 'to dictate', etc. *ɛarraf* 'to introduce' is idiomatically derived from *ɛeref* 'to (come to) know' and is never used with two objects, but always with a prepositional complement: *bəddi ɛarrfak ɛala ṣāḥbi...* 'I want to introduce you to my friend...'.

Further examples of causative constructions:

byəfham ʔaxūk šū lāzem yaɛmel? . 'Does your brother under- stand what he's supposed to do?'	*fahhem ʔaxūk šū lāzem yaɛmel.* 'Explain to your brother what he's supposed to do.'
hal-walad lē mū lābes kanze? ... 'Why isn't that child wearing a sweater?' [Act. Part., p.]	*lē mū mlabbse hal-walad kanze?* 'Why haven't you (f.) (or hasn't she) put a sweater on that child?'
ʔaxū ḥamal hamm ᵊwlādo .... 'His brother took on the care of his children'	*ḥammal ʔaxū hamm ᵊwlādo.* 'He saddled his brother with the care of his children'
l-wāḥed bidīɛ mən kətret *ᵊl-laff wəd-dawarān* .... 'One gets lost with so much turning and circling.'	*kətret ᵊl-laff wəd-dawarān* *bidayyeɛ.* 'So much turning and circling gets one lost' [On suppression of object, see p. 328.]

Further examples of the causative derivation:

Underlying Verb		Causative	
wəṣel	'to arrive'	waṣṣal	'to take' (someone some-where)
raʔaṣ	'to dance'	raʔʔaṣ	'to make...dance'
fāʔ	'to wake up' (intrans.) ...	fayyaʔ	'to wake' (someone)
dāx	'to get dizzy, nauseated' .	dawwax	'to make...dizzy, to nauseate'
šamm	'to smell'(trans.)	šammam	'to have(someone) smell'
ʔara	'to read'	ʔarra	'to have(someone) read'

Some caustatives are derived from adjectives: ʔawwa 'to strengthen' from ʔawi 'strong'; though in most cases these adjectives also have inchoative [p. 250] or descriptive [251] verbs from which the causative might also be said to be derived: ʔəwi 'to become strong' → ʔawwa 'to strengthen'.

xafīf	'light'	xaffaf	'to lighten'
bɛīd	'far away'	baɛɛad	'to remove, banish'
ṣaḥīḥ	'correct'	ṣaḥḥaḥ	'to correct'
ʔabyaḍ	'white'	bayyaḍ	'to whiten'
ʔaswad	'black'	sawwad	'to blacken'

Examples of causatives formed on patterns other than II:

Pattern IV

ẓeher	'to appear'	ʔaẓhar	'to reveal'
təlef	'to perish'	ʔatlaf	'to destroy'
ġani	'rich'	ʔaġna	'to make...rich'

Pattern I(a–e)

dār, bidūr	'to turn'(intrans.) .	dār, bidīr	'to turn'(trans.)
ʔām, biʔūm	'to get up'	ʔām, biʔīm	'to raise, remove'
dām, bidūm	'to last'	dām, bidīm	'to make...last'
ʔaɛma	'blind'	ɛama, byəɛmi	'to blind'

Underlying Word			Causative	

Pattern *FaɛLan:*

həlu	'sweet'	*halwan*	'to sweeten'
ʔaxraṣ	'mute'	*xarṣan*	'to shut(someone)up'

Others:

ṭəleɛ	'to come up, out' ...	*ṭālaɛ*	'to bring up, out (Pat. III),
		or *ṭaylaɛ*	(Lebanese)
raʔaṣ	'to dance'	*raʔwaṣ*	'to make dance, jiggle'
		(Pat. *FaɛwaL*),	cf. *raʔʔaṣ,* above.

ASCRIPTIVE VERBS

Ascriptive verbs, formed mainly on Pattern II, are derived from various kinds of words.

If the underlying word means 'X', or 'to do X', then the ascriptive verb means 'to impute or attribute X to...', or 'to treat...as X, or as having done X'.

Underlying Word			Ascriptive	
xān	'to betray'	*xawwan*	'to brand as a traitor'
byəšbah	'to resemble'	*šabbah*	'to liken'
ʔafḍal	'preferable, ... favorite'	*faḍḍal*	'to prefer, to favor'
sadaʔ	'to be true'; to .... tell the truth'	*saddaʔ*	'to believe'
kazab (or *kazzab*)	'to lie'	*kazzab*	'to disbelieve, consider... a liar'
ʔalīl	'little, few'	*ʔallal*	'to belittle, underestimate'
ḥmār	'donkey; stupid'	*ḥamran*	'to consider...stupid' (Pat. *FaɛLan* [p. 115])

The ascriptive derivation is a sort of specialization of the causative, used in a subjective sense: e.g. to disbelieve someone = to "make" a liar of him.

With most verbs, however, the ascriptive is virtually equivalent to the milder Estimative (see below).

ESTIMATIVE VERBS

Estimative verbs, formed on Pattern X *(staFɛuL)* [p.102], are derived mainly from simple adjectives.

If the underlying adjective means 'X', then the estimative verb means to consider or find (something) X'.

Underlying Word			Estimative Verb
ṣaɛᵃb	'difficult'	ṣṭaṣɛab	'to find...difficult'
həlu	'nice, pleasant'	staḥla	'to like, find...pleasant'
ktīr	'much, many'	staktar	'to consider...excessive'
ġarīb	'strange, odd'	staġrab	'to find...odd, be surprised at'
ẓġīr	'small'	ṣṭaẓġar	'to deem small, insignificant'
ʔaḥsan	'better, best'	staḥsan	'to prefer, consider...the best'
xān	'to betray', xāyen .	staxwan	'to consider...disloyal'
	'traitor'		

The estimative derivation is nearly equivalent to the ascriptive, though in some cases where the ascriptive implies social interaction, the estimative is more a matter of individual response: compare ascriptive *xawwan* 'to brand as a traitor' with estimative *staxwan* 'to consider disloyal'.

EDUCTIVE VERBS

Eductive verbs are formed mainly on Pattern X *(staFɛaL)* [p.102]. Most are derived from transitive verbs, a few from nouns.

If an underlying verb means '(Y) does X (with respect to Z)', then its eductive derivative means '(Z) elicits for himself — or brings about, or seeks to bring about for himself — (Y's) doing X'.

Underlying Word			Eductive Verb
ġafar	'to forgive'	staġfar	'to seek forgiveness'
ɛān	'to help'	staɛān	'to have recourse to'
šār	'to advise'	stašār	'to consult'
radd	'to return, give back'	staradd	'to ask (or get) back'
fād	'to be of use to'	stafād	'to benefit (from)'
		(mən)	

Underlying Word	Eductive Verb
xabbar 'to inform'	*staxbar* 'to seek (or get) information'
fahham 'to explain, make... .... understand'	*stafham* 'to seek (or get) clarification'
ʔaǧǧar 'to rent, hire out'	*staʔǧar* 'to rent, hire'
ǧāwab 'to answer'	*staǧwab* 'to question, interrogate'
walla 'to put...in charge'	*stawla* 'to take over'
Ɛamel 'to do, operate'	*staƐmal* 'to use'
dall 'to indicate, guide'	*stadall* 'to find the way'
samar 'fruits, profit'	*stasmar* 'to exploit, profit from'
ḥaʔʔ '(the) right (to)'	*staḥaʔʔ* 'to deserve'

CONATIVE VERBS

Conative verbs, with rare exceptions, are formed on Pattern III (*FāƐaL*) [p. 80].

The kind of activity designated by a conative verb has as its implicit goal the kind of event designated by its underlying simple verb.[1]

Underlying Verb	Conative
sabaʔ 'to overtake, pass'	*sāباʔ* 'to race' (trans.)
laḥeʔ 'to catch up with'	*lāḥaʔ* 'to chase after'
raḍa 'to please, satisfy'	*rāḍa* 'to ingratiate one's self with'
manaƐ 'to prevent'	*mānaƐ* 'to object to, forbid' (b-)
ṭaraḍ 'to expel, get rid of'	*ṭāraḍ* 'to chase away'
naṣar 'to secure the victory of' ..	*nāṣar* 'to back, support'
Ɛakas 'to reverse, upset'	*Ɛākas* 'to oppose, contradict'
baṭaḥ 'to throw down'	*bāṭaḥ* 'to wrestle'
laḥaẓ 'to catch a glimple of'	*lāḥaẓ* 'to watch; to notice'

---

[1] It should be noted that carrying on "goal-directed activity" does not necessarily imply an attempt or desire to attain that goal: one may chase without trying to catch, etc.

Underlying Verb		Conative
ḥakam 'to judge, pass sentence'	...	*ḥākam* 'to try, prosecute'
laha 'to amuse, divert'	....	*lāha* 'to entertain'
laʔa² 'to encounter'	....	*lāʔa* 'to (go to) meet, (look for and) find'

The Pattern II verb *ṣawwab* 'to aim at' is the conative of *ṣāb* 'to hit, attain'.

Highly idiomatic derivations include *xānaʔ* 'to scold, quarrel with' from *xanaʔ* 'to strangle'. Note also the reciprocative [p.248] *tʔātalu* 'to quarrel, fight' from *ʔatal* 'to kill'.

The subject of a conative verb is normally animate (since the verb designates goal-directed activity), while with an underlying simple verb this is not necessarily so: *šū manaɛ zawāžo?* 'What prevented his getting married?', but *mīn mānaɛ b-zawāžo* 'Who objected to his getting married?'

PARTICIPATIVE VERBS

Participative verbs are formed on Pattern III *(Fāɛal)* [p.80].

Participatives, which usually imply personal interaction, are commonly derived from simple verbs which do not necessarily imply interaction. If a simple verb underlying a participative means 'to do X', then the participative means 'to do X to or with (Y)', Y representing a personal object:

Simple Verb		Participative
katab 'to write (something)'	......	*kātab* 'to write to (someone)'
ḍəḥek 'to laugh'	....	*ḍāḥak* 'to laugh with (some- one)'
ḥaka 'to talk, to tell (some- thing)	....	*ḥāka* 'to talk to (someone)'
kašaf 'to reveal (something)'	.....	*kāšaf* 'to reveal...to (some- one)'
ʔasam 'to divide (something)'	.....	*ʔāsam* 'to share...with (some- one)'
zād 'to bid (on)' (b-)	....	*zāwad* 'to bid against'

---

²Perfect tense only; imperfect is *bilāʔi,* like the conative.

The personal object in a participative construction may correspond to a prepositional complement (usually with *maɛ* 'with' or *la-* 'to') of the simple verb:

bəddi ʔəhkī-lak ší	*bəddi hākīk*
'I want to tell you something'	'I want to talk to you'
katab maktūb la-ʔabū	*kātab ʔabū*
'He wrote a letter to his father'	'He wrote his father'
lɛabna maɛ mantáxab bērūt	*lāɛabna mantáxab bērūt*
'We played against the Beirut all-stars'	'We played the Beirut all-stars'

The inanimate object of a simple verb may correspond to a prepositional complement (usually with *b-*) of the participative:

faṣal səɛr ᵊs-sayyāra	*fāṣálon b-səɛr ᵊs-sayyāra*
'He haggled over the price of the car'	'He haggled with them over the price of the car'
hasáb ᵊt deni	*hāsabton b-dēni*
'I figured up my debt'	'I settled my debt with them'

> Idiomatic examples: *ɛəmel* 'to do (something)': *ɛāmal* 'to treat (someone some way)'; *samah* 'to allow (something)': *sāmah* 'to forgive (someone)'; *rahan* 'to pawn (something), put up as security': *rāhan* 'to bet (someone)'. Note also *hasab* and *hāsab*, above.

Some participatives are derived from simple nouns, which designate either a kind of participant or a kind of participation:

Noun (Participant)	Participative Verb
ṣāheb 'friend'	*ṣāhab* 'to make or be friends with'
rfīʔ 'companion'	*rāfaʔ* 'to accompany'
ɛadəww 'enemy'	*ɛāda* 'to treat with hostility'

Noun (Participation)	
həžže 'argument'	*hāžaž* 'to argue with'
xlāf 'difference, opposition' .	*xālaf* 'to oppose, differ with'
ṣədfe 'coincidence, unexpected encounter'	*ṣādaf* 'to encounter... unexpectedly'

RECIPROCATIVE VERBS

Reciprocative verbs, formed on Pattern VI (*tFāⁱaL*) [p.88], are derived mainly from participatives (see above). If the underlying verb means '(X) does Y to or with (Z)', then the reciprocative means '(X and Z) do Y to or with one another'. Since the subject denotes both or all interacting parties, which are generally animate, a true reciprocative verb normally occurs only in the plural.

	Underlying Verb		Reciprocative
ḥāka	'to talk to'	*tḥāku*	'to talk (together)'
kātab	'to write to'	*tkātabu*	'to write one another'
ṣāfaḥ	'to shake hands with'	*tṣāfaḥu*	'to shake hands'
sābaˀ	'to race' (trans.)	*tsābaˀu*	'to race' (intrans.)
lāˀa	'to(go to) meet (some- ... one)'	*tlāˀu*	'to meet, rendezvous'
nāsab	'to suit, correspond ..... to'	*tnāsabu*	'to match, correspond'

The verbs *nāsab* and *tnāsabu* do not require an animate subject, hence the reciprocative may occur in the third-person feminine singular [423] as well as in the plural: *hal-ˀalwān mā btatnāsab* 'these colors don't match'.

Some reciprocatives have no underlying participative verb, but are derived from simple verbs — combining the reciprocative derivation with the participative or conative [p.245]: *ḍḍārabu* 'to hit one another, fight', from *ḍarab* 'to hit'; *tˀātalu* 'to fight, quarrel', from *ˀatal* 'to kill'.

The reciprocative derivation is a specialized kind of mediopassive [p.238]. Some participatives have ordinary mediopassive derivatives, however, which differ from reciprocatives in that they occur, freely in the singular, and only express interaction when explicitly complemented by a phrase with *maⁱ* 'with' *sawa* 'together', or the like. For example *tšārak maⁱ ⁱammo* 'He went into partnership with his uncle' (mediopassive), from the participative *šārak ⁱammo* 'He took his uncle into partnership'.

Some of these derivatives may be construed either as ordinary mediopassives or as reciprocatives: *kān ⁱam-yatsābaˀ maⁱ sayyāra tānye* 'He was having a race with another car' (mediopassive); but *s-sayyārtēn kānu ⁱam-yatsābaˀu* 'The two cars were racing' (reciprocative).

SIMULATIVE VERBS

Simulative verbs are formed with the prefix *t-:* mainly on Pattern VI (*tFāɛaL*) [p. 88], in a few cases on quadriradical [p. 123] or *n*-suffix [p. 116] patterns. Most are derived from adjectives, some from nouns or verbs.

If the underlying word means 'X', then the simulative verb means 'to act X' (or 'to act like an X', or 'to act as if X'):

Underlying Word			Simulative Verb	
šāṭer	'smart, clever'	......	*tšāṭar*	'to act smart'
marīḍ	'ill'	....	*tmārad̞*	'to malinger'
ġašīm	'naive'	....	*tġāšam*	'to act naive'
šēṭān	'devil'	....	*tšēṭan*	'to be naughty'
walad	'child'	....	*twaldan*	'to be childish'
žāhel	'ignorant'	....	*tžāhal*	'to ignore, act ignorant of'
nəsi	'to forget'	....	*tnāsa*	'to act forgetful of'
ẓəher	'to appear'	....	*tẓāhar*	'to feign, simulate'
kasūl	'lazy'	....	*tkāsal*	'to loaf, be lazy'

Note that the element of pretense or simulation that is found in the verbs derived from qualitative adjectives is not found in those derived from adjectives which are themselves essentially behavioral rather than qualitative.[1] For example 'to <u>act</u> rude' is the same thing as 'to <u>be</u> rude':

ġalīẓ	'rude, crude, gross'	....	*tġālaẓ*	'to be rude, crude, gross'
raẓīl	'bad, wicked'	....	*trāzal*	'to be bad, wicked'
raxu	'lax, loose'	....	*trāxa*	'to relax'

---

[1] In such cases the contrast between simulative and descriptive [p. 251] is neutralized.

INCHOATIVE VERBS

If an adjective means 'X', then its inchoative paronym means 'to become X'.

Inchoatives of Pattern ʔaFɛaL color-adjectives [p. 130] are formed on Pattern IX (*FɛaLL*) [101]:

Adjective			Inchoative Verb
ʔaḥmar	'red'	....	ḥmarr	'to become red, to blush'
ʔaṣfar	'yellow'	....	ṣfarr	'to become yellow, turn pale'
ʔaswad	'black'	....	swadd	'to become black'

The defect-adjective [p. 130] ʔaɛwaž 'bent, crooked' also has a Pattern IX inchoative: ɛwažž 'to become bent, crooked'.

Some adjectives of Pattern məFɛeL [p. 133] have inchoatives of the pseudo-quadriradical ʔaFɛaL pattern [116]:

məslem	'Moslem'	....	ʔaslam 'to become a Moslem'
məžher	'having blossoms, ... flowering'		ʔažhar 'to bloom'
mūreʔ	'having leaves, ... leafy'		ʔawraʔ 'to leaf out'

Note the contrast of these adjectives with the participles: mʔažher 'in bloom', mʔaslem 'having become a Moslem' [p. 117].

Inchoatives from other kinds of adjectives are mostly formed on simple patterns: FəɛeL, byəFɛaL [p. 117] for sound and defective verbs; FaɛaL, byəFɛeL [pp. 59, 63] for geminate and hollow:

kbīr	'large, adult'	......	kəber	'to become large, grow up'
ḍɛīf	'weak, ill'	....	ḍəɛef	'to weaken, become ill'
ʔaɛma	'blind'	....	ɛəmi	'to go blind'
xafīf	'light'(in weight) ..		xaff	'to become light(er)'
dayyeʔ	'narrow, tight'	.....	dāʔ	'to become narrow'

Some inchoatives, derived mainly from words other than adjectives, are formed on Pattern V *(tFaɛɛaL)* [p. 86]:

Underlying Word		Inchoative Verb	
ʔaḥsan	'better'............	*tḥassan*	'to improve'
ʔəddām	'ahead'............	*tʔaddam*	'to progress'
səhel, byəshal	'to be easy'........	*tsahhal*	'to become easier'
byaʔrab	'to be related'[1]....	*tʔarrab*	'to become related (by marriage)'
byəmlok	'to own, possess'[1]..	*tmallak*	'to acquire, take possion of'
fəhem, byəfham	'to catch on, to understand'.......	*tfahham*	'to begin to understand, to come to understand better'

DESCRIPTIVE VERBS

If a simple adjective means 'X', then its descriptive verb means 'to be X'.[2]

Most descriptive verbs are formed on Pattern *FəɛeL, byəFɛaL* [p. 71], and occur mainly — in some cases always — in the imperfect tense and usually with a prepositional complement.

Adjective		Descriptive Verb	
sahªl 'easy'..............	*byəshal (ɛala)*	'to be easy'	(for)
ṣaɛªb 'difficult'........	*byəṣɛab (ɛala)*	'to be difficult'	(for)
bxīl 'stingy, miser'.....	*byəbxal (ɛala)*	'to be stingy'	(with s.o.)
bɛīd 'distant, far'......	*byəbɛod (ɛan)*	'to be distant, far'	(from)
ṣaḥīḥ 'correct, all right'..	*biṣaḥḥ*	'to be all right'	

The descriptive verb *byaʔrab (la-)* 'to be kin(to)' is correlative to the noun *ʔarāyeb* 'relative, kin'.

The relationship between a simple adjective and its inchoative or descriptive verb is very similar to that between an active participle and its underlying verb. The only functional difference is that while a participle normally depicts a state, a simple adjective depicts states, dispositions, or qualities indiscriminately. Insofar as a simple adjective is inherently stative (e.g. *mayyet* 'dead'), and if the correlative verb (*māt* 'to die') has no participle on the usual patterns (*Fāɛel* or *FaɛLān*), then the adjective does, in fact, function as a participle.

---

[1] Some verbs, especially "descriptive" verbs, are not normally used in the perfect tense. See below.

[2] In Classical Arabic, many descriptive verbs and simple inchoative verbs fall together into one class, meaning roughly 'to be or become X' (where the simple adjective means 'X'). These are double-aspect verbs, having — like those discussed in the section on participles — an inceptive and a durative aspect [p. 271].

ABSTRACTIVE VERBS

Abstractive verbs are formed mainly on Pattern VIII (*FtaCaL*) [p.95],
and are derived mainly from simple verbs.

Abstractives differ from their underlying verbs by a metaphorical shift
in meaning from concrete to abstract, or from animate to inanimate, or
physical to psychological, immediate to mediate, etc.; these shifts in
meaning generally involve the type of subject or complement the verb takes.

Underlying Verb			Abstractive Verb	
kašaf	'to uncover, expose'	...	*ktašaf*	'to discover'
ḥamal	'to pick up, carry'	....	*ḥtamal*	'to bear, put up with'
fataḥ	'to open' (e.g. a door)	......	*ftataḥ*	'to open' (e.g. a meeting)
xatam	'to seal'	....	*xtatam*	'to conclude, close'
ɛānaʔ	'to embrace' (some- one)	....	*ɛtanaʔ*	'to embrace' (e.g. a faith)
ḥawa	'to contain; to keep'	....	*ḥtawa* (*ɛala*)	'to include, contain'
naxab	'to pick out, choose'	..	*ntaxab*	'to elect'
maṣṣ	'to suck'	....	*mṭaṣṣ*	'to absorb'
lahab	'to flame, blaze'	......	*ltahab*	'to be inflamed'
xalaʔ	'to create'	....	*xtalaʔ*	'to dream up, fabricate'
ʔaxad	'to take, get'	....	*ttaxaz*[1]	'to take on, undertake'
ṭalab	'to ask for'	....	*ṭṭallab*	(Pat. V) 'to require'

In a few cases, Pattern VIII verbs are simultanously
abstractive and mediopassive: *waṣaf* 'to describe' → *ttaṣaf*
(*b-*) 'to be characterized (by)'; *waṣal* 'to connect' → *ttaṣal*
(*b-*) 'to have to do with, to be in touch with'; *labes* 'to
put on, wear' → *ltabas* 'to be obscure'.

---

[1]As a classicism, this derivative has *z* for Classical δ (which corresponds
to *d* in words inherited via spoken channels).

AUGMENTATIVE (Frequentative and Intensive) VERBS

Augmentative verbs are formed on Pattern II (*FaƐƐaL*) [p. 77] or on one of the pseudo-quadriradical patterns *FaƐwaL*, *FaƐFaL*, *FarƐaL*, or *FōƐaL* [p. 109].

Augmentatives are mainly derived from sound and geminate simple verbs of the *FaƐaL* patterns (and rarely from hollow or *FəƐeL*-pattern verbs).

A simple verb designating a kind of action does not specify whether the action is single or multiple, limited or extensive, restrained or forceful. An augmentative verb, on the other hand, indicates that the action is enhanced in one way or another — repeated, extended, or intensified.

Simple Verb	Augmentative Verb
safaˀ 'to clap, slap' . . . . (once or more)	*saffaˀ* 'to clap' (e.g. in applause or rhythm)
ˀataf 'to pick' (e.g. a . . . . flower)	*ˀaṭṭaf* 'to pick' (e.ę. many flowers)
kasar 'to break' (e.g. in two)	*kassar* 'to break' (e.g. to pieces)

One may say, for example, *lā ṭəˀṭof haz-zhūr* 'Don't pick those flowers' or, with the augmentative *lā ṭˀaṭṭef haz-zhūr*. But in reference to a single flower, the simple verb only may be used: *lā ṭəˀṭof haz-zahra* 'don't pick that flower' (not *lā ṭˀaṭṭef...*).

Augmentatives may be divided into FREQUENTATIVES, which indicate repeated or distributed action, and INTENSIVES, which indicate forceful action. (Intensives are more common in the pseudo-quadriradical patterns than in Pattern II, while frequentatives are the most common in Pattern II, and are more common in general than intensives.) Most augmentatives may be taken in whichever sense is compatiple with the meaning of the underlying simple verb, and with the context and situation in which it is being used. Thus *daƐwas* 'to trample, tread on', from *daƐas* 'to step on, tread on', may indicate protracted or extensive action, or intensive action.

"Intensive action", however, tends to be a vague and subjective notion. Many augmentatives which are theoretically intensives are in actual usage virtually synonymous with their underlying simple verb: *raƐab* and *raƐƐab* 'to scare, startle', *fəreḥ* and *farfaḥ* 'to rejoice', etc.

The difference between many simple verbs and their "intensive" derivatives, then, is more often exploited for stylistic or connotative purposes that for objective indications of intensiveness; speakers may sometimes choose intensives for the sake of emphatic or colorful speech.

Examples, **Pattern II**:

	Simple		Augmentative	
ṭaraʔ	'to knock'	....	*ṭarraʔ*	
xasal	'to wash'	....	*xassal*	
xazaʔ	'to tear, rip'	....	*xazzaʔ*	
dabaḥ	'to slaughter'	....	*dabbaḥ*	
rabaṭ	'to tie, hitch'	....	*rabbaṭ*	
raɛab	'to scare, startle'	....	*raɛɛab*	(intensive or synonymous)
dafaš	'to push'	....	*daffaš*	
žamaɛ	'to bring together, gather'	....	*žammaɛ*	
šaxaṭ	'to draw (a) line(s), scribble'	....	*šaxxaṭ*	(cf. *šaxwaṭ*)
žadal	'to braid'	....	*žaddal*	(cf. *žōdal*)
baram	'to turn, twist' (trans.)	......	*barram*	(cf. *bōram*)
ṣarax	'to shout'	....	*ṣarrax*	(cf. *ṣarwax*)

Pattern *Faɛwal:*

baxaš	'to perforate'	....	*baxwaš*	
ḥakaš	'to pick at, fool with'	....	*ḥakwaš*	
daɛas	'to tread on'	....	*daɛwas*	
šaxaṭ	'to draw (a) line(s), scribble'	....	*šaxwaṭ*	
šakk	'to prick, pierce'	....	*šakwak*	
šalaḥ	'to take off' (e.g. clothes) ...		*šalwaḥ*	'take off and throw around' (cf. *šōlaḥ*)
ɛalak	'to chew'	....	*ɛalwak*	
ʔaraṣ	'to sting, bite'	....	*ʔarwaṣ*	
ʔaraṭ	'to crunch, gnaw'	....	*ʔarwaṭ*	(cf. *ʔarʔaṭ*)
laʔaṭ	'to pick up'	....	*laʔwaṭ*	(cf. *lōʔaṭ*)
nataɛ	'to jerk' (intrans.)	....	*natwaɛ*	
naṭṭ	'to jump'	....	*naṭwaṭ*	
šaxar	'to snort; snore'	....	*šaxwar*	

Reduplicative Pattern *(FaɛFaL):*

	Simple	Augmentative	
ṭaraš	'to splash'	ṭarṭaš	
ʔaraṭ	'to crunch, gnaw'	ʔarʔaṭ	
ṣaraɛ	'to startle'	ṣarṣaɛ	
fəreḥ	'to rejoice'	farfaḥ	
laff	'to turn; wrap'	laflaf	'to wrap up'
ḥall	'to untie; solve'	ḥalḥal	'to untie'
šamm	'to smell' (trans.)	šamšam	'to smell, sniff'
ʔaṣṣ	'to cut, snip'	ʔaṣʔaṣ	
fatt	'to crumble' (trans.)	fatfat	
kabb	'to pour, spill'	kabkab	
ʔaraɛ	'to hit with a bang'	ʔarʔaɛ	'to clatter'
lāḥ	'to wave'	lōlaḥ	

Pattern *FarɛaL:*

	Simple	Augmentative	
baɛaṭ	'to splash around in the water'	barɛaṭ	
xamaš	'to scratch'	xarmaš	
dabak	'to tap, drum'	darbak	
šabak	'to involve, entangle'	šarbak	'to entangle, complicate'
ṭabaʔ	'to slam'	ṭarbaʔ	
kadas	'to pile'	kardas	(also kaddas)

Pattern *FōɛaL:*

	Simple	Augmentative	
laʔaṭ	'to pick up'	lōʔaṭ	(cf. laʔwaṭ)
šaḥaṭ	'to drag'	šōḥaṭ	
žadal	'to braid'	žōdal	(also žaddal)
zaġal	'to cheat' (in games)	zōġal	
ḥazaʔ	'to hiccup'	ḥōzaʔ	
baram	'to turn, wind'	bōram	'to wind'

APPLICATIVE VERBS

Applicative verbs, which are denominative, i.e. derived from nouns, are mostly formed on Pattern II [p. 77], or on one of the quadriradical [117] or pseudo-quadriradical [109] patterns.

If a noun means 'X', then the applicative verb derived from it means 'to apply, give, put, make, take, (etc.), X':

Underlying Noun		Applicative Verb	
zēt	'oil'	zayyat	'to oil'
bōdra	'powder'	bōdar	'to powder'
baxšīš	'tip, gratuity'	baxšaš	'to tip'
ʔəšʔr	'peel, skin, shell, bark'	ʔaššar	'to peel, (etc.)'
ʔatāt	'furniture, furnishings'	ʔattat	'to furnish'
buxār	'steam'	baxxar	'to steam'
blāṭ	'flagstones, tile'	ballaṭ	'to pave with flag-stones, tile'
talifōn	'telephone'	talfan	'to telephone'
zərr	'button'	zarrar	'to button'
xāzūʔ	'stake'	xōzaʔ	'to impale'
ʔāleb	'mold'	ʔōlab	'to mold'
tārīx	'date' (day of year)	tarrax	'to date'
būẓ	'ice'	bawwaẓ	'to ice'
banž	'anesthetic'	bannaž	'to anesthetize'
bhār	'spice'	bahhar	'to spice'
bərwāẓ	'frame'	barwaẓ	'to frame'
bəsmār	'nail'	basmar	'to nail'
fəršāye	'brush'	farša	'to brush'
ʔasās	'foundation'	ʔassas	'to found, establish'

Some applicatives are formed on other patterns: *ʔahda* (Pat. IV) 'to give (as a gift)', from *hdiyye* 'gift'; *thāyal* 'to trick' (Pat. VI) from *ḥīle* 'trick'. A few are derived from formulaic phrases: *basmal* 'to say *bəsməllāh...*' ('in the name of God...').

Many denominatives, though not applicatives strictly speaking, are derived in comparable ways: *tsawwaʔ* 'to shop, go to market', from *sūʔ* 'market'; *sabbab* 'to cause', from *sabab* 'cause', etc.

CHAPTER 10:   ADJECTIVE DERIVATION

Index of Categories:

Color and defect adjectives constitute two more categories, but since they have no underlying bases they are dealt with in the chapter on adjective patterns, p. 130.

Elatives [p. 310] and ordinal numerals [316], though they are partly adjectival in function, are treated in Chapter 11, Noun Derivation.

The quasi-inflectional [p. 49] category of Participles occupies the largest part of this chapter, because of the importance and complexity of their relationship to the underlying verbs.

PARTICIPLES

Formation

Most simple triradical verbs [p.55] have active participles on the pattern *Fā€eL* [131] and passive participles on the pattern *maF€ūL* [132]:

Verb		Participles
ḥafaẓ	'to put away, keep'.........*ḥāfeẓ*	'having put away, keeping'
	maḥfūẓ	'having been put away, kept'
fataḥ	'to open'.................*fāteḥ*	'having opened'
	maftūḥ	'open, having been opened'
ləbes	'to put on'(clothes).......*lābes*	'having put on, wearing'
	malbūs	'having been put on, being worn'
wazan	'to weigh'.................*wāzen*	'having weighed'
	mawzūn	'having been weighed'
yəʔes	'to despair'..............*yāʔes*	'despairing, desparate'
	mayʔus	'despaired(of)'
	(*mənno*)	
ḥaṭṭ	'to put'..................*ḥāṭeṭ*	'having put'
	maḥṭūṭ	'having been put'
bā€	'to sell'.................*bāye€*	'having sold'

Hollow verbs [p. 188] generally do not have passive participles.[1] In the active participles, a medial radical *w* is changed to *y:* *xāf* 'to fear' (Root *x–w–f*), act. part. *xāyef* 'afraid'.

Defective verbs [p. 186] have active participles ending in *i* and passive participles on the pattern *məF€i* [133]. (Medial radical *w* remains intact):

ʔara	'to read'..................*ʔāri*	'having read'
	məʔri	'having been read'
bana	'to build'.................*bāni*	'having built'
	məbni	'having been built'
nawa	'to intend'................*nāwi*	'intending'
	mənwi	'intended'
məši	'to go, walk'..............*māši*	'going, walking'
	məmši	'walked(on)'
	(*€alē*)	

---

[1]There are some exceptions. In some areas, for instance, the form *mabyū€* 'sold' may be heard. The word *madyūn* 'in debt' is used without any under-lying verb (cf. *dēn* 'debt').

In some regions (especially Palestine) defective passive participles keep the vowel *a*: *maʔri, mabni,* etc.

Passive participles of the defective "impersonal" passive verbs *ġəmi (ɛalē)* 'to faint' and *quḍi (ɛalē)* 'to be
done for, be a goner' are formed on the pattern *muFɛa:
muġma ɛalē* 'fainted', *muqḍa ɛalē* 'done for'. [See p. 365.]

The anomalous verb *ʔəža* 'to come' has active participle *žāye* (both masc. and fem.) (see p. 76, footnote.)

Quite a few sound and defective verbs — especially intransitive verbs
on Pattern *FəɛeL, byəFɛaL* [p. 71], and especially verbs that usually take
animate subjects — have active participles on the pattern *FaɛLān* [132]:

Verb		Active Participle	
kəber 'to grow up'	*kabrān*	'(having) grown up'
ɛəteš 'to get thirsty'	*ɛatšān*	'thirsty'
təɛeb 'to get tired'	*taɛbān*	'tired'
barad 'to get cold'	*bardān*	'cold' (animate only; inani-mate *bāred*)
nəsi 'to forget'	*nasyān* (or *nāsi*)	'having forgotten'
səmeɛ 'to hear'	*samɛān* (or *sāmeɛ*)	'having heard; listening'
harab 'to flee'	*harbān* (or *hāreb*)	'having fled, fleeing'
rəwi 'to be watered, irrigated'	*rayyān*	'well-watered, irrigated'

The hollow verb *žāɛ* 'to get hungry' (Root *ž-w-ɛ*) has
participle *žūɛān* 'hungry', in some areas *žīɛān*.

Geminate verbs [189] do not have participles on this
pattern.

In most cases in which there are alternative participial
forms (e.g. *samɛān* and *sāmeɛ*), the *FaɛLān* pattern is typical
of Syria Proper, while the *Fāɛel* pattern is more cosmopolitan.

The participles of all augmented and quadriradical verbs are formed by
prefixation of *m-* (or *mə-* before two consonants, or *mu-* in certain classicisms). In the passive participle, the last vowel is always *a*. In the
active participle, it is *e* for sound verbs, *i* for defective:

Verb			Participles	
taržam	'to translate'..................	*mtaržem*	'having translated'
		mtaržam	'(having been) translated'
ʔarrar	'to decide'....................	*mʔarrer*	'having decided'
		mʔarrar	'(having been) decided'
samma	'to name, call'...............	*msammi*	'having named'
		msamma	'(having been) named'
staƐmal	'to use'......................	*mastaƐmel*	'having used, using'
		məstaƐmal	'(having been) used'
tbanna	'to adopt'....................	*mətbanni*	'having adopted'
		mətbanna	'(having been) adopted'

In participles of Pattern IV (*ʔaFƐaL*) verbs [p.82], *mə-* replaces *ʔa-*: *ʔakram* 'to honor', *məkrem* 'having honored, honoring', *məkram* '(having been) honored'. (Most words of Patterns *məFƐeL* [133] and *məFƐaL* [134] do not function as true participles, however. See Agentive Adjectives [278].)

The next-to-last vowel is changed to *ə* in the active participles of sound and defective (and initial-weak) Pattern VII [p.91] and VIII [95] verbs, except in classicisms, where it remains *a*:

Pattern VII

Sound: *nsaḥar* 'to be bewitched'.........*mənsə́ḥer* 'bewitched'

Defective: *nʔara* 'to be read'.............*mən?ə́ri* '(having been) read'

Sound: *nʔaṭaƐ* 'to be discontinued'......*mən?ə́ṭeƐ* 'discontinued'
(Classicism)

Pattern VIII

Sound: *Ɛtamad* 'to rely (on).............*məƐtə́med* 'relying (on)'
(*Ɛala*) (*Ɛala*)
məƐtə́mad 'relied on'
Ɛalē

Defective: *ḥtawa* 'to include'.............*məḥtə́wi* 'including'
(*Ɛala*) (*Ɛale*)
məḥtə́wa 'included'
Ɛalē

Initial- *ttaḥad* 'to be united'...........*muttáḥed* 'united'
Weak: (Classicism)

In the active participles of geminate and hollow verbs of Patterns VII and VIII, and of all Pattern IX verbs [p.101], the stem vowel remains *a* (or *ā*):

Geminate: VII: *nṣaff* 'to be lined up'.....*mənṣaff* 'lined up'

VIII: *ḍṭarr* 'to be required, obliged' .....*məḍṭarr* 'required, obliged to'

IX: *ṣfarr* 'to blanch, turn pale' .....*məṣfarr* '(having) turned pale'

Hollow: VIII: *nʔāl* 'to be told'.........*mənʔāl* '(having been) told'

VIII: *ḥtāž (la-)* 'to need'...........*məḥtāž (la-)* 'in need(of)'

These verbs generally do not have passive participles (which would be the same in form as the active participles).

In the active participles of all other augmented geminate verbs, the last stem vowel is *ə* [p.23]. (The next-to-last vowel in Pattern X is often lost):

Pattern IV: *ʔaṣarr* 'to insist, resolve'......*mṣərr* 'insistent, resolved'

Pattern X: *staḥaʔʔ* 'to deserved'............*məstḥəʔʔ* 'deserving'

staradd 'to ask(for...)back'......*məst(a)rədd* 'having asked... back'

Pattern
FɛaLaLL: *ṭmaʔann* 'to feel secure'.........*məṭmaʔann* 'feeling secure'

In the active participles of all other augmented hollow triradical verbs, the last stem vowel is *ī*. (The next-to-last vowel in Pattern X is sometimes lost):

Pattern IV: *ʔaḥāṭ (bi-)* 'to surround..........*muḥīt (bi-)* 'surrounding'
                                               (Pass. *muḥāṭ fī* 'surrounded')

Pattern X: *stafād (mən)* 'to benefit(from)'.....*məst(a)fīd* 'having benefitted'

stašār 'to consult'..........*məstašīr* 'having consulted'
                                               (Pass. *məstašār* 'having been consulted')

A few augmented verbs are suppleted by participles
formed on patterns corresponding to simple verbs, e.g.
štara 'to buy': act, part. *šāri* 'having bought' (also
maštóri); *sta²šar* 'to hire': pass. part. *ma²šūr* 'hired'
(in reference to persons only; cf. *masta²šar* 'leased,
chartered').

The Function of Participles in General

An Arabic participle, generally speaking, is an adjective depicting a
CONSEQUENT STATE. That is to say, it describes its referent as being in a
certain state of affairs as a necessary consequence of the kind of event,
process, or activity designated by the underlying verb. For example *fāye²*
'awake' from *fā²* 'to wake up', *warmān* 'swollen' from *warem* 'to swell',
metĆallem 'educated' from *tĆallam* 'to learn, be .educated'.[1]

Of the two kinds of participles, the ACTIVE PARTICIPLE (*ism l-fāĆil*)
depicts the consequent state of its underlying verb's <u>subject</u> referent,
while the PASSIVE PARTICIPLE (*ism l-mafĆūl*) pertains to the referent of its
<u>complement</u>. Thus the verb *fatah* 'to open' has an active participle *fāteh*
'having opened' and a passive participle *maftūh* 'open, having been opened'.
The verb *ttafa²* 'to agree, come to an agreement' has a.p. *mattáfe²* 'in
agreement' and p.p. *mattáfa²* (*Ćalē*) 'agreed (upon)'.

---

[1] The term 'consequent state' is defined to include only the necessary consequences — the logical entailments — of a <u>kind</u> of event (process, activity).
Verbs like *fā²*, *warem*, and *tĆallam* refer, by definition, to <u>changes</u> of
state; hence every event (process, etc.) referred to with these verbs introduces a state that could reasonably be indicated by means of their
participles.

Certain other verbs, however, e.g. *safa²* 'to clap', do not ordinarily
imply a significant change in state, and their participles are rarely or
never used. (But cf. p. 270 .)

Still other verbs, e.g. *darab* 'to hit', sometimes do — and sometimes do
not — imply a significant change of state (depending on context and circumstances); the participles *dāreb* 'having hit' and *madrūb* 'having been hit'
could be used for some, but not all, of the situations to which their
underlying verb applies.

Though hitting (*d-darb*) might be thought of as a <u>physical</u> act par excellence — entailing, of course, physical consequences — it is worth noting
that hitting is often also a <u>social</u> act. The situation involving *d-dāreb*
'the hitter' and *l-madrūb* 'the one hit' is a sort of evanescent social
relationship similar to that between winner and loser, giver and receiver,
wrong-doer and wronged, etc. Thus someone might be described as *madrūb*
even though he has suffered no significant physical injury or displacement.

Passive Participles

Most passive participles are derived from transitive verbs. The subject to which a passive participle is predicate corresponds to the underlying verb's <u>object</u>: *fataḥ ᵊl-bāb* '(He) opened the door' → *l-bāb maftūḥ* 'The door is open'. Examples:

1. *l-fanšān maɛmūl mən*
   ᵓaḥsan mālᵓi
   'The cup is made of the best china' (p.p. of *ɛəmel* 'to make')

2. *š-šaġle lassāta mū mᵓarrara*
   'The matter is not yet decided' (p.p. of *ᵓarrar* 'to decide')

3. *ᵓana maɛzūm ɛand ġērak* [AO-115]
   'I'm invited to [dinner at] someone else's [house]' (p.p. of *ɛazam* 'to invite')

4. *laᵓa fīha ᵓəmᵓon ᵊnḥās* [AO-115]
   təmmo maxtūm
   'He found in it a copper flagon whose mouth was sealed' (p.p. of *xatam* 'to seal').

5. *ᵓəxti l-ᵊkbīre mžawwaze* [AO-43]
   'My elder sister is married' (p.p. of *žawwaz* 'to marry off')

Passive participles are also used attributively [p. 501] like any ordinary adjective. Examples:

6. *maktūb ᵊmsōkar*
   'an insured letter' (p.p. of *sōkar* 'to insure')

7. *kūsa məḥši*
   'stuffed squash' (p.p. of *ḥaša* 'to stuff')

8. *l-madīne l-mashūra*
   'the enchanted city' (p.p. of *saḥar* 'to enchant')

9. *mažalle šahriyye maɛrūfe*
   'a (well-)known monthly magazine' (p.p. of *ɛəref* 'to know, come to know')

10. *...mašākel ᵊktīr məštdrake bēnāton*
   '...many problems in common', lit. '...shared between them' (p.p. of *štarak* 'to share')

11. *l-warde l-maḥṭūta b-šaɛᵊrha*
   'the flower worn in her hair' (p.p. of *ḥaṭṭ* 'to put, place')

"Impersonal" Passive Participles. Some passive participles are derived from intransitive verbs that have prepositional complements [p. 444]. These participles are always followed immediately by their complemental preposition with a suffixed pronoun [477]: *məmši ɛalēha* 'walked on(f.)'

The subject for this kind of predicate is the antecedent of the suffixed pronoun: *has-saǧǧāde məmši ɛalēha* 'This rug has been walked on' (literally: "This rug, [there has been] walked on it". [See **Entraposition**, p.431.] The participle itself does **not** show agreement with the subject [429], remaining always in the base form (masculine/singular). [See Impersonal Passive Verbs, p.237.] Examples:

12. *l-ᵊhkūme ǧ-ǧdīde mawsūq*
    fīha

'The new government is trusted', 'There is confidence in the new government' (*wasaq b-* [p.479] 'to have confidence, faith in')

13. *hal-ʔumūr muxtálaf fīha*
    mən zamān

'These matters have been disagreed over for some time' (*xtalaf b-* 'to differ over, disagree about').

14. *naẓarīto maškūk fīha*

'His theory is doubted (or dubious)'[1] (*šakk b-* 'to have doubts about, to suspect').

15. *biʔāmen.ʔənno fī baɛd*
    ᵊl-ʔarwāh mʔaddar ɛalēha
    bəl-ɛazāb ᵊl-ʔazali

'He believes that there are some souls [who are] foreordained to eternal torment' (*ʔaddar ɛala* 'to decree, foreordain for s.o.').

Examples of attributive use:

16. *l-ʔaḍāya l-mabhūs fīha*

'the cases investigated' (*bahas b-* 'to inquire into, to investigate')

17. *l-mašrūɛ ᵊl-məttáfaʔ*
    ɛalē

'the plan agreed upon' (*ttafaʔ ɛala* 'to agree upon')

18. *bēt məɛtána fī mnīh*

'a house well cared for' (*ɛtana b-* 'to look after, take care of')

19. *l-luǧa l-məttarǧam mənna*

'the language translated from' (*ttarǧam mən* 'to be translated from')[2]

---

[1] *maškūk fī*, *mawsūq fī*, and other participles of this sort are often used in a dispositional sense [see p.275]: *mawsūq fī* 'trustworthy, worthy of confidence', *maškūk fī* 'dubious, questionable'. This usage is especially common in classicisms or set phrases.

[2] Cf. *mtarǧam* 'translated', p.p. of *tarǧam* 'to translate': *l-kətob l-ᵊmtarǧame* 'the books translated'. The two types of construction are hybridized in a phrase such as *l-luǧa l-məttarǧame mənna hal-kətob* 'the language from which these books are translated'. (*məttarǧame*, as a passive participle of an intransitive verb, should not show agreement, but in fact it does agree here with *l-kətob*, which is construed as its subject.) This type of participial phrase is rare, being usually circumlocuted with an attributive clause [p.505]: *l-luǧa halli ttarǧamet mənna hal-kətob*, or *l-luǧa halli mtarǧame mənna hal-kətob*.

Active Participles

The subject of a predicative active participle corresponds to the subject of its underlying verb: *kallon ᵊttafaʔu* 'All of them agreed' → *kallon
mattafʔīn* 'All of them are in agreement'.
A predicative active participle has the same kind of complementation
[p. 437] as its underlying verb. Thus the participle of a transitive verb
takes an object: *labes tyābo š-šdīde* 'He put on his new clothes' → *lābes
tyābo š-šdīde* 'He's wearing his new clothes'.

Despite its adjectival inflection, then, the active participle is generally verb-like in syntax. It functions as
an additional tense, contrasting mainly with the perfect
[p. 330]. While the perfect *labes tyābo* 'He put on his
clothes' carries no implication whether or not he still has
them on, the participial predication *lābes tyābo* means definitely that he still has them on. (With durative verbs,
the contrast is mainly with the imperfect rather than the
perfect; see pp. 269, 322, 326.)

The participle-object construction is not to be confused
with a substantivized participle standing in construct with
its transformed object [p. 465], although *huwwe kāteb
hal-ᵊktāb* could be interpreted either as a participle-object
predication 'He's written this book', 'He's the one who wrote
this book' or a substantive construct predication 'He's the
writer of this book'. This ambiguity is resolved in the
feminine form, where the substantive construct is marked by
a connective *t* [163]: *hiyye kātbet hal-ᵊktāb* 'She's the
writer of this book', while the participle-object construction has the absolute form: *hiyye kātbe hal-ᵊktāb* 'She's
written this book', 'She's the one who wrote this book'.
With pronoun suffixes, however, connective *t* is used
for the feminine in any case: *hiyye kātəbto* 'She's the one
who wrote it' or 'She's the writer of it'.

As also with verbs, the complemental form (*-ni*) of the first-person
singular pronoun is used with transitive participles: *huwwe mᶜallómni*
'He's taught me', 'He's the one who taught me'; *hiyye mᶜallómtni* 'She's`
taught me', 'She's the one who taught me'. (Cf. the annexive form *-i* used
with the occupational noun in construct: *huwwe mᶜállmi* 'He's my teacher',
hiyye mᶜallómti 'She's my teacher'.) See Personal Pronouns [p. 544].

With the other pronoun suffixes, there is no distinction between complemental and annexive forms, hence *mᶜállmo*,
for instance, is sometimes to be interpreted as 'He's taught
him', and sometimes as 'his teacher'; similarly *mᶜallómto*
'She's taught him' or 'his teacher(f.)'.

Active participles (like some passive participles [p. 482]) also take
the suffixed forms of the preposition *la-* plus pronoun, rather than the
disjunctive forms [p. 479]: *mtaršóm-li* 'having translated(m.) for me',
mtaršəmt-ślli 'having translated(f.) for me'. (Cf. *mtaršem ʔəli* 'a trans-
lator(m.) for me', *mtaršme ʔəli* 'a translator(f.) for me'.)

Still another verb-like trait of active participles is that the subject of a participial clause sometimes comes between the participle and its complement: *məttəf ʔīn kəllayātna məʕ baʕdna* [PVA 16] 'We're all in agreement with one another', *tālʕa bəntak ʔz-zġīre šaʔra* [DA-234] 'Your youngest daughter has turned out(to be)blonde'. (See Verb-Subject word order, p.000.)

Miscellaneous examples of active participles in their predicative use:

20. *ʔana šāye ʔaddem ṭalab*
    'I've come to submit a request' (a.p. of *ʔəša* [p.76])

21. *fī zərr wāʔeʕ mən fəsṭānek*
    'There's a button (fallen) off your dress' (a.p. of *wəʔeʕ* 'to fall')

22. *mətmakken huwwe tamām mn ʔl-ʔəglīzi?*
    'Does have a good command of English?' (a.p. of *tmakkan* 'to master')

23. *ʔana šāybo b-līra w-rəbʔʕ* [adap. SAL-198]
    'I got it for a pound and a quarter' (a.p. of *šāb* 'to bring, get') The participle implies '...got it and still have it', in contrast to the perfect *šəbto* 'I got it (and may or may not still have it)'.

24. *katter xērak, nəḥna mətʕaššyīn ya bēk* [AO-91]
    'Thank you (but) we have (already) dined, sir' (a.p. of *tʕašša* 'to dine, sup').

25. *šəba ṣ-ṣānʕa mū māsḥa l-ʔarḍ?* [DA-212]
    'What's the matter with the maid (that) she hasn't scrubbed the floor?' (a.p. of *masaḥ* 'to scrub')

26. *ʔēmta mqarrer ʔtsāfer?* [DA-248]
    'When have you decided to leave?' (a.p. of *qarrar* 'to decide')

27. *ʔālət-lo lēš hēk zaʕlān* [AO-114]
    'She said to him, "Why (are you) so vexed?"' (a.p. of *zəʕel* 'to become angry, displeased, unhappy')

28. *ṣ-ṣəbʔḥ laʔēt marti, bənt ʕammi, lābse tyāb ʔl-ḥəzʔn w-ʔāṣṣa šaʕʔrha* [AO-118]
    'In the morning I found my wife, my uncle's daughter, dressed in mourning and with her hair cut' (a.p. of *ləbes* 'to put on' (clothes) and *ʔaṣṣ* 'to cut')

29. *ṭ-ṭaʔs ḥəlu wəš-šams tālʕa ʔūm la-rrūḥ ṣōb ʔl-marže* [DA-218]
    'The weather is nice and the sun has come out; come on, let's go down toward the Maržé' (a.p. of *ṭəleʕ* 'to come out')

30. *bəl-ʔāxir ṭaleʕ ᵊmxayyeb*
    ᵊmḥabbīno

'In the end he disappointed his friends' (lit. "...turned out having disappointed...") (a.p. of *xayyab* 'to disappoint')

The term 'active' is rather inappropriate when applied to the participles of certain kinds of intransitive verbs, especially passive verbs [p. 234]; for instance *məntə́si* '(having been) forgotten' is the "active" participle of *ntasa* 'to be forgotten'. (It would make better sense to speak of the 'subjective participle', as contrasted with the 'complemental participle', but the existing terms are too well established to be ignored.)

Not surprisingly, the "active" participle of a passive verb is often closely equivalent to the passive participle of the underlying active verb. Thus *məntə́si* is practically synonymous to *mənsi* 'forgotten', (passive participle of *nəsi* 'to forget'). In many such cases the passive participle of the active verb is the one normally used while the active participle of the passive verb (as *məntə́si*) is very rare or virtually never used at all (as in the case of *taršam* 'to translate': p.p. *mtaršam* 'translated'; passive verb *ttaršam* 'to be translated' whose active participle (theoretically *"məttaršem"*) is not heard. (But cf. *məttaršam mənna*, p. 264 ex. 19.)

A complemented active participle is generally not used attributively, but the participial clause – like a verbal clause – may be subordinated as a whole [p. 495]: *l-bənt ḥáṭṭa warde b-šaʕra* 'The girl has put (i.e. is wearing) a flower in her hair' → *l-bənt halli ḥaṭṭa warde b-šaʕra* 'the girl wearing a flower in her hair'. (Cf. the complemented passive participle, which can be subordinated like any adjective: *l-warde l-maḥṭūta b-šaʕra* 'the flower worn (i.e. put) in her hair'. See, however, p. 505.

Uncomplemented active participles may be used attributively, like ordinary adjectives: *walad ḍā́yeʕ* 'a lost child' (a.p. of *ḍāʕ* 'to get lost'), *rəǧǧāl sakrān* 'a drunken man', *wlādi ǧ-ǧūʕānīn* 'my hungry children', *s-səne l-māḍye* 'the past year' (a.p. of *maḍa* 'to pass'), *nās mətʕallmīn* 'educated people', *l-bāxra l-ġarʔāne* 'the sunken (or sinking) ship' [see p. 271] (a.p. of *ġareʔ* 'to sink').

When an active participle is used with its normal complementation suppressed, it becomes an agentive [p. 278] or dispositional [277] adjective: *mašrūʕ šāmel* 'a comprehensive plan' (*šamal* 'to include, comprehend', transitive); *kīmāwi fahmān* 'an able chemist', i.e. a chemist who understands (*byəfham*) his business. See p. 275.

Person Inflection in Feminine Active Participles

When a feminine participle is used with a suffix (pronoun, or-l- plus pronoun [p.479]), the connective t [163] is used: lābse '(f.) wearing' + -hon 'them' → lābə́sthon 'wearing them'; fātḥa '(f.) having opened' + -lna 'for us' → fātəḥt-ə́lna 'having opened...for us'.

If, however, a feminine participle with a pronoun suffix refers to the person spoken to ('you'), then -ī- is inserted between the connective t and the suffix: lābəstīhon '(you, f.) wearing them', fātəḥtī-lna '(you, f.) having opened...for us'. Examples:

31. ʔənti kātəbtī?

'Are you(f.) the one who wrote it (m.)?' (As contrasted with hiyye kātəbto? 'Is she the one who wrote it?' and ʔana kātəbto 'I(f.) am the one who wrote it')

32. mɛalləmtīni had-dars

'You(f.) have taught me that lesson' (As contrasted with mɛalləmtni had-dars 'She has taught me that lesson')

33. lēš ᵊmḥārəbtīha?

'Why are you(f.) quarreling with her?' (a.p. of ḥārab 'to pick a fight with, to quarrel with'. [On present-tense English translation, see p.269.]) (Cf. lēš ᵊmḥārəbtha? 'Why is she quarreling with her?')

34. ʔənti msāwītī-lo ḥayāto taɛāse taɛāse

'You(f.) have been making his life miserable for him' (cf. hiyye msāwīt-ə́llo...'She has been making... for him')

35. hiyye mədžawwəzto ɛala ḥalāwto w-ʔənti mədžawwəztī ɛala mālo

'She married him for his looks and you married him for his money' (Note that since participles designate a consequent state [p.262], the wording here implies that both women are still married to him. Otherwise, the perfect tense would be used: džawwazə́to 'she married him', džawwaztī 'you married him'.)

These second-person participial forms are created by analogy to verbs in the perfect tense, which have a suffix -ti [p.175]: lbəsti 'you(f.) put on', lbəstīhon 'you put them on'; katabti 'you(f.) wrote', katabtī 'you wrote it(m.)'; sāwēti 'you(f.) made', sāwētī-lo 'you made...for him', etc.[1]

---

[1]Note that in the perfect tense, t marks second person and i marks feminine, while in the participle this analysis must be reversed.

In non-suffixing forms, feminine participles are the same for all persons: *wēn ḥáṭṭa l-manāšef?* [DA-199] 'Where have you(f.) put the towels?' (Or, in other contexts, 'Where has she put...')

The Relation of Participles to Verbal Aspects

If a verb is PUNCTUAL (or MOMENTANEOUS), i.e. if it purports to designate a kind of event, then its participles generally depict the state of affairs SUBSEQUENT to that event:

fāˀ	'to wake up'.................*fāyeˀ*	'having waked up, awake'		
samma	'to name, call'..............*msammi*	'having named'		
		msamma	'(having been) named, called'	
məsek	'to take hold of'...........*māsek*	'having taken hold of, holding'		
		mamsūk	'having been taken hold of, being held'	

Likewise, if a verb is DEVELOPMENTAL, i.e. if it implies a process of change from one state to another (regardless whether the change is momentaneous or gradual), then its participles depict the state toward which the development leads, i.e. the subsequent state:

səker	'to get drunk'..........*sakrān*	'drunk'	
ġayyar	'to change' (trans.).....*mġayyer*	'having changed' (trans.)	
		mġayyar	'(having been) changed'
tεallam	'to learn, be educated'..*mətεallem*	'educated, having learned'	

On the other hand, if a verb is DURATIVE but not developmental, i.e. if it designates an activity or a situation — but not a process of change or a momentary event — then its participles generally depict the state of affairs CONCURRENT with (or identical with) that activity or situation:

nṭaẓar	'to expect, await'.......*mənṭáẓer*	'expecting, awaiting'	
		mənṭáẓar	'(being) expected, awaited'
šaġal	'to occupy, keep...busy'.*šáġel*	'occupying, keeping...busy'	
		mašġūl	'occupied, busy'
dawwar	'to look for'...........*mdawwer*	'looking for'	
(εala)		*(εala)*	
		mdawwar	'sought, looked for'
		εalē	
ḥtawa	'to include'............*məḥtáwi*	'including'	
(εala)		*(εala)*	
		məḥtáwa	'included'
		εalē	

No matter whether the state depicted by a participle is subsequent or concurrent, it must in any case be a <u>consequent</u> state; i.e. it must be a necessary consequence of whatever it is the underlying verb designates. Thus there is really only one kind of semantic relationship between verbs and participles, not two.

Verbal aspects, unfortunately, cannot actually be deduced from the nature of the phenomena referred to; one and the same phenomenon may be viewed from various perspectives, and it commonly happens that Arabic and English take different perspectives on it. These differences would cause no confusion except for the fact that they are often too subtle to be reflected in the usual glosses, translations, and definitions encountered in textbooks and reference books. See Psychological State participles, p. 272.

Examples of concurrent state participles:

36. *ləssāni mətradded*   'I'm still undecided' (a.p. of *traddad* 'to vacilate', durative)

37. *rākde wara t-təslāye bass*   'She's only out for a good time' (lit. "running after amusement") (a.p. of *rakad* 'to run', durative)

38. *haš-žnēne məɛtdna fīha mnīḥ*   'This garden is well kept' (p.p. of *ɛtana b-* 'to take care of', durative)

39. *n-nās kəllha farḥāne w-ḍaḥkāne* [adap. fr. DA-301]   'The people are all rejoicing and laughing' (a.p. of *fəreḥ* and *ḍəḥek*, durative)

40. *wlād ɛammna kānu mṣayyfīn ᵊhnīk* [DA-152]   'Our cousins were spending the summer there' (a.p. of *ṣayyaf* 'to (spend the) summer', durative)

41. *šū l-ᵊġrāḍ halli lāzəmtak?* [DA-128]   'What things do you need?' (*lāzem*, a.p. of *byəlzam* 'to be necessary to (s.o.)', durative)

42. *məstangrīnkon ɛal-ɛaša* [SAL-70]   'We're expecting you for dinner' (a.p. of *stangar* 'to expect, await', durative)

43. *ɛaᵖlo sābeḥ bəl-xayāl*   'He's daydreaming', lit. 'His mind is swimming in fantasy' (a.p. of *sabaḥ* 'to swim', durative)

44. *ᵖana māliyyan məɛtémed ɛalē*   'I'm financially dependent on him' 'a.p. of *ɛtamad ɛala* 'to depend on', durative)

45. *mašġūl bāli ɛand ʔaḥmad bēk xēr šəbo?* [DA-217]

'I'm concerned about Ahmed Bey; he's all right, I hope?', lit. "My attention is occupied with..." (p.p. of *šaġal* 'to occupy, concern', durative)

Some verbs may be either punctual or durative, for instance *sāwa* 'to do, to make', *ġərəʔ* 'to sink'. The participles of such verbs may indicate either the subsequent state (*msāwi* 'having made', *ġarʔān* 'sunken') or the concurrent state ('making', 'sinking').

Verbs with an Inceptive Aspect. Some verbs that are used (duratively) in reference to an activity or a situation are also used (punctually) in reference to its INCEPTION, i.e. to the event which marks the beginning of that activity or situation. For example *nām* 'to sleep' (durative, as in *nəmᵊt sāɛtēn* 'I slept two hours') and 'to go to sleep, or 'to lie down to sleep' (punctual, as in *nəmᵊt bakkīr* 'I went to bed early'). Thus the participle *nāyem* 'asleep' is subsequent with reference to the inception and concurrent with reference to the duration. Other inceptive-aspect verbs:

Verb	Durative	Inceptive	Participle	
ʔaɛad	'to sit'............	'to sit down'..........	*ʔāɛed*	'sitting, seated'
rəkeb	'to ride'..........	'to mount, get on'......	*rākeb*	'mounted, riding'
sakat	'not to talk'......	'to stop talking'.......	*sāket*	'not talking'
ləbes	'to wear'..........	'to put on'............	*lābes*	'wearing'
			malbūs	'being worn'
ḥamal	'to carry'.........	'to pick up, load on'...	*ḥāmel*	'carrying'
			maḥmūl	'(being)carried'
sāfar	'to travel'........	'to set out on a trip'..	*msāfer*	'traveling'
rtāḥ	'to rest, be at..... ease'	'to relax, put one's.... self at ease'	*mərtāḥ*	'at ease'

Examples in use:

46. *ṣ-ṣaʔᵊr kān ḥāmel fāra b-maxālbo*

'The hawk had (i.e. was carrying) a mouse in its claws'

47. *kənt lāzəm təbʔa mərtāḥ bəl-bēt* [DA-218]

'You should have stayed resting at home'

48. *brīd šūfo, šūfī-li yā ʔāɛed yəmma nāyem?* [DA-217]

'I'd like to see him; (would you) see for me whether he's up or in bed?'

Psychological State Participles. Arabic verbs of perception, cognition, affect, and the like[1] are predominantly punctual while the corresponding English verbs are predominantly durative. Compare, for instance, Arabic *Ɛəref* 'to find out, to recognize, to become acquainted with' with the English verb *to know*.

The participles of this kind of Arabic verb are perfectly regular, depicting the psychological state consequent upon (and subsequent to) the event: *Ɛāref* (or *Ɛarfān*) 'having found out, having become acquainted with'. But since the corresponding English verbs are mainly durative – with simple present tense forms used for actuality [p. 320] as well as for dispositions or generalities – the Arabic participles are commonly rendered in English with the simple present tense: *ʔana Ɛāref* 'I know' (not "I am knowing" nor 'I have known').

Similarly in reference to the past, a participle that is complemental or attributive to a verb in the perfect [p. 340] may be translated into English with the simple past tense: *kənt Ɛāref* 'I knew' (in contrast to the simple perfect *Ɛrəft* 'I found out').[2]

Examples of "psychological" verbs and their active participles:

šāf	'to see'(momentarily).......	*šāyef*	'to see, be looking at' (dur.)
ħass	'to feel'(momentarily)......	*ħāses*	'to feel, be feeling' (dur.)
ħabb	'to like, take a liking..... to'(momentarily)	*ħābeb*	'having taken a liking to, to like' (durative)
fəhem	'to catch on, understand'... (momentarily)	*fāhem, fahmān*	'to understand' (dur.)
səmeƐ	'to hear'(momentarily)......	*sāmeƐ, samƐān*	'to hear, be listening to'(dur.)[3]

---

[1] The verbs actually involved here are those which are commonly complemented either by a clause or by an object, excluding, therefore, words like *mbaṣaṭ* 'to enjoy one's self', *tƐazzab* 'to suffer', *fakkar* in the sense 'to cogitate' (but including e.g. *ftakar* 'to think', which is normally complemented by a clause or an object).

[2] The English simple present and past are also used, however, in translating Arabic dispositional [p. 326] and annunciatory [325] predications, e.g. *ʔana baƐref* 'I know', thus obscuring the sometimes crucial distinction between verb and participle in Arabic: *fāhem kalāmo?* 'Do you understand what he is saying (or what he said)?' vs. *btəfham Ɛarabi?* 'Do you understand Arabic?', *kənt təfham Ɛarabi (b-hal-waʔt)?* 'Did you understand Arabic (at that time?)'. The two latter sentences are dispositional, and cannot normally be expressed except by the imperfect tense.

[3] These translations of *sāmeƐ* or *samƐān* only apply to the purely <u>sensory</u> meaning of *səmeƐ*, as opposed to the <u>cognitive</u> meaning (as in 'to hear about', 'to hear from', 'to hear the news', etc.) Thus *kaʔanni samƐān ʔəsmo* '(It seems) as if I've heard his name', not "...as if I <u>hear</u> his name". In the cognitive sense, *sāmeƐ* means 'having heard(of), familiar with (the sound of)'.

xāf	'to fear, take fright(of)' .....*xāyef*	'afraid of, to fear'(dur.)
	(momentarily)	
dzakkar	'to remember, recall'(mom.)....*madzakker*	'to remember' (dur.)[1]
rād	'to wish, want' (momentarily)..*rāyed*	'to wish, want' (dur.)
Ɛažab	'to please' (momentarily)......*Ɛāžeb*	'to please' (dur.)
hamm	'to interest, concern' (mom.)..*hāmem*	'to interest' (dur.)

Psychological participle clauses (Present state):

49. *šāyef hal-ʔarāḍi ʔaddēš xaḍra*
    [DA-235]
    '(Do you) see how green this land is(?)'

50. *ʔana xāyef la-ykūn maƐi z-zāyde*
    [DA-217]
    'I fear (I'm afraid) I may have appendicitis'

51. *hāses kaʔanni xalʔān ᵊždīd*
    'I feel as though I'm newly born'

52. *hal-ʔaqtirāḥ mū Ɛāžabni*
    'I don't like that suggestion', lit. 'That suggestion doesn't please me.'

53. *mū hāmóma ʔalla rāḥéta*
    'Nothing concerns her but her own comfort'

54. *rāyed baddel dolārāt ʔamērkiyye b-lērāt*
    'I wish to change some American dollars into pounds'

55. *sāmeƐ ṣōṭ ᵊn-nawaƐīr Ɛal-Ɛāṣi?* [DA-252]
    'Do you hear the sound of the water wheels on the Orontes?'

Past state:

56. *kān fī zalame hāseb hālo šāṭer u-Ɛālem* [AO-83]
    'There was a fellow who considered himself clever and learned' (a.p. of *hasab* 'to reckon, count, consider')

57. *w-ḍarab rās ᵊt-tamsāl halli huwwe maftakro bant ᵊt-tāžer* [AO-114]
    'And he struck (off) the head of the statue he though (was) the merchant's daughter' (a.p. of *ftakar* 'to think')

58. *ʔana mā kent matṣawwer ʔanno waṣlet haṣ-ṣināƐa Ɛandkon la-had-daraže* [DA-251]
    'I didn't imagine that this industry among you had reached such a level' (a.p. of *tṣawwar* 'to imagine')

59. *ʔana Ɛmalt hāli māli sāmeƐ* [AO-118]
    'I pretended not to hear'

---

[1] Note that while we translate *ʔana madzakker* consistently as a durative in English: 'I remember', *ʔana nāsi* on the other hand is more often rendered as a punctual: 'I've forgotten' (less often durative: 'I forget').

Antecedent State Participles. The active participles of some of the more common TRANSLOCATIVE verbs (verbs having to do with going, coming, etc. to and from places)[1] may be used to indicate not only a subsequent state (e.g. *rāžeɛ* 'having returned', from *ražeɛ* 'to return'), but also an ANTECEDENT state (*rāžeɛ* 'going to return, returning').

Verb		Participle	Subsequent State	Antecedent State
rāḥ	'to go'...........*rāyeḥ*		'gone'..............	'going, going to go'
ʔəža	'to come'.........*žāye*		'(having)come'......	'coming, going to come'
ṭaleɛ	'to go up, out'...*ṭāleɛ*		'gone up, out'......	'going up, out, etc.'
nəzel	'to descend'......*nāzel*		'having descended'..	'descending, going to descend'
tarak	'to leave'........*tārek*		'having left'.......	'leaving, going to leave'
daxal	'to enter'........*dāxel*		'having entered'....	'entering, going to enter'
xaraž	'to go out'.......*xārež*		'gone out'..........	'going out, going to go out'
wəṣel	'to arrive'.......*wāṣel*		'having arrived'....	'arriving, going to arive'
bəʔi	'to remain, stay'.*bāʔi*		'remaining, left'...	'going to remain, stay'
ʔaɛad	'to stay'.........*ʔāɛed*		'staying'...........	'going to stay'
sāfar	'to set out on a trip'..........*msāfer*		'(having)set out, traveling'........	'going to set out'

Examples of antecedent state participles:

60. *l-ɛēle wāṣle baɛəd bəkra* [DA-243] — 'The family is arriving tomorrow'

61. *šu blāʔīkon rāyḥīn ʔabəl ma tāxdu l-ʔahwe?* [DA-199] — 'You mean you're going before having coffee?!' (lit. "Do I find you about to go...")

62. *ʔana tārek əl-yōm* — 'I'm leaving today'

63. *ʔənte nāzel bəl-mubārā?* — 'Are you competing in the tournament?', lit. "Are you descending into...(e.g. the arena)"

---

[1] Sometimes inappropriately called 'verbs of motion'.

64. *mīn ᵊmṭāleɛ ᵊl-yōm ɛašiyye?* 'Who are you taking out this evening?' (a.p. of *ṭālaɛ*, causative [p. 243] of *ṭəleɛ*)

65. *huwwe lāḥᵖak* 'He's out to get out', lit. "He's catching up with you" (a.p. of *ləḥeᵖ* 'to catch up with, catch')

66. *ᵖana kənt rāyeḥ la-ɛandak šufak* [DA-243] 'I was going (to go) to see you'

Non-Stative Participles

Certain participles may be used in a dispositional sense [p. 277], for example:

Verb		Participle	Stative	Dispositional
ṭharrak	'to move'......	*məṭharrek*	'moving'..........	'movable'
tžawwal	'to travel'....	*mətžawwel*	'travelling'......	'disposed to travel'
ᵖəbel	'to accept'....	*maᵖbūl*	'accepted'........	'acceptable'
ᵖara	'to read'......	*maqrūᵖ* (classicism)	'(having been) read'..........	'legible'

The dispositional sense is sometimes more or less limited to set phrases, e.g. *tāžer mətžawwel* 'traveling salesman' (i.e. a salesman who travels, not a salesman who is traveling); *kəlᵊmto masmūɛa* 'His opinion is taken seriously; what he says goes' (lit. "His word is heard").

Participles are also often used in making generalizations about recurrent states [cf. p. 321]:

67. *ᵖəntu fātḥīn ᵊs-sabᵊt?* 'Do you open (or are you open) on Saturday(s)?'

68. *lābse ᵖawāɛi ḥəlwe* 'She wears pretty clothes'

69. *l-kamyōnāt māšye rāyḥa rāžɛa bēn l-ᵊmḥaṭṭa w-bētna* 'The buses run both ways (lit. "coming, going") between the station and where we live'

Participles are also sometimes used dispositionally in emphatic negative statements of this sort:

70. *waḷḷa māli mədžawwəza!* 'I certainly <u>wouldn't</u> marry her!'

71. *ɛālama ᵖante ɛam-ᵊtḥākīni ɛala haš-šaġle, māni mxayybak* 'Since you're speaking to me (personally) about this matter, I won't let you down'.

Some active participles may be used in an agentive [p. 278] or characteristic [279] sense:

Verb		Participle	Stative	Agentive or Characteristic
šamal	'to include'.....	*šāmel*	'including'.......	'inclusive, comprehensive'
barad	'to get cold'....	*bāred*	'(having gotten) cold'..........	'(characteristically) cold'
fəhem	'to understand'..	*fāhem, fahmān*	'who under- stands...'......	'understanding, knowledgeable'

Most agentive adjectives of Pattern *məFƐeL* [p. 133] are
etymologically active participles of Pattern IV verbs [260],
but have lost their complementation (if any) and their
strictly stative sense.

Substantivized active participles designating human
beings are often used in the occupational sense [p. 305]
(which corresponds – for nouns – to dispositional adjectives):
mƐullem 'teacher', *ħāyek* 'weaver'. Inanimate active participles are sometimes used in an agentive sense: *māneƐ* 'hindrance' (from *manaƐ* 'to prevent, hinder'), *bāƐes* (classicism)
'motive', from *baƐaθ* 'to send, to induce'.

Many passive participles are substantivized in a result-
ative sense (generally involving some idiomatic specialization of meaning): *maktūb* 'letter' (from *katab* 'to write'),
maxlūʔ 'creature' (from *xalaʔ* 'to create').

Substantivization as such does not necessarily destroy
the stative sense of a participle, however. Note *mwaẓẓaf*
'employee', *mƐaẓẓem* 'host', *lāžeʔ* 'refugee', etc., which are
normally always stative, and *mʔallef* 'author, composer',
which may be either stative (as in *mʔallef hal-ᵊktāb* 'the
one who wrote this book') or occupational (as in *mʔallef
kətob* 'a writer of books').

DISPOSITIONAL ADJECTIVES

A dispositional adjective indicates that the person (or thing) referred to is especially inclined or habituated or qualified to do what is designated by the underlying verb. Patterns $Fa\mathcal{E}\bar{u}L$ [p. 128], $Fa\mathcal{E}\mathcal{E}\bar{a}L$ [129], and $Fa\mathcal{E}\mathcal{E}\bar{\imath}L$ [129] are the ones generally used.

Underlying Verb		Dispositional Adjective

Pattern $Fa\mathcal{E}\bar{u}L$:

ḥasad	'to envy'.........................	ḥasūd	'envious, inclined to envy'
xəžel	'to be embarrassed, ashamed'......	xažūl	'shy, bashful'
ṣabar	'to be patient'..................	ṣabūr	'patient' (in disposition)
sakat	'not to talk, be silent'..........	sakūt	'silent, taciturn'
ġafar	'to forgive'.....................	ġafūr	'forgiving' (in disposition)
ʔakal	'to eat'.........................	ʔakūl	'gourmand'
ḍəḥek	'to laugh'.....................∴.	ḍaḥūk	'jolly, always laughing'

With medial radical semivowel, the Pattern is $Fayy\bar{u}L$: *ġayyūr* 'jealous' (in disposition), from *ġār* 'to be jealous'.

kasūl 'lazy' and *žasūr* 'daring' have no underlying simple verbs, but correspond to *tkāsal* 'to loaf' and *džāsar* 'to dare', respectively [p. 249].

Pattern $Fa\mathcal{E}\mathcal{E}\bar{a}L$:

ḥass		'to feel..................	ḥassās	'sensitive'
ṭəmeɛ		'to be greedy'............	ṭammāɛ	'greedy'
kazab,	kazzab	'to lie'..................	kazzāb	'liar'
ġašš		'to cheat'...............	ġaššāš	'cheater'
bəki		'to weep, cry'...........	bakka	'cry-baby, weeper'

Note the close relationship between dispositional adjectives of Pattern $Fa\mathcal{E}\mathcal{E}\bar{a}L$ and Occupational Nouns of the same Pattern [p. 305].[1]

---

[1]There is no clear-cut noun-vs.-adjective distinction in human designations formed on Patterns $Fa\mathcal{E}\mathcal{E}\bar{a}L$ and $Fa\mathcal{E}\mathcal{E}\bar{\imath}L$ (among others). [See p. 382.] There is, however, a clear enough distinction in meaning between the dispositional and occupational categories; all dispositional derivatives have here been included with adjectives, while occupationals are obviously to be classified as nouns.

Underlying Verb		Dispositional Adjective	

Pattern *FaɛɛīL:*

barad	'to get cold'..........................	*barrīd*	'sensitive to cold'
balaf	'to bluff'.............................	*ballīf*	'bluffer'
štaġal	'to work'.............................	*šaġġīl*	'(good)worker'
ṣaraf	'to spend'............................	*ṣarrīf*	'spendthrift'
laɛeb	'to play'.............................	*laɛɛīb*	'player'

      A slightly different pattern *(FəɛɛīL)* [p.129] is used for some dispositionals: *səkkīr* 'drunkard' from *səker* 'to get drunk'.

      It is important to distinguish between dispositional and stative adjectives; the English translations do not always express this distinction: *sakūt* 'quiet' (i.e. un-talkative in disposition) vs. *sāket* 'quiet' (i.e. untalka-tive for the moment); *ṣabūr* 'patient' (i.e. in disposition) vs. *ṣāber* 'patient' (i.e. waiting patiently); *kasūl* 'lazy' (i.e. habitually) vs. *kaslān* '(feeling or acting) lazy'.

      On the use of certain participles in a dispositional sense, see p. 275.

      On the adjective-like use of verbs in a dispositional sense, see p. 328.

AGENTIVE ADJECTIVES

      Agentive adjectives, formed on Pattern *məFɛeL* [p.133], depict their referent as doing — or tending to do — what is designated by a paronymous transitive verb: *ʔaraf* 'to disgust': *məʔref* 'disgusting'.

      Most typically, the object of the underlying verb is animate, and its subject, inanimate; the agentive adjective characterizes a stimulus as eliciting a certain kind of response.

      Agentive adjectives are not to be confused with Pattern IV participles [p. 260]. The active participle of a transitive verb takes an object [265], while an agentive adjective does not; and the participle designates only states [262], while the agentive designates states, dis-positions, or qualities indiscriminately.

Transitive Verb		Agentive Adjective	
taɛab	'to tire'.........................matɛeb		'tiring, tiresome'
zaɛaž	'to bother, disturb'............mazɛež		'bothersome, disturbing'
raḍa	'to please, satisfy'............marḍi		'satisfactory'
ʔaza	'to harm'........................maʔzi		'harmful'
hamm	'to concern, be important to'.....mhamm		'important'
mall	'to bore'.......................mmall		'boring'
wažaɛ	'to hurt, inflict pain'..........mūžeɛ		'painful, hurtful'[1]
ʔatlaf	'to ruin, annihilate'...........matlef		'ruinous, destructive'
ḍaḥḥak	'to make...laugh'...............maḍḥek		'funny, laughable'
rayyaḥ	'to make...comfortable'..........maryeḥ		'comfortable' (e.g. chair)
hayyab	'to inspire with awe, fear'.......mahyeb		'awesome, fearsome'
mawwat	'to kill, cause death'...........mumīt		'deadly, lethal'

CHARACTERISTIC ADJECTIVES[2]

Characteristic adjectives, formed on the pattern maFɛeL [p. 133], are derived from simple nouns. They depict their referents as being characterized by, or notably endowed with, the thing designated by the underlying noun:

Underlying Noun		Characteristic Adjective	
zōʔ	'taste'............................mazwe ʔ		'having good taste'
xaṭar	'danger'..........................maxṭer		'dangerous'
sann	'age'.............................msann		'aged'
šams	'sun'.............................mašmes		'sunny'
dahᵊn	'grease, oil'.....................madhen		'greasy, oily'
hawa	'air, breeze'.....................mahwi		'draughty, airy'
lsān	'tongue'..........................malsen		'articulate, eloquent'

---

[1] Note that mūžeɛ — like the subject of wažaɛ — refers to an external agent, while the subject of wažeɛ 'to hurt, pain' refers to an "internal" agent: rāsi byūžaɛni 'my head hurts me'. The agentive mūžeɛ does not correspond to wažeɛ — it does not mean 'painful' is this sense.

[2] Characteristic and Agentive can probably be analyzed structurally as alternants of a single category, since the former are all derived from nouns, the latter from verbs; the difference in the categories' "meanings" is perhaps merely a function of this grammatical difference in underlying words.

Underlying Noun		Characteristic Adjective	
ḥaʔʔ	'right'	*mḥəʔʔ*	'in the right'
waraʔ	'leaves'	*mūreʔ*	'in leaf, leafy'
zahᵊr	'blossoms'	*məzher*	'blooming, flowering'
ʔərᵊš	'piastre'	*məʔreš*	'well off'
baṭᵊn	'belly'	*məbṭen*	'paunchy, potbellied'

RELATIVE ADJECTIVES
(*an-nisba*)

A relative adjective indicates something characteristic of, or having to do with, what the underlying word designates. Most relative adjectives are formed by suffixing *-i* or sometimes *-āni* to a noun base; a few are derived from words other than nouns.

Underlying Noun		Relative Adjective	
žanūb	'south'	*žanūbi*	'southern'
ʔaṣᵊl	'origin'	*ʔaṣli*	'original'
ražžāl	'man'	*ražžāli*	'men's' (e.g. clothes)
ṭəbb	'(profession of) medicine'	*ṭəbbi*	'medical'
məšmoš	'apricot(s)'	*məšᵊmši*	'apricot-colored'
š-šam	'Damascus'	*šāmi*	'Damascene'

With suffix *-āni* [See also p. 282]:

žəsᵊm	'body'	*žəsmāni*	'bodily'
rōḥ, rūḥ	'soul, spirit'	*rūḥani* (and *rūḥi*)	'spiritual'
nafs	'self, psyche'	*nafsāni*	'psychological'

Relative derivatives showing stem changes

Nouns with the suffix *-e/-a* [p. 138] lose this suffix when *-i* is added:

zirāɛa	'agriculture'	*zirāɛi*	'agricultural'
ḥaʔīʔa	'truth'	*ḥaʔīʔi*	'true, real'
ɛāṭfe	'feeling, emotion, sentiment'	*ɛāṭfi*	'emotional, sentimental'
ɛāde	'custom, usage, habit'	*ɛādi*	'customary, usual'
ḍarūra	'necessity'	*ḍarūri*	'necessary'

Relatives derived from defective nouns [p. 211], or nouns ending in a radical semivowel, have *-w-* representing the semivowel before the *-i*. Other stem modifications may also occur:

Underlying Word			Relative Adjective
naša	'starch',,	*našawi*	'starchy'
luġa	'language'	*luġawi*	'linguistic'
nabi	'prophet'	*nabawi*	'prophetic, of the prophet(s)'
naḥu	'(Arabic) morphology, grammar'	*naḥawi*	'(Arab) grammarian'
tāni	'second'	*tānawi, sānawi*	'secondary'
ḥama	'Hama' (a city)	*ḥamwi*	'of Hama'
šəte	'winter'	*šətwi*	'of winter, wintry'
ʔaxx	(annex. form *ʔaxu*)	*ʔaxawi*	'brotherly'
sama	'sky'	*samāwi*	'of the sky, sky blue'

> Note also the forms *damawi* 'of blood, bloody', from Cl. *dam* (Colloq. *damm*) 'blood'; *yadawi* 'manual', from Cl. *yad* (Colloq. *ʔīd*) 'hand', *sanawi* 'annual' from Cl. *sana* (Colloq. *səne*). In these biradical words [p. 40] *-aw-* is a stem-formative and does not represent a radical.

Grammatical Types of Underlying Words

Relative adjectives derived from ethnic collectives [p. 301]:

Ɛarab	'Arabs'	*Ɛarabi*	'Arab, Arabic'
tərk	'Turks'	*tərki*	'Turkish'
kərd	'Kurds'	*kərdi*	'Kurdish'
ʔarman	'Armenians'	*ʔarmani*	'Armenian'
ʔamērkān	'Americans'	*ʔamerkāni*	'American'
ʔafranž	'Westerners'	*ʔafranži*	'Western'
badu	'Bedouins'	*badawi*	'Bedouin'
ʔəbṭ	'Copts'	*ʔəbṭi*	'Coptic'

> When substantivized, these relatives function as unit nouns [p. 301].

Derived from noun plurals:

Underlying Word				Relative Adjective	
sətt	'lady',	pl.	səttāt............	səttāti	'ladies' (e.g. clothes)
nəkte	'joke',	pl.	nəkat............	nəkati	'full of jokes, funny'
dawle	'nation',	pl.	duwal............	duwali	'international'

See also Occupational Nouns [p. 306].

Derived from prepositions [p. 485]:

fō̌	'above, over, up'..............	fō̌ʔāni	'upper'
taḥᵊt	'below, under, down'...........	taḥtāni	'lower'
ʔəddām	'in front (of)'................	ʔəddamāni	'front, fore(ward)'
wara	'behind'.......................	warrāni[1]	'back, hind'
xalf	'behind, rear'.................	xalfāni	'back, rear'
waṣṭ	'among, amid, in the middle'....	waṣṭāni	'middle, mid'
žuwwa	'inside'......................	žuwwāni	'inner'
barra	'outside'.....................	barrāni	'outer'

Derived from miscellaneous noun-type words [p. 382]:

ʔawwal	'first'........................	ʔawwalāni	'first, primary',
		ʔawwali	'initial'
ʔāxer	'last'.........................	ʔāxrāni	'last, final'
ʔaṣfar	'yellow'......................	ʔaṣfarāni	'yellowish'
ʔaswad	'black'.......................	ʔaswadāni	'blackish'
xamse	'five'........................	xamsāwi	'of five, of the fifth'
ʔarbϵīn	'forty'......................	ʔarbϵīni	'of the fortieth' (as in ϵīd ʔarbϵīni 'fortieth anniversary')

---

[1]Doubling of the r is an anomalous stem change.

CHAPTER 11: NOUN DERIVATION

Index of Categories

The substantivization of adjectives [p. 276] and the materialization of abstract nouns [284] are semantic types of noun derivation, which, however, do not involve any consistent kinds of change in the form of word bases.

ABSTRACT NOUNS (including GERUNDS)

Most verbs and adjectives, and some nouns, have an abstract noun derived from them — a noun which serves to name the kind of event, function, state, or quality predicated by means of the underlying word. The adjective *ʔamīn* 'honest', for instance, has an abstract derivative *ʔamāne* 'honesty'; the noun *ʔaxx* 'brother' has a derivative *ʔuxuwwe* 'brotherhood'; and the verb *ṭār* 'to fly' has a derivative *ṭayarān* 'flight, flying'.

An abstract noun derived from a verb is called a GERUND or VERBAL NOUN (*maṣdar*)[1].

The relationship between an underlying word and its abstract derivative is based on the syntactical transformation of a predicative clause [p. 401] into a construct phrase [464]: *l—walad šāṭer* 'the boy is clever' → *šaṭāret ᵊl—walad* 'the boy's cleverness'; *r—rəžžāl māt* 'the man died' → *mōt ᵊr—rəžžāl* 'the man's death'.

> On the syntax of gerunds, see Active and Passive Use of Gerunds [p. 296], Objects [440], Adverbial Noun Complements [p. 442], Derived Constructs [464].

Concretization of Abstract Nouns. Many abstract nouns are converted, without change in form, into CONCRETE nouns, in one or both of these ways:

1.) **Materialization.** Some abstract nouns may be used to refer to the outward manifestations or material concomitants of the abstract function. Thus the gerund *ʔakᵊl* 'eating' is also used to mean 'food'; the gerund *ktābe* 'writing' may designate the resulting inscription as well as the act.

> Very similar to materialization is HYPOSTASIS, whereby some immaterial result or concomitant of the function is conceptualized as if it had a regular kind of tangible manifestation though it actually hasn't. Cf. Hypostatic Nouns, p. 309.

2.) **Particularization.** Some abstract nouns may be used to designate separate or individual instances of the abstract function. Thus the gerund *zyāra* 'visiting' is also used to mean 'a visit', *ṣɛūbe* 'difficulty', to mean 'a difficulty'.

> Particularization converts a mass noun into a count noun [p. 366]: *tlatt ᵊṣɛūbāt* 'three difficulties', *zyārtēn* 'two visits'.
> Those gerunds from which instance nouns [297] are formally differentiated and derived, are not themselves so apt to be used in a particularized sense: *ḍarb* 'hitting, striking' (not 'a blow', for which the instance noun *ḍarbe* is used).

---

[1] The literal meaning of *maṣdar* is 'source', which would seem to imply that a verb is derived from its abstract noun instead of the reverse. This term was probably arrived at by way of metaphysical — rather than linguistic — considerations, perhaps under the influence of Platonism.

Some gerunds, however, are <u>not</u> used in a particularized
sense even though a true instance noun is also lacking:
ṭayarān 'flying, flight' (not 'a flight').

Many abstract nouns are simultaneously materialized and particularized.
Thus *nabāt* means not only 'growing, vegetating' (abstract),[1] and
'vegetation' (materialized), but also 'a plant' (materialized <u>and</u>
particularized). Likewise *šaxṣiyye* 'personality' means not only the
state or function of being a person (*šaxṣ),* but more often 'a personality'.

In some cases, different gerundial forms from the same
verb are concretized in different senses. The verb *daras*
'to study, learn' has two gerunds, *dars* and *dirāse; dars* is
used in the passive sense as 'lesson', *dirāse* in the active
sense as '(a) study'.
The verb *ḥakam* 'to judge' and 'to govern' has a gerund
ḥəkᵊm which is used abstractly in both senses, but concretely only in the sense 'judgement, decision'; the form *ḥkūme*
'government', on the other hand, is used only in the one
sense, usually concretely.

It may be noted that the derivational processes of
abstraction and concretization described here apply to
English and other languages as well as to Arabic. This is
no guarantee, however, that the languages will have parallel
derivations in any particular instance.

Abstract Derivatives of Adjectives and Nouns.

Abstract nouns derived from simple nouns and adjectives are mostly
formed on the patterns *FaƐāLe, FƐūLe,* and *FəƐL(e).*
Those derived from relative adjectives (ending in *-i*) are formed by
suffixing *-(yy)e* [p. 280]. Examples:

Pattern *FaƐāLe* [p. 146]:

Underlying Word		Abstract Noun	
šəžāƐ	'brave'	*šažāƐa*	'bravery'
bəšeƐ	'ugly'	*bašāƐa*	'ugliness'
Ɛaduww	'enemy'	*Ɛadāwe*	'enmity'
sadīʔ	'friend'	*sadāʔa*	'friendship'
ʔamīn	'honest'	*ʔamāne*	'honesty'
ʔāsi	'cruel'	*ʔasāwe*	'cruelty'
bāred	'stupid'	*barāde*	'stupidity'

---

[1] *nabāt* is seldom used abstractly except as paronymous complement [p. 442]:
byənbot nabāt "it grows a growth", i.e. 'it grows (considerably)'.

Underlying Word		Abstract Noun	
sālem	'safe, sound'.....	*salāmo*	'safety'
ḥārr	'hot'	*ḥarāra*	'heat'
ʕarāyeb	'kin'	*ʕarābe*	'kinship'

Pattern *FƐūLe* [p. 151]:

xəšen	'coarse'	*xšūne*	'coarseness'
rəṭeb	'damp, humid'.........	*rṭūbe*	'dampness, humidity'
ṭəfᵊl	'child, infant'.......	*ṭfūle*	'childhood, infancy'
sahᵊl	'easy'...............	*shūle*	'ease, facility'
ṣaƐᵊb	'difficult'..........	*ṣƐūbe*	'difficulty'
ʕabb	'father'.............	*ʕubuwwe*	'fatherhood'
bāred	'cold'...............	*brūde*	'coldness' (Cf. *barāde,* above)

Abstract nouns of Pattern *FƐūLe* are mostly derived from words of Patterns *FəƐL* [141], and *FaƐL* [139, 126].

Pattern *FəƐL* [p. 141]:

kbīr	'large'...............	*kəbᵊr*	'large size'
ẓġīr	'small'...............	*ẓəġᵊr*	'small size'
tʕīl	'heavy'..............	*təʕᵊl*	'heaviness; weight'
bƐīd	'far'................	*bəƐᵊd*	'distance'
bxīl	'stingy, miser'.......	*bəxᵊl*	'stinginess'
ṭawīl	'long'	*ṭūl*	'length'

	Underlying Word		Abstract Noun	

Pattern *FəɛLe* [p.142]:

	ʔalīl	'little, few'.........	*ʔəlle*	'small quantity, scarcity'
	šadīd	'intense'.............	*šədde*	'intensity'
	ʔawi	'strong, powerful' ...	*ʔuwwe*	'strength, power'
	ktīr	'much, many'..........	*kətra*	'large quantity'
	ṣāḥeb	'friend'	*ṣəḥbe*	'friendship, companionship'

Abstract nouns of Patterns *FəɛL* and *FəɛLe* are derived mainly from adjectives of Pattern *F(a)ɛīL* [p.127]. Those which have a final radical semivowel or the last two radicals alike have the final *-e;* most others do not.

Various other patterns are less commonly used for abstract derivatives of simple adjectives and nouns: Pattern *FaɛāL,* as in *žamāl* 'beauty' (from *žamīl* 'beautiful'); Pattern *FaɛaL,* as in *ṣaġar* 'childhood, youth' (from *ṣġīr* 'child, young'); Suffix *-iyye,* as in *ḥerriyye* 'freedom' (from *ḥərr* 'free'); and others.

Note that some abstract nouns – like their English counterparts – do not always indicate the positive quality or condition predicated by the underlying adjective, but rather the range of values defined by the adjective and its antonym: *ṭūl* 'length' (not necessarily 'longness'), *təʔəl* 'weight' (not necessarily 'heaviness').

Some adjectives and nouns are correlatives (or participles) of descriptive verbs [p.251]; their abstract nouns are also gerunds to those verbs: adj. *bxīl* 'stingy', verb *byəbxal* 'to be stingy', abstr. noun *bəxˀəl* 'stinginess, being stingy'; noun *ʔarāyeb* 'kin', verb *byəʔrab* 'to be kin to', abstr. noun *ʔarābe* 'kinship'; adj. *ṣaḥīḥ* 'correct', vb. *biṣaḥḥ* 'to be correct', abstr. noun *ṣəḥḥa* 'correctness'.

Abstract nouns derived from relative adjectives (or nouns) [p. 280] are formed by the suffixation of -(yy)e [139]:

Underlying Word			Abstract Noun	
waṭani	'patriot(ic)'..............		*waṭaniyye*	'patriotism'
ʔummi	'illiterate'..............		*ʔummiyye*	'illiteracy'
ɛabqari	'ingenious, genius'.......		*ɛabqariyye*	'ingenuity, genius'
ʔazali	'eternal'................		*ʔazaliyye*	'eternity'
nəsbi	'relative'...............		*nəsbiyye*	'relativity'
ɛaṣabi	'nervous'................		*ɛaṣabiyye*	'nervousness'
ʔanāni	'egotist(ical), selfish'..		*ʔanāniyye*	'egotism, selfishness'

Many derivatives of this sort are less often used abstractly than in a concretized sense [p. 284]; especially common are those designating institutions (either organized or implicit, and either universal or particularized):

Underlying Word			Concretized Derivative	
masīhi	'Christian'.............		*masīhiyye*	'Christianity'
bašari	'human'.................		*bašariyye*	'mankind'
šuyūɛi	'communist'.............		*šuyūɛiyye*	'communism'
ʔəštirāki	'socialist'.............		*ʔəštirākiyye*	'socialism'
žamhūri	'republican'............		*žamhūriyye*	'republic'
naẓari	'theoretical'...........		*naẓariyye*	'theory'
šaxṣi	'personal, individual'...		*šaxṣiyye*	'personality'
riyāḍi	'mathematical'..........		*riyāḍiyyāt*	'mathematics' (pl. only)

Some abstract or concretized derivatives are formed by suffixing -iyye to words of various other kinds. In some cases a change in the base pattern accompanies the suffixation:

masʔūl	'responsible'........		*masʔūliyye*	'responsibility'
ɛabd	'slave, enslaved'....		*ɛbūdiyye*	'enslavement, slavery'
huwwe	'he, it'.............		*hawiyye*	'identity'

A number of abstract nouns are formed by suffixing *-iyye*
to elatives: *ʔahammiyye* 'importance' (from *ʔahamm* 'more
important', from *mhəmm* 'important'), *ʔaktariyye* and
ʔaġlabiyye 'majority' (from *ʔaktar* 'more, most', and *ʔaġlab*
'most, major portion'), *ʔafḍaliyye* 'preference', (from *ʔafḍal*
'preferable'), etc.

Abstract derivatives of Pattern *ʔaFɛaL* adjectives
[p.130] and miscellaneous augmented words are not formed in
any very consistent ways: *sawād* 'blackness' (from *ʔaswad*
'black'), *ɛami* 'blindness' (from *ʔaɛma* 'blind' and *ɛəmi* 'to
go blind'), *ružūle* 'manliness' (from *ražžāl* 'man'), etc.

Gerunds

The gerunds of simple triradical verbs are formed on a variety of patterns; there is no sure way of telling which pattern is to be used for the
gerund of any particular verb, so each must be learned individually. The
gerunds of augmented verbs and quadriradical verbs, on the other hand, conform in almost every case to patterns which may be inferred from the pattern of the underlying verb.

Simple Gerundial Patterns. The most common of all is Pattern *FaɛL;* other
common patterns are *FəɛL, FaɛaL, Fɛāle, FaɛāL, FɛūL, FaɛLe, FəɛLe, FəɛLān,*
FaɛaLān. Examples:

Pattern *FaɛL* [p.139]:

Verb		Gerund	
žaraḥ 'to cut, wound'	....	*žarªḥ*	'wounding, cutting'
kasar 'to break'	....	*kasªr*	'breaking, breakage'
fəhem 'to understand'	....	*fahªm*	'understanding, comprehension'
ʔaxad 'to take'	....	*ʔaxªd*	'taking'
hazz 'to shake'	....	*hazz*	'shaking'
başaṭ 'to please'	....	*başṭ*	'pleasure, pleasing'
xāf 'to fear'	....	*xōf*	'fear'
bās 'to kiss'	....	*bōs*	'kissing'
bāɛ 'to sell'	....	*bēɛ*	'selling, sale'
rama 'to throw'	....	*rami*	'throwing'
wəɛi 'to become conscious'	.....	*waɛi*	'consciousness, becoming conscious'
ġaza 'to raid'	....	*ġazu*	'raiding'

Pattern *FəƐL* [p. 141]:

Verb		Gerund	Verb		Gerund
baġaḍ	'to hate'	*bəġḍ*	*ḥass*	'to feel'	*ḥəss*
ḥakam	'to judge'	*ḥəkəm*	*ḥafaẓ*	'to keep'	*ḥəfẓ*
ləƐeb	'to play'	*ləƐəb*	*labes*	'to wear, put on'	*ləbs*

ḥabb 'to like, love' ...... *ḥəbb*

Pattern *FəƐL* is not used for gerunds of hollow or defective verbs.

Patterns *FaƐaL* [p. 143]:

Verb		Gerund	Verb		Gerund
ḥasad	'to envy'	*ḥasad*	*ḥaṭṭ*	'to put'	*ḥaṭaṭ*
Ɛəmel	'to do, make'	*Ɛamal*	*ḍarr*	'to damage'	*ḍarar*
Ɛaraʔ	'to sweat'	*Ɛaraʔ*	*ṭalab*	'to request, order'	*ṭalab*

ġəleṭ 'to make a mistake' ...... *ġalaṭ*

Pattern *FaƐaL* is not used for gerunds of hollow or defective verbs.

Patterns *FaƐāL* [p. 146]:

Verb		Gerund	Verb		Gerund
nažaḥ	'to succeed'	*nažāḥ*	*Ɛaṭa*	'to give'	*Ɛaṭāʔ, Ɛaṭa*
nabat	'to grow, vegetate'	*nabāt*	*səxi*	'to be generous'	*saxāʔ, saxa*
fasad	'to corrupt'	*fasād*	*dəfi*	'to get warm'	*dafa*
dām	'to last'	*dawām*			

Pattern *F(i)ƐāL(e)* [pp. 147, 148]

Verb		Gerund	Verb		Gerund
Ɛabad	'to worship'	*Ɛbāde*	*ḥama*	'to defend'	*ḥmāye*
waled	'to bear (child)'	*wlāde*	*zād*	'to increase'	*zyāde*
ḥaras	'to guard'	*ḥrāse*			
zār	'to visit'	*zyāra*	*ḥakk*	'to itch'	*ḥkāk*
ʔara	'to read'	*ʔrāye*	*ġāb*	'to be absent'	*ġyāb*
zaraƐ	'to cultivate'	*zirāƐa*[1]	*raḍi*	'to be pleased, satisfied'	*raḍa* [p. 147]
daras	'to study'	*dirāse*[2]	*šəfi*	'to be cured'	*šifa* [p. 148]

Pattern *F(u)ƐūL* [p. 150]:

Verb		Gerund	Verb		Gerund
nəzel	'to descend'	*nzūl*	*sakat*	'not to talk'	*skūt*
daxal	'to enter'	*dxūl*	*marr*	'to pass'	*mrūr*
šaƐar	'to feel'	*šƐūr*	*ṭəleƐ*	'to come up or out'	*ṭlūƐ*
wəṣel	'to arrive'	*wṣūl*	*lazem*	'to be necessary'	*lzūm*
waṭi	'to be low'	*wṭuww*			

Pattern *FaƐaLān:*

Verb		Gerund	Verb		Gerund
ražaf	'to tremble'	*ražafān*	*ṭār*	'to fly'	*ṭayarān*
xafaʔ	'to beat, stir'	*xafaʔān*	*lām*	'to blame'	*lawamān*
nəšef	'to get dry'	*našafān*	*žāb*	'to bring'	*žayabān*
žara	'to run, flow'	*žarayān*	*dāʔ*	'to taste'	*dawaʔān*

Pattern *FəƐLān:*

Verb		Gerund	Verb		Gerund
nakar	'to deny'	*nəkrān*	*ġafar*	'to forgive'	*ġəfrān*
nəsi	'to forget'	*nesyān*	*Ɛəref*	'to know'	*Ɛərfān*
ʔaḍa	'to accomplish'	*ʔəḍyān*	*Ɛəṣi*	'to disobey'	*Ɛəṣyān*

---

[1] Two different gerunds of *zaraƐ* correspond to two different meanings of the verb: *zaraƐ* 'to sow, plant', has the gerund *zarʔƐ*.

[2] Another gerund is *dars;* see p. 285.

Pattern *FaƐLe* [p. 140]:

Verb		Gerund	Verb		Gerund
zalaʔ	'to skid, slide'	....*zalʔa*	*xāb*	'to fail, be disappointed'	...*xēbe*
raḥam	'to have mercy on'	..*raḥme*	*fāʔ*	'to wake'	...............*fēʔa*
waṣaf	'to prescribe'	......*waṣfe*[1]	*rāḥ*	'to go'	..................*rōḥa*

Pattern *FəƐLe* [p. 142]:

xadam	'to serve'	.........*xədme*	*Ɛāš*	'to live'	................*Ɛīše*
ʔəder	'to be able'	........*ʔədra*	*ġār*	'to be jealous'	............*ġīre*
saraʔ	'to steal'	.........*sərʔa*	*kasa*	'to clothe'	................*kəswe*

Pattern *F(a)ƐīL* [pp. 148, 149]:

Verb		Gerund	
raḥal	'to leave, emigrate'	.........*raḥīl*	'departure, moving away'
ʔann	'to moan'	....................*ʔanīn*	'moan, moaning'
šaxar	'to snore'	....................*šxīr*	'snore, snoring'
ṭann	'to ring, tinkle'	.............*ṭnīn*	'tinkle, ringing'
ḍažž	'to be noisy, to clamor'	......*ḍžīž*	'noise, clamor'
rakad	'to run'	....................*rkīd*	'running'

This pattern is specialized to some extent for gerunds designating sounds or noises.

Various other patterns are used less commonly for the gerunds of simple verbs, for example Pattern *FaƐaLe* as in *šafaʔa* 'pity' (from *šafaʔ* 'to pity'); Pattern *ʔəFƐāL* as in *ʔəhrāž* 'embarrassment' (from *haraž* 'to embarrass'; the anomalous defective pattern of *bəke* 'crying, weeping' [p. 147] (from *bəki* 'to cry, weep'), etc.

For *al-maṣdar l-mīmī*, see p. 309.

---

[1] *waṣaf* also means 'to describe', for which the gerund is *waṣ²f* 'description'.

Augmented Gerundial Patterns

Verbs of Pattern II(*FaƐƐaL*) [p.77] have gerunds of Pattern *taFƐīL*, excepting defective verbs, which have Pattern *təFƐāLe*, or sometimes, *taFƐiLe:*

Verb		Gerund	Verb		Gerund
Ɛallam	'to teach'	.... *taƐlīm*	*sažžal*	'to record'	.... *tasžīl*
ṣallaḥ	'to repair'	.... *ṭaṣlīḥ*	*faḍḍal*	'to prefer'	.... *ṭafḍīl*
daffa	'to heat'	.... *tədfāye*	*naʔʔa*	'to choose'	.... *tənʔāye*
wadda	'to take, guide'	.. *tūdāye*	*rabba*	'to educate'	...... *terbāye* or *tarbiye*

sawwa 'to fix, equalize' .... *taswiye*

Verbs of Pattern III *(FāƐaL)* [p.80] have gerunds of Pattern *mFāƐaLe;* (Defective form: *mFāƐā* [81]):

Verb		Gerund	Verb		Gerund
fāṣal	'to bargain (with)'	...... *mfāṣale*	*sāƐad*	'to help'	.... *msāƐade*
kātab	'to write to'	..... *mkātabe*	*Ɛāmal*	'to treat (s.o.)'	.. *mƐāmale*
sāwa	'to make'	.... *msāwā*	*lāʔa*	'to find'	.... *mlāʔā*

Verbs of Pattern IV *(ʔaFƐaL)* [p.82] have gerunds of Pattern *ʔəFƐāL* (defective form *ʔəFƐāʔ* or *ʔəFƐa);* (for hollow verbs, *ʔiFāLe):*

Verb   Gerund

ʔaƐlan 'to announce' .... *ʔəƐlān* 'announcement'

ʔaḍrab 'to go on strike' .... *ʔəḍrāb* 'going on strike, a strike'

ʔakram 'to honor, treat hospitably' .. *ʔəkrām* 'honoring, hospitality'

ʔažra 'to perform, execute' .... *ʔəžrāʔ, ʔəžra* 'performance, execution

ʔaḥāl 'to transfer, transform' ...... *ʔiḥāle* 'transfer, transformation'

The initial-weak verb *ʔāman* 'to believe' [p.85] has the gerund *ʔīmān* 'belief'

Verbs of Patterns V and VI (*tFaƐƐaL* and *tFāƐaL*) [pp. 86, 88] have gerunds of Patterns *taFaƐƐoL* and *taFāƐoL* respectively. (Defective forms *taFaƐƐi, taFāƐi.*):

Verb	Gerund	Verb	Gerund
tˀaddam 'to progress'.....	*taˀaddom*	*thāmal* 'to neglect'..........	*tahāmol*
tƐallam 'to learn'........	*taƐallom*	*tƐāwan* 'to cooperate'........	*taƐāwon*
thadda 'to provoke'......	*tahaddi*	*tsāwa* 'to be equalized'.....	*tasāwi*

    Many verbs of these patterns, however, share the gerund of an underlying verb of Pattern II or III: *tkātabu* 'to correspond with one another' and *kātab* 'to correspond with (someone else')' are both served by the gerund *mkātabe* 'correspondence'; the actual Pattern V or VI gerund in such cases is rare. See Active and Passive use of Gerunds [p. 296].

    Verbs of Patterns VII and VIII (*nFaƐaL* and *FtaƐaL*) [pp. 91, 95]: have gerunds of Patterns *ˀanFiƐāL* and *ˀaFtiƐāL* respectively. (Defective forms *ˀanFiƐāˀ* or *ˀanFíƐa, ˀaFtiƐāˀ* or *ˀaFtíƐa*):

nṣaraf 'to be dismissed'....	*ˀanṣirāf*	*ktašaf* 'to discover'......	*ˀaktišāf*
nfaƐal 'to be agitated'.....	*ˀanfiƐāl*	*žtamaƐ* 'to meet'..........	*ˀažtimāƐ*
nhaṭṭ 'to decline'........	*ˀanhiṭāṭ*	*ttafaˀ* 'to agree'........	*ˀattifāˀ*
nzawa 'to withdraw, be by one's self'........	*ˀanziwāˀ*	*htāl* 'to use trickery'..	*ˀahtiyāl*

              Ɛtana 'to take care of'...... *ˀaƐtína*

    Many verbs of these patterns, however, share the gerund of an underlying simple verb: *štagal* 'to be busy, to work' and *šagal* 'to busy', 'to occupy', are both served by the gerund *šagᵊl* 'work, busying'. In some cases of Pattern VIII, a simple gerund is used even though the underlying simple verb itself is not used: *ftakar* 'to think': gerund *fakᵊr* 'thought'; *štara* 'to buy': gerund *šᵊre* 'buying, purchase'.

    Gerunds of Pattern IX (*FƐaLL*) verbs [p. 101] have the Pattern *ˀaFƐiLāL:*

Verb	Gerund
hmarr 'to redden, to blush'........	*ˀahmirār* 'reddening, blush'

Verbs of Pattern X (*staFƐaL*) [p. 102] have gerunds of Pattern *ʔəstəFƐāL* (sound and geminate):

Verb	Gerund	Verb	Gerund
staƐmal 'to use'......	*ʔəstəƐmāl*	*stafham* 'to enquire'..........	*ʔəstəfhām*
staqbal 'to receive'..	*ʔəstəqbāl*	*stamadd* 'to procure supplies'..	*ʔəstəmdād*

With initial radical semivowel, the pattern is *ʔəstīƐāL*:

    stawrad 'to import'........*ʔəstīrād* 'import, importation, importing'

For hollow verbs, the pattern is *ʔəstiFāLe*:

    stafād 'to benefit'.......*ʔəstifāde* 'usefulness, benefit'

For defective verbs, the pattern is *ʔəstəFƐāʔ*:

    stasna 'to exclude'.......*ʔəstəsnāʔ* 'exclusion, exception'

Defective with initial radical semivowel:

    stawla 'to seize'.........*ʔəstīlāʔ* 'seizure'

Quadriradical and Pseudo-quadriradical verbs generally have gerunds of Pattern *FaƐLaLe* [p. 159] (*FaƐLane, FarƐaLe,* etc.):

Verb	Gerund
taržam 'to translate'........	*taržame* 'translation'
xarbaṭ 'to mess up'..........	*xarbaṭa* 'mess, messing up'
wašwaš 'to whisper'..........	*wašwaše* 'whispering'

Verbs with *t-* formative [p. 85]:

twaldan 'to be childish'..............	*waldane* 'childishness'
ddōšan 'to be dazed, astonished'......	*dōšane* 'astonishment, stupefaction'
tšēṭan 'to be naughty, mischievous'...	*šēṭane* 'mischief, naughtiness'

    In a few classicisms, the pattern *taFaƐLoL* is used for the gerunds of *t-* formative verbs: *tadahwor* 'decline, decadence' from *ddahwar* 'to decline, become decadent'.

Pattern *FƐaLaLL* verbs [p. 123] have gerunds on the pattern *ʔəFƐəL₁L₂āL₂*:

ṭmaʔann 'to feel confident, secure'....... *ʔəṭməʔnān* 'confidence, security'

Active and Passive Use of Gerunds

A gerund in construct [p 464] with a following term may correspond either to a verb its subject, or to a verb with its object: *mōt rəžžāl* 'a man's death' ← *māt rəžžāl* 'a man died'; *ʔakl ᵊl-laḥᵊm* 'the eating of meat, eating the meat' ← *ʔakal ᵊl-laḥᵊm* 'ate the meat' (or *byākol əl-laḥᵊm* 'eats the meat').

In the case of transitive verbs, therefore, a gerund may be used either in an active or a passive sense: *ʔatl ᵊr-rəžžāl*.... 'the man's killing (someone)' or 'the man's being killed'. Hence a single abstract noun commonly serves as the gerund of an active verb and of its passive derivative as well: *ʔatᵊl* 'killing' for both *ʔatal* 'to kill' and *ʔətel* (or *nᵊatal*) 'to be killed'; *ʔakᵊl* 'eating' for both *ʔakal* 'to eat' and *ttākal* (or *nᵊakal*) 'to be eaten'; *šəġᵊl* 'work, being busy' for both *šaġal* 'to occupy, to busy' and *štaġal* 'to work'.

Gerunds of transitive verbs are syntactically unique among nouns: A transitive gerund in construct with the transformed verbal subject (or first object) may retain the object (or second object) as such: *ʔatl ᵊr-rəžžāl ᵊl-ḥarāmi* 'the man's killing (of) the thief'; *taɛlīm ᵊl-ʔabb ᵊwlādo* 'the father's teaching (of) his children'. See p. 440.

SINGULATIVES

A singulative noun designates an individual unit or instance of what its underlying noun designates collectively or in general.[1] Singulatives are usually formed by suffixing *-e/-a* [p. 138]:

Underlying Noun			Singulative	
xass	'lettuce'	....	*xasse*	'a head of lettuce'
šaɛⁱr	'hair'	....	*šaɛra*	'a hair'
fəkⁱr	'thought, thinking'	....	*fəkra*	'a thought, an idea'
ṣarx	'shouting'	....	*ṣarxa*	'a shout, a cry'
bōs	'kissing'	....	*bōse*	'a kiss'
baʕar	'cattle'	....	*baʕara*	'a cow'
dəbbān	'flies'	....	*dəbbāne*	'a fly'
baḥⁱṣ	'gravel, pebbles'	....	*baḥṣa*	'a pebble'

A singulative derived from a gerund [p. 284] is called an INSTANCE NOUN (*ism l-marra*). A singulative derived from a mass noun [p. 368] designating some kind of material thing is called a UNIT NOUN (*ism l-waḥda*), and the noun it is derived from is called a COLLECTIVE (*ism l-ǧamɛ*).

It should be clearly understood that collectives (except for ethnic collectives [p. 301]) are grammatically singular, though the English translation may be plural: *dəbbān* 'flies'. Collectives — since they are mass nouns — may have plurals of Abundance or Variety [368]: *dababīn* 'many flies', while singulatives are of course count nouns: *dəbbāne* 'one fly', *dəbbāntēn* 'two flies', *tlətt dəbbānāt* 'three flies'.

Almost all singulatives are derived either from gerunds or from material mass nouns; an exception is *lēle* 'a night', from *lēl* 'nighttime'.

---

[1]To avoid misunderstanding this statement, it should be noted that 'designate', as used in this book, does not mean 'refer to'. A collective or an abstract noun may, of course, be used to <u>refer</u> <u>to</u> a particular instance of what it designates (*e.g.* *hal-xass* 'this lettuce', *fəkri ʔana* 'my idea'); it is not restricted to speaking in generalities or universals. But if a particular instance is referred to with a collective or abstract noun, its separateness or individuality is to be inferred from the context, and is an incidental matter; while an instance referred to with a singulative is explicitly and relevantly a <u>separate</u> instance.

Collectives and Units

1.) Almost all kinds of vegetables, fruits, grains, flowers, fruit trees, grasses, and the like, are designated by collectives and units:

Collective		Unit Noun	
badənžān	'eggplant'..................	*badənžāne*	'an eggplant'
baṭāṭa	'potato(es)'................	*baṭāṭāye*	'a potato' [cf. p. 212]
məšmoš	'apricot(s)'................	*məšᵊmše*	'an apricot' [p. 31]
lōz	'almond(s)'.................	*lōze*	'an almond'
ʔamᵊh	'wheat'..:..................	*ʔamḥa*	'a grain of wheat'
banafsaž	'violets'...................	*banafsaže*	'a violet'
ward	'roses; flowers'............	*warde*	'a rose, a flower'
fəlfol	'pepper'....................	*fəlᵊfle*	'a pepper, peppercorn'
naxᵊl	'date palms'................	*naxle*	'a date palm'
Ɛəšᵊb	'grass, weeds, herbs'.......	*Ɛəšbe*	'a blade of grass, a weed, an herb'
ʔašš	'straw'...:.................	*ʔašše*	'a straw'

Note also the generic terms *ḥabb* 'grain' (unit *ḥabbe*), *zahᵊr* 'blossoms' (unit *zahra*), *sažar* 'trees, shrubs' (unit *sažara*), *waraʔ* 'leaves' (unit *waraʔa*), *bəzᵊr* 'seed(s)', (unit *bəzre*), *ʔaṣab* 'cane, stalk(s)' (unit *ʔaṣabe*).

A few plant designations have the same form for both collective and unit: *fəṭᵊr* 'fungus, mushroom(s)', the generic term *nabāt* 'a plant' or 'plants, vegetation', *təmm ᵊs-samake* 'snapdragon(s)' (lit. "fish mouth"); etc.

Quite a few mass nouns designating plants, however, either have no unit derivative at all, or have one that is seldom used. In such cases a periphrastic phrase may be used, consisting of a generic unit term in construct with the specific mass term [p. 462]:

tūm	'garlic'............	*rās tūm*	'a garlic bulb'
ṣnōbar	'pine'..............	*sažaret ᵊṣnōbar*	'a pine tree'
(ḥabb) ᵊṣnōbar	'pine nuts'.........	*ḥabbet ᵊṣnōbar*	'a pine nut'
Ɛəneb	'grapes'............	*Ɛənbe* or *ḥabbet Ɛəneb*	'a grape'

2.) **Some** kinds of animals are designated collectively, including: Four kinds of domestic mammals:

Collective		Unit Noun	
baʔar	'cattle'.........	*baʔara*	'a cow'
ġanam	'sheep'..........	*ġaname*	'a ewe'
məɛze	'goats'..........	*məɛzāye*	'a (nanny) goat'
xēl	'horses'.........	(none)	

The unit derivatives for domestic mammals (as for domestic fowl) designate the female of the species only.

The term *xēl* has no unit derivative of its own, but is suppleted by the term *faras* 'mare'.[1]

Periphrastic unit constructs for these collectives may be formed (as in English) with *rās* (pl. *rūs*) 'head': *rās baʔar* 'a head of cattle', *rās xēl* 'a horse'.

Several kinds of bird (mainly fowl):

žāž	'chicken(s)'...........	*žāže*	'a hen'
baṭṭ	'duck(s)'..............	*baṭṭa*	'a duck'
wazz	'geese'................	*wazze*	'a goose'
ḥažal	'partridge(s)'.........	*ḥažale*	'a partridge'
ḥamām	'pigeons'..............	*ḥamāme*	'a pigeon'
būm	'owls'.................	*būme*	'an owl'

Also:

samak	'fish'.....................	*samake*	'a fish'
ṣadaf	'shellfish, oyster(s)'......	*ṣadafe*	'an oyster, a shellfish'
sfənž	'sponge(s)'................	*sfənže*	'a sponge'

---

[1] There is also, of course, the ordinary count noun *ḥṣān* 'horse' (pl. *ʔəḥᵊṣne*).

Several kinds of insect:

Collective			Unit Noun	
dəbbān	'flies'....................	dəbbāne	'a fly'
nāmūs	'mosquitos'..............	nāmūse	'a mosquito'
naḥᵊl	'bees'....................	naḥle	'a bee'
namᵊl	'ants'....................	namle	'an ant'
farrāš	'butterflies, moths'.......	farrāše	'a butterfly, moth'
Ɛətt	'clothes moths'...........	Ɛətte	'a clothes moth'
dūd	'caterpillars, worms'......	dūde	'a caterpillar, worm'
žarād	'locusts'.................	žarāde	'a locust'
baʔʔ	'bedbugs'.................	baʔʔa	'a bedbug'
ʔamᵊl	'lice'....................	ʔamle	'a louse'

3.) Collectives designate miscellaneous other sorts of material things which are familiar both in the aggregate and piecemeal:

bēḍ	'eggs'....................	bēḍa	'an egg'
žamᵊr	'embers, coals'...........	žamra	'an ember, a coal'
faḥᵊm	'charcoal, coal'..........	faḥme	'a piece of charcoal, coal'
ṣaxᵊr	'rock'....................	ṣaxra	'a rock'
kaƐᵊk	(a kind of) 'cake'.........	kaƐke	'a cake'
šabak	'netting'.................	šabake	'a net'
Ɛaḍᵊm	'bone(s)'.................	Ɛaḍme	'a bone'
ʔəšᵊr	'bark, peel(s), shell(s)'..	ʔəšra	'a peel, a shell'
fašak	'cartridges'..............	fašake	'a cartridge'
blāṭ	'tile, flagstone(s)'.......	blāṭa	'a flagstone'
səžžād	'rugs, carpeting'..........	səžžāde	'a rug'
ġēm	'clouds'..................	ġēme	'a cloud'
ṣābūn	'soap'....................	ṣābūne	'a bar of soap'
səkkar	'sugar'...................	səkkara	'a lump of sugar'
zmərrod	'emerald(s)'..............	zmərrde	'an emerald'

4.) A special type of collective is that which designates a kind of people (mainly ethnic groups). The unit noun, which designates one (male) person of the group, is the substantivized relative adjective [p. 281], formed with the suffix -*i*: *ɛarabi* 'an Arab', from the collective *ɛarab* 'Arabs'.

These ETHNIC COLLECTIVES differ from ordinary collectives in that they function in almost the same way as plurals; verbs and adjectives show · plural agreement with them [p. 426]: *l-ɛarab ᵊs-sūriyyīn* 'The Syrian Arabs', *ᵊᵊžu l-ɛarab* 'The Arabs have come'.
The only respect in which they differ from true plurals is that they are not used in numeral constructs [p. 471], but must stand in apposition to the numeral: *tlāte ɛarab* 'three Arabs' [501]. That is to say, the absolute form of the numeral – not the construct form [170] – must be used before these collectives.

The unit noun in many cases has no plural (since the ethnic collective serves this function quite adequately), while in other cases a true plural exists in addition to the collective: *tərk* 'Turks' (coll.): *tərki* 'a Turk' (unit): *ᵊatrāk* 'Turks' (pl.). Thus *tlāte tərk* 'three Turks', but *tlətt ᵊatrāk* (same translation).
All ethnic unit nouns have, of course, feminal derivatives [p. 304]: *ɛarabiyye* 'an Arab woman', *tərkiyye* 'a Turkish woman'.

Further examples:

Collective		Unit	
ᵊamērkān	'Americans'	*ᵊamērkāni*	'an American'
ᵊanglīz	'English'	*ᵊanglīzi*	'an Englishman'
ᵊalmān	'Germans'	*ᵊalmāni*	'a German'
rūs	'Russians'	*rūsi*	'a Russian'
badu	'Bedouins'	*badawi*	'a Bedouin'
nawar	'gypsies'	*nawari*	'a gypsy'
kərd	'Kurds'	*kərdi*	'a Kurd' (pl. *ᵊakrād*)
ᵊarman	'Armenians'	*ᵊarmani*	'an Armenian'
šarkas	'Circassians'	*šarkasi*	'a Circassian'
yūnān	'Greeks'	*yūnāni*	'a Greek' (pl. -*yyīn*)
rūm	'Greek (Catholic or Orthodox)'	*rūmi*	'a Greek (C. or O.)'
ᵊəbṭ	'Copts'	*ᵊəbṭi*	'a Copt' (pl. *ᵊbāṭ*)
yahūd	'Jews'	*yahūdi*	'a Jew'

Ethnic designations on internal plural patterns [p. 218] such as *maṣārwa* 'Egyptians' (sg. *maṣri*), *naṣāra* 'Christians'[1] (sg. *naṣrāni*), etc. may generally be used either as collectives or as true plurals: *tlāte maṣārwa* or *tlətt maṣārwa* 'three Egyptians'.

Some speakers treat the word *drūz* 'Druzes' as a collective rather than a plural (sg. *dərzi*). Similarly *frəsawiyye* 'French (pl.)' is generally used as a collective, while the singulative *frənsāwi* 'Frenchman' also has a true plural *frənsāwiyyīn*.

Some speakers tend to assimilate almost all the ethnic collectives to true plurals, using either the construct or absolute forms of numerals before them: *tlətt ʔamērkān* (or *tlāte ʔamērkān*), etc.

Many ethnic designations, of course, have no collectives (in Colloquial use, at least), but only a singular and plural: *həndi* 'Indian', pl. *hnūd; sūdāni* 'Sudanese', pl. *sūdāniyyīn*.

Gerunds and Instance Nouns

The gerunds of many simple triliteral verbs have singulatives derived from them. For example:

Verb		Gerund		Instance Noun	
ḍarab	'to hit, strike'..*ḍarb*	'hitting, striking'...*ḍarbe*	'a blow'
laƐeb	'to play'........*laƐb*	'playing'............*laƐbe*	'a play'
Ɛaṭaṣ	'to sneeze'.......*Ɛaṭ ᵊṣ*	'sneezing'...........*Ɛaṭṣa*	'a sneeze'
dāx	'to be nauseated,..*dōx* dizzy'	'nausea, dizziness'...*dōxa*	'an attack or wave of nausea'
daʔar	'to touch, feel'..*daʔ ᵊr*	'touching, feeling'...*daʔra*	'a touch'
māt	'to die'.........*mōt*	'death, dying'........*mōte*	'a death'
dafaƐ	'to push'........*daf ᵊƐ*	'pushing'............*dafƐa*	'a push'
takk	'to click, tick'..*takk*	'clicking, ticking'...*takke*	'a click, tick'
naṭṭ	'to jump'........*naṭṭ*	'jumping'............*naṭṭa*	'a jump'
bās	'to kiss'........*bōs*	'kissing'............*bōse*	'a kiss'
ġaza	'to raid'........*ġazu*	'raiding'............*ġazwe*	'a raid'

---

[1]Often derrogatory; the polite term is (sg.) *masīḥi*, pl. *masīḥiyyīn* (no collective).

Though most instance nouns are formed simply by suffixing *-e/-a* [p. 138] (with any automatic changes that entails), others have a base pattern different from that of the gerund. Gerunds of Pattern *F€ūL* [291], for instance, have singulatives of Pattern *Fa€Le* [140]:

Verb		Gerund		Instance Noun	
nəzel	'to descend.........*nzūl* go down'		'descent'.........*nazle*	'a descent'	
wə?e€	'to fall'...........*w?ū€*		'falling'.........*wa?€a*	'a fall'	
rəže€	'to return'.........*ržū€*		'return(ing)'......*raž€a*	'a return'	

Note also:

ġəleṭ	'to make a mistake'..*ġalaṭ*		'being mistaken'...*ġalṭa*	'a mistake'	
nazar	'to look, glance'....*nazar*		'looking, sight'...*nazra*	'a look'	
sāfar	'to travel'.........*safar*		'travel(ling)'.....*safra*	'a trip'	
ġāb	'to be absent'.......*ġyāb*		'absence'.........*ġēbe*	'an absence'	
ħarak	'to move'...........*ħarᵊk*		'movement'.........*ħarake*	'a movement'	
štaġal	'to work'...........*šəġᵊl*		'work'.............*šaġle*	'a job'	

A few Pattern II (*taF€īL*) gerunds [p. 293] have singulatives derived from them:

lammaħ	'to hint'...........*talmīħ*		'hinting'.........*talmīħa*	'a hint'	
warraṭ	'to involve'........*tawrīṭ*		'involvement'......*tawrīṭa*	'an involvement'

Otherwise, augmented gerunds do not have instance nouns, though many of them may function in a particularized sense [p. 284] as well as in the abstract sense: *?əttifā?* (ger. of *ttafa?* 'to agree') 'an agreement'; *?ə€lān* 'an announcement' (ger. of *?a€lan* 'to announce').

FEMINAL NOUNS

Many nouns designating male persons, and some designating male animals, may be converted into female designations by the suffixation of *-e/-a* [p. 138]:

Male		Female	
ɛamm	'(paternal) uncle'	*ɛamme*	'(paternal) aunt'
žār	'neighbor'	*žāra*	
žōz, zōž	'husband'	*žōze, zawže*	'wife'
zbūn	'customer, client'	*zbūne*	
təlmīz	'student'	*təlmīze*	
malek	'king'	*malike, malake*	'queen'
ʔarmal	'widower'	*ʔarmale*	'widow'
ɛəḍu	'member'	*ɛəḍwe*	
ḍēf	'guest'	*ḍēfe*	
ṣabi	'boy'	*ṣabiyye*	'girl'
ṣāḥeb	'friend'	*ṣāḥbe*[1]	
ṭafəl	'child, infant'	*ṭafle*	(See p. 372)
kalb	'dog'	*kalbe*	'bitch'

The feminal derivation may be applied freely to substantivized personal adjectives, including participial [276], occupational [305], and relative [301] derivatives: (Cf. Adjective Inflection):

mɛallem	'teacher'	*mɛallme*	
mwazzaf	'employee'	*mwazzafe*	
maslem	'Moslem'	*masəlme*	
ṭabbāx	'cook'	*ṭabbāxa*	
badawi	'Bedouin'	*badawiyye*	
ʔanglīzi	'Englishman'	*ʔanglīziyye*	'Englishwoman'

For nouns other than substantivized adjectives, the feminal derivation may or may not apply – each case must be learned individually. Note, for example, *ṣəhʔr* 'brother(or son)-in-law', but *kənne* 'sister(or daughter)-in-law', *tōr* 'bull, steer', but *baʔara* 'cow', etc. See Gender of Nouns [p. 372].

---

[1] *ṣāḥbe* usually implies 'mistress' when in construct with a term referring to a man.

OCCUPATIONAL NOUNS

An occupational noun indicates a person whose occupation it is to do what is designated by the underlying verb, or to work with, or tend, what is designated by the underlying noun. Occupational nouns are formed on Pattern *FaɛɛāL* [p.151], or on active participial patterns [258], or by suffixation of *-ži* or *-i:*

Underlying Word		Occupational Noun	
Pattern *FaɛɛāL*:			
raʔaṣ	'to dance'	*raʔʔāṣ*	'dancer'
ṭabax	'to cook'.....................	*ṭabbāx*	'cook'
rasam	'to draw, design, sketch, paint'	*rassām*	'designer, painter, artist'
falaḥ	'to till, cultivate'...........	*fallāḥ*	'farmer, peasant'
bana	'to build'....................	*banna*	'builder'
šaḥad	'to beg'......................	*šaḥḥād*	'beggar'
bāɛ	'to sell'.....................	*bayyāɛ*	'seller, merchant'
ṣ(ṭ)ād	'to hunt'.....................	*ṣayyād*	'hunter'
sāʔ	'to drive'....................	*sawwāʔ*	'driver, chauffeur'
laḥᵊm	'meat'........................	*laḥḥām*	'butcher'
ḥadīd	'iron'........................	*ḥaddād*	'blacksmith, ironsmith'
blāṭ	'tile, flagstone(s)'..........	*ballāṭ*	'tile mason'
xēl	'horses'......................	*xayyāl*	'horseman'
bāb	'door, gate'...................	*bawwāb*	'doorman, gatekeeper'
Active Participial Patterns:			
ḥāk	'to weave'....................	*ḥāyek*	'weaver'
xadam	'to serve'....................	*xādem* (also *xaddām*)	'servant'
nāb	'to represent'................	*nāʔeb*[1]	'representative'
ʔaḍa	'to judge, pass sentence'......	*ʔāḍi*	'judge'
dār	'to direct, manage'...........	*mudīr*	'director, manager'
ṣāraɛ	'to wrestle'..................	*mṣāreɛ*	'wrestler'
katab	'to write'...................	*kāteb*	'writer'
šaɛᵊr	'poetry'......................	*šāɛer*	'poet'

---

[1]Classicism: *ʔ* replacing medial *y* in Pattern *FāɛeL*.

Underlying Word		Occupational Noun	

Suffix *-ži:*

xəḍar	'vegetables'..................	*xəḍarži*	'greengrocer'
bōya	'shoe polish'................	*bōyaži*	'bootblack'
kəndara	'shoe'.......................	*kəndarži*	'cobbler'

Suffix *-i:*

sāɛāt	'watches'....................	*sāɛāti*	'watchmaker'
žnēnāt	'gardens'....................	*žnēnāti*	'gardener'
ġālāt	'locks'......................	*ġālāti*	'locksmith'
luġa	'language'...................	*luġawi*	'linguist'

Occupational nouns in *-i* are mainly formed on an *-āt* *plural* stem; see, however, Relative Adjectives [p. 280].

Note that the English suffix *-er* is often used more broadly than the Arabic occupational derivation. To say 'She's a good dancer' does not imply that dancing is her occupation, whereas *hiyye raʔʔāṣa mnīḥa* would only be said of a professional dancer.

INSTRUMENTAL NOUNS (*ism l-ʔāla*)

An instrumental noun indicates an implement or apparatus used in doing what is designated by the underlying verb. Patterns *FaɛɛāLe* [p. 152], *məFɛāL(e)* [156], *maFɛaL(e)* [153] and *məFɛaL* [155] are used:

Pattern *FaɛɛāLe:*

Underlying Verb		Instrumental Noun	
sār	'to go, travel'.............	*sayyāra*	'automobile'
ṭār	'to fly'....................	*ṭayyāra*	'airplane'
maḥa	'to erase'..................	*maḥḥāye*	'eraser'
kamaš	'to grasp'..................	*kammāše*	'pincers'
bara	'to sharpen, point'.........	*barrāye*	'pencil-sharpener'
barad	'to cool'...................	*barrāde*	'refrigerator'

Pattern *məFƐāL*, (for defective verbs: *məFƐāLe*):

Underlying Word	Instrumental Noun
fataḥ 'to open'........................ *məftāḥ*	'key'
ḥarat 'to plow'........................ *məḥrāt*	'plow'
naʔar 'to peck'........................ *mənʔār*	'beak'
wazan 'to weigh'........................ *mīzān*	'scale balance'
ʔala 'to fry'........................ *məʔlāye*	'frying pan, skillet'
kawa 'to iron'........................ *məkwāye*	'(flat)iron'
dara 'to winnow'.................... *mədrāye*	'winnowing fork'

Patterns *maFƐaL, maFƐaLe:*

laʔaṭ 'to pick up'................... *malʔaṭ*	'tongs'
barad 'to file'...................... *mabrad*	'file'
ḍarab 'to hit, strike'............... *maḍrab*	'bat'
našaf 'to wipe, dry'................. *manšafe*	'towel'
saṭar 'to line, draw straight lines'..*masṭara*	'ruler, straight-edge'

Patterns *məFƐaL, məFƐaLe* (for geminate verbs):

ʔaṣṣ 'to cut, snip'................. *mʔaṣṣ*	'scissors'
fakk 'to undo, take apart, unscrew'..*mfakk*	'screwdriver'

LOCATIVE NOUNS (*ism l-makān*)

A locative noun indicates a place or installation for doing what is designated by the underlying verb, or for getting or putting what is designated by the underlying noun. Locatives are formed on Patterns *maFɛaL* [p. 153], *maFɛaLe* [153], and *maFɛeL* [154].

Underlying Word	Locative Noun

Pattern *maFɛaL:*

ʔaɛad	'to sit'	*maʔɛad*	'seat'
laɛeb	'to play'	*malɛab*	'playground'
ṣanaɛ	'to manufacture'	*maṣnaɛ*	'factory'
xaraž	'to go out'	*maxraž*	'exit'
marr	'to pass'	*mamarr*	'aisle'
məši	'to go, walk'	*mamša*	'passageway, hall'
rəɛi	'to graze'	*marɛa*	'pasture'
ṭār	'to fly'	*maṭār*	'airport'
ḥažar	'stone'	*maḥžar*	'stone quarry'

Pattern *maFɛaLe:*

ḥakam	'to try, sentence'	*maḥkame*	'court'
daras	'to study'	*madrase*	'school'
ġasal	'to wash'	*maġsale*	'washstand'
xāḍ	'to wade'	*maxāḍa*	'ford'
ḍēf	'guest'	*maḍāfe* (also *maḍāf*)	'reception room'
ktāb	'book'	*maktabe*	'library'

Pattern *maFɛeL:*

wəʔef, waʔʔaf	'to stop'	*mawʔef*	'stop, station'
waḍaɛ	'to place'	*mawḍeɛ*	'position'
žalas	'to sit'	*mažles*	'meeting chamber, session room'

HYPOSTATIC NOUNS[1]

A hypostatic noun indicates the abstract result or object of the activity designated by its underlying verb: *maksab* 'profit, earning', from *kəseb* 'to make, earn'. These nouns are formed on Patterns *maFɛaL(e)*, *maFɛ(i)Le, məFɛaL(e), məFɛaL, məFɛ(i)L(e)* [p. 153-156].

Underlying Verb		Hypostatic Noun
balaġ 'to attain, amount to'.......	*mablaġ*	'amount, sum'
ʔaṣad 'to intend, aim at'..........	*maʔṣad*	'intent, goal'
ɛana 'to mean'....................	*maɛna*	'meaning'
nagar 'to look at'.................	*mangar*	'view, sight'
farr 'to flee, escape'............	*mafarr*	'flight, escape'
lām 'to blame'...................	*malām*	'blame, censure'
nām 'to sleep'..................	*manām*	'dream'
wəled 'to be born'...............	*mawled, mīlād*	'birth, birthday'
waɛad 'to promise'...............	*mawɛed, mīɛād*	'date, appointment'
ṣār 'to become'.................	*maṣīr*	'destiny'
ḥabb 'to like, love'.............	*maḥabbe*	'love, affection'
sabb 'to curse'..................	*msabbe*	'curse, invective'
ʔəder 'to be able'...............	*maʔdira*	'ability'
ɛəref 'to know'..................	*maɛʾrfe*	'knowledge, acquaintance'
waɛaẓ 'to preach, lecture'........	*mawɛiẓa*	'lecture, reprimand'
rād 'to wish, want'.............	*murād*	'wish, desire, intent'
ṣāb 'to hit, befall'............	*mṣībe*	'calamity'

Hypostatic nouns are similar in meaning to gerunds [p. 284] and in some cases function virtually as such (e.g. *maɛʾrfe* 'knowledge, acquaintance'). In general, however, they do not share the syntactical peculiarities of gerunds, nor (by the same token) do they designate "action" or "activity".

---

[1]Including what is sometimes called *al-maṣdar l-mīmī* "the *m*- gerund", and also *ism z-zamān* "the noun of time". The Locative [p. 308] is a "spatially concretized" version of the abstract *ism l-makān waz-zamān*.

DIMINUTIVES (*ism t-taṣġīr*)

Only a few Syrian Arabic nouns have diminutives derived from them. The basic pattern is *FƐayyeL*, or – if the underlying noun has a long vowel between the first and second radicals – *FwayƐeL*.

Underlying Word		Diminutive	
ġġīr	'child, young one'..........	ġġayyer	'little one'
ṣabi	'boy'......................	ṣbayy	'little boy'
ʔabᵊn	'son'......................	bnayy(-i)	'(my) little son'
bᵊnt	'daughter, girl'............	bnayye	'little daughter, little girl'
ši	'thing, something, some'....	šwayy(e)	'a little'

> Mainly in Lebanon, the following are also used (as terms of affection, and sometimes in a more general sense as well): *bayy* 'father', *xayy* 'brother', *xayye* 'sister', *dayye* 'hand', *ǧrᵊyye* 'foot', *dayne* 'ear'.

> Patterns *FaƐƐūL* and *FaƐƐūLe* are also used, mainly to form nicknames and terms of affection (again, especially in Lebanon): *Ɛabbūd, Ɛabbūde* (from *Ɛabdaḷḷa* and other names beginning with *Ɛabd-*); *laṭṭūf* (from *laṭfaḷḷa); ḥammūd* (from *ʔaḥmad); marrūm* (from *maryam* 'Mary'), etc.
> Note also: *nattūfe* 'a tiny bit' (from *naṭfe* 'a little bit'), *laʔʔūme* 'a little bite, a little mouthful' (from *laʔme* 'a bite, mouthful').

ELATIVES (*ism t-tafḍīl*)

Elatives, derivable mainly from adjectives, are formed on the pattern *ʔaFƐaL* for triliteral roots; *ʔaFaƐLaL* for quadriliteral.

If an underlying adjective means 'X', its elative means 'more or most X'. For example: *ṣaƐᵊb* 'difficult' → *ʔaṣƐab* 'more (or most) difficult'; *ʔadīm* 'ancient' → *ʔaʔdam* 'more (most) ancient'; *mnāseb* 'suitable' → *ʔansab* 'more, most suitable'; *zangīl* 'rich' → *ʔazangal* 'richer, richest'.

Underlying Word		Elative (Sound)
sahªl	'easy'......................	*ʔashal* 'easier, easiest'
bəšeɛ	'ugly'.....................	*ʔabšaɛ* 'uglier, ugliest'
sexªn	'hot'.......................	*ʔasxan* 'hotter, hottest'
txīn	'thick, fat'..............	*ʔatxan* 'thicker, fatter, etc.'
ṭawīl	'long, tall'..............	*ʔaṭwal* 'longer, taller, etc.'
bāred	'cold'.....................	*ʔabrad* 'colder, coldest'
wāseɛ	'broad, roomy'...........	*ʔawsaɛ* 'broader, roomier, etc.'
yābes	'dry, hard'................	*ʔaybas* 'drier, harder, etc.'
mašhūr	'famous'..................	*ʔašhar* 'more, most famous'
mədhen	'greasy'..................	*ʔadhan* 'greasier, greasiest'
zaɛlān	'displeased'..............	*ʔazɛal* 'more, most displeased'
dayyeʔ	'narrow, tight'...........	*ʔadyaʔ* 'narrower, tighter, etc.'
mufīd	'useful, beneficial'........	*ʔafyad* 'more useful, beneficial, etc.'

If the underlying adjective is formed on a pattern requiring *y* in place of medial radical *w* (*FāɛeL* [p. 258], *FaɛɛeL* [128]), the radical *w* is in some cases restored in the elative: *xāyef* 'afraid' → *ʔaxwaf* 'more, most afraid'; *rāyeʔ* 'clear, undisturbed' → *ʔarwaʔ* 'more, most clear, etc.'; *žayyed* 'good, excellent' → *ʔažwad* 'better, best, etc.'; *sayyeʔ* 'bad, unfortunate' → *ʔaswaʔ* 'worse, worst, etc.', *zāyed* 'abundant, extra' → *ʔazwad* (or *ʔazyad*) 'more, most abundant, etc.'

With final radical semivowel (Elative defective):

raxu	'loose, lax'...................	*ʔarxa* 'looser, more lax, etc.'
ḥelu	'sweet, pretty, nice'..........	*ʔaḥla* 'sweeter, prettier, etc.'
ʔawi	'strong'.....................	*ʔaʔwa* 'stronger, strongest'
zaki	'intelligent'.................	*ʔazka* 'more, most intelligent'
šaʔi	'hoodlum, delinquent'..........	*ʔašʔa* 'more, most delinquent, etc.'
ġani	'rich'.......................	*ʔaġna* 'richer, richest'
ṣāfi	'clear'......................	*ʔaṣfa* 'clearer, clearest'
ʔāsi	'solid, hard'................	*ʔaʔsa* 'solider, solidest, etc.'
ṣaḥyān	'wide awake'..................	*ʔaṣḥa* 'more, most wide awake'

With second and third radicals alike (Elative usually geminate):

Underlying Word			Elative	
ḥadd	'sharp'	ʔaḥadd	'sharper, sharpest'
fažž	'unripe'	ʔafažž	'more, most unripe'
mərr	'bitter'	ʔamarr	(or ʔamrar) 'bitterer, bitterest'
ždīd	'new'	ʔažadd	(or ʔaždad) 'newer, newest'
xafīf	'light'	ʔaxaff	(or ʔaxfaf) 'lighter, lightest'
daʔīʔ	'precise, exact'	ʔadaʔʔ	'more, most precise, etc.'
šadīd	'intense, vehement'	ʔašadd	(or ʔašdad) 'more, most intense, etc.'
ʔalīl	'little, few'	ʔaʔall	'less, least'
ġaššāš	'cheater'	ʔaġašš	'more of a cheater, etc.
xāṣṣ	'special, private'	ʔaxaṣṣ	'more, most special, etc.'
mhəmm	'important'	ʔahamm	'more, most important'
mməll	'boring'	ʔamall	(or ʔamlal) 'more, most boring'

Quadriradical (Pattern ʔaFaELaL):

zangīl	'rich'	ʔazangal	'richer, richest'
šaršūḥ	'sloppy'	ʔašaršaḥ	'sloppier, sloppiest'
mbaḥbaḥ	'abundant'	ʔabaḥbaḥ	'more, most abundant'
mšarṭaṭ	'ripped, tattered'	ʔašarṭaṭ	'more, most tattered'
mbahdal	'shabby, dirty'	ʔabahdal	'shabbier, dirtier, etc.'
mEanṭaẓ	'stuck up, haughty'	ʔaEanṭaẓ	'haughtier, haughtiest'

Note, however, that the hollow quadriradical šēṭān 'devil, naughty' has a triradical elative ʔašṭan 'naughtier, naughtiest', the radical semivowel being lost.

Types of Underlying Word. Though the vast majority of elatives are derived from simple adjectives or from the more common augmented adjectives a few are derived from nouns, or adverbs, or are of indeterminate derivation:

Underlying Word			Elative	
bəl-Eažale	'quickly, hurriedly'	ʔaEžal	'more, most quickly, etc.'
šōb	'hot weather'	ʔašwab	'hotter, hottest (weather)'
šwayye	'little, few'	ʔašwa	'less, least, fewer, etc.'
rəžžāl	'man'	ʔaržal	'more of a man, most manly, etc.'

The elative *ʔaḥsan* 'better, best' is derived from
Classical *ḥasan*, which is not normally used in Colloquial
but is displaced by *mnīḥ* 'good'. Thus *ʔaḥsan* serves as a
suppletive elative to *mnīḥ*.

When two or more adjectives with the same root have
elatives, then of course a single elative form must serve in
more than one sense: *ʔabṣaṭ* 'more, most pleased, contented'
(from *mabṣūṭ* 'pleased, contented'), but also meaning
'easier, simpler, etc.' (from *baṣīṭ* 'easy, minor, simple').
Likewise *ʔatɛab*, elative of both *taɛbān* 'tired' and *mətɛeb*
'tiring'.

Often, however, the elative form is allocated to <u>one</u> of
the adjectives - usually to the most common one, or to the
one whose meaning is the most susceptible of gradation:
ʔaʔall 'less, least', elative of *ʔalīl* 'little, few', but
<u>not</u> used as the elative of *məstʔall* 'independent'; likewise
ʔaǧraḥ 'more dangerous, sharper, etc.', elative of *ǧāreḥ*
'dangerous, sharp', but not used as the elative of *ǧarīḥ*
or *maǧrūḥ* 'wounded'.

Elative Syntax

An elative may be used attributively, as an adjective: *ʔūḍa ʔaḥsan* 'a
better room', *l-ʔūḍa l-ʔaḥsan* 'the better (or best) room'.

An elative may also be used in construct, as a noun: *ʔaḥsan ᵊl-ʔuwaḍ*
'the best of the rooms', *ʔaḥsan ʔūḍa* 'the best room'.

In an elative construct, a definite [p.494] following term is always
identificatory [458]: *ʔaḥsan ᵊl-madrase* 'the best of (/in) the school',
while an <u>indefinite</u> following term is always classificatory: *ʔaḥsan
madrase* '<u>the best school</u>'. See Elative and Ordinal Annexion [473].

Note that an elative in construct with an indefinite
term is rendered in English as if it were definite: *ʔaḥla
bənt* 'the prettiest girl' (same translation as the attributive construction: *l-bənt ᵊl-ʔaḥla*). *ʔaḥla bənt* is nonetheless indefinite; its sense might be more exactly rendered
as "a girl who is prettiest". (But see p.406.)

The English comparative (-er, more...) is normally used
in translating an indefinite attributive elative: *talamīz
ʔazka* 'brighter students', or an indefinite elative with a
mən ('than') phrase: *ʔazka mn ᵊt-tānyīn* 'brighter than the
others'.

Otherwise, the English superlative (-est, most...) is
normally used if the referent is being compared with more
than one other thing, while the comparative is used (in
standard English, at least) if it is compared with only one
other thing: *hal-ʔuḍa ʔaḥsan* 'This room is better (or best')',
hāy ʔaḥsan ʔūḍa 'This is the best (or better) room'.

A COMPARATIVE PHRASE is formed with an elative complemented by the preposition *mən* 'than': *bēton ʔawsaƐ mən bētna* 'their house is larger than
ours', *hyaƐmel xamsīn līra ʔaħtar mənni* 'He makes fifty pounds more than 1',
ʔasxaf fəkra mən hēk ʔaḷḷa mā xalaʔ 'A sillier idea than that God never
allowed!' (lit. 'created').

> When the elative is definite, it is generally translated
> as a superlative (-est, most), and the *mən* is generally
> translated as 'of': *ṣ-sarāya l-ʔafxar mn əl-kəll* [RN-II.15]
> 'the most elegant (*faxᵊr*) palace of all'.

The word *ʔaktar* 'more, most' (elative of *ktīr* 'much, many') may be used
to form comparative phrases in supplementation to adjectives, especially
with adjectives which have no elatives of their own: *ʔabyaḍ ʔaktar mn
ət-talž* [RN-I.49] 'whiter than snow'; *ʔana barrīd ʔaktar mənnak* 'I'm more
sensitive to the cold than you'; *maƐžūʔ ʔaktar baƐd ᵊḍ-ḍəhᵊr mən Ɛala bəkra*
'more crowded in the afternoon than in the morning'.

> The *mən*-phrase (like the <u>than</u>-phrase in English) may of
> course be suppressed: *ʔabyaḍ ʔaktar* 'whiter', *maƐžūʔ ʔaktar*
> 'more crowded', etc.

Elatives with -*l*- suffixes

Like verbs and participles, some elatives complemented by a pronominal
la- phrase [p.479] take the suffix forms (-*lo*, etc.), not the disjunctive
forms (*ʔəlo*, etc.): *ʔafýdd-lak* 'more useful to you', *ʔaħsál-lo* [p.27]
'better for him', *ʔaṣƐáb-ᵊlkon* 'more difficult for you (pl.)'.

> Others, however, take the disjunctive forms: *ʔahdmm
> ʔə́lna* 'more important for us'.

Exclamations with *ma*-

Elatives are used after the particle *ma*-, in the sense 'How...!',
'Isn't that...!':

> | | |
> |---|---|
> | *ma-ʔaħla ləbsa!* | 'How pretty her clothes are!' |
> | *ma-ʔaṭyab hal-ʔakle!* | 'How good this food is!' |
> | *ma-ʔaẓġar hal-kərsi!* | 'How small this chair is!' |
> | *ma-ʔašalban ħakyo!* | 'How sweetly he speaks!' |

Elatives in this construction take a nominal complement
which may be pronominalized like a verbal object: *ma-
ʔaħlāha* 'How pretty she is!', *ma-ʔaẓġaro* 'How small it is!'

Lack of Inflection

Elatives in Colloquial Arabic are generally not inflected; the form *ʔawsaɛ* 'wider, roomier, larger', for instance, serves attributively as feminine (*ǧnēne ʔawsaɛ* 'a larger garden') and plural, as well as for masculine (*bēt ʔawsaɛ* 'a larger house').

There are, however, a few Classicisms in which the feminine pattern *FaɛLa* is used, as in *qaṣwa* (fem. of *ʔaqṣa* 'most remote, extreme') *tadabīr qaṣwa* 'extreme measures'.

Elatives are occasionally used in the dual: *l-ʔaḥsanēn* 'the best two'; *ʔalɛanēn* 'So much the worse!' (*ʔalɛan*, elative of *malɛūn* 'damnable').

Miscellaneous Examples of the Use of Elatives

1. *šū ḥabbēt ʔaktar ši?*
   'What would you (or did you) like the most?'

2. *mən ʔalɛan ᵊxṣālo, t-taraddod*
   'Indecisiveness is one of his worst qualities' (*ʔalɛan*, el. of *malɛūn* 'damnable')

3. *byəmlok šī ʔašwa mən bala*
   'He owns next to nothing' (*ʔašwa*, el. of *šwayy*; lit. 'less than nothing')

4. *šāf ʔiyyām ʔaḥsan*
   'He's seen better days'

5. *maɛāšo ʔazwad mən maɛāši*
   'His salary is larger than mine' (*ʔazwad*, el. of *zāyed* 'abundant' [311])

6. *ɛažbətni ʔawwal nəmre ʔaktar ᵊl-kəll*
   'I liked the first number most of all'

7. *ʔaxi ʔaṣġar mənnak b-ɛašr ᵊsnīn* [DA-157]
   'My brother is ten years younger than you'. (*ʔaṣġar*. el. of *ṣġīr* 'young', lit. '...younger than you by ten years'.)

8. *l-ʔəstāz ʔəža ɛal-madrase ʔabkar mn ᵊt-talamīz* [DA-158]
   'The teacher came to school earlier than the students'. (*ʔabkar*, el. of *bakkīr* 'early')

9. *ɛandkon ʔaḥsan* [DA-100]
   'With you would be better'

10. *ʔaḥsál-lak təži bukra*
    'It would be better for you to come tomorrow'

11. *mā wažadt ʔafyad mən hēk* [RN-II.15]
    'I haven't found anything more useful than that'

12. *kəllma kān ʔašṭar zādet kəbriyā* [RN-II.15]
    'The smarter he is, the more arrogant he becomes'

NUMERAL DERIVATIVES

Ordinals

The numerals from two through ten have ordinals derived from them, formed on the Pattern *FāɛeL* [p. 144]:

Cardinal Numeral		Ordinal	
tnēn	'two'...................	*tāni*	'second, other'
tlāte	'three'.................	*tālet*	'third'
ʔarbɛa	'four'...................	*rābeɛ*	'fourth'
xamse	'five'..................	*xāmes*	'fifth'
sətte	'six'...................	*sādes*	'sixth' (see below)
sabɛa	'seven'.................	*sābeɛ*	'seventh'
tmāne	'eight'.................	*tāmen*	'eighth'
tesɛa	'nine'..................	*tāseɛ*	'ninth'
ɛašara	'ten'...................	*ɛāšer*	'tenth'

The ordinal corresponding to *wāḥed* 'one' is irregular in form: *ʔawwal* 'first'. Its antonym *ʔāxer* 'last' also belongs with the ordinals.

Besides the irregular form *sādes* 'sixth', the regular (but less elegant) *sātet* is also sometimes heard.

The ordinals are like elatives [p. 313] in forming classificatory constructs with indefinite nouns: *ʔawwal marra* 'the first time', *tālet rəžžāl* 'the third man', *ɛāšer sane* 'the tenth year', *ʔāxer dars* 'the last lesson'. See Elative and Ordinal Constructs [p. 473].

Ordinals may also be used attributively, as ordinary adjectives, and with adjectival inflection: *s-sane l-ɛāšra* 'the tenth year', *d-dars ᵊl-ʔawwal* 'the first lesson', *bənto t-tālte* 'his third daughter', *marra tānye* 'a second time, again', *wlād tānyīn* 'other children', *dars tālet* 'a third lesson'.

ʔawwal and *ʔāxer*, however, are less often used attributively than the other ordinals, since the relative adjectives *ʔawwalāni* and *ʔaxrāni* [p. 282] often take their place, and because the adjective *ʔaxīr* is also often used instead of *ʔāxer*. In the feminine, the Classicism *ʔūla* is commonly used instead of *ʔawwale*.

Ordinals may also be used in identificatory construct as ordinary nouns: *ʔawwal has-sǝne* 'the first of this year', *tālet ᵊr-ržāl* 'the third (one) of the men', *ʔāxer ᵊz-zuwwār* 'the last of the visitors'; or with pronoun suffixes [p.541]: *ʔawwála* 'the first of it (f.)', *tálᵊton* 'the third of them', *rābǝɛna* the fourth (one) of us'.

For numbers above ten, the cardinal form [p.509] is used attributively to a singular in the ordinal sense: *d-daraže t-ṭnaɛᵊš* 'the twelfth grade, step', *l-marra l-ɛǝšrīn* 'the twentieth time', *d-dars ᵊl-xamse w-ʔarbɛīn* 'the forty-fifth lesson'.

A more formal alternative is to put the units in ordinal form, as in Classical Arabic: *l-qarn ᵊs-sābeɛ ɛašᵊr* 'the seventeenth century' (Note that *ɛašᵊr* is used, not *ɛašara* [p.170]). For 'first', *ḥādi* replaces *ʔawwal* in these phrases: *l-ḥādi w-ɛǝšrīn* 'the twenty-first'.

Fractions

The numerals from three through ten have fractions derived from them, formed on the pattern *Faɛl* [p.139]:

Cardinal Numeral		Fraction	
tlāte	'three'	*tǝlt*	'a third'
ʔarbɛa	'four'	*rǝbᵊɛ*	'a fourth'
xamse	'five'	*xǝms*	'a fifth'
sǝtte	'six'	*sǝdᵊs*	'a sixth'
sabɛa	'seven'	*sǝbᵊɛ*	'a seventh'
tmāne	'eight'	*tǝmᵊn*	'an eighth'
tǝsɛa	'nine'	*tǝsᵊɛ*	'a ninth'
ɛašara	'ten'	*ɛašᵊr*	'a tenth'

The fraction corresponding to *tnēn* 'two' is irregular: *nǝṣṣ* (or *nǝṣᵊf*) 'a half'.

The plurals of these fractions are formed on the pattern *Fɛāl*: *tlǝtt ᵊrbāɛ* 'three fourths', *ʔarbaɛ(t) ᵊxmās* 'four fifths'.

Fractions beyond the tenths are expressed periphastically with the cardinal numerals: *žǝzᵊʔ mn ᵊṭnaɛᵊš mǝn...* 'the twelfth part of'; *sabɛa ɛala ṭnaɛᵊš* 'seven twelfths' (lit. 'seven over twelve').

CHAPTER 12: TENSE

In Arabic, as in English, verbs are inflected for two tenses only: the PERFECT or PAST *(al-māḍi)*, and the IMPERFECT or NON-PAST *(al-muḍāriɛ)*.[1]

> On the formation of the tenses, see Verb Inflectional Forms [p. 173].

The verb of an independent clause is put in the perfect usually to designate past events or states: *katab* 'he wrote', *nām* 'he slept'. The imperfect, on the other hand, designates events, states, or dispositions that are <u>not</u> past: *byəktob* 'he writes, will write, would write'; *binām* 'he sleeps, will sleep, would sleep'.

> In the case of complemental verbs, the terms 'past' and 'not past' must be understood relatively to the time reference of the main clause. The time reference of a complemental verb in the imperfect can be past, relative to the moment of utterance, but cannot be past, relative to the time reference of the main clause. [p. 340].

Time reference in the imperfect is rendered more specific by the Particle of Actuality *ɛam–* [p. 320] or the Particle of Anticipation *raḥa–* [322]: *ɛam–yəktob* 'he is writing', *raḥa–yəktob* 'he's going to write'.
Without these particles the imperfect *(byəktob)* is used mainly to predicate generalities ('he writes'), potentialities ('he would write, he can write'), and assumed future events ('he'll write') [p. 324].

---

[1]The term 'tense', with reference both to Arabic and to English, is best limited to actual <u>inflectional</u> categories, excluding the numerous syntactic combinations involving auxiliaries, proclitics, etc. These syntactic "tenses", nevertheless, are dealt with in the course of this chapter.

It is often said [e.g. AO-25] that the Arabic perfect and imperfect are more properly called 'aspects' than 'tenses' – implying that these categories have more to do with perspective than with temporal sequence. This contention is perhaps based, in part, on a faulty analysis of such matters as the use of the imperfect in complemental clauses [p. 340] and the use of the perfect in conditional clauses [331], and in part, on the literary conventions of Classical Arabic (and even of other Semitic languages).

USES OF THE IMPERFECT

The Imperfect with Proclitics

The particles of actuality *(Ɛam-)* and anticipation *(raḥa-)* are prefixed, unaccented [p.18], directly to the imperfect verb form, but differ from true prefixes in that a single particle may serve more than one verb at a time in coördinations [392]: *raḥa-yākol w-inām* 'he's going to eat and go to bed', *mā Ɛam-yākol ulā yašrab* 'he's neither eating nor drinking'. (The indicative prefix *b-* [180] of the simple imperfect, on the other hand, is generally repeated with each verb: *mā byākol ulā byašrab* 'He neither eats nor drinks'.[1])

The Particle of Actuality

There are several forms of this particle: *Ɛam-* is the most generally used, but in Damascus *Ɛamma-* is also heard, and sometimes also *Ɛamm-, ʔam-,* and the full word *Ɛammāl.* In various parts of Lebanon, the forms *Ɛan-, Ɛa-, man-,* and *ma-* are also used. Most forms of the particle may be followed by the verb either with or without the indicative *b-*: *Ɛam-byākol* or *Ɛam-yākol* 'he is eating'; the Lebanese forms *Ɛan-, man-,* and *ma-,* however, are never followed by *b-*.[2] In Damascus, *Ɛam-* + *-b-* is most common in the first person singular *(Ɛam-bākol* 'I am eating', more common than *Ɛam-ʔākol); otherwise the forms without *b* are predominant: *Ɛam-nākol* 'we're eating', *Ɛam-yāklu* 'they're eating', etc.)

The particle of actuality is used to designate a state or an activity actually going on at the moment – the true "present" – as opposed to generalities and dispositions, for which the simple *b-* imperfect is used [p.326]. This particle is usually translatable into English with the "progressive" -ing forms (though not in the case of some psychological-state verbs [272] and certain others.) Examples:

1. *l-ʔmʔadden Ɛam-iʔadden*   'The muezzin is giving the call to
   ʔl-ʔadān   prayer'

2. *xalīl Ɛam-yatḥāka maƐ ʔr-raʔīs*   'Khalil is talking with the boss'

---

[1] There are certain parts of Greater Syria in which *b-* is more like the proclitics *Ɛam-* and *raḥa-,* i.e. one may say either *mā byākol ulā byašrab* or *mā byākol ulā yašrab.*

[2] The form *Ɛam-* is said [SPA-38] to result from the consistent assimilation of *n* [p.27] in *Ɛan-* to the following *b*: *Ɛan-* + *byākol* → *Ɛam-byākol* (then with *b* elided: *Ɛam-yākol).* This would explain why *b-* is not used after *Ɛan-;* it would also seem to imply that *Ɛam-* is unrelated in origin to the forms *Ɛamm(a)-, Ɛammāl.*

3. *bitamm...Ɛamma-yəbki w-yəmnaɛni*
   mn ᵊn-nōm [AO-119]

'He keeps on crying and keeping me
from sleeping'

4. *ʔəbni Ɛam-iṣīr rəžžāl*

'My son is getting to be a man'

5. *hallaʔ Ɛam-bədzakkar*

'It's(all) coming back to me now!'
'lit. "now I'm remembering")

A verb with *Ɛam-*, like the English -ing forms, may denote interrupted, off-and-on activities, as long as they
are viewed as constituting a time-limited <u>state</u> <u>of</u> <u>affairs</u>,
as opposed to a mere disposition or generality:

6. *Ɛamma-bixayyəṭ-lak ṭaʔm*
   ᵊždīd? [AO-47]

'Is he making you a new suit?'

7. *Ɛam-iṣammed maṣāri mənšān*
   taqāɛdo

'He's saving money for his retire-
ment'

8. *Ɛam-bədros bəž-žāmƐa*

'I'm studying at the university'

9. *mā Ɛādu Ɛam-yəthāku maƐ*
   baƐdon

'They're no longer speaking to one
another'

10. *Ɛamma-ʔəftəker b-šarwet*
    šantet ʔīd [DA-251]

'I'm thinking of buying a handbag'

Certain kinds of English verbs do not ordinarily occur in the -ing form
to indicate actuality, but the corresponding Arabic verbs (English notwith-
standing) are used with *Ɛam-* when appropriate, just like other verbs:

11. *māli Ɛam-lāʔi bayyāƐ išūf šū*
    bəddi

'I can't find a clerk to wait to me',
lit. "I'm not finding a clerk to see
what I want"

12. *šū Ɛam-təƐni?*

'What do you mean?', i.e. 'What are
you getting at?'

13. *māli Ɛam-bəʔder bakkel ᵊʔšāṭi*

'I can't buckle my belt', i.e. right
now, as opposed to *mā bəʔder...*'I
(generally) can't...'

14. *māli Ɛamma-ʔaƐref ṭarīʔi*
    [AO-116]

'I don't know my way', i.e. 'I can't
find my way just now'.

15. *Ɛam-ʔəsmaƐ mənno bēn waʔt*
    u-waʔt

'I hear from him from time to time',
i.e. nowadays, as opposed to *bəsmaƐ
mənno...*'I (generally) hear from
him...'

16. *Ɛam-iʔakked ʔənno kān ᵊhnīk*

'He maintains he was there'

17. *d-doktōr Ɛam-iʔūl ʔənno zāl*
    ᵊl-xaṭar Ɛanha hallaʔ

'The doctor says she is out of danger now'

With durative [p. 269] and translocative [274] verbs, whose participles are used (sometimes or always) indicating present actuality, the imperfect with *ɛam-* normally designates repetitive instances, in contrast to the participle which is generally used for an uninterrupted state:

18. *kəll marra ɛam-ʔəži la-ɛando*   'Every time I come to see him (i.e.
    ɛam-ikūn mašġūl   these days) he's busy'

19. *ɛam-inām bi-ɛālē kəll sabt*   'He sleeps over in Aley every Sat-
    u-ʔaḥad   urday and Sunday' (or 'He's been
                                        sleeping...')

20. *ṣāyer ɛam-ixāf haṣ-ṣabi kəll*   'This boy has started being afraid
    ma nṭafa ḍ-ḍaww   whenever the light is put out'.

Verbs like *ʔāl* 'to say', *ɛəref* 'to know', *ʔəder* 'to be able', etc., which are commonly complemented by a clause, are not so often used with *ɛam-* as with the simple *b-* imperfect in the annunciatory sense [p. 325]: *biʔakked ʔənno* ...(cf. ex. 16) *d-doktōr biʔūl*...(cf. ex. 17).

A notable difference between Arabic verbs with *ɛam-* and English "progressive" verbs with *-ing* is that the latter may be used in reference to the future, while the imperfect with *ɛam-* is never so used[1]: 'We're leaving tomorrow': *msāfrīn bukra;* 'If you're going with us tomorrow...': *ʔiza bətrūḥ maɛna bukra...* .

The Particle of Anticipation

There are several forms of this particle: *raḥ-, raḥa-, laḥ-, laḥa-,* and *ḥa-,* in addition to the full word *rāyeḥ.* The forms beginning with *l* are typical of Damascus and certain other areas, while the other forms may be heard in various regions (including Damascus). The particle is always followed by the imperfect without *b-: raḥa-yākol, laḥa-ʔākol,* etc.

The particle of anticipation generally indicates that what the following verb refers to is impending in the future, as a consequence of present intentions or a course of events already under way. It is most commonly translatable as 'going to...'. Often, however, it carries a sense of imminence or immediacy, best translated as 'about to...'. Examples:

1. *raḥa-šəf-lak yāha w-rədd-əllak*   'I'm going to see her (for you) and
   xabar [DA-80A]   let you know.'

2. *byəġhar laḥa-tənzel maṭar*   'It looks as though there's going to
   ʔawiyye [DA-153]   be a heavy rain.'

---

[1]Unless, of course, it is complementary to a future main clause [341].

3. *ʔaddēš raḥ-təbʔa hōn?* [EA-59]   'How long are you going to stay here?'

4. *ʔēmta laḥa-yṣór-lak fərṣa tšūfo?*   'When are you going to have a chance to see him?'

5. *ʔoɛa l-ʔaṭṭa laḥa-txarmšak!*   'Look out, the cat will scratch you!'

6. *taʔrīban laḥa-xalleṣ*   'I'm nearly finished' (Lit. 'I'm almost about to finish')

7. *šu byəghar raḥa-nəṣal* [DA-44]   'Well, it looks as though we're almost there' (Lit. '...we're about to arrive')

8. *ʔiza laḥa-tšatti l-ḥafle l-mūsīqiyye bəṭṣīr žuwwa*   'If it looks like rain the concert will be indoors' (Lit. 'if it's going to rain...')

9. *ʔana raḥa-rūḥ, nšālḷa tāni marra bšūfak bəl-bēt* [DA-218]   'I must go; I expect I'll see you at home next time' (Lit. 'I'm about to go....')

10. *l-məfti ḥa-yəɛlen fatwā ž-žəmɛa ž-žāye*   'The *mufti* is to deliver his opinion next week'

Many future events may be referred to either with the particle of anticipation or with the simple (*b–*) imperfect (see below); but in some contexts where the simple imperfect would more naturally be taken to indicate a generality or disposition [p. 326], *raḥa–* is used to make it unambiguously future:

11. *mīn raḥa-yṭaɛmi w-yəksi kəll hal-ʔaṭfāl əl-fəʔara?*   'Who will clothe and feed all those poor children?' (*mīn biṭaɛmi w-byəksi*...would be understood as 'Who clothes and feeds...'.)

12. *l-bəʔɛa mā laḥa-ṭəṭlaɛ*   'The stain won't come out' (i.e. '...isn't going to come out', as opposed to *mā bṭəṭlaɛ* '...won't come out', i.e. '...isn't disposed to come out')

Uses of the Simple Imperfect

The imperfect indicative without a proclitic *Ɛam-* or *raḥa* is used in several different senses: 1) Future, 2) Annunciatory, 3) Generalizing and Dispositional.

Almost all examples in the following sections are in the indicative mode (*b-*). Much of what is said here about the simple imperfect applies to both modes, but the subjunctive involves factors that tend to obscure (and in some cases override) considerations of tense as such. See p. 359 ex. 21, 22.

Future

In contrast to the particle of anticipation (see above), the simple imperfect is commonly used in reference to what is <u>assumed</u> will take place in the future, but with no special emphasis on immediacy or on present involvement in the course of events leading up to it.

Since the simple imperfect is also used in other senses, it is usually the context, or the circumstances of the utterance, which make the time reference explicit: *brūḥ bukra* 'I('ll) go tomorrow' or 'I'm going tomorrow'. Examples:

1. *bkūn Ɛandak Ɛal-ʔaktar baƐd sāƐa* [DA-197]
'I'll be at your place within an hour at the latest'

2. *ʔēmta btəbda d-drūs?* [DA-173]
'When does school ('lit. 'lessons') start?'

3. *baƐəd bəkra birūḥ Ɛal-madrase* [DA-197]
'The day after tomorrow he's going to school'

4. *nšāḷḷa brūḥ ʔs-səne š-šāye w-ʔbšūfak ʔhnīk* [DA-128]
'God willing, I'll go next year and see you there'

5. *ḍ-ḍarb ʔt-tāni mā bifūtak* [AO-112]
'The next blow won't miss you!'

6. *bḥətt-əllak ʔl-bāʔi b-kīs waraʔ* [DA-107]
'I'll put the rest in a paper bag for you'

7. *lēš mā byāxədhon maƐo lamma byeržaƐ?* [DA-75]
'Why doesn't he take them with him when he goes back?'

8. *baƐəd ma yəntṭbeƐ bəbƐat-lak nəsxa* [EA-259]
'After it's printed I'll send you a copy'

9. *hallaʔ ʔs-ṣānƐa btəži w-bətsāwī* [DA-103]
'The maid will come and do it right away'

10. *t-təmsāl byənsóbek bəl-brōnz*
'The statue is to be cast in bronze'

Annunciatory

The simple imperfect (like the English simple present) is often used to make (or elicit) an <u>announcement</u> or <u>sign</u> or <u>token</u> of a purported fact — as distinct from an ordinary report or statement of it: *bisallmu ɛalēk* 'They send you greetings', *mnəškor ʔaḷḷa* 'We thank God'.[1]

1. *būɛdak ḥa−ʔədros*	'I promise you I'm going to study'
2. *bhannīk*	'Congratulations!' (lit. 'I congratulate you')
3. *ʔana hallaʔ bəftə́teḥ ʔž̌-žalse*	'The meeting will come to order' (lit. 'I now open the session')
4. *bətkūn madāmti*	'This is my wife' (An introduction, as contrasted with a simple informative statement: *hayy madāmti*)

Besides its use in the set phrases of social formalities, the simple imperfect is commonly used to announce what someone says, thinks, knows, wants, etc. — generally with verbs complemented by clauses:

5. *biʔūl ʔənno ʔaxū mū žāye* [DA-95]	'He says that his brother isn't coming'
6. *huwwe byənkor ʔəlo ʔīd fīha*	'He denies he had a hand in it'
7. *bənṣaḥak ʔnsāha*	'I advise you(to) forget it'
8. *mətli mətlak mā baɛref*	'I don't know either'
9. *bžənn baɛʔrfo*	'I think I know him'
10. *blāʔi ɛala ġafle bəddak ʔtrūḥ* [DA-172]	'And now all of a sudden you have to go?!' (lit. 'I find all of a sudden...')
11. *šū btəʔmor ǧēro, ya bēk?* [DA-130]	'What else do you wish, sir?' (lit. 'What else do you order, sir?')
12. *hādi tāni marra byəntəxbū ɛəḍu barlamān* [EA-159]	'This is the second time they've elected him member of parliament'

---

[1]With verbs in the first person designating linguistic (or partly linguistic) acts, an annunciatory utterance in appropriate circumstances actually constitutes an integral part (if not the whole) of the announced event, rather than a mere token or sign of it: *ʔana btanni ɛal-ʔəqtirāḥ* 'I second the motion' (To <u>say</u> it is to <u>do</u> it.)

As distinct from annunciatory predications, reportorial predications may employ the particle of actuality (*Ɛam-*) [p. 320], a participle [272], or the perfect tense [330], or – in the case of linking verbs [452]– a non-verbal clause [402] (See ex. 4, above.)

For instance: *Ɛam-byənkor ʔəlo ʔīd fīha* (cf. ex. 6, same translation); *ʔāl ʔənno ʔaxū mū šāye* 'He said his brother wasn't coming' (cf. ex. 5); *māli Ɛāref* 'I don't know' (cf. ex. 8).

Since a report and an announcement are in certain respects equivalent, there are many situations in which there is little to choose between them.

Generalities and Dispositions

The generalizing and dispositional uses of the simple imperfect are by no means always distinct from one another; they are separated here more by virtue of their English translations than by intrinsic differences. In those cases where they <u>are</u> clearly distinct, furthermore, the dispositional use tends to merge with the future [p. 324] and the generalizing use, with the annunciatory [325].[1]

Generalizing. Like the simple present in English, the simple imperfect is used to make (or elicit) generalizations and non-temporal statements:

1. *l-mazarīb bṭənṭəšem lamma*   'The drains clog up when it rains'
   baṭmaṭṭer

2. *š-šāšat bibīḍu bēḍ*   'Hens lay eggs'

3. *ʔarbƐa w-xamse byaƐʔəmlu təsƐa*   'Four and five make nine'

4. *b-ʔawāxer ʔr-rabīƐ l-ḥabb*   'Late in spring the grain ripens'
   byəstəwi [AO-39]

5. *bināmu Ɛal-ʔəṣṭūḥ bəl-lēl*   'They sleep on the roof at night
   b-sabab ʔš-šōb [AO-39]   because of the heat'

6. *yōm bikūn fī fərṣa l-madāres*   'On a day that's a holiday the
   mā btəftaḥ [DA-239]   schools don't open'

---

[1]The simple imperfect indicative is functionally the base, or residual (or neutral) tense-mode, i.e. we are dealing with the non-past non-subjunctive non-actual non-anticipatory inflection, whose uses, structurally speaking, are exactly that. It is to be expected, therefore, that any positive characterization of these uses will involve partially merging or overlapping categories. That such characterization can be done with some semblance of simplicity and completeness however, shows up the falsity in any purely negative definition of residual categories.

7. wṣiyye bala ʔəmḍa bətkūn bāṭle   'A will without a signature is invalid' (or '...would be invalid')

8. ɛala ʔayy ṭarīʔa biṣīr ʔl-ʔəntixāb? [SAL-153]   'By what method does election take place?'

9. bi-ɛālē mā biṣīr bard matʔl hōn [DA-173]   'In Aley it doesn't get so cold as (it does) here'

10. mnəži la-ɛandkon ɛəšrīn marra la-təžu la-ɛanna marra   'We come to your house twenty times for every time you come to ours'

Dispositional. The simple imperfect is commonly used to indicate potentialities, dispositions, and propensities. The English equivalents are variously rendered, usually with 'can', 'would', 'will', or adjectives:

1. btəstaʔžər-lak ɛarabiyye ʔərʔb l-ʔmḥaṭṭa   'You can hire a car near the station'

2. btaɛref wēn blāʔi ʔmāš ʔmnīḥ? [EA-105]   'Do you know where I can find some good cloth?' (The main verb btaɛref is annunciatory [p.325].)

3. ʔēmta ma kān btədfaɛ-li [DA-107]   'You can pay me anytime'

4. waḷḷa mā bədfaɛ fī wlā ʔərš   'I wouldn't pay a piastre for it!'

5. r-rəžžāl byəɛʔžbak [EA-158]   'You'd like the man'

6. b-ḥayāti mā bəštəġel maɛ žamāɛa mən han-nəmre   'I would never work for people of that sort'

7. mā bəddi kūn maṭraḥo   'I wouldn't want to be in his place' (The quasi-verb bəddo 'to want' [p.412] is often translated as a dispositional, though it is not inflected for tense.)

8. hal-ʔmnaḍḍef bizīl ʔl-bəʔaɛ   'This cleaner will remove the spots'

9. l-xašab nāšef la-daraže byəštéɛel fīha b-ʔshūle   'The wood is dry enough to catch fire easily'

10. huwwe biġār ʔktīr   'He's very jealous (in disposition)', i.e. 'He gets jealous a lot'

11. hal-walad byəstéḥi   'That boy is bashful', i.e. '...gets embarrassed'

12. mā byətlāɛab [EA-161]   'He isn't deceitful', i.e. He doesn't (or won't) deceive'

13. *mā fī šī byənɛ́mel?*   'Is there nothing to be done?'

14. *hal-ᵊ?māš byəngə́sel?*   'Is this material washable?', i.e.
'Can this material be washed?'

15. *waḷḷa hal-manẓar mā byəntásа*   'This view is unforgetable', i.e.
'This view cannot be forgotten'

16. *huwwe xaṣᵊm byənxāf mənno*   'He's an adversary to be feared'

17. *kān fərṣa mā btəttamman ?əli*   'It was a very lucky break for me',
i.e. '...an occasion(that) cannot
be evaluated...'

Note that the verbs in the last eight examples above (ex. 10-17), most of which are translated into English with adjectives, do in fact function much like dispositional adjectives [p.277]; thus *bigār* in example 10 is (or at least can be) equivalent to the adjective *ġayyūr* 'jealous' (in disposition). Like dispositional adjectives, they are all intransitive and most are not complemented at all.

This ADJECTIVAL USE of dispositional verbs contrasts overtly with the ordinary use, in the case of verbs that are normally transitive, since the object is suppressed: *haz-zalame bigəšš* 'That fellow cheats', i.e. 'He's a cheater' = *haz-zalame ġaššāš;* as contrasted with *haz-zalame bigəššak* 'That fellow will (or would) cheat you', which shows the true verbal construction. Further examples with object suppressed:

18. *hal-kalb mā biɛaḍḍ*   'That dog won't (or doesn't) bite'

19. *?akl ᵊl-būẓa mā bəḍḍərr*   'Eating ice cream won't do any harm'

20. *haš-šaġle bətmallel*   'This job is boring', lit. "...bores"

21. *hayy mas?ale mā bəḍḍaḥḥek*   'This is no laughing matter', i.e.
'...a matter that doesn't cause
laughter'

22. *lā təsraɛ ɛala ṭər?āt bədzaḥle?*   'Don't speed on slippery roads', i.e.
'...on roads that cause skidding'

Examples 19-22 show verbs with inanimate subjects; these (being transitive with object suppressed) generally correspond to agentive adjectives [p.278] rather than to dispositionals: *bətmallel* = *mməlle,* *bəḍḍaḥḥek* = *məḍᵊḥke.*

See also p.409.

Note that English adjectives ending in -able (or -ible) are mostly <u>passive</u> dispositionals, e.g. 'washable' = 'can be washed'. Since Arabic dispositional and agentive adjectives are not normally formed from passives, it follows that the usual translation of these English adjectives will be with verbs: *byəngə́sel* '(is) washable'. This is all the more true in the case of adjectives with a negative prefix un-, in-, etc., since Arabic has no such formative, thus *mā byəntə́sa* '(is) unforgetable'. (There is, however, a limited use of passive participles in the dispositional sense [p. 275], mainly in Classicisms: *gēr maqrūʔ* 'illegible', more colloquially: *mā byənʔə́ra*.)

USES OF THE PERFECT

Past Time Reference

While indicating that an event or state referred to is in the past, the perfect tense implies nothing, one way or another, about the definiteness or the current relevance of that event or state. It may, therefore, be rendered in English either by the simple past (*katab* 'he wrote') or by the present-perfect ('he has written'), depending on context and circumstances.

Examples translated with the simple past:

1. *dəhek ᵊl-malek ᵊktīr* [AO-88]   'The king laughed heartily'

2. *fēn štagalt baʕᵊd ma txarrašt?* [EA-206]   'Where did you work after you were graduated?'

3. *kān mən ʔadīm ᵊz-zamān tāžer ʕando bənt* [AO-113]   'There was once upon a time a merchant who had a daughter'

4. *ʔabū kān faʔīr, w-bāʕ ʔarāḍī* [EA-160]   'His father was poor, and sold his land'

5. *lamma ṣāret l-ᵊntixābāt, ntaxabū raʔīs baladiyye* [EA-161]   'When the elections took place, they elected him mayor'

Examples translated with the present perfect:

6. *ʔaxadᵊt dawāk, walla ləssa?*   'Have you taken your medicine yet?'

7. *štamaʕt maʕo ʕəddet marrāt* [EA-158]   'I've met him several times'

8. *mā fī šī tgayyar*   'Nothing has changed'

9. ṣinā£et ᵊṣ-ṣābūn ṣāret ᵊl-yōm   'The soap industry has become the
   ᵓa£ẓam ṣinā£a fi-ṭrablos   biggest industry in Tripoli today'
   [PAT-183]

10. šū ṣār ma£ak?   'What's happened to you?' (also
                                           'What happened to you?')

    A participle [p. 262], in contrast to a verb in the per-
fect, may be used in reference to past events only if the
consequent state is currently in force: *šū ṣāyer ma£ak?*
'What's happened to you? (that you should be in this state)',
while *šū ṣār ma£ak?* can be said regardless whether the consequent state is still in effect or not.

    Some Arabic verbs which are basically momentaneous are usually trans-
lated with English <u>stative</u> (or <u>durative</u>) verbs. (This happens most commonly with verbs of cognition, affect, etc. See p. 272.) In such cases the
Arabic perfect – when used in reference to past events whose consequent
state is still in effect – is translated by the English present:

11. halla? ᵊrtāḥ bāli   'Now I feel relieved' (i.e. 'Now my
                                           mind has been relieved')

12. £rəft kīf?   'Do you know how it is?' (i.e. 'Have
                                           you found out how it is?')

13. fhəmt ᵓənnak msāfer bukra   'I understand you're leaving tomor-
                                           row' (i.e. 'I've been given to under-
                                           stand...')

14. ba£d ma halla? ᵓəlt-əlli ᵓəsmo   'Now that you've told me his name I
    dẕakkarto tamām   remember him perfectly' (i.e. '...
                                           I've brought him to mind perfectly')

15. mən malāmeḥ wəššak bə?der ᵓūl   'From the expression on your face I
    ᵓənnak mā ḥabbēto   can tell that you don't like it'
                                           (i.e. '...that you haven't taken a
                                           liking to it')

    Similarly, some English verbs are put in the present in
the annunciatory sense [p. 325], while the Arabic counterparts remain in the perfect:

16. ttafa?na   'We're agreed', 'It's a deal' (i.e.
                                           'We've agreed')

17. tšarrafna   'I'm (we're) honored' (i.e. 'We've
                                           been honored')

18. xaǰǰaltni   'You embarrass me' (i.e. 'You've
                                           embarrassed me')

19. baṣaṭṭni b-hal-xabar [DA-243]

'I'm glad to hear that' (i.e. 'You've gladdened me with this news')

20. šū hī š-šrūṭ ᵊlli ʔtaraḥta?
[SAL-170]

'What terms do you propose?' (i.e. 'What are the terms that you've thought up?')

Conditional Clauses

The perfect tense is commonly used in conditional clauses, usually associated with the particles ʔiza, law, ʔən (all translated 'if') and ma (translated '-ever' as in fēn ma 'wherever...').

With ʔiza 'if'. The perfect is used to indicate a condition which is presumably not fulfilled at present and may or may not be fulfilled in the future: ʔiza rəhᵊt maɛna, mā btətʔaxxar 'If you went with us, you wouldn't be late' or 'If you go with us, you won't be late'.

> The English translation with 'went...wouldn't...' is used if the main verb (btətʔaxxar) is interpreted as dispositional [p. 327], and 'go...won't...', if it is interpreted as future [324]. The English past tense in the 'if'-clause is required whenever the main verb is conditional ('would...'), but the Arabic perfect in the ʔiza-clause does not depend on its main verb.

Examples:

1. ʔiza daʔart fīha btəfroṭ

'If you touch it, it'll come to pieces' or 'If you touched it, it'd come to pieces'

2. mnəṣal la-natāyeš ʔahsan ʔiza ttabaɛna haṭ-ṭarīʔa

'We'll get better results if we follow this method' or 'We'd get... if we followed..'

3. məmken rūḥ ʔiza ɛazamūni

'I might (or may) go, if they invite me'

4. ʔiza ʔəwi l-wašaɛ, bɛāt wara doktōr

'If the pain gets stronger, send for a doctor'

5. nṭəẓərni ʔiza ṣār u-tʔaxxarᵊt ʔana

'Wait for me if I happen to be late' (lit. "...if it happened and I was late")

6. ʔiza mā kān ḥāḍer haṭṭ ɛalāme ʔəddām ʔəsmo

'If he's not present put a mark by his name'

7. ʔiza ḍallet haḍ-ḍōše laha-žənn

'If that noise keeps up I'll go crazy'

8. raḥa-nəži ʔəlla ʔiza nəzlet maṭar

'We'll come unless it rains' (lit. "...except if it rains")

In English the <u>present</u> tense must be used after 'if'
when the main verb is imperative (ex. 4,5,6) or future (ex.
7, 8), while in Arabic the perfect may be used in these
cases as well as in the others.

Note that in examples 1 and 2 the main verb is in the
simple imperfect, which, in this type of sentence, can depict either a "real" future situation or (dispositionally)
a hypothetical situation. The imperatives may also be used
for both real and hypothetical situations, though in their
case the English translation is the same for both.

Examples 7 and 8 differ from all the others in that they
could <u>not</u> be used to depict a hypothetical situation; the
particle of anticipation (*raḥa-, laḥa-*) [p. 322] – unlike
the simple imperfect – is not used dispositionally. Therefore the English translation is again limited to the present
and future verb forms, but in this case the limitation is
set by the Arabic meaning and not – as with the imperatives
– by English grammatical constraints.

The perfect is not obligatory after *ʔiza*, however, unless the situation
depicted is definitely hypothetical. When applied to a real situation, the
ʔiza-clause may have a verb in the imperfect or no verb at all: *ʔiza baṭrūḥ
maᶜna, mā btatʔaxxar* 'If you're going with us, you won't be late'; *btamm
ʔiza lā badd manno* 'I'll stay if necessary'.

An imperfect or non-verbal *ʔiza*-clause sometimes implies that the condition is expected to be fulfilled – as contrasted with the perfect, which implies no particular expectations one way or the other.

Examples:

9. *nšāḷḷa mā fī māneᶜ ᶜandak ʔiza*   'I hope you don't mind if I go now'
    *brūḥ halla*ʔ

10. *ʔiza t-taqrīrēn byatnāqaḍu lā*   'If the two reports conflict, don't
    *tsadde*ʔ *lā hād u-lā hād*   believe either one'

11. *ʔiza btastannāni šī yōmēn*   'If you'll wait for me a couple of
    yamken ʔaṭlaᶜ maᶜak [DA-172]   days I might go up with you'

12. *ʔiza baddak raʔyi hāda tanāzol*   'If you want my opinion, this is a
    ᶜan mabādʔak   backsliding from your principles'[1]

13. *ʔiza ᶜalēk šī lā tatʔaxxar*   'If there's something you have to do,
    manšāni [DA-243]   don't delay on my account'

---

[1]This is a pseudo-conditional construction, i.e. *hāda tanāzol*...is not a
genuine apodasis; it is logically independent of the protasis.

In example 13, the verbless clause ʔiza ɛalēk šī (theoretically) implies an expectation that you probably <u>do</u> have some pressing engagement or other, which makes it easier for you to excuse yourself than it would be if the speaker said ʔiza kān ɛalēk šī... (with the perfect kān which cancels out this expectancy) thereby putting more pressure on you <u>not</u> to excuse yourself. Thus the element of expectancy is converted into an element of politeness. Similarly, ʔiza bətrūḥ maɛna...is more of an invitation than ʔiza rəhᵊt maɛna..., and btamm ʔiza lā bədd mənno is more of an offer than btamm ʔiza kān lā bədd mənno.

Past Conditionals. The present tense after ʔiza may, of course, simply indicate past time:

14. ʔiza sāfar ᵊmbārḥa, byəṣal   'If he left yesterday, he'll arrive
    ᵊl-yōm   today'

Note also ʔiza sāfar ᵊmbārḥa, bikūn wəṣel ᵊl-yōm 'If he'd left yesterday, he'd have arrived today' or 'If he left yesterday, he'll have arrived today' [p. 341].

With ʔiza there is no distinction between <u>possible</u> conditions and <u>contrary-to-fact</u> conditions. The latter are indicated in English by a past-perfect phrase in the protasis ('if he'd left...') couples with a conditional phrase in the apodasis ('he'd have arrived...'), but in Arabic the same sentence (ʔiza sāfar...bikūn wəṣel) is used in either case — whether it is known that he has <u>not</u> arrived, or <u>not</u> known whether he has arrived or not.

ʔiza **with the Linking Verb** kān [p. 452]. A hypothetical condition with ʔiza is often expressed by the verb kān in the perfect, followed by a complemental verb: ʔiza kān šāfha, biḥākīha 'If he saw her, he'd talk to her'.

15. xāf ʔənno yətrok ᵊš-šəġᵊl   'He was afraid that he'd quit work-
    ʔiza kān rafaḍ ṭalabo [AO-103]   ing if he denied his request'

The complemental verb may be in the simple imperfect indicative (i.e. with the b- prefix) to indicate a disposition or a generalization [p. 326]:

16. šī rxīṣ, ʔiza kān byəštᵊġel   'That's cheap, if he does good work'
    ᵊmnīḥ [AO-47]

17. *lāzem ᵊtkūn bala ḥass ʔiza mā*
    kənt ᵊbtətʔassar b-hal-manẓar

    'You must be devoid of feeling if
    you're not moved by that sight'
    (i.e. 'You'd have to be if you
    weren't disposed to be moved...')

The hypothetical *kān* may likewise be followed by a verb in the imperfect with the particle of anticipation [p.322]:

18. *xallīni ʔaɛref ʔabl ᵊb-salaf*
    ʔiza kənt raḥa-təǧi

    'Let me know ahead of time if you're
    coming' (i.e. '...if you anticipate
    coming')

Note, however, that the simple imperfect is never used after *kān* in reference to a hypothetical future event. While a **main** clause may use the simple imperfect in the future sense *(mənlāʔī bukra* 'We're meeting him tomorrow'), this is an "assumed" future event [p.324], corresponding to a "positive-expectancy" conditional clause [332]: *ʔiza mənlāʔī bukra* 'If we're meeting him tomorrow...'. A "hypothetical" future event, on the other hand, requires the perfect tense in a conditional clause, with or without *kān:* *ʔiza (kān) lāʔēnā bukra* 'If we meet(met) him tomorrow...'. Examples:

19. *ʔiza kān mā mətᵊt bəddi*
    ʔaʔṭaɛ rās hal-kazzāb [AO-95]

    'If I don't die, I intend to cut
    that liar's head off'

20. *ʔiza kān laʔēt wāḥed ɛaṭ-ṭarīʔ*
    halli ʔal-lak sᵊʔīni, xallī
    yəšrab... [AO-99]

    'If you meet someone on the road
    who says to you "Give me water",
    let him drink' (Note the perfect
    tense of the attributive verb
    ʔal(-lak), as well as *laʔēt;* the
    attributive clause is also part of
    the hypothetical condition.)

The hypothetical *kān* may be used with *ʔiza* in two ways: either inflected, as in examples 17 and 18, or uninflected, as in examples 19 and 20. When uninflected, *kān* must come right after *ʔiza;* when inflected, it may be separated from *ʔiza* by the subject or by a negative particle [p.383]. Further examples of the uninflected *kān:*

21. *ʔiza kān ᵊl-ɛaṣāye ʔazharet*
    u-warraʔet ᵊl-yōm ᵊt-tāni,
    ɛrēf ʔənno ʔaḷḷa ġafar xaṭāyāk
    [AO-99]

    'If the stick has grown blossoms and
    leaves by the next day, know, then,
    that God has forgiven your sins'

22. *ʔiza kān māli ʔaḥsan bətǧībī-li*
    l-ḥakīm [AO-51]

    'If I'm not better you'll bring the
    doctor to (see) me'

23. *bḥūn ɛandak...baɛᵊd sāɛa...*
    ʔiza kān ᵊl-ḥallāʔ mū maɛǧūʔ
    [DA-197]

    'I'll be at your place in an hour,
    if the barber's isn't crowded'

24. *ʔiza kān fī balkōnāt bikūn*
    ʔafḍal [DA-290]

    'If there are(were) balconies, that
    will(would) be preferable'

Compare the inflected versions: *ʔiza l-ɛaṣāye (kānet) ʔazharet...*(cf. 21); *ʔiza mā kənt ʔaḥsan...*(cf. 22); *ʔiza l-ḥallāʔ mā kān maɛšūʔ...*(cf. 23).

With *ʔən, n-* **'if'**. The perfect is always used in conditional clauses expressed with *ʔən:*

1. *ʔən mā sakatt baḍərbak*   'If you don't shut up I'll hit you!'

2. *w-ʔn mā ʔəša, šū mnaɛmel?*   'And if he doesn't come, what'll we do?'

3. *r-rāḥ brūḥ maɛo, w-ʔn mā rāḥ brūḥ waḥdi*   'If he goes, I'll go with him, and if he doesn't go, I'll go alone' (*r-* for *n-* before *r* [p. 27])

4. *nšāḷḷa mā fī māneɛ ʔn-daxxant*   'I trust there's no objection if I smoke (?)'

Note also the set phrases *n-šā ʔaḷḷāh* and *n-rād ʔaḷḷāh* 'If God wills', and *n-ʔaḷḷa sahhal* "If God eases (the way)".

Like *ʔiza, ʔən* is often followed by *kān: n-kān mā ʔəša...* 'If he doesn't come...'

With *law* **'if'**. Most conditions expressed with *law* are hypothetical, and most, furthermore, are contrary to fact or to expectation. The verb of a *law*-clause is generally in the perfect tense:

1. *law kənt ʔb-maḥallak bəbʔa bəl-bēt*   'If I were in your shoes, I'd stay at home'

2. *law kān ʔl-manāx ʔanšaf b-ʔšwayye bikūn ʔaḥsan b-ʔktīr* [DA-151]   'If the climate were a little drier, it would be a lot better'

3. *w-law mā daras, byanšaḥ*   'Even if he didn't study, he'd do well'

4. *mənraššəɛ-lak ʔl-maṣāri ḥatta w-law kənna bəddna nəšḥad*   'We'll(we'd) pay you back the money even if we have(had) to beg'.

5. *w-lu ʔalaḥḥēt ɛaliyyi māli laḥ-ʔə̌zi*   'Even if you insist, I won't go' (The form *-lu* is commonly used instead of *law* after emphatic *w-* [p. 390].)

In desiderative ('if only', 'would that') conditions, however, *law* is commonly followed by verbs in the imperfect (indicative or subjunctive), or by non-verbal clauses. The apodasis is often suppressed:

6. *law btaᶜref ʔəddēš ᵊbḥəbbak*   'If you only knew how much I love
[SPA-27]   you!'

7. *law yəḥki kəlme wāḥde*   'If he would just speak up once, the
btənḥall ᵊl-məškle   problem would be solved'

8. *law ᶜandha šwayyet ḥēl bass!*   'If she only had a little strength!'

9. *ʔāx law ʔəʔʔtlo ᶜala hēk*   'I could kill him for doing such a
ᶜamal saxīf!   stupid thing!'("Oh, if I'd kill him...")

        The desiderative *law* is often used in a milder sense, to express invitations:

10. *law bətšarrəfna ᶜal-ġada*   'Why don't you have lunch with us?'
                                 ("if you would honor us for lunch")

Hypothetical *kān* in the Apodasis. When a conditional clause is introduced by *law*, the apodasis (main clause) is commonly introduced by the linking verb *kān* in the perfect: *law šəftha kənt ᵊbʔəl-lha* 'If I saw her, I'd tell her'.

        Note that the *b* prefix of a verb in the imperfect is <u>not</u> dropped after the hypothetical *kān*, as it is, usually, when *kān* is used for past time reference [p.341].

This use of *kān* is not obligatory if the main verb is in the imperfect. Its omission makes the apodasis more vivid: *law šəftha, bʔəl-lha* (same translation). (See examples 1-5.)

11. *law kənt ᵊb-maḥallak, kənt*   'If I were in your shoes, I'd stay
bəbʔa bəl-bēt   home' (Cf. example 1)

12. *kān byəṭlaᶜ b-ʔīdo ykūn*   'He could be the first in his class
ʔawwal wāḥed bəṣ-ṣaff law rād   if he wished'

13. *law kənti məštāʔtī-li*   'If you(f.) really wanted to see me
kənti btəži laᶜanna   you'd come to our house' [p.268]

But if the main verb is in the perfect — indicating a hypothetical event in the past — then it must be introduced either by *kān* (also in the perfect) or by the particle *la-*, or by *la-* plus *kān*: *law šəftha, kənt ʔəlt-əlha* (or *la-ʔəlt-əlha,* or *la-kənt ʔəlt-əlha*) 'If I had seen her, I'd have told her'.

14. *law ʔəlt-əlli kənt rəḥt maᶜak*   'If you'd told me, I'd have gone with
[DA-171]   you'

15. *law kan-li l-ʔəxtiyār la-kənt*   'If the choice had been mine, I'd
rəḥt bəṭ-ṭayyāra   have gone by plane'

16. *law tarak ᵊmbārḥa, la-wᵊṣel*   'If he'd left yesterday, he'd have
    ᵊl-yōm   arrived today'

17. *law biḷᵊbbu baɛdon ᵊl-baɛᵊḍ*   'If only they liked one another,
    kānu tɛāmalu sawa mᵊn zamān   they'd have gotten together long ago'

18. *law fahhamna ʔᵊnno hōn kᵊnna*   'If he'd let us know that he was
    daɛēnā ɛal-ʔᵊžtimāɛ   here, we'd have invited him to the
                                          meeting'

19. *w-law mᵊn hēk, ʔaḷḷa hū*   'And if it hadn't been for that, God
    ʔaɛlam šū kān ṣār fīna   knows what would have happened to us'
    [SAL-140]

With *law-la* 'if it were not for', 'but for':

20. *law-la l-ᵊwlād la-kān tarak*   'If it weren't for the children, he
    marto mᵊn zamān   would have left his wife long ago'

21. *law-la l-bōṣle kᵊnna ḍaɛna*   'Without the compass we'd have got-
                                          ten lost'

22. *law-lāhon la-kᵊnna mᵊnkūn*   'If it weren't for them, we'd be in
    halla? ᵊb-bārīz   Paris now'

23. *law-lāha kᵊnt šaḥḥād ᵊl-yōm*   'But for her, I'd be a beggar today'
    ʔana

        (The form *law-la* is also commonly used before *mā,* in a
    negative verbal clause:)

24. *law-la mā staxaff ᵊl-mawḍūɛ*   'If he hadn't made light of the mat-
    mā kān ṣār fī hēk   ter, that wouldn't have happened to
                                          him'

25. *law-la mā waržaɛ ġabā?o mā*   'If he hadn't displayed his stupid-
    kānu stažhalū   ity, they wouldn't have thought him
                                          ignorant'

Quasi-Conditional Clauses

The perfect is used in its hypothetical sense in certain constructions
similar to *law* conditionals, but which do not involve the conditional particle itself.

        A prepositional phrase may occur in place of the
    protasis:

1. *bidūn ṭawṣiyyāto mā kᵊnt*   'Without his recommendations, I
   ᵊstaḥsant ᵊl-fᵊkra ʔabadan   wouldn't have approved of the idea
                                          at all.' (Cf. *law-la ṭawṣiyyāto...*)

2. *baɛ̄d hal-maṭar ṣaret ʔasɛ̄ar*   'After this rain, grain prices should
l-ᵊḥbūb ᵊbtənzel [DA-238]   go down' (Cf. *law baṭmaṭṭer...* 'If it
    would rain...')

    The expression *w-ʔalla* 'or else...!' is itself a condi-
tional protasis (← *w-ʔan laʔ* 'and if not'), and is commonly
followed by a verb in the perfect:

3. *ʔaṣhak baɛdēn təržaɛ la-hōn,*   'Don't come back here again, or I'll
w-ʔalla ʔataltak [AO-119]   kill you!'

    Some clauses may be analyzed as an apodasis without a
protasis:

4. *kənt ᵊktīr baṭmanna rūḥ, bass*   'I'd very much like to go, but you'll
ᵊbtaɛzrūni [SAL-115]   (have to) excuse me' (Cf. *kənt ᵊktīr
baṭmanna rūḥ law ɛazamūni, bass...*
'I'd very much like to go if they('d)
invite(d) me, but...')

    The perfect is commonly used after *rēt-* 'would that...':

5. *rētni matᵊt ʔabᵊl ma ɛabbart*   'I'd sooner <u>die</u> than express my
ɛala raʔyi   opinion' (on a given matter) (Cf. *law
ɛabbart...*)

With *ma* '-ever'. The perfect is used for hypothetical conditions introduced
by *kəll ma* and *ʔēmta ma* 'whenever', *šū ma*, *ʔaš-mən, ʔē-mən* and *mah ma* 'whatever', *mīn ma* 'whoever', *wēn ma (fēn ma)* 'wherever', *kīf ma* 'however', *ʔadd
ma* 'however much':

1. *šū ma ṣār lā təftaḥ had-darᵊž*   'Whatever happens, don't open that
drawer!'

2. *mā bihəmmni šū ma ḥaka yəḥki*   'I don't care, let him say whatever
[DA-213]   he will'

3. *lāzəmni bēt fēn ma kān ykūn*   'I need a house, no matter where it
[DA-213]   is' (lit. "...wherever it be, let it
be")

4. *kəll ma daʔʔ ᵊl-kūz bəž-žarra*   'At every drop of the hat he threat-
bihaddədna b-ʔastiʔālto   ens us with his resignation' (lit.
"Whenever the mug hits the jar...")

5. *fīki təsʔali wēn ma kān*   'You (f.) can ask anywhere' (lit.
[SAL-192]   "You can ask wherever it may be")

6. *bəţḥadda mīn ma kān yaɛmel ḥaš-šī!*
'I challenge anyone to do that!' (lit. "I challenge whoever it may be... ")

7. *šū ma ʔəlt ḥa-nrūḥ*
'No matter what you say, we're going'

8. *ʔadd ma ɛažžaltni ḥaš-šaġle mā btəxloṣ ʔabkar*
'No matter how much you hurry me, this job won't be done any sooner'

9. *biləḥḥu ɛaz-zāyer kəll ma rād irūḥ məšān yəʔɛod šwayye zyāde* [PAT-199]
'They urge the visitor, every time he wants to go, to stay a while longer'

10. *biḥabb mīn ma šāf w-byəḥki šū ma səmeɛ* [RN-41]
'He takes a liking to whomever he sees and tells whatever he hears'

Some of these forms may be preceded by *law:*

11. *hal-žamāɛa mā byəstɛīdu žənsīton law šū ma ɛəmlu*
'That bunch won't get back their citizenship no matter what they do'

12. *law mah ma ɛməlt māli laḥ-ʔaɛṭīk maṣāri*
'No matter what you do, I'm not going to give you money'

13. *law ʔəš-mən ṣār, māli ʔāyem mən ʔarḍi*
'No matter what happens, I won't budge.'

With the attributive forms *ʔayy* and *ʔanu* 'any, whatever' [p.573], the perfect is also used, but without *ma:*

14. *ʔaɛṭīni ʔayy mašrūbāt kānu* [RN-41]
'Give me whatever beverages there are'

15. *xōd ʔanu ktāb ɛažabak*
'Take any book you like'

ma can also be used with the imperfect, in the generalizing or dispositional senses, or for "expected" conditions (or courtesy) [p.332].

16. *kəll ma bšūfo ʔaktar kəll ma bḥabbo ʔaktar*
'The more I see of him, the more I like him'

17. *ʔadd ma byaɛṭīk, xōd mənno* [DA-215]
'As much as he'll give you, get from him'

18. *wēn ma bətrīd tākol ʔana bākol* [DA-213]
'Wherever you'd like to eat, I'll eat'

19. *la-wēn ma bəddak brūḥ* [DA-215]
'I'll go wherever you want' (The tenseless *bəddak*, without a linking verb *kənt*, is equivalent to the imperfect.)

The *ma* forms may also be used with *kān* for past time reference plus a complemental verb in the imperfect for generalization [p. 326]:

20. *kəll ma kān ifakker fīha kān*   'Every time he thought about it he
    yətkarkar   would chuckle'

TENSE SUBORDINATION

Time reference in a main clause is relative to the moment of utterance: *Єam-yəktob maktūb* 'He's writing a letter' (at the present moment); *katab maktūb* 'He wrote a letter' (before the present moment). In an Arabic complemental clause [p. 449], however, time reference is relative to that of the main clause: *šəfto Єam-yəktob maktūb* 'I saw him writing a letter' (or 'I saw he was writing a letter'). Since the clause *Єam-yəktob maktūb* is complemental to the main clause *šəfto* 'I saw him', the present actuality of his writing applies, not to the moment of utterance, but to the prior moment indicated by the perfect tense in *šəfto*. Likewise in *šəfto katab maktūb* 'I saw he had written a letter', the past time of his writing indicated in the complemental clause *katab maktūb* is prior to the past moment referred to in the main clause *šəfto*. Similarly: *šəfto ḥa-yəktob...* 'I saw he was going to write...', *ḥa-tšūfo katab* 'You'll see that he'll have written...', etc.

In English — as in many other European languages — tense subordination of this sort does not exist. Either the tense of the complemental verb is shifted to agree with that of the main verb ("sequence of tenses"): 'I saw he <u>was</u> writing', or else the complemental verb is reduced to a "non-finite" form: 'I saw him writing', 'I saw him write'.

Examples (Main verb in perfect):

1. *ḥakā–lha šū šāf* [AO-113]   'He told her what he had seen'

2. *ftakart ʔənnak ᵊbtaЄref* [EA-150] 'I thought that you knew'

3. *ʔāl bəʔder rūḥ*   'He said I could go'

4. *baЄdēn ʔāl ʔənno raḥa-yənṭəẓer*   'Then he said that he was going to
   ʔawāmer ždīde   await new orders'

5. *tāni yōm šāf ʔənha warraʔet*   'The next day he saw that it had
   u-ʔaẓharet [AO-100]   leafed out and blossomed'

6. *bass ᵊmbāreḥ sməЄt ʔənnak*   'Just yesterday I heard that you
   marīḍ [EA-149]   were ill' (Verbless complemental
                                        clause [p. 403])

7. *kənt ᵊmḥasseb ʔənno bəddo yrūḥ*   'I was under the impression that he
                                        wanted to go'

8. *zənta b-ɛaˀli ˀiza brūḥ*   'I weighed it in my mind whether I
   wəlla laˀ   should go or not'

9. *lāˀēnā mā byəswa xabaro*   'We found him not all he was cracked
                                    up to be'

10. *kaˀənni sməɛt ˀl-ˀəfˀl*   'I thought I heard the lock click'
    ɛam-iṭaˀṭeˀ

In accordance with this principle of tense subordination, the tense of
a main verb may be "compounded" by making it complemental to the linking
verb *kān* 'to be':

kān 'he was' + *ɛam-yəktob* 'he is writing' → *kān ɛam-yəktob* 'he was writing'

kān 'he was' + *raḥa-yəktob* 'he's going to write' → *kān raḥa-yəktob* 'he was
                                                                   going to write'

kān 'he was' + *katab* 'he wrote' → *kān katab* 'he had written'

kān 'he was' + *byəktob* 'he writes' → *kān yəktob* 'he used to write'

> The *b-* prefix of the simple imperfect is usually drop-
> ped after *kān* for past time reference, but is kept intact
> for the hypothetical sense [p. 355]: *kān byəktob* 'he would
> write'.

bikūn 'he will be' + *ɛam-yəktob* 'he is writing' → *bikūn ɛam-yəktob* 'he'll be
                                                                    writing'

bikūn 'he will be' + *katab* 'he wrote' → *bikūn katab* 'he will have written'

(Etc.)

> It should be noted that the linking verb and the com-
> plemental verb do not constitute a "verb phrase", properly
> speaking. The linking verb stands in construction with
> the whole predicate (exactly as it does with a non-verbal
> predicate), not with the verb as such. See p. 452.

Examples of *kān* with verbal complement:

1. *t-trēn kān ləssā ɛam-yətḥarrak*   'The train was still moving'

2. *kānet təštə́ǵel b-maktab*   'She used to work in an office'

3. *lamma wṣəlt, kānet ˀl-maṭar*   'When I arrived, the rain had
   ˀnˀaṭɛet [AO-67]   stopped'

4. *bəkra nšāḷḷa bə́ǰi bzūrak*   'Tomorrow I'll come see you and I
   w-ˀnšāḷḷa bətkūn ṣaḥḥēt   trust you'll have recovered'
   [DA-217]

5. *mən yōmēn tlāte kānet sāƐti*
   Ɛamma-tˀaṣṣer [AO-71]

'For two or three day my watch was losing time'

6. *kəll ma Ɛərfet šū bəddo, kānet*
   tərkod u-təẍhad la-taƐməl-lo
   yā [AO-111]

'Whenever she found out what he wanted, she would run and take pains to do it for him' (i.e. 'she used to run...')

7. *la-bēn ma təlbes badəltak*
   əẍ-ẍdīde bikūn ḅāḅa wəṣel
   [DA-298]

'By the time you've put on your new suit, Daddy will have arrived'

8. *ˀakīd bikūnu ˀahlak stawḥašū-lak*
   b-ǧēbtak

'Your family certainly must have missed you when you were away' (*bikūnu* is dispositional [p.327].)

9. *lā tədros əd-dars ət-tālet*
   ˀabəl ma tkūn ˀatˀant əd-dars
   ət-tāni

'Don't study the third lesson before you've mastered the second' (*ˀatˀant* is in the perfect to emphasize the completion of mastery, but *ˀabəl ma* requires the subjunctive [p.358], hence *tkūn.*)

10. *bass yā rētak kənt maƐi, kənt*
    əmbaṣaṭṭ ˀaktar [DA-171]

'But if only you'd been with me, I'd have had a better time' (The second *kənt* is used here for a hypothetical apodosis [p.336], not for past time reference.)

11. *law šəftha bər-rabīƐ, kənt*
    bətˀūl ǧēr hēk [DA-250]

'If you saw it in springtime, you wouldn't say that' (*kənt* for hypothetical apodosis)

Tense subordination is also commonly shown in certain kinds of attributive clauses [p.495], annexion clauses [p.490], and supplemental clauses [p.531]:

1. *ẍ-ẍamƐ əstaˀbalo b-barbara*
   bəddəll Ɛal-əmwāfaˀa

'The gathering greeted him with a murmur of approval' (i.e. '...that indicated approval')

2. *b-hal-maṣāri l-rəbḥūha Ɛammaru*
   byūton [PVA-30]

'With this money they had earned, they built their houses'

3. *stahlakna kəll əṣ-ṣābūn halli*
   bəl-bēt

'We've used up all the soap we had in the house' (Verbless attributive clause [   ])

4. *Ɛamel kəll halli byəṭlaƐ b-ˀīdo*

'He did everything he could'

5. *tnazzaht u-ˀana Ɛam-bəˀra*
   [RN-I.227]

'I walked while I was reading'

CHAPTER 13: MODE

Verbs in the imperfect tense are inflected for three modes: Indicative, Subjunctive, and Imperative.

The INDICATIVE, used in assertive predications [p. 347], is expressed by a prefix *b-* or a proclitic *ɛam-* or *raḥa-* preceding the person prefix: *byəftaḥ* 'he opens', *ɛam-yəftaḥ* 'he is opening', *raḥa-yəftaḥ* 'he's going to open'. See p. 320 ff.

The SUBJUNCTIVE, used in optative predications and in various subordinate syntactic positions, is expressed by a bare person-prefix (i.e. a prefix **not** preceded by *b-*, *ɛam-*, or *raḥa-*): *yəftaḥ* '(that)he open'.

The IMPERATIVE, used in commands or requests, is expressed by the imperfect stem without a person-prefix, and in some cases also by internal modification of the stem: *ftāḥ* 'open' [p. 198].

> The uses of the indicative mode are treated only insofar as they contrast with the subjunctive; that is to say, the indicative is taken as the "standard" or "neutral" mode which is used whenever the other modes are **not** used.[1] The indicative is fully exemplified, however, on p. 320 ff.

---

[1] It makes better sense morphologically, and is perhaps structurally more satisfactory on the whole, to take the subjunctive as the neutral or unmarked mode (non-assertive). Then the function of "assertion" is signalled 1.) by the subordination of a subjunctive verb to any non-subjunctive main term, including the proclitics *ɛam-* and *raḥa-* [p. 320], or 2.) by prefixation of *b-* to the subjunctive form. (Non-verbal predications, together with verbal predications in the perfect tense, are generally — though by no means always — assertive.) For ordinary expository purposes, however, the fact remains that little needs to be said about assertion, while quite a bit needs to be said about non-assertion.

The subjunctive and indicative of Syrian Arabic should not be identified with the so-called subjunctive (*al-muḍāriɛ l-manṣūb*) and indicative (*al-muḍāriɛ l-marfūɛ*) of classical Arabic *ʔiɛrāb*, though there is, of course, some similarity in use between the Syrian subjunctive and the combined subjunctive and jussive of Classical Arabic. (The latter, however, are not full-fledged grammatical categories at all, but only automatic syntactic alternants.)

The Subjunctive in Independent Optative Clauses

While the indicative is used to express or elicit assertions, the subjunctive is used to express or elicit exhortations, suggestions, and
invocations:

Assertive   Optative

mənrūḥ Ɛas-sinama.................................*nrūḥ Ɛas-sinama*
'We'll go to the movies'   'Let's go to the movies'

bətrūḥ Ɛas-sinama maƐna?.........................*trūḥ Ɛas-sinama maƐna?*
'Are you going to the movies with us?'   'Will you go to the
                                                      movies with us?'

blā?i taksi b-haš-šareƐ?.........................*lā?i taksi b-haš-šareƐ?*
'Can I find a taxi on this street?' [p. 327]   'Shall I find a taxi on
                                                      this street?'

?aḷḷa biwaff?ak................................*?aḷḷa ywaff?ak*
'God will grant you success'   'May God grant you
                                                      success'

Further examples of the independent subjunctive:

1. *?aƐmel ?ahwe, wəlla šāy?*   'Shall I make coffee, or tea?'

2. *šāyef ?mnīḥ, wəlla*   'Can you see all right, or shall I
   ?əftaḥ-lak ?ḍ-ḍaww?   turn on the light for you?'

3. *rūḥ žīb kam ?annīnet bīra?*   'Shall I go get a few bottles of
                                       beer?'

4. *nərtaḥ-?lna nətfe hōn?*   'Shall we rest a bit here?'

5. *tfət-lak ši da?ī?a?*   'Will you come in for a minute?'

6. *yalli lāḥeš tyābo yəži yšīlon*   'Whoever has strewn his clothes
                                       around shall come pick them up'

7. *?aḷḷa yəžmaƐna sawa marra tānye* 'May God bring us together again'
   [DA-253]

8. *ṭəṣbeḥ Ɛala xēr*   'Good night' (lit. 'May you be well
                                       in the morning').

9. *yəxrab bēto*   'A curse upon his house!' (lit.
                                       'May his house be ruined').

10. *lā ykən-lak fəkre*   'Don't give it a thought' (lit.
                                       "Let there not be a thought to you").

See also p. 355, example 17, and the paragraphs preceding and following it.

Note the formulaic phrases *sallem ʔīdēk* and *katter xērak*
(both translated 'thank you'; the first for work performed).
The verbs are subjunctive (not imperative) aphaeretic forms
for *ysallem...* 'May He protect (your hands)' and *ykatter...*
'May He increase (your well-being)'. (Cf. English 'Bless
you' for 'God bless you', 'Thank you' for 'I thank you').

In the second person after the negative particle *lā* (or *mā*) [p. 389],
the use of the subjunctive extends to include direct commands and requests,
in lieu of the non-existent negative imperative construction:

Positive Command (Imperative)		Negative Command (Subjunctive)	
rūḥ	'Go!'	*lā trūḥ*	'Don't go'
taɛa	'Come!'	*lā taǧi*	'Don't come!'
ǧībī-li yā	'Bring(f.)it to me'	*lā dǧībī-li yā*	'Don't bring it to me.'

The Particle *la-* [cf. p. 353] is sometimes used before a main verb in the
first person subjunctive, expressing exhortation ('let...'):

la-nərǧaɛ la-masʔalt ʔl-bēt [DA-244]	'Let's go back to the matter of the house'
la-ḥadder-lak tyābak [DA-181]	'Let me get your clothes ready for you'
ʔiza bəddak ʔtrūḥ tədzaḥlaʔ ɛat-talǧ, la-ɛīrak ṭaʔmi	'If you intend to go skiing, let me lend you my suit'

The Subjunctive in Subordinate Clauses

In various kinds of subordinate clause, the mode of a verb depends — as
it does in independent clauses — on whether the clause is assertive or optative. The indicative is used if the subordinate clause is assertive, i.e.
if it depicts an objective state of affairs (actual, hypothetical, or antic-
ipated): *ʔāl ʔannak ʔbtəǧi* 'He said that you would come'. The subjunctive,
on the other hand, is used if the clause expresses an exhortation, suggestion, wish, fear, intention, or the like: *ʔal ʔannak təǧi* 'He said that you
should come'. [See p. 347.]

In Complemental Clauses [p. 449]. The subjunctive is used after overt ex-
pressions of exhortation, suggestion, wish, fear, intention, etc. Many such
clauses are introduced by *ʔanno* 'that':

After *ṭalab* 'to ask(for), request':   1. *ṭalab mən rəfaʔāto yəstannū* 'He asked his companions to wait for him'

ʔamar 'to order, command':   2. *l-malek ʔamar ᵃṣ-ṣayyad ʔənno yžəb-lo ʔarbaɛ samakāt* [AO-117] 'The king ordered the fisherman to bring him four fish'

ttafaʔ 'to agree':   3. *ttafaʔna nətbādal ᵃd-dōr* 'We agreed to take turns'

waɛad 'to promise':   4. *wɛədni ʔannak mā taɛməla tāni marra* 'Promise me not to do it again'

naṣīḥa 'advice':   5. *naṣīḥti ʔənno nətrok ḥālan* 'My advice is that we leave immediately'

xāf 'to fear':   6. *xāf ʔənno yətᵃrku š-šəġᵃl* [adap.fr. AO-103] 'He was afraid they would quit the job'

xaṭar 'danger':   7. *fī xaṭar ʔənno yəxṣar waẓīfto* 'There's danger that he'll lose his job'

staḥaʔʔ 'to deserve':   8. *ʔənti mā btəstḥəʔʔi ʔənno ḥākīki* [AO-119] 'You(f.) don't deserve that I should speak to you'

kəreh 'to hate':   9. *bəl-ḥaʔīʔa bəkrah ʔezᵃɛžak* 'I really hate to bother you'

ḥabb 'to like':   10. *bətḥəbbu ʔəržaɛ ʔāxədkon?* [DA-129] 'Would you(pl.)like me to come back and pick you up?'

rād 'to wish, want':   11. *kān marra malek smīn ktīr w-rād yənḥaf* 'There was once a very fat king, and he wanted to reduce'

ʔəbel 'to accept, agree to':   12. *farīʔna ʔəbel ināzəlon* 'Our team agreed to play them'

The indicative, on the other hand, is generally used after expressions of knowledge, assurance, supposition, assumption, and the like[1]:

---

[1]Note that the complemental verb may be indicative even though the superordinate predication is interrogative (ex. 1), negative (ex. 2), or optative (ex. 3) (below).

žann 'to think, suppose':

1. bəṭžann ʔənno byaɛref l-ᵊḥkāye?
'Do you suppose he knows the story?'

ɛtaʔad 'to believe':

2. mā baɛtᵊʔed ʔənnek btaɛᵊrfi ṭəṭᵊbxi
'I don't believe you(f.) know how
to cook'

faraḍ 'to suppose, assume':

3. nəfroḍ ʔənno mā byəži 'Let's suppose
he doesn't come...'

ṭṣawwar 'to imagine':

4. mā ʔədret təṭṣawwar ʔənno byəkᵊzbu
ɛalēha 'She couldn't imagine that
they would lie to her'

ḥalaf 'to swear':

5. ḥalaf ᵊl-malek ʔənno mā byəržaɛ
[AO-117] 'The king swore that he
wouldn't return'

šāf 'to see':

6. maɛi has-salle bass šāyəf-lak mā
laḥa-təsaɛhon [DA-106] 'I have this
basket but I see that it's not
going to hold them'

From the foregoing examples it should be clear that the difference in meaning between assertive and optative predications is not a difference between fact and hypothesis, nor between likelihood and unlikelihood. It is more like the psychological distinction between <u>objective</u> and <u>subjective</u>: an assertive predication depicts a (real or imaginary) state of affairs, while an optative predication projects a state of mind.

Not surprisingly, there are borderline cases in which speakers may choose either indicative or subjunctive: waɛadni ʔənno byəržaɛ 'He promised me that he would come back' (assertive), but waɛadni ʔənno yəržaɛ 'He promised me to come back' (optative).

Further examples of expressions complemented by subjunctive verbs:

bəddo 'to want, require, be supposed to, intend to, be going to':

1. ʔana bəddi ʔəržaɛ ɛal-bēt   [DA-77]
'I want to go back home'

2. r-rəžžāl halli bəddna nzūro šū
byəštāġel? [DA-75] 'The man we're
going to visit — What's his work?'

3. kān bəddi ʔəštrīha 'I wanted to buy
it' (or 'I was going to buy it')

4. bəddak yāha təʔra w-təktob? [DA-80]
'Do you want her (to be able) to
read and write?'

lāzem 'must, ought to, have to,
  necessary to'; byəlzam 'to
  be necessary for (s.o.):

yəmken 'may, might, maybe,
  perhaps'; məmken 'possible':

ʔəder 'to be able':

5. bəddo l-bēt ikūn mafrūš? – ʔēwa
   w-ikūn ʔarīb Ɛal-mufawwaḍiyye
   [DA-289] 'Does he want the house to
   be furnished? – Yes, and (that) it
   should be near the legation'

6. bəddha tšatti 'It's going to rain'

7. lāzem ʔūfi b-waƐdi [AO-116] 'I
   must keep my promise'

8. lāzem ᵊnkūn bəl-maṭār ʔabl ᵊb-sāƐa
   [DA-249] 'We ought to be at the
   airport an hour ahead of time'

9. kənt lāzem təbʔa mərtāḥ bəl-bēt
   [DA-218] 'You ought to have stayed
   and rested at home'

10. byəlzamak mara kbīre w-ᵊtkūn
    Ɛaššiyye [DA-80a]: 'You need an
    older woman who would be a house-
    keeper' (lit.'...and (that) she be
    a housekeeper')

11. yəmken təṣal maƐ l-ᵊwlād baƐᵊd
    xamṣtaƐšar yōm [DA-198] 'She may ar-
    rive with the children in two weeks'

12. Ɛala hal-lōn yəmken ʔəštéri t-ṭaʔᵊm
    mən bērūt [DA-199] 'In that case I
    might buy the suit in Beirut'

13. yəmken yəʔbal ižawwzak yāha[AO-114]
    'Perhaps he'll agree to give her to
    you in marriage'

14. yəmken tkūn mā ḥabbēt ʔakᵊlna
    [DA-199] 'Maybe you don't like our
    food!' [p.330]

15. ʔāl məmken rūḥ 'He said I might go'

16. məmken tətwaṣṣat-li ʔābel ᵊl-mudīr
    hallaʔ? [DA-295] 'Is it possible
    that you might arrange for me to
    see the director now?'

17. btəʔʔədru təsbaḥu ʔēmta ma kān
    u-tətraṭṭabu [DA-151] 'You can swim
    anytime and refresh yourselves'

18. mā ʔəder lā yākol u-lā ynām
[DA-107] 'He could neither eat
nor sleep'

19. btəʔder b-layāli kawānīn təʔεod
bəẓ-ẓalt mən ġēr nār? [AO-87]
'Could you, on December and Janu-
ary nights, sit in the nude without
a fire?'

fī 'to be able' [p.415]

20. mā fī yətεawwad εan-niẓām ʔl-ʔāsi
'He can't get used to the strict
discipline'

21. fīni sāεdak b-ʔayy ṭarīʔa? 'Can I
help you in any way?'

εəref 'to know how to':

22. btaεˀrfi ṭəṭˀbxi ṭabˀx ʔafranǯi?
[DA-99] 'Do you(f.)know how to
cook European style?' (Cf. εəref
ʔənno...'to know that...', followed by an assertive clause)

nəsi 'to forget to':

23. nəsi yʔarrex ʔl-maktūb 'He forgot
to date the letter'

24. lā tənsa ma tḥəṭṭ ʔl-mōzāt fōʔ
ˀt-təffāḥāt [DA-107] 'Don't
forget to put the bananas on top
of the apples'

After the negative command lā tənsa 'don't forget', the
particle ma commonly introduces the subjunctive verb. (Do
not confuse this with the negative particle mā.)
Cf. nəsi (ʔənno) 'to forget that...', followed by assertive clause.

dzakkar 'to remember to':

25. dzakkar ṭəṭfi ḍ-ḍaww 'Remember to
put out the light'

(Cf. dzakkar (ʔənno) 'to remember
that...', followed by assertive
clause.)

bada 'to begin':

26. b-ʔawwal ˀš-šahˀr l-ˀfεāle badu
yəhˀfru ʔasāsāt ʔl-bēt [AO-75] 'On
the first of the month the workers
began to excavate (for) the foundations of the house'

ballaš 'to begin':

27. l-bannāyīn biballšu yəbnu l-ḥīṭān
[AO-75] 'The masons will begin to
build the walls'

baṭṭal 'to stop, cease':

28. hal-walad ʾēmta ha-ybaṭṭel yəbki? 'When is that child going to stop crying?'

29. ḍall rūḥ w-ᵊržāɛ laḥatta ybaṭṭel ḥada yəṭlob mᵊnnak [AO-99] 'Keep going back and forth until everybody has stopped asking you (for it)'

yā rēt 'would that, I wish':

30. yā rētak ᵊtšūf ᵊr-rabīɛ ɛanna b-bērūt 'I wish you could see the springtime we have in Beirut!'

31. yā rēt ʾəʾder ʾəʾra har-rmūz ᵊṣ-ṣīniyye 'I wish I could read those Chinese characters'

(May also be used with the perfect: yā rēto kān hōn! 'If only he were here!' [p. 338])

nšāḷḷa 'God willing', 'I hope':

32. nšāḷḷa mā ykūn ɛando wlād ᵊẓġār [DA-243] 'I hope he doesn't have any small children'

33. nšāḷḷa kūn mā ʾasaʾt-ᵊllak 'I hope I didn't hurt you' [cf. ex. 9, p. 342]

(Also used with the indicative, in the sense 'I trust': nšāḷḷa bṭəmbᵊṣṭi ɛanna [DA-81a] 'I trust you'll have a good time here'

ɛalē 'to have to, be obliged to': [p. 415]

34. ləssa ɛalē yḥəṭṭ wadīɛa bᵊl-ḅaṇk 'He still has to make a deposit at the bank'

35. ʾəlkon ɛaliyyi kūn hōn ʾabl ᵊb-ɛašᵊr daʾāyeʾ [DA-29] 'I'm to be here for you (pl.) ten minutes early' (lit.: 'I owe it to you to be here...')

ḍṭarr 'to be forced, obliged, required':

36. ḍṭarrēt ʾeštᵊġel sāɛāt ʾᵊḍāfiyye 'I had to work extra hours'

məḥtᵊmal 'probable':

37. məḥtamal ʾᵊnno hal-ɛawāmel ᵊtʾazzem ᵊl-waḍᵊɛ 'It is probable that these factors will precipitate a crisis'

məstaḥīl 'improbable, impossible':

38. mn ᵊl-məstaḥīl ᵖənno yəži 'It's highly improbable that he would come'

xalla 'to let, allow':

39. xallīna nāxod ᵊl-bāṣ [DA-44] 'Let's take the bus'

40. xallīhon yəṣṭəflu maᴱ baᴱdon [AO-83] 'Let them thrash it out between them'

41. šlōn xallētī· yəṭlaᴱ b-hal-bard? [DA-198] 'How could you let him go out in this cold?'

ᵖaḥsan 'better':

42. laᵖa ᵖənno ᵖaḥsan yəftaḥo [AO-115] 'He found that it would be better to open it'

fəkr 'idea':

43. fəkro tāni səne yəži ləl-blād ᵊl-ᴱarabiyye [DA-173] 'His idea is to come some other year to the Arab countries'

faḍḍal 'to prefer':

44. n-nās hōn w-ᵊhnīk bifaḍḍlu yəštəru lᵖaḥsan [DA-129] 'People both here and over there prefer to buy the best'

ᵖarrar, qarrar 'to decide':

45. ᵖēmta mqarrer ᵊtsāfer? [DA-248] 'When have you decided to leave?'

ᴱazam 'to invite':

46. r-raᵖīs ᴱazdmon yətᴱaššu maᴱo [AO-91] 'The boss invited them to dine with him'

hamm 'to be important (to)':

47. biḥəmmni təḥkī-lha šwayyet ᵖənglīzi [DA-80] 'It's important to me that she (be able to) speak a little English'

ᵖəšha(k) 'be careful not to'

48. ᵖəšhak...tətrok ᵖīd maryam [DA-301] 'Be careful you don't let go of Mary's hand'

žarrab 'to try, attempt':

49. žarreb taᴱmel ᵖaḥsan l-marra ž-žāye 'Try to do better the next time'

ḥāwal 'to try, strive':

50. ḥāwel ikūn sardak mawḍūᴱi ᴱan ᵊl-ḥādes 'Try to give an objective account of the incident' (Lit. 'strive that your account be...')

tḥāša 'to avoid':

51. tḥāšēt ʔəzkor ši   I took care
not to mention anything...'

tḥadda 'to defy':

52. bətḥaddāk ᵊdžāweb Eala suʔāli
'I defy you to answer my question'

xāyef 'afraid' (commonly followed
by the particle la-:)

53. huwwe xāyef la-ykūn maEo z-zāyde
[DA-203] 'He's afraid he has
appendicitis'

54. ʔana xāyef la-mā yəži   [RN-I.248]
'I'm afraid he isn't coming'

55. xāyəf-lak ᵊl-bēt yəhboṭ 'I'm
afraid the house will cave in'

kallaf 'to entrust, ask a favor of':

56. baddi kallef ḥaḍᵊrtak təsEā-li
b-waẓīfe [SAL-92] 'I'd like to
ask you to see about a job for me'

yā dōb 'hardly':

57. yā dōbi ʔūm bi-maṣārīfi 'I can
hardly keep up with my expenses'

bəl-kād 'hardly':

58. kān hal-ʔadd daʔīʔ bəl-kād ᵊtšūfo
'It was so tiny you could hardly
see it'

Eēb Eala 'shame on...for':

59. Eēb Ealēk təḥki ḥēk 'Shame on
you for talking that way!'

mā baʔa ʔəlla 'it only remains to':

60. ḥaḍḍer ḥālak mā baʔa ʔəlla nəṣal
[DA-250] 'Get ready, we're almost
there'

Eaṭa məhle 'to give...time to':

61. Eaṭīni məhle fakker bəl-mawḍūE
[DA-297] 'Give me some time to
think the matter over'

Translocative verbs (and their participles) [p. 274] are often complemented by optative clauses:

1. Eammi žāye yzūrna l-yōm [DA-172]   'My uncle's coming to visit us today'

2. ʔžīt ʔāxdak la-Eand wāḥed ʔəža   'I've come to take you to see some-
mən yōmēn mən ʔamērka [DA-75]   one who came two days ago from
                                        America'

3. bāba rāḥ iṣalli ṣalāt ᵊl-Eīd   'Daddy has gone to pray the holiday
[DA-298]   prayer'

4. rāyeḥ žībha w-ʔəži [AO-115]   'I'm going to get it and come back'

5. *baɛd kam yōm, ʔən šā ḷḷāh,*
   btəšfa w-bətrūḥ təštəǵel
   [AO-51]

   'In a few days, God willing, you'll get well and go to work'

6. *nāzel waʔʔəf-lak bəš-šams*
   ʔəddām bāb ʔl-ʔotēl [DA-218]

   'I'm going down to wait for you in the sun in front of the hotel entrance'

7. *halla ʔ bəbɛat-lak əṣ-ṣānɛa*
   tāxədhon [DA-129]

   'I'll send the maid to you right away to get them'

Optative clauses like those above are equivalent to clauses introduced by *la-, ta-, ḥatta,* or *laḥatta* '(in order) to', 'so that', which may complement any sort of main clause:

1. *ʔəža la-yšūf ɛēlto* [DA-75]

   'He came to see his family'

2. *bəftəker ɛandi waʔʔət la-ʔəšš*
   [DA-180]

   'I think I have time to shave'

3. *tfaḍḍal ləl-bēt la-tšūf əl-ɛarūs*
   [AO-114]

   'Come to the house to see the bride'

4. *ḥaṭṭəthon ɛan-nār bəl-meʔlāye*
   la-təʔlīhon [AO-117]

   'She put them on the fire in a frying-pan to fry them'

5. *kīf bəddi ʔaɛmel la-yəǵfor ʔaḷḷāh*
   xaṭiyyāti [AO-99]

   'What should I do so that God will forgive my sins?'

6. *halla ʔ bətrīd təftaḥ əṭ-ṭard*
   la-nšūf šū fī? [DA-245]

   'Now will you open the package so we can see what's in it?'

7. *ʔaddēš baddo ta-yəxlaṣ?*
   [Leb.: SAL 169]

   'How long will it take to finish?'

8. *ʔžīt la-hal-balad ḥatta ʔətrāfa ʔ*
   maɛo [AO-114]

   'I've come to this town so that I may accompany him'

9. *kallafni dabbər-lo bēt ḥatta*
   yəskon fī [DA-289]

   'He's asked me to find him a house to live in'

10. *tfaḍḍal laḥatta ʔaržīk halli*
    ɛandi [AO-79]

    'Come in, so that I may show you what I have'

Besides their use in optative clauses, these conjunctions are used in the sense 'until'. See p. 358.

In complementation to *kān* and other linking verbs [p.452] the subjunctive is used in <u>assertive</u> complemental clauses:

1. *ċand mɪn kəntɪ təštəġlɪ mən ʔabᵊl?* [DA-81]   'For whom were you working before?'

2. *w-kān har-rāɛi yəṭlaɛ kəll yōm... maɛ ᵊl-ġanam w-yərɛāhon* [AO-103]   'And this shepherd would go out every day with the sheep and let them graze'

3. *kəll žəsmi kān yūžaɛni, xṣūṣan ʔəžrayyi* [AO-51]   'My whole body ached, especially my legs'

4. *kānet tərkoḍ w-təžhad la-taɛməl-lo yā* [AO-111]   'She would run and strive to do it for him'

5. *l-bənt ʔəžet la-ɛando w-ṣāru yətlāʔu marrāt ᵊktīre* [AO-107]   'The girl came to him, and they began meeting often'

6. *ṣār yəḥki maɛon ʔašya ɛəlmiyye* [AO-83]   'He began talking with them (on) scientific matters'

7. *l-xārūf...ṣār imāɛi wəs-saɛdān yəḍḥak ɛalē* [AO-96]   'The sheep started to bleat, and the monkey, to laugh at him'

8. *ṣərt taɛref l-ᵊblād ʔaktar mənni* [DA-172]   'You've come to know the country better than I'

9. *w-kān yərmi l-baṣalāt bəl-ʔarḍ lamma yūṣal ɛal-barriyye* [AO-104]   'And he would throw the onions on the ground when he got out in open country' (Note that *yūṣal*, after *lamma*, is still governed by the linking berb *kān.*)

10. *w-tammet ᵊṭġūro w-təbki kəll yōm la-məddet səntēn* [AO-118]   'And she kept on going to see him and crying every day for two years'

11. *ḍallet ᵊtnəʔʔ ɛaliyyi*   'She kept on nagging me'

12. *l-mākina ražɛet təštáġel*   'The machine is working again' (lit. "...has returned to work")

13. *ʔām ᵊt-təlifōn idəʔʔ*   'The telephone began ringing'

14. *mā ɛād iṭāwəɛni ʔabadan*   'He never obeys me any more'

15. *ḍalḷ rəbᵊɛ sāɛa mā yəṣṭaṭɛem bəl-ʔakᵊl*   'He didn't touch his food for a quarter of an hour' (lit. "He remained... not tasting the food")

16. *btəsboʔ w-ᵊtšūfni*   'You'll already have seen me' (lit. "You'll go ahead and see me")

A subjunctive verb sometimes stands independently in a generalizing or hypothetical sense (as if *kān* or some other linking verb had been suppressed):

17. *hēk yaɛməl-lo...; baɛdēn*   'Here's the way he would do with
hadāk iʔəl-lo rūḥ ʔaḷḷa   him...; then that one would tell him
yəblīk..., yʔəl-lo šūf   "Go on, may God affict you...",
ṃhammad, hal-ḥaki hāda   (and) he'd say to him "Look, Moham-
bəl-ġərbe mū ḥəlu...   med, that kind of talk (when you're)
                                abroad isn't nice..."'

A similar but special use of the subjunctive is that of the verb *bəʔi* (or *baʔa*) 'to keep on', in the imperfect with a complement. The indicative is used for generalizations, in the usual way with no time limitations: *ʔaḥmad byəbʔa yəzūrna kəll ʔaḥad* 'Ahmed visits (i.e. keeps on visiting) us every Sunday'; *hal-maṭɛam byəbʔa fī ʔakəl ṭayyeb* 'This restaurant always has good food'. The subjunctive, on the other hand, indicates that the generalization applies to the past and not to the present: *ʔaḥmad yəbʔa yəzūrna kəll ʔaḥad; baṭṭal, lē?* 'Ahmed used to visit us every Sunday; why did he stop?'; *hal-maṭɛam yəbʔa fī ʔakəl ṭayyeb, mā ɛād fī* 'This restaurant used to have good food, but not any more'.

The subjunctive is also sometimes used in circumstantial complements [cf. pp. 448, 531]:

18. *w-maḍḍēt ʔarbaṭaɛšar šahər*   'And I spent fourteen months travel-
sāfer mən əmḥaṭṭa la-mḥaṭṭa   ing from station to station'
[SAL-137]

19. *ṣār-lak zamān təštəġel fi rās*   'Was it a long time you spent work-
əl-məšɛab? [SAL-136]   ing in Ras el-Mish'ab?'

20. *ʔəsmaɛo yəxṭob fəl-masāʔel*   'Listen to him speak on national
əl-waṭaniyye [EA-159]   problems...'

While the subjunctive is normally used in these complemental clauses in the generalizing sense (e.g. ex. 2, 5, 8, 18, etc. above), the indicative (with *b-*) is used in the dispositional sense [p. 327]:

1. *ṭ-ṭābe kānet mā btənṭāl*   'The ball was out of reach (*mā btənṭāl*
                               'it cannot be reached': *kanet mā
                               btənṭāl* 'it could not be reached').
                               [p. 328].

2. *ɛan ʔarīb biṣīr bisāɛdak*   'Soon he'll be able to help you'
                               (*bisāɛdak* 'he's disposed to help you':
                               biṣīr bisāɛdak 'he'll become disposed
                               to help you')

3. ṣāret ᵊṭ-ṭayyārāt bətwaddīk   'It's gotten so that planes will
   la-wēn ma bəṭḥəbb   take you wherever you like'
        (ṭ-ṭayyārāt bətwaddīk 'the planes
        will/would/can take you')

The indicative is also sometimes used – instead of the
subjunctive – in the generalizing or actualizing sense after
linking verbs, especially when something intervenes between
the linking verb and the complemental verb, or when the
linking verb is in the imperfect:

4. ṣār ʔəbn ᵊl-mīna byət ʔammal   'The inhabitants (lit. "the son") of
   yūžed šəġᵊl bəl-marfaʔ [PAT-181]   El-Mina have begun hoping to find
   [PAT-181]   work in the port'

5. kān rāsi kəllo byūžaɛni   'My whole head ached'

6. bəḍḍall ᵊbtəḥki w-ᵊbtəḥki   'She keeps on talking and talking
        [cf. ex. 45, p.453.]

In Attributive Clauses [p.497]. A term that is indefinite – in reference as
well as in grammar – may be qualified by a clause with a subjunctive verb:

1. mā fī taksi nrūḥ fī?   'Isn't there a taxi we can go in?'

2. mā ɛandi šī ḍīf ɛala hāda   'I have nothing to add to that'

3. fī hada yaɛṭi bālo ɛaẓ-ẓġār?   'Is there anyone to look after the
   ɛaẓ-ẓġār?   children?'

4. lāzem ᵊndawwer ɛala šī   'We must look for some way to help
   ṭarīʔa nɛāwno fīha   him'

5. bəddi wāḥde taɛref təḥkī-lha   'I want someone(f.) who can speak a
   šwayyet ʔənglīzi [DA-98]   little English'

6. lāzem muḥāmi ʔāder ydāfeɛ   'He needs an able lawyer to defend
   ɛanno   him'

7. ləssa ɛalēna šī ktīr naɛᵊmlo   'There's still a lot we have to do'

8. šū fī ɛandek ṭabᵊx thəṭṭī-lna?   'What have you(f.) in the way of
   [DA-198]   food to offer us?'

9. btaɛref hada ydabbər-li šī kīs,   'Do you know anyone who will prepare
   w-iwaṣṣəl-li yā ɛal-bēt?   me a sack(ful) and deliver it to the
   [SAL-195]   house?'

10. hada ġērak ykūn fī nəʔṭet damm   'Anybody else but you who had a drop
    mā byaʔbəl-š hal-ɛār [SPA-30]   of blood in him would not accept this
         disgrace'

A noun may, of course, be grammatically indefinite
[p.494] while referring to something quite definite; in such
cases an attributive verb is normally in the indicative:
ɛandi wāḥde btaɛref ʔanglīzi 'I have someone(f.) who knows
English' (Cf. ex. 5).

The subjunctive is not always obligatory, however, even
if the reference is indefinite: *mā baɛref ḥada bibīɛ swād*
[SAL-195] 'I don't know anyone who sells fertilizer';
b-ḥayāti mā šəft ḥada byākol xəbᵊz hal-ʔadd 'I've never in
my life seen anybody who eats so much bread'.[1]

In Prepositional Complement Clauses. After a preposition plus *ʔənno* 'that',
the subjunctive is used:

1. *huwwe ʔaɛla mən ʔənno*   'He's above cheating people' (lit.
   yġəšš ᵊn-nās   "He's higher than that he cheat
                                   people")

2. *wāfaʔ ɛala ʔənno yəbʔa*   'He agreed to stay' (lit. "He agreed
                                   on that he stay.")

3. *l-ḥašwe kafīle b-ʔənno*   'The charge is sufficient to blow us
   ṭṭayyərna kəllna   all up' (lit. "...in that it blow us
                                   all up")

4. *mā ṣəfi bēno w-bēn ʔənno*   'It came within a hair's breadth of
   yṣībni ʔəlla šaɛra   hitting me' (lit. "There didn't re-
                                   main between it and between that it
                                   hit me but a hair")

Most complemental prepositions are lost when the complement is a clause [p.449].

In Supplemental Clauses [p.528]. The subjunctive is used after certain subordinating conjunctions, mainly in reference to future or hypothetical events:

After *ʔawwal ma* 'as soon as':   1. *ʔawwal ma təǰi, fatteš ɛalē* 'As soon
                                         as you get here, look it over'

la-bēn ma 'while, until, by   2. *xalli l-ᵊmšadd la-bēn ma yənšaf*
  the time that':   *ᵊl-ġəre* 'Leave the clamp on until
                                          the glue dries'

                                  3. *w-la-bēn ma təlbes badᵊltak ᵊž-ždīde*
                                  bikūn bāba wəṣel [DA-298] 'And by
                                  the time you've put on your new suit
                                  Daddy will be here'

bass 'as soon as'; 'provided that':   4. *bass yəǰi byākol* 'As soon as he
                                         comes, he'll eat'

---

[1] The indicative in this sentence, however, distinguishes the attributive
clause from a circumstantial complement: *mā šəft ḥada yākol...* 'I
haven't seen anyone eat...'

5. *l-ʔažra mā bəthəmm ᵊktīr bass ᵊtkūn*
   maɛʔule [DA-290] 'The rate doesn't
   matter so much provided that it's
   reasonable'

mən ǧēr ma, bidūn ma, bala ma
'without'

6. *l-balad ᵊttāxadet mən ǧēr ma*
   təndəreb wlā rṣāṣa 'The town was
   taken without a shot's being fired'

7. *btədxol ᵊl-ʔašya b-ɛaʔlak bdūn ma*
   taɛref [PVA-60] 'The things will
   enter your mind without your knowing (it)'

baɛᵊd ma 'after':

8. *baɛd ma xalleṣ šəḡli biṣīr ɛandi*
   waʔt [DA-249] 'After I finish my
   work I'll have time'

9. *məntalfən-lak baɛᵊd ma nrasteʔ*
   ḥālna 'We'll phone you after we
   get ourselves organized'

ʔabᵊl ma 'before':

10. *salamāt, mnīḥ halli ʔžit ʔabᵊl ma*
    ʔəṭlaɛ [DA-243] 'Greetings; it's
    good that you've come before I left'

11. *šu blāʔīkon rāyḥin ʔabᵊl ma tāxdu*
    l-ʔahwe? [DA-199] 'What's this? Are
    you leaving before having coffee?'

12. *ʔabᵊl ma mūt bəddi mənnak ḥāže*
    [AO-116] 'Before I die there's some-
    thing I want from you'

la-, ta-, ḥatta, laḥatta 'until':
[cf. p. 353]

13. *rūḥ dəḡri la-tšūf ᵊl-bināye l-ḥamra*
    [DA-45] 'Go straight ahead til you
    see the red building'

14. *mā bbaṭṭel ʔəṭlob ta-mūt* [adap. fr.
    SPA-30] 'I won't stop pleading till
    I die'

15. *ḥalaf ᵊl-malek ʔənno mā byəržaɛ...*
    ḥatta yaɛref ʔaṣᵊl hal-baḥra [AO-117]
    'The king swore that he would not re-
    turn until he discovered the origin
    of that lake'

16. *w-kīf w-ʔiza stannētak laḥatta*
    təxloṣ [DA-197] 'How about it if I
    wait till you finish?'

After *baɛᵊd ma, la-bēn ma, ḥatta*, and other expressions, the perfect
tense is used in reference to accomplished facts, and the imperfect indicative for generalizations:

17. *lāha l-ᵃwlād la-bēn ma ḍahret*   'He entertained the children until
    ᵊmmon   their mother came in'

18. *w-baᵉᵃd ma biṣalli, byāxod*   'And after he prays, he takes his
    zuwwātto w-birūḥ la-šᵊġlo   provisions (viz. lunch) and goes to
    [PAT-195]   work'

19. *stannēna bᵊs-sayyāra la-rᵊžᵉet*   'We waited in the car till she came
                               back' (Cf. *stannēna bᵊs-sayyāra
                               la-tᵊržaᵉ* 'We waited in the car for
                               her to come back'.)

After *ᵊabᵊl ma*, however, the subjunctive is almost always used, not
only in generalizations but even in reference to accomplished facts:

20. *ᵊamma kasr ᵊṣ-ṣafra...byāxdúwa*   'As for breakfast, the Tripolitanians
    ṭ-ṭrabᵊlsiyye ᵊabᵊl ma yaṭlaᵉu   have it before they leave the house'
    mᵊn bēton [PAT-195]

21. *ᵊabᵊl ma yūṣal ᵉal-balad laᵊa*   'Before he got to the town he met a
    rāᵉi [AO-83]   shepherd'

22. *ᵊabᵊl ma tᵊži b-ᵊšwayye kānet*   'A little while before you came, my
    marti maᵉ l-ᵃwlād hōn [DA-218]   wife was here with the children'

       In the Palestinian area, the subjunctive is used some-
what more broadly after subordinating conjunctions that it
is further north; after *lamma(n)* 'when', for example, (in
reference to the future): *lēš mā byāxᵊdhom maᵉo lamman
yᵊržaᵉ* 'Why doesn't he take them with him when he goes
back?' (Cf. DA-75: ...*lamma byᵊržaᵉ*); after *baᵉᵃd ma* for
generalization: *kᵊll wāḥed mᵊnna baᵉᵃd ma yᵊūm fᵊṣ-ṣabḥ
byᵊlbas tyābo* [Cr-36] 'Every one of us, after getting up
in the morning, puts on his clothes'.

THE IMPERATIVE (*al-ᵊamr*)

       The imperative is used in ordering, requesting, or inviting the person
addressed to do whatever the verb designates: *ftāḥ ᵊl-bāb* 'Open(m.)the
door', *ᵉᵊdi* 'sit down(f.)', *šarrfūna* 'visit(pl.)us' (lit. 'honor us').

       Imperatives are inflected only for number/gender (mas-
culine, feminine, plural).
       On the formation of imperatives, see Verb Inflectional
Forms [p.198].

       Imperatives cannot be used in the negative. Prohibitions and negative
requests are expressed by *lā* (or *mā*) with the second-person subjunctive
[   ]: *lā tᵊftaḥ ᵊl-bāb* 'Don't open(m.)the door', *lā tᵊᵊᵊdi hōn* 'Don't
sit(f.)here', *mā trūḥu* 'Don't go(pl.)'.

Examples:

1. xōd hal-ɛaṣāye w-ᵊnṣəbha   'Take this stick and plant at where-
   b-maṭraḥ ma bəddah [AO 99]   ever you wioh'

2. b-ᵊhyātek ḥətti ḥaṭab bəl-ʔāẓān, 'Please put(f.)wood in the heater
   w-šaɛɛlī-li l-ḥammām [DA-180]   and light (it for) my bath'

3. xallūkon ɛam-ᵊtrattbu l-mawādd   'Keep on (pl.) arranging the mat-
   ɛala han-namaṭ   erials in this way'

4. xtār, ya ṣayyād, l-ʔatle halli   'Choose, O fisherman, the way you'd
   bətrīdha [AO-116]   like to be killed'

5. ʔūmi ya mara, kəli [AO-112]   'Get up, woman, (and) eat!'

6. balla žəb-ᵊlna wāḥed ʔahwe   'Please bring us one coffee and one
   w-wāḥed bīra [DA-45]   beer'

7. zkōr ʔəsmi, bidaxxlūk   'Mention my name (and) they'll let
                                     you in'

8. ʔɛadi šwayye nṭəgri [AO-113]   'Sit down(f.) a while (and) wait'

9. xallīni ʔaɛref ʔabl ᵊb-salaf   'Let me know ahead of time if you
   ʔəza kənt raḥa-təži   decide to come'

10. šūf ʔiza ʔəžet ᵊl-bōṣṭa   'See if the mail has come'

11. ʔiza mā kān ḥāḍer ḥaṭṭ ɛalāme   'If he's not present put a mark by
    ʔəddām ʔəsmo   his name'

12. yalla rūḥ sāwīha w-ᵊltəɛen   'Go ahead, do it and be damned!'

13. starži w-xəda   '(Just) dare and take it!'

14. rkōd būs ʔīdo w-ɛāyed ɛalē   'Run kiss his hand and wish him a
    [DA-302]   happy holiday'

15. ɛmēl maɛrūf, ʔəl-li mīn   'Please tell me who you are' (lit.
    ʔənte [AO-108]   'Do a favor, tell me...')

   Note that a coördination of imperatives is often used
where the sense would seem to require complementation by a
subjunctive [p.345]. See example 13, above (syndetic).
Most such coördinations are asyndetic [p.398]:

16. dall rūḥ w-ᵊržāɛ lahatta   'Keep on going back and forth until
    ybaṭṭel hada yəṭlob mənnak   everyone has stopped asking (of)
    [AO-99]   you' (Lit. "Continue, go and return
                                     return...")

   Similarly, an imperative is often used in complementation to
an annunciatory verb [p.325]:

17. *bənṣaḥak ᵊnsāha*
    'I advise you to forget it' (lit. 'I advise you, forget it')

18. *bətraǧǧāk dəllni Ɛal-ʔotēl*
    [DA-16]
    'Please direct me to the hotel' (lit. 'I beg of you, direct me...')

    A rather peculiar imperative construction is its use in complementation to the verb *kān* [p. 341] in the second-person perfect. This construction produces an exclamatory hypothetical command, generally translatable into English as 'you should have...!' (The main stress of the sentence falls on the imperative):

19. *kənt šūfo ʔabᵊl ma təǧi!*
    'You should have <u>seen</u> him before you came!'

20. *kənt kōl lamma kənt fəl-bēt!*
    'You should have <u>eaten</u> when you were at home!'

    As in English, imperative in Arabic are sometimes used with subject pronouns (*ʔante, ʔanti, ʔantu* 'you') for emphasis:

21. *ʔántu rūḥu ḥkū maƐo*
    '<u>You</u>(pl.) go talk with him'

22. *ʔánti ḥaḍḍri l-Ɛaša l-yōm*
    '<u>You</u>(f.) prepare dinner today'

23. *rūḥ ʔante w-hiyye ǧību š-šanta*
    'You(m.) and she go get the bag'.

    Note, in the last example, that the first imperative is singular, applying only to *ʔante*, while the second (*ǧību*) is plural, its subject being the coordination *ʔante w-hiyye*.

CHAPTER 14: PERSON, NUMBER, AND GENDER

Person

Arabic verbs, like those of many other languages, are inflected for three "persons" called FIRST (*al-mutakallim*), SECOND (*al-muxāṭab*), and THIRD (*al-ǧāʔib*). See Verb Inflectional Forms, p. 175.

Of the eight personal pronouns, each belongs inherently to one of the three persons. See Personal Pronouns [539].

All nouns and other nominal terms belong inherently to the third person.[1]

The use of the Arabic person categories is basically identical with that of English. The first person designates the person speaking ('I') or — in the plural — the person speaking plus anyone else ('we'), either including or excluding the person spoken to. The second person designates the person or persons spoken to ('you') or — in the plural — the person(s) spoken to plus anyone else except the speaker. The third person designates anyone or anything excluding the speaker and person spoken to, or, in the case of "impersonal" predications [p. 365], nothing at all.

> The person of a pronoun is determined by agreement with its antecedent, if any [p. 535]; if there is no antecedent, then it is determined directly by the role of its referent in the discourse.
>
> A verb's person inflection is determined by agreement with its subject, if any; if there is no subject expressed, person is determined directly by the role of its subject-referent (if any) in the discourse; if there is no subject-referent, then the verb stands in the third (i.e. neutral) person.

Generalizing in the Second Person. As in English, the second person (masculine/singular) is often used to make generalizations that are applicable to anyone:

1. *lāzem tədros ʔhʔūʔ ḥatta tṣīr kāteb ɛadəl b-sūriyya*
   'You have to study law in order to become a notary public in Syria.'

2. *ṣaɛʔb taləʔzmo b-šī*
   'It's hard to nail him down to anything' (lit. "It's hard for you to obligate him in anything")

3. *mā bətšūfo ʔəlla ɛam-yədzammar*
   'You never see him but what he's grumbling'

> This usage is mainly limited to verbs in the imperfect, and does not in any case apply to the disjunctive pronoun *ʔənte* [p. 378].

---

[1]Except insofar as they are used vocatively [p. 378].

Also as in English, the third-person plural is often
used with vague or unknown reference: *ḥēk biʔūlu* 'That's
what they say'; *ṭafu n nār ᵊb-sᵊrƐa* 'The fire was put out
quickly' (lit. 'They put out the fire quickly').

The term *l-wāḥed* (3rd p. sing.) is also used similarly
to 'one' in English for indefinite or generalizing reference: *l-wāḥed šū biƐarrfo* 'One never knows' (lit. "What
will let one know?").

Except in baby-talk, the third person is rarely used to
designate the speaker or person spoken to; there is very
little tendency de-personalize for the sake of formality or
deference in Syrian Arabic. One may sometimes hear expressions like *l-bēk byaʔmor šī?* 'Does the bey order something?'
(for *btaʔmor šī?*) or *šū byaqtᵊreḥ ᵊl-ʔaxx?* 'What does our
colleague suggest?' (for *šū btaqtᵊreḥ?*); such usage is
limited to highly formal or stilted discourse.

A more ordinary formal or deferential reference to a
person addressed is *ḥaḍᵊrtak* (f. *ḥaḍᵊrtek*, pl. *ḥaḍratkon*),
literally "your presence", which is sometimes substituted
for *ʔante* (f. *ʔanti*, pl. *ʔantu*). This form, however, constitutes a "partitive" construct [p.467]; that is, the
leading term *(ḥaḍret...)* is subordinate to the following
term *(-ak)*, which is second person and requires second-
person agreement in the predicate: *ḥaḍᵊrtak šū btaʔmor?*
'What would you like, sir?'.[1]

Agreement. There are very few complications in the person-agreement of a
verb with its pronoun subject, or of a pronoun with its pronoun antecedent:
ʔante wēn kᵊnt? 'Where were you?', *ʔana mā baƐref* 'I don't know', *nᵊḥna
mā Ɛanna maṣāri* 'We have no money'. In coördinations [p.391], 1st p. + 2nd
or 3rd p. → 1st p. pl.; and 2nd p. + 3rd p. → 2nd p. pl.:

4. *ʔana w-ʔante mᵊrrūḥ sawa*   'You and I will go together'

5. *wlā ʔana wlā huwwe laḥa-nkūn*   'Neither he nor I will be there'
   ᵊhnīk

6. *la-wēn rᵊḥtu ʔanti w-huwwe?*   'Where did you(f.) and he go?'

Note, however, *la-wēn rᵊḥti ʔanti wiyyā?* 'Where did
you and he go?' or 'Where did you go with him?'.

---

[1]The difference between *ʔante* and *ḥaḍᵊrtak* is of course **not** like the difference in European languages between (for example) 'tu', and 'vous',
'du' and 'Sie'. *ḥaḍᵊrtak* is limited to polite initial encounters with
strangers, or the like; *ʔante* (*ʔanti*, *ʔantu*) may be used by anyone to
anyone, like English 'you'.

A verb attributive to a predicate such as *ʔawwal wāḥed* 'the first one', *l-waḥīd* 'the only one', or the like, commonly agrees with a first person pronoun <u>subject</u> of that predicate. (See Equational Sentences, p. 405.)

7. *ʔana kǝnt ʔāxer wāḥed tarakt*
 ᵊl-bēt

'I was the last one to leave the house'

8. *nǝḥna l-waḥīdīn yalli mnaɛref*
 ᵊnsāwīha.

'We're the only ones who know how to do it'

9. *šu ʔana ʔawwal rǝžžāl bǝstek?*

'Am I the first man to kiss you?'

Impersonal Verbs. Verbs that have no subject and no subject-referent remain in the third (i.e. neutral) person (masculine/singular). These verbs include passives of intransitive verbs [p. 237], and certain other complemented expressions:

10. *ġǝmi ɛalēha*

'She fainted' ("There came a fainting upon her")

11. *hal-kalb lāzem yǝnḥaṭṭ-ǝllo*
 kammāme

'That dog ought to have a muzzle put on him'

12. *byāxǝdni žǝmɛa la-ḥatta*
 ʔǝṭṭǝleɛ ɛala kǝll hal-mašākel

'It would take me a week to look into all these problems'

Verbs with a clausal subject [p. 451] are likewise in the third-person masculine; this construction is equivalent to that of an impersonal verb with a clausal complement:

13. *bižūz ʔǝži maɛkon*

'Perhaps I'll come with you(pl.)' (lit. "That I come with you is possible" or "It is possible that I come with you")

14. *bihǝmmni tǝḥkī-lha šwayyet*
 ʔǝnglīzi [DA-80]

'It's important to me that she speak a little English'

Certain impersonal verbs are used in the feminine: *mā btafreʔ maɛi ʔǝnni rūḥ waḥdi* 'It doesn't matter to me that I go alone'. See p. 428.

NUMBER

Pure number inflection occurs in Syrian Arabic only for nouns [p. 209] (and rarely adjectives [201]). Verbs, pronouns, and generally also adjectives have number and gender combined in a single system; their number/gender inflection is determined by agreement with the nouns to which they are predicate [401], attribute [493], or sequent [535], or else by the "natural" number and gender of their referents. See Number/Gender Agreement [p. 427].

Count Nouns

Singular *(al-fard)*. The singular of nouns that purport to designate discrete (countable) entities is commonly used to indicate that the number is exactly <u>one</u>, in contrast to the dual and to numeral constructs with the plural: *ktāb* 'a book', i.e. 'one book' (vs. *ktābēn* 'two books' vs. *tlətt kətəb* 'three books').

In a non-enumerative capacity, the singular of a count noun is used as a classificatory term [p. 458] in certain kinds of annexion:

1). After numerals above ten: *Ɛəšrīn əktāb* 'twenty books', *ʔarbaṭaƐšar səne* 'fourteen years', *xamsā Ɛəšrīn ʔərš* 'twenty-five piastres'.

2). After the words *kamm* and *kəll* [p. 467]: *kamm əktāb* 'several books' or 'how many books'; *kəll əktāb* 'every book'.[1]

3). Sometimes after substantives: *žəld Ɛəžəl* 'calf skin', *wažaƐ rās* 'headache'.

> The singular (with the article prefix) is often used for generalizing: *tarbiyet əṭ-ṭəfəl* 'child rearing' (lit. "bringing up the child"); *l-marʔa ʔəlha ḥʔūʔ*... 'women have rights' (lit. "the woman has..."); *mən ṣanƐ əl-ʔənsān* 'man-made' (lit. "of the man's making").
> In construct with a collective [p. 279] or a plural, a singular is sometimes used distributively: *ʔarn əl-baʔar* 'the horns of cattle' (lit. "the horn..."), *Ɛāyšīn mən Ɛəbbon la-təmmon* 'They're living from hand to mouth' (lit. ..." from their pouch to their mouth"). The partitives meaning '-self' [p. 468] are also used in this way: *xallīna nsāwīha b-nafəsna* 'Let's do it by ourselves' (lit.... "by our self").

---

[1] *kəll* may be used with the plural, of course, in identificatory constructs: *kəll əl-kətəb* 'all the books'; *kamm*, however, is only used with the indefinite singular.

Dual (*at-taθniya*). The dual is used to specify exactly <u>two</u> of whatever the noun base designates: *ktābēn* 'two books'.

  Use of the numeral *tnēn* 'two' in construct with a plural puts somewhat more emphasis on the number then does the use of the dual inflection: *tnēn kətᵊb* 'two books'. Still more emphasis is achieved by using the dual noun with the numeral following in apposition: *ktābēn ᵊtnēn* '<u>two</u> books'.

The dual inflection is more comparable in function to the numerals than to the plural. The dual need not be used every time two of anything are referred to. If the number happens to be two but is beside the point, or to be taken for granted, then the <u>plural</u> is used, just as in English: *Eando banāt bass* 'He has daughters only' (applicable though he may have exactly two); *l-manţo dayyeʔ Eand l-ᵊktāf* 'The coat is tight in the shoulders'. Cf. *Eando bəntēn bass* 'He only has two daughters'; *l-manţo dayyeʔ Eand ᵊl-kətfēn* 'The coat is tight in both shoulders'.

 In reference to things that normally come in a pair, the dual is not ordinarily used in contrast to the plural, but only in contrast to the singular. Such duals (when definite) are usually translatable into English with 'both': *l-kaffēn* 'both gloves' (cf. plural *l-ᵊkfūf* 'the gloves', in reference to a pair); *ʔəžᵊrtēno* 'both his legs' (cf. plural *ʔəžrē* [p.170] 'his legs').

  Note that the forms *ʔəžrēn* 'feet, legs', *ʔīdēn* 'hands, arms', *Eēnēn* 'eyes', and *ʔadanēn* 'ears' are not duals in colloquial usage, but plurals: *ʔarbaE ʔəžrēn* 'four legs'. The true duals of these words have connective *t* [p.163] before the suffix: *ʔəžᵊrtēn ʔittēn, Eēntēn, ʔədᵊntēn*.

Most duals tend not to be used with pronoun suffixes; such constructions are generally circumlocuted by using the <u>plural</u> with the suffix, followed by the numeral *tnēn: kətbi t-tnēn* 'my two books'.

  Notable exceptions include the duals of nouns designating paired parts of the body: *Eēntēni* 'both my eyes'.

Plural (*al-žamE*). If the singular of a noun designates <u>one</u> of something, then its plural designates <u>more</u> than one: *ktāb* '(one) book', *kətᵊb* '(two or more) books'. If the number is specified by a numeral in construct [p.471], however, the following term is put in the plural only if the number is between two and ten: *tnēn kətᵊb* 'two books', *tmann kətᵊb* 'eight books'.

  With numerals above ten, the following term is put in the singular: *ţnaEšar ᵊktāb* 'twelve books' [p.472]. If the number is two, the dual, of course, may generally be used instead of *tnēn* with the plural.

Abstract[1] and Mass Nouns

Many nouns which do not purport to designate discrete (countable) entities are normally used only in the singular, e.g. *ʔəstəqlāl* 'independence', *dawām* 'duration, permanence', *zəft* 'tar', *ṣəde* 'rust'.

Certain others, contrariwise, are normally used only in the plural: *maɛlūmāt* 'information', *maḥāṣen* 'good points, advantages', *riyāḍiyyāt* 'mathematics', *maṣāri* 'money'.[2]

Some singular abstract and mass nouns may be put in the plural to indicate abundance, variety, or indefinite quantification: sg. *ramᵊl* 'sand', pl. *rmāl* 'sands', another plural *ramlāt* '(a batch, or batches, of) sand'; singular *taṣarrof* 'behavior, pl. *taṣarrofāt* '(various kinds or instances of) behavior'.

> These are not count plurals — they are not used after numerals — and are not to be confused with the plurals of <u>particularized</u> abstract and mass nouns [p. 284], which <u>are</u> count plurals. While *ramlāt,* for instance, might sometimes be understood to mean 'a batch, or batches, of sand', this translation should not be taken to imply that one could say *tlətt ramlāt* to mean "three batches of sand". (*ramlāt* as a count plural only means 'grains of sand'). See p. 297.

No abstract or mass nouns are normally used in the dual.

Further examples of mass noun plurals, indicating abundance or variety:

Singular		Plural
zēt	'oil'	*zyūt*
ḥabb	'grain, seeds'	*ḥbūb*[3]
ṃayy	'water'	*ṃayāya*[4]
zbāle	'trash, garbage'	*zabāyel*
laḥᵊm	'meat, flesh'	*lḥūm*[5]
žaww	'air, atmosphere'	*ʔažwāʔ*

---

[1]The term 'abstract' here denotes a <u>semantic</u> category, broader than the <u>derivational</u> category of abstract nouns [p. 284].

[2]Also *məṣriyyāt*. There is, actually, a singular *məṣriyye* — a defunct monetary unit referred to figuratively in expressions like *mā ɛandi w-lā məṣriyy* 'I haven't a cent'.

[3]Also used as a count plural of *ḥabbe* 'pill'.

[4]The plurals *ṃayyāt* and *miyāh* are also used [p. 370], but *ṃayāya* is more strongly connotative of abundance or variety.

[5]The plural *laḥmāt* belongs more specifically to the singular *laḥme* 'meat', and, in the identificatory use [p. 370], also to *laḥᵊm* in the sense 'flesh' *laḥmāto* 'his flesh'. As a count noun, *laḥmāt* means 'pieces of meat' (sg. *laḥme* 'a piece of meat').

Plural of Abundance and Plural of Paucity (*ǧamɛ l-kaθra wa-ǧamɛ l-qilla*).

Sometimes the plural of a singulative [p. 297] — a count plural — stands in contrast to the plural of the underlying collective or gerund, which indicates abundance or variety, and which is not used after numerals:

		Singular		Plural	
Unit	*samake*	'a fish'....*samakāt*	'fish, fishes'
Collective	*samak*	'fish'......*ʔasmāk*	'(many or various) fish'
Unit	*dəbbāne*	'a fly'.....*dəbbānāt*	'flies'
Collective	*dəbbān*	'flies'.....*dababīn*	'(many or various) flies'
Unit	*mōǧe*	'a wave'....*mōǧāt*	'waves'
Collective	*mōǧ*	'waves'.....*ʔamwāǧ*	'(many or extensive) waves'
Instance	*ġalṭa*	'an error'..*ġalṭāt*	'errors'
Gerund	*ġalaṭ*	'error'.....*ʔaġlāṭ*	'(various kinds or instances of) error'

When there is both a plural of abundance and a plural of paucity (i.e. a count plural), the plural of abundance is formed by a base pattern change [p. 218] while the plural of paucity is usually formed by suffixation of -*āt*. An exception is *ʔālāf* 'thousands', the count plural of *ʔalf* 'thousand' which also has plurals of abundance *ʔlūf* and *ʔalafāt*. When a plural of paucity is used without a numeral (2-10), it still usually implies that the things referred to are few in number and individually discriminated.

In some cases, the distinction between plurals of abundance and paucity is not clearly maintained. The form *wrāʔ* 'leaves', for instance, may serve as a plural of abundance — as the plural of the collective *waraʔ*, but also as a count plural — as the plural of the unit noun *waraʔa* 'a leaf': *tlətt ᵊwrāʔ* 'three leaves'. There is also a plural of paucity *waraʔāt*. Likewise the plural *wrūd(e)* 'flowers, roses' may serve as the plural of abundance (coll. sg. *ward* 'flowers, roses') and also as a count plural: *xams ᵊwrūd* 'five roses', while *wardāt* is a plural of paucity (unit sg. *warde* 'a flower, a rose').

A plural of abundance which stands in contrast to a plural of paucity but which is also used with numerals may be called an "all-purpose plural".

Some count nouns ending in -*e*/-*a* have a plural of paucity in -*āt* and also an internally formed all-purpose plural, but no collective: *sigāra* 'cigarette', pl. of paucity *sigārāt*, all-purpose plural *sagāyer*; *xēme* 'tent' pl. of paucity *xēmāt*, all-purpose pl. *xiyam*; *ḥayye* 'snake', pl. of paucity *ḥayyāt*, all-purpose pl. *ḥayāya*.

Plural of Identification and Indefinite Quantification

Some nouns which in the singular designate a substance in general, or as a sample of its kind, have plurals (in *-āt*) designating a certain batch or indefinite quantity of that substance: sg. *ramᵊl* 'sand', pl. *ramlāt;* sg. *ḥalīb* 'milk', pl. *ḥalībāt;* sg. *zēt* 'oil', pl. *zētāt;* sg. *ʔamᵊḥ* 'wheat', pl. *ʔamḥāt.*

Examples of usage: (sg.) *har–ramᵊl mā byᵊswa lᵊl-bāṭōn* 'This sand (i.e. this kind of sand) is no good for concrete' vs. (pl.) *xōd har–ramlāt mᵊn hōn* 'Get this sand (i.e. this batch of sand) out of here'. Or, in reference to the milkman, one might say *žāb ᵊl–ḥalībāt* 'He brought the milk' while in reference to the waiter in a restaurant one would say *žāb ᵊl–ḥalīb.*

> In the case of the waiter, milk is considered qualita-tively, i.e. in contrast to the other kinds of things he brings to the table; but since it goes without saying that the milkman brings milk, the milk he brings is viewed quan-titatively, as a batch.
> This is indefinite quantification, however, and is not to be confused with quantification by numerals. To specify a certain number of batches or orders of milk, the numeral is used (in its absolute form [p. 170]) followed by an ap-positive [510] singular: *tlāte ḥalīb* 'three (orders of) milk, three milks'.

This type of plural is also used in an indentificatory sense, as op-posed to the singular, which is qualitative, i.e. classificatory. That is to say, while the singular is commonly used in classificatory constructs, the plural usually marks an identificatory construct [p. 458] (whether it is leading term or following term):

Classificatory		Identificatory	
ḥalīb ᵊl–maɛze	'(the) goat's milk' (indicating the kind of milk)	*ḥalībāt ᵊl–maɛzāye*	'the goat's milk' (i.e. the milk of a par-ticular goat)
mayyet ᵊl–baḥᵊr	'(the) sea water'	*mayyāt ᵊl–baḥᵊr*	'the sea's water'
zēt ᵊz–zētūn	'the olive oil'	*zētāt ᵊs-sammān*	'the grocer's oil'
ṭaḥn ᵊl–ʔamᵊḥ	'the grinding of wheat'	*ṭaḥn ᵊl–ʔamḥāt*	'grinding the wheat'

The plurals of unit nouns [p. 298] are generally also used in this identificatory sense, as opposed to collec-tives, which are generally classificatory: *ɛaṣīr ᵊl–bᵊrdʔānāt* 'the juice of the oranges' vs. *ɛaṣīr ᵊl–bᵊrdʔān* 'the orange juice'.

Since pronouns are always identificatory terms, it is usually the plural of identification (if any) that is used with pronoun suffixes, rather
than the singular: *ʔamḥātna* 'our wheat', *z̄ētāton* 'their oil', *ḥalībāta*
'her milk', *laḥmāto* 'his flesh', *ɛ̄ɛnbāto* 'his grapes', *bərdʔānāti* 'my
oranges', *ṃayyāta* 'its water'.

All this is not to say that the singular in such cases
<u>cannot</u> be used in identificatory constructs, but only that
<u>it tends</u> not to be so used, at least when an actual spe-
cific batch of something is referred to. The singular is
more apt to be used in a (grammatically) identificatory
construct if the reference is actually to a generality or a
hypothetical case: *ʔaḥmad byəḥleb ʔl-baʔarāt w-bibīɛ̄*
ḥalībon bəl-madīne 'Ahmed milks the cows and sells their
milk in the city', *š-šāšāt bibīḍu bēḍ w-ʔaḥmad byākol kamān
laḥmon* 'The hens lay eggs, and Ahmed also eats their flesh'
[AO-63].

———————

Concerning plurals in general, one should keep in mind
that it is not always possible to determine the Arabic number inflection by meaning, or by translation from English.
Many kinds of "thing" may be regarded either as wholes or
as aggregates of discrete parts. Compare *ṣabbāṭ* '(a pair
of) shoes', which is singular, with *kfūf* 'gloves' (in ref-
ence to a pair), which is plural; *ɛ̄ɛdde* 'tools', which is
singular, with *maṣāri* 'money', which is plural; *baʔar*
'cattle', which is singular, with *šmāl* 'camels', which is
plural. See Collectives and Units [p. 298].
Not only the <u>form</u> of a plural, but also the <u>kinds</u> of
plural a noun will have, or whether it will have a plural
at all, are to a considerable extent questions of lexical
idiosyncracy.
Some nouns lack one or another inflection for no obvious reason. *šī* 'thing', for instance, is a count noun
(*tlətt ʔašya* 'three things'), but it has no dual. (Its
more elegant doublet *šēʔ*, however, does have a dual: *šēʔēn*
'two things'). The noun *mara* 'woman' has neither dual nor
plural, though the plural is suppleted by the word *nəswān*
'women'.
Many nouns have different plurals corresponding to different meanings: *lsān* 'tongue', pl. *lsānāt* 'tongues' (literal anatomical sense), plurals *ʔəlson* and *ʔalsine* 'tongues'
(figurative linguistic senses).
Sometimes different plurals are stylistically significant: sg. *ʔəsᵊm* 'name', plurals *ʔasāmi* (informal) and
ʔasmāʔ (more formal). In still other cases, different plural forms may be virtually equivalent, or a matter of person or regional variation: sg. *lḥāf* 'blanket, cover', pl.
lḥāfāt or *ləhᵊf*; sg. *šahᵊr* 'month', pl. *šhūr* or *ʔəšhor*.

GENDER OF NOUNS

Arabic nouns (in the singular) belong either to the masculine or to the
feminine gender, or, in a few cases, to both genders. It is the function
of noun gender to govern the gender inflection of verbs and adjectives and
the gender selection of pronouns [pp. 420, 428, 501, 535].

Natural Gender

A noun that designates human beings is masculine if the person is male,
and feminine if the person is female:

Masculine		Feminine	
ʔabb	'father'	ʔəmm	'mother'
ʔabᵊn	'son'	bənt	'daughter, girl'
ʔaxx	'brother'	ʔəxt	'sister'
ɛarīs	'bridegroom'	ɛarūs	'bride'
zalame	'man, fellow'	sətt	'lady'

Certain animal designations (mainly domestic animals) are also limited
by sex:

tōr	'bull, steer'	baʔara	'cow'
kabᵊš	'ram'	ġaname	'ewe'
tēs	'billy goat'	ɛanze	'nanny goat'
xārūf	'young male sheep'	məɛzāye	'nanny goat'
dīk	'cock' (male of any fowl)	faras	'mare'

The masculine noun ṭəfᵊl 'child, infant' is used to refer to children in the abstract (tarbiyet ᵊṭ-ṭəfᵊl 'bring-
ing up a child') or to predicate childishness of a person
of either sex (ləssāta ṭəfᵊl 'She's still a child'); otherwise it is used only in reference to a male, or a child
whose sex is not known. The specifically female counter-
part is ṭəfle: hayy ṭəfle ḥəlwe 'She's a pretty child'.
Similarly: kalb 'dog' (male or sex unspecified) and kalbe
'bitch', ḥṣān 'horse' and faras 'mare'. On the other hand
ʔaṭṭ 'cat' is used mainly to specify the male, while the
feminine ʔaṭṭa may be applied not only to females but also
when the sex is unspecified: hal-ʔaṭṭa dakar wəlla ʔəntāye?
'Is that cat male or female?'
The nouns ɛažūz 'elderly person'[1] and bēbē 'baby' have

---

[1] Some speakers, however, tend to pair off ɛažūz as 'old woman' with ʔəxtyār
'old man'. The forms ɛažūze and ʔəxtyāra are used exclusively in reference
to females.

fluctuating gender depending on their reference: *l-bēbē bəddo yərḍaɛ* 'The baby (boy, or sex unspecified) wants to nurse', and *l-bēbē bədda ṭərdaɛ* 'The baby (girl) wants to nurse'.

Some nouns, though often or usually applied to human beings, do not actually designate human beings as such; their gender generally does not fluctuate even though they may denote persons of either sex: *maxlūʔ* 'creature' (masculine), *ḍaḥiyye* 'victim' (feminine), *wāṣṭa* 'intermediary, mediator, means' (f.), *šaxṣiyye* 'personality' (f.), *šaxʔṣ* 'person' (m.).

Some noun stems are used with and without the suffix -*e/-a* [p.138] to designate female and male respectively: *ṭabbāx* 'cook' (m.) and *ṭabbāxa* (f.), *ṣabi* 'boy' and *ṣabiyye* 'girl, young lady', *xāl* '(maternal) uncle' and *xāle* '(maternal) aunt'. See p.304. Unless paired in this way, however, the -*e/-a* suffix is not a sign of feminine gender for human beings: *zalame* 'man, fellow', *xalīfe* 'caliph', *ṭāġye* 'tyrant', etc. For animals, it indicates feminine gender but not necessarily female sex (except as qualified above).

Gender of Names

Names of towns, cities, etc., and most countries, states, etc., are feminine. Note the feminine agreement in these examples:

š-šām kəbret ʔktīr mən ɛašr ʔsnīn la-halla?   'Damascus has grown a lot in the last ten years'

maṣʔr maʔhūle ʔaktar mən sūriyya   'Egypt is more populous than Syria'

The names of a few countries and regions, however, may be construed either as masculine or feminine: *ləbnān* 'Lebanon', *nažʔd* 'Nejd', *l-ʔḥžāz* 'The Hejaz', *l-yaman* 'Yemen', *l-ʔərdon* 'Jordan', *l-ɛirāq* 'Iraq', *l-maġreb* 'Morocco' or 'Northwest Africa', *l-barazīl* 'Brazil'. E.g. *ləbnān žamīl, məš hēk?* 'Lebanon is beautiful, isn't it?' [PVA-30].

Names of ships (and planes, automobiles) are feminine: *l-šampolyōn žanḥet ɛal-ʔwzāɛi* 'The Champollion ran aground off Ouzai'.

Names of the letters of the alphabet are feminine: *sāwi n-nūn mžawwafe ʔaktar mən hēk* 'Make the *nūn* deeper than that'.

It is said that the names of cities, countries, ships, etc., are feminine because they are elliptical for construct or appositive phrases [pp.462,506] headed by feminine words such as *madīne* 'city', *blād* 'land, country', *bāxra* 'ship', etc.: *madīnet berūt* 'the city of Beirut', *blād ʔl-yūnān* 'The land of Greece', *l-bāxra šampolyōn* 'the ship Champolion'.

This explanation does not hold true for the names of the
letters, however, since *ḥarf* 'letter' is masculine: *ḥarf*
ᵊl-bē. 'the letter *bē*'.

Formal Gender

For nouns that are neither names nor human designations, gender cannot
be inferred from meaning, but can usually be inferred from form. Those
which (in the singular) have a suffix *-e/-a* [p.138], *-a* [165], *-ā* [164],
or *-t* [164] are feminine. Most others are masculine:

Masculine		Feminine	
maktab	'office'	*maktabe*	'library'
daraž	'staircase'	*daraže*	'step, degree'
xaṭaʔ	'wrong, transgression'	*xaṭīʔa*	'sin'
zəkᵊr	'mention'	*zəkra*	'commemoration, memory'
nəsᵊr	'eagle'	*būme*	'owl'
namᵊl	'ants' (collective)	*namle*	'an ant'
ʔəstəqlāl	'independence'	*ḥərriyye*	'freedom'
murād	'desire, intention'	*mubārā*	'match, game'
nabāt	'plant(s)' (Here *t* is part of the Root: *n–b–t*, Pattern *FaƐāL*)	*ḥayāt*	'life' (Here *t* is a suffix; Root *ḥ–y–y*)

Defective [p.43] nouns ending in *a* or *e*, however, are generally masculine;
the vowel is part of the stem, not a suffix:

Ɛaša 'supper' (masc.):   Root *Ɛ-š-y* with Pattern *FaƐāL* [p.146]

šəte 'winter, rain' (masc.): Root *š-t-w* with alteration of Pattern
                             FƐāL [147]

maƐna 'meaning' (masc.):   Root *Ɛ-n-y* with Pattern *maFƐaL* [153]

> Note that *səne* 'year' and *mara* 'woman' are biradical
> nouns [p.162]; the *-e/-a* is a suffix (cf. construct forms
> *sənt, mart* [168]), hence these words are feminine. (And
> *mara* is feminine par excellence in any case, by virtue of
> its meaning.)
>   The ending *-āʔ* is usually not a suffix (*ʔ* replacing a
> final radical semivowel, as in *duƐāʔ* 'supplication', mas-
> culine, Root *d-Ɛ-w*, Pattern *FuƐāL*), but in the rare cases
> where it is actually a suffix the noun is feminine: *kəbriyāʔ*
> 'pride, arrogance' (Root *k-b-r*).

Exceptions

There are a few feminine nouns whose gender is not indicated either by form or by meaning:

ɛ̄n	'eye', 'waterhole'	*rīḥ*	'wind' (also masc.)
ʔīd, yadd	'hand, arm'	*ʔarḍ*	'land, ground, earth'
ʔəžʼr, rəžʼl	'foot, leg'	*šams*	'sun'
ʔədʼn	'ear'	*sama, samāʔ*	heaven' (also m.)
daʔʼn	'chin, beard'	*ɱayy*	'water' (also ɱayye)
raḥʼm	'womb'	*səkkīn*	'knife' (also səkkīne)
ṭīẓ	'backside, arse'	*dəkkān*	'shop'
nafs	'spirit, self'	*ʔəṣbaɛ*	'finger' (also ʔəṣbaɛa)
rōḥ	'soul, spirit'	*ṭāḥūn*	'mill' (also ṭāḥūne)
dār	'house'	*maṭar*	'rain'
balad	'town, community, country'	*ḥarb*	'war' (also masc.)
blād	'country'	*ṭarīʔ*	'road, way' (also masc.)

The noun *sū̲ʔ* 'market' is generally feminine in its abstract or general sense, e.g. *s-sū̲ʔ ʼs-sōda* 'the black market', otherwise masculine.

ʔarḍ is masculine in its sense 'floor'.

rōḥ is masculine in the sense 'ghost, disembodied spirit'.

The feminine gender of *žhannam* 'Hell' might be attributed to its being a place name [p. 373].

The words *nās* 'people' and *xēl* 'horses' are feminine, though they often take plural agreement. See p. 426.

In the case of ethnic collectives [p. 301] the question of gender does not come up, since they consistently have plural agreement.

The gender of other kinds of collectives depends on their form as in the case of ordinary singulars: *baʔar* 'cattle' (masculine), *məɛze* 'goats' (feminine); *ɛadas* 'lentils' (masculine), *fāṣūliyye* 'kidney beans' (feminine).

All questions of number/gender function in verbs, adjectives, and pronouns are dealt with under Number/Gender Agreement, including the number/
gender of verbs and adjectives without subjects [p. 427].

CHAPTER 15: SYNTACTICAL PRINCIPLES AND CONSTRUCTIONS

Sentences and Clauses (*al-ǧumla*)

A sentence is not just a string of words, but a string of words pronounced as a "prosodic unit". A prosodic unit has rhythmic, melodic, and dynamic features which contribute to the phrasing and meaning of the word string.

A COMPOUND sentence is a coördination [p.391] of word strings each of which could be used to form a complete sentence by itself. These potentially sentence-forming word strings are called CLAUSES.[1]
In the sentence *huwwe ʔādami w-ʔana bḥabbo* 'He's a nice person and I like him', there is a non-verbal clause [402] *huwwe ʔādami* coördinated by the conjunction *w-* 'and' with a verbal clause [407] *ʔana bḥabbo*.

A COMPLEX sentence consists of a (prosodically unified) SUPERORDINATE CLAUSE which contains, as one of its parts, a SUBORDINATE CLAUSE.
In the sentence *bəxṭəb-lo yāha lamma byətxarraž* 'I'll ask her hand in marriage for him when he graduates', the (one-word) clause *byətxarraž* 'he graduates' is subordinated to the rest of the sentence in a supplemental (adverbial) capacity [528] by the conjunction *lamma* 'when'.
A superordinate clause may in its turn be subordinated, as in *baddi ʔəl-lo ʔanno bəxṭəb-lo yāha lamma byətxarraž* 'I intend to tell him that I'll ask her hand in marriage for him when he graduates'. The clause *bəxṭəb-lo yāha lamma byətxarraž* is subordinated to the rest of the sentence in a complemental capacity [449] by the conjunction *ʔanno* 'that'.[2]

A sentence containing only one clause is a SIMPLE SENTENCE.

---

[1]The definition of 'clause' depends, of course, on that of 'complete sentence', which is simply a sentence whose word string can be analyzed in terms of one of the clause-forming constructions. The circularity of these definitions is perfectly tolerable, so long as all those utterances which do not qualify as complete sentences can either be 1.) analyzed as incomplete sentences, i.e. analyzed in terms of complete sentences, or 2.) dismissed as trivial for present purposes.
In this book 'clause' designates a much more abstract entity than 'sentence', since the latter is defined as a prosodic unit while a clause is defined merely as a word string, stripped of prosody. If this grammar dealt systematically with intonation (prosody) it would probably be better also to define 'clause' as a kind of prosodic unit, but since intonation is not dealt with, the present definition - being in accord with traditional usage - should be less confusing for most readers.
Note that the Arabic concept of *ǧumla* includes both 'sentence' and 'clause'. In fast uninterrupted monologue especially, it is often impossible to distinguish between a coördination of clauses and a coördination of simple sentences.

[2]A supplemental clause may be contrasted with the MAIN clause, which is complete in itself, while a complemental clause is an integral part of the superordinate clause.

Sentence Types

Syrian Arabic has six main types of complete sentence, insofar as conversational function may be correlated with clause structure and prosodic structure: 1.) Exclamations, 2.) Calls, 3.) Commands, 4.) Declarations, 5.) Yes/No Questions, and 6.) Substitution Questions.

Exclamations. Many kinds of clause may be used in exclamations, but the simplest and only exclusively exclamatory kind consists of an INTERJECTION, which is a word that neither undergoes inflection nor enters into construction with other words: *Éafārem!* 'Bravo!', *mašāḷḷa!* 'Isn't that wonderful!'. Some exclamations consist of the vocative particle *ya* plus an adjective or noun: *ya laṭīf* 'Good grief!', *ya Éēb ᵊš-šūm!* (expression with which a host at dinner disclaims guests' praise).

Calls. A call generally consists of a noun or noun phrase – very often a personal name – which may or may not be preceded by the vocative particle *ya* (or sometimes *ʔa*): *(ya)ḥasan!* '(O) Hassan!'

Most interjections and Vocative phrases, of course, are more often used in supplementation to a main clause than as full sentences: *šlōnkon ya ṣabāya* 'How are you, girls?', *Éaẓīm waḷḷa!* '(That's) great, by golly!'.

Declarations. The clause of a declarative sentence may be a predication [p.401] or an extraposition [429]: *maddēt ʔawwal šahrēn Éand xāli* 'I spent the first two months at my uncle's', *ʔawwal šahrēn maddēthon Éand xāli* 'The first two months, I spent (them) at my uncle's'.

The category of declarative sentences includes <u>statements</u>, which are characterized by verbs in the indicative or by a non-verbal clause [402]: *mərrūḥ sawa* 'We'll go together', *ʔana maÉak* 'I'm with you'; and also <u>exhortations</u> and <u>invocations</u>, which are characterized mainly by verbs in the subjunctive, but sometimes also by non-verbal clauses: *nrūḥ sawa* 'Let's go together', *ʔaḷḷa maÉak* 'God be with you'. (See p. 344.)

Yes/No Questions. A yes/no interrogative sentence generally has the same kind of clause as the corresponding declarative sentence, but the intonation is different. (See p. 379.) *maddēt ʔawwal šahrēn Éand xālak?* 'Did you spend the first two months at your uncle's?', *ʔawwal šahrēn, maddēthon Éand xālak?* 'The first two months – did you spend them at your uncle's?', *mənrūḥ sawa?* 'Will we be going together?', *nrūḥ sawa?* 'Shall we go together?'

The particle *ši* is often used to indicate a question: *ṭʔūmti ʔəžet mən Éand ᵊl-kawwa ši?* [DA-237] 'Have my suits come back from the cleaners?'. The interrogative particle may come at the end of the sentence, as above, or it may precede a complement, thereby setting it off and emphasizing it: *Éam-təʔṣod ši ʔənni kazzāb?* 'Are you implying that I'm a liar?', *zərt b-ᵊhyātak ši l-Éāṣme?* 'Have you ever visited the capital?'

Yes/no questions may be pronounced with a rising intonation similar to that of (American) English questions, or
else with a level or slightly rising medium-high pitch and
a long drawl on the last syllable [p. 17].

Substitution Questions. Sentences formed with the question-words *šū* 'what',
mīn 'who', *wēn* 'where', etc., are also derivable from declarative sentences
by substitution of the question word for some particular part of the clause,
and by certain changes in word order: *wēn maddēt ʔawwal šahrēn?* 'Where did
you spend the first two months?', *ʔawwal šahrēn, wēn maddēthon?* 'The first
two months – where did you spend them?' (See p. 566.)

Substitution questions are commonly pronounced with
level medium or medium low final pitch, and a drawl. The
question usually begins with with high pitch, on the
question word itself.

Commands. A declarative sentence may generally be converted into a (positive) command by dropping the subject (if any) and changing the verb to
imperative [p. 359]: *maddi ʔawwal šahrēn ɛand xālak* 'Spend the first two
months at your uncle's'. (A negative command, however, is formed with
the subjunctive: *lā tmaddi ʔawwal šahrēn...* 'Don't spend the first
two months...'.)

Predication: The Basic Clause Type

The sort of clause that can be made into both a declarative and a
(yes/no) interrogative sentence is called a PREDICATION.[1] For example:

Declarative	Interrogative
šāyīna dyūf ʔl-yōm .... 'We're having guests today' (lit. "Guests are coming to us today")	*šāyīna dyūf ʔl-yōm (ši)?* 'Are we having guests today?'
lāzem nahtáfel fīhon .... 'We must give them a big welcome'	*lāzem nahtáfel fīhon (ši)?* 'Must we give them a big welcome?'
ʔaxūk mā byaži .... 'Your brother isn't coming'	*ʔaxūk mā byaži?* 'Isn't your brother coming?'
maẓbūṭ .... '(That's) right'	*maẓbūṭ?* '(Is that) right?'

---

[1] This does not mean that every declarative sentence can be converted, as it
stands, into a normal interrogative sentence (or vice versa), but only
that every one has the same grammatical structure as other sentences which
can be so converted, or (if compound), that it can be broken down into
simple clauses which can be so converted. For instance the compound declarative sentence *sažžalna hala?a w-bukra batšūfūha* 'We've recorded a
[television] spot and tomorrow you'll see it' could not be made into a
normal interrogative as it stands, but the two coördinate clauses could be
converted separately.

Declarative	Interrogative

mā ɛandak maṣāri. . . . .   *mā ɛandak maṣāri?*
'You have no money'   'Don't you have any money?'

nəržaɛ ɛal-bēt.   *nəržaɛ ɛal-bēt?*
'Let's go back to the house'   'Shall we go back to the house?'[1]

Predication is the most important and basic clause-forming construction type, since not only does it account for all declarative and interrogative sentences, but indirectly also for commands [p. 359], and substitution questions [566], as <u>derivative</u> from predications. Only the most peripheral sentence types — calls and interjections [378] — are fundamentally independent of predication.

The Parts of a Predication

A predication consists of a PREDICATE, with or without a SUBJECT: *r-ražžāl šāf ᵊl-kalb* 'The man saw the dog' or *šāf ᵊl-kalb* 'He saw the dog'; *ʔante mətʔakked?* 'Are you sure?' or *mətʔakked?* '(Are you) sure?'

A simple predicate consists of a word or phrase, which is ordinarily:

(1.) a verb or verb phrase: *fhəmᵊt* 'I understand' (lit. "I have understood"), *fhəmᵊt kalāmak* 'I understand what you say', *fhəmᵊt ɛalēk* 'I understand you'.

(2.) an adjective or adjective phrase: *(ʔana) zaɛlān* 'I am displeased', *(ʔana) zaɛlān mənnak* 'I'm displeased with you'.

(3.) a preposition or a prepositional phrase: *huwwe ʔəddām* 'He is in front', *huwwe ʔəddām ᵊl-bēt* 'He is in front of the house'.

(4.) a noun or noun phrase: *hāda maktūb* 'This is a letter', *hāda maktūb ʔəlak* 'This is a letter for you', *hāda ʔawwal maktūb* 'This is the first letter'.

The subject of a simple predication is usually a noun, or a noun phrase, or a pronoun: *r-ražžāl šāfo* 'The man saw it', *ʔabᵊn har-ražžāl mū hōn* 'That man's son isn't here', *hāda ʔabno* 'That's his son'.

---

[1] Independent optative clauses [p. 344] are marginally predicative; in the first-person plural they may be used freely as either declarative or interrogative, while in first-person singular and the second person they are usually interrogative, and in the third person normally declarative.

Phrase-Forming Constructions

A PHRASE, roughly speaking, is a constituent of a clause that consists of more than one word but is generally not itself a clause. In this book most of the many ways in which words are combined in phrases come under one or another of several major headings, including:

ATTRIBUTION [Ch. 19], whereby the elements of a predication are converted into a noun phrase: *l-bēt l-ᵊkbīr* 'the big house' (cf. *l-bēt ᵊkbīr* 'the house is big').

COMPLEMENTATION AND SUPPLEMENTATION [Ch. 17, 20], which account for almost all verb phrases and many noun and adjective phrases: *šāf ᵊl-bēt* 'saw the house', *trūḥ ʔawām* '(that)you go quickly', *mabṣūṭ fī* 'pleased with it', *kamān wāḥed* 'one more'.

ANNEXION [Ch. 18], which forms many noun-type phrases and all preposi- tional phrases: *farš ᵊl-bēt* 'the furniture of the house', *ʔawwal bēt* 'the first house', *šuwwāt ᵊl-bēt* 'inside the house'.

The Parts of Speech

The so-called parts of speech are syntactical form classes – categories based on the way words function in clauses and phrases.[1]

The broadest category is that of PREDICATORS – words which may normally be used as the main term of a predicate. In Arabic, predicators include verbs, adjectives, nouns, and free prepositions.

Non-predicators include adverbs and all kinds of particles, such as conjunctions and bound prepositions.

NOUNS are distinguished as the only predicators that may normally also be used as the main term of a <u>subject</u>.

ADJECTIVES are distinguished by their use as <u>attributes</u>.

FREE PREPOSITIONS are also used as <u>supplements</u>.

VERBS have no use other than predication and command.[2]

Of the non-predicators, ADVERBS are distinguished from particles by their use as main terms in supplements.

---

[1] A clear-cut part of speech system commonly also depends, to some extent, on correlation with non-syntactical matters such as inflection [p. 35]. It is a mistake to suppose that any single criterion can establish the mem- bership of every word that obviously belongs to a particular form class. By the same token, certain words belong to different classes, depending on which (usually convergent but sometimes divergent) criteria are used.

[2] This is not to say that a verbal <u>clause</u> (which may be a one-word clause) cannot be subject, attribute, complement, etc.

Pronouns and other substitutes are a special case, not adequately definable in terms of syntactical form classes [p.535].

Noun-Type Words (*al-ism*). Nouns in the strict sense — SUBSTANTIVES — may be distinguished syntactically from other NOUN-TYPE WORDS such as elatives [p.310], numerals [170], pronouns, and adjectives.

Numerals and elatives are distinguished by the fact that they are used freely as attributes as well as in the more typical noun-like capacities: *l-walad ᵊl-ʔakbar* 'the oldest boy' (cf. *ʔakbar walad*).

> Certain substantives may also be used attributively: *l-waṭan ᵊl-ʔǝmm* 'the mother country' [p.506]. Certain others may be used adverbially: *šǝfto marra* 'I saw him once' (lit. "...a time"). [p.521].

Adjectives are typically quite different from nouns in that they do not normally occur as subject, but do occur as attribute. There are, however, many adjectives applicable to human beings which are also freely used in a substantive capacity: *zġīr* 'small, young' or 'child'; *kazzāb* 'lying' or 'liar' [p.201]. This widespread overlapping of the two syntactic classes — plus their morphological similarities — makes it desirable to include adjectives also under the category of 'noun-type word'.

Pronouns clearly qualify as noun-type words since they are used as subject [p.548], though they only marginally qualify as predicators at all [551].

> The rest of this chapter is devoted to two types of construction and not dealt with elsewhere in the book: negation and coördination.

NEGATION

The most common negative particles are *mā,* used mainly with verbs and a few other expressions, and *mū,* used mainly with non-verbal predicates. *lā* is used mainly with the independent subjunctive [p. 389]. These particles come immediately before the negated term and are usually accented more strongly than the negated term. For *la⁹* 'no', see p. 536.

Commonly in Palestine and to a lesser extent in southern and central Lebanon, *mā* is paired with a suffix -*š* which is attached to the negated term (cf. French ne...pas). (In some dialects -*š* may be used without *mā,* or with *⁹a-* instead of *mā.* Thus *mā baɛref* 'I don't know' = *mā baɛráf-š* = *baɛráf-š* = *⁹a-baɛráf-š.*) The -*š* form corresponding to *mū* is *məš* or *muš.*

The Particle *mā.* Examples with verbs:

1. *mā žarrabᵊt li⁹anno mā kān maɛi wa⁹ᵊt ⁹aɛɛod u-⁹əsfon*
'I haven't tried (it) because I haven't had time to sit and think'

2. *mā səfi ġēr ɛašᵊr da⁹āye⁹*
'There's not but ten minutes left'

3. *hayy mā bətsəḥḥ-əlli hnīk*
'That won't do me any good over there'

4. *lāzem təḥləf-li mā taɛmel maɛha šī* [AO-114]
'You must swear to me not to do anything to her'

5. *l-wāḥed mā bilā⁹i mətᵊl balado*
'There's no place like home' (lit. "One doesn't find the like of his community")

6. *mā bəṭlaɛ ɛal-ḥāra bəl-bižāma*
'I wouldn't go out on the street in pajamas'

7. *mā byaɛᵊžbo šī, šū ma žəbt bi⁹əl-lak mā bikaffi, mā byənfaɛ, lēš mā sāwēto hēk u-hēk*
'Nothing pleases him; whatever you bring he tells you it isn't enough, it's won't do, why didn't you do it thus and so'

8. *fī tlətt ⁹aɛtibārāt lāzem mā nədžāhálon*
'There are three considerations we should not overlook'

9. *⁹əl-li, baɛᵊd mā zərt ⁹āsārāt labnān?* [SAL-115]
'Tell me, haven't you visited the ruins of Lebanon yet?'

10. *hayy ḥāle mā btənhámel*
'It's an unbearable situation' [p. 328]

11. *ṭ-ṭābe kānet mā btənṭāl*
'The ball was out of reach'

12. *l-ʔaġlab mā laḥa-yəḥṣal*   'Chances are, he won't get the job'
    ɛaš-šaġle

13. *yəlli ʔaxatto laḥadd ᵊl-māster*   'What I took for the master's isn't
    mā ḥa-yzîd ᵊktîr ɛal-Ph.D.   going to add much to the Ph.D.'

14. *ʔana mā ɛam-bḥākîk* [SPA-221]   'I'm not talking to you'

15. *ʔabūk mā ɛam-yākol*   'Your father is not eating'

16. *ʔana mā ɛam-bəštáġel hal-ʔiyyām*   'I'm not working these days'

      Verbs with *ɛam-* and *raḥa (laḥa, ḥa-*, etc.) [p. 320] are
also often negated with *mū, mālo* [pp. 387, 388].

      Active participles are sometimes negated with *mā*:

17. *kîf, mā məštāʔ ləš-šām?*   'Aren't you homesick for Damascus?'

18. *mā bərmi šabᵊkti ġēr ʔarbaɛ*   'I don't cast my net more than four
    marrāt u-mā ṣafyān-li ʔəlla   times, and there isn't but one time
    marra wāḥde [AO-115]   left to me'

mā **with Other Verb-like Expressions.** The words *bəddo* 'to want, intend,
(etc.)' [p. 412], *fî* 'there is' and 'to be able', *ɛando, maɛo*, and *ʔəlo*
'to have' [413], and a few similar expressions, are negated with *mā*:

19. *mā bəddak ᵊl-ɛarāḍa?*   'Don't you want the publicity?'

20 *mā bəddha tākol*   'She doesn't want to eat'

21. *hal-ᵊktāb mā baddo*   'This book doesn't require hard
    wala taɛᵊb [PVA-56]   work'

22. *mā fî ʔəxtilāf ᵊktîr*   'There's not much difference'

23. *šu mā fî hada bəl-bēt?*   'Isn't there anyone home?'

24. *b-mūžeb ʔānūn l-ᵊḥkūme l-ᵊždîd*   'According to the government's new
    mā fî l-wāḥed yəstamlek ʔaktar   law, one may not own more than four
    mən ʔarbaɛ byūt   houses'

25. *mā fîna naɛᵊmlo halla?*   'We can't do it now'

26. *mā fîkon wala wāḥed ᵊmnîḥ*   'There's not a good one among you'

      In the last example *fîkon* stands for *fî* 'there is' +
fîkon 'among you', collapsed into a single form; cf. *mā fî
wala wāḥed ᵊmnîḥ fîkon* (same translation).

27. *mā bo šî* [p. 415]   'He's all right' or 'There's noth-
                      ing the matter with him'

28. *l-ḥaʔîʔa mā ɛandi waʔᵊt ʔəlha*   'The truth is, I haven't time for it'

29. mā ʕando dars ᵊl-yōm   'He has no lesson today'

30. mā ʕalēk; ʔana bḥākī   'It's not your responsibility; I'll
                                          talk to him' (lit. "It's not on
                                          you...")

31. mā ʔəlkon ḥaʔʔ   'You (pl.) are in the wrong' (lit.
                                          "You have no right.")

32. mā ʔəli ʕalāʔa bət-ṭawgīf   'I have nothing to do with hiring'
    [SAL-92]

        Instead of the disjunctive forms ʔəlo, etc. [p.479], the
    suffixing forms may be used with mā:

33. ʕīd l-ᵊkbīr mā-lo tārīx ᵊmʕayyan   'Easter has no fixed date'
    [DA-303]

34. l-ᵊmḥāžaže mā-la ʔāxer   'There's no end to the argument'

35. l-yahūd biṣallu b-ᵊknīs wāḥed,   'The Jews pray in one synagogue,
    mā-lhon ǧēro [Bg. 1]   they have no other'

mā with pronouns. In equational sentences [p.406], mā may be used before
personal pronouns (especially third person)

36. mā huwwe l-masʔūl ʕan ᵊl-ḥādes   'He's not the one responsible for
                                          the accident'

37. mā hənnen halli rafaʕu d-daʕwa   'It is not they who initiated the
                                          suit'

38. mā hiyye halli kasret ᵊl-vāz   'She's not the one who broke the
                                          vase'

39. mā huwwe ʔəlla t-tanāzoʕ   'It's nothing else than the eternal
    ᵊl-ʔazali bēn ᵊl-xēr waš-šarr   conflict between good and evil'

40. mā ʔana yalli ḥakēt   'It's not I who spoke'

        mā huwwe and mā hiyye are sometimes apocopated to mā-hu,
    mā-hi, or mā-u, mā-i: mā-hu huwwe [Bart.-776] 'It's not
    he'; mā-u ʔabūk.., ʔabūyi ʔana [DS] 'It's not your father,
    it's my father!'

        mā is used with the indefinite noun ḥada 'anyone, someone' (translated
    'no one, nobody'):

41. mā ḥada šāfna   'No one saw us'

42. mīn ḥaka ʕat-talifōn?   'Who was it (lit. "Who spoke") on
    – mā ḥada; wāḥed galṭān   the phone?' – Nobody...somebody who
    bən-nəmre   got the wrong number'

Similarly, *mā* is sometimes used with *šī* 'something, any-thing' (translated 'nothing'), but this locution is limited mostly to answers ("incomplete predications"):

43. *šū ɛam-taɛmel? - mā šī* 'What are you doing?' - 'Nothing'

The Particle *mū*

Practically any non-verbal predicative term may be negated with *mū*:

1. *l-ḥaʔīʔa mū ḥāṭeṭ bi-bāli t-taɛlīm* 'The truth is, I haven't seriously considered teaching' (*ḥāṭeṭ* is a participle [p. 265].)

2. *ʔaxdet ʔl-bakalōryus, mū hēk?* 'She's gotten her bachelor's degree, hasn't she?' (lit. "isn't is so?")

3. *hal-ḥaki hāda mū ḥəlu* 'That (kind of) talk isn't nice'

4. *ɛēna mū šūɛāne, mā bəddha tākol šī* 'She doesn't have a hungry look; she doesn't want anything to eat' (lit. "Her eye isn't hungry..")

5. *fa-maɛnāta kəll ʔl-ɛamaliyye mū zyādet maɛlūmāt* 'So the significance of the whole business is not acquisition of more knowledge'

6. *mū masʔalet mā bəddi hal-ɛarāḍa* 'It's not a question of my not want-ing the publicity'

7. *ʔana ḥabbēt ʔəži la-hōn mū bass məšān ʔš-šahāde, bass məšān ʔl-xəbra* 'I wanted to come here not only for the degree, but for the experience'

8. *mū hāda yalli waṣṣēt ɛalē* 'This isn't what I ordered'

9. *ʔana mū mabṣūṭ ʔl-yōm* 'I'm not feeling well today'

10. *kānu mū mawžūdīn lamma daʔʔēnā-lon talifōn* 'They were out when we phoned them' (lit. "They were not-to-be-found...") Cf. *mā kānu mawžūdīn...* 'They were not in...'

11. *hayye fəkra mū ɛāṭle* 'That's not a bad idea' (lit. "an idea [that is] not bad")

12. *huwwe sālek ṭarīʔ mū mnīḥ* 'He's following a bad course' (lit. "...a road [that is] not good")

13. *mū mətʔl ʔaxi l-ʔkbīr, ʔana rəḥʔt ɛaž-žāmɛa* 'Unlike my older brother, I went to the university'

14. *mū mən zamān šəfto*   'Not long ago I saw him' (Cf. *mā šəfto mən zamān* 'I haven't seen him for quite a while')

15. *mū lāzem təstaxfef b-naṣāyeḥ wāldak*   'You shouldn't take your father's advice lightly'

      Logically, *mū lāzem* should mean 'needn't' or 'it is not necessary', while 'mustn't' or 'shouldn't' would be expressed as *lāzem mā...* (as in example 8, p.   ). Actually, however, *mū lāzem* usually means 'mustn't, shouldn't, ought not to'.

      mū is sometimes used with *raḥa–* and *ɛam–* verb forms. (Cf. examples 12-16, p.   ):

16. *mū raḥa–tkūn ᵊmṣībe kbīre ʔiza mā ḥṣəlt ɛalē*   'It won't be a great misfortune if I don't get it'

17. *mū ɛam–yəštə́ḡel halla?*   'He's not working now'

      mū may also occur before other kinds of verb forms, when they form part of a clause to be negated emphatically as a whole, or as a quotation, or the like:

18. *l–yōm bēt ɛammtak ǧāyīn yəsharu ɛanna; mū taɛməl–li nādi w–rəfaʔāti...*   'Today your aunt and her family are coming to spend the evening with us; there'll be none of your [excuses to go out such as] "club and companions"'

      The use of *mū* before *ɛand,* etc. [p. 413] generally indicates a true prepositional phrase with a subject rather than the quasi-verbal expression with a complement: *ktābak mū ɛandi* 'Your book is not at my place' or '...among my things' (vs. *mā ɛandi ktābak* 'I don't have your book').

      Before personal pronouns, *mū* focuses more emphasis on the pronoun than *mā* [p. 385]: *mū hiyye halli ǧābet walad, ʔəxta* 'She's not the one who had the baby; it's her sister'; *mū ʔana yalli ḥakēt* 'I'm not the one who spoke' (Cf. ex. 40, p. 385).

      mū šī 'nothing' may be used as well as *mā ši* [p. 386], but *mū* is not ordinarily used with *ḥada* (: *mā ḥada* 'no one').

The Negative Copula

      Instead of using an independent subject pronoun with *mū,* pronoun suffixes may be attached to the stem *māl–* or *mān–*: *māli rāyeḥ* or *māni rāyeḥ* 'I'm not going' (instead of *ʔana mū rāyeḥ*). These forms constitute a sort of quasi-verb, like *bəddo,* etc. [p. 412], with pronoun suffixes for subject-affixes.

The form *māl-* is typically Damascene; the most usual
Lebanese form of the negative copula is *mann-: mannak šāyef?*
'Don't you see?'. (There are other variants, e.g. *maynak,*
mənak.) In some areas this type of form is not used in the
third person at all, for which *mā-hu, mā-hi,* etc. are used
[p.385]. The most usual Palestinian forms have *ma-* +
apocopated "independent" pronoun form + *-š* [383]: *mahūš* 'he
is not', *mahīš* 'she is not', *mantiš* 'you(m.) are not', *mantīš*
'you(f.) are not', *mahnāš* 'we are not', etc.; but *mantīš* 'I
am not'.

Examples:

1. *mālak ɛāməl-lak šī bēt šəɛ³r?*   'Haven't you composed any verse of
                                        poetry?'

2. *ɛam-yədros handase ?aw fīzya,*   'He's studying engineering or
   māli ?akīd mənna   physics – I'm not sure about it'

3. *lēš hal-labake?...mālna ġəraba*   'Why [go to all] this bother? We're
                                        not strangers'

4. *šlōnak ya ḥasan? wəššak mālo*   'How are you, Hassan? You don't
   mnīḥ [AO-51]   look well' (lit. "your face isn't
                                        good")

5. *lamma bfī?, ?iza kān māli ?aḥsan* 'When I wake up, if I'm not better
   bətžībī-li l-ḥakīm [AO-51]   you can get the doctor for me'

6. *w-təlɛet w-³tləɛ³t maɛha w-hiyye* 'And she went out, and I went out
   mālha šāɛra [AO-118]¹   along with her, without her notic-
                                        ing' (lit. "...and she was not per-
                                        ceiving")

      The *māl-* forms are commonly also used before verbs with
ɛam- and *raḥa-* [p.320]:

7. *halla? māli ɛam-rūḥ ɛaž-žāmɛa*   'I'm not going to the university
                                        now(adays)'

8. *ṣar-lon zamān mālon ɛam-yəsmaɛu* 'They haven't been hearing from him
   mənno   for a long time'

9. *mālo ɛam-yə?der yətṣawwar ³š-šī* 'He can't imagine what it is we're
   yalli ɛam-naɛ³mlo   doing'

10. *mālna raḥa-nəttáfe? ?abadan*   'We're not ever going to reach an
                                        agreement'

---

¹The AO text actually reads *w-hīye mā-lha šaɛ³rha* ('not having her hair')
which seems not to make sense in the context.

Note that *māl-* + pronoun suffix is indistinguishable in form from *mā* + *-l-* + pronoun suffix. See examples 33-35, p. 385. Thus in Damascus *māli* means both 'I am not' and 'I haven't (got)', but in many other parts of Syria *māli* means only 'I haven't got', while *māni* means 'I am not'.

The Particle *lā*

Verbs in the independent subjunctive [p.345] (especially in negative commands) are negated with *lā:*

1. *lā tətˀaxxar* — 'Don't be late'

2. *lā tˀāxzūni* — 'I'm sorry', 'Excuse(pl.) me', lit. 'Don't blame me, Don't hold it against me'

3. *lā trawweḥ ɛalēna šammet ˀl-hawa* — 'Let's not miss the outing', lit. "Don't let the outing get away from us" (*rawwaḥ* 'to let go, make go', causative of *rāḥ*)

In many parts of Greater Syria, however, *mā* is generally used in negative commands rather than (or as well as) *lā: mā tətˀaxxar* 'Don't be late', *mā tˀāxzūni* 'I'm sorry', etc.

4. *lā ykəl-lak fəkre* — 'Don't give it a thought', lit. "Let there not be a thought to you"

5. *ˀaḷḷa lā yˀadder* — 'God forbid!' lit. "May God not decree"

lā is used before the second-person perfect of *ɛād* and *baˀa* 'to keep on (doing something), to do...again', as a negative command 'don't...any more':

6. *lā ɛədtu dzūrū* — 'Don't(pl.) visit him any more'

7. *lā baˀēt ˀtḥākīhon* — 'Don't talk to them any more'

Cf. *mā ɛədna nzūro* 'We don't visit him any more', *mā baˀēt ḥākīhon* 'I don't talk to them any more'. Though *ɛād* and *baˀa* in these locutions are inflected as full-fledged verbs, they function syntactically as a sort of intrusive adverbial element, coming between the negative particle and the verb it really applies to. Thus *lā...dzūrū* 'Don't visit him...', *lā...tḥākīhon* 'Don't talk to them...'.

lā also occurs with a verb in the perfect in the expression *lā samaḥ ˀaḷḷa* 'God forbid!', lit. "May God not have allowed!"

There are a number of classicisms in which *lā* is used with a verb in the imperfect without *b-* (but as an indicative):

8. *mḥassbe ʔənno lā yustaġna ɛanna*   'She thinks she is indispensable'

9. *hāda ʔamᵊr lā yəḥtāž la-bərhān* [SPA-214]   'That's a matter that needs no proof'

Also in classicisms, *lā* is used before nouns, in the sense of *mū* 'no' or *mā fī* 'there is no' (*lā li-nafyi l-žins* "the generic *lā*"):

10. *lā šakk ʔənno ʔaḥsan*   'There's no doubt that it's better'

11. *lā šəkᵊr ɛala wāžeb*   'You're welcome', lit. "There's no thanks for [something done as a] duty"

12. *xnāʔa maɛo lā bədd mənna halla?*   'An argument with him is inevitable now'

13. *žamāl hal-bənt lā šēʔ bən-nəsbe la-ʔəxwāta*   'That girl's beauty is nothing compared to her sisters' '

In coördinations: *lā...w-lā* 'neither...nor':

14. *lā ʔana w-lā huwwe laḥa-nkūn ᵊhnīk*   'Neither he nor I will be there'

15. *lā baɛᵊrfo w-lā byaɛrəfni*   'I don't know him and he doesn't know me'

16. *ʔaddēš ḥəlwe hal-ʔiyyām, lā fī bard u-lā fī šōb* [DA-239]   'How nice it is these days, there is neither cold nor hot weather'

The first term of a coördination with *w-lā* can have *mā* or one of the other negativizers instead of *lā;* see ex. 21, p.384. Also:

17. *ʔana māli maɛ ᵊl-ʔəqtirāḥ w-lā ḍəḍḍo*   'I am neither for the proposal nor against it'

lā is used with the "emphatic *w-*" in the sense 'not even': *w-lā* (or *wala*). See p.384, ex. 26. (Cf. *w-law* 'even if', p.335.)

18. *w-lā wāḥed mn ᵊd-dakātra ʔəder išaxxeṣ ᵊl-maraḍ*   'Not one of the doctors could diagnose the disease'

19. *w-lā žawāb mn ᵊž-žawābēn maẓbūṭ*   'Neither of the two answers is correct'

If a complement or a post-posed subject [p. 407] has *w-lā,* the main term of the predicate must also be preceded by a negative particle:

20. *mā fī w-lā nətfet xəbᵊz bəl-bēt*   'There's not even a piece of bread in the house'

21. *s-sama ɜraʔʔet w-lā ɛād fī w-lā* 'The sky became blue and there *ġēme* [AO-67]   wasn't a single cloud left'

22. *mā ɛād naṭaʔ w-lā b-ḥarf w-lā*   'He neither pronounced another *tkallam w-lā kəlme* [AO-118] letter nor spoke another word' (The *w-lā* before *tkallam* is 'nor', in coördination with *mā ɛād...,* while the *w-lā* before *b-ḥarf* and before *kəlme* is the emphatic particle.)

COORDINATION

Coordination is a type of construction in which none of the two or more terms is grammatically subordinate to – or dependent on – the other (or others). SYNDETIC coordinations are marked by a conjunction between the co-ordinated terms, such as *w-* 'and', *ʔaw* 'or', *lāken* 'but', etc., while ASYN-DETIC coordinations [p. 398] simply have their terms juxtaposed with no conjunction. (POLYSYNDETIC coordinations [396] have a conjunction before the leading term as well as before the following terms: *yā...yā...* 'either... or...'.)

The Conjunction *w-* 'and'. This conjunction is a proclitic, i.e. it is pronounced as a prefix on the following word [p. 18], though the coordinated term may be whole clause or phrase. The use of *w-* in coordinations is similar to the use of English 'and', but unlike 'and', *w-* is also used as a subordinating conjunction [p. 531] and as a particle of emphasis [390, 335].

In close phrasing [p. 21] between a word ending in a consonant and a word beginning with a single consonant, this conjunction is regularly transcribed '*u-*' in this book: *təffāḥ u-mōz* 'apples and bananas'; otherwise it is transcribed as a consonant: *w-mōz kamān* 'and bananas too', *ʔalam w-ᵊktāb* 'a pencil and a book'.[1] In combination with the article [493], the conjunction is written in our transcription without the hyphen and with a following *ə* (rather than *ᵊ*): *l-ʔalam wəl-ᵊktāb* 'the pencil and the book'. See p. 476.

---

[1] In actual pronunciation, there is a good deal of free variation and indeterminancy as between *w* and *u* in some positions, since the difference between them is subtle and non-phonemic [p. 9].

Examples.   Coordination of noun-type words and phrases:

1. *šlōn ᵊl-ɛarūs wəl-ɛarīs?*   'How are the bride and groom?'

2. *maɛi nəmret talifōno w-ɛənwāno*   'I have his telephone number and
                                        address'

> Note, in the foregoing examples, that the article pre-
> fix and the pronoun suffixes must be repeated for each co-
> ordinated term to which they apply, while in English 'the'
> and 'his' can apply to the coordination as a whole.
> See also ex. 1, p. 394.

3. *bəddna šī badle w-ṣabbāṭ*   'I (lit. "we") want a suit and (a
   u-ʔəmṣān, w-šī šwayyet ᵊġrāḍ   pair of) shoes and shirts, and a
                                        few [other] things'

> Multiple coordinations like that in example 3 are in
> English often converted into a <u>listing</u>, with 'and' kept
> only before the last term: '...a suit, shoes, shirts, and
> a few other things'.   In Arabic, however, *w-* is usually
> kept between all the terms.

4. *huwwe w-samīr kānu b-fard ṣaff*   'He and Samir were in the same class'

> For further examples of personal pronouns in coordina-
> tions, see pp. 364, 551.

5. *l-marḥale t-tālte wəl-ʔaxīre...*   'The third and final stage...'
   [DA-305]

6. *ɛandi baṭṭīx ʔaḥmar u-ʔaṣfar*   'I have watermelon and canteloupe'
                                        (lit. "...red and yellow melon")

7. *la-ʔawwal u-ʔāxer marra, laʔ!*   'For the first and last time, no!'

8. *...ɛaɡamet u-faxāmet farš byūt*   '...the magnificence and elegance of
   ᵊl-ʔaġᵊnya [PAT-191]   the furnishings in the houses of the
                                        rich'

> Examples 7 and 8 illustrate coordinations as leading
> term in annexion; see p. 456.

Coordination of verbs and verb phrases:

9. *...badu yənᵊɛšu w-yəḥyu l-ʔadab*   'They began to stimulate and revive
   ᵊl-ɛarabi l-ʔadīm [DA-304]   the old Arab culture'

10. *ʔana rāyeḥ ʔəšlaḥ ʔawāɛiyyi*   'I'm going to take off my clothes
    w-ʔəlbes bižāmti   and put on my pajamas'

> See also p. 320, top.

Coordination of clauses and sentences:

11. ʔāl mudīr ʔl-barāmež ʔanna   'The program director said it was
    ḥalwe w-ɛažʔbto ktīr   nice and he liked it a lot'

12. biḥabb banāt ɛammto w-biḥabb   'He likes his aunt's daughters and
    yashar maɛhon   he likes to spend the evening with
                                    them'

13. waḷḷa šāṭer w-ɛēn ʔaḷḷa ɛalē   'He is certainly clever, and God's
                                    eye is upon him'

14. rūḥ ʔasʔal ʔammak baddha šī,   'Go ask your mother if she wants any-
    w-baɛdēn sāwi yalli baddak yā   thing, and then do what you wish'

15. byaghar ʔannak kaslān w-ʔbtatrok   'It seems that you're lazy and you
    ʔl-wagīfe yōmēn wara baɛʔdhon   leave your assignment [undone] for
    w-kall yōm batʔūl "bakra"   two days in a row, and every day you
                                       say "tomorrow".'

16. ḥaṭṭeṭ ʔl-ɛaša ʔaddāmo, w-mā   'She set the dinner before him, but
    radyet tākol maɛo [AO-111]   wouldn't eat with him'

   Followed by the negative mā, as in example 16, w- is
sometimes better translated 'but' than 'and'.

17. šaft falm ʔz-zahra? fī šī   'Have you seen the picture at the
    garīf? — rawɛa, w-bal-ʔaxaṣṣ   Zahra? Is there anything good in
    l-ʔmmassle. — wal-ʔaṣṣa?   it? — It's great, especially the
                                    [leading] actress. — And [what
                                    about] the story?'

18. mfakker taržaɛ laš-šām b-ʔšbāṭ?   'Are you planning to go back to
    — laʔ, baržaɛ b-ʔḥzērān. —   Damascus in February? — No, I'm
    w-battamm ɛala ṭūl baš-šām?   going back in June. — And will you
                                     stay permanently in Damascus?'

   Like English 'and', w- is often used to link clauses
in a significant sequence — the order of coordinated terms
representing a time sequence or a cause-and-effect sequence
of events:

19. nḥana w-tarak ʔl-masraḥ   'He bowed and left the stage'

20. zaḥlet ražlo w-waʔeɛ la-wara   'His foot slipped and he fell over
                                    backwards'

21. bass ʔkbēs hal-maske wal-bāb   'Just press this handle and the door
    byanfáteḥ   will open'

22. ɛmal-lak taṭlīɛa b-sarɛa   'Take a quick look and see if the mail
    w-šūf ʔiza ʔažet ʔl-bōṣṭa   has come'

Like 'and' again, w- is used in **ANAPHORIC** coordinations.
The following term is a repetition of the leading term, and
has augmentative [p. 253] significance:

23. *bəḍḍall ᵊbtəḥki w-ᵊbtəḥki*   'She keeps on talking and talking'

24. *l-ᵊmnāqaše stamarret sāɛāt   'The argument went on for hours and
    u-sāɛāt*   hours'

25. *kəll šī ɛam-yəġla ʔaktar   'Everything is getting more and more
    u-ʔaktar*   expensive'

      SYNONYMIC coordinations are commonly used for rhetorical
emphasis:

26. *ɛāšu b-taɛāse w-bəʔs*   'They lived in misery and wretchedness'

      See also examples 8 and 9, above.

Conjunctions translated 'or'

      ʔaw 'or' is used mainly to coordinate words or phrases, more rarely
clauses. Examples:

1. *byəʔbaḍ ᵊl-fallāḥ taman ᵊḥbūbo   'The farmer collects the price of his
   ʔaw fwākī ʔaw xəḍrāto mn   grain or fruit or vegetables from the
   ᵊs-səmsār* [PAT-185]   broker'

2. *l-yōm mā fī rōḥa ɛal-ʔahwe   'Today there's [to be] no going to
   ʔaw ɛas-sīnama ʔaw la-hōn   the coffeehouse or to the movies or
   u-la-hon*   hither and yon'

3. *səntēn ʔaw tlāte bən-nəsbe   'Two or three years for an engineer
   la-mhandes ktār*   are a lot'

4. *l-malābes ᵊl-franžiyye hiyye   'The Western outfit consists of
   ɛibāra ɛan banṭalūn u-sūka   trousers and jacket with or without
   maɛ ʔaw bidūn ṣəḍriyye* [PAT-197]   a vest'

      Example 4 shows a coordination of prepositions, which
is a rather uncommon construction in Arabic. Cf. p.456.

5. *ʔiza mū ḥāṭeṭ bi-bālak   'If you don't have your mind set on
   ᵊt-taɛlīm bəž-žāmɛa ʔaw ma   teaching in a university or something
   ʔašbah mā-la ṭaɛme*   similar there's no sense in it'

      Like English 'or', *ʔaw* is used in synonymic coordinations:

6. *l-madīne mʔassame la-ɛəddet   'The city is divided into a number
   ʔaʔsām ʔaw ʔaḥya* [PAT-179]   of sections or quarters'

7. *bisammū l-ɛaṣr ᵊl-ɛabbāsi ʔaw   'They call it the Abbasid Period or
   ᵊl-ɛaṣr ᵊz-zahabi*   the Golden Age'

The conjunction *yā* 'or' is used similarly to *ʔaw*, but not for synonymic coordinations. (See also polysyndetic coordinations, below.) Examples:

8. *žāye l-yōm yā bəkra*   'He's coming today or tomorrow'

9. *baɛd ᵊl-ʔakᵊl byāxod šəkᵊl*
   fwāki yā šəkᵊl ḥəlu [PAT-195]

   'After eating [the main courses] he has some kind of fruit or some kind of sweet'

10. *z-zyāra fi ṭrāblos bəddūm waʔᵊt*
    ṭawīl, sāɛtēn yā tlatt sāɛāt
    w-ʔiyyām ʔaktar [PAT-197]

    'Visiting in Tripoli takes a long time, two or three hours and sometimes longer'

11. *kəll yōm žəmɛa w-ʔaḥad baɛd*
    ᵊd-dəhᵊr bətšūfon rāyḥīn
    ɛal-ʔaḥāwi, yā ɛa-šamm ᵊl-hawa
    ɛal-bəddāwi, yā ɛal-mīna, yā
    ɛa-zġarta, yā ɛal-mənye, yā
    ɛal-ʔalmūn, yā ɛa-bərž rās
    ᵊn-nahᵊr [PAT-187]

    'Every Friday and Sunday afternoon you see them going to the coffee houses, or on an outing to el Beddawi, or to el Mina, or to Zghorta, or to Méniye, or to Almoune, or to Bordj Râs en Nahr'

The conjunctions *yəmma* (or *yamma*) and *wəlla* 'or, or else' are to some extent synonyms of *yā* and *ʔaw*, but are used most commonly in ALTERNATIVE QUESTIONS:

12. *ɛaṭīna warᵊʔtēn. – daraže*
    ʔūla yəmma daraže tānye?
    [DA-26]

    'Give me two tickets. – First class or second class?'

13. *w-hallaʔ mnēn mərrūḥ? mən*
    hōn yəmma mn ᵊhnīk? [DA-77]

    'And now which way do we go? This way or that way?'

14. *ṭləɛt mən bērūt raʔsan, wəlla*
    mn ᵊš-šām?

    'Did you leave directly from Beirut, or from Damascus?'

15. *w-lah-təržaɛ ɛaš-šām wəlla*
    lah-ᵊḍḍall hōn?

    'And are you going back to Damascus, or will you stay here?'

16. *bḥaṭṭ-əllak zēt šaɛᵊr wəlla*
    bass mayy? [DA-180]

    'Shall I put hair tonic on, or just water?'

Alternative questions are commonly pronounced with an intonation similar to that of substitution questions [p. 379]. The first term (which ends just before the conjunction) has a slightly rising pitch, while the following term may end on a medium-low level pitch; or else – as in English – fall all the way to the "bottom".

17. *s-səne fīha...šahᵊr wāḥed ʔəlo*
    bass tmāna w-ɛəšrīn wəlla
    təsɛa w-ɛəšrīn yōm [AO-71]

    'There is one month in the year which has only twenty-eight or else twenty-nine days'

18. *staɛžel wəlla btətʔaxxar*   'Hurry up or you'll be late'

19. *mā tšədd ʔīdak, walla mā byədxol*
    ᵊd-dawa [PVA-60]

    'Don't tense your arm, or the medi-
    cine won't go in'

20. *skōt walla bədᵊrbak* [SPA-431]

    'Hush up or I'll hit you'

21. *rūḥ ʔəl-lo ʔənt yamma ʔana brūḥ*
    [SPA-433]

    'You go tell him or else I'll go'

    Examples 18-21 illustrate another common use of *walla*
(less common for *yəmma, yamma*), namely the coordination of
a command with a predication. The predication depicts the
consequence of not obeying the command.

Polysyndetic Coordinations. *yā*, and sometimes also *yəmma* (or *yamma*) and *ʔaw*,
may be used before the first term of a coordination and repeated before the
following term (or terms), thus constituting a conjunction set like 'either
...or...' in English:

1. *yā ʔana brūḥ yā huwwe*

    'Either I go or he goes!'

2. *ʔēmta bəddak ᵊdžība? — yəmken*
   yā bəkra yā baɛᵊd bəkra [DA-99]

    'When do you want to bring her? —
    Perhaps either tomorrow or the day
    after'

3. *ʔamma l-laḥme la-ḥāla huwwe*
   byākᵉla məšwiyye yā kəfta
   bəl-fərn yā bəs-sīx [PAT-195]

    'As for meat by itself, he eats it
    roasted, either as meatballs [done]
    in the oven, or on a spit'

4. *lāzem ʔāxod hal-bənt, yamma*
   b-rəḍa mɛallmi yamma b-ģəṣmen
   ɛanno [AO-107]

    'I must have that girl, either with
    my master's approval or in spite of
    him'

5. *ʔaw byəšrab ḥalībon, ʔaw bisāwi*
   mənno žəbne w-zəbde [AO-63]

    'He either drinks their milk, or
    makes cheese and butter from it'

    The form *ʔəmma* or *ʔamma* is often used as part of an
'either...or...' conjunction set, in various combinations,
for contrastive emphasis. In some cases it is preceded by
yā or *w-*:

6. *ʔamma ʔana w-ʔamma ʔante*
   b-hal-bēt!

    'It's either you or I in this house!'
    (i.e. One of us has to go)

7. *ʔəmma btəṭlaɛ mən hōn ʔaw*
   bʔawwṣak!

    'Either you get out of here or I'll
    shoot you!'

8. *ʔana msāfer yā l-yōm yā ʔəmma*
   bəkra

    'I'll be leaving either today, or
    tomorrow'

'Neither...nor...' coordinations are expressed with *lā*
...*w-lā*..., literally 'not...and not...'.[1] See p. 390.
Further examples:

9. *byāklu b-ʔīdon w-mā byəstaɛʔmlu*
   lā šawke w-lā səkkīn [PAT-193]

   'They eat with their hand(s), using
   neither fork nor knife'

10. *ṭūl ḥayāto mā šāf lā haž-žabal*
    u-lā hal-barriyye [AO-117]

    'In all his life he had never seen
    either that mountain or that plain'

11. *maṣrūfo ʔalīl; lā sīnama w-lā*
    ʔahwe w-lā taman ət ʔūme
    franžiyye [PAT-195]

    'His expenses are slight; no movies,
    no coffeehouse, and no cost of West-
    ern clothes'

Clause Conjunctions

The conjunction *fa-* 'so, and' differs from *w-* in that it is only used
to conjoin sentences or clauses, and always implies significant sequence
[p. 393] or some sort of conclusion or summation:

1. *ṭ-ṭayyāra tāhet fa-thaṭṭamet*
   bəl-barriyye

   'The plane got lost and crashed in
   the desert'

2. *ʔasās ṭarīʔet ət-taɛlīm*
   btətġayyar ɛalēk fa-kəll šī
   bikūn əždīd

   'The basis of the teaching method
   will be different for you, so everything will be new'

3. *kān ɛanna ḍyūf, w-šāyīhon ḍyūf*
   mən ɛammān, fa-ʔəžu səhru
   ɛanna

   We had guests, and they had guests
   from Amman, and they [all] came and
   spent the evening with us'

4. *mā beʔder ʔəṭlaɛ la-ykūn maɛi*
   ʔbūl mən žāmɛa ɛrəft kīf;
   fa-maɛi, ʔəžāni ʔbūl mən
   žāməɛtēn

   'I wouldn't be able to leave until I
   had acceptance from a university, you
   see; and I have; I've got acceptance
   from two universities'

lāken and *bass* 'but':

5. *maḥmūd byəʔrabo la-ḥsēn,*
   lāken ʔərbe šwayye bɛīde

   'Mahmoud is related to Hussein, but
   it's a rather distant relationship'

6. *waḷḷa ʔana bḥəbb əl-fətuwwe*
   lāken bəddi rūḥ ɛas-sinama

   'I do like the Youth Club but I want
   to go to the movies'

---

[1] These coordinations are not exactly polysyndetic, since *lā* is a negative
particle, not a conjunction. The fact that the leading term has *lā* rather
than *mā* or *mū*, however, does constitute a mark of coordination.

7. *kənt bəddi ʔəʔrā-li šwayye*
   lāken maɛlēš, mənfəzz bakkīr
   bukra

'I was going to do some reading, but never mind, we'll get up early tomorrow'

8. *taɛlīqo ɛal-ʔaxbār kān məxṭḍṣar*
   lāken wāḍeḥ

'His commentary on the news was brief but clear'

9. *ballašt ᵊs-səne, bass b-ᵊšbāṭ*
   ᵊž-žāye bxalleṣ

'I've started the year, but next February I'll finish'

10. *ʔana baɛᵊrfo mn ᵊš-šām*
    bəl-madrase, bass kān faṣɛūn
    ᵊẓġīr

'I know him from Damascus at school, but he was just a little kid'

11. *bəddha xams ᵊsnīn, bass xams*
    ᵊsnīn madrasiyye..., fa-badawwmu
    ʔarbaɛ ᵊsnīn bass ᵊbtəntᵊʔel
    la-xams ᵊṣfūf, ɛrəft kīf

'It takes five years, but five school years...; so they stay four years but you go though five classes, you see'

Asyndetic Coordinations

Certain kinds of terms are often coordinated without a conjunction. Consecutive numerals (including nouns in the dual), for instance, are commonly juxtaposed in the sense '...or...':

1. *š-žamāɛa kəllhon ṣar-lon ʔarbaɛ*
   xams ᵊsnīn, w-mū zalame zalamtēn,
   kān fī xams sətt ālāf zalame
   ʔāɛdīn mən kəll nawāḥi ʔamērka

'The whole group had been [here] four or five years, and it wasn't just one or two people; there were five or six thousand people present from all parts of America'

2. *baɛdēn bəddi ʔəržaɛ ləš-šām*
   ʔəʔɛəd-li šahrēn tlāte

'Then I expect to go back to Damascus to stay two or three months'

3. *d-doktōr ʔāl lāzem nəstanna*
   tlāta rbaɛt iyyām [DA-217]

'The doctor said we'd have to wait three or four days'

Note in ex. 3 the special form *tlāta rbaɛ* (instead of *tlāte ʔarbaɛ*)

Adjectives and nouns are often coordinated asyndetically in sentences like the following:

4. *mā btəfreʔ maɛi bēḍa sōda*

'I don't care whether it's black or white'

5. *ʔalla yərḥǎma ḥayye mayyte*

'God have mercy on her, alive or dead'

6. *hal-ʔakle mā baɛref šū nāʔᵊṣa,*
   məlᵊḥ fəlfol, mā baɛref

'I don't know what it is this food lacks; salt? pepper? I don't know'

As in English, attributive adjectives [p.502] are coordinated asyndetically in the sense '...and...' more often than not: *bənt laṭīfe ḥelwe* 'a nice pretty girl' (for *bənt laṭīfe w-ḥelwe*). The *w-* is kept, however, if the adjectives apply <u>distributively</u> — contrastively to different instances of something referred to by a plural or collective: *mənšaʔāt Ɛaskariyye w-ṣināɛiyye* 'military and industrial installations', *samak ʔabyaḍ u-ʔaḥmar u-ʔazraʔ u-ʔaṣfar* [AO-117] 'white, red, blue, and yellow fish'.

Note also the set phrase *ʔaṭraš ʔaxras* 'deaf and dumb, deaf-mute'.

Verbal clauses with the same subject-referent are often conjoined asyndetically in the sense of 'and', but such clauses are usually in significant sequence [p.393] and may often be interpreted as complemental:

7. *ḥākā kamm kəlme xallā yəstəḥi*
   'He said a few words to him and embarrassed him'

8. *staḥkamto b-ḍarbe xalaɛt-əllo nīɛo*
   'I aimed a blow at him and loosened his jaw for him'

9. *tfaḍḍalu ya šamāɛa kəll wāḥed imədd ʔīdo yətsallā-lo šwayy*
   'Come on, folks, everybody help himself and have a good time'

10. *l-ʔkbīr hallaʔ mawžūd bi-ʔamērka biɛāwen ʔabū* [DA-75]
    'The eldest is now in America and helps his father'

11. *w-ʔbtəržaɛ Ɛənd ʔṣ-ṣəbʔḥ btənfox Ɛala wəššo, bətrawweḥ Ɛanno l-banž* [AO-118]
    'And she comes back in the morning and blows on his face, and drives the anesthetic away from him'

This kind of construction is particularly common when the first clause has a translocative verb [p.274]:

12. *bəmroʔ bāxdak mn ʔl-ʔotēl s-sāɛa xamse w-nəṣṣ* [DA-249]
    'I'll come back and pick you at the hotel at half past five'

13. *ʔante ʔūm la-taxtak strəḥ-lak šwayye* [DA-217]
    'You go on up to bed and rest a while'

14. *bəkra bəži bətžadda Ɛandek*
    'Tomorrow I'll come and have lunch with you'

15. *rāyeḥ bžəb-lak yāha* [AO-115]
    'I'll go and get her for you'

16. *žāye bəddo yāha ṭṭarreḥ ḥāla*
    'He comes along and wants her to have an abortion'

17. *byəržaɛ Ɛal-bēt biɛāyed Ɛalēna w-byəfṭar maɛna* [DA-300]
    'He'll come back home and wish us holiday greetings and break his fast with us'

The *w*- in ex. 17 links *biɛāyed ɛalēna* with *byəfṭar maɛna,* while this coordination is linked asyndetically as a whole with *byərǧaɛ ɛal-bēt.*

Asyndetically linked phrases and words:

18. *məṭli məṭlak mā baɛref, bass*   'I don't know any more than you do,
    ʔalḷa kbīr mā byənsa ḥada   but God is great and forgets no one'
    [DA-243]

19. *s-samakāt ṣāru sūd sūd* [AO-117]   'The fish became very black' (Cf.
                                         p. 394, ex. 23-26).

20. *zəɛel ktīr ᵊktīr* [AO-115]   'He got very, very angry' (Cf. *zəɛel
                                         ʔaktar u-ʔaktar* [AO-115])

Miscellaneous further examples of asyndetic coordination:

21. *ʔannaɛto ktīr, mā ʔtanaɛ*   'I did all I could to persuade him,
    [Bart. 685]   but he wouldn't be persuaded'

22. *maɛʔūl ʔəbʔa hōn, maɛʔūl mā*   'It would be reasonable for me to
    ʔəbʔa   stay here, but also reasonable for
                                         me _not_ to stay'

23. *mā taɛmel ḥarake bʔawweṣ!*   'Don't make a move or I'll shoot!'

24. *šlōnkon ya ṣabāya ya šabāb?*   'How are you, young ladies and
                                         gentlemen?'

25. *hal-bərnāmeǧ biwarǧi...kīf*   'This program shows...how they should
    lāzem yətṣarrfu, kīf lāzem   act, how they should manage their com-
    idīru šərkəthon, kīf lāzem   panies, and how they should treat
    iɛāmlu mwaẓẓafīnhon w-iḥassnu   their employees and improve their
    ʔawḍāɛhon   conditions'

CHAPTER 16: PREDICATION AND EXTRAPOSITION

Predication — defined in Chapter 15 [p.379] — is the
basic clause-forming construction. The constituents of a
predication are the SUBJECT and the PREDICATE. The subject, however, is commonly suppressed, especially in verbal predications, so that many predications consist of a
predicate alone: *bɒtrūḥ ɛal-bēt?* 'Are you going home?'
(for *ʔɒnte bɒtrūḥ ɛal-bēt?*), *rāḥ išūfak* 'He went to see
you' (for e.g. *ʔaxūk rāḥ išūfak* 'Your brother went to see
you').[1]

The relationship of subject and predicate is expressed mainly by number/
gender agreement [p.420]. The predicate (if inflectible for number/gender)
usually agrees with the subject.

The word order of subject and predicate varies, depending partly on what
the subject and predicate consist of, and partly on emphasis, stylistic considerations, etc.

---

[1] The subject-affix of a verb [p.175] is sometimes analyzed as a pronoun,
and as subject of the verbal clause. Since it is an obligatory part of
the verb, however — since it must be present whether or not a syntactic
subject is also present — it is in fact a genuine inflectional affix and
cannot be counted as a pronoun or a subject-surrogate in the full sense of
these terms. (In this respect subject-affixes differ fundamentally from
the complemental pronoun suffixes [p.539], which generally occur in place
of — not in addition to — a syntactical complement. [But see p.434].)
Traditional Arabic grammar makes a fundamental distinction between the
construction of a verbal clause (*ǧumla fiɛliyya*) and that of a nominal
clause (*ǧumla ʔismiyya*). The subject (*al-fāɛil* "the agent") of a verbal
clause is treated in effect as another kind of complement, since it normally follows — or may follow — the verb (while preceding the object or
other complements) and since a verb often shows no agreement with a following indefinite subject [421].
A nominal (or a non-verbal) clause, on the other hand, is traditionally
analyzed in terms of the topic-comment construction (*al-mubtada? wal-xabar*),
since the subject normally precedes the predicate. The type of topic-comment construction here called 'extraposition' [p.431] has an anaphoric pronoun in the comment whose antecedent is the topic; note that when verbal
subject-affixes are considered pronouns, then the subject of a following
verbal predicate also qualifies as an extrapositive topic, since it is antecedent to the subject "pronoun" in the verb.

Arabic predications are more diverse (both in constituency and in word order) than predications in English. The main differences are 1.) that in Arabic the subject may be suppressed in many cases where English requires a subject pronoun; 2.) that the Arabic subject in many cases follows the predicate — or a part of the predicate — where in English it generally must come first; 3.) that in Arabic the predicate may consist of a prepositional, adjectival, or nominal phrase as well as a verbal phrase, while in English it is always verbal.

Non-Verbal Predications

An indefinite [p.494] nominal, adjectival, or prepositional predicate is used to depict a present (or permanent) state or characteristic of the subject referent. The subject ordinarily comes first (but see pp. 414, 419) and is usually definite. In the English translations the predicate (or in questions, the subject) is usually introduced by 'is', 'are', or 'am'.

Prepositional Predicates:

1. *ʔabūk bəl-bēt wəlla barra?* 'Is your father in the house, or outside?' (On "free" prepositions, see p. 485.)

2. *bēto ḥadd ᵊs-sīnama* 'His house is next to the movie theater'

3. *l-ᵊblād taḥt ᵊl-ḥəkm ᵊl-ɛərfi* 'The country is under martial law'

4. *sayyāra halla? barrāt ʔəmkānītna bəl-marra* 'A car just now is altogether beyond our means' (Indefinite subject.)

5. *ʔana bēn ᵊl-ʔayādi* [DA-197] 'I'm at your service' (lit. "I'm between the hands")

6. *ḥkāyti maɛak mətl ᵊhkāyet malek ᵊl-yūnān maɛ ᵊl-ḥakīm rayyān* [AO-116] 'My experience (lit. 'my story') with you is like the story of the king of Greece with the doctor Rayyan'

7. *hal-ᵊktāb tabaɛ ṣāḥbi* 'This book belongs to my friend' [p. 489]

8. *ṭūl ɛəmra ʔaḷḷa fōʔ u-bēta taḥᵊt* 'All her life [her only concern has been that] God is above and her house is below' (i.e. She's a homebody)

Most cases in which a prepositional predicate precedes its subject come under the heading of 'quasi-verbal predications', e.g. *ɛanna ḍyūf* 'We have guests', lit. "With us (Fr. chez nous) are guests". See p. 413. To translate an English sentence with an indefinite subject such as 'A plate is on the table' or 'On the table is a plate', the impersonal predicator *fī* 'there is' [p. 415] is used: *fī ṣaḥ²n ɛaṭ-ṭāwle* or *ɛaṭ-ṭāwle fī ṣaḥ²n* 'There is a plate ...', etc.

Note, however: *taḥt ²īdi wāḥde mā fī mənha* [DA-80A] 'I have one(f.) that can't be beat' (lit. "Under my hand is one of which there are none"). The idiomatic sense of *taḥt ²īdi* is similar to that of the quasi-verbal *ɛandi, maɛi*, etc.; perhaps for that reason it is also assimilated to them syntactically.

Note also: *mən ²alɛan ²xṣālo t-taraddod* 'One of his worst qualities is indecision', which has a prepositional predicate preceding a definite subject. In this case the phrase *mən ²alɛan ²xṣālo* ("of the worst of his qualities") functions like a nominal phrase, and the sentence is similar to an equational predication [p. 405] (cf. *²alɛan ²xṣālo, t-taraddod* 'His worst quality is indecision'), in which the first term is interpreted as subject and *t-taraddod,* as predicate.

> On the predicative use of the prepositional-phrase substitutes *hōn* 'here', *hnīk* 'there', *wēn* 'where', etc., see Ch. 21.

Adjectival Predicates:

9. *maṣrūfo ²alīl*   'His expenses are slight'

10. *l-maɛkarōna xafīfe ɛal-məɛde*   'Macaroni is easy on the stomach'

11. *xzāntak matrūse tar²s*   'Your wardrobe is chock full' (pass. participle with paronymous complement [p. 442])

12. *manẓar ²l-baḥ²r ktīr ḥəlu* [PVA-20]   'The view of the sea is very beautiful'

13. *²əntu mabṣūṭīn?*   'Are you(pl.) well?'

14. *ḥāret ²l-²aslām dayy²a ktīr, lāken ²andaf mən ḥāret ²n-naṣāra* [Bg. I.1]   'The Muslim quarter is quite crowded but is cleaner than the Christian quarter'

15. *hēkal māmūt maɛrūḍ bəl-matḥaf*   'The skeleton of a mammoth is on exhibit in the museum' (Note that the Arabic subject is indefinite.)

Nominal Predicates:

16. *²axū ḥallā², ²əsmo ḥasan*   'His brother is a barber; his name is Hassan' (*ḥasan* is definite; see p. 405.)

17. *bēt ²l-xūri ɛēle kbīre* [SAL-65]   'The Khourys are a large family'

18. *hāda maktūb mn ᵊš-šarke*   'This is a letter from the company'

19. *mašrūɛi ʔastaxrāž ᵊzyūt*   'My plan is [for the] extraction of
    nabātiyye [DA-296]   vegetable oils'

20. *d-doktōr xayyāṭ doktōr šāṭer*   'Dr. Khayat is a good doctor'
    [DA-202]

21. *žāmaɛt* Indiana *žāmɛa ktīr halu*   'Indiana University is a very pretty
                                              place' (lit. '...a very pretty
                                              university')

22. *d-danye ɛažʔa ktīr* [DA-301]   'It's very crowded (outside)' (lit.
                                              "The world is much a crowd")

23. *l-ʔaslām fal-balad ʔasmēn,*   'The Muslims in the town are [in]
    sanniyye w-ɛalawiyye [PAT-179]   two parts: Sunnis and Alawis'

24. *wan-naṣāra šiyaɛ ᵊktīre* [Bg.I.1]   'And the Christians are [of] many
                                              sects'

Examples 23 and 24 illustrate a use of nominal predicates
that is unlike English; the predicate designates those things
which the subject-referent is composed of or divided into.

Arabic lacks the distinction sometimes made in English
between **CLASSIFICATORY** and **DEFINITIONAL** predications by
changing the article of the subject: 'The eagle is a large
bird' (classificatory) vs. 'An eagle is a large bird' (definitional). In Arabic the subject takes the article prefix
in either case: *n-nasᵊr ṭēr ᵊkbīr*. Similarly:

25. *l-ʔansān haywān nāṭeq*   'Man is a rational animal'

26. *l-mūs sakkīn ᵊbtatsakkar*   'A jackknife is knife that can be
                                              closed'

A nominal predicate may be definite. In that case, the predication is usually EQUATIONAL, i.e. the subject and predicate are interchangeable and refer to the same thing[1]:

27. *ʔabūhon Ɛādel / Ɛādel ʔabūhon* 'Their father is Adel' / 'Adel is their father'

28. *raʔīs ᵊl-wazāra, raʔs ᵊl-ḥukūme l-ḥaqīqi / raʔs ᵊl-ḥukūme l-ḥaqīqi, raʔīs ᵊl-wazāra* 'The prime minister is the actual head of the government'/ 'The actual head of the government is the prime minister'

> Sentences like those in ex. 28 are usually pronounced with a considerable prosodic break between the subject and the predicate: the end of the subject is drawled, usually with a rising intonation, and there is often a pause before the beginning of the predicate. (Alternatively, the predication may be transformed by extraposition: *raʔīs ᵊl-wazāra huwwe raʔs ᵊl-ḥukūme l-ḥaqīqi* "The prime minister, he is...". See p. 434.) Similarly:

29. *l-ʔāḍi, yəlli byəḥkom / yəlli byəḥkom, l-ʔāḍi* 'The judge is the one who makes the decision' / 'The one who makes the decision is the judge'

> Or better: *l-ʔāḍi huwwe lli byəḥkom / yəlli byəḥkom, huwwe l-ʔāḍi.*

30. *dāʔiman maƐbūdak ᵊl-maṣrūf wəl-maṣāri* 'All you ever care about is expenses and money' (lit. "Always your idol is...")

---

[1] A predication that is equational in the strictest sense cannot be said to have a subject and a predicate; the two terms are grammatically (as well as referentially) equivalent. The word order in a nominal predication depends entirely upon definiteness (or pronominalization, see below), hence when both terms are definite the word order is irrelevant.

Actually, however, these predications are rarely if ever equational in the strictest sense. That is to say, the permutation of terms usually carries with it a change of meaning, such that while *abūhon ʔaḥmad* is felt to be a statement about their father, *ʔaḥmad ʔabūhon* is a statement about Ahmed. We continue to speak, therefore, of the leading term as 'subject' and the following term as 'predicate' even while calling the predication 'equational'.

The term 'equational sentence' has sometimes been used in Arabic grammar more broadly, to denote all non-verbal predications. Though this may seem a gratuitous abuse of the concept of 'equation', it might also be argued (rightly or wrongly) that 'equational predication' in the narrow sense is merely a semantic category for Arabic, while in the broader sense it is formal.

Elatives and ordinals in construct with an indefinite term [p.473] may
also enter into an equational predication. That is to say, they may occur
either as following term or as leading term in a predication where the
other term is definite (even though they are indefinite by the criterion of
agreement [494]):

31. *Eali ʔaḥsan laεεīb bəl-farīʔ* /   'Ali is the best player on the team'/
    ʔaḥsan laεεīb bəl-farīʔ, Eali   The best player on the team is Ali'

32. *š-šokolāṭa ʔaṭyab šī Eandi* /   'Chocolate is my favorite flavor'
    ʔaṭyab šī Eandi š-šokolāṭa   (lit. "Chocolate is the tastiest
                                             thing with me") / 'My favorite flavor
                                             is chocolate'

33. *ʔəbni tālet wāḥed bəṣ-ṣaff* /   'My son is the third one in the line'
    tālet wāḥed bəṣ-ṣaff, ʔəbni   / 'The third one in the line is my
                                             son'

> Cardinal numerals, likewise, count as definite terms in
> arithmetical statements such as *tlāte w-sətte təsEa* 'Three
> and six is nine'.

> A statement to the effect that X is the name of Y is
> grammatically an equational predication (though of course
> the two terms do not refer to the same thing): *ʔəsmo ḥasan/
> ḥasan ʔəsmo* 'His name is Hassan'/'Hassan is his name':

34. *ʔəsᵊm blādna ž-žamhūriyye*   'The name of our country is "The
    l-ləbnāniyye [SAL-152] /   Lebanese Republic"'/'"The Lebanese
    ž-žamhūriyye l-ləbnāniyye   Republic" is the name of our country'
    ʔəsᵊm blādna

> There are some nominal predications in which both terms
> are definite, but which are nevertheless classificatory, not
> equational: *tnēnna wlād ᵊṣ-ṣaḥra* [SAL-138] 'We are both sons
> of the desert'. The predicate *wlād ᵊṣ-ṣaḥra* is a classifi-
> catory construct [p.458], depicting something characteristic
> of the subject-referent, not something identical with it.
> The subject and predicate therefore cannot be interchanged.
> Similarly, *ḥasan ṣāḥbi* 'Hassan is my friend' does not nec-
> essarily mean that he is my only friend; therefore it is not
> always permutable to *ṣāḥbi ḥasan* 'My friend is Hassan'.

The most common type of equational predication is that in which the
subject is a personal or demonstrative pronoun [pp.539,552]:   *hāda ʔabūhon*
'That's their father', *huwwe r-raʔīs* 'He's the boss', *hāda huwwe* 'That's
him' A pronominal predicate is rarely used with a definite nominal subject, however (as in *ʔabūhon, hāda* 'Their father is that one'); the two terms
are therefore not generally interchangeable.

35. *hayy ʔəxti ẓ-ẓ̌ġīre*   'That's my little sister'

36. *hadōl ᵊl-kətᵊb halli ṭalabton?*   'Are these the books you ordered?'

37. *huwwe raʔīs ʔl-baladiyye*   'He's the mayor'

38. *hāda ʔabǧaḍ šī ɛandi*   'That's what I dislike most of all'

39. *ʔana ʔawwal wāḥed wṣəlṭ*   'I was the first to arrive' (lit. "I am the first one that arrived")

40. *hādi tālet waẓīfe ʔaxadha*   'This is the third job he's had'
    [EA-181]

    The pronoun subject usually appears to agree with the predicate in number/gender; actually this is not grammatical agreement but merely a consequence of the fact that the two terms have the same referent. (Predicates agree with subjects, not vice-versa [p.420].) When there is a conflict between the number/gender of the predicate and the "natural" number and gender of the pronoun's referent, then the natural number/gender usually prevails:

41. *ʔanti z-zalame w-ʔana l-ɛarūs*   'You(f.) are the man and I'm your
    ʔəlek [AO-115]   bride' (as in a masquerade)

Verbal Predications

    The placement of the subject in verbal predications depends on a number of different factors, and is to a considerable extent optional.

    All the statements about word order in these sections apply only to "normal" or basic word order; for the predicate-subject inversion, see p. 419.

    If the subject is indefinite, it usually follows the verb: *šāfha raǧǧāl* 'A man saw her'. If it is definite, it may generally either precede or follow: *r-raǧǧāl šāfha / šāfha r-raǧǧāl* 'The man saw her'. If the verb has complements (other than pronoun complements), a post-verbal subject ordinarily precedes them: *šāf ʔr-raǧǧāl ʔl-bənt* 'The man saw the girl'.

    Examples, indefinite subject following verb (subject underscored):

1. *nəzel zalame ǧarīb ɛənd wāḥed*   'A strange man came to stay with one
   mən ʔahāli d-dēɛa [AO-108]   of the villagers'

2. *ʔəǧāni ʔbūl mən ǧāməɛtēn*   'I was accepted by two universities'
        (lit. "Came to me acceptance from...")

3. *daxal fallāḥ mən dawāhi l-ʔəds*   'A peasant from the outskirts of
   bəl-ɛaskariyye [AO-91]   Jerusalem joined the army'

4. *lā tənzel mən ɛar-raṣīf,*   'Don't get off the sidewalk; a car
   btədɛasak sayyāra   will run over you'

5. *mā ṣəfi ǧēr bākētēn bəl-bēt*   'There are not but two packs left
   <u>   </u>   in the house'

The subject commonly follows a complemental preposition
with pronoun suffix:

6. *mā rāḥ ɛalēk šī*   'You haven't missed anything' (lit.
                     <u> </u>   "There has not gone by you a thing")

7. *wəṣəlni mənha ʔəɛlām ᵊmbāreḥ*   'I got a note from her yesterday'
                   <u>   </u>   (lit. "Reached me from her a note
                                            yesterday")

8. *nša ʔʔ ᵊl-ḥēt w-ṭəleɛ mənno ɛabd*   'The wall opened up and out of it
   ʔaswad byəšbah ᵊt-tōr [AO-117]   came a black slave who looked like a
   <u>   </u>   bull'

Examples, definite subject following verb:

9. *nṣarafu wlād ᵊl-madrase*   'The children have gotten out of
            <u>   </u>   school' (lit. "The school children
                                            have been let out")

10. *bətǧīb ᵊš-šams ᵊs-sāɛa xamse*   'The sun sets at approximately five
    taʔrīban [AO-71]   <u>   </u>   o'clock'

11. *byəltdʔa ǧaraḍna bi-hal-maxzan*   'What we need can be found in this
    [DA-252]   <u>   </u>   store'

12. *ḥamlət-li marti š-šarāb mətl*   'My wife brought me the drink as
    ᵊl-ɛāde [AO-118] <u>   </u>   usual'

13. *labbaset ᵊl-bənt təmsāl*   'The girl dressed the candy statue
    ᵊl-ḥalāwe rōb ᵊl-ɛərs [AO-114]   in the wedding gown'
             <u>   </u>

14. *waḷḷa byətrōḥan ʔalbi*   'It certainly does my heart good to
    b-ḥakyo   <u>   </u>   hear him talk' (lit. "By God my heart
                                            is revived by his talk")

15. *mā ɛād ᵊl-wāḥed yəsmaɛ ʔaxbār*   'One no longer hears the news from
    balado   <u>   </u>   his home town' (The subject precedes
                                            the complemental verb *yəsmaɛ* but fol-
                                            lows the "linking" verb *ɛād*.)

Examples, definite subject preceding verb:

16. <u>*d-doktōr waddā*</u> *dəǧri*   'The doctor took him directly to the
    ɛal-məstašfa [DA-202]   hospital'

17. *halla ʔ* <u>*sayyārt ᵊš-šərke*</u>   'The company car will take us there
    bətwaṣṣəlna [DA-251]   now'

18. *bāba rāḥ iṣalli ṣalāt ᵊl-Ɛīd*   'Daddy has gone to perform the holi-
   [DA-298]   day prayer'

19. *bər-rabīƐ kəll ᵊl-bəzᵊr byəṭlaƐ*   'In the spring all the seeds sprout
   mn ᵊl-ᵊarḍ [AO-59]   from the ground'

20. *l-fallāḥ byəḥṣədhon bəl-manžal*   'The farmer harvests them with a
   b-ᵊawwal ᵊṣ-ṣēf [AO-59]   scythe early in the summer'

21. *ᵊahli w-ᵊahlo byaƐᵊrfu baƐḍon*   'My family and his are acquainted
                                        with one another'

22. *hallaᵊ ᵊabi bikūn ᵊāƐed la-ḥālo*   'Now my father will be all by himself'

A verb in the simple imperfect functioning adjectivally [p.328], or usually in any characterizing sense, is like a non-verbal predicate; i.e. it is normally only preceded, not followed, by a definite subject:

23. *haš-šabb byəštə́ǵel*   'That young man (really) works' (=
                                        haš-šabb šaǵǵīl 'That young man's a
                                        good worker')

24. *šəǵlo byətmallal*   'His work is boring' (= *šəǵlo mmalle*)

25. *hal-manžar mā byəntdsa*   'That sight is unforgetable'

26. *r-rəžžāl byəƐᵊžbak* [EA-158]   'You'd like the man' (i.e. 'The man
                                        is likeable', lit. "The man would
                                        please you")

27. *walḷāh sayyədna byəswa təᵊlo*   'Our master is certainly a good man'
   [AO-118]   (lit. "By God, our master is worth
                                        his weight")

28. *l-walad byəšbah ᵊabū*   'The boy resembles his father'

29. *Ɛala kəll ḥāl ᵊz-zāyde mā*   'Anyway, appendicitis isn't serious'
   bəthəmm [DA-217]   (lit. "...doesn't matter")

Under certain conditions, the subject usually precedes the verb regardless whether it is definite or not. A long subject phrase, for instance, is usually not inserted between a verb and its complements. It may follow pronominalized complements, as in ex. 8 above, but if there are non-pronominal complements, the subject normally comes before the verb:

30. *ḥayyaḷḷa rādyo mōže ᵊaṣīre*   'Any short wave radio can get Cairo
   bižtb ᵊl-qāhira bi-kəll ᵊshūle   quite easily'

31. *w-lā dawa mn ᵊl-ᵊədᵊwye halli*   'None of the medicines that the doc-
   waṣafū-lo yā l-ḥəkama mā naḥḥaf   tors prescribed for him reduced the
   ᵊl-malek [AO-95]   king['s weight]'

32. *ɛīd l-ᵊkbīr ʔaw ɛīd ᵊl-ʔaḍḥa*   'Greater Bairam or the Feast of Im-
    byūʔaɛ bi-ɛašara zᵊl-ḥᵊžže   molation falls on the tenth of Dhu'l
    [DA-302]   Hijjah'

    This constraint is not a hard and fast rule. In narra-
tive style, particularly, there are exceptions as in example
3, above.

    A subject phrase consisting of only two words often counts
as a "long subject phrase", particularly if the complement
consists of a single word:

33. *lazʔa bārde bᵊtxaffef ᵊl-wažaɛ*   'A cold compress will reduce the pain'

34. *wᵊl-yōm ǧrūf saɛīde žamɛᵊtna*   'And today happy circumstances have
    sawa [SAL-60]   brought us together'

    An indefinite subject may also be put first for emphasis:

35. *žamɛ ᵊkbīr ᵊštamaɛ bᵊs-sāḥa*   'A large crowd gathered in the plaza'

36. *b-hadāk ᵊl-waʔt šī ʔalīl kān*   'At that time very little was known
    maɛrūf ɛan bawāɛso l-ḥaʔīʔiyye   about his real motives'

37. *ṭᵊmbor bikaffi la-naʔlet ᵊǧrāḍak*   'A cart will suffice for moving your
     things'

38. *mīt sᵊne maḍet w-mā ḥada*   'A thousand years passed and no one
    nažžāni [AO-116]   let me out' (Note also that *ḥada*
     ordinarily precedes the verb.)

39. *kān ᵊb-balad ʔᵊxtēn, l-wāḥde*   'There were in a certain town two sis-
    ɛāʔle wᵊt-tānye mɛᵊžže; šabbēn   ters, one well-behaved and the other
    rādu yᵊtšawwazūhon [AO-111]   intolerable; two young men wanted to
     marry them'[1]

---

[1] In example 39 considerations of narrative style determine the placement
of the subjects; *šabbēn* comes before its verb perhaps for emphasis ("there
were a certain town two young men who...") or perhaps to counterbalance
the structure of the first sentence. In the first sentence the subject
ʔᵊxtēn follows the complement *b-balad* (a characteristically narrative construction, cf. the English translation), especially in order not to be
separated from the following coordinated clauses, to whose subjects it is
the antecedent. The coordination *l-wāḥde ɛāʔle wᵊt-tānye mɛᵊžže* is
actually a separate sentence, but its referential dependence on the antecedent *ʔᵊxtēn* gives it much the force of an attributive clause.

In subordinate clauses, certain conjunctions tend to be followed mostly by verbs; verb-subject word order is favored in such clauses. The verb-favoring conjunctions include the particle *ma* (as in *baɛᵊd ma* 'after', etc.), *ʔiza, law, ʔᵊn* 'if', and to a lesser extent *lamma, waʔt*, etc. 'when', and *ḥatta*, etc. 'until, in order that'. As a conjunction, the particle *la-* 'in order that, until' can <u>only</u> be followed by a verb:

40. *kīf bᵊddi ʔaɛmel la-yᵊġfor ʔaḷḷa xaṭiyyāti?* [AO-99]

'What should I do in order that God will forgive my sins?'

41. *bᵊddak tᵊstaɛžel ʔabᵊl ma yṭᵊnn ᵊž-žaraṣ*

'You'd better hurry before the bell rings'

42. *ṭ-ṭabīx lāzem yᵊstᵊwi mᵊtᵊl ma dfīt ʔana lamma kᵊnt bᵊg-ġalṭ ɛala rās ᵊž-žabal* [AO-88]

'The food must get done the same way I got warm when I was naked on top of the mountain'

43. *nṭᵊġer lamma byᵊržaɛ ʔabūha mn ᵊl-ḥažž* [AO-114]

'Wait till (when) her father returns from the Pilgrimage'

44. *w-lamma žāb ᵊl-xādem hal-ᵊġrād, ṭabxᵊthon ᵊl-bᵊnt ᵊb-ḥalle kbīre* [AO-114]

'And when the servant brought those things, the girl cooked them in a large pot'

45. *ḍall mᵊdde ṭawīle w-mā sāfar, ḥatta tdāyaʔ l-ᵊmɛazzem mᵊnno* [AO-108]

'He stayed a long time and didn't leave, until the host got fed up with him'

46. *mā rᵊḍyet taɛmel ᵊl-ɛᵊrs ʔᵊlla ʔiza ḥᵊḍru lēlātha ʔarbɛīn bᵊnt* [AO-113]

'She wouldn't agree to go through with the wedding unless forty girls would attend that night'

47. *w-ḥallaʔ bᵊtšūf ʔaddēš byᵊfraḥu waʔt ᵊbyᵊži l-laḥḥām* [DA-299]

'And now you'll see how happy they are when the butcher comes'

The subject of an attributive clause [p. 495] also generally comes after the verb (except for anaphoric pronouns [p. 497]):

48. *ɛaṭᵊto lᵊl-mara halli baɛatha ɛali z-zēbaʔ* [AO-114]

'She gave it to the woman Ali Quicksilver had sent'

Examples of pre-verbal subject after *lamma, ḥatta,* and *ma:*

49. *lamma lūṭ ʔaxṭa, rāḥ laɛᵊnd ɛammo brāhīm* [AO-88]

'When Lot sinned, he went to his uncle Abraham'

50. *w-naṭar ḥatta l-ʔaḍiyye ntaset* [AO-88]

'And he waited until the matter was forgotten'

51. *baɛᵊd ma l-kᵊll ᵊtɛaššu, ʔaɛlan ᵊs-sᵊlṭān ʔᵊbtidāʔ l-ᵊmžādale* [EA-249]

'After everyone had eaten, the sultan announced the beginning of the debate'

After the complemental conjunction *ʔənno* [p.449], the subject usually precedes the verb:

52. *drīt ʔanno ʔaxi māt bəž̆-ž̆ihād*   'I've learned that my brother died
    [AO-118]   in the holy war'

53. *w-ᵊftakar ʔanno d̲-d̲ēf*   'And he thought that in this way the
    b-haṭ-ṭarī̆ʔa yamken yəfham   guest might get the point and leave'
    w-isāfer [AO-108]

Quasi-Verbal Predications

The noun stem *bədd-* is used with pronoun suffixes to form a verb-like predicator meaning 'to want, require, intend, be going to':

bəddo	'he wants, etc.'	*bədd(h)a*	'she wants, etc.'
bəddak	'you(m.)want, etc.'	*bədd(h)on*	'they want, etc.'
bəddek	'you(f.)want, etc.'	*bəddkon*	'you(pl.)want, etc.'
bəddi	'I want, etc.'	*bəddna*	'we want, etc.'

The pronoun suffixes function as subject-affixes, agreeing with the subject (if any), which usually comes first: *l-walad bəddo ʔalam* 'The boy wants a pencil'. The complement may be either nominal (as *ʔalam*, above) or verbal: *bəddo yrūḥ* 'He wants to go'. The verbal complement may be suppressed: *mā bəddo* 'He doesn't want to'; the nominal complement may be pronominalized on the stem *yā-*: *mā bəddo yāha* 'He doesn't want it(f.)'.

> *bəddo*, then, is syntactically verbal in almost every respect for most speakers (but see ex. 8, below), though in some parts of Greater Syria it enters certain constructions as a noun: *bəddi hiyye* 'I want it(f.)' [Bart. 31], *mā baʔa bədd* 'There's no more need (for it)' [ibid.]. If *bəddo* is construed as a noun, then *bəddo ʔalam* is a nominal predication meaning literally 'His requirement is a pencil', and *l-walad bəddo ʔalam* has to be interpreted as an extraposition [431] "The boy, his requirement is a pencil". These interpretations do not apply, however, insofar as pronominalizations are in the complemental form: *bəddo yā* 'He wants it' rather than the subject (or predicate) form: *bəddo huwwe*.

Examples of the use of *bəddo*:

1. *bəddi ʔaržać ləš̆-š̆ām*   'I want (or intend) to go back to
                                        Damascus'

2. *ʔaxi l-ᵊkbīr bəddo yətž̆awwaz*   'My older brother wants (or is going
    [AO-55]   to) get married'

3. *zalamtēn bəddhon Ɛal-ʔaʔalli*   'Two men(would)need at least two
   žəmƐa la-yəhᵊṣdu ḥaʔlet   weeks to harvest that wheatfield'
   hal-ʔamᵊḥ

4. *mā bəddak yāhon?*   'Don't you want them?'

5. *ʔēmta ma bəddi, bāxod sayyāra*   'Whenever I want, I'll take a car
   w-ᵊbṣīr bəš-šām   and I'll be in Damascus'

6. *bəddna la-nəṣal šī nəṣṣ sāƐa*   'It'll take us about half an hour to
                                        get there' (lit. "We'll require...")

7. *bəddha xams ᵊsnīn, bass xams*   'It takes five years, but that's five
   ᵊsnīn madrasiyye   <u>school</u> years' (Feminine impersonal
                                        predication [p. 428])

8. *kənt bəddi ʔəʔrā-li šwayye*   'I wanted to read a little'

Note that the linking verb [p. 452] in ex. 8 is inflected
in agreement with *bəddi* (as with a verbal subjective complement [448]. This usage is optional, however; the linking verb before *bəddo* may also remain uninflected: *kān
bəddi ʔəʔrā-li šwayye*, lit. "It was my intention to read a
little"; in this respect, at least, *bəddo* may be construed
as a noun.

9. *mā bəddha l-masʔale maṭāƐem,*   'There's no question of restaurants,
   mnākol Ɛanna bəl-bēt [DA-197]   we'll eat at home' (lit. "The ques-
                                        tion doesn't require restaurants...")

Note the verb-subject word order in ex. 9: *mā bəddha
l-masʔale...*

10. *šū bəddkon yāni ʔaƐmel?*   'What do you(pl.)want me to do?'

The prepositions *Ɛand, maƐ,* and *la- (ʔəl-)* [p. 476ff] are used with pronoun suffixes to form verb-like predicators meaning approximately 'to have':
Ɛando Ɛēle 'He has a family' (lit. "With him [Fr. chez lui] is a family");
maƐak maṣāri? 'Have you any money?' (lit. "Is there with you money?");
ʔəla Ɛyūn ḥəlwe ktīr 'She has beautiful eyes' (lit. "There are to her, beautiful eyes").

These prepositional predicators are less thoroughly verb-like than *bəddo*
in two main respects:

1.) The nominal term that follows them may usually be suppressed (like
a subject [p. 418]) rather than pronominalized on the stem *yā-* (like an object [438]): *maƐi* 'I have it' or 'I have some', etc. In the case of *Ɛando,*
however, the following term may either be suppressed or pronominalized:
Ɛandi 'I have some, I have it', or *Ɛandi yā* 'I have it'.

2.) The prepositions are sometimes used in the same sense and same construction except with a noun rather than with a pronoun suffix: *la-ʔəmmi
ʔəxwe ktīre* [AO-43] 'My mother has many brothers and sisters' (lit. "To my

mother there are many... "). The verb-like construction is *ʔəmmi ʔəla ʔəxwe ktīre*, in which the pronoun suffix of *ʔəla* is like a verbal subject-affix, agreeing with the subject *ʔəmmi*.

The verb-like nature of these prepositional constructions, then, consists in the predominance of pronoun suffixes over nouns after the prepositions, and the fact that a nominal subject (or quasi-object) almost always <u>follows</u> the prepositional predicator, while the case of ordinary prepositional predications, the subject, which is usually definite, usually comes first. (But see p. 403.)

Secondly, the prepositional quasi-verbs are negativized with the particle *mā*, which is used before verbs, rather than with *mū*, etc., which is used with ordinary non-verbal predicates [p. 384 ff].

Examples:

11. *maɛi nəmret talifōno w-ɛənwāno*   'I have his telephone number and address'

12. *šu ʔəlak marā? bəš–šəɛ²r*   'You must have a mania for poetry'

13. *ɛādatan bikūn ɛandhon tlətt*
    ²fṣūle   'They usually have three terms' (in an academic year)

14. *kān ɛanna dyūf*   'We had guests'

Examples 13 and 14 illustrates another non-verb-like feature of the prepositional predicators: the linking verb [p. 452] remains uninflected for number/gender when complemented by *ɛando, maɛo*, etc., whereas with verbs (and optionally with *bəddo*) it is inflected to agree with the complement: *kənna nzūr* 'we used to visit', *kənna bəddna* (or *kān bəddna*) 'we wanted', but *kān ɛanna* 'we had' (<u>not</u> *"kənna ɛanna"*).

15. *mā ʔəlkon ḥa??*   'You're wrong' (lit. "There is not to you right")

16. *ṣəhrak ɛando ržāl ²l–yōm, mā*
    byə?der yəži   'Your son-in-law has some men [visiting him] today, he can't come'

17. *bass lā tənsa ʔənno ɛandkon*
    ²l–baḥ²r [DA-151]   'But don't forget that you(pl.) have the sea'

18. *maɛak ²kmālet ɛaš²r lērāt?*
    — maɛi, tfaḍḍal [DA-46]   'Have you change for ten pounds? — Yes, I have; here you are'

19. *ṭ-ṭāwle ʔəla ʔarbaɛ rəžlēn*   'The table has four legs'

20. *žəddi kan–lo tlətt ²byūt*   'My grandfather had three houses'

QUASI-VERBAL PREDICATES 415

Note, in example 20, that ʔəlo generally takes the form
of a suffix when complementing a linking verb. [p.482.]
Similarly: ʔəli žəmɛa mā šəftak 'I haven't seen you for a
week' (i.e. I've had a week of not seeing you), or ṣar-li
žəmɛa mā šəftak 'It's been a week now that I haven't seen
you' (lit. "It's become for me a week..."). The suffix
form is also commonly used with the negative mā [p.385]:
š-šawāreɛ mā-lon ʔərəṣfe 'The streets have no sidewalks'.

Three more prepositional quasi-verbs are ɛalē 'to have to, to have as a
responsibility or a debt'; fī 'to be able to' or, in impersonal predications
[p.365], 'there is, there are'; and bo 'to be the matter with' (used only
with šū or šə- 'what' and mā-...šī 'nothing'):

21. šu ɛalēk šəġəl əl-yōm? [DA-173]   'Do you have work to do today?'

22. ʔana kamān ɛaliyyi məšwār   'I have to go there too' (lit. "I
     la-hnīk [DA-248]   also, there is on me an errand to
         there")

     Note also the set phrase maɛlēš or maɛlē-ši 'never mind,
     that's all right' (→ mā ɛalē-š[ī] "There's nothing on it");
     mā ɛalēk 'never mind, it's not your responsibility'.

23. šš-bo? — mā-bo šī   'What's the matter with him (or it)?
         — Nothing'

24. mā fīhon yaɛəmlū-lo šī   'They can't do a thing for him'

25. fīni sāɛdak əb-kamm lēra?   'Can I help you with a few pounds?'

26. ḥayaḷḷa wāḥed fī yəfham   'Anybody can see through that fel-
     ḥaʔīʔet haš-šaxṣ   low' (lit. "...can understand the
         truth of that person")

27. š-šahāde fīk tāxədha b-səne   'You can get the degree in a year
     w-nəṣṣ   and a half'

     Examples of the impersonal fī 'there is, there are':

28. fī wāḥed xalaṣ w-wāḥed   'There's one who's finished and one
     ɛam-yədros   studying'

29. l-yōm mā fī šī mən hād   'Today there's none of that, thank
     l-ḥamdəlla   God'

30. mā bəɛtəʔed fī waʔət ləl-ḥādse   'I don't think there's time for [me
     yəlli baɛrəfa   to recount] the incident I know of'

31. kīf mərrūḥ ɛal-ʔaṣṣāɛ? — fī   'How shall we go to Qassaa? — There's
     l-bāṣ wət-trāmwāy wət-taksi   the bus, the streetcar, and taxis'
     [DA-45]

32. *kān fī žamāɛa ktār ᵊhnīk*   'There were a lot of people there'

33. *mā fī fīha ᵖᵊrne la—maḥrame*   'There isn't even room in it for a
                                        handkerchief' (lit. "There isn't
                                        in it a corner for...")

Example 33 illustrates the juxtaposition of the impersonal predicator *fī* and a supplemental phrase *fīha* 'in it
(f.)'. In such cases the impersonal *fī* is often elided,
thus: *mā fīha ᵖᵊrne la—maḥrame.* (See also p. 384, ex. 26.)

fī is often complemented by *ɛando, maɛo, ᵖᵊlo,* etc.:

34. *fī ᵖᵊlo muɛžabīn ᵊktīr w—fī*   'He has a lot of admirers and he has
    ᵖᵊlo nās nāqidīn ᵊktīr   a lot of critics' (lit. "There are
                                        to him...")

35. *nᵊḥna maɛlūmak halla? fī ɛanna*   'We of course now have industriali-
    taṣnīɛ bᵊš—šām   zation in Damascus' (lit. "...there
                                        is with us...")

The quasi-complement of *fī* may come first, for emphasis
(like a true subject), especially when negative:

36. *bᵊkra l—žᵊmɛa, šᵊǧᵊl mā fī*   'Tomorrow's Friday; no work!'
    [DA-199]

37. *ᵖaḥla mᵊn hēk mā fī* [DA-150]   'There's nothing prettier than that'
                                        (Cf. object-verb inversion, p. 439.)

The quasi-complement may of course be suppressed, as
in the case of the other prepositional predicators:

38. *šū fī ḥᵊlu? — l—yōm mā fī*   'What is there for dessert? — There
                                        isn't any today'

The construction with question-word and complement as
in *šū fī ḥᵊlu* is treated on p. 569.

Participial Predicates. Participles are like verbs and unlike ordinary adjectives, in that the subject of a participial predicate often follows it. (Subject underscored in examples):

1. *ṭāleɛ hawa barra* [DA-199]   'A wind is coming up outside'

2. *žāye maɛhon ᵊṣ-ṣahr ᵊž-ždīd*   'The new son-in-law is coming with them'

3. *ʔāyəl-li ɛaʔli ʔətfarraž ɛala ḥalab* [DA-248]   'I'd like to take a look around Aleppo' (lit. "My mind has told me to...")

4. *mɛawwad yāmo kəll yōm mā ɛando dars byəži byəɛɛod ɛandi*   'Sonny[1] is accustomed to coming and spending some time with me every day he has no lesson'

Further examples of participial predicates — mostly with subject first or subject suppressed — are given on pp. 263-75. (See especially p. 266.) Others with subject following are given on p. 422.

Clausal Subjects

The subject of a predication may be clause introduced by *ʔənno* (more rarely *halli*, etc.), or a paratactic verbal clause. Subject clauses virtually always follow the predicate, and are often also susceptible to analysis as complemental clauses. Some examples are given here, others on p. 451.

1. *xaṭṭet l-ᵊḥkūme ʔənnha tʔayyed ᵊl-ʔadāya l-ɛarabiyye* [EA-232]   'The government's plan is to support the Arab cause(s)'

2. *maš maɛʔūl ʔansākon* [EA-264]   'It's inconceivable that I should forget you' (lit. "It's not reasonable that...")

3. *yalli ɛam-bəḥki ʔənno tə̌ži tāxod doktōra bəl-handase*   'What I'm saying is that you should come and take your doctorate in engineering'

4. *labake ʔənno rūḥ ᵊxṣūṣi*   'It's a bother for me to go personally'

---

[1] The word *yāmo* — like *ḅāba* 'daddy' and certain other kinship terms associated with endearment and baby-talk — is used reciprocally; i.e. *yāmo* is used by children to address their mother and by the mother to address her children, and in other relationships assimilated to that between mother and children. In this instance a paternal aunt (*ɛamme*) is referring to her nephew.

Suppression of the Subject

In English, the subject of an otherwise complete predication is rarely omitted except in certain kinds of casual conversational exchanges, where first and second person pronouns are sometimes suppressed, e.g. 'Didn't see him' (for 'I didn't...'), 'Want to go?' (for 'Do you want...'), etc. In Arabic, on the other hand, it is usual in all styles to omit the subject whenever it is clear from the context or the circumstances what the predicate applies to (and that it is in fact a predicate). See pp. 548-549.

Verbal and quasi-verbal predicates are the ones most commonly used without a subject: *rāḥ išūfak* 'He went to see you', *baddo yšūfak* 'He wants to see you', *ɛando yā* 'He has it', etc.

Adjectival predicates, however, are also very commonly used without a subject, and nominal predicates, too, to a lesser extent. Examples of non-verbal predications with subject suppressed:

1. *ɛali, tarak waẓīfto fi dāʔərt*
   ʔṣ-ṣaḥḥa; w-halla, kāteb ʔẓġīr
   fi ʔotēl ʔš-šarq. — bass, mabṣūṭ
   ʔb-šaġlo? [EA-168]

   'Ali left his job in the Department of Health; and now, he's a petty clerk in the Orient hotel. — But does he like his work?' (lit. "... pleased with...")

2. *ʔaxdet ʔl-bakalōrya mū hēk?*
   — laʔ, bass brōvē, bass ḥalwe
   w-manṭaʔha sales

   'She's gotten her batchelor's [degree] hasn't she? — No, just her [teacher's certificate, but she's pretty and articulate'

3. *l-ḥāṣel ʔāxed waẓīfe žaddan*
   ʔmnīḥa

   'The fact is, he's gotten a very good job'

4. *ɛiṣām bēk žāye maɛhon, walla*
   xaṭwe ɛazīze

   'Issam Bey is coming with them?! Well, that's a notable step!' (i.e. up the social ladder)

5. *šu lāʔi ḥāmel žarīde l-yōm*

   'Well, I see you have a newspaper with you today' (lit. "[I] have found [you] carrying...") Both the main predicate *lāʔi* and the complemental predicate *ḥāmel*... are without subjects.

6. *kān ɛanna ḍyūf. — mn ʔš-žəns*
   ʔn-nāɛem ḥatman. — lā walla,
   ʔrāybīnna

   'We had guests. — Of the fair sex, no doubt. — No indeed, they were relatives of ours'

In ex. 6 the phrase *mn ʔš-žəns ʔn-nāɛem* might perhaps be analyzed as a prepositional predicate with no subject: 'They were of the fair sex...'; Here we count it merely as an "incomplete" predication, supplemental to *ḍyūf* in the preceding sentence (cf. the English translation).

In general, prepositional predicates without subjects are uncommon except in response to questions or the like: *wēn ḥasan?* 'Where is Hassan?' — *bəl-bēt* 'In the house'

A predication with its subject suppressed is not to be confused with intrinsically subjectless or "impersonal" predications. See pp. 237, 365, 415.

The Predicate-Subject Inversion

Besides the basic kinds of word order in which the subject follows the main term of the predicate, there is also an **INVERTED** word order, in which a definite subject may be placed after the whole predicate, with the main sentence accent remaining on the predicate: *šā́ṭer hal-walad* 'That boy is smart', *raḥ-tākol ʾátle ʾənte* 'You're going to get a beating', *bəl-bḗt ʾabū́k?* 'Is your father in the house?'

This inversion gives the impression that the subject was at first suppressed (to be "understood" from context), then restored later as an afterthought. Its effect is to put relatively more emphasis on the predicate, less on the subject. In declarative sentences the inverted subject is usually spoken at a pitch considerably lower than that of the predicate where the main sentence accent falls, but in questions the subject remains at a medium-high pitch or may rise higher. [See p. 379.] Examples (with ´ marking main accent of sentence):

1. *waḷḷa zakíyye hal-bənt*	'That girl is certainly intelligent'
2. *mū́ ḥəlu hal-ḥaki*	'That [kind of] talk isn't nice'
3. *ẓarīf ᵊktī́r nabīl*	'Nabil is a lot of fun'
4. *šu mā́ btətzakkar šī ʾənte?*	'Can't you remember anything?'
5. *btaɛ́ref byə́nsa l-wāḥed*	'One forgets, you know'
6. *hallaʾ laḥa-dəʾʾ talefṓn mən hṓn ʾana*	'Now I'm going to make a phone call from here'
7. *kān kātab-li ɛanwāno hṓn b-wāšᵊnṭon huwwe*	'He'd written me his address here in Washington'
8. *tā́za xaḍᵊrtak ᵊl-yṓm?* [DA-105]	'Are your vegetables fresh today?'
9. *bəl-kabī́n tábaɛo huwwe, waḷḷa ɛaḍ-ḍahᵊr?*	'Is he in his cabin, or on deck?'
10. *hṓn bēt ᵊs-sayyed salā́me?* [EA-243]	'Is this Mr. Salameh's house?'
11. *mᵊ́tlak ᵊḥkāyti*	'It's the same with me as with you' (lit. "Like you, my story is")
12. *b-xamsīn ʾᵊ́rš dazzīnt ᵊl-bēḍ*	'A dozen eggs [sells] for fifty piastres'
13. *ṣáɛb ᵊš-šᵊǧᵊ́l maɛ nās ǧᵊšᵊm*	'Working with inexperienced people is difficult'

Predicate-subject inversion should not be confused with the permutation of terms in an equational predication [p. 405].

Number/Gender Agreement

A predicate that is inflectible for number/gender usually agrees with its subject. That is to say, the number and gender of the subject (if any) usually determine whether a predicate adjective or verb will be masculine, feminine, or plural.

> The subject also determines whether a verb will be in the first, second, or third person, but this a much simpler matter, treated in Ch. 14 [p. 364].

The general rules of number/gender agreement given here must be qualified and modified by more specific rules given later:

(1) A masculine singular subject requires a masculine predicate:

hal-ᵊktāb ǧāli   'This book is expensive'

wəṣel ᵊktābi?   'Has my book arrived?'

l-walad žūɛān   'The child is hungry'

(2) A feminine singular subject requires a feminine predicate:

hal-bərnēṭa ǧālye   'This hat is expensive'

wəṣlet bərnēṭṭi?   'Has my hat arrived?'

l-bənt žūɛāne   'The girl is hungry'

(3) A dual subject requires a plural predicate:

hal-bərnēṭṭēn ǧālyīn   'Both these hats are expensive'

wəṣlu l-ᵊktābēn tabaɛi?   'Have my two books arrived?'

l-bəntēn žūɛānīn   'Both girls are hungry'

(4) A w- coordination of singulars requires a plural predicate [See p. 502]:

l-ᵊktāb wəl-bərnēṭa ǧālyīn   'The book and the hat are expensive'

wəṣlu ṣ-ṣabi wəl-bənt?   'Have the boy and the girl arrived?'

(5) A plural pronoun subject requires a plural predicate:

hadōl ǧālyīn   'These are expensive'

wəṣlu hənne?   'Have they arrived?'

(6) Most animate[1] plural subjects require a plural predicate:

l-ᵊwlād žūɛānīn   'The children are hungry'

wəṣlu l-banāt?   'Have the girls arrived?'

---

[1]The term 'animate' should here be understood in a sort of theological sense, to include words designating human beings, but generally excluding animals [p. 424].

(7) Most inanimate plural subjects require either a plural or a feminine
predicate, depending partly on whether the subject referents are viewed
(respectively) as separate, particular instances, or as a collectivity
or generality:

wəṣlu kətbak? or wəṣlet kətbak?	'Have your books arrived?'
hal-baranîṭ ǧāylîn	'These hats are expensive'
l-baranîṭ ǧālye	'Hats are expensive'

(8) A clausal subject requires a masculine predicate:

byəghar ʔənnha ǧālye	'It seems that it's expensive'
mnîḥ halli wəṣlu	'It's good that they've arrived'

Since masculine is the base or neutral number/gender,
intrinsically subjectless ("impersonal") predications also
have masculine predicates [p. 365].

A predicate noun — as well as a verb or adjective —
often seems to agree in number and gender with the subject:
Ɛmūmi dakātra 'My uncles are doctors'; ʔaxta, mart ṣāḥbi
'Her sister is my friend's wife'. This agreement, however,
is not grammatically necessary; it is determined by the nature of the subject referent rather than by the grammatical category of the subject itself. Thus, for instance,
ʔaxūha mart ṣāḥbi 'Her brother is my friend's wife' is not
ungrammatical, only "unnatural". Note also: maƐbūdak
ᵊl-maṣāri 'Your idol (m.) is money (pl.)'; hayy modēl ᵊždîd
'This one (f.) is a new model (m.)', where hayy substitutes
for e.g. has-sayyāra 'this car', as contrasted with hāda
modēl ᵊždîd 'This [thing you see before you] is a new model'.
See also p. 407, ex. 41.

Non-Agreement with Post-Verbal Subject

A verb followed by an indefinite feminine or plural noun subject does
not necessarily agree with that subject, but may remain in the masculine
form: wəṣel banāt (or wəṣlu banāt) 'Some girls arrived', wəṣel bənt (or
wəṣlet bənt) 'A girl arrived'. Examples:

1. maḍa taʔrîban səne — 'Almost a year has passed'

2. bukra bižîni šatlāt ᵊmlāḥ — 'Tomorrow I'll have some good plants'
   [SAL-197] — (lit. "...will come to me good plants")

3. *kān ᵊb-balad ʔəxtēn* [AO-111]

'There were in a [certain] town two sisters'

4. *lēlt ᵊmbārḥa ʔəžāna zuwwār*

'Last night we had visitors' (lit. "...came to us...")

5. *txarraž fīha ʔaṭəbba w-ʔavokātiyye w-ᵊmhadsīn* [PIPL-XIX]

'Doctors and lawyers and engineers have graduated there'

6. *mən zamān kān yəži nās ᵊktīr la-hal-maṭɛam* [DA-238]

'A long time ago lots of people used to come to that restaurant'

7. *mā ṣəfi ġēr ɛašᵊr daʔāyeʔ*

'There's only ten minutes left'

8. *lā ykəl-lak fəkre*

'Don't give it a thought' (lit. "Let there not be to you a thought")

Participles with a following subject may be uninflected in the same way as verbs:

9. *bāʔī-lna mašye ṭawīle ʔəddāmna*

'We have a long walk ahead of us' (lit. "There remains for us...")

10. *ṣafyān tlətt əšhor la-ḥzērān*

'There are three months to go before June' (lit. "Are left three months...")

11. *žāyīni ḥawāle mən ʔafrīqya l-žunūbiyye* [DA-245]

'I've received a money order from South Africa' (lit. "Has come to me...")

12. *mabɛət-lak makatīb*

'Some letters have been sent to you'

13. *mawžūd ᵊhnīk ᵊwlād ɛarab ᵊktīr* [DA-237]

'There are many Arabs [to be] found there'

14. *ṭāləɛ-lo ḥarāra b-kəll žəsmo*

'He has a rash all over his body' (lit. "Has broken out for him...")

Less commonly, a verb fails to agree with a following underline{definite} subject, when something intervenes between the verb and its subject, or when the subject is a coordination:

15. *ʔassar ɛalēhon ᵊl-mursalīn ᵊl-ʔamērkān* [PIPL-XVII]

'The American missionaries have influenced them'

16. *kān ᵊb-ṣəḥᵊbto kibār ḍəbbāṭ ᵊž-žēš*

'He was accompanied by the top army brass' (lit. "Were in his company...")

17. *bikūn ᵊhnīk hēʔet ᵊl-wazāra wəl-ᵊmwaẓẓafīn wal-ʔakāber* [DA-300]

'The cabinet ministers and officials and big shots will be there'

18. *bəl-ᵊkrūm byəltđ?a l-wāwi wət-taƐlab wəḍ-ḍabᵊƐ* [PIPL-XIV] — 'In the vineyards are found the jackal, the fox, and the hyena'

A subject phrase formed with *ʔəlla* or *ġēr* 'except, but' does not affect the preceding verb even though the phrase is definite:

19. *mā bihəmmha ġēr ᵊl-ʔašyāʔ ᵊl-māddiyye* — 'Nothing interests her but material things'

20. *mū hāmə́ma ʔəlla rāḥə́ta* — 'She's only concerned with her own comfort'

21. *rəḥt ʔana w-ʔabi la-nzūrkon* [DA-238] — 'My father and I went to see you' (The verb *rəḥt* agrees in person, but not in number. Cf. p. 364.)

Feminine Agreement with Plurals and Collectives

Most inanimate plurals, and some animate plurals and collectives, have feminine agreement in the predicate when collectivity or generality is emphasized rather than heterogeneity or particularity. Examples, inanimate (with feminine predicate underscored):

1. *l-ᵊmġāmarāt kəlla <u>bəṭlet</u> maƐi mən zamān* — 'All adventures ceased with me quite a while ago'

2. *Ɛala ḥasab ma <u>Ɛam-təḥki</u> ž-žarāyed fī ʔazme wazāriyye* — 'According to what the papers are saying, there's a cabinet crisis'

3. *mā <u>Ɛādt</u> maƐi maṣāri* — 'I have no more money' (lit. "Does not continue with me money". The form *Ɛādt* is a syncopation of *Ɛādet.*) Note that *maṣāri* is construed here as a full-fledged subject, not as a complement of *maƐi* [p. 413].

4. *waʔᵊt mərrūḥ la-Ɛandon ṭūl ᵊs-sahra mā <u>btəxloṣ</u> ʔaḥadīsa l-ḥəlwe* — 'When we go to their house, there's no end all evening to her charming conversation(s)' (*ʔaḥadīs,* pl. of *ḥadīs)*

5. *hēk <u>bəṭṣīr</u> maƐlūmātkon ʔawsaƐ* [PVA-42] — 'Thus your knowledge will become broader' (*maƐlūmāt* 'knowledge, information', plural only [p. 368])

6. *hal-ᵊmġallafāt halli žəbthon <u>ᵊkbīre</u>* [DA-238] — 'These envelopes you brought are too large'

In many circumstances it makes little or no difference
whether one chooses the feminine or the plural; thus in ex.
6 the predicate could be *ħbār* as well as *kbīre*. Sometimes,
however, the difference in agreement can show whether a
subject with the article prefix is meant generally or specifically: *l-kətᵊb mā bəthəmmo* 'Books don't interest him'
vs. *l-kətᵊb mā bihəmmū* 'The books don't interest him'. If
the sentence begins with *hal-kətᵊb* 'these books', the spec-
ificity of the reference is already established, and then it
makes no crucial difference whether the predicate is feminine or plural.

Further examples with specific subject, in which feminine and plural
predicates are interchangeable:

7. *l-krafatāt bəl-wāžha laftet*   'The neckties in the display window
   (or *lafatu*) *naẓari*   caught my eye' (lit. "turned my
                                     glance")

8. *snāni Eam-ᵊṭṭaʔteʔ* (or *Eam-*   'My teeth are chattering'
   iṭaʔᵊtʔu)

Note that plural animal designations commonly take feminine agreement:

9. *bəž-žabal bətEīš ᵊd-dyāb*   'In the mountains live wolves'

10. *n-nsūra kānet ħāyme fōʔ*   'The vultures were soaring above in
    bəs-sama   the sky'

A number of collective or plural human designations may be used with
feminine verbal predicates. These include *nās* and *ʔahᵊl* 'people, folks',
and plurals ending in *-e/-a* [pp. 213, 229]:

11. *rāħet ᵊn-nās ʔabᵊl nəṣṣ ᵊl-lēl* 'The people left before midnight'
    [DA-238]

12. *ya tara n-nās šū raħa-tʔūl?*   'I wonder what people will say?'

13. *kəll ᵊn-nās Eənda xabar*   'All the people know about it' (lit.
    [SPA-308]   "...have news")

14. *ʔahl ᵊd-dēEa bətʔūl ʔannon*   'The villagers say that they are not
    mū mədžauwzīn   married'

15. *Eala nafxet ᵊl-bōragān,*   'At the sound of the horn, the workers
    š-šaggīle tfarṭaEet bi-kəll   scattered in all directions'
    ᵊž-žihāt

16. *lāken bəddi nafs ᵊl-ʔasātze*   'But I'll expect the same professors
    tEalləmni   to teach me'

Plural Agreement

A verbal or adjectival predicate is put in the plural to agree with a plural subject, whenever the subject referents are thought of as diverse or individually discriminated:

1. *ʔawā€īha kānu mlaḥwašīn ḥawāli*   'Her clothes were strewn all over
   l-maḥall kəllo   the place'

2. *kəll hal-makatīb wəṣlu sawa*   'All these letters arrived at once'

> Note, in ex. 2, that if the letters were not thought of
> in terms of their separateness, there would be little moti-
> vation for remarking that they arrived all together.

3. *wrāʔo maẓbūṭīn*   'His papers are correct'

4. *s-safāyen ʔltammuʔ*   'Have the notebooks been collected?'

5. *hal-ʔalwān mā bināsbu ba€ḍon*   'These colors don't go together'
                                      (lit. "...don't suit each other")

> In ex. 5 the reciprocity that is made explicit by the
> object *ba€ḍon* requires that the colors be thought of indi-
> vidually. The same situation, however, could be referred
> to with a reciprocative verb in the feminine: *hal-ʔalwān
> mā btətnāsab* [p. 248] 'These colors don't match', in which
> the colors are considered in their overall effect rather
> than separately.

Plurals of paucity [p. 369], and especially plurals of unit nouns [297], almost always have plural agreement in the predicate, except that inanimate unit noun plurals do not take adjective agreement in *-īn:*

6. *hal-kūsāyāt mū mnāḥ ʔktīr*   'These squashes are not very good'

7. *t-təffāḥāt €am-yəbdu yəntəz€u*   'The apples are beginning to go bad'

> Cf. *l-fawāki €am-təbda təntə́ze€* 'The fruit is beginning
> to go bad' (*fawāki* is a mass noun plural: sg. *fākye.*);
> *t-təffāḥ €am-yəbda yəntə́ze€* 'The apples (collective) are...'.

If an adjective has no internal plural [p. 205], however, then the feminine is used, or else the uncommon feminine/ plural [p. 201]:

8. *had-dərrāʔnāt māwiyye* or   'These peaches are juicy'
   had-dərrāʔnāt māwiyyāt

Many singular nouns designating (or sometimes designating) groups of people are commonly used with plural verbal (and participial) predicates. These nouns include, again, ʔahᵃl and nās (if this be considered a feminine singular noun) and their synonyms. Ethnic collectives [p.301] have plural agreement almost exclusively. Names of various kinds of institutions are often applied to the sum of their members:

9. š-šǝrta <u>fattašu</u> l-balad mǝn   'The police searched the town from
    ʔawwdla la-ʔāxǝ́ra   one end to the other'

10. fī ɛālam ᵃktīr ɛam-<u>yǝstannūk</u>   'There's a large crowd awaiting you'
                                            (ɛālam 'world', Fr. 'monde')

11. bēt ʔǝxtak bǝddhon <u>yǝšu</u>   'Your sister and her family are com-
    <u>yǝsharu</u> ɛanna   ing to spend the evening with us'
                                            (lit. "The house of your sister...")

12. fī nās ɛam-<u>imūtu</u> šūɛ   'There are people dying of hunger'

13. ʔahl ᵃl-balad <u>šāfū</u> ɛālem   'The people of the town took him for
    [AO-83]   a learned man' (lit. "...saw him a..."

14. l-ǧawǧāʔ kānu raha-<u>yǝšᵃnʔū</u>   'The mob was about to lynch him'

15. l-kǝll <u>byaɛᵃrfu</u> ʔǝnno ǧaššāš   'Everyone knows he's a swindler'

These words may also be used with singular agreement, however. For example:

16. l-kǝll <u>ʔaddar</u> ʔaɛmālo   'Everyone appreciated his work'
                                            (cf. ex. 15)

17. š-šǝrṭa ɛam-<u>ᵃddawwer</u> ɛalē   'The police are looking for him'
                                            (cf. ex. 9)

Note also the singular agreement in the following:

18. šēš mā <u>byākǝ́lon</u> hadōl   'An army wouldn't eat all these!'

19. ɛēlto <u>sākne</u> ʔarīb la-bētna   'His family lives near our house'

Agreement with Constructs and Other Noun Phrases

Generally speaking, it is the leading term of a noun construct [p.456] that determines agreement: *bənt ṣāḥbi ḥəlwe* 'My friend's daughter is pretty (f.)'; in the case of partitive constructs and certain others, however, the following term determines agreement: *kəll ᵊl-banāt ḥəlwīn* 'All the girls are pretty'. See p.466ff.

In some cases a prepositional supplement (in periphrasis of annexion [p.460]) determines agreement rather than the supplemented term: *byaᵊrūḥa ɛadad ᵊkbīr mən l-ᵊmsaqqafīn* 'A large number of intellectuals read it'. Though *ɛadad* (masc. sing.) is formally the main term of the subject, the agreement (as in English) is with the supplemental term, which is plural.

In some abstract and gerundial constructs [p.464], the following term sometimes determines the agreement of a verbal predicate: *ʔakl ᵊl-būẓa mā bəḍḍərr* 'Eating ice cream does no harm' (cf. *ʔakl ᵊl-laḥᵊm mā biḍərr* 'Eating meat does no harm'). A coordination as following term does not produce plural agreement, however, but the verb may be masculine or feminine depending on the gender of the last term: *kətret ᵊl-laff wəd-dawarān biḍayyeɛ ᵊl-wāḥed* 'So much turning and circling gets one lost'.

In the case of numeral constructs [471], the agreement of a verbal predicate may be plural or feminine, depending to some extent on the same considerations as in the case of nouns without numerals: *tlətt ᵊržāl ᵊəžu ʔāmūha* 'Three men came and took it away' (plural) but *tlətt waᵊɛāt bəl-yōm mā bətkaffi* 'Three meals a day are not enough' (feminine). In the latter sentence *waᵊɛāt* is of course inanimate, and the phrase *tlətt waᵊɛāt bəl-yōm* 'three meals a day' stands for a significant whole rather than disparate parts, and the sentence is a generalization [cf. p.424].

In some cases a numeral construct is merely the name of a sum, so to speak, and the predicate is masculine: *ʔarbaɛ līrāt byəkfi* [SAL-39] 'Four pounds will suffice'.

Number/Gender with Subject Suppressed

When there is no subject expressed [p.418], the number/gender of a verbal or adjectival predicate is usually "natural", i.e. not determined by the rules of agreement with the suppressed subject as if it were present, but by the more direct semantic classification of the referent by which pronouns are selected when they have no antecedent [p.363].

Thus, if instead of saying *n-nsūra kānet ḥāyme fōʔ bəs-sama* 'The vultures were soaring above in the sky' we wish to say 'They were soaring...' (still in reference to the vultures), the linking verb and predicate adjective would probably be made plural: *kānu ḥāymīn...* . (Usually, however, a subject referent of this sort will have been recently enough mentioned so that the noun may still serve as <u>antecedent</u> — though not subject — to the predicate; if its antecedence is clear enough in the context, then the feminine agreement may still hold.) Similarly in the case of certain collectives and other singulars used in a collective sense; if the subject is dropped from e.g. *žēš mā*

byākóla 'An army couldn't eat it', the verb would probably have to be made
plural to preserve the sense: *mā byāklūha* 'They couldn't eat it'.

In the choice between masculine and feminine when there is no question
of a plural, the suppressed subject is more likely to have an influence,
even if the word has not yet come up in the discourse. Thus someone might
say, looking at an automobile, *ḥalwe, mū ḥǝk?* 'Pretty,isn't it?', with the
feminine predicate adjective under the influence of the familiar feminine
noun *sayyāra* — the suppressed subject. On the other hand, if no particular
word is lurking in the speaker's mind in association with what he is referring to, he is perhaps more likely to use the masculine: *ḥalu, mū ḥǝk?*
(except, of course, if an animate referent is evidently female [p.372]).

Note that in certain expressions concerning the day, the weather, etc.,
a feminine predicate is used with the subject *d-dǝnye* 'the world' suppressed:
bǝṣ-ṣēf bǝtɛattem mǝtʔaxxra 'In summer is gets dark late', i.e. ...*d-dǝnye
bǝtɛattem...*; *ɛam-ᵊtšatti* 'It's raining', i.e. *d-dǝnye ɛam-ᵊtšatti.*

There are certain kinds of "impersonal" expressions, usually with complements, in which the feminine is normally used, even though masculine is
generally the base or neutral inflection [cf. p.365]:

1. *mā btǝfreʔ maɛi ʔǝnni rūḥ wāḥdi*   'I don't mind going alone' (lit.
                                            "It(f.) does not differ with me
                                            that...")

2. *mū mǝhᵊrze tkasser rāsak*   'It's not worth while for you to
   b-hal-mawḍūɛ   knock your brains out over this
                                          matter'

3. *rāyeḥ maɛna? — btǝtwaʔʔaf*   'Are you going with us? — It all
                                          depends'

4. *bǝddha xams ᵊsnīn*   'It takes five years'

5. *hallaʔ zādet šwayye ɛan ḥadda*   'Now [matters] have gone a bit too
                                          far'

6. *mā kānet laṭīfe mǝnno ʔabadan*   'That wasn't very nice of him'

Uninflected Adjectives

There are a numer of adjectives which show no agreement, for example
ɛāl 'fine, excellent', *ḍǝgri* 'straight', etc. (See p.501 for others):

ʔalfēn u-xams miyye ɛāl lǝž-žihtēn   'Two thousand five hundred is fine
[DA-291]   for both sides'

dāʔiman kānet ḍǝgri maɛi   'She has always been straight with
                                          me'

EXTRAPOSITION

Topic and Comment *(al-mubtada? wal-xabar)*

Several different kinds of clause come under the heading of TOPICAL, or TOPIC-COMMENT, clauses. The "topic" is a noun-type word or phrase which introduces the "comment" and delimits its scope or application. The comment itself is a predication: *Éali, baÉ*rfo mn *hdaÉšar sane* 'Ali — I've known him for eleven years'.

> A subject-predicate clause (i.e. a predication with a subject preceding the predicate) is also traditionally analyzed as a special kind of topical clause. Thus in the sentence *Éali byaÉrafni* 'Ali knows me', *Éali* is called *al-mubtada?* (topic) and *byaÉrafni* is called *al-xabar* (comment).[1]

Topical clauses other than ordinary subject-predicate clauses differ from the latter, in that the comment itself has a subject — or subject-referent — of its own, and therefore a main verb or adjective in the comment is not inflected to agree with the topic. Examples:

1. *l-*hsāb *l-žāri, bathatt masāri w-*btashab manhon* [DA-293]
   '[In] a checking account you deposit money and withdraw (from) it'

2. *?ana, l-*mžāmarāt kānet bēn Éamr *?s-sabataÉ*š wal-ÉašrÄ«n*
   '[For] me, the age of adventures was between seventeen and twenty'

3. *basal žassant ?azra?, fÄ« Éandi xamse mazrūÉÄ«n bi-faxxār* [SAL-197]
   '[As for] blue hyacinth bulbs, I have five, planted in pots'

4. *hal-bēdāt *d-dazzÄ«ne b-xamsÄ«n ?arš*
   'These eggs are fifty piastres a dozen' (lit. "These eggs, the dozen is at fifty piastres")

5. *žnēnti w-*žnēnto l-hēt bal-hēt*
   'My yard adjoins his' (lit. "My yard and his yard — the wall is at the wall")

---

[1] Since comments are predications, the traditional analysis in effect equates 'predication' with 'predicate'. Though it is true as a general rule that predicates may stand alone as predications (i.e. that subjects may be suppressed), it is strictly speaking invalid to collapse the two levels into one, because that would imply that *al-xabar* (the comment) is a recursive element, which is not the case. In other words: if a comment may consist of a subject and predicate, and if a comment is a predicate, then there is no theoretical limit to the containment of predicates within predicates (just as there is no limit to the containment of annexion phrases within annexion phrases [p.456]). In fact, however, a predication may serve as comment to a topic, but the resulting topical clause may not serve, in its turn, as comment to still another topic. See also footnote on p.401.

6. *š-šətwiyye b-bērūt mā fī ʔaḥla*   'The winter season in Beirut –
   mən hēk [DA-152]   there's nothing nicer than that!'[1]

7. *hayy mā baɛref*   '[As for] that, I don't know'

8. *hēʔtak mū mabṣūṭ*   'You don't look well', lit. "[With
                                            respect to] your appearance, [you're]
                                            not well"

9. *žənsīti ʔamērkāni, lāken ʔaṣli*   'I'm American by nationality, but
   ləbnāni   Lebanese by blood' (lit. "My nation-
                                            ality – [I'm] American, but my origin
                                            – [I'm] Lebanese")

In example 9, the fact that *ʔamērkāni* (m.) does not agree with the feminine *žənsiyye* shows that this is not an ordinary subject-predicate sentence, which would be *žənsīti ʔamērkiyye lakēn ʔaṣli ləbnāni* (same translation). In ex. 8, *mabṣūṭ* likewise does not agree with the feminine *hēʔa*. Cf. *hēʔtak mū mnīḥa* (same translation, but lit. "Your appearance is not good"), which is an ordinary subject-predicate sentence.

Resumptive Pronoun in the Comment *(al-ɛāʔid)*

Examples 1-9 above illustrate the fairly uncommon kinds of topical clauses in which topic and comment are not linked grammatically by any means other than juxtaposition and "prosody" [p. 377]. A far more important kind of clause is the kind with a pronoun somewhere in the comment whose antecedent is the topic:

a.) *hal-bənt, btaɛrə́fa ʔənte?*   "That girl – do you know her?"

b.) *hal-bənt, tɛarraft ɛalēha?*   "That girl – have you been intro-
                                        duced to her?"

c.) *hal-bənt, ʔəsma faṭma*   "That girl – her name is Fatima"

d.) *hal-bənt hiyye əl-ʔaḥla*   "That girl – she is the prettiest"

---

[1]A disputable contention. Prospective visitors should be warned that the Lebanese winter normally has long spells of rainy, chilly weather. Note that the word *šəte* means both 'wintertime' and 'rain'.

Topical clauses with a resumptive pronoun are related by **EXTRAPOSITION**[1] to more or less equivalent <u>predications</u>, which have the topical noun phrase in place of the pronoun. Thus example (a) above is an extraposition from *btaɛref hal-bənt ʔənte?* 'Do you know that girl?'; ex. (b), from *tɛarraft ɛala hal-bənt?* 'Have you been introduced to that girl?'; (c), from *ʔəsᵊm hal-bənt faṭma* 'That girl's name is Fatima'; and (d), from *hal-bənt, l-ʔaḥla* 'That girl is the prettiest'. The effect of extraposition is to focus attention on the **EXTRAPOSITIVE** (or **EXTRAPOSED**) term, i.e. the part of the predication which is made a topic and replaced in the predication by a pronoun.

In the case of many equational predications, however, extraposition is commonly used not so much to emphasize the extrapositive subject, but simply to identify the predication as such. For example the predication *l-bənt, l-ʔaḥsan* 'The girl is the best' might in some circumstances be confused with the noun phrase *l-bənt ᵊl-ʔaḥsan* 'the best girl'; therefore the predication tends to be replaced by a topical sentence even when no special emphasis is intended: *l-bənt hiyye l-ʔaḥsan*. See p. 405.

Examples of extrapositive object (Resumptive pronoun underscored):

1. *kəll ᵊṣ-ṣēfiyye maḍḍēnā<u>ha</u> maɛo*   'The whole summer we spent with him'

2. *ʔaktar ʔašɛāri kənt ʔəkt<u>ŝba</u> bi-dars ᵊl-fīzya ʔaw ᵊl-kīmya*   'Most of my poetry I wrote in physics or chemistry class'

3. *samīr, sməɛt bəddhon iraʔʔ<u>ū</u>* [EA-169]   '[As for] Samir, I hear they intend to promote him'

4. *faḍᵊlkon mā bəns<u>ā</u> ṭūl ḥayāti* [EA-264]   'I'll never forget your kindness'

5. *l-hawa bṭəḍgaṭ<u>o</u> ṭrəmbe*   'The air is compressed by a pump' (lit. "The air, compresses it a pump")

6. *hal-maẑalle byəʔrū<u>ha</u> ɛadad ᵊkbīr mən l-ᵊmsaqqafīn*   'This magazine is read by a large number of intellectuals' (lit. "This magazine, read it a large number...")

Note that extraposition may have an effect on the word order of subject and predicate. In example 6, the subject *ɛadad ᵊkbīr mən l-ᵊmsaqqafīn* is too long to fit comfortably in the "original" predication between *byəʔru* and *hal-maẑalle* [p.409], therefore it is more likely to precede the verb: *ɛadad ᵊkbīr mən l-ᵊmsaqqafīn byəʔru hal-maẑalle*.

---

[1] The term 'extraposition' is taken from Chaim Rabin (*Arabic Reader*, Lund Humphries, London, 1947; and other works). The term 'resumptive pronoun' is from Frank A. Rice (personal communication) and the terms 'topic' and 'comment' from Charles F. Hockett (*A Course in Modern Linguistics*, Macmillan, New York, 1958).

7. *žōz ᵊtwār ləl-ḥart bisammūhon*
   faddān [AO-63]

   'A pair of oxen for plowing are
   called a yoke [of oxen]' (lit. "A
   pair...they call them...")

8. *hāda banū ždīd la-ᵓərwāᵓ*
   hal-ᵓarāḍi l-wāsɛa [DA-253]

   'This was built recently for the ir-
   rigation of this large area' (lit.
   "This they have built new for irri-
   gating these broad lands")

   Note, in examples 5-8, that extraposition of the object
   in Arabic is often rendered in English by the passive construction. See p. 236.

9. *w-ᵓana žāyīni ṭarḍ la-ᵓaxdo*
   [DA-244]

   'And I have a package to pick up'
   (lit. "And I — there has come to
   me a package...")

   In example 9 the extraposed term is itself a personal
   pronoun, which takes the "independent" form *ᵓana* as topic,
   and *-ni* as object. The ordinary predication, then, is
   simply *žāyīni ṭarḍ la-ᵓaxdo; -ni* is extraposed as *ᵓana* but
   the resumptive pronoun must again be *-ni*.

10. *halli bətrīdi bžəb-lek yā*
    [AO-115]

    'Whatever you(f.) want I'll bring
    you(it)'

11. *yəlli byəži bi-bālo biḥəṭṭo*

    'Whatever comes to his mind he puts
    (it) down'

12. *halli bixalləṣni bəddi ᵓaġnī*
    la-wəld ᵊwlādo [AO-116]

    'Whoever rescues me, I shall make
    him and his descendants rich'

Examples of extraposed annex (following term) in noun constructs:

1. *s-sayyāra dūlāb mən dawalība*
   banšar

   'One of the car's tires is flat'
   (lit. "The car, a tire of its tires
   has been punctured")

2. *l-buḥayra žəmᵓa mīt ᵓadam*

   'The lake is a hundred feet deep'
   (lit. "The lake, its depth is...")

3. *ṣāḥbi dāyman ɛaᵓlo sābeḥ*
   bəl-xayāl

   'My friend always has his head in
   the clouds' (lit. "My friend, always
   his mind is swimming in fantasy")

4. *hāda mū maɛnāto bəd-ḍarūra ᵓənno*
   lāzem ᵊtrūḥ la-hnīk

   'This doesn't necessarily mean that
   you'll have to go there' (lit. "This,
   it is not its meaning necessarily..."

5. *hal-makīnāt bəṭel ᵓastaɛmāla*

   'These machines are obsolete'
   ("These machines, has ceased their
   use")

6. *hēk ʔašya mū məmken šarḥa* 'Such things cannot be explained'
      ("Such things, is not possible their explanation")

7. *l-manṭoyāt ᵊmxaffaḍ səɛᵊrhon* 'Coats have been reduced from forty
   mən ʔarbɛīn dōlār la-tlātīn dollars to thirty' ("The coats, has been reduced their price...")

8. *taṣarrofāto ṣaɛᵊb fəhᵊmha* 'His behavior is hard to understand'
      ("...is difficult its understanding")

9. *ʔana kān fəkri rūḥ bət-trēn* 'I was thinking of going by train'
   [DA-249] ("[As for] me, it was my idea to go by train")

10. *ʔahᵊl hal-žazīre kəllon ṣayyādīn* 'The people of this island are all
    samak (of them) fishermen'

Examples of extraposed annex ("object") of a preposition:

1. *hal-ᵊmlāḥaẓa kān huwwe l-maʔṣūd* 'That remark was aimed at him' (lit.
   fīha "That remark, he was the target in it")

2. *haṣ-ṣənᵊf mā ɛād ᵊltaʔa mənno* 'That brand hasn't been on the market
   bəs-sūʔ mən sane for a year' ("That brand, there has not been found [any] of it...")

3. *r-raʔīs fī ḥawalē ržāl maʔtədrīn* 'The president has able men around him'

4. *dastūr ᵊl-wilāyāt ᵊl-məttáḥide* 'Work began on the constitution of
   bada l-ɛamal fī sənt ʔalf u-sabᵊɛ the United States in the year 1789'
   miyye w-təsɛā w-tmānīn ("The constitution..., began the work on it...")

5. *š-šakkāt ləssa mā txallaṣ* 'The checks still have not been
   ɛalēhon cleared'

6. *hal-ɛamal ḥa-ykən-lo natāyeš* 'That act will have numerous conse-
   mətɛaddede quences' ("...there will be to it...")

7. *halli xəḍᵊrto ʔaḥsan bəštəri* 'The one whose vegetables are best, I
   mənno [DA-128] buy from (him)'

8. *halli bixallaṣni bəftaḥ-lo knūz* 'Whoever rescues me, I shall open to
   ᵊl-ʔarḍ [AO-116] him the treasures of the earth'

9. *bass hāda ɛanna mənno ktīr* 'But that [is something] we have a
   bi-ʔamērka [DA-251] lot of in America'

10. *huwwe handase madaniyye maɛo* 'He has [a degree in] civil engineering'

11. *ʔana mā ḥada byəsʔal ɛanni* 'Nobody asks about me!'

Examples of extraposed subject (with equational comment [p. 405]):

1. *hāda huwwe l-bās halli byəmši*
s-sāɛa təntēn?   'Is this the bus that leaves at two
o'clock?'

2. *kəll ma hunālek huwwe laha-ykūn*
ɛibāra ɛan seminārēn ʔaw tlāte   'All there is to it will consist of
two or three seminars'

3. *ʔahamm ṣināɛa fi-trablos hiyye*
ṣināɛet ʔṣ-ṣābūn [PAT-185]   'The most important industry in Tri-
poli is the soap industry'

4. *hal-ʔaġʔnya hadōl hənne l-mallāke*
wət-təžžār [PAT-191]   'These rich men are the landowners
and merchants'

5. *ʔaʔsām ʔl-madīne d-dāxliyye...*
hiyye buwwābet ʔl-ḥəddādīn,
l-ʔmxātra, n-nūri... [PAT-179]   'The interior sections of the city
are: Buwwêbet el-Heddêdîn, El-
Mhêtra, En-Nouri, etc.'

6. *ʔašhar ʔasar tārīxi fəl-balad*
huwwe l-ʔalɛa [PAT-179]   'The most famous historical monument
in town is the fortress'

7. *ʔahamm šī bi-kəll doktōrā hiyye*
l-ʔəṭrūḥa   'The most important thing in every
doctorate is the dissertation'

Note, in example 7, that the resumptive pronoun is feminine, agreeing with its predicate *l-ʔəṭrūḥa* rather than
with its antecedent *ʔahamm šī*. (Cf. ex. 6, in which the
agreement goes according to the rules.) Inconsistencies of
this sort are common when a resumptive subject pronoun stands
between an antecedent and a predicate that differ in number/
gender.

Comment-Topic Inversion

An extraposition is sometimes inverted, i.e. the topic is put after the
comment, just as a subject may be put after the predicate [p. 419]: *mḥammad*
baɛʔrfo 'Mohammed I know (him)' → *baɛʔrfo, mḥammad*.

1. *baɛrəfa ʔana, l-bənʔt?*   'Do I know her, the girl?'

2. *huwwe yalli mʔalləfa hal-madrase*   'He's the one who organized it, that
school'

3. *žēš mā byāksəlon hadōl yəlli*
ɛaddēton   'An <u>army</u> wouldn't eat all those that
you counted off'

Another construction somewhat similar to the comment-topic inversion is often used with reference to human beings: the preposition *la-* [p.479] introduces the inverted topic:

4. *kant šūfo kəll yōm la-ʔaḥmad* 'I used to see(him,) Ahmed, every day'

5. *nabīl byəʔrabo la-mḥammad lāken* 'Nabil is related to Mohammed but
 ʔərbe šwayye bɛ̄īde   somewhat distantly'

6. *huwwe ṣāḥbo ktīr la-ʔaxi*   'He's a good friend of my brother's'

  In ex. 6, *ʔaxi* could not come first, in a normal topic position, because it would sound as if *huwwe* (rather than the *-o* of *ṣāḥbo*) were the resumptive pronoun: *ʔaxi huwwe ṣāḥbo ktīr* 'My brother is a good friend of his'.

  Extraposition is used not only with predications, but also with other constructions derived from predication: In substitution questions: *ʔante šū mašrūɛak?* 'What is your plan?' *šū huwwe mašrūɛak?* 'What is your plan?', *ʔaxūk wēno?* 'Where's your brother?', *wēno ʔaxūk* 'Where is your brother', etc. See p.566.

  Less commonly, the comment is a command: *yəlli bətlāʔi bəs-sūʔ žība* 'Whatever you can find in the market bring (it)'.

  See also Attribution, p.496.

CHAPTER 17:   COMPLEMENTATION

Complementation is a type of construction which in Syrian Arabic is expressed by word order only.[1] The leading, or COMPLEMENTED, term is followed — not necessarily immediately — by its COMPLEMENT or COMPLEMENTS.

> The word order is generally reversed when the comple-
> ment is a question-word [p. 566]. Otherwise, inverted word
> order is rare [pp. 439, 452, 453.]

The several kinds of complementation are treated separately as follows:

> The kind of complementation that goes with any partic-
> ular complemented term is largely determined by lexical
> idiosyncrasy, and must be learned as a matter of vocabu-
> lary. Translation equivalents may be misleading.

A complemented term may have one, two, or three complements.

A verb (or participle or gerund) may be complemented by one or two noun
phrases; if two, the first must be an object.

Adjectives and nouns, as well as verbs, may be complemented by one or
two prepositional phrases, or by a clause, or by a phrase and a clause.

> The word order of prepositional phrases in respect to
> other complements depends on various specific consider-
> ations [p. 445].
> On the distinction between complements and supplements,
> see p. 444 (footnote).

---

[1] In Classical Arabic, complementation is also expressed by *an-naṣb* (the "accusative case" for noun-type complements, the "subjunctive mode" for verbs).

OBJECTS *(al-maf£ūl bihi)*

An OBJECT is a pronominalizable complement to a verb (or to a participle or gerund). That is to say, it is a noun-type word or phrase of any
kind whose referent (if definite) may subsequently be referred to by a
pronoun suffixed directly to the verb, or to the stem *yā-* [p.545]: *šaft
ᵃl-bənt* 'Did you see the girl?', *laᵓ, mā šaftha* 'No, I didn't see her';
šaft-əllak yāha 'I saw her (for you)'.

> The verb-object construction is practically the same in
> Arabic as in English; but in many individual cases, an Ara-
> bic verb with an object is translated by an English verb
> with prepositional complement, and vice versa.

Examples:

1. *ᵓəmḍi kəll ᵃn-nəsax*   'Sign all the copies'

2. *ḥḍərt ᵃl-£ašа b-ᵓāxr   'Did you attend the dinner at the
   ᵃl-ᵓəštimā£?*   end of the meeting?'

3. *mā šafᵃt hada bəl-bēt*   'I didn't see anyone in the house'

4. *£am-yəstġəll ṭībet nafsak*   'He's imposing on your good nature'
                                       (In this case the Arabic object is
                                       translated with a prepositional com-
                                       plement 'on your good nature'.)

5. *ḥakət-ᵃlna ᵓəṣṣa mā btətsadda?*   'She told us an incredible story'
                                       (In this case the English first ob-
                                       ject 'us' corresponds to an Arabic
                                       prepositional phrase -ᵃlna 'to us'.)

6. *tammam yalli kān nāwi ya£ᵃmlo*   'He accomplished what he had in-
                                       tended to do' (Substantivized
                                       yalli-phrase [p.494])

First and Second Objects. In Arabic as in English, some verbs take two objects. The first of them usually represents a person (or something comparable to a person), to or for whom an act is performed, while the second
represents something used in the act or resulting from it:

7. *lāzem ᵃtwarǰi š-šərṭi biṭāqet   'You must show the policeman your
   hawītak*   identity card'

8. *bəddi ᵓəsᵓal l-ᵃm£allem suᵓāl   'I want to ask the teacher another
   tāni*   question'

9. *£ār ṣaḥbo badᵃlto š-ǰdīde*   'He lent his friend his new suit'

10. *žawwaz wāḥed ṣāḥbo bənto*
    ž-žamīle

    'He married off his beautiful daughter to a friend of his', lit. "He gave-in-marriage (to) a friend of his his beautiful daughter"

Also as in English, the first object may be pronominalized alone, or both may be pronominalized at the same time, but the second object cannot be pronominalized unless the first is too:

First Object Pronominalized | Both Objects Pronominalized

11. *Ɛaṭāni hdiyye*...................*Ɛaṭāni yāha*
    'He gave me a gift'   'He gave it to me' lit. "He gave me it"

12. *labbəstīhon tyābon?*...............*labbəstīhon yāhon?*
    'Did you(f.)put their clothes on them?'   'Did you put them on them?'

13. *fahhəmni d-dars*...................*fahhəmni yā*
    'Explain the lesson to me'   'Explain it to me'

14. *ballaġto r-risāle?*...............*ballaġto yāha?*
    'Did you give him the message?'   'Did you give it to him?'

15. *btəʔder ʔtsalləfni šwayyet*
    maṣāri?.........................*btəʔer ʔtsalləfni yāha?*
    'Could you lend me a little money?'   'Could you lend it to me?'

In order to pronominalize a second object without pronominalizing the first, the first object must be converted into a prepositional complement (generally with *la-*) and the order of complements reversed. Here again, Arabic and English are grammatically alike:

16: *bāƐ ʔəbno l-bēt*...................*bāƐo l-bēt*
    'He sold his son the house'   'He sold him the house'

17. *bāƐ ʔl-bēt la-ʔəbno*...............*bāƐo la-ʔəbno*
    'He sold the house to his son'   'He sold it to his son'

Object-Verb Inversion. The word order of verb and object is rarely reversed, though in certain kinds of exclamations with the elative an inverted order is usual: *ʔaƐžab šī ʔalla mā xalaʔ* 'A more marvelous thing God has never created!', *ʔažnan mən hēk Ɛəmri mā šəft* 'I've never seen anything crazier than that!'

See also Extrapostion of Object [p.431] and Question-word Inversion [p.566].

Objects of Active Participles. The active participle [p. 265] of a transitive verb takes an object just as the verb itself does:

18. ḥáṭṭe warde b-šáɛra . . . . ḥáṭṭáta b-šáɛra
    'She's wearing (i.e. she's   'She's wearing it in her hair'
    put) a flower in her hair'

19. mīn ᵊmɛallem l-ᵊwlād had-dars? . . . . . . mīn ᵊmɛallémon yā?
    'Who taught the children   'Who taught it to them?'
    this lesson?'

> But an active participle functioning as a noun (e.g.
> mɛallem in the sense of 'teacher') or as an ordinary adjec-
> tive (e.g. šāmel 'comprehensive') does not, of course, take
> an object. See p. 276.

Objects of Gerunds. If a verb with one object is transformed into a gerund, then – provided that the gerund is in construct with the transformed subject of the verb [p. 464] – the object may remain as such:

20. dirāset ᵊabno l-mūsīqa . . . . dirāsto yāha
    'His son's study of music'   'His studying it'

21. ᵊakl ᵊn-nās ᵊl-laḥᵊm . . . . ᵊaklon yā
    'the people's eating of meat'   'their eating it'

But if the transformed subject is not expressed, then the object does not remain as such but becomes following term to the gerund in construct: dirāset ᵊl-mūsīqa 'the study of music', ᵊrāyet ᵊl-qurᵊān 'reading the Koran'. See p. 296.

If the gerund of a verb with two objects is in construct with the transformed first object, then the second object remains as such:

22. taɛlīm ᵊwlādon l-ᵊᵊrāye . . . . taɛlīmon yāha
    'teaching their children to   'teaching it to them'
    read'

> The object of a gerund may, however, be replaced by a
> prepositional complement with la- [p. 479]: dirāset ᵊabno
> lal-musīqa 'His son's study of music'.
> A concretized gerund [p. 284] does not take an object,
> but a prepositional complement instead: zyārti ᵊalon 'my
> visit to them' (not "zyārti yāhon").

ADVERBIAL NOUN COMPLEMENTS

Verbs (and participles) are sometimes complemented by a noun-type word or phrase similar to an object (or, more exactly, to a second object), but which is not pronominalizable.[1]

An adverbial complement serves to specify something used or involved in the act or situation referred to, or to specify some aspect of it:

1. *byəzraɛu ʔarāḍīhon ʔam³ḥ* — 'They sow their land with wheat'

2. *zādet ³š-šāy səkkar* — 'She added sugar to the tea', i.e. "...added to the tea with sugar"

3. *mallēt ³l-ʔannīne mayy* — 'I filled the bottle with water'

4. *l-ʔannīne malāne mayy* — 'The bottle is full of water' (Complemented participle)

5. *bikallfak ʔaktar mən hēk* — 'It'll cost you more than that'

6. *ḍṭarrēt ʔəštəǧel sāɛāt ʔəḍāfiyye* — 'I had to work extra hours'

7. *rāyḥīn fərṣet tlatt əšhor* [SAL-68] — '(We're)going on a three months' vacation' (Complemented participle)

8. *baɛatū məšwār mafxūt* — 'They sent him on a wild goose chase'

9. *mənbīɛ naʔdi bass* — 'We only sell for cash'

10. *l-³ḥsāb nāʔeṣ tlətt dolārāt* — 'The account is three dollars short' (Complemented participle)

11. *šaʔʔo nəṣṣēn* — 'He cut it in two' (lit. '...two halves')

In some cases there is an alternative construction with object and prepositional complement: *byəzraɛu ʔam³ḥ b-ʔarāḍīhon* 'They sow wheat in their fields' (Cf. example 1); *mallēt mayy bəl-ʔannīne* "I filled water into the bottle" (Cf. example 3).

---

[1]Not pronominalizable, because not definitizable [p. 494].

Adverbial Noun Complements: Gerundial and Paronymous
(al-maf⁀ɛūl l-muṭlaq, the "Absolute Object")

Verbs (and participles) are sometimes complemented by a gerund [p. 284], with or without modifiers. The most common kind of gerundial complement is the PARONYMOUS COMPLEMENT or "COGNATE OBJECT"), in which the complemented verb's own gerund is used.

Without modifiers, a paronymous complement is used for emphasis:

1. kān ɛam-biẓəṭṭ ẓaṭṭ bēn
   ᵊš-šawāreɛ

   'He was racing wildly through the streets', lit. "He was chasing a chase through the streets"

2. l-xiṭāb hazz ᵊš-žamhūr hazz

   'The speaker moved the crowd profoundly', lit. "The speaker shook the crowd a shaking"

3. ṣāḍafto mṣāḍafe

   'I ran across him by chance', lit. "I encountered him an encounter"

4. kānet ᵊs-sayyāra ɛam-tākol
   ᵊz-zəfᵊt ʔakᵊl

   'The car was really burning up the road', lit. "...was eating the asphalt an eating"

5. waḷḷa maskūbe sakᵊb!

   'She really has a beautiful figure!', lit. "By God (she is) moulded (with) a moulding"

With modifiers, a paronymous complement serves to show how something referred to by the verb is done:

6. staʔbalūna ʔəstəʔbāl bāred

   'They received us coldly', lit. "They received us a cold reception"

7. ɛaraḍ ʔaḍīto ɛarḍ ᵊmnīḥ

   'He presented his case well', lit. "He presented his case a good presentation"

8. š-šaġle kəlla kānet
   ᵊmnaẓẓame tanẓīm ɛāṭel

   'The whole job was poorly organized', lit. "...was organized a bad organization"

9. bṭəṭṣarraf ṭaṣarrof ᵊl-xānmāt

   'She conducts herself like a lady', lit. "She behaves (with) the behavior of ladies"

10. ṭ-ṭayyāra habṭet ᵊhbūṭ
    ʔəḍṭirāri

    'The plane made a forced landing', lit. "...landed an obligatory landing"

11. btərsom rasᵊm zēti

    'She paints in oils', lit. "She draws (by) oil drawing"

12. mīn štaġal ʔaktar ᵊš-šəġᵊl?

    'Who has done the most work?', lit. "Who has worked most of the work?"

13. *l-ʔəxtēn byəxtəlfu ɛan baɛḍon*
    kəll ʔl-ʔəxtilāf

'The two sisters are altogether different from one another', lit. "... differ from one another all the difference"

14. *byūton mafrūše farš ʔmnīḥ*
    [adap. from PAT-191]

'Their houses are well furnished', lit. "...furnished a good furnishing"

Instance nouns [p. 297] are sometimes used as paronymous complements:

15. *ġləṭṭ ġalṭa fagīɛa*

'I've made an awful mistake'

16. *ḍarabo ḍarbe ʔawiyye*

'He struck him a mighty blow'

17. *dərna dōra kāmle ḥawāli l-balad*

'We made a complete tour around the town'

18. *xaṭa xaṭwe kəllha dahāʔ*

'He made a very shrewd move', lit. "He stepped a step (which was) all shrewdness"

19. *lammaḥət-ʔlna talmīḥa wāḍḥa*

'She gave us a broad hint', lit. "She hinted to us a clear hint"

Sometimes the gerund of an underlying verb is used to complement a derived verb:

20. *tɛāmal ʔmɛāmale wāṭye*

'He got a raw deal', lit. "He was treated (with) a low treatment" (*mɛāmale*, ger. of *ɛāmal* 'to treat', complementing the passive *tɛāmal* 'to be treated')

21. *darraso dirāse mhīḥa*

'He taught him well' (*dirāse*, ger. of *daras* 'to study' complementing the causative *darras* 'to make... study, to instruct')

22. *ɛadad ʔs-səkkān ʔzdād zyāde*
    hāʔile

'The population has increased tremendously' (*zyāde*, ger. of *zād* 'to increase' [trans. and intrans.], complementing the mediopassive *zdād* 'to increase' [intrans. only].)

In some cases a paronymous complement is not a gerund at all: *kānu raḥa-yšaʔʔfū šəʔaf* 'They were about to tear him to pieces' (figuratively). The complement *šəʔaf* is the plural of *šəʔfe* 'piece', a simple noun, paronymous to *šaʔʔaf* 'to break in pieces'. In *txānaʔna xnāʔa kbīre* 'We had a big argument', the paronymous complement *xnāʔa* may be considered the participative noun [p. 247] underlying the reciprocative verb [248] *txānaʔu* 'to argue', or alternatively, its suppletive gerund. See also example 12 above.

Non-paronymous gerundial complements:

23. rəžeε rakªḍ la-εarabīto
    [PVA-22]

'He ran back to his car', lit. "He returned (by) running to his car" (ger. of rakaḍ 'to run')

24. ṭəleε šarḥaṭa mn ªl-madrase

'He was expelled from school', lit. "He came out – (by) expulsion – from school" (ger. of šarḥaṭ 'to expel')

25. nəzel maεªṭ bəž-žāṭ

'He ate voraciously from the platter', lit. "He came down (with) voracity at the platter" (ger.of maεaṭ 'to devour')

26. bətražžāk lā təfhamni ġalaṭ

'Please don't misunderstand me', lit. "I beg of you, don't understand me (by) mistake" (ger. of ġaleṭ 'to make a mistake')

27. bisāwi ṭʔūmto ṭafṣīl

'He has his suits tailor made', lit. "He makes his suits (by) tailoring" (ger. of faṣṣal 'to cut out, make to measure')

PREPOSITIONAL COMPLEMENTS

Many verbs, nouns, and adjectives are complemented by prepositional phrases, involving some particular preposition[1]:

1. safrətna btətwaffaʔ εaṭ-ṭaʔs

'Our trip depends on the weather'

2. mīn raha-yʔūm bəd-difāε?

'Who's going to take on the defense?'

3. sammūha səεād εala ʔəsªm səttha

'They named her Suad after her grandmother'

4. baddi kallef haḍªrtak təsεā-li b-waẓīfe

'I'd like to ask you to help me find a job' [SAL-92] (Two prepositional complements)

5. l-maḥkame ḥakmet εalē bəl-ʔəεdām

'The court sentenced him to death' (Two prepositional complements)

---

[1]Prepositional complements are often difficult to distinguish from preposi-tional supplements [p.523]. The essential difference is that a complement is expected – and sometimes required – to go with some particular word, or some particular kind of word, in the complemented phrase; a supplement, on the other hand, goes with the phrase as such. The speaker is not under constraint to use a supplement because of any particular word or kind of word in the phrase. Supplements in general, furthermore, do not have to follow the supplemented term; their word order is relatively free.

6. *Ɛam–ᵊtxabbi Ɛanni ši?*   'Are you hiding anything from me?'

7. *mā bəddi ᵓāxod maṣāri mən*   'I don't want to take money from
   hal-məskīn   the poor thing'

8. *huwwe rfīᵓ ᵓadīm ᵓəlna*   'He's an old companion of ours'
                                                       (Prepositional complement to noun
                                                       rfīᵓ)

9. *sāknīn byūt məlk ᵓəlon*   'They live in houses they own'
   [PAT-191]   (Prep. Comp. to noun *məlk:* lit.
                                                       "They inhabit houses [which are]
                                                       property to them")

10. *hiyye b-ḥāle mayᵓūs mənha*   'She's in a desparate situation',
                                                       lit. "She's in a situation (that's)
                                                       despaired of " [p.263].

11. *haš-ši xāṣṣ ᵊb-Ɛaṣᵊrna*   'It's something peculiar to our
                                                       times'

12. *l-bēt lāḥet ᵊl-ᵓəhmāl Ɛalē*   'The house showed signs of neglect'
                                                       (*ᵓəhmāl Ɛala* 'neglect of')

13. *ᵓana mayyet mn ᵊt-taƐab*   'I'm dead tired' (*mayyet mən* 'dead
                                                       of', *māt mən* 'to die of')

14. *...la-sabab mn ᵊl-ᵓasbāb*   'for some reason or other'

15. *š-šām ᵓabrad mən bērūt*   'Damascus is colder than Beirut in
    bəš-šəte   winter' (Comparative phrase [p.314])

16. *ᵓaxi ᵓaġġar mənnak b-Ɛašr*   'My brother is ten years younger
    ᵊsnīn   than you' (Comparative phrase, fol-
                                                       lowed by second prep. compl. 'by
                                                       ten years')

The position of prepositional phrases (complemental or supplemental) relative to other complements varies, depending on a number of different factors.

Generally speaking, a preposition with pronoun suffix [p.477] comes before an object (unless, of course, the object itself is a pronoun suf- fixed to the verb): *Ɛam–ᵊtxabbi Ɛanni ši?* 'Are you hiding anything from me?' (Cf. *Ɛam–ᵊtxabbī Ɛanni?* 'Are you hiding it from me?'). If, on the other hand, the preposition is followed by a noun(or noun phrase), then the object usually comes first: *Ɛam–ᵊtxabbi ši Ɛan ᵓaxūk?* 'Are you hid- ing anything from your brother?' (See also Example 7 above.)

A prepositional phrase tends to precede an adverbial complement if it is shorter, and follow it if it is longer: *tᵓaddam b-məhᵊnto ta ᵓaddom Ɛažīb* 'He's made remarkable progress in his career'; *ṭaleƐ šarḥaṭa mn ᵊl-madrase* 'He was expelled from school' [ex. 24, p.444].

This principle of relative length of complements (the shorter having word-order priority) applies generally whenever other principles of priority are not in effect. It is not, of course, a hard-and-fast rule.

It applies also to predicative complements [See examples, below], except that a complement must <u>follow</u> whatever element of the sentence it is predicative <u>to</u>, regardless of length.

PREDICATIVE COMPLEMENTS

Many verbs (and other verb-type expressions [p.412]) are complemented by <u>predicates</u> [p.380] which are applicable — contingently upon the verb[1] — to the verb's subject, object, or (less commonly) prepositional complement.

Like adverbial complements, a predicative complement is always preceded by the object, if any, and is sometimes preceded by a prepositional complement [p.444].

Subjective Complements (Complements predicative to the subject, or subject "understood" [p.418]):

1. *l-maktūb wəṣel <u>mət²axxer šwayye</u>*   'The letter arrived a bit late'

2. *²aɛadna ²rāb la-baɛdna*   'We sat near each other'

3. *s-sa²²f madhūn <u>²abyaḍ</u>*   'The ceiling is painted white' (Subject of passive participle corresponds to object of active verb)

4. *mīn ṭaleɛ <u>²l-ġāleb</u> bəl-²m²ātale?*   'Who came out the winner in the fight?'

5. *l-²kmāle ²alak <u>baxšīš</u>*   'Keep the change', lit. 'The change (is) for you (as) a tip' (*²alak* is a verb-type expression [p.414].)

6. *btəštáġel <u>manukān</u> b-maḥall fax²m ləl-²albisa*   'She works as a model in an elegant dress shop'

---

[1]Predicative complements differ from <u>attributes</u> — which are also transformed predicates [p.493] — in this respect: The predication implied by an attribute is not <u>contingent</u> on anything else in the clause; it is assertive and unconditional, while the predication implied by a predicative complement is in a sense optative [p.347], conditioned by the main verb. Compare the attributive adjective *žamīl* , in *la²ēt ²l-bēt ²ž-žamīl ?* 'Did you find the pretty house?' with the complemental *žamīl* in *la²ēt ²l-bēt žamīl ?* 'Did you find the house pretty?'

7. *nƐalnet madīne makšūfe waʔt*   'It was declared an open city during
   ʔl-ḥarb.   the war'

8. *šū Ɛəndak fwāki?* [SAL-43]   'What have you (in the way of) fruit?'

9. *kamm fī mətr ʔmrabbaƐ fi*   'How many square meters are there in
   had-dāyra?   this circle?' [p.572]

10. *fī Ɛāṣfe ṭālƐa*   'There's a storm coming up'

Complements to linking verbs are — strictly speaking —
subjective complements, but they are treated here along
with other paratactic complemental clauses [p.450].

All complemental verbs that have the same subject-
referent as the complemented term, furthermore, may be
analyzed as subjective complements. For examples, see
p.348ff.

Objective Complements (Complements predicative to the object):

1. *Ɛaṭēṭo yā ḥdiyye*   'I gave it to him as a gift'

2. *ḥassabūni ʔənglīzi*   'They took me for an Englishman'

3. *bəddo tfaṣṣəl-lo yāha badle*   'He wants you to make it into a suit
   [EA-118]   for him', lit. "...to cut for him it
                                      (as) a suit"

4. *hādi tāni marra byəntəxbū*   'This is the second time they've
   Ɛəḍu barlamān [EA-159]   elected him member of parliament'

5. *nžabart ḥəṭṭ xams ʔʔrūš*   'I was required to put five piastres
   taʔmīn Ɛal-ʔannīne   deposit on the bottle'

6. *ʔaddēš Ɛam-tāxod ḥaʔʔ*   'How much are you getting for these
   haṣ-ṣabbāṭ?   shoes?' (lit. "...(as)price(of)
                                      these shoes")

7. *ttaxaz ʔṭ-ṭəbb ʔš-šarƐi*   'He made forensic medicine his
   məhne ʔəlo   career'

8. *byəbƐatu ʔəsm əkbīr*   'They send a large part of it to
   ləl-əmṣāben məšān yəƐəmlū   the soap factories to have it made
   ṣābūn [PAT-183]   (into)soap'

9. *hāda bsammī Ɛamal Ɛaẓīm*   'That's what I call a great deed'

10. *ḥaṭṭēt ḥāli wāṣṭa bəl-xilāf*   'I acted as mediator in the dispute',
                                    lit. "I put myself (as) mediator..."

11. *bəƐtabərha wāžeb maƐnawi*   'I consider it a moral obligation'

12. *šū ḥāmel šahādāt?* [SAL-96]   'What diplomas have you?', lit. "What do you carry (in the way of) diplomas?"

13. *zayyanet ᵊl-bēt ktīr ḥalu ɛala ɛars bantha*   'She decorated the house very nice-(ly) for her daughter's wedding'

14. *batḥabb ᵊl-ʔahwe ḥalwe walla sāda?*   'Would you like the coffee sweetened or straight?'

15. *lāzem txalli l-bēt ᵊnḍīf*   'You've got to keep the house clean'

16. *tarakᵊt ballōra wāḥde šāɛle b-ʔūḍet ᵊl-ʔāɛde*   'I left one lamp lit in the living room'

17. *laḥa-tlāʔi ṭ-ṭalɛa wāʔfe w-ṣaɛbe*   'You'll find the climb steep and difficult'

18. *ḥāses ḥāli ʔaḥsan b-ᵊktīr ᵊl-yōm*   'I'm feeling much better today', lit. "I'm feeling myself (as) much better...

19. *šāyef ḥāli matl ᵊz-zaft ᵊl-yōm*   'I feel terrible today', lit. "I see myself like pitch today"

20. *xalli ɛēnak ɛal-ᵊwlād*   'Keep your eye on the children'

21. *šaft ᵊl-žunūd māšyīn?*   'Did you see the troops marching?'

22. *mā blāʔiha ɛaṭ-ṭarẓ ᵊl-ɛarabi ṣ-ṣarf*   'It doesn't seem to me to be in the pure Arab style', lit. "I don't find it in the..."

Many objective complements are verbal. It is convenient to treat these complements in the section on paratactic complemental clauses (p.450, ex. 10), but note also:

23. *xallīna nalḥoš ᵊfrank la-nšūf mīn birūḥ*   'Let's toss a coin to see who goes'

24. *mḥassbe ʔanno fīha taʔmᵊron isāwu šū ma batḥabb*   'She thinks she can order them to do whatever she likes'

Prepositional Objective Complements (Complements predicative to the object of a preposition):

1. *bamroʔ ɛalēk bal-bēt b-hal-kam yōm*   'I'll stop by (and see) you at home one of these days'

2. *ṣār-ᵊlhon madzawwžīn sane w-ᵊšwayye*   'They've been married a little over a year', lit. "It has become to them married..."

3. *ṣar-li xams ᵊsnīn baɛᵊrfo*   'I've known him for five years', lit. "It's become for me five years (that) I know him"

COMPLEMENTAL CLAUSES

Many verbs, nouns, adjectives, and miscellaneous other predicative terms
[p.412] are commonly (in some cases almost always) complemented by a clause.

Some complemental clauses are HYPOTACTIC, i.e. introduced by a conjunction: *ʔāl ʔənno bəddo yrūḥ* 'He said that
he wanted to go', while others are PARATACTIC, having no
conjunction: *ʔāl bəddo yrūḥ* 'He said he wanted to go'. The
usual complemental conjunctions are *ʔənno* 'that' [p.543],
ʔiza 'whether, if', *la–, ḥatta,* etc. 'in order to' [p.353].

Examples of hypotactic clauses:

1. *ftakart ʔənnak l-ᵊmɛallem*
   [PVA-32]

   'I thought that you were the teacher'

2. *raḥa–ʔūl la-samīr ʔənno mā
   yətʔaxxar*

   'I'm going to tell Samir not to be
   late'

3. *ləssa ʔana mū mətʔakked ʔiza
   brūḥ wəlla laʔ*

   'I'm still not sure whether I'll go
   or not'

4. *w-rāḥ la-balad tānye la-yšūf
   ʔiza bilāʔi zalame šāṭer ʔaw
   ɛālem mətlo* [AO-83]

   'And he went to another town to see
   if he could find a man as clever or
   as learned as himself'

In example 4 the main verb *rāḥ* is complemented by the
clause introduced by *la–;* the complemental verb *yšūf* is
complemented in its turn by the *ʔiza* clause.
Both *ʔiza* and *la–,* etc. are also used in supplemental
clauses. See pp.331, 358.
The forms *yalli, ᵊlli,* etc. [p.494] are sometimes used
as a complemental conjunction in sentences like the following:

5. *fraḥt ᵊktīr ᵊlli ražeɛ ʔəbᵊn
   ɛammak* [RN-II.51]

   'I'm very glad that your cousin has
   returned'

6. *w-ʔana mabṣūt ᵊlli kān hēk, ʔaw
   ᵊlli ṣār maɛi hal-ʔəmtiḥān hāda*
   [SVSA-124]

   'And I'm pleased that that's the way
   it was — that I had that examination'

Some clauses complement transitive verbs, i.e. verbs
that can take an object, while others complement intransitive verbs, or nouns or adjectives — which are otherwise
complemented by prepositional phrases. In colloquial Arabic the complemental preposition is usually lost before a
clause, so that the distinction between objects and prepositional complements is lost when the complement is a

clause (but see p. 357). Examples of clauses corresponding
to prepositional complements:

7. *bəɛtə́ref ʔənni kənt ġalṭān*   'I admit that I was mistaken' (cf.
                                        bəɛtə́ref bi-ġalᵊṭṭi 'I admit my mis-
                                        take')

8. *waɛadna ʔənno raḥ-isāɛədna*   'He promised us that he was going to
                                        help us' (cf. *waɛadna bəl-ᵊmsāɛade*
                                        'He promised us help')

9. *l-ləžne ḥakmet ɛal-bināye ʔənna*   'The committee ruled that the build-
   mū ṣālḥa ləs-səkne   ing was not fit for habitation' (cf.
                                        l-ləžne ḥakmet ɛal-bināye bət-tahbīṭ
                                        'The committee slated the building
                                        for demolition')

      Note also example 3 (cf. *mətʔakked mən* 'sure of') and
example 6 (cf. *mabṣūt mən, mabṣūt b-* 'glad of, pleased
with'). In example 2, the complemental clause may be
equated with an object since the verb *ʔāl* 'to say, tell'
is transitive. Similarly in ex. 4, the *ʔiza* clause functions like an object of the transitive verb *šāf* 'to see'.

Examples of paratactic clauses:

10. *w-ʔamar ᵊž-žənn yərmūni b-nəṣṣ*   'And he ordered the Jinn to throw
    ᵊl-baḥᵊr [AO-116]   me into the middle of the sea'

11. *bḥəbb kəll šahᵊr təbɛatū-li*   'I want you(pl.)to send me a state-
    bayān b-ᵊḥsābi [DA-294]   ment of my account every month'

12. *rūḥ ᵊsʔāl ʔəmmak bəddha šī*   'Go ask your mother if she wants
                                         anything'

13. *l-ḥaʔīʔa bfaddel mā rūḥ*   'The truth is, I'd prefer not to go
    la-maḥall balāk [DA-172]   anywhere without you'

14. *ʔənti ʔlī-lo fāyze žāye*   'You(f.) tell him Faiza is coming'

15. *xāyəf-lak ᵊlᵣbēt yəhboṭ*   'I'm afraid the house will cave in'

16. *kān bəddi ʔəštrīha, bass ʔal-li*   'I wanted to buy it, but he told me
    mā ʔəštrīha   not to'

17. *marra w-marrtēn ʔəlt-əllo*   'Time and again I've told him not to
    lā təlɛab bəṭ-ṭarīʔ   play in the street'

      In Arabic there is no distinct line drawn between di-
rect and indirect quotation. Example 17, translated literally, is '...I told him, don't play in the street', while
in ex. 16 the quotation is made indirect, and in 14 the
clause *fāyze žāye* could be either direct or indirect quota-

tion. Direct quotation (as in ex. 17) is used more liberally than it is in English, is less apt to be set off
intonationally, and has less dramatizing force.

Subject Clauses. Many predicative terms are followed by a clause which functions as the subject [p.417] of the predication. A subject clause is superficially just the same as a true complemental clause, since it is inherently
indefinite [407] and therefore normally follows the main term of the predicate. By the same token, the predicative term is normally neutral (3rd p.
sing.) in inflection [p.365]:

18. *byəghar ʔənno ʔafḍal šī*   'It appears that the best things is
    l-ʔəttifāʔ ɛala ḥall waṣaṭ   to agree on a compromise solution'

19. *ʔabadan mā xaṭar ɛala bāli*   'It never crossed my mind that he
    ʔənno laḥa-yəɛtéreḍ   was going to object'

20. *l-muhəmm ʔənnak təhḍar w-kəll*   'The important things is that you at-
    šī ʔənšāḷḷa bikūn tamām   tend, and everything (God willing)
                                          will be all right'

21. *məɛᵊžze ʔənnon bəʔyu ɛāyšīn*   'It's a miracle that they are still
                                          alive'

22. *wāḍeh mn ᵊl-maktūb ʔənno mālo*   'It's clear from the letter that he
    raḍyān   isn't satisfied'

23. *mnīḥ halli ʔžīt ʔabᵊl ma*   'It's good that you've come before
    ʔəṭlaɛ [DA-243]   I left' (cf. examples 5 and 6.)

Paratactic subject clauses:

24. *byəghar kənt ʔākel šī tᵊīl*   'It seems you must have eaten some-
    [DA-217]   thing indigestible' (lit. 'heavy')

25. *fəkro yəbɛatni ɛal-məstašfa*   'His idea is to send me to the
    [DA-217]   hospital'

26. *mā biḥəʔʔ-əllak tāxod žāye*   'You don't deserve to get a prize'
    [AO-88]   (lit. 'It isn't right for you...')

27. *lāzem nām kamān šwayye* [AO-51]   'I must sleep a while longer' (lit.
                                          'It is necessary that I sleep...')

28. *masməḥ-li ʔəlɛab tanes ma dām*   'I'm allowed to play tennis as long
    mā zīd fīha   as I don't overdo it' (lit. "It's
                                          allowed to me to play...")

29. *b-ʔəmkānak tsāwī-li talifōn?*   'Could you give me a phone call?'
                                          (lit. "Is it in your power to...")

Many very common expressions are complemented by paratactic clauses; see the examples in Chapter 13, p.347 ff.

Linking Verbs (*kān wa-ʔaxawātuhā*)

The verbs *kān* 'to be', *ṣār* 'to become', *ḍall* 'to remain', and a few others are almost always complemented, paratactically, by a <u>predicate</u> [p.380]. The subject of the complemental clause, if any, is the same as that of the linking verb. The predicate may be of any sort (i.e. verbal, adjectival, nominal, or prepositional: *kānet ɛam-təḥki* 'she was talking', *kānet taɛbāne* 'she was tired', *kānet bənt ᵊgġīre* 'she was a little girl', *kānet bəl-bēt* 'she was in the house'.

> There are other verbs that are always complemented by a predicate but with which the predicate is limited to a certain kind; e.g. *ʔəder* 'to be able' is always complemented by a <u>verbal</u> predicate.

Examples, *kān:*

30. *kān ʔaḥsan-lak təstašīrna*

   'You should have consulted us' (lit. "It was better for you to consult us")

31. *kənna šāyfīn malāmeḥ ᵊǰ⁺ᵊžbāl*

   'We could see the outlines of the mountains'

32. *bəddi kūn ᵊġfīt b-ᵊġyābak* [SPA-30]

   'I must have dozed off in your absence'

33. *bižūz kān ᵊl-bōṣṭaži*

   'It was probably the postman'

34. *žnēnᵊta bətkūn zāhye b-hal-waʔt mn ᵊs-səne*

   'Her garden is colorful this time of year'

35. *kān wāḥed bāša ʔāɛed fi balkōn sarāyto* [PVA-28]

   'A certain pasha was sitting on the balcony of his palace'

With complement-verb inversion:

36. *nšāḷḷa baṣīṭa kānet* [SAL-137]

   'Nothing serious, I trust!' (lit. "God willing, minor it was")

Examples, *ṣār:*

37. *šū ɛməlt ḥatta ṣāret martak hēk, mətl ᵊl-malāyke?* [AO-112]

   'What did you do, that your wife became so, like the angels?'

38. *ṣār ᵊl-masa?*

   'Is it evening already?' (lit. "Has it become...")

39. *kān ṣār baɛd nəṣṣ ᵊl-lēl lamma ržəɛna ɛal-bēt*

   'It was after midnight when we got back home' (lit. "It had become after ..."; the linking verb *kān* is complemented by the linking verb *ṣār*, which in its turn is complemented by a prepositional predicate.)

40. ṣərt təḥki Ɛarabi mnīḥ
[PVA-26]

'You speak Arabic well now' (lit.
"You have become that you speak...")

41. kəll šī biṣīr tamām

'Everything will be all right' (lit.
"...will become all right")

With complement-verb inversion:

42. mažmūɛti kāmle ṣāret halla?

'My collection has now become complete'

Examples, ḍall:

43. ḍallēna sahranīn la-waʔət
mətʔaxxer bəl-lēl

'We stayed up till late in the night'

44. ḍallet ʔtnəʔʔ Ɛaliyyi

'She kept nagging at me'

45. biḍall yəḥki Ɛan ʔl-ḥawādes
ʔl-māḍye

'He keeps talking about past events'

Examples, bəʔi, baʔa:

46. s-səkkīne ž-ždīde dāyman
ʔbtəbʔa ṭayybe

'A new knife always stays good'
(saying)

47. mā baʔa fī Ɛəndi ġēr nəṣṣ
ʔannīnet zēt [PVA-44]

'I haven't got but a half bottle of
oil left' (the ġēr phrase is subject, fī Ɛəndi the predicate and
complement of the linking verb.)

48. byəbʔa yzūrha kəll yōm

'He keeps on visiting her every day'

49. bʔīt ʔhnīk kamm šahʔr

'I stayed there several months'

Examples, mā Ɛād 'no longer':

50. mā Ɛād iṭāwəɛni ʔabadan

'He no longer obeys me at all'

51. l-bənt mā Ɛādet ʔẓġīre təlɛab
bəl-ləɛab

'The girl is no longer little
(enough) to play with dolls'

52. mā Ɛād fiyyi ʔəthammála

'I can't stand it any more'

53. ʔiza bəttamm ʔtɛāmlo hēk mā
laḥa-yɛūd yəsmaɛ mənnak

'If you keep on treating him like
this he won't listen to you any
more' (bəttamm is also a linking
verb.)

CHAPTER 18: ANNEXION *(al-ʔiḍāfa)* AND PREPOSITIONS

A CONSTRUCT, or ANNEXION PHRASE, is composed of two immediately adjacent nominal or noun-type terms [p. 382], of which the leading term *(al-muḍāf)* is generally qualified by the following term *(al-muḍāf ʔilayhi):*

šawāreɛ bērūt '(the) streets(of)Beirut'

bēt nažīb '(the) house(of)Najeeb': 'Najeeb's house'

ʔəsʔm bənt '(the) name(of a)girl': 'a girl's name'

waraʔ ɛəneb 'leaves(of) grapes': 'grape leaves, vine leaves'

> Most constructs can be rendered roughly in English by inserting 'of' between the translated terms, preserving the word order of the original. In normal English, however, the Arabic following term is often translated as a possessive (Najeeb's, girl's), or as the first constituent of a noun compound (grape leaves), resulting in a word order that is the reverse of the Arabic.

When some words occur IN CONSTRUCT (i.e. as leading term in an annexion phrase), they appear in a CONSTRUCT FORM which differs from the ABSOLUTE FORM used otherwise. Construct forms are treated in Chapter 5, p. 162ff.

Absolute Form (Illustrating use of word not in construct) — Construct Form

madrase sānawiyye 'secondary school'....*madrast ᵊl-balad* 'the town school'

ž-žarīde l-ʔaḥsan 'the best newspaper'..*žarītt ᵊl-yōm* 'today's paper'

l-ʔaxx ʔaḥmad 'Brother Ahmed'.......*ʔaxu ʔaḥmad* 'Ahmed's brother'

xamse mənhon 'five of them'........*xams ᵊržāl* 'five men'

> There are various kinds of annexion, depending on the types of leading term: substantive, adjective, partitive, cardinal numeral, and elative/ordinal.

> Prepositional phrases are also conveniently considered a type of annexion phrase, though the more typical prepositions are quite unlike noun-type words, and prepositional phrases are un-noun-like in function (not normally used as subject of a clause). See p. 476.

For annexion clauses, see p. 491.

SUBSTANTIVE ANNEXION

The leading term of an ordinary noun construct cannot have an article prefix [p.493], regardless whether it is definite or indefinite: *šərket zēt* '(an) oil company': *šərket ᵊz-zēt* '<u>the</u> oil company'; *šawāreɛ madīne* 'city streets': *šawāreɛ ᵊl-madīne* '<u>the</u> city streets'.

There are a few set phrases which are exceptions to this rule: *l-bēt mūne* 'the storeroom, pantry' (but also regular: *bēt ᵊl-mūne*), *l-bani ʔādam* 'the human being', *l-ʔəmm ʔarbɛā w-ʔarbɛīn* 'the centipede', *l-ṃayy ward* 'the rose water', etc.

Occasionally the leading term is a coördination [p.392]: *šawāreɛ u-ḥārāt ᵊl-madīne* 'the streets and quarters of the city', *ḥərriyyet u-ʔəstəqlāl ᵊl-fəkᵊr* 'freedom and independence of thought'.

Often, however, such coordinations are avoided by the use of an anaphoric pronoun: *šawāreɛ ᵊl-madīne w-ḥārātha* 'the streets of the city and its quarters'.

Except for coördinations, the leading term of an annexion phrase is limited to a single word.

The following term, on the other hand, may be any sort of noun-type word or phrase [p.381,382]: *šawāreɛ madīne kbīre* '(the)streets(of a) large city', *ḥərriyyet ᵊl-fəkᵊr wər-raʔi* 'freedom (of) thought and opinion', *ḥārāt ʔakbar mədon ʔafrīqya* '(the)quarters of Africa's largest cities'.

Since the following term may be any sort of noun-type phrase, it may, of course, be another annexion phrase, as in the last example above (which is, in fact, a construct within a construct within still another construct). Note also: *taḥsīn ṣifāt taḥammol ᵊl-ḥarāra* 'improvement (in) qualities (of) resistance (to) heat'; *farš ʔaɛgam byūt ʔaǧᵊnya ʔurubba* [PAT-191] '(the) furniture (of the) greatest (of the) houses (of the) rich (of) Europe'.

Definite and Indefinite Constructs. If the following term of a construct is definite, the leading term is treated as definite also; and if the following term is <u>in</u>definite, the leading term, likewise, is treated as indefinite.[1] (On Definiteness, see p.494.)

---

[1] Instead of speaking here of the leading term, one might say 'the construct as a whole'. The leading term is generally the main term and the following term is subordinate, i.e. agreement is with the leading term. (But see p.466ff.)

Definite	Indefinite

fənžān ᵊl-ᵓahwe 'the cup of coffee'......*fənžān ᵓahwe* 'a cup of coffee'

ɛaṣîr ᵊl-bərdᵓān 'the orange juice'......*ɛaṣîr bərdᵓān* 'orange juice'

səkkān baladna 'our town's inhabitants'..*səkkān balad* 'a town's inhabitants'

ᵓasᵊm bənto 'his daughter's name'........*ᵓasᵊm bənᵊt tānye* 'another girl's name'

To say that the leading term is "treated as definite" means that if it has an attribute, the attribute shows definite agreement with it; and to say it is "treated as indefinite" means the attribute shows indefinite agreement with it.

An attributive adjective (or noun) shows definite agreement by having the article prefix; an attributive clause, by having the clause definitizer *yalli (halli, etc.). See p. 493.

Definite	Indefinite

bənt ᵊl-xabbāz ᵊl-həlwe...................*bənt xabbāz həlwe*
'the baker's pretty daughter'   'a baker's pretty daughter'

bənt ᵊl-xabbāz yalli šəfnāha bəl-balad....*bənt xabbāz šəfnāha bəl-balad*
'the baker's daughter we saw in town'   'a baker's daughter we saw in town'

bêt nažîb ᵊl-faxᵊm........................(Cannot be made indefinite be-
'Najeeb's stately house'   cause the following term, a proper name, is inherently definite.)

By the same token, if the last term in a series of constructs within constructs is definite, then all the other terms are likewise treated as definite, and if the last term is indefinite, so are all the others. [p. 456]

Constructs with Pronouns. A pronoun can never be leading term in annexion, but it <u>can</u> be following term: *ᵓasᵊm hāda* '(the)name(of)this'; *ᵓasᵊm mîn* '(the)name(of)whom?', i.e. 'whose name?'.

A personal pronoun [p. 541] as following term in annexion takes the form of a suffix: *ᵓəsmo* '(the)name(of)him', i.e. 'his name'; *šawārəɛha* '(the) streets(of)it', i.e. 'its streets'; *madrasətna* '(the)school(of)us', i.e. 'our school'.

The personal pronouns are inherently definite; thus any noun to which a pronoun is suffixed is — as leading term — also treated as definite: *bənto l-həlwe* 'his pretty daughter'.

A noun with a pronoun suffix, then, constitutes an annexion phrase as it stands; and the pronoun in its turn
<u>cannot</u> stand in construct with another following term.
Therefore a noun with a pronoun suffix — like a noun with
the article prefix — can only be the <u>last</u> word in a con-
struct-within-construct series. Avoid trying to interrupt
a construct like *ʔūḍet nōm* 'room (of)sleeping', i.e. 'bedroom' with a pronoun suffix as in *ʔūḍətna* 'our room'. To
say 'our bedroom', the suffix may be attached to *nōm:* *ʔūḍet
nōmna* "(the)room (of the)sleep(of)us", or periphrastically:
ʔūḍt ʔn-nōm tabaɛna [p. 460].

Identificatory and Classificatory Annexion. There are two ways in which the
following term may qualify the leading term:

In an IDENTIFICATORY construct — if it is definite — the following term
generally answers the question 'which?' (or 'whose?') applied to the leading
term. For instance in the phrase *walad ǧāri* 'my neighbor's boy', *ǧāri* shows
<u>which</u> (or <u>whose</u>) boy is referred to.

In a CLASSIFICATORY construct — whether it is definite or not — the following term generally answers the question 'what kind of...?' applied to the
leading term. Thus in *ɛaṣīr ʔl-bardʔān* 'the orange juice', *l-bardʔān* shows
<u>what</u> <u>kind</u> <u>of</u> juice is meant.

The main grammatical difference between the two kinds of annexion is
this: In identificatory constructs the following term — if it is definite
— can generally be <u>pronominalized</u>; i.e. whatever the following term refers
to may subsequently (or alteratively) be referred to by a pronoun, suffixed
to the leading term: *walad ǧāri* 'my neighbor's boy' → *walado* 'his boy'.
With classificatory constructs this cannot be done.

Identification is fundamentally a function of definiteness [p. 494]; and classification, a function of indefinite-
ness. But since the article prefix is added to the following term only — even when its function is really to definitize
the leading term — it is not possible simply to equate
identificatory terms with definitizable terms.
The personal pronouns, of course, are inherently identificatory.

The rules of thumb involving 'which?' and 'what kind
of?' do not apply equally well to all kinds of construct:
in *fənǧan ʔl-ʔahwe* 'the cup of coffee', *l-ʔahwe* does not,
strictly speaking, tell "what kind of" cup is meant, but
it is classificatory nevertheless: *l-ʔahwe* is not pronominalizable.
There are, also, some inherently definite following
terms which are not pronominalizable: *ǧarīdet bukra*
'tomorrow's paper', *ǧazīret baḥrēn* 'the Island of Bahrain'
[p. 462].

Many annexion phrases, taken out of context, can be understood either as classificatory or as identificatory: *wlād ᵊl-madrase* 'the schoolchildren' (classificatory) or 'the children of the school' (identificatory).

The Demonstrative Proclitic in Annexion Phrases. Unlike the article, the demonstrative *hal-* 'this, that, these, those' [p.556] may generally be attached to the leading term of a definite classificatory construct:

hal-ᵊwlād ᵊl-madrase	'these schoolchildren'
hal-fənžān ᵊl-ᵓahwe	'this cup of coffee'
hal-ɛaṣīr ᵊl-bərdᵓān	'this orange juice'
hal-ᵓālt ᵊṭ-ṭaṣwīr	'this instrument (of) picturing', this camera
hal-ḥadwet l-ᵊḥṣān	'that horseshoe'
hal-waraᵓ ᵊl-karbōn	'this carbon paper'
hal-ᵊmḥaṭṭet ᵊl-ᵓiẕāɛa	'this broadcasting station'

Alternatively, however, *hal-* is sometimes attached to the <u>following</u> term, merging with the article; (unless doing so would create an undesirable ambiguity with respect to an <u>identificatory</u> construct [see below]):

fənžān hal-ᵓahwe	'this cup of coffee'
ɛaṣīr hal-bərdᵓān	'this orange juice'
ᵓālet haṭ-ṭaṣwīr	'this camera'
waraᵓ hal-karbōn	'this carbon paper'

With identificatory constructs, on the other hand, *hal-* can never be attached to the leading term. When attached to the following term, moreover, its meaning applies strictly to that of the following term:

wlād hal-madrase	'the children of this school'
ɛaṣīr hal-bərdᵓānāt	'the juice of those oranges' [p.370]
ḥadwet hal-ᵊḥṣān	'that horse's shoe'

To apply a demonstrative modifier to the leading term of an identificatory construct, the full words *hāda, hayy,* etc. [p.557] may be added after the following term:

ḍaffet ᵊn-nahr hayy	'this bank of the river'
ṭaraf ᵊṭ-ṭāwle hāda	'this edge of the table'

Cf. *ḍaffet han-nahᵊr* 'the bank of this river'

Periphrasis of Annexion. Annexion is not the only construction in which one noun-type term is used to identify or classify another. Instead of standing in construct with the qualifying term, a noun may often he linked to that same qualifier more loosely – by a preposition, usually *tabaɛ* [p.489], *la–* [479], *mən* [478], or *b–* [479]:

haš-šəʔfet ʔl-ʔarḏ 'that piece of land' <u>or</u> *haš-šəʔfe mn ʔl-ʔarḏ*

šrūš haš-šažara 'the roots of that tree' <u>or</u> *š-šrūš tabaɛ haš-šažara*

ṣānəɛtna 'our maid' <u>or</u> *ṣ-ṣānɛa tabaɛna*

ʔəmmet haš-žabal 'the summit of that mountain' <u>or</u> *l-ʔəmme b-haš-žabal*

xārṭeṭ ṭəroʔ 'a road map' <u>or</u> *xārṭa ləṭ-ṭəroʔ*

Since the leading term in annexion is subject to somewhat rigid limitations (e.g. it can only consist of a single word or coördination, and can only be definite or indefinite by agreement with the following term), there are certain situations in which a construct cannot be used at all, but may be circumlocuted by a prepositional construction.

1.) If the leading term is to be indefinite while the following term is definite: *xārṭa la-ṭəroʔ ləbnān* 'a road map of Lebanon' (i.e. 'a map for the roads of Lebanon'); the construct *xārṭeṭ ṭəroʔ ləbnān* '<u>the</u> road map of Lebanon' can only be definite, because the last term *ləbnān,* a proper name, is inherently definite.

A classificatory term following an elative or an ordinal [p.473], for instance, has to be indefinite: *ʔaḥsan šəʔfe mn ʔl-ʔarḏ* 'the best piece of land', *ʔawwal raʔīs ləl-žəmhuriyye* 'the first president of the republic'.

If this kind of term is followed by a definite construct, its meaning would be distorted to that of identification: *ʔaḥsan šəʔfet ʔl-ʔarḏ,* for instance, would mean 'the best (part) of the piece of land'.

2.) If both the leading term and the following term are to have modifiers: *l-ʔasɛār ʔl-ɛālye tabaɛ ʔl-kətob ʔl-madrasiyye* 'the high prices of school books'; cf. the construct *ʔasɛār ʔl-kətob əl-madrasiyye* 'the prices of school books'.

Adjectives coming after the last noun in a construct may apply to either term, depending on the sense and the agreement [p.503]: *farš ʔl-bet ʔž-ždīd ʔž-žamīl* 'the furniture of the beautiful new house' or 'the beautiful new furniture of the house'. But two contiguous adjectives are not used to modify two <u>different</u> terms; for 'the beautiful furniture of the new house', one must have recourse to the *tabaɛ* construction: *l-farš ʔž-žamīl tabaɛ ʔl-bēt ʔž-ždīd.*

A construct is always possible if there is only one adjective attribute involved: *fars ʔl-bēt ʔž-ždīd;* but even so it is often preferable to use a periphrasitic construction to resolve an ambiguity in the annexion phrase: *l-farš ʔž-ždīd tabaɛ ʔl-bēt* 'the new furniture of the house' or *l-farš tabaɛ ʔl-bēt ʔž-ždīd* 'the furniture of the new house'; *ṭ-ṭaraf ʔt-tāni mn ᵊš-šāreᶜ* 'the other side of the street' (rather than *ṭaraf ᵊš-šāreᶜ ᵊt-tāni,* which would more likely be understood as 'the side of the other street').

    3.) If one wishes both to classify <u>and</u> to identify the referent of a term, it is usually the classification that is done by annexion, while the identification is relegated to a *tabaᶜ* phrase: *farᶜ ᵊl-falsafe tabaᶜ šāmᶜᵊtna* 'our university's philosophy department', *ᵓᵊnšāyet ᵊl-ᵓᵊnglīzi tabaᶜak* 'your English composition', *mḥaṭṭet ᵊl-banzīn tabaᶜ ᶜammi* 'my uncle's gasoline station'.

        This rule may be reversed to lay constrastive emphasis on the classificatory term: *mḥaṭṭet ᶜammi tabaᶜ ᵊl-banzīn* 'my uncle's <u>gasoline</u> station'.

    Alternatively, in some cases, a classificatory following term may itself be put in construct with an identificatory term: *ᵓūḍet nōm ᶜabdalla* 'Abdullah's bedroom' (or *ᵓūḍt ᵊn-nōm tabaᶜ ᶜabdaḷḷa); makīnt ᵊḥlāᵓet ᵓaxi* 'my brother's electric shaver' (or *makīnet l-ᵊḥlāᵓa tabaᶜ ᵓaxi); ᶜaṣīr bᵊrdᵓāno* 'his orange juice' (or *ᶜaṣīr ᵊl-bᵊrdᵓān tabaᶜo).*

        This type of compound construct cannot be used very freely because in many cases the intended classificatory term would have its sense distorted to that of identification [p. 458]: *farᵊᶜ falsafet šāmᶜᵊtna,* for instance, would seem to mean 'the branch of our university's philosophy'. Note, however, that *ᶜaṣīr bᵊrdᵓāno* would <u>not</u> generally be taken to mean 'the juice of his oranges', because collectives are usually classificatory [p. 370].

Relationships Expressed by Substantive Annexion.[1] Ordinary noun constructs are used to express widely varied relationships of meaning between leading and following terms. For example:

Unit and Collective [p. 297] (Generally classificatory; periphrasis usually with *mᵊn):*

    kᵊtlet laḥᵊm 'a piece of meat'

    šᵊᵓfet xᵊbᵊz 'a piece of bread'

    ḥabbet ᶜᵊneb 'a grape' (lit. 'a berry of grapes')

    rās baṣal 'an onion' (lit. 'a bulb of onions')

    rūs baᵓar 'heads of cattle'

---

[1] The categories of relationship given here are merely intended to suggest the semantic scope of this construction, and are not meant to constitute a definitive classification (or kind of classification).

Genus and Differential Description (Classificatory; periphrasis various):

laḥ³m ba⁹ar 'beef' (lit. 'meat of cattle')

ḥakīm ⁹ɛyūn 'eye doctor'

ḥāsset ³š-šamm 'the sense of smell'

ɛa⁹rab da⁹āye⁹ 'minute hand'

⁹alam ḥəb³r 'fountain pen' (lit. 'pen of ink')

ṭāleb ṭəbb 'student of medicine'

kəllīt ³l-ḥ⁹ū⁹ 'the law school' (college of the law')

zahr ³l-lēmūn 'the orange (or lemon) blossoms'

Genus and Specific Name (Classificatory; no periphrasis):

žoz hənd 'coconuts' (lit. 'nuts of the Indies')

šažar zān 'beech trees'

sayyāret fōrd 'a Ford car' (Also appositive [p. 506]: *sayyāra fōrd*)

dīk ḥabaš 'a turkey cock' (lit. 'cock of Abyssinia')

Genus and Individual Name (Identificatory but no pronominalization; no periphrasis)

blād ³l-yūnān 'the Land of Greece'

buḥayret lūṭ 'the Dead Sea' ('Lot's Lake')

sənt ⁹arbɛīn 'the year '40' (i.e. 1940)

ḥarf ³r-rē 'the letter *rā⁹*'

kəlmet šaṭranž 'the word *šaṭranž*'

> In some cases the individual name is originally an adjective: *nahr ³l-ɛāṣi* 'The Orontes River', literally *n-nahr ³l-ɛāṣi* 'the unruly river'. As the adjective becomes less a description and more a name, the tendency is to drop the article prefix from the leading term, changing the construction from attribution to annexion. The same tendency may be seen in phrases like *sənt ³l-māḍye* 'last year' for *s-səne l-māḍye*.

Part (or Aspect) and Whole (Generally identificatory, periphrasis usually with *tabaɛ* or *la-*):

šaṭṭ ³l-baḥ³r 'the seashore'

⁹afa r-rās 'the back of the head'

rās ᵊs-səne 'New Year's' (lit. 'head of the year')

ʔažrayyi 'my feet'

šāšet ᵊt-təlefizyōn 'the television screen'

Ɛəḍwīt ᵊn-nādi 'the membership of the club'

Relation and the Related Object (Generally identificatory, periphrasis usually with *tabaƐ* or *la-*):

ʔəmm ṣāḥbi 'my friend's mother' (Both *ʔəmm* and *ṣāḥeb* are relational terms)

mwaẓẓafīn ᵊs-safāra 'the embassy employees'

wlād žīrānna 'our neighbors' children' (both *wlād* and *žīran* are relational)

ʔəsm ᵊṣ-ṣabi 'the boy's name'

raʔīs ᵊž-žəmhuriyye 'the president of the republic'

rəzᵊʔ farīd 'property of Fareed'

Associated Object and its Association (Generally identificatory, periphrasis usually with *tabaƐ* or *la-*):

bēt tāžer 'a merchant's house'

maḥramtek 'your handkerchief'

wlād ᵊl-ḥāra 'the neighborhood children'

madīnet ᵊn-nabi 'the city of the prophet'

žazīret ᵊl-Ɛarab 'the Arabian Peninsula' (lit. 'island of the Arabs')

There are many other kinds of relationship expressed by annexion, for example: Container and Contents: *ṣaḥᵊn təffāḥ* 'a bowl of apples', *ḥaʔlet ʔamḥ* 'a wheatfield'; Qualification and Object Qualified: *baṣīṣ fəkra* 'an inkling' (lit. 'a glimpse of an idea') *Ɛadam ᵊl-mubālā* 'carelessness' (lit. 'lack of care'); etc.

Derivative Constructs

Some clauses [p. 377] may be transformed into annexion phrases, by deriving a noun from the main term of the predicate and putting it in construct with the erstwhile subject or object: *l-ɱayy ʔalīle* 'Water is scarce' → *ʔallet ʔl-ɱayy* 'the scarcity of water'; *ḥažaz ʔūḍa* 'He reserved a room' → *ḥažᵊᵶ ʔūḍṭo* 'his room reservation'; *bibīɛ dəxxān* 'He sells tobacco' → *bayyāɛ dəxxān* 'a seller of tobacco, tobacconist'.

The leading term of most derivative constructs is an abstract noun [p. 284], derived from an adjective or noun, or (as gerund) from a verb. Others are substantivized participles [276], occupational nouns [305], instrumental nouns [305] or locative nouns [308].

Abstract Noun with Subject:

ṣ-ṣxūr ᵊktīre
  'rocks are abundant'

→ *kətret ᵊṣ-ṣxūr*
  'the abundance of rocks'

ṭ-ṭərᵊʔāt dayyʔa
  'the roads are narrow'

→ *ḍīʔ ᵊṭ-ṭərᵊʔāt*
  'the narrowness of the roads'

huwwe (l-)masʔūl
  'he is responsible (or in
  charge)'

→ *masʔūlīto*
  'his responsibility'

ṭaʔʔ ᵊl-ʔəfᵊl
  'the lock clicked'

→ *ṭaʔʔet ᵊl-ʔəfᵊl*
  'the click of the lock' (*ṭaʔʔa* is
  an instance noun [p. 297].)

byūžaɛ(ni) rās(i)
  'my head aches'

→ *(maɛi) wažaɛ rās*
  '(I have) a headache'

Abstract Noun (Gerund) with Object:

bisāwu fəxxār
  '(they) make pottery'

→ *msāwāt fəxxār*
  'pottery making'

byəḥsob ᵊt-takalīf
  '(He) calculates the expenditures'

→ *ḥasb ᵊt-takalīf*
  'calculation of the expenditures'

ṣannafu han-nabatāt
  '(they) classified these plants'

→ *taṣnīf han-nabatāt*
  'the classification of these
  plants'

ɛam-idarrbu ž-žunūd
  '(they')re training the troops'

→ *tadrīb ᵊž-žunūd*
  'the training of troops'

Occupational Noun with Object:

biʔallef mūsīqa
  'he composes music'

→ *mʔallef mūsīqa*
  'a composer of music'

biṣīd samak
  'he catches fish'

→ *ṣayyād samak*
  'a fisherman'

(*bāxra, btəḥmel ṭayyārāt*
  '(a ship which) carries air-
  planes'

→ *ḥāmlet ṭayyārāt*
  'an aircraft carrier'

These constructs are classificatory, while active participial constructs (see below) are identificatory. Some
nouns that are participial in form may be used in either
way: *hal-ᵊmᶜallef ᵊl-mūsīqa* 'this composer of music' (occupational noun: classificatory construct) vs. *mᶜallef
hal-mūsīqa* 'The composer of this music' (participial noun:
identificatory construct). See p. 458.

Substantivized Active Participle with Object:

saraᶜ ᵊs-sayyāra
  'he stole the car'

→ *sāreᶜ ᵊs-sayyāra*
  'the one who stole the car'

ᶜallafet l-ᵊktāb
  'she wrote the book'

→ *mᶜallfet l-ᵊktāb*
  'the author (f.) of the book'

Substantivized Passive Participle with Subject:

waẓẓafᵊto l-ᵊḥkūme
  'the government employed him'

→ *mwaẓẓaf l-ᵊḥkūme*
  'the government employee'

hal-bakēt məḥtᵊwi ᶜalēha
  'this package contains them'

→ *məḥtawayāt hal-bakēt*
  'the contents of this package'

Instrumental Noun with Object:

byəftaḥu fīha ᶜəlab
  '(they) open cans with it'

→ *fattāḥet ᶜəlab*
  'a can opener'

byəšklu fīha waraᶜ
  '(they) clip paper with it'

→ *šakkālet waraᶜ*
  'a paper clip'

byəftaḥu fī l-bāb
  '(they) open the door with it'

→ *məftāḥ ᵊl-bāb*
  'the door key'

Locative Noun with Subject or Object:

byəǧri fī nahᵊr
  'a river runs in it'

→ *maǧra nahᵊr*
  'a river bed'

byəṣnaᶜu fī ṣābūn
  'they manufacture soap in it'

→ *maṣnaᶜ ṣābūn*
  'a soap factory'

ADJECTIVE ANNEXION (*al-ʔiḍāfa ġayr l-ḥaqīqīya*)

A few adjectives are used in construct with nouns, mostly in set phrases applicable to human beings. For example:

ʔalīl (ʔl-)ʔadab   'ill-mannered, uncivil', lit. 'meager of manners'

ktīr (ʔl-)ġalabe   'prying, busybody', lit. 'excessive of inquiry'

tʔīl ᵊd-damm   'unlikeable, boorish', lit. 'heavy of blood'

xafīf ᵊd-damm   'likeable, pleasant', lit. 'light of blood'

maʔṭūɛ ᵊr-rās   'beheaded', lit. 'cut off of the head'

ṭawīl ᵊl-bāl   'patient', lit. 'long of attention'

ɛadmān ᵊl-ɛāfye   'run down, sickly', lit. 'deprived of vitality'

Feminine forms: *ʔalīlet ʔadab, ktīret ġalabe, ɛadmānt ᵊl-ɛāfye,* etc.

Adjective constructs are classificatory [p.458]; the following term cannot be pronominalized.

Unlike substantives [p.456], adjectives in construct may be definitized by prefixation of the article: *l-ᵊktīr ᵊl-ġalabe* 'the busybody'; *mīn haš-šabb ᵊt-tʔīl ᵊd-damm?* 'Who's that unpleasant young man?'

Adjective constructs are generally derived from subject-predicate constructions or verb-object constructions: *tʔīl ᵊd-damm ← dammo tʔīl; rābeṭ ᵊš-šaʔš* 'calm, composed' (lit. 'controlled of spirit') ← *rabaṭ šaʔšo* 'He composed himself' (lit. '...his spirit'). Cf. p.464.

Note the difference between the participial construct *rābeṭ ᵊš-šaʔš* (fem. *rābṭet ᵊš-šaʔš*) and a participle-object phrase *rābeṭ šaʔšo* 'in control of himself' (fem. *rābṭa šaʔša* 'in control of herself') [p.265].

A construct adjective transformed from a predicate adjective does not show agreement with its following term (its erstwhile subject), but with the new subject (or the term it modifies): *hiyye xafīft ᵊd-damm ← dammha xafīf.*

PARTITIVE ANNEXION

Certain nouns — PARTITIVES — are generally subordinate to the terms they stand in construct with; that is to say, agreement [p.427] with the construct is determined by the following term, not by the leading term: *nᵊṣṣ ᵊs-sᵊkkān harabu w-baʔīton mātu* 'Half of the inhabitants fled and the rest of them died': *harabu* and *mātu* agree with the plurals *sᵊkkān* and *-on,* respectively, not with the leading terms *nᵊṣṣ* (masc./sing.) 'half' and baʔiyye (fem./sing.) 'rest'; kəll hal-ʔakle ṭayybe 'all this food is good': ṭayybe agrees with the fem. ʔakle 'food', not with the masculine kəll 'all'.

Partitives include nouns designating indefinite proportions and quantities, sometimes fractions from halves to tenths, and a few other terms. For example:

kəll	'all, whole, every'	məƐẓam	'majority, most'
baƐḍ	'some', 'each other'	ʔaktariyye	'majority'
ğēr	'other'	ʔağlabiyye	'majority'
šwayye	'a few, a little'	baʔiyye	'rest, remainder'
šī	'some, a'	nafs	'same, -self'
kamm	'several, a few'	ẓāt	'same, -self'
Ɛədde	'a number'	ḥāl–	'-self'
fard	'a single one'	waḥd–	'by... -self, alone'
žōz	'a pair'	haḍra	(honorific)
žamīƐ	'all, whole'	syāde	(honorific)
Ɛāmme	'generality, mass'		

The term šī, šwayye, kamm, and Ɛədde, in their partitive senses, are normally used in construct only with classificatory indefinite terms:

šī laḥme	'some meat'	kamm šahər	'a few (or how many?) months'
šī bənt ḥəlwe	'a (or some) pretty girl'	kamm marra	'several times' (See p. 366.)
šwayyet mayy	'a little water'	Ɛəddet marrāt	'a number of times'

Some of the others are used in construct mainly with identificatory (usually definite) terms:

žamīƐ əš-šaƐb	'the whole nation'	məƐẓam ət-talamīẓ	'most of the students'
Ɛāmmet ən-nās	'the masses (of people)'	baʔīt səkkān baladna	'the rest of the inhabitants of our town'

Still others are commonly used with either classificatory (indefinite) or identificatory (definite) terms:

Indefinite (Classificatory)		Definite (Identificatory)	
rəbəƐ sāƐa	'a quarter hour'...........rəbəƐ mālo	'a quarter of his wealth'	
baƐḍ nās	'some (certain) people'.....baƐḍon	'some of them'	

Note especially the term *kəll,* whose English translation varies, depending on whether the following term is
definite or indefinite, singular or plural, etc.:

Indefinite (Classificatory)	Definite (Identificatory)

kəll balad 'every (or each) town'......*kəll ᵊl-balad* 'the whole town'

kəll šaxṣ 'every (or each) person'....*kəll ᵊn-nās* 'all the people'

kəll šī   'everything'...............*kəllo*   'all of it'

  kəll with a pronoun suffix is not generally used as
object to a verb, nor as following term to a noun in construct or to a preposition; but is used in apposition
[p.511] to the pronoun, which is repeated: *šəfton kallon*
(not *"šəft kəllon"*) 'I saw all of them'; *tyābna kəllna* (not
"tyāb kəllna") 'The clothes of all of us'; *fīha kəllha* (not
"fi kəllha" or *"b-kəllha"*) 'in all of it'.

  The relationship of *kəll* (and *ġēr,* see below) to classificatory and identificatory following terms is like that
of elatives and ordinals [p.473].

  The term *ġēr* also requires various translations, depending on whether the following term is definite or indefinite,
etc.:

ġēr marra 'another time'.............*ġēr hal-marra* 'not this time, some
                      other time' (i.e.
                      'other than this time')

ġēr ᵊwḷād 'other children'...........*ġēr ᵊwlādna* 'except our children'
                     (i.e. 'other than our
                     children')

ġēr šaxṣ 'someone else'.............*ġērak* 'someone else (than
   i.e. 'another person'   you)' i.e. 'other than
                     you'

  nafs and *zāt* in construct with a pronoun are translated as '-self':
nafsi 'myself', *zāto* 'himself'; in construct with a noun, they are usually
translated as 'same': *nafs ᵊl-wa�* 'the same time', *nafs ᵊl-balad* 'the same
town' (though the latter might also be 'the town itself' = *l-balad nafsa*).
With pronoun suffixes, these terms are most commonly used as appositives:
�na nafsi 'I myself', *r-rəžžāl zāto* 'the man himself'.

  The partitive *waḥd-* stands in construct with pronoun suffixes only,
usually as appositive: *ᵊnti waḥdek* 'you (f.) alone', or adverbially: *brūḥ
waḥdi* 'I'll go alone'.

  The term *ḥāl* as a partitive stands in construct with pronoun suffixes
only: *ḥāli* 'myself', *ḥālkon* 'yourselves'. It is most commonly used as

object: *šaraḥᵃt ḥāli* 'I cut myself', *ɛᵊmel ḥālo nāyem* 'He pretended to be asleep', lit. "He made himself asleep".

All the partitives meaning '-self' may occur after certain prepositions: *la-ḥālak* 'for yourself', *ɛan ḥāli* 'about myself', *b-nafsi* 'to myself' (lit. 'in myself'), *la-waḥdo* 'for (or by) himself alone'.

> In their partitive uses, these terms stand in construct with definite (identificatory) terms only.

The "honorifics" *ḥaḍra* (lit. 'presence'), *syāde, saɛāde, faxāme*, etc. are partitives: *haḍᵊrtak btᵊži maɛna?* 'Are you coming with us, sir?'; *šarraf ḥaḍret ᵊr-raᵊīs, walla lᵊssa?* 'Has the president arrived yet?'

Examples of partitive constructs in context:

kᵊll:

1. *ṣār ᵊr-rāɛi yᵊmsek kᵊll rāsēn ġanam sawa* [AO-104] — 'The shepherd started picking up every two head of sheep together'

2. *kᵊll hal-ḥēwānāt hādōl bišaġġlu ᵊaḥmad ᵊktīr* [AO-63] — 'All these animals keep Ahmed quite busy'

3. *ᵊana kᵊlli tballalt* [AO-67] — 'I got all wet' (lit. "I, all of me ...")

4. *kᵊll ᵊl-bᵊzᵊr byᵊṭlaɛ mn ᵊl-ᵊarḍ* [AO-59] — 'All the seeds sprout from the ground'

5. *b-kᵊll mamnūniyye* — 'With pleasure', lit. 'in all gratitude'

6. *kīf hal-ᵊᵊmᵊom ᵊz-zġīr...wᵊsɛak kᵊllak?* [AO-116] — 'How could that little bottle hold all of you (m./sg.)?' (i.e. '...your whole body')

7. *xāf ᵊktīr w-ražaf kᵊll žᵊsmo* [AO-116] — 'He took fright and his whole body trembled'

ġēr:

8. *ɛar-raff mā fī kᵊtᵊb ġēr kᵊtbi* — 'On the shelf there are no books but mine' (lit. '...other than my books')

9. *ɛan ᵊarīb bāyne tamām ġēr šᵊkᵊl* — 'From close up it looks altogether different' (lit. "...(of) another kind")

10. *ᵊana mā bḥᵊbb ġēr ᵊl-baṣal* [AO] — 'I don't want anything but onions'

11. mīn ʔəlna ǧērkon? [DA-245] — 'Who (is there) for us (to count on) but you?'

12. btəʔmor šī ǧēro? [SAL-81] — 'Would you like anything else?' (lit. "Do you order a thing other than it?")

baɛḍ:

13. ləssa fī baɛḍ nəʔaṭ bədda taswiye — 'There are still some points that need to be ironed out'

14. baɛḍon ʔəžu w-baɛḍon mā ʔəžu — 'Some of them came and some didn't'

15. baɛḍ ʔṭ-ṭəllāb mā byədərsu — 'Some of the students don't study'

16. lā tʔalldu baɛḍkon ʔl-baɛḍ — 'Don't copy one another' (lit. "Don't some of you imitate the some (others)"

šī, šwayye, kamm:

17. štarēt ʔs-sayyāra mn ʔl-wakīl wəlla mən šī šaxʔs? — 'Did you buy the car from a dealer or from some (private) individual?'

18. bətrīd naɛmel šī məšwār sawa? [PVA-12] — 'Would you like for us to take a walk (or ride) together?'

19. mnəšrab šī fənžān ʔahwe [PVA-34] — 'We'll have a cup of coffee'

20. naʔʔī-li mən ɛal-wəšš šī tlətt banadōrāyāt [DA-129] — 'Pick out (some) three tomatoes for me from on top'

21. fəkərna haṣ-ṣēfiyye nrūḥ ṣōb ʔš-šmāl šī šahər zamān [DA-152] — 'This summer we're thinking of going up north for about a month('s time)'

22. ʔiza btəʔrāon šī kamm marra btəhfdzon b-ʔshūle [PVA-56] — 'If you read them over a few times you'll memorize them easily'

23. rūḥ žīb kamm ʔannīnet bīra? — 'Shall I go get a few bottles of bear?'

24. biḥəṭṭu bəl-ʔawwal šwayyet ṭīn w-biḥəṭṭu ɛalē ḥažara [AO-75] — 'They first lay on a little mud and set a stone on it'

25. d-dənye šwayyet bard barra — 'It's a little cool outside'

ḥāl, waḥd, nafs, zāt:

26. l-banāt lamma ṣəfyu la-ḥālhon ṣāru ydūru bəl-bēt [AO-113] — 'When the girls were left to themselves they started looking around the house'

27. *walla ya bēk mā bəddi ʔəḥki*   'Well, sir, I don't want to talk
    ɛan ḥāli [DA-99]   about myself'

28. *ḥaḍḍer ḥālak mā baʔa ʔəlla*   'Get ready (lit. prepare yourself),
    nəṣal [DA-250]   we're almost there'

29. *kān fī zalame ḥāseb ḥālo šāṭer*   'There was a man who considered
    u-ɛālem [AO-83]   himself clever and learned'

30. *rāḥ ʷṣ-ṣayyād la-nafs ʷl-baḥra* 'The fisherman went to the same
    w-ṣād ʔarbaɛ samakāt [AO-117]   pond and caught four fish'

31. *s-sawāḥel waḥda kānet taḥt*   'The coasts alone were under the
    ʷl-ḥəkm ʷt-tərki [SAL-151]   Turkish rule'

32. *xallīna nsāwīha b-nafsna*   'Let's do it ourselves'

Fractions:

33. *təlt ʷl-balad ḥtarʔet* (or   'A third of the city burned'
    ḥtaraʔ)

34. *rəbʷɛ ʔamwālo nɛaṭet la-mašarīɛ* 'A quarter of his wealth was given
    xēriyye   to charitable causes'

But if the following term is indefinite, agreement is usually with the leading term: *rəbʷɛ sāɛa mā bikaffi* 'A half hour is not enough'.

NUMERAL ANNEXION

There are various irregularities and complexities in the construct forms of numerals. See p.170.

Unlike substantives, cardinal numerals in construct may be definitized by prefixation of the article:

Indefinite   Definite

xams ʷrǧāl   'five men'............*l-xams ʷrǧāl*   'the five men'

ʔarbaɛ bēḍāṭ 'four eggs'...........*l-ʔarbaɛ bēḍāṭ* 'the four eggs'

ɛəšrīn təlmīz 'twenty students'.....*l-ɛəšrīn təlmīz* 'the twenty students'

Numerals from two to ten stand in construct with nouns
in the plural: *tnēn ᵊwlād* 'two children', *Ɛašr ᵊwlād* 'ten
children'; above ten the following term is put in the singular: *ʔarbƐīn walad* 'forty children'[1] [p.367].

Cardinal numerals generally stand in construct with indefinite terms
(which classify the things enumerated), but those between two and ten are
also sometimes put in construct with definite terms (which identify the
things enumerated): *tlatt ᵊwlādon* 'their three children', *tlātətna* 'the
three of us'.

With definite terms, it is common for the numeral to
stand in apposition rather than in construct: *wlādon ᵊt-tlāte*
'their three children', *r-ržāl ᵊl-xamse* 'the five men', *nəhna
t-tlāte* 'we three'.
Collectives and other mass nouns stand in apposition to
numerals: *tlāte ʔamērkān* 'three Americans', *tnēn ʔahwe* 'two
coffees' [p.510].
wāḥed 'one' never stands in construct except in the
syncopated form *waḥd–* with a pronoun suffix: *brūḥ waḥdi*
'I'll go alone' (lit. "I'll go, the one of me"). The ordinary uses of *wāḥed* are with an appositive: *wāḥde bənt* 'a
girl' or in apposition: *bənt wāḥde* 'one girl'.

Examples of cardinal numeral constructs:

1. *fī tlətt waršāt ᵊmhəmmīn* [Bg. 1]   'There are three important factories'

2. *kān b–ʔīdi tlətt ᵊžwēzāt
w–ᵊtnēn ʔaxṭyāriyye*   'Three deuces and two kings were in
my hand'

3. *lāzem nəstanna tlat–arbaƐt
iyyām* [DA-217]   'We must wait three (or) four days'
[p.171]

4. *ramāha w–ṭālaƐ fīha ʔarbaƐ
samakāt* [AO-117]   'He cast it and brought up four fish
in it'

5. *ṣār kəll yōm iṭaƐmī ʔarbaƐ
xams rūṣ baṣal* [AO-103]   'He began feeding him four (or) five
onions every day'

6. *ʔawwal kīlo b–Ɛašr ᵊʔrūš w–kəll
kīlo bizīd ᵊb–sətt ᵊʔrūš*
[DA-225]   'The first kilogram is (for) ten
piastres and each (additional) kilogram adds six piastres'

7. *kam səne ṣar–lak biʔamērka? –
tmənn snīn*   'How many years have you been in
America? – Eight years'

8. *ʔēmta btədba d–drūs? – baƐᵊd
Ɛašᵊrt iyyām* [DA-173]   'When does school begin? – In ten
days'

---

[1]In Classical Arabic numerals above ten do not stand in construct with their
following term, because it is in the accusative case rather than the geni-
tive. This consideration does not apply to Colloquial Arabic, of course.

9. *yəmken təṣal maε l-ᵊwlād baεᵊd xamṣṭaεšar yōm* [DA-198]   'She may arrive with the children in a fortnight'(lit. "after fifteen days")

10. *fī xamsā w-εəšrīn kəlme* [DA-226]   'There are twenty-five words in it'

11. *s-səne fīha sabᵊεt əšhor ᵊalhon wāḥed w-ᵊtlātīn yōm* [AO-71]   'There are seven months in the year which have thirty-one days'

12. *kān taḥt ᵊīdo ᵊarbεīn zalame* [AO-113]   'There were forty men under his command'

13. *kəll hal-ᵊġrāḍ b-ᵊtlətt lērāt u-sabεīn ᵊərš* [DA-129]   'All these things come to three pounds and seventy piastres'

14. *w-laᵊu syūf ᵊt-tmānīn režžāl* [AO-113]   'And they found the swords of the thirty men'

15. *mā xalla lā kbīr w-lā ġġīr mn ᵊl-ᵊarbaε mīt rās ġanam tabaε mεallmo* [AO-114]   'He left none, either small or large, of the four hundred head of sheep of his master's'

16. *māt mən məddet ᵊalf w-ᵊtmān mīt səne* [AO-116]   'He died one thousand eight hundred year ago'

17. *...ṣīġet εāᵊalti btəswa šī xamst ālāf lēra* [DA-297]   'My wife's (lit. family's) jewelry is worth some five thousand pounds'

ELATIVE AND ORDINAL ANNEXION

An elative [p.310] may be used in construct either with a definite or an indefinite term: *ᵊahla l-banāt* 'the prettiest of the girls', *ᵊahla banāt* '(the) prettiest girls'.

> When an elative construct is translated into English with a superlative (-est, most...), the superlative is usually accompanied by 'the', even when the construct is indefinite [p.456].

A definite following term makes an elative construct identificatory; i.e. the definite term *l-banāt,* (in *ᵊahla l-banāt*) shows <u>which</u> prettiest things are meant. Conversely an indefinite following term makes the construct classificatory: the indefinite term *banāt,* in *ᵊahla banāt,* shows <u>what kind of</u> prettiest things are meant.

Elatives, which are uninflected, fluctuate in number/gender [p.420]. In a definite (identificatory) construct, the number and gender of an elative depend entirely upon its reference, regardless of the following term: *hayy ᵊahla l-banāt* 'This (f./sg.) is the prettiest of the girls'; *hadōl ᵊahla l-banāt* 'These (pl.) are the prettiest of the girls'; *hāda ᵊahla l-ᵊbyūt* 'This (m./sg.) is the prettiest of the houses'.

With an indefinite (classificatory) following term, on the other hand, the number and gender of the construct depends entirely upon that of the following term; i.e. an elative leading term is <u>subordinate</u> to an indefinite following term: *hayy ʔaḥla bənt* 'This (f./sg.) is the prettiest girl'; *hāda ʔaḥla bēt* 'This (m./sg.) is the nicest house'; *hadōl ʔaḥla banāt* 'These are the prettiest girls.'

> While elatives often stand in construct with an indefinite singular count noun [p. 366], they seldom stand in construct with a <u>definite</u> singular count noun, and then only if the elative is substantivized: *ʔaḥsan bēt* 'the best house', but *ʔaḥsan ᵊl-bēt* would mean 'the best part of the house' or 'the best thing about the house'. Thus in order to say 'our best house', one must avoid *ʔaḥsan bētna*, which would mean 'the best thing about our house', and say either *ʔaḥsan bēt mən byūtna*, 'the best (house) of our houses', or *ʔaḥsan byūtna* 'the best of our houses', or *ʔaḥsan bēt ʔəlna* 'the best house (belonging) to us'. See Periphrasis of Annexion [p. 460].

Ordinal numerals [p. 316] are like elatives in their function as uninflected subordinate nouns in construct with indefinite following terms: *tālet bēt* '(the) third house'; *tālet bənt* '(the) third girl' (*hayy tālet bənt* 'This (f./sg.) is the third girl').

Unlike elatives, however, ordinals do not stand in construct with indefinite plurals, and seldom do so with definite terms of any kind. Thus *tālet l-ᵊbyūt* 'the third (one) of the houses' is usually circumlocuted with a phrase such as *tālet bēt mən l-ᵊbyūt*, or *t-tālet mən l-ᵊbyūt*. In definite (identificatory) constructs, furthermore, an ordinal is generally inflected for number/gender: *tālətt ᵊl-banāt* 'the third (one) of the girls', *tālətton* 'the third (one) of them'; (or by periphrasis *t-tālte mn ᵊl-banāt, t-tālte mənhon*).

The terms *ʔawwal* 'first' and *ʔāxer* 'last' are used freely in identificatory constructs, however, in the sense 'first part of' and 'last part of': *ʔawwal waɛgo* 'the first part of his sermon'; *ʔāxr ᵊs-səne* 'the last part of the year'; *mən ʔawwálla la-ʔāxéra* 'from (its) beginning to (its) end'. In this sense *ʔawwal* and *ʔāxer* function as substantives, and are not inflected for gender.

> Elatives, too, may occur in this substantival function, when followed by a definite count noun [p. 366] in the singular: *ʔaḥsan ᵊs-səne* 'the best (part) of the year'.

Examples of elative and ordinal constructs in context:

1. *bi-hal-waʔt ʔaktar ᵊn-nās byəžū-lha* [DA-172]
    'That's when most people go there' (lit. "At that time most of the people come to it")

2. *ṣār ʔaġna ʔahᵊl zamāno* [AO-119]
    'He became the richest of the people of his time'

3. *ləbset ʔaḥsan ʔawāɛi ɛəndha* [AO-118]

'She put on the best clothes she had' (Cf. *ʔaḥsan ʔawāɛīha* 'the best of her clothes')

4. *baɛ*d ʔāxer ramaḍān yaɛni bi-ʔawwal šawwāl* [DA-302]

'After the last of Ramadan, that is to say, on the first of Shawwal'

5. *hāda ʔaḥsan šī mawǧūd bəl-balad* [DA-129]

'This is the best thing (to be) found in town'

6. *waʔʔəf-*lna ɛala ʔawwal bāb ɛala yamīnak* [DA-45]

'Stop (for us) at the first door on your right'

7. *fəkro tāni səne yəǧi ləl-blād *l-ɛarabiyye* [DA-173]

'His idea is to come some other year to the Arab countries'

8. *l-fallāḥ byəḥsədhon...b-ʔawwal *ṣ-ṣēf* [AO-59]

'The farmer harvests them early in the summer'

9. *ʔaddēš bəddak *tḥəṭṭ ʔawwal dafɛa?* [DA-294]

'How much do you want to put in as a first deposit?'

10. *tālet wāḥed ḥasan*

'The third one is Hassan' [p. 406]

11. *ḥāwalt ʔāxer ḥēli*

'I tried my utmost' (lit. '...the last of my strength')

12. *ʔawwal dars ɛandi byəbda s-sāɛa tmāne w-nəṣṣ*

'My first lesson begins at half past eight' (Cf. *ʔawwal darsi* 'the beginning of my lesson')

13. *ʔaddēš ʔaʔall šī lāzem ḥəṭṭo?* [DA-294]

'What's the minimum amount (lit. the least thing) I must deposit?'

PREPOSITIONS

The prepositional construction is a special kind of annexion [p.455], differing from nominal annexion only by virtue of its leading term's being a preposition rather than a
noun-type word. A PREPOSITION is a word or proclitic [p.18]
that occurs mainly or always as leading term in a phrase
whose following term is a noun-type constituent and whose
function can be that of supplement [523], complement [444],
attribute [500]or predicate [402], but not subject.

Among the most common and important prepositions in Syrian Arabic are
the following:

la–	'to, for'	*ɛala*	'on, about, to, against'
mən	'from, of, than'	*ɛan*	'about, from'
b–	'at, in, by, with'	*ɛand*	'with, at, Fr. *chez*'
fi	'in, on, at'	*maɛ*	'with'

No attempt will be made here to deal with the various
meanings and translations of these prepositions, for which
see a dictionary.
The prepositions listed above are very common, and
examples of their use may be found on almost every page of
this book where full sentences are given. This section
will be devoted only to certain special features of their
forms and functions.

Alterations in Form

In combination with the article [p.493], some of the prepositions are
slightly altered in form:

la–	+ *l–* → *ləl–*:	*ləl–walad*[1]	'to the boy'
b–	+ *l–* → *bəl–*:	*bəl–ᵊktāb*	'with the book'
fi	+ *l–* → *fəl–*:	*fəl–bēt*	'in the house'
ɛala	+ *l–* → *ɛal–*:	*ɛal–maktab*	'to the office'

---

[1] These combinations with *ə* are sometimes considered to have the helping
vowel: *lᵊl–walad, bᵊl–ᵊktāb,* etc. This use of the helping vowel, however,
is not allowed for in the rules of anaptyxis given here [p.29]. According
to these rules, we would get *lᵊl–walad,* but "*bl–ᵊktāb*", not *bᵊl–ᵊktāb.*
Our transcription with the large *ə* simply implies that *ə* in these combinations remains in all environments.

The preposition *b-* is sometimes assimilated to an initial *m* or *f*: *m-maḥallak* (or *b-maḥallak*) 'in your place', *f-faršti* (or *b-faršti*) 'in my bed'. Sometimes this preposition is pronounced *bi*: *bi-ʔawwal ᵊš-šahᵊr* 'on the first of the month'.

fi may also be pronounced with a short *i* in close phrasing [p.19]: *fi-bēti* (or *fi bēti*) 'in my house', or sometimes with no vowel at all: *f-bēti*.

The *ə* of *mən* 'from' is generally lost before a vowel: *mn ᵊl-bēt* 'from the house'.[1]

Especially in Lebanon, *ʕala* is sometimes shortened to *ʕa-* even when not in combination with the article: *ʕa-bēti* 'to my house' (for *ʕala bēti*). Sometimes, on the other hand, *ʕala* keeps its longer form even before the article: *ʕala ṭ-ṭāwle* (or *ʕaṭ-ṭāwle*) 'on the table'.

ʕand is generally pronounced *ʕənd* in some parts of Greater Syria.

la- is commonly reduced to *l-* in parts of Lebanon [p.13].

Pronoun-Suffixing Forms. When the "object"[2] of a preposition is a personal pronoun, it is the suffixed form of the pronoun which is used [p.539]:

maʕo	'with him, it'	*ʕando*	'with him'(Fr. *chez lui*)
maʕak	'with you(m.)'	*ʕandak*	'with you(m.)'
maʕek	'with you(f.)'	*ʕandek*	'with you(f.)'
maʕi	'with me'	*ʕandi*	'with me'
maʕha	'with her, it'	*ʕandha*	'with her'
maʕhon	'with them'	*ʕandhon*	'with them'
maʕkon	'with you(pl.)'	*ʕandkon*	'with you(pl.)'
maʕna	'with us'	*ʕanna*	'with us'

---

[1] The *ə* of *mən* is probably best analyzed as a helping vowel; to be perfectly consistent we should transcribe *mᵊn-bēto*, *mnᵊl-bēt*, rather than *mən bēto*, *mn ᵊl-bēt*. Our transcription here follows a tradition based on Arabic spelling, which connects only one-letter proclitics to the following word. Since *mən* is written as a separate word, one's tendency is to transcribe its only vowel as an integral part of the word rather than as a helping vowel.

[2] The use of this traditional term for the following term in a prepositional phrase does not, of course, imply that the prepositional construction is a kind of complementation.

Note that the d of *Ɛand* is usually elided with the suffix *-na* 'us': *Ɛanna* (for *Ɛandna*).

maƐha and *maƐhon* are sometimes pronounced *maḥḥa* and
maḥḥon, respectively. The *h* of *-ha* and *-hon* may also be
dropped, as is the case generally [p. 541]: *maƐa* 'with
her', *maƐon* 'with them', *Ɛanda* 'with her', *Ɛandon* 'with
them'.

On the quasi-verbal use of these prepositions, see p. 413.

The suffixing forms of *mən* and *Ɛan* have a double *n* before a vowel:

mənno	'from him, it'	*Ɛanno*	'from him, it'
mənnak	'from you(m.)'	*Ɛannak*	'from you(m.)'
mənnek	'from you(f.)'	*Ɛannek*	'from you(f.)'
mənni	'from me'	*Ɛanni*	'from me'
mənha	'from her, it'	*Ɛanha*	'from her, it'
mənhon	'from them'	*Ɛanhon*	'from them'
mənkon	'from you(pl.)'	*Ɛankon*	'from you(pl.)'
mənna	'from us'	*Ɛanna*	'from us'

Note that *Ɛanna* 'from us' is pronounced the same as
Ɛanna 'with us' (see above), though the latter is sometimes also pronounced *Ɛənna*.

When the *h* of *-ha* and *-hon* is elided, the *n* is commonly doubled as before the other suffixes beginning with
a vowel: *mənna* 'from her', *mənnon* 'from them', *Ɛanna* 'from
her', *Ɛannon* 'from them'; note that the 'her' forms are
then pronounced the same as the 'us' forms. In some parts
of Greater Syria, however, the *h* is more often elided without a doubling of the *n*, thus: *məna* 'from her', *mənon*
'from then', etc.

The suffixing form of *Ɛala* is *Ɛalē-*, except in the first person singular, where it is *Ɛaliyy-* (or in some areas *Ɛalayy-*):

Ɛalē	'on him, it'	*Ɛalēha*, *Ɛalēa*	'on her, it'
Ɛalēk	'on you(m.)'	*Ɛalēhon*, *Ɛalēon*	'on them'
Ɛalēki	'on you(f.)'	*Ɛalēkon*	'on you(pl.)'
Ɛaliyyi (*Ɛalayyi*)	'on me'	*Ɛalēna*	'on us'

The suffixing form of *fi* is *fī-* (a regular sound change [p. 27]):

fī	'in him, it'	*fīha*	'in her, it'
fīk	'in you(m.)'	*fīhon*	'in them'
fīki	'in you(f.)'	*fīkon*	'in you(pl.)'
fiyyi	'in me'[1]	*fīna*	'in us'

With loss of *h* in *-ha* and *-hon:* *fiya* or *fiyya* 'in her', *fiyon* or *fiyyon* 'in them'.

The preposition *b-* is not normally used with pronoun suffixes (but see p. 415); the stem *fī-* is used in its stead. Conversely, in some parts of Greater Syria *fi* is not often used <u>without</u> pronoun suffixes, *b-* taking its place most of the time. Thus *b-* and *fi* are not merely partial synonyms but are virtually alternants of the same preposition: *b-ʔūṭṭi* 'in my room' vs. *fīha* 'in it', *b-səkkīn* 'with a knife' vs. *fīha* 'with it'.

    In certain other areas, however, most speakers make a distinction between non-suffixing *b-* and *fi*, preferring *fi* in the sense 'in': *fi ʔūṭṭi* (or *fi-ʔūṭṭi* or *f-ʔūṭṭi*) 'in my room', while *b-* is obligatory in certain other senses, e.g. 'by, with': *b-səkkīn* 'with a knife'. In any case, *fi* is optional in most of its non-suffixing contexts, being generally replaceable with *b-*, while *b-*, on the other hand, is by no means always replaceable with *fi* (e.g. *b-sərɛa* 'fast', lit. "with speed").

The Preposition *la-* 'to, for'. *la-* has two kinds of form with pronoun suffixes: a DISJUNCTIVE form, like the other prepositions, and a CONJUNCTIVE form, which is suffixed to verbs and participles [p. 482], and sometimes also to elatives [314] and the negative *mā* [385].

The disjunctive suffixing form is *ʔəl-*:

ʔəlo	'to him, it'	*ʔəlha, ʔəla*	'to her, it'
ʔəlak	'to you(m.)'	*ʔəlhon, ʔəlon*	'to them'
ʔəlek	'to you(f.)'	*ʔəlkon*	'to you(pl)'
ʔəli	'to me'	*ʔəlna*	'to us'

---

[1] In the quasi-verbal use, usually *fīni* 'I can' ("[I have it] in me to...").
See p. 547.

Examples of the disjunctive form in context:

1. *mā ɛandi waʔʔt ʔəlha*   'I don't have time for it'

2. *ṣāret dāyman əmṭīɛa ʔəlo* 'She started being always obedient to him'

3. *huwwe ṣāḥeb ḥamīm ʔəli* 'He's a close friend of mine' (lit. "...friend to me")

4. *ʔəlak maktūb əmsōkar* [DA-223] 'There's a registered letter for you'

5. *xalli l-qarār ʔəlo*   'Leave the decision to him'

6. *ɛam-ʔaɛmel ṭaʔʔm ʔəli* 'I'm having a suit made for me'

   In examples 5 and 6, the disjunctive forms *ʔəlo, ʔəli* are used, for the sake of emphasis, rather than conjunctive forms suffixed to the verbs (*xallī-lo* 'leave...to him', *ɛam-ʔaɛməl-li* 'I am making...for myself').

On the quasi-verbal use of these forms, see p.413.

   There is a limited use of certain other disjunctive forms, notably *lē-*, used sometimes as in *štaʔʔt lēk* 'I've missed you' (instead of the conjunctive *štaʔt-əllak*). Note also: *ʔawwal ṣadīʔ lina fi bayrūt* [SAL-59] 'our first friend in Beirut' (for *ʔəlna*). (Cf. Classical forms with *ʔila* and *li-*.)

   The conjunctive forms vary, depending on the preceding and following sounds:

-lo, -əllo 'to him, it'	*-lha,*	*-la,*	*-əlha, -əlla*	'to her, it'
-lak, -əllak 'to you(m.)'	*-lhon,*	*-lon,*	*-əlhon, -əllon*	'to them'
-lek, -əllek 'to you(f.)'	*-lkon,*	*-əlkon*		'to you(pl.)'
-li, -əlli 'to me'	*-lna,*	*-əlna*		'to us'

   -l- is sometimes assimilated to the *n* of *-na* 'us' *žāb-ənna* (for *žāb-əlna*) 'he brought...to us'.

1.) -*śll*- is used after two consonants and before a vowel:

   žəbt-śllak   'I've brought (for) you(m.)...'

   ḥaṭṭ-ślli   'Put(m.)...for me'

   -*śll*- is also used optionally (instead of -*l*-) after the subject-affix -*t* [p.193] even when the -*t* is preceded by a vowel: *ḥaṭṭēt-əllak* 'I put...for you(m.)' (or *ḥaṭṭēt-lak*).

2.) -*śl*- is used after two consonants and before a consonant:

   žəbt-ślkon   'I've brought (for) you(pl.)...'

   ḥaṭṭ-ślna   'Put...for us'

3.) -*l*- is used otherwise:

   bžśb-lak   'I'll bring...(for) you(m.)'

   žībī-lna   'bring(f.)...(for)us'

   After a single consonant and before a consonant, however, the helping vowel *ə* must come before -*l*-, by the rule of anaptyxis [p. 29]:

   bžśb-əlkon   'I'll bring...(for) you(pl.)'

   žśb-əlna   'He brought...(to) us'

   After *l*, the helping vowel is generally not used:

   ʔśl-lna   'tell(m.) (to) us'

   byaɛmśl-lkon 'he'll make...for you(pl.)'

   The two *l*'s, furthermore, are generally reduced in pronunciation to one: *ʔśl-na, byaɛmśl-kon*. See pp. 23, 24.

   On accentuation, see pp. 18-19.

Reduction of Preconsonantal Stem Vowel before −*l*−. When an −*l*− suffix is added to a word ending in a long vowel + a single consonant, the long vowel is generally shortened; *ā* commonly becomes *a*, and *ī*, *ē*, *ū*, and *ō* almost always become *ə* [p. 23]:

ṣār	+ −lak → ṣar−lak	'it has been for you...'
ʔāl	+ −li → ʔal−li	'he said to me...'
ɛmēl	+ −lo → ɛməl−lo	'do for him...'
ṣrōf	+ −lak → ṣrəf−lak	'spend for yourself...'
ʔūl	+ −lon → ʔəl−lon	'say to them...'
ǰīb	+ −lna → ǰəb−əlna	'bring (for) us...'
masmūḥ	+ −li → masməḥ−li	'allowed (to) me'

Note also the optional loss of *ū* in the fem. *ʔūli* + −*l*− + pn. sfx.: *ʔlī−lo* 'tell(f.) (to) him' (or *ʔūlī−lo*).

Examples of −*l*− suffixes:

1. smaḥū−lna mnəstaʔzen
'Excuse(pl.) us, we must go' (lit. "Allow (to) us, we ask permission")

2. ʔaddēš bāʔī−lak hōn?
'How much longer do you have here?' (lit. "How much is left to you here?")

3. baɛd əd̦−dəhər bǰəb−əlkon yāhon
'This afternoon I'll bring them for you(pl.)'

4. nšāḷḷa ʔal−lkon šəkran u−bass
'I suppose he said to you(pl.) "thanks" and that was all?'

5. bʔəl−lon ənsīt
'I'll tell them I forgot'

6. lamma yərǰaɛ laḥ−ikəl−lo maǰāl ʔawsaɛ
'When he returns there's going to be broader scope for him' (laḥ−ikūn + −lo → laḥ−ikəl−lo)

7. ṣar−la tārke ʔamērka tlətt iyyām [DA-198]
'She left the States three days ago' (lit. "It's been for her having left America three days")

8. ʔālət−lo bənto xədni maɛak
'His daughter said to him, "Take me with you'

9. lamməɛ−li ṣ−ṣabbāṭ mnīḥ [DA-180]
'Shine the shoes for me well'

10. bdawwər−lak w−əbrədd−əllak xabar bəkra ṣ−ṣəbəḥ [DA-290]
'I'll look around (for you) and let you know tomorrow morning' (lit. "and send back news to you...")

11. *wēn bəṭḥəbbu waʔʔəf-ᵊlkon?*   'Where would you(pl.) like me to
    [DA-45]   wait for you?'

12. *halli bətrīdi bžəb-lek yā*   'I'll bring (to) you (f.) what you
    [AO-115]   want'

13. *yōm baɛᵊd yōm biɛəd-ᵊlna nafs*   'Day after day he repeats the same
    ᵊl-ʔəṣṣa   story to us'

14. *ʔana məštaʔt-əlkon*   'I've(f.) missed you(pl.)' ('I've
                                    been yearning for you')

15. *hiyye madyənt-əllo b-kəll ši*   'She's indebted to him for everything'

The "Ethical Dative" and Redundant -*l*- Suffixes. Almost all constructions involving pronouns are also applicable to nouns (since pronouns are, by definition, noun "substitutes" [p.535]). Thus *žab-ᵊlhon ᵊhdiyye* 'He brought (to) them a present' is a substitute for sentences such as *žāb ləl-ᵊwlād ᵊhdiyye* 'He brought (to) the children a present'.

In Syrian Arabic, however, there are certain very common uses of conjunctive -*l*- phrases which apply to pronouns only; there are no corresponding uses of *la*- with nouns. For instance:

16. *bžann-əllak hēk bəddo yaɛmel*   'I think that's what he wants to do'
    [DA-75]

> The suffix -*əllak* is functionally a sentence supplement [p.526], though in form it seems to be a supplement or complement to the verb *bžann*. Therefore it does not mean "I think for you...", but merely betokens an assumed relevance or interest of the statement to the person addressed; or as a stylistic feature it may be used simply to give a more intimate or personal tone to a discourse — emphasizing the conversational relationship between speaker and person spoken to. Further examples:

17. *xāyəf-lak hal-ʔəxtiṣārāt mā*   'I'm afraid these abbreviations are
    tənfáhem   incomprehensible'

18. *šāyəf-lak ᵊs-siyāse l-ᵊmɛāṣra*   'I find contemporary politics very
    bəthayyer ᵊktīr   confusing'

19. *btaɛrə́f-li ši bənt ᵊbtəʔɛod*   'Do you know any girl who would work
    ṣānɛa? [DA-80]   as a maid?'

> Note also example 10, above. The -*l*- phrase is an "ethical dative" in *bdawwər-lak,* but a complement in *brədd-əllak.*

Similarly, conjunctive -*l*- phrases are often used with
a pronoun that is redundant upon the subject-affix of the
verb (or in the second-person with an imperative verb); the
verb and the pronoun have the same referent:

20. *l-marra l-mādye sməɛt-əlli kamm*   'The last time, I heard a few like
    wāḥde hēke   that'

21. *bəddna nəḥkī-lna šī sīre ṭawīle*   'We must have a good long talk'

22. *žəddi kān ɛando ɛāde yāxəd-lo*   'My grandfather had the habit of
    ġafwe baɛd əl-ġada   taking a nap after lunch'

23. *ɛədū-lkon šī nəṣṣ sāɛa tānye*   'Stay (pl.) another half hour!'
                                          (lit. "sit...")

24. *dzakkar-lak šī wāḥed ʔənte*   'You think of one'

25. *bəddi ʔaʔrā-li šwayye*   'I want to do a little reading'

26. *mā laḥa-yɛəš-lo ʔaktar mən*   'He won't live more than five days'
    xaməst iyyām

Another use of redundant pronouns with -*l*- is in anticipation of a pronoun suffixed to the verb's complement:

27. *taɛažt-əlla bāb sayyārəta*   'I dented (for her) the rear door of
    l-warrāni   her car'

28. *raššēt-əllo šwayyet mayy ɛala*   'I sprinkled a little water on his
    wəššo   face'

29. *ʔakl əs-səkkar əktīr bisawwəs-lak*   'Eating sugar too much will decay
    əsnānak   your teeth'

30. *makatībo dāyman bətʔammət-li*   'His letters always depress me'
    ʔalbi   (lit. "...oppress my heart")

31. *haṭ-ṭaṭawwor xayyab-əlna ʔāmālna*   'This development has dashed our
                                          hopes'

Free Prepositions

There are several locative prepositions which can be used predicatively without an "object".[1]

fōʔ	'above, over, upstairs'
taḥt	'below, under, downstairs'
žuwwa	'inside' (annexing form *žuwwāt*)
barra	'outside' (annexing form *barrāt*)
ʔəddām	'in front(of)'
wara	'behind, in back'

Examples without objects:

1. *hənne barra bəž-žnēne*   'They're outside in the garden'

2. *l-ḥafle l-mūsīqiyye bətṣīr žuwwa*   'The concert will be indoors'

3. *fī makātīb ʔəlak taḥʔt Ɛand ʔs-sammān*   'There are some letters for you downstairs at the grocer's'

4. *mīn hāda yalli taḥʔt?*   'Who's that down there?'

5. *samīra fōʔ maƐ ʔəmma*   'Samira is upstairs with her mother'

6. *ʔoƐa s-sayyāra yalli wara!*   'Look out for the car behind!'

7. *Ɛarabāt ʔr-rəkkāb ʔəddām wəš-šaḥʔn wara*   'Passenger cars are forward and freight (cars) to the rear'

Examples with noun objects:

1. *byəskon barrāt ʔl-balad*   'He lives outside the city'

2. *žuwwāt ʔd-dār Ɛəndo žāž u-dīk* [AO-63]   'Inside the house he has chickens and a rooster'

3. *fī malža taḥt ʔl-ʔarḍ*   'There's a shelter under the ground'

4. *ʔūḍti fōʔ ʔl-matbax*   'My room is over the kitchen'

---

[1]These expressions cannot be analyzed as "adverbs" or the like, since they can stand alone as predicate, as well as in various supplemental and complemental capacities. Adverbs are by definition non-predicative [p. 381].

'Predicative use', of course, includes use in constructions derived from predication, viz. attribution [493] and predicative complementation [448].

5. *naṭṭ wara n-nōl u-ṣār iḥayyek*   'He jumped behind the loom and began
   ʔawām [AO-96]   to weave quickly'

6. *xallīna nažtớmeε ʔaddām ᵊl-bōṣta*   'Let's meet in front of the post
                                             office'

Prepositional Combinations with *la-* and *man*

    la- 'to' and *man* 'from' may precede any of the free prepositions as well
as *εand* 'at, with', to convert a locative phrase into a TRANSLOCATIVE phrase:

1. *εazᵈmon la-εando εal-εaša*   'He invited them to his house for
                                             dinner'

2. *badžīb-li hal-ᵊġrāḍ man εand*   'Would you bring me those things from
   ᵊl-laḥḥām?   the butcher's?' (lit. "...from at the
                                             butcher")

3. *ṣār...yarmīhon man fōʔ ᵊl-ḥēṭ*   'He started throwing them out over
   la-barra [AO-104]   the wall'

4. *ʔarreb haṭ-ṭarabēẓa la-ʔaddām*   'Move that table over in front of
   εammtak   your aunt'

5. *ʔana žāye man barrāt ᵊl-balad*   'I'm coming from out of town'

6. *ḥāwel talʔớṭa man taḥt*   'Try to get at it from underneath'

7. *ržāε šwayye la-wara*   'Back up a little'

    man (but not *la-*) is also used before *εala* 'on':

8. *žīb ᵊṣ-ṣaḥᵊn man εala ṭ-ṭāwle*   'Get the dish from off the table'

9. *naʔʔī-li man εal-wažš šī kīloyēn*   'Pick out about two kilos of toma-
   banadōra [DA-106]   toes from on top for me'

        εala serves both in the locative sense 'on' and in the
translocative senses 'onto' and 'to': *ḥaṭṭo εaṭ-ṭāwle* 'Put
it on the table' *rāḥ εal-bēt* 'He went to the house'.
        In other cases as well, *la-* is often omitted in trans-
locative phrases when the preposition has an object: *ṭlaεt
barrāt ᵊl-balad* 'I went out of town', but not when there is
no object: *ṭlaεt la-barra* 'I went outside'.

        It should be noted that *man* in translocative phrases
means not only 'from', but also 'through', 'over', 'by':

10. *ṭlaεt barrāt l-ᵊmdīne man bāb*   'I came out of the Old City through
    tūma lᵊl-ʔaṣṣāε [AO-67]   Bâb Touma to Qassaa.'

11. *l-bāṣ byəmroʔ mən ʔəddām bābna* 'The bus goes by in front of our
    [DA-104]   door'

    Note also ex. 3, above: *mən fōʔ* 'over' (not 'from on top of').

    baƐᵊd 'after' and *ʔabᵊl* 'before' may be preceded by *mən* 'since', and
    baƐᵊd may also be preceded by *la-* 'until':

12. *l-ʔasƐār ġəlyet mən baƐd*   'Prices have gone up since the
    ᵊš-šafāf   drought'

13. *trōk hal-masʔale la-baƐd ᵊl-Ɛīd*   'Leave that matter till after the
                                          holiday'

14. *mən ʔabl ᵊžwāzo kān yəskar*   'Before his marriage he used to get
                                     drunk' (Here *mən* does not mean 'from'
                                     or 'since' a certain time, but rather
                                     'during' a certain length of time:
                                     cf. the spacial sense 'through', 'by'.)

      baƐᵊd and *ʔabᵊl* are also used adverbially with no "ob-
    ject", with or without a preceding *mən* (or *la-*): *mā kənt*
    ʔəštəġel Ɛand hada mən ʔabᵊl [DA-81] 'I've never worked for
    anyone before', *halli byəxloṣ ʔabᵊl byəstanna t-tāni Ɛand*
    ᵊl-bāb [DA-244] 'Whoever finishes first will wait for the
    other at the door'.
      baƐᵊd and *ʔabᵊl* are not to be considered "free prep-
    ositions", however, since they are not normally used pre-
    dicatively without an object.

    fōʔ, *taht*, *wara*, *ʔəddām*, *baƐᵊd* and *ʔabᵊl* may all either take pronoun
    suffixes directly, or else they may be followed by *mən* with suffixes: *baƐdi*
    or *baƐᵊd mənni* 'after me', *fōʔo* or *fōʔ mənno* 'above it'. Commonly, however,
    the *m* of *mən* is doubled (or in some areas, preceded by *l*): *baƐd ᵊmmənni*
    (or *baƐd ᵊlmənni*) 'after me', *fōʔ ᵊmmənno* (or *fōʔ ᵊlmənno*) 'above it':

15. *huwwe byəži dōro ʔabl ᵊmmənni*   'His turn comes before mine'

16. *kənt māši wara mmənno*   'I was walking behind him'

17. *hanne sāknin taht ᵊmmənna*   'They live below us' (i.e. downstairs)

18. *w-ʔamᵊt ʔante ʔəlt-əlla ʔəddām*   '...and you told her, in front of me,
    ᵊmmənni Ɛandi rəfaʔāti   that you had your companions with you'
                                       [p. 450, bottom]

Other Special Prepositions

ka- 'as' forms phrases which are limited to supplemental use [p. 524], and does not take pronoun suffixes:

1. *kān marġūb ᵊktīr ka-mḥāḍer huwwe*   'He was much in demand as a lecturer'

2. *bəḥsen ʔəržaℰ ka-ʔəstāz*   'I could go back as a teacher'

3. *ka-wāḥed ʔamērkāni byəḥki ℰarabi*   'For an American, he speaks Arabic
   mnīḥ   well'

On *kaʔənno* 'as if' see p. 491.

Certain other prepositions are also not used with pronoun suffixes: *ḥasab* 'according to', *ʔāṭeℰ* 'across', *badaL* and *ℰawaḍ* 'instead of' (but *badāl* and *ℰawāḍ*, same meaning, can take suffixes), *ʔərb* and *ʔarīb* 'near' (but *b-ʔərbo* 'near it', *ʔarīb mənno* 'near it').

bēn 'between, among' has a form *bēnāt,* used with plural suffixes, (and sometimes also with nouns) in the sense 'among' (or 'between' if the plural refers to two only): *bēnāton* 'among them' or 'between (the two of) them'. In coordinations, 'between...and...', the preposition never takes the *-āt* form — and must be repeated if one or both of the following terms is a pronoun suffix, since the suffixes themselves cannot be coordinated: *bēni w-bēnak* 'between you and me'.

1. *šū l-farᵊʔ bēn ᵊt-tnēn?*   'What's the difference between the
   [DA-293]   two?'

2. *kānet ᵊl-bənt bēn ᵊl-ḥərrās,*   'The girl was among the guards,
   lābse badle ℰaskariyye [AO-115]   dressed in a military uniform'

3. *ḥəms u-ḥama wāʔℰīn bēn ᵊš-šām*   'Homs and Hama lie between Damascus
   u-ḥalab   and Aleppo'

4. *mīn ℰali bēnāton?*   'Which of them is Ali?' ("Who is
        Ali among them?")

5. *ℰtamadna ℰalēha bēnātna*   'We decided (on) it among ourselves'

6. *fəḍḍūha bēnāt baℰᵊdkon*   'Settle it among yourselves'

7. *dawwart bēn* (or *bēnāt*) *l-ᵊbyūt*   'I went around among all the houses'
   kəllon

8. *ʔəža ṣaldḥa bēni w-bēn marti*   'He came and patched things up between
        me and my wife'

9. *bēnna w-bēnkon mā fī farᵊʔ*   'Between you and us there's no
        difference'

10. *bēnon u-bēn ℰəmmālon fī ʔəxtilāf*   'There's a disagreement between them
         and their workers'

tabaε 'of, belonging to' forms phrases which function as predicate
(*has-stīlo tabaε farīd* 'This pen belongs to Fareed') or attribute (*wēn
ᵊs-stīlo tabaε farīd?* 'Where is Fareed's pen?'); but unlike ordinary
prepositions is does not form adverbial phrases [p.523]. Examples:

1. *hayy tabaεna* — 'This is ours'

2. *l-ḥādes ṣār εand ᵊs-sūke tabaεna* — 'The accident happened on our corner'

3. *tabaε mīn hal-ᵊktāb?* — 'Whose is this book?'

4. *hal-bərǧi tabaε šū?* — 'Where does this screw belong?'

5. *l-mūs tabaεak ḥadd?* — 'Is your razor (or jacknife) sharp?'

6. *wēn ᵊl-ballōra tabaε ᵊl-kāz?* — 'Where's the chimney for the lamp?'

7. *hal-ᵊgrāḍ tabaεhon (or tabaḥḥon)* — 'These things are theirs'

8. *hayy baṭṭāriyye tabaε bīl* — 'This is a flashlight battery'

    Some speakers rarely use *tabaε* with an indefinite fol-
lowing term (as in ex. 8), preferring in such cases an annexion phrase (*baṭṭāriyyet bīl*) or a *la–* phrase (*baṭṭāriyye
la-bīl*). Note the definitized following term in expressions
like *waraʔa tabaε ᵊl-xams miyye* 'a five hundred [pound] note'.

    In agreement with a plural, the forms *tabaεāt* and *tabaεūl* are sometimes
used[1]:

9. *xōd l-ᵊǧrāḍ tabaεātak mən hōn* — 'Get your things out of here'

10. *tabaεūl mīn hal-kətᵊb?* — 'Whose books are these?'

11. *hal-barāǧi tabaεāt ʔēš?* — 'What are these screws for?' (or 'Where do these screws go?')

12. *bfaḍḍel habbel ᵊl-xəḍar tabaεāti* — 'I prefer to steam my vegetables'

13. *tabaε mīn haṣ-ṣuwar? – tabaεūli* — 'Whose pictures are these? – Mine'

14. *hal-ʔarāḍi tabaεāt εammi* — 'This land (lit. 'these lands') belongs to my uncle'

---

[1]The existence of these plural forms is a measure of the noun-like (and
un-preposition-like) character of the word *tabaε*. Regardless how it is
classified, *tabaε* is grammatically unique; as a noun, it would be exceptional in that it must always stand in construct. There are, of course,
many prepositions which are etymologically – and sometimes functionally –
nouns, e.g. *mətᵊl* 'like' (or 'the like of'), *žamb* 'beside' (or 'side'),etc.
    As for the plural form *tabaεūl*, the final *l* is presumably a variation
from *n* (cf. Pal. *tabεūn*), perhaps reinterpreted as a quasi-verbal form
with an *–l–* suffix [p.480]: *tabaεū-lo* 'belonging (pl.) to him' (cf. Classical *tābiε lahu*).

In various parts of Greater Syria, certain other words
are used in the same way as *tabaɛ*. In parts of Lebanon and
Palestine, the form *btāɛ* is used, generally with full adjectival inflection: fem. *btāɛet...*, *btāɛti* 'mine', etc.; pl.
btūɛ or *btāɛūn*; in Palestine the plural form of *tabaɛ* is
tabɛūn (rather than *tabaɛūl*). In Damascus the word *šīt* is
common: *l-mōtōr šīt ᵊs-sayyāra xarbān* 'The engine of the
car is out of order'; the plural of *šīt* is *šyāt: lā tāxod
hal-ᵊġrād, šyāti hadōl* 'Don't take these things, they're
mine'. The Palestinian form of this word is *šēt*, pl. *šayyūt*.

In the periphrasis of annexion [p.460], an attributive
tabaɛ phrase is commonly preferred to annexion when the
leading term is a recent loan word, or a substantive ending
in a vowel (not counting the *-e/-a* suffix): *r-rādyo tabaɛi*
'my radio' (rather than *rādyōyi*), *l-ᵊabartmān l-ᵊždīd
tabaɛna* 'our new apartment' (rather than *ᵊabartmānna l-ᵊždīd*).
The *tabaɛ* construction is also common in expressing a looser
sort of relationship than what is implied by annexion, e.g.
s-sūke tabaɛna 'our corner' (ex. 2, above) rather than
sūkətna, which would sound more like a matter of ownership
or some sort of intimate association.

Prepositional Clauses and Annexion Clauses

A number of prepositions and nouns may be followed by a clause as well
as by a nominal phrase. In most such cases, the clause is introduced by
the particle *ma: ᵊabᵊl ma nākol* 'before we eat' (cf. *ᵊabl ᵊl-ᵊakᵊl* 'before
eating'), *b-maṭraḥ ma bikūn* 'Wherever it is' (cf. *b-maṭraḥo* 'in its place,
where it belongs'). For example:

baɛᵊd ma	'after'	*waᵊᵊt ma, sāɛet ma,*	'at the time(hour,
mᵊtᵊl ma	'as'	*yōm ma, sᵊnt ma,*	day, year, minute)
		daᵊīᵊet ma	that...', 'when'
bala ma, bidūn ma	'without'	*ᵊadd ma*	'as much as'
badal ma, badāl ma	'instead of'	*bēm ma, la-bēn ma*	'while'

Most phrases composed of a noun or preposition plus *ma*
plus a clause function as adverbial supplements. For examples
of their use, see p.528; also p.357.
Note, however, the expression *mᵊmma* 'than' (*mᵊn + ma*),
which is used mostly in complementation to an elative [p.314]:

1. *hiyye ᵊaḥla b-ᵊktīr mᵊmma kᵊnᵊt
   mᵊnṭᵊẓer*   'She is much prettier than I
                                                  expected'

2. *lā tɛaᵊᵊed ᵊl-ᵊumūr ᵊaktar mᵊmma
   hiyye mɛaᵊᵊade halla?*   'Don't make things more complicated
                                                  than they already are'

Note also:

3. *ʔūmi, xalliṣī məmma huwwe fī*
   [AO-119]

'Get up (f.) and release him from
what he is in' (i.e. from the spell
he is under)

Similarly, with a noun (substantive):

4. *daxlet mən maṭraḥ ma ʔəžet mn*
   ᵊl-ḥēṭ [AO-117]

'She went back through the wall the
same way she had come' (lit. "She
entered through the place she had
come through the wall")

With elatives:

5. *hayy mən ʔaḥsan ma ykūn*

'This is (of) the best there is'

With *kəll* 'every' [p. 339]:

6. *kəll ma mənḥəbb nəṭlaɛ la-barra*
   btənzel maṭar

'Every time we want to go outside,
it rains'

A few nouns and prepositions may be followed by a clause introduced by
ʔənno (which more usually introduces <u>complemental</u> clauses [p. 449]):
la-daražet ʔənno 'to such an extent that...' (also complemental: *la-daraže
ʔənno...*); *maɛ ʔənno* 'although' (one of the meanings of *maɛ* is 'despite').
Some examples of prepositions with an *ʔənno* clause are given on   .
Note also *ka-ʔənno* 'as if', *la-ʔənno* (or *la-ʔanno* or *li-ʔanno*) 'because':
la- 'for' + *ʔənno* 'that...' [see p. 543]:

7. *biṣawwer ᵊl-marʔa kaʔənno naḥḥāt*

'He describes women as if he were
a sculptor'

8. *mā ʔəža laʔənno kān ᵊdɛīf*

'He didn't come, because he was sick'

9. *s-saɛdān mā rədi yətɛallam maɛ*
   ʔənno mɛallmo ṣār yəḍᵊrbo [AO-96]

'The monkey wouldn't learn even
though his master began beating him'

10. *kānet mətʔassra la-daražet ʔənno*
    mā ʔədret təḥki

'She was so deeply affected that she
couldn't speak'

The particles *la-* and *mənšān* 'for, to, in order that' are used both as
prepositions and as conjunctions, i.e. their following term may be either a
nominal phrase or a clause (without any particle such as *ma*): *rāḥu ɛal-bēt
la-yāklu* or ... *mənšān yāklu* 'they went home to eat': cf. *rāḥu ɛal-bēt
ləl-ʔakᵊl* or ... *mənšān ᵊl-ʔakᵊl* '...for (the) food'.

Certain nouns may also stand in construct with a clause
without benefit of a subordinating conjunction. See ex. 6,
p. 386 (*masʔalet...* 'a question of...').

CHAPTER 19: ATTRIBUTION

An ATTRIBUTE[1] *(an-naɛt)* is a subordinated predicate [p.380] or comment [429]. The term it is attributive to *(al-manɛūt)* corresponds to the subject of that predicate, or the topic of that comment. The attribute follows the term it is attributive to, and generally agrees with it in definiteness (as well as in number/gender, when applicable):

Predication or Extraposition	Attribution (Indefinite)	Attribution (Definite)
l-madīne kbīre	*madīne kbīre*	*l-madīne l-ᵊkbīre*
'The city is large'	'a large city'	'the large city'
laʔāhon ṣabi	*ṣabi laʔāhon*	*ṣ-ṣabi yalli laʔāhon*
'A boy found them'	'a boy who found them'	'the boy who found them'
l-madīne mā šəftha	*madīne mā šəftha*	*l-madīne yalli mā šəftha*
'The city, I haven't seen (it)'	'a city I haven't seen'	'the city I haven't seen'

Note the resumptive pronoun *(-ha)* in the last example, which is characteristic of attribution phrases derived from extraposition, just as it is of the underlying extrapositional clause itself [p.430].

The Article Prefix *(ʔadāt t-taɛrīf).* Adjectives and certain other attributes are usually definitized with the article prefix, whose basic form is *l-: l-hawa l-bāred* 'the cold air', *l-ᵊhṣān ᵊl-ʔadham* 'the black horse'. The article is totally assimilated, however, to dental and front palatal consonants *(al-ḥurūf š-šamsiyya): t, d, s, z, ṭ, ḍ, ṣ, ẓ, š, ž, n, r.* Examples of the assimilated article, in noun-adjective attribution phrases:

ṣ-ṣaff ᵊt-tālet	'the third row'	*l-lḥāf ᵊž-žamīl*	'the pretty quilt'
š-šōraba s-smīke	'the thick soup'	*ṭ-ṭāleb ᵊz-zaki*	'the bright student'
r-rasm ᵊd-daʔīʔ	'the fine drawing'	*ẓ-ẓābeṭ ᵊḍ-ḍaḥūk*	'the jolly officer'

s-samne n-nabātiyye 'the vegetable shortening'

The article is not invariably assimilated to *ž;* one may sometimes hear, for instance, *l-žāmeɛ l-ᵊždīd* 'the new mosque' instead of *ž-žāmeɛ ᵊž-ždīd.*

---

[1] The term 'attribute' is sometimes used in a broader sense in American linguistics, to denote subordinate terms in general. In French, on the other hand, 'attribut' generally means 'predicate', while 'épithète' means 'attribute' in our sense.

The Clause Definitizer. The particle *halli* or *yalli* (or *yəlli* or *ᵊlli*) — rather than the article prefix — is used to definitize an attributive comment or verbal predicate, while in the case of non-verbal predicates, attribution to a definite term may or may not involve *halli* (etc.), depending on other considerations. (See p. 500.)

A term is DEFINITE if (1) it is introduced by the article *l–* or the demonstrative prefix *hal–* [p. 556] or by *halli* (etc.); or (2) if it is a pronoun or a proper name; or (3) if it is in construct [p. 456] with a definite term. Otherwise it is INDEFINITE. Thus *l-bənt* 'the girl', *hal-bənt* 'this girl', *hādi* 'this(f.)', *hiyye* 'she', *maryam* 'Mary', *bənt ᵊt-tāžer* 'the merchant's daughter', *bənto* 'his daughter' are definite; while *bənt, wāḥde bənt, ši bənt* (all translated 'a girl'), *bənᵊt tāžer* 'a merchant's daughter', *ᵊakbar bənt* 'the oldest daughter' are all indefinite, regardless whether or not they <u>refer</u> to a definite person.

Thus in *fī wāḥde bənt bəddo yətžawwazha* 'There's a certain girl he wants to marry', the attributive comment *bəddo yətžawwazha* 'he wants to marry her' is not introduced by *halli* even though *wāḥde bənt* would presumably have a quite definite reference; similarly, in *hayy ᵊaḥla bənt šəftha* 'That's the prettiest girl I've seen', the attributive comment *šəftha* is likewise indefinite.

Like the article prefix, the particle *halli* (etc.) is not limited to use in attributes; it is also used to convert any sort of predication into a definite noun phrase which may function as subject, predicate, complement, or annex. Examples of non-attributive *halli*–phrases:

1. *halli bṭaᶜṭī bikūn ᵊmnīḥ* [DA-100] — 'Whatever you give will be fine'

2. *tfaḍḍal la-ḥatta ᵊaržīk halli ᶜəndi* [AO-79] — 'Come, let me show you what I have'

3. *btaᶜref halli ḍarabak?* [AO-115] — 'Do you know the one who hit you?'

4. *byākol ᵊdtle yəlli byəstahzel kalām ᵊabū* — 'He who makes fun of what his father says will get a beating!' (Pred.-Subj. inversion [p. 419])

5. *ḥakā–lha kəll halli ṣār maᶜo* [AO-115] — 'He told her all that had happened to him'

6. *baᶜd ᵊlli ᵊālo kərhū n-nās* — 'After what he said, people hated him'

7. *hāda yalli kān lāzəmni b-ᶜēno* — 'This is what I needed exactly'

8. *yəlli baᶜᵊrfo, ᵊanno rtafaḍ ṭalabo* — 'All I know is that his request was denied' (or 'As far as I know...')

As shown in the examples above, non-attributive *halli* (etc.) can generally be translated into English as 'what', 'whatever', 'who', 'whoever', 'he who', 'that which', etc.

In its attributive use, the particle may often be translated as 'who', 'which', or 'that', but it should be kept in mind that *halli* does not really correspond to these English words (relative pronouns); its presence or absence is a matter of definiteness, while the use or non-use of the relative pronouns has nothing to do with definiteness: *bənt ᵊbtaɛref ṭəṭbox* 'a girl who knows how to cook'; *r-rǧāl halli šəfton* 'the men I saw'. (But see ex. 21 and 22, p. 499)

Definite Attributive Clauses *(aṣ-ṣila)*

Examples, attributive verbal predicates:

1. *ʔabl ᵊšwayye smaɛt ᵊl-madāfeɛ halli bəddəll ɛala nihāyt ᵊṣ-ṣalā* [DA-298]

   'A little while ago I heard the cannon(s) which signal the end of the prayer'

2. *l-ɛaṣāye kānet tabaɛ wāḥed mn ᵊl-malāyke halli ʔəǧu la-ɛənd ᵊbrāhīm* [AO-99]

   'The stick belonged to one of the angels who came to Abraham'

3. *bəddāri wlād ʔaxūha yəlli byəštəǧel ɛənd ᵊǧ-ǧarrāḥ* [AO-44]

   'She looks after the children of her brother who works for the surgeon'

4. *laʔu syūf ᵊt-tmānīn rəǧǧāl halli haǧamu ɛalēhon* [AO-113]

   'They found the swords of the eighty men who had attacked them'

5. *bʔarǧīk kamān maṣāṭer mn ᵊt-ṭalabiyye halli ʔəǧətni mbāreḥ* [AO-79]

   'I'll also show you some samples from the consignment that came (to me) yesterday'

6. *kīf hal-ʔəmʔom ᵊǧ-ǧǧīr halli mā byəsaɛ ʔəlla ʔəṣbaɛtak wəsɛak kəllak?* [AO-116]

   'How did that little flagon that wouldn't hold any more than your finger hold the whole of you?'

Attributive quasi-verbal predicate [p. 412]:

7. *r-rəǧǧāl ʔaxad xanǧaro w-ʔaṭaɛ rās ᵊl-ʔaṭṭ halli ɛəndo* [AO-112]

   'the man took his dagger and cut off the head of the cat he had'

8. *b-hal-ʔəṭaɛ yalli maɛak mā fīk tmauwət-li šāhi*

   'With those pieces you have you can't checkmate me'

Attributive non-verbal predicates [p. 402]:

9. *stahlakna kəll ᵊṣ-ṣābūn halli bəl-bēt*

   'We've used up all the soap (that was) in the house'

10. *raḥa-ʔəstannāk bəl-ʔahwe halli*
    ɛala žanab ʾl-maržе [DA-197]

    'I'll wait for you in the coffeehouse
    (that's) on the Marjé'

11. *ktōb ʾəsmak bəl-ɛāmūd yalli*
    ɛal-yamīn

    'Write your name in the right-hand
    column'

12. *s-sayyāra yalli ʾəddāmi waʾʾafet*
    ɛala ġafle

    'The car (that was) in front of me
    stopped suddenly'

13. *ɛam-ʔəštəǧel ɛawāḍ ʾaxi halli*
    marīḍ

    'I'm working in place of my brother
    who is sick'

14. *šū l-ʾġrāḍ halli lāzəmtak?*
    [DA-128]

    'What things do you need?' (lit.
    "What are the things that are neces-
    sary to you?")

15. *šūf hāda halli žāy, hāda ʾabu*
    ɛafīf [DA-134]

    'See that man coming? That's Abu
    Afif' (lit. "Look at that who is
    coming, ...")

Non-verbal attributes to a definite term are not by any
means always introduced by the clause definitizer. Compare
ex. 12 with *s-sayyāra ʾəddāmi* 'the car in front of me', ex.
13 with *ʾaxi l-marīḍ* 'my sick brother', ex. 14 with *l-ʾġrāḍ*
ʾl-lāzme 'the necessary things', ex. 15 with *š-šahr ʾž-žāye*
'the coming month'. See p. 500.

Examples of definite attributive comments (i.e. attributive clauses with
their own subjects or with subject-referents different from the terms they
are attributive to):

16. *hayy ʾl-bənt yalli ʾəlt-ʾllak*
    ɛanha [DA-99]

    'This is the girl I told you about'

17. *rakḍet u-ɛānaʾet ʾl-malek halli*
    ẓannto ṣāḥəbha [AO-119]

    'She ran and embraced the king, whom
    she thought [to be] her lover'

18. *ṭalab ʾl-malek mn ʾṣ-ṣayyād*
    ʾənno ydəllo ɛal-maṭraḥ halli
    ɛamma-yṣīd fī s-samak [AO-117]

    'The king asked the fisherman to di-
    rect him to the place where he was
    catching the fish' (lit. "...the
    place he was catching in it the fish")

19. *s-sadīʾ yalli ɛaṭēto yāha kān*
    məhtaž-la ktīr

    'The friend I gave it to needed it
    badly'

20. *wēn ʾt-tnēn halli rəhʾt maɛon*
    ɛal-madrase?

    'Where are the two you went to school
    with?'

21. *ʾaddēš ḥaʾʾ ʾs-sayyāra lli*
    bəddak təštrīha? [EA-180]

    'What's the price of the car you
    want to buy?'

22. *lāzem baddel haṭ-ṭaʾṣīr halli*
    ʾaṣṣarto fīk [AO-108]

    'I must make up for this neglect with
    which I have treated you'

23. *ʔahᵊl l-ᵊmdīne halli sāwētīhon samak, kᵊll yōm byədɛu ɛalayyi w-hāda sabab ḍaɛafi* [AO-119]

'The townspeople that you(f.) turned into fish curse me every day, and that is the cause of my illness'

24. *laha-tᵊtrok ᵊn-nās halli ʔāɛde ɛandhon* [DA-98]

'She's going to leave the people she's staying with'

25. *kᵊnt mᵊṭṣaṭṭeḥ ɛala hat-taxt ḥalli ʔana fī halla?* [AO-118]

'I was lying on this bed that I'm in now'

26. *byəd²rsu l-wuqūd yalli byəstaɛᵊmlu ləṣ-ṣawarīx u-hal-masāʔel*

'They study the fuel used for rockets, and things like that'

Sometimes, as in ex. 26, the resumptive pronoun [p.430] after a verb is ommitted; i.e. *l-wuqūd yalli byəstaɛᵊmlu* 'the fuel they use' rather than ...*yalli byəstaɛᵊmlū* "the fuel they use (it)". This construction is of course more like an English relative clause than the more common one is.

27. *lāʔi l-ʔaɛdād yalli hiyye ʔaḍɛāf ᵊl-xamse*

'Find the numbers that are multiples of five'

28. *hal-kᵊtob ᵊntašaru fᵊl-qāhira lli hiyye l-ʔān ᵊl-markaz ᵊl-ʔadabi lᵊl-ɛālam ᵊl-ɛarabi*

'These books were published in Cairo, which is now the cultural center of the Arab world'

Examples 27 and 28 show attributive comments with re-sumptive subject pronouns [p.434]. This construction is usual in the case of nominal predicates, especially definite predicates. (Cf. p.405.) Thus, 'I want to introduce you to my friend, who is the mayor': *bᵊddi ɛarrfak ɛala ṣāḥbi yᵊlli huwwe raʔīs ᵊl-baladiyye.*

Indefinite Attributive Clauses (*aṣ-ṣifa*)

In attribution to an indefinite term, a predicate or comment is usually paratactic; i.e. there is usually no particle like *yalli*, etc. to mark its subordination, and it is indistinguishable from an independent sentence ex-cept for its inclusion in, or prosodic unity with, the superordinate clause. Examples (attributive clause underscored):

1. *fī ɛandi sadīʔ ʔamērkāni ʔᵊža* <u>*ždīd ɛal-ᵊblād*</u> [DA-289]

'I have an American friend who has just recently come to this country'

2. *rᵊḥna la-ɛand fallāḥ byᵊskon* <u>*b-ḍēɛa ʔarībe mn ᵊl-madīne*</u> [AO-59]

'We went to see a farmer who lives in a village near the city'

3. *baɛᵊd bᵊkra fī bēt ᵊmnīḥ bᵊddo* <u>*yᵊfḍa*</u> [DA-244]

'The day after tomorrow there's a good house that's going to be vacated'

4. mā fī šī tg̀ayyar

'Nothing has changed' (lit. "There is not a thing that has changed")

5. mnaɛref bəl-madīne ɛēle mnīḥa ɛəndha bənt ḥəlwe bəddon ižawwzūha [AO-55]

'We know a good family in the city who have a pretty daughter they want to marry off'

Example 5 shows one attributive clause within another. bəddon ižawwzūha 'they want to marry her off' is attributive to bənt ḥəlwe, while ɛəndha bənt ḥəlwe bəddon... 'they have a pretty daughter they want...' is all attributive to ɛēle mnīḥa. Similarly in ex. 2, ʔarība mn əl-madīne '[it is] near the city' is attributive to ḍēɛa, while byəskon əb-ḍēɛa ʔarība... 'he lives in a village near...' is all attributive to fallāḥ.

6. fī ʔəli ʔəbən ɛamm tāžer hnīk [DA-245]

'I have a cousin who's in business there' (lit. "...a cousin [he iš] a merchant there")

7. kān fī ṣayyād ʔəxtyār u-faʔīr əktīr, ɛəndo mara w-tlətt əwlād [AO-115]

'There was a poor old fisherman who had a wife and three children'

8. ʔəli ḥkāye ɛažībe ktīr, bətkūn ɛəbra la-halli bəddo yəɛtəber [AO-118]

'I have a very strange story, that will be a lesson for him who will take heed'

9. hayy šəgle bəddi qarrəra baɛəd šahrēn tlāte

'That's something I'll decide in two or three months'

10. baɛatt-əllak əzbūn ḍərso ɛam-yūžaɛo w-ɛam-bidawwer ɛala kammāše la-yəxlaɛo

'I sent you a patient whose tooth was hurting him and he was looking for a pair of pliers to pull it'

11. w-mā bətlāʔi maṭraḥ əthəṭṭ rəžlak fī mən kətr əz-zaḥme [DA-302]

'And you can't find a place to put your foot down because of the crowd' (lit. "...to put your foot in (it)")

12. hayy ʔawwal marra bəštəg̀el fīha [DA-81]

'This is the first time I've worked' (i.e. "...first time in which I work")

13. ḥaket kalām mā fhəmt mənno šī [AO-118]

'She said some words of which I understood nothing'

14. šāf fīha barmīl əkbīr, fī raməl w-ṭīne [AO-115]

'He saw a large barrel with sand and clay in it' (lit. "...[there was] in it sand...")

15. dabbaru xəṭṭa kəlla makər

'They conceived a very clever plan' ("...a plan all of which was cleverness")

16. *ḥāwal kəll šī məmken taṣawwuro* 'He tried everything imaginable'
    <u>*məmken taṣawwuro*</u>   ("everything whose imagining is
                                   possible")

17. *l-lēle t-tānye šāf ʔaṣᵊr ʔaswad* 'The next night he saw a black castle
    bābo maftūḥ [AO-117]   whose door was open'

18. *šū ɛandak ḍamānāt ᵊtʔaddəmha* 'What collateral do you have to offer
    ləl-bank liqāʔ hal-mablaḡ?   the bank against this amount?'
    [DA-296]

19. *byətɛaššu l-masa ɛaša ʔaktar* 'In the evening they have a supper
    ᵊl-ʔawʔāt huwwe mn ᵊl-bāʔi ɛan which is usually (of) food left over
    <u>*ᵊl-ḡada mn ᵊl-ʔakᵊl*</u> [PAT-197] from dinner'

> Note the resumptive subject pronoun (*huwwe*) in ex. 19.
> (Cf. ex. 27 and 28, p. 497.) In this case the attributive
> predicate is prepositional (*mn ᵊl-bāʔi...*); the subject
> pronoun confirms the attributive (and predicative) role of
> what follows its antecedent *ɛaša* 'supper' [cf. p. 549].
> Without *huwwe*, *mn ᵊl-bāʔi...* might be construed as supple-
> mental to the verb *byətɛaššu:* 'they usually sup on left-
> overs from...' (with *ɛaša* as an unmodified paronymous com-
> plement [p. 442]).

20. *mā byəstāhel mara razīle mətᵊl* 'He doesn't deserve a wicked woman
    marto halli kəll yōm bṭaɛṭī   like his wife, who gives him a drink
    šarāb bətbannžo fī [AO-118]   to anesthetize him every day' (lit.
                                      "...a drink she anesthetizes him
                                      with (it)")

> In ex. 20 the indefinite clause *bətbannžo fī* is attribu-
> tive to *šarāb*, which is part of another subordinate clause
> *halli kəll yōm...*, which is attributive to the definite noun
> *marto*.

Some speakers occasionally use *yalli*, etc. to introduce clauses that are
attributive to an indefinite term:

21. *b-hadāk ᵊl-waʔᵊt kān fī ktīr* 'At that time there were a lot of
    nās yəlli staḡallu l-mawʔef   people who took advantage of the
    <u>*yəlli staḡallu l-mawʔef*</u> situation'

22. *fī wāḥde yalli bətzakkára fīha* 'There's one I remember that has her
    <u>*yalli bətzakkára fīha*</u>   name in it'
    ʔəsma

> Example 22 has two subordinate clauses, both attributive
> to the indefinite term *wāḥde*. The first is introduced by
> *yalli*, while the second, *fīha ʔəsma* 'her name is in it', is
> paratactic.

Attributive Words and Phrases

Adjectival, nominal, and prepositional predicates – unlike verbal predicates and extrapositional comments – can often be made attributive in two
ways: either as clauses, or as simple words or phrases.   As clauses, they
are definitized with the particle *yalli* (etc.) [p.494]; as simple words or
phrases, adjectives and (usually) nouns are definitized with the article prefix, while prepositional phrases are not definitized at all:

Clause Attribution	Word or Phrase Attribution
ʔəbno yalli žūɛān..................... 'his son who is hungry'	*ʔəbno ž-žūɛān* 'his hungry son'
ʔəbno yalli (huwwe) sammān........... 'his son who is a grocer'	*ʔəbno s-sammān* 'his son the grocer'
l-bāb yalli ɛal-yamīn................ 'the door that's on the right'	*l-bāb ɛal-yamīn* 'the door on the right'

Prepositional Attributes

Examples, prepositional phrases attributive to definite terms:

1. *n-naǧme ɛala watīre wāḥde*
   naɛɛasətni

   'The monotonous tune made me sleepy'
   (lit. "The melody on one tone...")

2. *n-nās ḥawalēna kānu ɛam-yəḥku*
   bəl-ɛālī

   'The people around us were talking
   loudly'

3. *l-maḥallāt ʔəddām ʔaḥsan mən*
   wara

   'The seats in front are better than
   [those] in back'

4. *l-krafatāt bəl-wāžha lafatu*
   naẓari

   'The neckties in the display window
   caught my eye'

5. *xōd hal-ʔmmawwaže ɛala lōn*
   ʔōṣ ʔl-ʔadaḥ [adap. from AO-79]

   'Take this rainbow-colored moiré'
   (lit. "Take this wavy [one] on the
   color of the rainbow")

6. *šāyef has-sadd ɛala buḥayret*
   ʔl-ʔaṭṭīne? [DA-253]

   'Do you see that dam on Lake
   Qattinah?'

There are a few prepositional set phrases with the force
of adjectives, which in attribution to a definite term are
sometimes preceded by the article: *fōʔ ʔṭ-ṭabīɛa* 'super-
natural', *fōʔ ʔl-ɛāde* 'extraordinary', etc.: *ẓ-ẓawāher*
ʔl-fōʔ ʔṭ-ṭabīɛa '(the)supernatural phenomena' (or *ẓ-ẓawāher*
fōʔ ʔṭ-ṭabīɛa).

Adjective Attributes

Examples. Single adjective, attributive to single noun (or noun with pronoun suffix):

1. *wərte ẓġīre*   'a small inheritance'

2. *waḍᵊɛ məstaḥīl*   'an impossible situation'

3. *nās ġəšᵊm*   'ignorant people'

4. *l-xaṭar ᵊl-ḥaʔīʔi*   'the real danger'

5. *l-mašrūbāt ᵊl-məsᵊkra*   '(the) intoxicating beverages'

6. *l-ɛarab ᵊs-sūriyyīn*   'the Syrian Arabs'

7. *han-naṣb ᵊl-faxᵊm*   'this imposing monument'

8. *raʔīsi l-ᵊmbāšar*   'my immediate superior'

9. *ḥāžātak ᵊl-ḥāliyye*   'your present needs'

10. *zōʔo l-xāṣṣ*   'his personal taste'

Number/gender agreement for attributes is much the same as for predicates [p. 420], though there are a few minor exceptions and additional points about agreement noted in the following sections. One point is that an adjective attribute to an inanimate dual noun is sometimes put in the feminine, in the same way as with plurals:

11. *s-səntēn ᵊl-ʔawwalāniyyīn,*   'the first two years'
     or *s-səntēn ᵊl-ʔawwalāniyye*

Examples of feminine/plural adjectives [p. 201]:

12. *n-nəswān ᵊl-xāynāt* [AO-118]   'treacherous women'

13. *nəswān məsᵊlmāt sāfrāt* [PAT-197]   'unveiled Moslem women'

Examples of uninflected adjectives:

waṣaṭ 'medium':   14. *ʔyāsāt waṣaṭ*   'medium sizes'

tāza 'fresh':   15. *bēḍ tāza*   'fresh eggs'

ṣərf 'authentic':   16. *ʔahwe ɛarabiyye ṣərf* 'authentic Arab coffee'

ḥlēwa 'good-looking': 17. *haš-šabb l-ᵊḥlēwa*   'that good-looking young man'

See also pp. 428, 520.

Adjective attributes to a coördination:

18. *roǧǧāl u mara ǧūɛānīn*   'a hungry man and woman'

19. *marti w-waladi t-taɛbānīn*   'my tired wife and child'

> The adjective is always plural in agreement with an additive coordination of singular nouns, but it may be feminine in agreement with a coördination of plurals, provided that each of the plurals could itself take feminine agreement [p. 423]:

20. *kətᵊb w-ṣuwar w-ᵊkwānāt ǧālye*   'expensive books, pictures, and records'

21. *š-šuɛūb wəl-žuyūš ᵊl-ɛarabiyye*   'the Arab peoples and armies'
    [DA-305]

> Feminine agreement with a coördination of plurals is not limited to adjective attributes, but applies to any kind of predication or attribution. Note, for example: *šū fī b-hal-makatīb wəl-muxābarāt ᵊlli žəbtha l-yōm?* 'What's in those letters and announcements you brought today?' *l-kətᵊb wəṣ-ṣuwar wəl-kwānāt ǧālye* 'Books, pictures, and records are expensive'.

Coördinated adjective attributes, with different referents:

22. *mənšāʔāt ɛaskariyye w-ṣināɛiyye*   'military and industrial installations'

23. *s-səfara l-briṭāni wəl-ʔamērkāni wəl-frənsāwi*   'the British, American, and French ambassadors'

24. *l-luǧatēn ᵊl-ɛarabiyye wəl-ʔanglīziyye*   'the Arabic and English languages'

25. *l-žənsēn l-ᵊmzakkar wəl-ᵊmʔannas*   'the masculine and feminine genders'

> As illustrated in examples 23-25, coördinated attributes that apply distributively to different single referents of a plural or dual noun do not agree with that plural or dual, but with their <u>singulars</u>. In example 22, however, the reference is presumably to more than one installation of each kind mentioned, so the agreement is still with the plural *mənšāʔāt* (whose singular, it so happens, is not ordinarily used in any case).

When attributes to the same term have coinciding reference, then their coördination is more often asyndetic than syndetic [p. 398]:

26. *bənt həlwe laṭīfe* (or *bənt həlwe w-laṭīfe*)   'a lovely (and) charming girl'

27. *Ɛaša ṣəxᵊn tᵊꞮl*   'a hot (and) copious evening meal'

28. *l-baṣṣāt ᵊl-wəṣxa l-maƐšūᵊa*   'the dirty (and) crowded busses'

One attribution phrase may contain another; thus the last in a string of attributive adjectives may apply to the whole preceding phrase, and so on:

29. *l-ᵊadab ᵊl-Ɛarabi l-ᵊadīm*   'the old Arab culture'

30. *hawa šmāli ᵊawi*   'a strong north wind'

31. *l-ḥarb ᵊl-Ɛālamiyye t-tānye*   'the Second World War'

32. *haṭ-ṭāwle l-ᵊmfaṣṣaṣa l-ḥəlwe*   'this beautiful inlaid table'

33. *l-maƐāhed ᵊl-Ɛəlmiyye*   'the important foreign scientific
    l-ᵊažnabiyye l-ᵊmhəmme   institutes'

> Note that the attribute closest to the noun in such cases is often a relative adjective [p. 280].

Adjective attributes to (the leading term of) a noun construct:

34. *sayyāret ᵊəbni l-ᵊždīde*   'my son's new car'

35. *ṣāḥeb maṭƐam mašhūr*   'a famous restaurant owner'

> Example 35 is ambiguous: since both *ṣāḥeb* and *maṭƐam* are masculine, the attribute *mašhūr* could apply to either term; the phrase could therefore also mean 'the owner of a famous restaurant'.

36. *sayyāret ᵊəxti l-ᵊkbīre l-ᵊždīde*   'my sister's big new car'

> Theoretically this could also mean 'my big sister's new car', but in actual usage contiguous adjectives after a noun construct virtually always apply to the same term. (The theoretical possibility of 'my new big sister's car' is not ruled out grammatically, but the situations to which it would apply are unusual enough to make this interpretation unlikely.)
> See p. 460.

Adjective attributes to a numeral construct [p. 471]:

37. *tlətt ᵊašxāṣ tānyīn*   'three other persons'

38. *ᵊarbaƐ nesax tānye (or tānyīn)*   'four other copies'

39. *xams fiyaš zərᵊᵊ (or zarᵊa)*   'five blue chips'

40. *xams ʔiṣābāt malārya žədad*   'five new cases of malaria'
    (or *ždīde*)

41. *tlətt ʔʔlām ᵊmnāḥ* (or *mnīḥa*)   'three good pencils'

42. *sətt bēḍāṭ ᵊmnāḥ*   'six good eggs'

      In ex. 42 the (internal) plural adjective is obligatory
because *bēḍāt* is the plural of a unit noun [p.425], while
in ex. 37 the adjective must be plural because *ʔašxāṣ* is
animate. In the other cases (38-41) the adjective may be
either plural or feminine (as according to rule 7, p.421).

      With numerals over ten the following noun is in the
singular, and the adjective may either be plural (in agreement with the numeral) or singular (in agreement with the
noun):

43. *ḥdāšar ʔalam ᵊmnāḥ* (or *mnīḥ*)   'eleven good pencils'

44. *ṭnaɛšar fīše zərᵊʔ* (or *zarʔa*)   'twelve blue chips'

      In a phrase with *kamm* 'several' [p.467], a noun must be
singular, but an attribute is plural:

45. *kamm ʔalam ᵊmnāḥ*   'several good pencils'

    An attributive adjective may be preceded by *mū, lā,* or *ǧēr* 'not, non-,
un-' or by *ktīr* 'very'. In attribution to a definite term, the article is
prefixed to *mū, lā,* or *ktīr* rather than to the adjective; in the case of
ǧēr it is prefixed to the adjective but may or may not also be prefixed to
ǧēr:

46. *šarāha mū maɛʔūle ləl-maṣāri* . . . . *šarāhto l-mū maɛʔūle ləl-maṣāri*
   'an abnormal desire for money'   'his abnormal desire for money'

47. *ḥarake lā šuɛūriyye* . . . . *hal-harake l-lā šuɛūriyye*
   'an unconscious impulse'   'that unconscious impulse'

48. *ɛamal ǧēr qānūni* . . . . *l-ɛamal ǧēr ᵊl-qānūni*
   'an illegal act'   'the illegal act'

49. *ɛaša ǧēr rasmi* . . . . *l-ɛaša l-ǧēr ᵊr-rasmi*
   'an unofficial dinner'   'the unofficial dinner'

50. *qawāɛed ʔaxlāʔiyye ktīr ṣārme* . . . . . . *l-qawāɛed ᵊl-ʔaxlāʔiyye l-ᵊktīr ṣārme*
   'a very strict moral code'   'the very strict moral code'

A complemented passive particle is generally susceptible to phrase attribution:

51. *lāzem Eawweḍ ᵊn-nōm ᵊl-maksūr*   'I have to catch up on my sleep' (lit.
    Ealiyyi   "...to make up the sleep lost to me")

A complemented active particle is generally construed as a verb, and is therefore not susceptible to phrase attribution [p. 267]. There are exceptions, however:

52. *ləssa mā mnaEref kəll ᵊg-grūf*   'We still don't know all the facts
    ᵊl-muḥīṭa bəl-ḥādes   concerning the accident' (or "...
                                the circumstances surrounding...")

      In certain parts of Greater Syria — notably Lebanon —
the clause definitizer [p. 494], ordinarily taking the form
(ᵊ)lli, is often reduced to the form *l-* and is therefore
not always distinguishable from the article. The distinction between clause attribution and phrase attribution thus
tends to be lost in the definite form as well as in the
indefinite.
      The reduced clause definitizer, however, is often not
assimilated to a following dental or palatal consonant:
l-ləbnāniyye l-rāǰEīn mən ʔamērka [PVA-30] 'the Lebanese
(who have) returned from America'. (But cf. also *waladi
s-sāken fi bārīz* [PVA-2] 'my son (who is) living in Paris'.)

    The article, rather than the clause definitizer, is also sometimes
used with an attributive extrapositional clause [p. 496] whose adjectival
predicate (usually a passive participle) comes first:

53. *l-mandūbīn ᵊl-mazkūra ʔasmāʔhon*   'the aforementioned delegates', 'the
                                   delegates whose names have been mentioned'

      This construction, (oddly named *an-naEt s-sababī* "the
causal attribute")[1] is mainly limited in colloquial Arabic
to rather pedantic usage. A phrase such as *l-walad
ᵊl-maksūra rəkᵊbto* [RN-II.49] 'the boy with the broken
knee' would more usually be paraphrased as *l-walad ᵊlli
rəkᵊbto maksūra.* Cf. also *l-mara l-sāken Eənda ʔaxūk*
[RN-II.51] 'the woman at whose house your brother is living'
(in which *l-* however, is better interpreted as the reduced
clause definitizer since it is not assimilated to the *s*).

---

[1] *sababī* is perhaps to be interpreted here is some such sense as 'relational',
'supporting', or 'intermediary, indirect', rather than 'causal'.
    The derivation of this construction may be illustrated as follows:
rəkbet ᵊl-walad maksūra 'The boy's knee is broken', with extraposition of
the annex [p. 432] → *l-walad rəkᵊbto maksūra,* with participle-subject word
order in the comment [top 433, ex. 7] → *l-walad maksūra rəkᵊbto,* with
attribution of the comment [p. 496] → *l-walad ᵊl-maksūra rəkᵊbto.*

Noun Attributes or Appositives (*al-badal wa-Ɛaṭf l-bayān*)[1]

Examples involving proper names and other human designations:

1. *ʔaxūk ᵊd-doktōr*   'your brother the doctor'

2. *ṣāḥbi Ɛabd ᵊl-xāleʔ*   'my friend Abdul Khaleq'

3. *l-ʔaxx Ɛali ʔabu zēd*   'our friend (or colleague) Ali Abu Zaid' (lit. "[the] brother Ali...")

4. *ḥasan ᵊl-kəndaržī*   'Hassan the shoemaker'

5. *ḥabībāti l-ᵊwlād*   'my darling(s the) children'

6. *ṣāḥabna ʔaḥmad ᵊl-fallāḥ*   'our friend Ahmed the peasant'
   [AO-63]

7. *ṣ-ṣəhr ᵊž-ždīd Ɛiṣām bēk*   'the new son-in-law, Issam Bey the doctor'
   ᵊd-doktōr

Examples 6 and 7 each consist of three terms, the first being a relational term, the second a name, and the third an "epithet" (in these cases, an occupational term). In ex. 7 the first term itself consists of a noun-adjective attribution phrase.

8. *hiyye kənnto žōzet ʔəbno, mū*   'She's his daughter-in-law, not his
   kənnto žōzet ʔaxū   sister-in-law'

The words *kənne* and *ṣəhᵊr* are less specific than most Arabic kinship terms, especially in that they apply indiscriminately to one's own generation or to one's children's generation. *kənne* designates the wife of a son or of a brother, and *ṣəhᵊr*, the husband of a daughter or a sister. Thus the phrases *žōzet ʔəbno* 'his son's wife' and *žōzet ʔaxū* 'his brother's wife' in ex. 8 are put in apposition to *kənnto* in order to specify the relationship more exactly.

---

[1] In the traditional analysis *al-badal* (not to mention *al-Ɛaṭf*) does not come under the category of *an-naƐt* 'attribute', probably because of the inclusion of such extraneous sub-categories as *badal l-baƐḍi mina l-kull* 'partitive apposition', *badal l-ištimāl* 'inclusive apposition', and *al-badal l-mubāyin* 'corrective apposition'. Partitive and inclusive apposition (which are of little or no importance in colloquial Arabic) belong with *at-tawkīd l-maƐnawī* [p. 511] as constructions derived from partitive annexion [466], while corrective apposition is not properly a grammatical category at all.

No attempt is made her to distinguish between *al-badal l-muṭābiq* 'congruent apposition' (noun attribution) and *Ɛaṭf l-bayān* 'explicative apposition' (asyndetic noun coördination).

Nouns designating the material of which something is composed are often used attributively:

dahab	'gold':	9. *sənsle dahab*	'a gold chain'
fəḍḍa	'silver':	10. *s-sakakīn ᵊl-fəḍḍa*	'the silver knives'
mālˀi	'china(ware)':	11. *ṣ-ṣḥūn ᵊl-mālˀi*	'the china dishes'
ṣūf	'wool':	12. *kanze ṣūf*	'a wool sweater'
faru	'fur, pelt':	13. *kabbūd ˀəmmi l-faru*	'my mother's fur coat'

In example 13 the leading term is an annexion phrase.

Alternatively, in many cases, collocations of this type can be made by annexion rather than by attribution: *kanzet ṣūf* 'a sweater of wool', *sənsəlt ᵊd-dahab* 'the chain of gold'. (Note also the construction with a relative adjective [p. 280]: *kanze ṣūfiyye* 'a woolen sweater', *sənsle dahabiyye* 'a golden chain'.)

Note also:

bōdra	'powder':	14. *səkkar bōdra*	'powdered sugar'
xām	'something in an unprocessed state':	15. *maɛāden xām*	'metal ores'
taˀlīd	'imitation':	16. *žəlᵊd taˀlīd*	'imitation leather'
təhfe	'object of great value':	17. *ktāb təhfe*	'a wonderful book, a gem of a book'
zyāde	'increase, excess':	18. *rāteb zyāde*	'more pay, extra pay'
kfāye	'sufficiency':	19. *ˀakl ᵊkfāye*	'enough food'
šmāl	'left':	20. *ˀīdak ᵊš-šmāl*	'your left hand'
yamīn	'right':	21. *fardet ṣabbāt yamīn*	'a right shoe'

Apposition phrases like these are distinguished from annexion phrases by the fact that the leading term may be definitized with the article prefix (ex. 10, 11) or with a pronoun suffix (ex. 20). If the leading term has the *-e/-a* suffix [p.138], it keeps the absolute form with an appositive (ex. 9, 12). An appositive noun is distinguished from an ordinary adjective by the fact that it need not agree with the leading term in number/gender (ex. 11, etc.). An appositive noun is distinguished from an uninflected adjective [501] by that fact that it is also normally used in the typically noun-like constructions: *xām ᵊl-ḥadīd* 'iron ore', *ɛal-yamīn* 'on the right'.

Attributive noun phrases:

ʔabᵊn ɛarab 'Arab, someone of
Arab descent' (fem. *bᵊnt ɛarab*,
pl. *wlād ɛarab*)

22. *ʔʊʊtāʊ ʔabᵊn ɛarab* 'an Arab
teacher'

Since *ʔabᵊn ɛarab* is itself an annexion phrase, it is
made definite by prefixing the article to its following term
only: *l-ʔastāẓ ʔabn ᵊl-ɛarab* 'the Arab teacher'.

mōže ʔaṣīre 'short wave':

23. *rādyo mōže ʔaṣīre* 'a short wave
radio'

Since *mōže ʔaṣīre* is a noun-adjective attribution phrase,
both of its terms take the article when it is definitized:
r-rādyo l-mōže l-ʔaṣīre 'the short wave radio'.

ʔyās waṣaṭ 'medium size':

24. *ʔᵊmṣān ᵊʔyās waṣaṭ* 'medium-size
shirts' (def. *l-ʔᵊmṣān l-ᵊʔyās
ᵊl-waṣaṭ*. *waṣaṭ* is an uninflected adjective.)

ṣāḥeb zᵊmme 'conscientious'
(fem. *ṣaḥbet zᵊmme*, pl. *ṣḥāb
zᵊmme*):

25. *ṭāleb ṣāḥeb zᵊmme* 'a conscientious student'

Basically *ṣāḥeb zᵊmme* is an substantive construct, lit.
"master (or owner) of conscience", thus only the following
term takes the article in apposition to a definite term:
ṭ-ṭāleb ṣāḥeb ᵊz-zᵊmme 'the conscientious student'. When
not attributive, however, this phrase is usually treated
more like an adjectival construct [p.466], with *ṣāḥeb* also
taking the article: *ṣ-ṣāḥeb ᵊz-zᵊmme* 'the conscientious
person'.

Attributive Numerals. The cardinal numerals from two to ten are commonly used in apposition to definite terms [p.494]:

n-nəswān ᵊt-tlāte	'the three women'
l-ʔaṣābeɛ ᵊl-xamse	'the five fingers'
ṣanaɛīto t-tnēn	'his two apprentices'
ʔəntu t-tlāte	'you three'
d-dōltẹ̄n ᵊt-təntēn	'the two countries'

The numeral tnēn 'two' agrees in gender with the (singular of) term it is attributive to: fem. təntēn. (The feminine form is also commonly used in <u>construct</u> with a feminine term: təntēn nəswān 'two women'.)

The numeral wāḥed (fem. wāḥde) 'one' is unlike the other cardinal numerals in that it is used attributively like an ordinary adjective, with an indefinite term as well as a definite one:

ʔūḍa wāḥde	'one room'
rəžžāl wāḥed	'one man'

Cardinal numerals above ten are used attributively in an ordinal sense:

l-bēt ᵊṭ-ṭnaɛᵊš	'the twelfth house'

All cardinal numerals are used attributively in an ordinal sense in the numbering of pages and the like; neither term takes the article:

ṣafḥa xamse	'page five'
ṣafḥa xamsīn	'page fifty'

The cardinal numerals 1-12 are used in telling time, attributively to s-sāɛa 'the hour', but without the article prefix:

s-sāɛa ɛašara	'ten o'clock
s-sāɛa təntēn u-nəṣṣ	'half past two'

Since the article prefix is not used with the numeral, the attribution phrase is indistinguishable in form from the predication: s-sāɛa ɛašara 'It's ten o'clock'.

Elatives [p.313] and ordinals [316] are also used attributively, the latter agreeing in number/gender like ordinary adjectives.

Numerals with Appositives. Ethnic collectives [p.301] and singular mass
nouns [368] are used after the absolute form of numerals [170]:

1. *tlāte ɛarab u-xamse ʔamērkān*   'three Arabs and five Americans'

2. *ʔarbɛa ʔahwe w-ʔtlāte ḥalīb*   'four coffees and three milks'

> *wāḥed* and *tnēn* do not agree in gender with a feminine
> mass noun in apposition: *wāḥed bīra* 'one beer', *tnēn ʔahwe*
> 'two coffees'. *wāḥed,* however, is also used as an indef-
> inite substantive designating a person (usually translated
> 'someone' or 'somebody' when it has no appositive); in this
> use it is inflected for gender: *wāḥde bant* 'a girl, some
> girl, a certain girl', *wāḥed ʔamērkāni* 'an American(m.)'.
> (*wāḥed* is of course not used with ethnic collectives, but
> with their unit derivatives [p.301].)
> Note also the phrases *wāḥed ṣāḥbi* 'a friend of mine'
> and *nās ʔṣḥābi* 'friends of mine'; here the appositive is
> definite though its leading term is indefinite. (Cf. p.406,
> after ex. 34.)

Anaphoric suppression [p.537] of a noun after a numeral leaves the numeral in its absolute form, sometimes with an appositive:

3. *kilōyēn lūbye w-ʔtlāte bētanžān*   'two kilos of beans and three of
   [DA-129]   eggplant'

4. *šū ṭ-ṭawābeɛ halli batrīdha?*   'What stamps do you want?' – Four
   – *ʔarbɛa barīd žawwi tabaɛ*   twenty [-piastre] air mail'
   ʔl-ɛašrīn [DA-245]

Specificative Apposition (or Specificative Complementation, *at-tamyīz*[1]**).**
The appositives in examples 2 and 3 above are not true attributes, but
rather COMPLEMENTS OF SPECIFICATION (*at-tamyīz*)[1]; they differ from true
attributes in that they do not agree with their leading term in definition,
but remain always indefinite: *l-ʔarbɛa ʔahwe* 'the four coffees, *t-tlāte*
bētanžān 'the three [kilos] of eggplant'. (Cf. the definite attribution
phrase *t-tlāte l-ɛarab* **'the three Arabs'**[2], or better, *l-ɛarab ʔt-tlāte*
[p.509].)

---

[1] Most of the constructions that come under the heading of *at-tamyīz* in
Classical Arabic correspond in Colloquial to annexion phrases (as with
numerals above ten [p.366]), or are included in what are here called predicative complementation [446] and adverbial noun complementation [441]. The
specificative appositives treated here are, for nouns, what "adverbial noun
complements" are for verbs.

[2] Another possibility is *t-tlātet ʔl-ɛarab;* this type of annexing form [171]i
sometimes used with ethnic collectives and other nouns as well as with pronoun suffixes.

Besides mass-noun appositives with terms of quantification or measurement, specificative complements are sometimes used in phrases like the following:

1. *ǧarāme ʔəžmāliyye ɛašʔrt ālāf lēra* — 'a collective fine of ten thousand pounds'

2. *mažmūɛa žamīle rsūm maṭbūɛa* — 'a beautiful collection of prints' (lit. "...[of] printed drawings")

3. *haṣ-ṣaniyye l-həlwe nḥās ʔaṣfar* — 'this lovely brass tray' (lit. "this lovely tray [of] yellow copper")

In each of these examples, an adjective attribute intervenes between the main term and the appositive. If the adjective is eliminated, then the appositive becomes either a true attribute — agreeing with the main term in definition — or else the main term is put in construct with it: *haṣṣaniyye n-nḥās ʔl-ʔaṣfar* 'this brass tray' [cf. p.507]; *mažmūɛet ʔrsūm maṭbūɛa* 'a collection of prints'.[1]

Except as illustrated above, substantives in Syrian Arabic rarely take complements of specification; an isolated case is the noun *ṣifa* 'quality, attribute, capacity' as used in phrases like *b-ṣifato mɛallem* 'in his capacity as a teacher'.

Emphatic Apposition, *(at-tawkīd)*[2]. Definite partitive constructs [p.468] with *kəll* 'all, whole' and *zāt* and *nafs* 'self' are susceptible to extraposition [cf. p.431]; the following term of the construct is moved in front and replaced in the construct by a pronoun:

kəll ʔl-banāt 'all the girls' → *l-banāt kəllon* "the girls, all of them"

kəll ʔž-žəmɛa 'the whole week' → *ž-žəmɛa kəlla* "the week, all of it"

kəll bētna 'our whole house' → *bētna kəllo* "our house, all of it"

zāt ʔs-sayyāra 'the very car' → *s-sayyāra zāta* 'the car itself'

nafsi 'myself' → *ʔana nafsi* 'I myself'

---

[1] Specificative complementation, then, is another kind of annexion-periphrasis [p.460]. Cf. *mažmūɛa žamīle mn ʔr-rsūm ʔl-maṭbūɛa*.

[2] More exactly, *at-tawkīd l-maɛnawī* 'emphasis by meaning', as distinct from *at-tawkīd l-lafẓī* 'emphasis by repetition'. See p.394. *At-tawkīd* is not true attribution, but rather a kind of complementation or supplementation.

In the last example the following term of the construct
is a pronoun, therefore its extraposition as an independent
pronoun requires its replacement by a resumptive pronoun,
which is of course the same as the original [p.541].

Indefinite constructs with *ǧēr* 'other' [p.468] are similarly susceptible to extraposition: *ǧēr kətᵊb* 'other books'
→ *kətᵊb ǧērhon* "books other than them".

A suffix pronoun may be emphasized (or fitted for attributes [p.550])
by following it with the corresponding independent pronoun:

bēto	'his house'	→	*bēto huwwe*	'his house'
maɛi	'with me'	→	*maɛi ʔana*	'with me'
ḍarabak	'he hit you'	→	*ḍarabak ʔante*	'he hit you'

Order of Attributes

An attributive word or phrase precedes an attributive clause:

1. *w-naʔlet ᵊl-ɛabd ᵊl-mažrūḥ |*
   halli tamm ḥayy. . . [AO-118]

   'And she moved the wounded slave,
   who was still alive'

2. *ʔəli ḥkāye ɛažībe ktīr |*
   bətkūn ɛəbra la-halli bəddo
   yəɛtᵊber [AO-118]

   'I have a very strange story, that
   can be a lesson for whoever is willing to learn'

A single attributive noun or adjective usually precedes an attributive
phrase:

3. *hayy ʔətɛa fanniyye | waḥīde*
   mən nōɛa

   'It's a work of art unique among its
   kind'

4. *byaɛmel kəll ᵊš-šaḡlāt ᵊl-lagane |*
   l-mətɛallʔa bəl-bēt

   'He does all the odd jobs around the
   house' (*lagane* is a noun, used attributively in an idiomatic sense,
   'casual'.)

5. *l-kāteb ɛam-yəẓhar ʔədrāk*
   ɛamīq | ləl-wəḍɛ ᵊs-siyāsi

   'The author shows profound insight
   into the political situation'

In example 6 the phrase *ləl-wəḍɛ ᵊs-siyāsi* is not strictly
speaking an attribute, but rather a complement. It generally
makes no difference in word order whether a prepositional
phrase is attributive, complemental, or supplemental to a
given term.

A prepositional attribute (or complement, or supplement) usually follows an adjectival (or nominal) attribute, if any:

6. *Ɛam-yən²šru ʔišāƐāt <u>bəšƐa</u>* | 'They're spreading ugly rumors about
   <u>Ɛanno</u>   him'

7. *hāda kān Ɛamal ᵊktīr ṭāyeš* | 'That was a very imprudent act on
   <u>mənnak</u>   your part' (lit. "...from you, by
                                            you")

   A pronominal *tabaƐ* phrase [p. 489], however, may precede an adjective attribute:

8. *kīf ᵊmlāʔi mdarreb ᵊs-sawāʔa*   'How do you like your new driving
   <u>tabaƐak</u> | <u>ᵊš-ᵊdīd?</u>   instructor?'

CHAPTER 20: SUPPLEMENTATION

The term 'supplementation' is used in this book to designate any of the various subordinating constructions that
do not come under the more definite categories of attribution [p.493], annexion [455], or complementation [437].[1]
Supplementation is a "loose" type of construction, which is
often syntactically vague or unmarked, in some cases requiring no particular word order.

The most important kinds of supplement are ADVERBIAL,
which modify verbs or verb phrases, and CLAUSE SUPPLEMENTS,
which modify clauses as such. There are also supplements
to nouns, adjectives, adverbs, etc., and to sentences as
such. Many supplements are used to modify terms of various
kinds.

Adverbs and Other Supplemental Words

Strictly speaking, an adverb is a single word that is used mainly or
always to modify verbs or verb phrases. More broadly, words that are used
mainly to supplement clauses or adjectives are also called adverbs. Examples:

kamān 'also, too, more, again':

1. *žəb-ᵊlna kamān šwayyet lēmūn*   'Bring some lemons (or oranges) too'
   (or: 'Bring a few more lemons')

2. *marwān bəddo šī šwayyet ᵓawāɛi,*   'Marwan wants a few clothes, and so
   w-ᵓana kamān   do I'

3. *w-ɛandi kamān ṣīǧet ɛāᵓəlti,*   'And I also have my wife's (lit.
   btəswa šī xamst ālāf lēra   family's) jewelry; it's worth about
   [DA-297]   five thousand pounds'

4. *w-ᵓəm-li ɛala žanab šī wᵓītēn*   'And put aside for me a couple of
   bəftēk kamān [DA-109]   okes of beefsteak, too'

5. *lāzem nām kamān šwayye* [AO-51]   'I must sleep a little more'

6. *hāda mawḍūɛ tāni kamān*   'That's something else again'

7. *ɛaṭīni ᵓannīntēn ᵊnbīt kamān*   'Give me two more bottles of wine,
   ᵓiza bətrīd   if you will'

---

[1]Ideally, the contrast between complementation and supplementation is a
difference between non-subordinating (exocentric) and subordinating (endo-
centric) constructions that are otherwise similar. Actually, however, the
difference between them cannot be sharply drawn; many of the constructions
included under complementation are subordinating in one sense or another.

ʔawām 'quick(ly)':

8. *rāḥet marti ʔawām, w-baɛᵊd*   'My wife went quickly, and after a
   šwayye raǧɛet [AO-51]   while she came back'

9. *ḥaṭṭi ɛēnek ɛala ɛēni ʔawām*   'Look (f.) me in the eye now, quick!'

10. *naṭṭ ʔawām!*   'Quick, hop to it!'

sawa 'together':

11. *šaftkon fāytīn ɛal-bēt sawa*   'I saw you going into the house
                       together'

12. *ʔiza mā fī māneɛ mnatrāfaʔ*   'If there's no objection, we can go
    sawa [DA-248]   together'

    The word *sawa* is sometimes also used predicatively:
batšūfon sawa ʔaktar ᵊl-waʔt 'You see them together most of
the time' (Predicative complement [p. 447]).

bakkīr 'early':

13. *ʔana bfīʔ bakkīr, ɛaṣ-ṣabᵊḥ*   'I wake up early in the morning'
    [AO-34]

14. *man faḍlak taɛa ʔadd ma fīk*   'Please come as early as possible'
    bakkīr

15. *ʔǧīna bakkīr ɛal-ḥafle*   'We arrived early at the party'

    The word *bakkīr* is occasionally used predicatively:
waḷḷa bakkīr, ɛadū-lkon šī naṣṣ sāɛa tānye 'Why it's early!
Stay another half hour'.

hallaʔ 'now, right now, just now':

16. *ʔabu samīr hallaʔ byaǧi*   'Abu Samir is now on the way here'

17. *hallaʔ ṣarṭi ṣabiyye*   'You're a big girl now'

18. *šū ɛam-yadros hallaʔ?*   'What's he studying now?'

19. *ʔiza baddak taržaɛ hallaʔ*   'If you want to go back now you'll
    lāzmak santēn [AO-119]   need two years'

20. *hallaʔ babɛat-lak ᵊṣ-ṣānɛa*   'I'll send you the maid right now
    tāxadhon [DA-129]   to get them'

21. *w—halla⁹ ba£⁹d ⁹alf w—⁹tmān*   'And now after eighteen hundred years
    mīt sane ⁹ante xallaṣtni   you have rescued me and I must keep
    w—lāzem ⁹ūfi b—wa£di [AO-116]   my promise'

22. *⁹ante raḍyān halla⁹?*   'Are you satisfied now?'

23. *⁹ana halla⁹ ⁹wṣalt*   'I've just now arrived'

The demonstratives *hōn* 'here', *hnīk* 'there', and *hēk* 'so, thus, like that' are commonly used adverbially, but are basically predicators [p. 381]. See 559ff. The words *bəkra* 'tomorrow' and *mbāreḥ* 'yesterday' are basically nouns [p. 521].

On *ləssa* and *ba£⁹d* 'still, yet', see p. 546.

Adverbs in *-an.* Many adverbs (and other supplemental words) are derived from adjectives or nouns by suffixation of *-an.*[1] For example:

⁹asāsan	'basically'............	*⁹asās*	'basis'
ḥa⁹ī⁹atan	'truly, really'.........	*ḥa⁹ī⁹a*	'truth, reality'
£ādatan	'usually, customarily'..	*£āde*	'habit, custom, usage'
fə£lan	'actually'.............	*fə£l*	'act'
dā⁹iman, dāyman	'always'...............	*dāyem*	'lasting, permanent'
⁹axīran	'finally'..............	*⁹axīr*	'final'
mwa⁹⁹atan	'temporarily'..........	*mwa⁹⁹at*	'temporary'
yōmiyyan	'daily'................	*yōmi*	'daily' (adj.)
nəsbiyyan	'relatively'...........	*nəsbi*	'relative'
nəsbatan	'relatively'...........	*nəsbe*	'relationship'
māliyyan	'financially'..........	*māli*	'financial'

[1]Most of these forms are classicisms, though some are very solidly established in Colloquial usage. Classical Arabic itself, of course, has no such thing as adverb derivation; *-an* is merely the indefinite accusative suffix.

Adverbs in *-an* most often precede the supplemented term, though they often come between subject and predicate of a supplemented clause. Examples of usage:

1. *Ɛādatan mənkūn barra bər-rīf*
   b-hal-faṣᵊl mn ᵊs-səne

   'We're usually out in the country at this time of the year'

2. *s-sama ᵓaxīran Ɛam-ṭəṣḥa*

   'The sky is finally clearing'

3. *ᵓana māliyyan məɛtə́med Ɛalē*

   'I'm financially dependent on him'

4. *byətɛāmal raᵓsan maɛ ᵊš-šərke*

   'He deals directly with the company' (*raᵓsan* 'directly': Cl. *raᵓs* 'head')

5. *dāyman huwwe biġə́šš*
   bəl-ᵊfḥūṣe

   'He always cheats on examinations'

6. *tyāba dāyman Ɛala ᵓāxer mōḍa*

   'Her clothes are always in the latest style'

7. *kəll žəsmi kān yūžaɛni,*
   xṣūṣan ᵓəžrayyi [AO-51]

   'My whole body ached, especially my legs' (*xṣūṣan* 'especially': *xṣūṣ* 'specialness')

8. *l-fəᵓara xāṣṣatan tɛazzabu*
   ktīr

   'The poor, especially, suffered a lot' (*xāṣṣatan* 'especially: *xāṣṣa* 'special characteristic')

9. *ᵓanu sāɛa bəṭṭīr ᵊṭ-ṭayyāra?*
   — yōmiyyan ᵊs-sāɛa sabɛa
   ṣ-ṣəbᵊḥ [DA-249]

   'When does the plane leave? — Daily at seven in the morning'

10. *taᵓrīban xalaṣᵊt*

    'I'm almost finished' (*taᵓrīban* 'almost, about, approximately': *taᵓrīb* 'approximation')

11. *ṣal-li hōn taᵓrīban ᵊḥdaɛšar*
    šahᵊr

    'I've been here about eleven months'

12. *ᵓaddēš bə́ddha taᵓrīban?*
    [DA-80A]

    'About how much does she want?'

13. *d-dars kān ḥáyyen nəsbatan*

    'The lesson was relatively easy'

Adverbs in *-an* following the supplemented term are often unaccented: *ḥáyyen nəsbatan* 'relatively easy'. (Cf. predicate-subject inversion [p.419].)

A special case of derivation is the clause supplement *baɛdēn* 'then, afterwards', from the preposition *baɛd* 'after'[1]:

14. *bākol bət-tax²t w-baɛdēn ²b²ūm u-bəlbes* [AO-34]

'I eat in bed and then I get up and dress'

15. *halla² ɛamma-tna²²eṭ..., baɛdēn bətšatti* [AO-67]

'Now its sprinkling a few drops; later it will rain'

16. *bəḥki maɛak baɛdēn*

'I'll talk with you later'

17. *rəḥ²t ɛal-fətuwwe baɛdēn?*

'Did you go to the Youth Club after-wards?'

18. *²aṣḥa, baɛdēn ²btə²leb ²l-²əbrī²*

'Be careful or you'll upset the pitcher'

In ex. 18 *baɛdēn* is used in a <u>consequential</u> sense rather than in a purely temporal sense; in such cases the English translation is generally 'or, or else'.

baɛdēn is also used in an <u>additive</u> sense 'then, also, then too':

19. *ɛali baɛ²rfo mən ²ḥdaɛšar səne la²anno ²ahli w-²ahlo byaɛ²fu baɛḍon, w-baɛdēn mən ṭūl ḥayāto ɛali kān bəl-²amērkiyye*

'I've known Ali for eleven years be-cause our families know one another, and then too, all his life Ali has been in the American [school]'

A few adverbs are formed by attaching an enclitic *ma* to a noun or adjective, which may also have the suffix *-an:*

20. *hal-xəṭṭa ²arībe noɛan-ma la-halli b-bālna*

'That plan is pretty close to what we had in mind' (*noɛ* 'kind, sort')

21. *huwwe noɛan-ma xabīr b-hal-ḥaq²l*

'He's something of an expert in that field'

22. *²əllet-ma baɛref haž-žamāɛa*

'I hardly know those people' (*²əlle* 'scarcity, small amount')

Cf. subordinating conjuction *ma*, p. 490.

---

[1] The suffix *-ēn* of *baɛdēn* is presumably a special alteration of *-an;* note that the Lebanese form in areas where general Syrian *ē* is usually changed to *ay* [p. 14] is *baɛdēn* (not "*baɛdayn*"). Note also the forms *baɛdan* [SPA-462] and *²ablan* 'before' (adverbial) [SAL-96]: *šū štaġalt ²ablan?* 'What did you work at previously?'. Feghali [SPA] always writes *baɛden* (= *baɛdan*), never *baɛdēn;* perhaps he interprets the length of the vowel as a feature of phrasing or intonation [p. 17].

Adverbial Adjectives. Certain adjectives are commonly used supplementally, uninflected:

ṭayyeb	'well'	*tamām*	'entirely, perfectly, exactly'
mnīḥ	'well'	*maẓbūṭ*	'right, correctly, straight, perfectly'
ḍaġri	'straight, directly'	*ktīr*	'much, a lot, very, too'

Most supplemental adjectives always follow the supplemented term, but *ktīr*, and sometimes *tamām*, may either precede or follow.

Examples in use:

1. *btaɛrəfni ṭayyeb, ya bēk* [DA-128]

   'You know me well, sir'

2. *ʔana brīdak taɛref ᵊmnīḥ kəll šī bi-hal-balad* [DA-128]

   'I want you to become well acquainted with everything in this town'

3. *lā twāxəzni, mā fhəmt ɛalēk ᵊmnīḥ* [DA-17]

   'I'm sorry, I didn't understand you very well'

4. *xallīna nrūḥ ḍaġri ɛal-ʔotēl*

   'Let's go straight to the hotel'

5. *qanaɛni tamām*

   'He convinced me completely'

6. *mən yōmēn tlāte kānet sāɛti ɛamma-tʔaṣṣer, hallaʔ waʔʔafet tamām* [AO-71]

   'For two or three days my watch had been losing time; now it's stopped altogether'

7. *s-sāɛa xamse tamām*

   'It's exactly five o'clock'

8. *ɛməlᵊt tamām ɛaks halli ʔəlt-əllak yā*

   'You've done exactly the opposite of what I told you'

9. *mā fhəmᵊtni maẓbūṭ*

   'You didn't understand me rightly'

10. *mbaṣaṭᵊt ᵊktīr b-rəfᵊʔtak* [DA-235]

    'I very much enjoyed your company'

11. *baɛtᵊʔed haš-šanta btaɛžeb žōžti ktīr* [DA-252]

    'I believe this bag will please my wife very much'

12. *ʔaɛṣābi mətʔaθθre ktīr*

    'My nerves are strongly affected'

13. *tʔaxxarna ktīr, lāzem nəmši*

    'We're very late, we must go'

14. *mabṣūṭīn ᵊktīr*

    'They're quite well'

15. *bass ḥaʔīʔatan ktīr ẓarīfe,*
    w-baɛdēn maɛānīha mākne tamām

'But it's really very nice, and then too, its meaning is perfectly clear'

16. *ktīr ʔarībe ləl-ḥayāt ɛrəft kīf*

'It's very true to life, you see'

17. *farīd ktīr matɛalleʔ ᵊb-hal-*
    ʔarābe, ktīr ɛāžəbto

'Fareed is very fond of that kinship he likes it a lot'

Note also: *ṣāḥbi ktīr* 'a good friend of mine' (in which *ṣāḥeb* is construed as an adjective [cf. pp. 406, 508].

ktīr may also be used as a noun 'a lot, a large amount', in partitive annexion [466]: *ktīr nās* 'a lot of people' (cf. periphrasis [460] *ktīr mn ᵊn-nās*); or in apposition; *nās ᵊktīr* (same translation); cf. *nās ᵊktār* 'many people' (adjective attribute).

Adverbial Nouns and Noun Phrases. Many nouns and noun phrases are used supplementally, especially designations of time and of quantity. Examples:

bəkra (or *bukra*) 'tomorrow'

l-yōm 'today'

l-masa 'this evening'

l-lēle 'tonight'

mbāreḥ (or *mbārḥa*) 'yesterday'

ʔawwal ᵊmbāreḥ (or *ʔawwalt ᵊmbāreḥ*) 'the day before yesterday'

s-səne l-mādye (or *sənt ᵊl-mādye*) 'last year'

šwayye 'a little'

s-sāɛa tmānye '(at) eight o'clock'

marra 'once', *marrtēn* 'twice'

marrāt ᵊktīre 'often, frequently'

baɛd ᵊl-ʔawʔāt 'sometimes'

ɛašᵊr daražat 'ten degrees'

ṭūl ᵊn-nhār 'all day'

miyye bəl-miyye 'one hundred percent'

hal-ʔadd 'so much'.

sāɛtēn 'two hours'

ʔawwal šī 'first of all'

Cf. Adverbial Noun Complements [p. 441].

Examples in use:

1. *sāfar ʔawwal ᵊmbāreḥ*

'He left the day before yesterday'

2. *šlōnak ᵊmbāreḥ bəl-muzākara?*

'How did you do yesterday in the home-work session?'

3. *la-nšūf šū bəddna natɛašša l-yōm*

'Let's see what we're having for dinner today'

4. <u>bəkra</u> mənṣə́ref <u>ə́d-dəhə́r</u>

'Tomorrow we get out at noon'

5. nāyem b-bēt xālti l-lēle

'I'm sleeping at my aunt's house tonight'

6. šū raha-nsāwi <u>l-yōm</u> Ɛašiyye?

'What are we going to do this evening?' (lit. "...today the evening")

7. bəsmaƐ ʔaxbārha bəs-səne <u>marra</u>

'I hear from her once a year' (lit. "I hear her news in the year once")

8. Ɛadad ʔs-səkkān zād xamse bəl-miyye

'The population increased five per-cent'

9. waʔʔtha ʔalbet ʔṣ-ṣabiyye l-məʔlāye [AO-117]

'Then (lit. "its time") the girl turned the frying pan over'

10. yōm mn ʔl-ʔiyyām kānu l-banāt Ɛaš-šəbbāk w-marəʔ bət-ṭarīʔ šēx [AO-113]

'One day (lit. "a day of the days") the girls were at the window when a sheikh went by on the road'

11. btəʔraf kəll ʔl-Ɛamaliyye, yaƐni ʔiyyām

'You get disgusted with the whole business, some days, that is'

12. tāni yōm ḍəƐef

'The next day, he got sick'

13. l-bard has-səne ʔəža Ɛala bakkīr [DA-197]

'The cold weather this year has come early'

14. byəflaḥ ʔl-ʔarḍ kəll ʔs-səne [AO-59]

'He tills the soil the whole year'

15. ḥālə́ton mū baṭṭāle <u>hal-ʔadd</u>

'They're not so badly off' (lit. "Their condition is not bad that amount")

16. lā tkūn kəll hal-ʔadd mū mbāli

'Don't be so indifferent'

17. l-fatḥa mū kbīre kfāye

'The opening isn't big enough' (cf. p. 507)

18. lāzem nām kamān <u>šwayye</u> [AO-51]

'I must sleep a little more'

19. ʔana <u>šwayye</u> bardān

'I'm a bit chilly'

20. tənʔāytak kānet <u>šwayye</u> mū mwaffaʔa

'Your choice was rather unfortunate'

21. bəddi rūḥ lāken mašɡ́ul <u>ʔšwayye</u>

'I want to go, but I'm rather busy'

22. bass hāda ktīr <u>ʔšwayye</u> [DA-297]

'But that's a little too much'

Note, in ex. 21 and 22, that *šwayye* in supplementation
to a preceding adjective is commonly unaccented.
šwayye, like its antonym *ktīr*, may be used in construct
with a noun [p.470]: *šwayyet xəbᵊz* 'a little bread', *šwayyet*
bard 'a little cold (weather)'.

23. *šwayye šwayye huwwe hədi*   'Little by little he calmed down'

24. *l-maɛāzīm ʔəžu wāḥed wāḥed*   'The guests arrived one by one'
    [PAT-169]

25. *ɛīd baɛd ᵊmmənni kəlme kəlme...*   'Repeat after me word for word...'

26. *mīn byəži la–ɛand ᵊt-tāni ʔaktar?*   'Who comes to visit the other most
    [often]?'

27. *l-maṭar btənzel ʔaktar u–ʔaktar*   'The rain comes down harder and
    [AO-67]   harder' (lit. "...more and more")

28. *bẓənn byəštᵊğel ʔaḥsan mən ʔabu*   'I believe he does better work than
    ʔaḥmad [AO-47]   Abu Ahmed' (lit. "works better
    than...")

ʔaktar and *ʔaḥsan* are commonly used supplementally, as
elatives of *ktīr* and *mnīḥ*, respectively [p.520].

Prepositional Supplements. Prepositional phrases of all kinds (except
tabaɛ [p.489]) are used adverbially:

1. *ʔana bfayyʔak baɛᵊd ṣalāṭ*   'I'll wake you after morning prayer'
    ᵊṣ-ṣəbᵊḥ

2. *ɛam-yəktob waẓīft ᵊl-fīzya*   'He's doing his physics assignment
    bəṣ-ṣaff   in the classroom'

3. *ɛal-ɛaṣr ᵊmnəšrab šāy w-ɛənd*   'Late in the afternoon we drink tea
    ᵊl-masa mnākol [AO-30]   and in the evening we eat'

4. *bšūf bəl-bēt šū bəddhon*   'I'll see in the house what they
    w-bəbɛat-lak xabar maɛ ᵊṣ-ṣānɛa   want, and send you word by the maid'
    [DA-130]

5. *ʔana b-ɛēni šəfta b-wādi l-ğūl*   'With my [own] eye[s] I saw her in
    [AO-107]   Ghoul Valley' (The phrase *b-wādi
    l-ğūl* is an objective complement
    [p.447].)

6. *btaʔmor təšrab šī ʔabl ᵊl-ʔakᵊl?*   'Would you like something to drink
    [DA-199]   before eating?'

7. ʔana ɛala kəll ḥāl mā bākol   'In any case I only eat at home'
   ġēr bəl-bēt [DA-198]   (bəl-bēt is supplemental to the verb
                                   ḥākol, while ɛala ḥəll ḥāl is supple-
                                   mental to the whole clause.)

8. lēš sāyeʔ b-has-sərɛa?   'Why are you driving so fast?' (lit.
                                   "...with this speed?")

9. bəš-šətwiyye byəsknu bət-ṭābeʔ   'In the winter they live on the upper
   ᵊl-fōʔāni, b-sabab ᵊl-bard   storey, because of the cold and damp'
   wər-rṭūbe [AO-39]   (The phrase b-sabab... is supple-
                                   mental to the whole preceding clause,
                                   while bəš-šətwiyye is supplemental
                                   only to the following verb phrase.
                                   bət-ṭābeʔ... is the prepositional
                                   complement to the verb.)

10. l-ᵊḥkūme bəl-ḥāl ṭālaɛet   'The government immediately issued a
    takzīb   denial'

11. waʔʔaf ᵊs-sayyāra ɛal-ʔāxīr   'He brought the car to a complete
                                   stop'

12. ɛan ḥaʔa ʔənte btəɛnīha?   'Do you really mean it?'

   Examples 10-12 illustrate several of the many idiomatic
prepositional phrases that are used adverbially; there are
many more, e.g. ɛala ġafle 'suddenly', ɛan ʔarīb 'soon',
ɛala ṭūl 'always, continuously', bəl-marra 'at all' (with
negative), bəl-kād 'hardly', etc.
   The forms ʔāxīr (ex. 11) and ḥaʔa (12) are anomalous,
used only in these set phrases (and bəl-ʔāxīr 'finally').
One would expect ʔaxīr or ʔāxer 'final, last, end', and
ḥaʔʔa 'its(f.)right, its truth'.

13. mənkannes ᵊl-bēt mən fōʔ   'We'll sweep the house from top to
    la-taḥt [AO-27]   bottom'

14. ḥaket kalām mā fhəmto w-sāwətni 'She said something I didn't under-
    baɛᵊdha mətᵊl ma bətšūf – nəṣṣi stand, and then made me the way you
    ḥažar w-nəṣṣi laḥᵊm[AO-118]   see me – half stone and half flesh'
                                   (baɛᵊdha lit. "after it(f.)")

   Free prepositions [p.485] may of course be used adverbially without an "object"; similarly baɛᵊd 'after' and ʔabᵊl
'before'. See p.487.

Examples of prepositional supplements to non-verbal clauses:

15. la-daraže huwwe masʔūl   'To a [certain] degree, he is
                                   responsible'

16. ka-walad ɛəmro xams ᵊsnīn huwwe 'For a five-year-old boy he's quite
    ṭawīl ᵊktīr   tall'

17. *baɛtáʔed hat-taqrīr ɛala waǯh*   'I believe this report is on the
    ʔl-ɛumūm ṣaḥīḥ   whole correct'

18. *ban-nāḥye n-naẓariyye mā fī*   'From a theoretical point of view
    ʔaxtilāf ʔktīr   there's not much difference'

Prepositional supplements to non-verbal words and phrases:

19. *huwwe doktōr fal-ʔaqtiṣād*   'He's a doctor of economics'

20. *baddhon ɛal-ʔaʔalli ǯamɛa*   'They'll need at least a week' (The
                                form *ʔaʔalli* is a classicism; col-
                                loquial *ʔaʔall* 'least'.)

21. *ktīr mn ʔl-xarāfāt ʔalha*   'Many myths have a historical
    ʔaṣʔl tārīxi   foundation'

22. *mā xalla ṣanf mn ʔl-fawāki*   'He didn't leave out any kind of
    wal-ḥalwiyyāt ʔalla ḥaṭṭo   fruit or sweet (but what he put it in)'

23. *hāda mū ǯī ǯdīd ɛaliyyi*   'This is not something new to me'

24. *bāxadhon tlatt marrāt bal-yōm*   'I take them three times a day' (lit.
    [DA-218]   "...in a day")

25. *l-wāḥed ɛand bēti wat-tāni*   'The one [of them] is by my house and
    baɛdo b-ʔtmann dakakīn [DA-125]   the other is eight doors beyond it'
                                (lit. "...after it by eight shops")

       In ex. 25, the phrase *b-ʔtmann...* is supplemental to
the prepositional predicate *baɛdo*. In ex. 24, *bal-yōm* is
supplemental (or complemental) to the nominal supplement
tlatt marrāt. The *man*-phrases in ex. 21 and 22 are annexion
periphrases [p. 460].

       Most prepositional phrases that are subordinate to
nouns are attributive [p. 500]; many of those subordinate to
adjectives are complemental.

Besides adverbs, nouns, adjectives, and prepositions, a few words of other kinds are used supplementally:

ḥatta 'even' (as a conjunction, 'until, in order that' [p.358]):

1. *ḥatta r-raǧol ᵊl-ɛādi byəfham*
   haš-šī
   'Even a layman understands that'

2. *mā ḥada ḥatta lāḥaẓ ᵊǧyābo*
   'No one even noticed his absence'

3. *mā ᵓdərᵊt šūfo ḥatta*
   'I didn't even get to see him'

bass 'only' (as a conjunction, 'but, as soon as' [p.398, 357]):

4. *ṣafyān ɛanna bass ᵊtnēn*
   'We only have two left'

5. *mū bass ḥəlwe, ẕakiyye kamān*
   'She's not only pretty; she's also intelligent'

6. *wṣəlt la-hōn mən daᵓīᵓa bass*
   'I only got here a minute ago'

byəṭlaɛ 'about, what amounts to' (as a verb, 'it comes out'):

7. *ᵓassarna byəṭlaɛ mīt ɛaskari*
   'We took about a hundred prisoners' (lit. "We captured it comes to a hundred soldiers")

Sentence Supplements

Certain words and phrases are commonly used to supplement a sentence as a whole rather than some constituent of it[1]; these supplements do not "modify" the meaning of anything in the sentence, but they modify or clarify the relationship of the sentence to its context, or to the circumstances of its utterance. Examples:

1. *bᵊl-munāsabe wēn ᵊd-dəxxānāt*
   ᵊlli waɛattna fīhon?
   'By the way, where are the cigarettes (lit. "smokes") you promised us?'

2. *mā bəṭᵓaxxar ᵓanšāḷḷa, šu yaɛni*
   bəddek ᵓərkab ṣārūx?
   'Don't worry, I won't be late; what do you(f.) expect, anyway — for me to get on a rocket?'

---

[1]This is not to say that the supplement is not a part of the sentence; prosodically it is as much a part of the sentence as any other kind of supplement. Note also the difference between a sentence supplement and a clause supplement; one of the immediate constituents of a sentence is the whole clause (word-string) which it embraces and prosodically unifies [p. 377].

3. *Ɛala haḷ-lōn byəlzamak šānƐa*   'In that case, you'll need a maid'
   [DA-98]

4. *btəftə́ker ba?a fəkra mnīḥa*   'So you think it's a good idea'

5. *bəškor ?alla mā bə?i fiyyi šī*   '[I] thank God, I'm all right now'
   [DA-218]

6. *lēš ya tara has-shūl žarda?*   'Why do you suppose these plains are
   [DA-250]   so barren?'

7. *daxlak šlōn ?l-ḥāle halla?*   'Say, how are things now in San
   bi-sān fransīsko? [DA-77]   Fransisco?'

8. *?ayyədhon lakān Ɛal-?ḥsāb*   'Enter them on your account, then'
   xāṭrak [DA-129]

9. *?šīt la-Ɛandak marrtēn*   'I came to your place twice to tell
   la-?əl-lak, bass maƐ ?l-?asaf   you, but unfortunately I didn't see
   mā šəftak [DA-171]   you'

10. *ṭabƐan ?l-xārūf mā tƐallam*   'Of course the sheep wouldn't learn
    w-ṣār imāƐi [AO-96]   and began to bleat'

11. *bi-nafs ?l-wa?ət ṣfōn fīha*   'At the same time — think of it — he's
    Ɛamm-irauweḥ Ɛala ḥālo mažāl   losing a big opportunity'
    ?kbīr

12. *nəḥna maƐlūmak halla? fī Ɛanna*   'Of course as you know we now have
    ṭaṣniƐ bəš-šām   industrialization in Damascus'

In ex. 12 the second person suffix with *maƐlūm* (lit.
'known') is a sort of "ethical dative" [p. 483], which im-
parts a note of intimacy to what would otherwise be a
starkly impersonal statement.

Supplemental Clauses

Supplemental clauses generally may either'precede or follow the main clause:

ʔawwal ma ṭəṣal Ɛaṭīna xabar......*Ɛaṭīna xabar ʔawwal ma ṭəṣal*
'As soon as you get there 'Let us know as soon as you
let us know'   get there'

ʔiza ʔǧīt, btəmbáṣeṭ ʔktīr........*btəmbáṣeṭ ʔktīr ʔiza ʔǧīt*
'If you come, you'll have a 'You'll have a very good time
very good time'   if you come'

Most supplemental clauses are <u>clause supplements</u>, i.e. they enter into construction with the main clause as such. A few, however, are sentence supplements or phrase supplements [p.529].

The main types of supplemental clause are CONDITIONAL clauses, which are amply illustrated in Chapter 12 [p.331ff]; CIRCUMSTANTIAL clauses [p.531]; and the rest, which may be called simply ADVERBIAL clauses.

Adverbial Clauses

Most clauses introduced by a word or phrase plus the particle *ma* [p.490] are supplemental. Examples of these clauses are given in Chapter 13 [p.357ff] (see also p.338); further examples:

1. *ʔabˀl ma təlbes biǧāmtak, təʔɛod <u>la-dirāstak</u>*
'Before you put on your pajamas, you must sit down and study' (lit. "... sit to your study")

2. *baɛˀd ma n-nās ġannū-lon <u>u-raʔaṣū-lon</u>, rāḥu w-daǧǧarūhon la-ḥālhon* [AO-111]
'After the people sang and danced for them, they went away and left them alone' [See p.411.]

3. *baɛˀd ma laʔu l-məzneb ʔənte halla? ˀtbarrēt*
'Since they've found the guilty one, you are now exonerated' (lit. "After they've found..., you have now been exonerated")

4. *mā ǧəfˀt ḥada mən waʔˀt ma rǧəɛt*
'I haven't seen anyone since I got back'

5. *btaˀder ˀtxallī maɛak <u>ʔadd ma</u> bəddak*
'You can keep it (lit. "leave it with you") as long as you want'

6. *b-ˀmǧarrad ma zakar ʔəsma ḥəḍret*
'No sooner had he mentioned her name than she appeared'

7. *bsāwī-lak talifōn ˀb-daʔīʔet ma <u>ʔaɛref</u>*
'I'll give you a phone call the minute I find out'

8. *lēǧ mā btaɛməl-lak ǧī Ɛawāḍ ma təʔɛod ṭūl ˀl-waʔˀt tətǧakka?*
'Why don't you do something instead of complaining all the time?'

9. *tarket ᵊl-ᵊūḍa bala ma taḥki*
   kᵊlme

   'She left the room without saying a word'

10. *fī nās ɛāyšīn lūks bēn ma l-ġēr*
    žūɛānīn

    'Some people live in luxury while others go hungry'

11. *w-mā fī rṭūbe mᵊtᵊl ma bisīr*
    ɛandkon [DA-150]

    'And there isn't the humidity you get there' (lit. "...like it is with you (pl.)")

12. *manfarrᵊo ɛalēhon la-ḥatta*
    yāklu b-ᵊiyyām ᵊl-ɛīd mᵊtᵊl ma
    byāklu l-ᵊaġniya [DA-299]

    'We distribute it among them so that they may eat during the holiday as the rich eat'

    mᵊtᵊl ma is more often used in supplementation to a word or phrase than to the whole main clause. In ex. 12 the *mᵊtᵊl ma* clause is supplemental to the verb *yāklu;* in ex. 11, to the noun *rṭūbe*.

    Examples of *ma* clauses as sentence supplements:

13. *ᵊabᵊl ma ᵊansa, ḥaṭṭ-ᵊlli šī*
    kilōyēn xōx w-ᵊtlāte nžāṣ
    [DA-130]

    'Before I forget – put in (for me) a couple of kilos of plums and three of pears'

14. *ḥasab ma baɛref mā fī ᵊᵊlak*
    bōṣṭa

    'As far as I know, there's no mail for you'

    For a sentence-supplement *ᵊiza* clause, see ex. 12, p. 332.

Adverbial clauses introduced by words or phrases other than *ma:*

15. *lamma xalṣet ᵊs-sane, ṭalab*
    ᵊr-rāɛi ᵊažᵊrto [AO-103]

    'When the year ended, the shepherd demanded his pay'

16. *l-yōm lamma faᵊᵊt kān maɛi*
    wažaɛ rās ᵊawi [AO-51]

    'Today when I woke up I had a severe headache'

17. *ṭṭaṣel fiyyi lamma baddak yāni*

    'Get in touch with me when you want me'

18. *balla sallᵊm-li ɛas-sᵊtt waᵊt*
    ᵊbtaṣal [DA-245]

    'Please give my regards to your wife when she arrives'

19. *waᵊᵊt maddēt šahrēn fi New York*
    kᵊnt šūfo kᵊll yōm

    '[During the] time I spent two months in New York I saw him every day'

20. *yōm kᵊnna rāžɛīn mᵊn bērūt*
    ᵊaxatt bard [DA-217]

    'The day we came back from Beirut I caught cold'

21. *bass ᵊtlāᵊi l-bēt mᵊnrūḥ ᵊana*
    wiyyāk la-nšūfo [DA-291]

    'As soon as you find the house you and I will go together to see it'

22. *w-fəreḥ əktīr laʔənno tʔakkad*
    ʔənno ʔalla ġafar-lo xaṭāyā
    [AO-100]

'And he was very glad because he was
certain that God had forgiven his sins'

23. *u-laʔanno māli ɛənwān sābet*
    bɛatū-li yā b-wāṣəṭṭ
    əl-mufawwaḍiyye l-ʔamērkiyye
    [DA-294]

'And since I have no permanent address,
send it to me in care of the American
Legation'

24. *b-ḥēs mā kān ɛandi l-maṣāri mā*
    ʔdərət rūḥ

'Since I didn't have the money I
couldn't go'

25. *b-ma ʔənno msāfer bəkra lāzem*
    nəstaɛžel

'Since he is leaving tomorrow, we must
hurry' (*b-ma ʔənno*, lit. "with [the
fact] that...")

26. *raḥa-kūn əhnīk, maɛ ʔənno*
    waʔti dayye?

'I'll be there, though my time is
short'

27. *ʔana bžəb-lak əl-ʔarbaɛīn bənt*
    la-bētak ɛala šarṭ taɛṭīni
    ʔarbaɛīn dīnār [AO-113]

'I'll bring the forty girls to your
house on condition that you give me
forty dinars'

Extraposition in Adverbial Clauses. Most conjunctions that introduce adverbial clauses tend not to be followed by noun-type words [p.411]; thus the
subject (less commonly the object, etc.) of an adverbial clause preceding
the main clause is often extraposed [p.431] — placed in front of the conjunction. (This type of extraposition requires no resumptive subject pronoun .)

1. *ʔalla taɛāla lamma farraʔ*
   əl-mawāheb ɛala bani ʔādam,
   kān əl-fallāḥ ġāyeb [AO-92]

'When Almighty God apportioned His
gifts among men, the peasant was
absent'

2. *l-banāt lamma ṣəfyu la-ḥālhon*
   ṣāru ydūru bəl-bet [AO-113]

'When the girls were left alone, they
started looking around the house'

3. *l-malek baɛd ma šafā mā kāfā*
   [AO-116]

'After he cured the king, he (the
king) didn't reward him' (Extrapositive object)

4. *ʔana ʔawwal ma ʔžīt sakanət*
   bəl-bēt ɛand hadōl əž-žamāɛa

'When I first came, I lived at the
house of those people'

5. *ktīr əmn əš-šabāb waʔət bikūnu*
   bi-ɛəmr əl-murāhaqa biḥāwlu
   ʔənno yaɛmlu nōɛ əmn əš-šəɛər

'Lots of young men, when they're
adolescent, try to compose some sort
of poetry'

6. *l-walad əg-ẓġīr lamma ykūn*
   zaɛlān mən ʔabū baɛdēn irāḍi
   ʔabū byaži biḥəṭṭ rāso hēke
   byəsəndo

'When a little boy is angry with his
father and them makes up with him,
he comes and leans his head [against
him] like this'

In most cases the extraposed term can also be construed as subject of the main clause, with the adverbial clause inserted between the subject and the predicate. (This analysis might apply to all but ex. 1 above.)

An adverbial clause is also sometimes inserted between a verb and its prepositional or clausal complement:

7. *sāfarᵃt ʔabᵃl ma ʔəǧi la-hōn la-ʔoroppa*   'Before I came here I went to Europe'

8. *w-ṣāret kəll ma fāt wāḥed mənhon ṭəʔṭaɛ rāso* [AO-113]   'And she started cutting off their heads every time one of them would come in'

Circumstantial Clauses *(al-ǧumla l-ḥāliyya)*

The conjunction *w-* [p. 391] introduces subordinate clauses with the sense 'while, when, with':

1. *šlōn mā bəddo yəṣʔoṭ bəl-faḥᵃṣ w-huwwe mā fataḥ ᵃktāb?*   'How could he help but fail in the test when he hasn't opened a book?'

2. *šaḥaṭᵃt rəfrāf ᵃs-sayyāra w-ʔana ṭāleɛ la-wara mn ᵃl-karāǧ*   'I scraped the fender of the car (while I was) backing out of the garage'

3. *w-huwwe māši w-mətɛaǧǧeb səmeɛ ʔanīn bəke* [AO-118]   '(As he was) walking alone and wondering, he heard the sound of weeping' (lit. "...a moan of weeping")

4. *šaɛha ḥalab bānet w-ʔalɛətha bən-nəṣṣ* [DA-250]   'See there, Aleppo has come into view, with its citadel in the middle'

As illustrated in examples 2 and 3, circumstantial clauses may sometimes be rendered in English with a participial phrase rather than with a clause. Circumstantial clauses are most often non-verbal (ex. 2, 3, 4) and quite often participial (2, 3).

Most circumstantial clauses follow the main clause (ex. 1, 2, 4), and most have a subject — often a pronoun subject (ex. 1, 2, 3) — right after the *w-*.

In some cases (ex. 4), subordinate *w-* clauses are not clearly distinguishable from coördinate clauses ('See there, Aleppo has come into view, and its citadel is in the middle').

Further examples:

5. *šlōn bəddo ṭ-ṭabīx yəstŵi wəṭ-ṭanāǧer ᵃmɛallaʔa fō? ɛas-saǧara?* [AO-88]   'How can the food get done with the pots hung up in the tree?'

6. *ḥaṭṭo ʔəddām ʔs-saɛdān w-ṣār*
   iɛallmo wəs-saɛdān yətfarraž
   [AO-96]

'He put him in front of the monkey
and started teaching him, while the
monkey looked on'

     Ex. 6 could also be construed as a coördination: '...
started to teach him, and the monkey, to watch' (with anaphoric suppression [p. 537] of *ṣār* before *yətfarraž*).

7. *l-fallāḥīn biḥəbbu yāklūhon*
   u-hənne xədʔr [PVA-18]

'The country people like to eat them
while they're green'

8. *kānet ʔl-bənt wara l-bāb*
   wəb-ʔīdha sēf [AO-113]

'The girl was behind the door with a
sword in her hand' (Or as a coördination: '...and a sword was in her
hand')

9. *w-rakḍet u-maɛha ṭāse fīha*
   mayye

'And she ran, carrying a bowl with
water in it' (lit. "...and with her
a bowl, in it water")

10. *bəṣ-ṣəbʔḥ w-ʔana rāyeḥ ɛala*
    šəġli bəštəri ɛādatan žarīde
    mn ʔž-žarāyed

'In the morning when I'm going to
work I usually buy one of the newspapers'

11. *də ?? ʔl-ḥadīd u-huwwe ḥāmi*

'Strike the iron while it's hot'

12. *mnēn bəʔder ʔəbɛat ḥawāle*
    barīdiyye? — tālet šəbbāk
    w-ʔante fāyet [DA-223]

'(From) where can I send a postal
money order?' — Third window as you
go in'

13. *l-bāb ʔnfataḥ w-kaʔənno fī*
    səḥʔr

'The door opened as if by magic'
(lit. "...and [it was] as if there
were magic [in it]")

14. *məmken ʔdžəb-li ʔahuti*
    w-fīha xēṭ konyāk?

'Could you bring me my coffee with a
dash of brandy in it?'

15. *kīf ya žənni bətʔūl slēmān*
    nabiyy aḷḷāh w-ʔslēmān māt mən
    məddet ʔalf w-ʔtmān mīt səne?
    [AO-116]

'How, O genie, can you say Solomon
is God's prophet, when Solomon died
eighteen hundred years ago?'

     A subject pronoun is sometimes extraposed (put before
the *w-*) at the beginning of a sentence, especially in a
clause with *rāyeḥ* 'going' or the like. (Cf. p. 530.):

16. *ʔnt ʔw-rāyeḥ xədni* [RN-I.228]

'Pick me up on your way'

17. *w-nəḥna w-rāyḥīn marrēna*
    b-šəllālāt nyāgara [SAL-67]

'And on our way, we went by Niagara
Falls'

Paratactic Supplemental Clauses. Sometimes the circumstantial *w–* (or some other supplemental conjunction) is omitted:

1. *daxalt Ɛalēha, b–ʔīdi sēf* [AO-118]

   'I broke in on her, a sword in my hand'

2. *huwwe Ɛam–yəḥki byākol nəṣṣ ʔl–kəlme*

   'When he talks he swallows half the word'

3. *wēnak ʔb–hal–ʔiyyām mā ḥada bišūfak?* [DA-197]

   'Where are you these days, that no one sees you?'

4. *kəll ši xāleṣ, raḥ–ikallef kaza dōlār* [SAL-171]

   'When everything is completed, it'll cost [so many] dollars'

CHAPTER 21: SUBSTITUTION

The main types of SUBSTITUTES in Arabic are personal pronouns [p.539], demonstratives [552], question words [566], and answer words [536].

These categories are not syntactical form classes [p.381], but are based on the way certain words or sets of words "re-place" or "stand·for" any expression of a particular gram-matical class under certain conditions. Thus the personal pronouns substitute for nouns or noun phrases, and the de-monstratives *hōn* 'here' and *hnīk* 'there' substitute for cer-tain kinds of prepositional phrases, etc.

Anaphoric Substitution

The third-person pronouns (*huwwe, hiyye, hənne; -o, -ha, -hon*) occur mainly in ANAPHORIC SEQUENCE: as SEQUENT to an ANTECEDENT.[1] The antec-edent is a noun or noun phrase which is subsequently replaced in the dis-course by the sequent pronoun: *btaɛref haš-šabb ʔənte?* 'Do you know that young man? – ʔē baɛ³rfo mnīḥ, ṣâḥbi huwwe* 'Yes, I know him well, he's my friend'.

In this type of anaphoric sequence the main differences between Arabic and English involve resumptive pronouns [p.430] and subject pronouns [548]. Arabic requires a sequent pronoun where English has none in sentences such as *mīn ³l-bənt ³lli šəftak maɛha?* 'Who's the girl I saw you with?'; whereas English requires a subject pronoun, and Arabic does not, in sequences like *šū ʔaxbār maḥmūd? – waḷḷa ktīr maḅṣūṭ* 'What's the news from Mahmoud? – Why, he's quite well'.

A sequent pronoun agrees in number/gender with its antecedent in the same way that a predicate agrees with its subject [p.420]. Thus, for example: *yalli lāḥeš tyābo yəǧi yšīlon* 'Whoever has strewn his clothes around shall come pick them up'; *fī ɛandak šī kət³b ǧēra?* 'Have you any other books?' (lit. "books other than them (f.sg.)"); *yōm bikūn fī fərṣa l-madāres mā btəftaḥ* [DA-239] 'The schools don't open on a holiday' (lit. "A day there is in it (m.) vacation...").

---

[1]The term 'antecedent' in this book is used only in connection with anaphoric sequences; elsewhere, however, it is sometimes also used to designate the leading term in attribution: "the antecedent of a relative clause" = the term to which a clause is attributive [p.495].

The term 'sequent' has sometimes been used as a translation of the Ara-bic 'tābiɛ', which designates the 'following term' in attribution and cer-tain other constructions (viz. those in which there is case agreement in Classical Arabic). This, of course, has nothing to do with anaphoric sequence.

When the antecedent is vague — or conceptual rather than strictly verbal — the feminine singular pronoun is often used as its sequent: *masməḥ-li ʔəlɛab tanes ma dām mā zīd fīha* 'I'm allowed to play tennis as long as I don't overdo it'. Neither the noun *tanes* nor the clause *ʔəlɛab tanes* is exactly the antecedent of *-ha* 'it'(f.); in either case the sequent would then have to be masculine. See p. 428.

The "answer words" *laʔ* 'no' and *ʔē, ʔēwa, naɛam, mbala* (all translated 'yes') are anaphoric predication-substitutes. They eliminate repetition, in an answer, of the predication in a question. The word *mbala* is used to assert the affirmative in answer to a negative question or in contradiction to a negative statement.

Besides their purely anaphoric use, these words are used as interjections, and in supplementation to a full or partial answering sentence. *ʔē, mbala,* and *laʔ,* especially, are commonly followed by something more; when used alone, they sometimes sound rather curt. Hence: *šəfət ʔaḥmad? — ʔē šəfto* 'Did you see Ahmed? — Yes, I did'; *mā šəfət ʔaḥmad? — mbala šəfto* 'Didn't you see Ahmed? — Yes, I did'; *— laʔ mā šəfto* 'No, I didn't' (in answer to either question).
    The word *naɛam* is more polite or deferential than *ʔē.* It is used, furthermore, (with falling intonation) in response to a call or a command: *ya ʔaḥmad... — naɛam.* 'Oh Ahmed... — Yes?', and (with rising intonation) to ask for repetition or continuation of something said: *naɛam?* 'What?', 'I beg your pardon?' 'Yes?'. Note also the combination *ʔē naɛam,* which is more deferential, or more affable, than *naɛam* alone.
    laʔ is used anaphorically in coördinations with *wəlla* 'or' [p. 395]: *btəži wəlla laʔ?* 'Are you coming, or not?'.
    The form *laʔ* is not much used in a purely exclamatory capacity; the usual negative interjection are *lā* and *lah: lā waḷḷa* 'No indeed!'; *lah, lah* 'No, no!' (reaction of dismay).
    There is also a form *laʔa,* sometimes used (anaphorically) instead of *laʔ.*

The demonstratives *hāda* 'this, that', *hēk* 'so, thus, this, that', and *hnīk* 'there' are often used anaphorically (but *hnīk* not so much as English 'there' [p. 561]). See p. 554 ff.

The interrogative substitutes or "question words" [p. 566] (*šū* 'what', *wēn* 'where', etc.) are used in a sort of reverse anaphoric sequence, with the substitute as antecedent, and the phrase it "stands for" — the answering phrase — as sequent.

First and second person pronouns and most demonstratives are seldom or never used anaphorically, but are DEICTIC or PRESENTATIONAL. Their reference depends entirely on the circumstances or the "scene" of the utterance: the time, the place, the persons taking part in the conversation. (Third person pronouns are also sometimes deictic rather than anaphoric.)

Anaphora and Suppression of Anaphora

Anaphoric substitution contrasts on the one hand with actual ANAPHORA, in which the sequent involves repetition of the antecedent, and on the other hand with ANAPHORIC SUPPRESSION, in which the sequent is partly or entirely left out, to be "understood" from context.

There are certain kinds of constructions in which anaphora is usual in Arabic, but generally avoided in English (by substitution, suppression, or different wording). In a nominal predication, for instance, the same word often occurs as the main term of both the subject and the predicate:

1. *l—masʔale mū masʔalt ʔs-saɛʔr*   'It isn't a question of the price' (lit. "The question isn't...")

2. *xāyəf—lak hal—maraḍ hāda maraḍ ɛaʔli*   'I'm afraid this illness is mental' (or 'I'm afraid this is a mental illness')

See also examples 20 and 21, p. 404.

In Arabic a noun is commonly repeated with different pronoun suffixes, while in English the independent possessives (mine, yours, etc.) usually substitute in the sequent:

3. *maɛāšo ʔazwad mən maɛāši*   'His salary is more than mine'

4. *ʔəsmi byəži baɛəd ʔəsma bəl—lĭsta*   'My name comes after hers in the list'

Another anaphoric construction characteristic of Arabic is the supplementation of a singular noun by a <u>mən</u> phrase with its plural or dual: *yōm mn ʔl—ʔiyyām* 'one day' (lit. "a day of the days"), *bənt mən banāt ʔabu ɛali* 'One of Abu Ali's daughters':

5. *mā brūḥ b—ʔayy ḥāl mn ʔl—ʔaḥwāl*   'I won't go on any condition'

6. *wlā šawāb mn ʔš—šawābēn maẓbūṭ*   'Neither of the two answers is correct'

In answers to questions the English auxiliary verbs 'to do', 'to be', and 'to have' are commonly used as sequent with the main verb suppressed. In Arabic these sequences usually have anaphora: *šāyef hal-bēt ᵊhnīk?* – (*ᵓē*) *šāyef* 'Do you see that house over there?' – Yes, I do'; *btəži maɛna?* – *laᵓ mā bəži* 'Are you coming with us? – No, I'm not'.

In rendering English expressions like 'so do I', 'more than I have', etc., the Arabic sequent is usually suppressed:

7. *ᵓana rāyeḥ halla?* – *w-ᵓana kamān*

'I'm going now. – So am I' (or 'I am too')

8. *ṭalab maṣāri ᵓazwad mən ᵓaxū*

'He asked for more money than his brother did'

After *mən* 'than', *matᵊl* 'like, as', *ᵓadd* 'as much as', and in certain similar cases, an Arabic leading term (noun, preposition, verb) is often suppressed, while in the English rendering there is usually an anaphoric substitute or anaphora:

9. *farɛ ᵊl-falsafe tabaɛ žāmɛətna ᵓaḥsan mən ᵊž-žāmɛa l-ᵊflāniyye*

'The philosophy department of our university is better than that of University X'

10. *ɛəmro taᵓrīban ᵓaddi* (or *ᵓadd ɛəmri*)

'He's almost the same age as I am' (lit. "His age is almost as much as me" or ...as much as my age")

11. *sᵓāl ɛan ᵊž-žār ᵓabl ᵊd-dār, w-ɛan ᵊr-rafīᵓ ᵓabl ᵊṭ-ṭarīᵓ* (Saying)

'Ask about the neighbor before you ask about the house, and about the traveling companion, before you ask about the road'

Similarly: *matl ᵊl-māḍi* 'as in the past' (cf. *bəl-māḍi* 'in the past'), *matl ᵊl-ᵓawwal* 'as in the beginning' (cf. *bəl-ᵓawwal* 'in the beginning, at first'). Note also: *msāwāt ᵊhᵓūᵓ ᵊl-marᵓa bər-ražol* 'equality of women's right with men's (or ...with those of men)'.

PERSONAL PRONOUNS (*aḍ-ḍamīr*)

There are eight personal pronouns in Syrian Arabic, each of them representing a person category combined with a number/gender category [p. 363].
Each pronoun has two main forms: The SUFFIXED form is used as object to a verb [p. 438] or as the following term in a construct [457] or a prepositional phrase [477] or after certain conjunctions, etc. [543]. The INDEPENDENT form is used otherwise, e.g. as subject [548], or as an appositive [512] or extrapositive [432].

The independent forms are:

	Third Person	Second Person	First Person
Masculine	*huwwe* 'he, it'	*ʔənte* 'you'	*ʔana* 'I' (m. and f.)
Feminine	*hiyye* 'she, it'	*ʔənti* 'you'	
Plural	*hənne* 'they'	*ʔəntu* 'you'	*nəḥna* 'we'

Stylistic and dialectal variants include the apocopated forms *hū* 'he', *hī* 'she', *ʔənt* 'you (m.)', and *nəḥᵊn* 'we'. Also *hənnen* 'they' (Damascus), *humme* or *humma* 'they' (Palestine), *ʔəhna* 'we' (Palestine), *ləhna* 'we' (Damascus).

The basic suffixed forms are:

	Third Person	Second Person	First Person
Masc.	−o 'him, it, his, its'	−ak 'you, your'	−ni, −i 'me, my'
Fem.	−ha 'her, it, its'	−ek 'you, your'	
Pl.	−hon 'them, their'	−kon 'you, your'	−na 'us, our'

In Palestine one hears −hom (or −hum) 'them, their', and −kom (or −kum) 'you, your' (pl.). Cf. *humma*, above. In Lebanon: −u 'him, his', etc. (and −hun 'them, their', −kun 'you, your' pl.).

Modifications of the Suffix Forms. The suffixes whose basic forms begin with a vowel (*-ak, -ek, -o*) occur in these forms only after a consonant; if the stem ends in a vowel, then *-ak* becomes *-k*, *-ek* becomes *-ki*; while *-o* disappears entirely – but leaving the stem in its suffixing form [p. 27], with the final vowel long and accented:

After Consonant

dzdkkar 'he remembered':

dzdkkar-ak 'he remembered you (m.)'

dzdkkar-ek 'he remembered you (f.)'

dzdkkar-o 'he remembered him'

ʔəddā́m 'ahead (of)':

ʔəddā́m-ak 'ahead of you (m.)'

ʔəddā́m-ek 'ahead of you (f.)'

ʔəddā́m-o 'ahead of him'

bifáhhem 'he'll explain':

bifáhhm-ak 'he'll explain to you (m.)'

bifáhhm-ek 'he'll explain to you (f.)'

bifáhhm-o 'he'll explain to him'

ʔəxt 'sister':

ʔə́xt-ak 'your (m.) sister'

ʔə́xt-ek 'your (f.) sister'

ʔə́xt-o 'his sister'

dars 'lesson':

dárs-ak 'your (m.) lesson'

dárs-ek 'your (f.) lesson'

dárs-o 'his lesson'

lā́ken 'but':

lākə́nn-ak 'but you (m.)...'

lākə́nn-ek 'but you (f.)...'

lākə́nn-o 'but he...'

After Vowel

nə́si 'he forgot':

nəsī́-k 'he forgot you (m.)'

nəsī́-ki 'he forgot you (f.)'

nəsī́ 'he forgot him'

wára 'behind':

warā́-k 'behind you (m.)'

warā́-ki 'behind you (f.)'

warā́ 'behind him'

bifáhhmu 'they'll explain':

bifahhmū́-k 'they'll explain to you (m.)'

bifahhmū́-ki 'they'll explain to you (f.)'

bifahhmū́ 'they'll explain to him'

ʔdxu 'brother (of)' [p. 169]:

ʔaxū́-k 'your (m.) brother'

ʔaxū́-ki 'your (f.) brother'

ʔaxū́ 'his brother'

ddwa 'medicine':

dawā́-k 'your (m.) medicine'

dawā́-ki 'your (f.) medicine'

dawā́ 'his medicine'

ldwla 'but for...'

lawlā́-k 'but for you (m.)'

lawlā́-ki 'but for you (f.)'

lawlā́ 'but for him'

The suffixes -ha and -hon may lose their h after consonants, and sometimes (especially in Lebanon) after long vowels. These variants require the
same stem form [20, 22] that the forms with h do:

dʒakkɑ́r-ha or dʒakkɑ́r-a   nəsí-ha or nəsíy-a (i.e. nəsía)[1]
'he remembered her'   'he's forgotten her'

dʒakkɑ́r-hon or dʒakkɑ́r-on   nəsí-hon or nəsíy-on
'he remembered them'   'he's forgotten them'

ʔə́mm-ha or ʔə́mm-a   ʔabū́-ha or ʔabúw-a
'her mother'   'her father'

ʔə́mm-hon or ʔə́mm-on   ʔabū́-hon or ʔabúw-on
'their mother'   'their father'

              ɛalḗha or ɛalḗa   'on her, it'
              ɛalḗhon or ɛalḗon 'on them'

The suffix -i becomes -yi when the stem ends in a vowel: dawā́-yi 'my
medicine', maṣāríy-yi 'my money' (i.e. maṣārī́-yi), fíy-yi 'in me'
(i.e. fī́-yi).

The first person singular form -ni is complemental [p.437]; -i is used
otherwise. See below.

USES OF THE SUFFIXED PRONOUNS

1.) As following term in an identificatory **construct** [p.458]

        Suffixed to ordinary nouns, the pronouns are generally
        rendered in English by the possessives: my, your, his, etc.
        With quantifiers, etc. [p.466ff], by an of-phrase: kəllon
        'all of them', baɛ́don 'some of them', tnēnā́tna 'the two of us'

1. ʔaxad maḥramto mən ǯēbto w-ɛaṣab   'He took his handkerchief from his
   ʔīdḫa [AO-115]   pocket and bandaged her hand'

2. ʔəxti l-ʔkbīre mǯawwaze w-ṣəhri   'My elder sister is married, and my
   ʔəsmo ḥasan [AO-43]   brother-in-law, his name is Hassan'

3. ǯəddak u-səttak ṭayybīn?   'Are your gradfather and grand-
   [AO-43]   mother living?'

---

[1]It is a convention of our transcription to write iy before a vowel or before y, and ī before a consonant or finally; the two spellings are equivalent, as also are uw and ū.

4. *bəddi msāεattak b-ʔaḍiyye ẓġīre* [DA-295] — 'I need your assistance in a small matter'

5. *z-zāyde ma bəthəmm. εamalītha salīme* [DA-217] — 'Apendicitis is not serious. The operation is safe', lit. "Its operation..."

6. *nəṣṣo l-fōʔāni mən laḥᵊm w-damm w-nəṣṣo t-taḥtāni mən ḥažar* [AO-118] — 'The top half of him (was) of flesh and blood and the bottom half of of him, of stone'

7. *tnēnātna msāfrīn la-ḥalab u-hayy tazākərna* [DA-250] — 'The two of us are going to Aleppo and here are our tickets'

8. *εmūmi kəllon mātu* [AO-43] — 'All my paternal uncles are dead', lit. "My uncles, all of them have died"

9. *bən-natīže kəllo mətᵊl baεḍo* — 'It's all the same in the long run', lit. "In the outcome, all of it is like each other of it"

10. *w-ʔəza tʔaxxart..., mnāxod ġērak* [DA-29] — 'And if you're late, we'll take someone else' (*ġēr* is a noun meaning '(some)other'; in identificatory construct [p. 468]: 'other than...'.)

11. *ʔāl b-nafso, 'ʔaḥsan mən bala...'* [AO-115] — 'He said to himself, "It's better than nothing"

Some nouns are commonly used with suffixes in special supplemental capacities: *εəmᵊrkon rəḥtu la-εālē?* 'Have you (pl.) ever gone to Aley?', lit. "(In) your life..."; *sāεə́ta, waʔta* 'then, at that time' [p. 521], etc.

2.) **After a preposition** [p. 477]. Examples:

1. *ḥakēna maεo mən šahᵊr* — 'We talked with him a month ago'
2. *šaεεlī-li l-ḥammām* [DA-180] — 'Light the bath (heater) for me'
3. *ṭlōb mənno ʔīd bənto* [AO-114] — 'Ask him for his daughter's hand (in marriage)' (lit. "ask of him...")
4. *bəttə́kel εalēk* [DA-290] — 'I'm depending on you'
5. *bayyəḍ-ᵊlna wəššna ʔəddāmo* [DA-291] — 'Put us in a favorable light with him', lit. "Whiten for us our face before him"
6. *š-šərke mā fīha barake* [DA-296] — 'There's no advantage in partnership', lit. "Partnership, there's no blessing in it".

7. *ɛandọ ɛēle?*

'Does he have a family?', lit. "(Is there) with him (*chez lui*) a family?"

8. *ʔizan byaɛmlū–lọ ɛamaliyye* [DA-203]

'They'll operate on him, then', lit. "Then they'll do for him an operation"

9. *mīn ɛali bēnāthon?* [DA-233]

'Which of them is Ali?', lit. "Who is Ali among them?"

10. *mǝtli̠ mǝtla̠k mā baɛref* [DA-243]

'I don't know either', lit. "Like me, like you, I don't know."

11. *mā mǝnrūḥ balā̠hon* [DA-153]

'We wouldn't go without them'

12. *biḥǝṭṭu kamān ṭīn w–fōʔọ ḥažara tānye* [AO-75]

'They lay on more clay, and on top of it, another stone.'

3.) As **subject** of a clause after *ʔǝnno* 'that', *laʔanno* (or *laʔǝnno*) 'because', *kaʔanno* (or *kaʔǝnno*) '(It's) as if'. The final *-o* of these conjunctions is a neutral or "dummy" third-person masculine pronoun, which disappears when other suffixes are attached:

1. *šu mā bǝṭṣadde? ʔǝnni̠ kǝnt fī?* [AO-116]

'Don't you believe that I was in it?'

2. *mǝɛʔǝžze ʔǝnno̠n bǝʔyu ɛāyšīn*

'It's a wonder that they stayed alive'

3. *ftakart ʔǝnna̠k l-ǝmɛallem* [PVA-32]

'I thought that you were the teacher'

4. *šāf ʔǝnnha̠ warraʔet u–ʔazharet* [AO-100]

'He saw that it had leafed out and bloomed'

5. *bḥǝṭṭ–ǝllak ǝl–bāʔi b–kīs waraʔ laʔannhon xfāf* [DA-107]

'I'll put the rest in a paper bag for you, because they're light'

6. *hēʔtak maḅṣūṭ, w–kaʔanna̠k mā sāwēt ɛamaliyye* [DA-218]

'You look well, as if you hadn't had an operation at all'

7. *wallāhi kaʔanna̠ bǝr–rabīɛ* [DA-149]

'Why, it's just like spring', lit. "It's as if we were in springtime"

As subjects in general are commonly suppressed [p.418], the neutral forms of these conjunctions (ending in *-o*) are commonly used before verbs in the first or second person, as well as third person: *ḥalaft ʔǝnno bǝʔtol...ḥalli bixallǝṣni* [AO-116] 'I swore that I would kill the one who released me': in contrast to the version with subject expressed: *ḥalaft ʔǝnni̠ bǝʔtol...* .

If the following verb is third person masculine/singular, however, there is of course no contrast between expression and supression of a pronominal subject, because of the dummy suffix *-o: ḥalaf ʔǝnno byǝʔtol...* .

Some speakers, especially in Lebanon and Palestine, do
not always use the dummy suffix: *l-mara ʔəla ḥaʔʔ ʔənn*
tantáxeb... [SAL-154] 'Women have a right to vote'.

The conjuction *lāken* 'but' may also be used with the suffixes; the
suffixing form is *lākənn-:*

8. *kənt ᵊmḥassbak zalame mnīḥ*   "I thought you were a nice guy, but
   lākənnak ṭlə€ᵊt €āṭel   you turned out to be no good'.

4.) **As a complement** [p.437], to verbs and a few other kinds of words. In
this function, the first-person singular suffix takes the form –*ni* (instead
of –*i*); all the other suffix forms are the same as with nouns and prepositions.

4. a) As object to verbs and active participles:

1. *ʔaxad ᵊt-təffāḥa w-ʔakalha*   'He took the apple and ate it'
   [AO-91]

2. *ʔa€€ddon b-maṭraḥ zarīf u-tarákon*   'He seated them in a nice place and
   [AO-88]   left them'

3. *baṣaṭṭni b-hal-xabar* [DA-243]   'I'm glad to hear that', lit.
                                         'You've gladdened me with this
                                         news'

4. *halla ʔ sayyārt ᵊš-šərke*   'The company car will take us there
   bətwaṣṣəlna [DA-251]   right away'

5. *l-malek €aṭā́ žāyze* [AO-88]   'The king gave him a prize'

6. *w-ʔiza mā ṣaddaʔtni, €mēl dōret*   'And if you don't believe me, go
   ᵊl-ʔarḍ w-ʔīs [AO-83]   around the world and measure (it).'

7. *tarᵊkto w-sabᵊʔto la-bēto*   'She left him and went on ahead of
   [AO-115]   him to his house'

8. *žāyīni maktūb*   'A letter has come for me' (*žāye* is
                                         the active participle of *ʔəža* 'to
                                         come' [p.76], which is sometimes
                                         transitive: 'to come *to* or *for*
                                         (someone)'.)

9. *ʔəl-li ʔiza lāzmak šī mən bērūt*   'Tell me if you need anything from
   [DA-245]   Beirut'

The English object 'me' is not an object in the Arabic,
but a prepositional complement - "tell *to* me";, while the
Arabic object -*ak* corresponds to an English subject - 'if
you need'. *lāzem* 'necessary' is the active participle of
byəlzam 'to be necessary to (someone)' - a transitive verb.

An object pronoun is suffixed to the stem *yā-* if the verb itself already has a pronominalized first object [p.438] or an *-l-* suffix [479]:

10. *ɛaṭāni yāha kəllha*   'He gave it all to me'

11. *ʔana bžəb-lak yā*   'I'll bring it to you'

12. *ʔaḷḷa yxallī-lna yāk*   'God keep you (for us)'

The pronouns are also suffixed to the stem *yā-* as objects of the quasi-verb *bəddo* 'to want', whose subject-affixes are in the form of pronoun suffixes [p.412]: *bəddi yāha* 'I want it (f.)', *bəddo yākon* 'He wants you (pl.)':

13. *ṭṭəşel fiyyi lamma bəddak yāni*   'Get in touch with me when you want me'

With the stem *yā-* either *-ni* or *-i* may be used: ... *lamma bəddak yāyi*.

The *yā-* forms are also sometimes also used after *ɛand* 'with' + suffix, thus construing *ɛand(o)* as a quasi-verb 'to have' [p.413]:

14. *bəṭṭallaɛ bəl-mawžūdāt ɛandi*   'I'll look through what I have in
    w-ᵊbšūf ʔiza ɛandi yāha   stock and see if I have it'

In the expression *ma dām* 'since, while, inasmuch as' *dām* is construed as a verb, hence *ma dāmni* 'since I...'. In the case of *ma ɛada* 'excepting, not counting, either *-ni* or *-i* may be used: *ma ɛadāni* or *ma ɛadāyi* 'excepting me'.

4. b) In exclamations with *ma-* and an elative [p.314]:

15. *šūf hal-maşāneɛ ᵊl-ḥadīse*   'See how fine those modern factories
    ma-ʔaɛžamha [DA-251]   are!'

16. *ma-ʔaḥlāni ʔəɛ³žmo hal-kalb!*   'Wouldn't that be something, for me
                                             to invite that (son-of-a) dog!'
                                             (lit. "How nice of me to invite
                                             him, that dog")

4. c) With the exclamatory demonstratives [p.564] *lēk-* and *šaɛ-*, 'there is..., here is, look there at..., (voici, voilà)', a suffix - usually third person - is usual (and obligatory after *šaɛ-*):

17. *šaɛo žāye*   'There he comes'

18. *šaɛha ḥalab bānet...* [DA-250]   'Look there, Aleppo has come into
                                               view'

19. *šaɛhon ᵊr-rəkkāb nāzlīn...*   'Here come the passengers disem-
    [DA-249]   barking'

20. *lēko ʔəža wāḥed* [DA-44]   'Here comes one'

Note the -ni forms in the first-person singular: šaɛni
hōn 'Here I am', lēkni žāye 'Here I come'.

4. d) With the words ləssa and baɛd 'still, yet':

21. ʾē ləssāk mā šəft šī [DA-173]   'Yes but you haven't seen anything
                                          yet'

22. ɛmūmi kəllon mātu, lāken ɛammāti   'My (paternal) uncles are all dead,
    ləssāhon ṭayybīn [AO-43]   but my aunts are still living'

23. ləssāni mā ɛaraḍtha bəl-wāžha   'I haven't yet put them on view in
    [AO-79]   the showcase'

24. ʾabno ṣ-ẓġīr baɛdo təlmīz [adap.   'His youngest son is still a
    fr. DA-77]   student'

25. ž-žəsʾr ləssā́ taḥt ʾt-taɛmīr   'The bridge is still under con-
                                          struction'

        ləssa also has the suffixing forms ləssāt-, ləssāɛ-, and
    ləssaɛt-: ləssāto təlmīz, etc.

        The suffixes are not obligatory in this construction.
    Note: bābā ləssa mā ʾəža [DA-299] 'Daddy still hasn't
    gotten here', ləssa ʾana mū mətʾakked... 'I'm still not
    sure...'.

4. e) With the expressions (ya)rēt 'I wish, would that...' and (ya)dōb
       'hardly'.

26. bass ya rētak kənt maɛi...   'But I wish you'd been with me...'
    [DA-171]

27. ya rēto kān hōn   'If only he were here'

28. rētni mətʾt ʾabʾl-ma ɛabbart   'I'd sooner die than express my
    ɛala raʾyi   opinion'

        With the imperfect subjunctive [p.350] ya rēt may be
    used without a suffix: ya rēt ʾəʾder ʾəṣal la-hnīk 'If I
    could only get there!'

29. dōbo yaɛmel maṣāri kfāye txalli   'He hardly makes money enough to
    ʾahlo ɛāyšīn   keep his family alive'

        With ya dōb the first-person singular form is -i, not
    -ni:

30. yā dōbi ʾūm bi-maṣarīfi   'I can scarcely meet my expenses'

4. f) With the expressions *fī* 'to be able' and *b-* 'to be the matter with' [p. 415]:

31. *fīk ᵊtsāɛᵊdni? - mā fīni sāɛdak*   'Can you help me?' - 'I can't help you.'

32. *šᵊbak? (šū bāk?) - mā bni šī*   'What's the matter (with you)?' - 'Nothing's the matter (with me)'

5.) With the question-words [p. 566] *wēn* 'where', *kīf* and *šlōn* 'how', and *ᵊaddēš* 'how much':

33. *wēno?, wēnni?*   'Where is he?', 'Where am I?'

34. *kīfak ᵊl-yōm?*   'How are you today?'

35. *šlōnkon ya ṣabāya ya šabāb*   'How are you, girls and boys?'

36. *šlōnek b-šᵊġl ᵊl-bēt?* [DA-99]   'How are you (f.) at housework?'

37. *law bᵊtšūf ᵊaddēšo kān mamnūn*   'You should have seen how grateful he was!'

The word *mīn* 'who' has a suffixing form *mᵊn-,* which is combined with apocopated forms of the "independent" pronouns: *-u* 'he', *-i* 'she', *-(h)ᵊn* 'they': *mᵊni yalli ᵊāɛde b-šambak* 'Who (f.) is sitting beside you?'; *mᵊnu raᵊīsak?* 'Who is your boss?'; *mᵊn(h)ᵊn rᵊfaᵊātak?* 'Who are your companions?' See p. 549.

USES OF THE INDEPENDENT PRONOUNS

1.) As subject:

1. *hiyye bəl-bēt*   'She's in the house'

2. *ʔənte wēn kənt š-žəmɛa l-mādye?*   'Where were you last week?'
   [DA-149]

3. *b-ʔanu farəɛ bəš-šēš ʔənte?*   'In which branch of the army are
                                          you?'

4. *ṭābxīn nəhna žāž ɛal-ɛaša*   'We're having chicken for dinner'

For Identification of the Referent. If the predicate is a prepositional phrase (as in examples 1 and 3), an independent pronoun may be needed to show the person and number/gender of the subject-referent. If the predicate is adjectival (as in example 4), a pronoun may be used to show the person of the subject-referent (though the adjective in any case shows its number/gender). A subject pronoun may also be used to resolve ambiguities in the inflectional form of a verbal predicate: *btaɛərfo ʔənte?* 'Do you know him?' (vs. *btaɛərfo hiyye?* 'Does she know him?').

> Otherwise in verbal predicates the subject-affixes [p.175] give complete person and number/gender information about the subject-referent: *byaɛərfu* 'They know'; in such cases an independent pronoun (as in *byaɛərfu hənne*) is redundant, and its inclusion in the clause must serve some function other than identification. (See below.)

For Contrastive Emphasis. If the predicate (or the context, or the circumstances) identifies the subject-referent by person and number/gender, then a subject pronoun may still be used to emphasize the contrast between its referent and other referents:

5. *hənne byədfaɛu l-əhrāse bass*   'They'll pay the taxes, but you
   ʔəntu btətkaffalu b-maṣrūf əl-mayy   (pl.) will take care of the water
   wəl-kahraba [DA-292]   and electricity expenses'

6. *ʔana mā baɛref bass bɡənn-əllak*   'I don't know, but I think my maid
   ṣāneɛti btaɛref [DA-98]   knows'

7. *walla mā btədfaɛ ʔənte* [DA-198]   'But you're not to pay!'

8. *ʔana ya bēk bəɡsel w-bəkwi*   'Sir, I wash and iron and scrub
   w-bəmsah w-əbsāwi t-txūt [DA-99]   and make the beds' (The contrast
                                          being with her mother, who cooks.
                                          Another function of *ʔana* here,
                                          however, is to introduce and help
                                          unify the coordinated predicates.)

For Emphasis on the Predication as Such. Subject pronouns in Arabic are often used, neither to identify nor to emphasize their referent, but rather to identify or emphasize the <u>predicate</u> (or, more exactly, the predication as such): *btəfham Ɛaliyyi ʔənte* 'You <u>do</u> understand me!'[1]

Since suppression of the subject [p.418] makes a predication more dependent on its context, and also makes it sound more casual, it follows that the inclusion of a suppressible subject pronoun may serve to make a predication "stand out" from its context, or to sound more insistent. The subject sets off the predicate as a frame does a picture.

9. *šukran Ɛala kəll ḥāl ʔana mā bdaxxen*
   'Thanks anyway, but I don't smoke'

10. *ʔənte btaƐref ʔaddēš xaǧǧaltna hadāk ʔl-yōm*
    'You <u>know</u> how much you put us to shame that day'[2]

11. *walla ʔana məštaʔt-əlhon w-bəddi šūfon*
    'I (f.) certainly do miss them and I'd like to see them'

12. *šlṓna hiyye?*
    'How <u>is</u> she?'

13. *ma huwwe fəl-mustašfa* [EA-150]
    'But he <u>is</u> in the hospital'

14. *məhʔrɛe hiyye walla laʔ?*
    '<u>Is</u> it worth while, or not?'

15. *šū huwwe mašrūƐak?* [DA-296]
    'What <u>is</u> your plan?'

In ex. 15, the effect of *huwwe* is simply to emphasize the question-word predicate *šū*. Cf. the less emphatic *šū mašrūƐak* 'What's your plan?' The contexts from which examples 12 and 13 were taken make it clear that no contrastive emphasis is intended. The latter comes in response to a question *lēš mā birūḥ Ɛal-mustašfa* 'Why doesn't he go to the hospital?' If the question had been e.g. *wēno huwwe?* 'Where is he?' the answer would probably have been simply *fəl-mustašfa,* with no subject expressed.

Similarly, the apocopated subject pronouns that are fused to the question word *mən–* 'who' [p.547] are used to make the question more emphatic than it would be with the simple form *mīn: mənu haz-zalame?* 'Who <u>is</u> that man?' vs. *mīn haz-zalame?* 'Who's that man?'

Note also example 2, above, and examples 21 and 22, below.

---

[1] A better English translation (for the context from which this was taken) would be '<u>You</u> know what I mean...' in a sort of cajoling intonation (high pitch on 'you', middle or low pitch on the rest, with a slight rise at the end). The important thing about this translation is that the high pitch on 'you' has nothing to do with identification or contrastive emphasis, just as *ʔənte* in the Arabic has nothing to do with them either.

[2] Or '<u>You</u> know how much you put us to shame that day...', with the intonation discussed in the preceding footnote.

2.) Independent pronouns are used in **apposition** [p. 512] to the corresponding suffix pronoun, for emphasis:

16. xallī huwwe yqarrer   'Let <u>him</u> decide'

17. rəfaʔa mən šīlon hənne   'companions of their own age group'

18. ʔəlak ʔənte mablaġ baṣīṭ lāken   'To you it's a small sum, but to
    ʔəlo huwwe maṣāri ktīr   him it's a lot of money'

In apposition, with modifiers:

19. žəb-li ʔana t-tāni laḥme w-baṭāṭa   'Bring <u>me</u> meat and potatoes, too'
    [DA-47]

20. ɛərfet ʔənni ʔana halli žaraḥt   'She realized that it was I who had
    ʔl-ɛabd [AO-118]   wounded the slave'

     In example 19 ʔana has an adjectival attribute t-tāni;
in 20 it has an attributive clause halli žaraḥt... . A
suffix pronoun itself cannot have modifiers, except as
mediated by its corresponding independent form.

3.) **In extraposition** [p. 431], antecedent to a suffix pronoun:

21. huwwe šar-lo ɛašr ʔsnīn bi-ʔamērka   'He's been in America for ten
    [DA-75]   years'

22. ʔana ləssāni mā baɛref ʔš-šām   'I still don't know Damascus well'
    ʔmnīḥ [DA-77]

23. w-ʔənte ya bēk šū bžəb-lak?   'And you, sir, what shall I bring
    [DA-46]   you?'

     An extrapositive pronoun – like an ordinary subject pro-
noun – may be used for contrastive emphasis on the referent,
as in example 23, or to emphasize the predication as such,
as in examples 21 and 22.

4.) As subject of a **circumstantial clause** with w- [p. 531]:

24. ṣār-lak zamān ɛəndi w-ʔana mā   'You've been staying with me for
    baɛref ʔəsmak ʔl-karīm [AO-108]   quite a while now and I don't even
                                           know your name'

25. byəthaddasu w-hənne ʔāɛdīn ḥawl   'They converse while seated around
    hal-bərke [PAT-187]   this pool'

26. mən ɛašr ʔsnīn w-ʔana bʔəšš   'For ten years I've been shaving
    daʔni la-ḥāli yom ʔē yōm laʔ   (my beard for) myself every other
    [DA-197]   day'

5.) In coordinations [p. 391]:

27. *rāyḥīn ʔənte w-Ɛali sawa?*   'Are you and Ali going together?'

28. *mā ṣəfi ġēr ʔana w-ʔənti.*   'Nobody's left but you (f.) and me'

29. *lā ʔənte w-lā huwwe, ʔana*   'Neither you nor he, but I will
    bāxéda.   get it'

30. *mīn bəddak, ʔana wəlla huwwe?*   'Whom do you want, him or me?'

31. *yā ʔana yā huwwe bitamm hōn.*   'Either he or I will stay here'

    Note that in coördinations, pronouns precede nouns,
first-person pronouns precede others, and second-person
generally precedes third.

6.) With an appositive [p. 506]:

32. *ʔəntu l-ʔamērkān bəthəbbu laḥm*   'You Americans like beef better'
    ᵊl-baʔar ʔaktar [DA-109]

33. *nəḥna l-Ɛarab hiyādiyyīn*   'We Arabs are neutralists'

34. *ḥənne ž-žamāƐa mā byəʔzu ḥada*   'That bunch wouldn't harm anyone'

35. *tfaḍḍalu ʔəntu t-tnēn*   'Come in, you two'

7.) Pronouns are seldom used as **predicate**, except in equational sentences
[p. 406], and then mainly when the predicate is a mere repetition of the subject.

36. *kīfak? – waḷḷa ʔana ʔana*   'How are you?'–'So-so'(lit. "I am I")

37. *ləssāta hiyye hiyye*   'She's still the same' (lit. "She
                              is still she")

38. *w-ᵊš-šəġᵊl huwwe huwwe ʔiza kān*   'And the work is the same, whether
    la-wāḥed u-ʔiza kān la-tnēn   it's for one or for two' (lit.
    [DA-198]   "And the work, it is it...")

    Note also the following sentence:

39. *ʔaddēš ṣār-lo ləbnān mətᵊl ma*   'How long has Lebanon been as it is
    huwwe l-yōm? [SAL-150]   today?'

    Cf. *...mətᵊl ma kān ᵊmbāreḥ* '...as it was yesterday'.
The conjunction *ma* is usually followed by a verb, but a predication of actuality [p. 402] corresponding to the verb *kān*
'to be' is of course non-verbal. Since *l-yōm* is merely supplemental ("adverbial") [521], it cannot stand alone as a
predicate; without *huwwe* to fill the breach, the subordinate
clause could not exist as such (though it could be collapsed
into a prepositional phrase *mətl ᵊl-yōm* [538]).

DEMONSTRATIVES

Pronouns *(ism l-ʔišāra)*

The main forms of the PROXIMAL demonstrative pronouns are:

Masculine	*hāda*	'this, this one, that, that one'
Feminine	*hādi, hayy*	'this, this one, that, that one'
Plural	*hadōl*	'these, those'

The main forms of the DISTAL demonstrative pronouns are:

Masculine	*hadāk*	'that, that one, that other'
Feminine	*hadīk*	'that, that one, that other'
Plural	*hadōlīk, hadōk, hadənk*	'those, those others'

    The distal demonstratives, which are much less used than the proximal, refer only to something (or someone) relatively far away from both the speaker and the person spoken to: *mənu hadāk?* 'Who's that over there?'.
    The proximal demonstrative correspond not only to English 'this, these', but also to 'that, those', whenever the reference is to something near (or associated with) the person spoken to: *šū hāda (yəlli maɛak)?* 'What's that one (you have there)?'
    The demonstrative pronouns are of course not limited to the presentation of objects in a spatial dimension, but may also indicate "distance" in time: *hadīk kānet ʔawwal sawra* 'That (other) was the first revolution'; or conceptual "distance" independent of space and time: *hādi kānet ʔawwal sawra* 'That was the first revolution', i.e. the revolution we're discussing now – and which is in that sense "present" to us now.

    Stylistic variants include the apocopated form *hād* (for *hāda*); the pronouns whose main forms end in a consonant also have forms with a final *-e:* *hayye, hadōle, hadīke, hadənke,* etc.
    In Lebanon the forms *hayda* (for *hāda*), *haydi* (for *hādi*), *hawdi* (for *hadōl*), *hawdīk* or *hudīk* (for *hadōlīk*) are commonly used. (*hawdi* also has an apocopated form *haw.*) In Palestine masc./pl. *hadōlāk* is sometimes distinguished from fem./pl. *hadōlīk*. The forms *hadənk(e)*, also *həndənk(e)*, are usual in Damascus, but are not heard in most other areas. Damascus also has a variant *hadōn*, for *hadōl*.

Examples of Usage:

1. *hāda nədᵊr mən sətti d̩-d̩ɛ̄ïfe*
   [AO-114]

   'This is a votive offering from my sick grandmother'

2. *hādi fatra bi-ḥayāt kəll šaxṣ, ɛādatan*

   'That's a stage in the life of every person, usually'

3. *hayy ᵊl-bənt yalli ʔəlt-əl-lak ɛanha* [DA-99]

   'This is the girl I was telling you about'

4. *hadōl ᵊl-kətᵊb ᵊl-maɣbūt̩īn?*

   'Are these the right books?'

5. *hayye masāʔel mā bətxəṣṣni*

   'Those are matters that don't concern me'

As subject to a nominal predicate (ex. 1-5), the demonstrative generally agrees with the predicate in number/gender. See, however, p. 421. In ex. 5, note the feminine demonstrative agreeing with the plural predicate noun [p. 423].

6. *šū hād?*

   'What's that?'

7. *fī ɛandkon dāyman t̩aʔṣ malɛūn mətᵊl hād?*

   'Do you always have weather as awful as this?'

8. *l-yōm mā fī šī mən hād l-ḥamdəlla*

   'Today there's none of that, thank goodness'

The apocopated form *hād* occurs mainly at the end of a phrase. It is especially common in anaphoric use after *mətᵊl, mən* (ex. 7, 8). Note also: *lā hād w-lā hād* 'neither one nor the other, neither this nor that'.

9. *hayy ɛala ḥarīr ʔaṣli, hayy ɛala šal, w-hayy ᵊmmauwaže* [AO-79]

   'This one (f.) is [of] pure silk, this one is [of] wool, and this one is a moiré' (antecedent: *krāve* 'necktie')

10. *mā btaɛref maḥramtak? mū hādi hiyye?* [AO-115]

    'Don't you recognize your hankerchief? Isn't this it?'

11. *wal̩l̩a mū ktār hadōle*

    'Why, those are not so many!'

12. *šū bisammu hāda?*

    'What do they call this?'

13. *bəži bəkra, hāda ʔiza mā šattet*

    'I'll come tomorrow, that is, if it doesn't rain'

Since masculine(/singular) is the neutral or bass number/gender [p. 421], the masculine demonstrative is generally used in reference to an object whose name the speaker does not know (ex. 12, 6), and commonly also as sequent to a clausal antecedent (ex. 13) or a vague or conceptual antecedent [p.536], as in ex. 8, The feminine, however, is also commonly used in the latter case [cf. p.428]: *šū hayye?* 'What's this?' (i.e. 'What's up?, what's happening?'), *hayy hiyye* 'That's it!' (i.e. 'You've hit the nail on the head'):

14. *kəll šī ʔəlla hayy waḷḷa*   'Anything but that!'

15. *lēš bəddak hāda? xōd hadāk*   'Why do you want this one? Take that other one'

16. *Ɛaṭīni kamm wāḥed mən hadōl*   'Give me a few of these and a few of *w-kamm wāḥed mən hadənk*   those others'

   In anaphoric use, the demonstratives are sometimes to be rendered in English by personal pronouns, or in more pedantic style, by 'the former' (distal) and 'the latter' (proximal):

17. *baƐdēn hadāk iʔəl-lo rūḥ ʔaḷḷa*   'Then he (the former) would tell him, *yəblīk*   "Go on, may God afflict you"'

18. *hāda bisāwi fiyyi hēk* [AO-111]   'He might do that to *me*'

19. *wēnha faṭma w-marwān? — waḷḷa*   'Where is Fatima, and Marwan? — Well, *marwān žāye, šaƐo taḥət*   Marwan is coming; he's down there lock- *Ɛam-yəʔfel ʔs-sayyāra w-hadīk*   ing the car, and she (the former) is *maƐo*   with him'

   Examples of demonstratives as topic [p.429]:

20. *hāda huwwe w-farīd kānu b-fard*   'He (the latter) and Fareed were in *ṣaff*   the same class' [cf. p.361, ex. 23]

21. *yəmken...təʔbaḍ-lak šī šwayyet*   'Maybe you'll get a little more money, *maṣāri zyāde, nšāḷḷa? — hayy*   I hope? — You're really sharp when it *šāṭer fīha, mā btənsāha ʔabadan!*   comes to that! You never forget it'

22. *ya ʔaxi l-Ɛazīz, hayy ʔənte*   'My dear friend, there you're wrong *ġalṭān tāni marra*   again' [cf. ex. 7, p.430]

23. *hāda mḥammad ʔaxūk, hāda bəddi*   'This is your brother Mohammed, I *ykūn ʔb-Ɛaṣʔbtak*   want him to be in your group'

24. *hāda ʔante halli kāteb ʔl-waraʔa?*   'Are you the one who wrote the paper?'
   [DA-188]

   Note (ex. 24) that first and second person singular sub- ject pronouns, as well as third person, may be extraposed as a demonstrative, for emphasis: *hāda ʔante..., hayy ʔanti..., hāda ʔana...* (cf. *hāda huwwe...,* ex. 20).

In some contexts it is necessary to make a distinction in Arabic like that in English between 'this', 'that' (in reference to something vague or conceptual, i.e. 'this matter'), and on the other hand 'this one, that one' (in reference to a particular thing or person). Generally speaking, the demonstrative pronouns are to be taken in the definite, material sense, except with *hāda* and *hayy* in certain kinds of context and in certain constructions and set phrases, e.g. *maɛ hāda* 'nevertheless, despite that', *fōʔ hāda* 'moreover' (lit. "above that"), *hāda ʔiza...* 'that is, if...' [ex. 13], *hayy hiyye* 'That's it!'. Further examples in which the context makes it clear that the reference is <u>not</u> to some material thing:

25. *šū hāda? blāʔi ṭ-ṭaʔṣ bada yətɡ̌ayyar* [DA-153]
    'What's this!? It looks as if the weather has begun to change'

26. *marti mā btəḥki ɛarabi ʔabadan. – hāda mā bihəmm ya bēk, ʔana baɛref šwayyet ʔəŋglīzi* [DA-99]
    'My wife speaks no Arabic at all. – That doesn't matter, sir. I know a little English'

See also examples 8, 14, and 22, above.

In other types of context English 'this' or 'that' used with reference to something vague or conceptual must be rendered in Arabic as *haš-šī* or *haš-šaɡ̌le*, lit. 'this thing', because *hāda* or *hayy* might be taken as referring to some particular person or object:

27. *haš-šī byāxod waʔt ʔktīr*
    'This takes (or will take) a long time' (cf. *hāda byāxod waʔt ʔktīr* 'This one will take a long time')

28. *šū raʔyak ʔb-haš-šī?*
    'What do you think of that?' (cf. *šū raʔyak ʔb-hāda?* 'What do you think of this one?')

29. *mā bəʔder ʔəšɡ̌el bāli b-haš-šaɡ̌le*
    'I can't concern myself with that' (cf. *...b-hāda* '...with that one' or '...with him')

30. *haš-šī ṣar-lo ɛam-idāyəʔni mədde*
    'This has been bothering me for some time' (cf. *hāda...* 'This one...' or 'He...')

See also *hēk* [p. 561].

Demonstrative Pronouns in Attribution Phrases

The demonstrative pronouns are used not only independently, but also in phrases with definite nouns. In some cases the pronoun comes first, and in other cases, it follows the noun: *hadāk ᵊl-bēt* (or *l-bēt hadāk*) 'that (other) house'.[1]

The Demonstrative Prefix. The proximal demonstratives (*hāda, hayy, hadōl*) are not often used before a noun with the article prefix, but are usually reduced to *ha-*, which in combination with the article forms a prefix (or proclitic) *hal-*: *hal-bēt* 'this (that) house', *hal-ᵊknīse* 'this (that) church', *hal-ʔalwān* 'these (those) colors'.

The *l* is assimilated to a following dental or palatal consonant, as in the case of the article alone [p. 493]: *har-ržāl* 'these (those) men', *han-nəswān* 'these (those) women', *haš-šəbbāk* 'this (that) window'.

Examples in context:

1. *wēn fī maṭɛam ᵊmnīḥ hōn?* —
   šāyef hal-bināye l-ḥamra?
   ...warāha. [DA-46]

   'Where is there a good restaurant around here? — Do you see that red building? Behind it.'

2. *w-kān har-rāɛi yəṭlaɛ kəll yōm*
   ɛal-barriyye maɛ ᵊl-ġanam
   w-yərɛāhon [AO-103]

   'And this shepherd would go out in the country every day with the sheep and let them graze'

3. *mā bəržaɛ...ḥatta ʔaɛref ʔaṣᵊl*
   hal-baḥra w-hal-barriyye
   w-haž-žabal [adap. fr. AO-117]

   'I won't go back until I find out the origin of that lake and that plain and that mountain'

The use of the demonstrative prefix in example 1 is deictic [p. 537], while in examples 2 and 3 it is anaphoric, with antecedents earlier in the respective narratives.

On the use of *hal-* in annexion phrases, see p. 459.

Note the use of *hal-* before *kamm* 'several': *b-hal-kamm yōm* 'one of these days, any day now'.

---

[1] Noun phrases with demonstrative pronouns are transforms of equational predications [p. 406]: *hadāk, ᵊl-bēt* 'That is the house' → *hadāk ᵊl-bēt* (or *l-bēt hadāk*) 'that house'. Just as in an equational predication there is no significant distinction between subject and predicate, so also in noun-pronoun (or pronoun-noun) phrases there is no point in calling one the attribute and the other the main term — except, somewhat arbitrarily, on the basis of word order. These constructions, then, are a kind of apposition [p. 506]; there is no justification for distinguishing between 'demonstrative pronouns' and 'demonstrative adjectives' in Arabic.

Occasionally, the full forms *hāda, hayy,* or *hadōl* are used in phrases before a noun with the article. Being longer and grammatically more explicit than the *hal–* phrases, their effect is to give extra emphasis or clarity[1]:

4. *mīn hadōl ᵊn-nās halli kənt*   'Who are those people you were talk-
   Ɛam-təḥki maƐon?   ing with?' (cf. *han-nās*)

5. *l-qaṣīde fīha ?asᵊm, w-hāda*   'The poem has a name in it, and that
   l-?asᵊm mā bəddi ?əzᵊkro   name I don't want to mention' (cf.
       hal-?asᵊm)

The distal demonstrative (*hadāk, hadīk, hadənk,* etc.) normally occur in their full form before a noun with the article:

6. *w-mā btə?der təsḥab mənhon*   'And you can't withdraw it before
   ?abᵊl hadāk ᵊl-wa?t [DA-293]   that time' (*mənhon,* lit. "of them",
       antecedent: *maṣāri* 'money', plural.)

7. *məni hadīk ᵊl-mara?*   'Who is that woman?'

8. *hadənk ᵊt-təffāḥāt ᵊmbayyen*   'Those other apples seem to be
   Ɛalēhon tāza ?aktar mən hadōl   fresher than these'

The form *hadōk(e)* is generally not used in noun phrases, but only independently.
Note the feminine form with a masculine noun in *hadīk ᵊl-yōm* 'That day' = *hadāk ᵊl-yōm.*

In Lebanon the distal demonstratives also have a reduced form *hāk (hēk* [p.14])used before the noun: *hāk ᵊl-bēt (hēk ᵊl-bayt)* 'that house' = *hadāk ᵊl-bēt.*

Both distal and proximal demonstratives may also <u>follow</u> the noun. This is the normal order in the case of proper names, nouns with pronoun suffixes, and generally with annexion phrases (but see p. 459):

9. *nizār ?abbāni hāda mənsammī*   'This Nizar Abbani we call "the first
   šāƐer ᵊl-mar?a l-?awwal   poet of Woman"'

10. *žawābo hāda ḥa?ī?atan mā kan-lo*   'That reply of his was really un-
    mūžeb   called for'

11. *Ɛammti hayye halli Ɛam-bəḥki-lak*   'This aunt of mine I was telling you
    Ɛanha džawwazet lamma kān Ɛəmra   about was married when she was four-
    ?arbaṭaƐšar səne   teen years old'

---

[1]Technically speaking, the difference is probably best analyzed as a difference in construction: the full forms represent the main term in an attribution phrase, with the following noun as its appositive (cf. p.506), while the prefix *hal–* (since it is a mere affix) is subordinate to its noun.

12. *bənt ṣāḥbak hadīke ṭəlɛet*   'That daughter of your friend has
    ḥəlwe žəddan   turned out to be very pretty'

13. *mnēn žāye ɛāmūd ᵊd-dəxxān hāda?*   'Where is that column of smoke com-
                                          ing from?'

14. *b-ɛəṭlet ᵊr-rabīɛ hayy rəhᵊt*   'This spring vacation I went to
    la-flōrida   Florida'

    Less commonly, the demonstrative follows a single noun
with the article prefix: *l-bēt hāda* 'this house', *l-ʔūḍa
hādi* 'this room'.

    Nouns with pronoun suffixes, and proper names, sometimes
follow a demonstrative; this inverted order is like that of
nouns with the article in ex. 4 and 5, above: *wēno hāda
marwān?* 'Where is this (fellow) Marwan?' *hāda xayyi mā
hāžar* [Nakh. I-80] 'This brother of mine didn't emigrate'.

    The most common way of emphasizing the demonstrative element in a noun
phrase (with the article, not with suffix pronoun or a proper name) is to
prefix *hal-* to the noun and follow it also with the full form of a demonstrative:

15. *məmken tafsīra b-haṣ-ṣūra hayye*   'It can also be interpreted in this
    kamān   way'

16. *mīn hal-bənt hadīk?*   'Who's that girl over there?'

17. *haš-šahᵊr hāda šahᵊr šəte*   'This month is a winter month'
    [AO-71]

18. *laha-šūfo b-hal-ʔiyyām hayy*   'I'll see him any day, now' (lit.
                                          "...in these days")

19. *kəll hal-ḥēwānāt hadōl bišaǧǧlu*   'All these animals keep Ahmed quite
    ʔaḥmad ᵊktīr, lāken biɛīš mən   busy, but he lives off them'
    warāhon [AO-63]

    Note that in ex. 19 the "emphasis" gained by using *hadōl*
after *hal-ḥēwānāt* is not contrastive, i.e. it is not to distinguish these animals from certain others, but simply to
strengthen the anaphoric link between this phrase and its
antecedents; the sentence is a sort of conclusion or summary
for a discourse on the various animals Ahmed keeps and what
he does with them.

Locative Demonstratives

The words *hōn* 'here' and *hnīk* 'there' are substitutes for prepositional phrases (or occasionally, noun phrases) denoting <u>places</u>.

The forms *hōne* and *hnīke* are also sometimes used (cf. p. 552). In Lebanon the forms *hunīk* or *hawnīk* are generally used instead of *hnīk* (and *hawn* for *hōn* [p. 14]), and in Palestine *hanāk* or *hunāk*.

Examples, predicative:

1. *nšāḷḷa ʔaxūk bǝl-bēt? — naɛam,*   'Is your brother in, please? — Yes,
   ʔaxi hōn [DA-76]   my brother's here. Come in'

2. *byǝɣhar xalīl mū hōn* [DA-46]   'It looks as if Khalil isn't here'

3. *wēn samīr u-ʔabu samīr, ʔǝnšāḷḷa*   'Where are Samir and Abu Samir, are
   hōne?   they here?'

4. *ɛali rāḥ la-kalifōrnya, mū hēk?*   'Ali went to California, didn't he?
   — ʔē halla? ǝhnīk   — Yes, he's there now'

5. *hōn ʔaḥmad bēk? — naɛam hōn*   'Is Ahmed Bey here? — Yes, he is'
   [DA-217]

> Examples 5 has predicate-subject inversion [p. 419] in the question, and suppression of the subject [418] in the answer. The English translation, contrariwise, has an anaphoric substitute as subject in the answer, but suppresses 'here' in the predicate.

Examples, attributive:

6. *šū hāda halli hnīk?* [DA-18]   'What's that over there?'

7. *hal-manāɡer hōn btǝsḥer ǝl-ʔǝnsān*   'This scenery here is enchanting'
   [DA-173]

> The form *hōne* (Leb. *hawni*) is in some areas used also preceding an indefinite noun, e.g. in narratives, in the sense 'a, a certain, this': *hawni xawāža* 'a (certain) gentlemen...', *hawni marra* 'once, a certain time' [PVA-22].

Examples, predicative complemental [p. 446]:

8. *ṭālbīn mǝnno ʔǝnno yǝbʔa*   'They've asked him to stay perma-
   ɛala ṭūl hōn bǝš-šǝrke   nently here in the company'

9. *ṣar-lo hnīk taʔrīban idaɛšar*   'He's been there almost eleven
   šahǝr   months'

10. *yəmken ikūnu baɛ²d šī sāɛa*   'They may be here in about an hour'
    hōne

Examples, adverbial:

11. *btaɛ²rfo mn ²š-šām, wəlla*   'Do you know him from Damascus, or
    tɛarraft ɛalē hōn?   did you meet him here?'

12. *bass hōne hal-masāfe məz²ɛže*   'But here, that distance is disturb-
                                          ing' (i.e. the thought of being far
                                          from home)

13. *baɛ²d ma xalleṣ ²hnīk bəddi*   'After I finish there, I'll go back
    ²əržaɛ ɛaš-šām   to Damascus'

Examples, with prepositional supplement:

14. *šū ɛam-tədros halla² hōn*   'What are you studying now here in
    b-waš²nṭon?   Washington?'

15. *bass ²hnīk ²b-bērūt ²aɛadt nəmt*   'But there in Beirut I stayed and
    ɛandon ²b-bēton   slept in their house'

16. *laḥa-žəb-lak ²ahwe. šū bət²ūl?*   'I'll bring you some coffee, how
    — hōn žuwwa!? l-²ūda šōb ²ktīr   about that? — Here inside? It's so
    [DA-172]   hot in this room'

hōn and *hnīk* are not used alone in complementation (or supplementation)
to translocative verbs [p. 274], but are preceded by *la-* 'to' or *mən* 'from',
'through' [cf. p. 486]: *la-hōn* 'hither', *la-hnīk* 'thither', *mən hōn* 'from
here, this way, hence', *mn ²hnīk* 'from there, that way, thence':

17. *²ana ḥabbēt ²əži la-hōn mū bass*   'I wanted to come here not just for
    məšān ²š-šahāde, li²anni bə²der   the degree, because I could get that
    ²axədha mn ²hnīk...   over there' (lit. "...from there")

18. *rūḥ ɛaš-šarīɛa w-žīb mən ²hnīk*   'Go to the Jordan and fetch water
    ṃayye [AO-99]   from there'

19. *mən hōn byəbɛatu ṭ-ṭrūḍ?*   'Is this where you mail packages?'
    [DA-225]   (lit. "From here do they send...")

20. *birūḥu la-hnīk la²ənno ²arxaṣ*   'They go there because it's cheaper'

21. *w-halla² mnēn mərrūḥ? mən hōn*   'And now which way shall we go?
    yəmma mn ²hnīk? [DA-77]   This way or that way?'

22. *šlōnek fāyze xānom, taɛi la-hōn*   'How are you, Miss Faiza? Come here
    la-žambi   beside me'

Note also the predicative use of *mən* + demonstrative:

23. *ʔana mən kalifōrnya – w-ʔana*   'I'm from California – 'And I'm from
    mn ʰhnīk kamān [DA-76]   there too'

Although *hnīk* is often used anaphorically, like English 'there' (as in example 23), there are many cases in which it is not so used. As an anaphoric substitute for the name of a city, town, etc., or a building, room, etc., a third-person pronoun is normally used in Arabic after a preposition or noun in construct, while 'there' is used in English:

24. *btaɛref sān fransīsko? – bēti*   'Do you know San Fransisco? – My home
    fīha [DA-76]   is there!' (lit. "...in it")

25. *bəl-ʔawwal ṭləɛ ət ɛala blūdān,*   'First I went up to Bloudâne, and from
    w-mənha ɛala ḍhūr ʰš-šwēr   there, to Dhour Choueir'
    [DA-171]

26. *rəḥt ɛala bērūt. – šlōn šəft*   'I went to Beirut. – How did you like
    ṣēfha? [DA-171]   the summer there?' (lit. "...its
                                          summer")

27. *mā fī ǧēr matɛam hōn? – fī,*   'Isn't there any other restaurant
    hayy wāḥed tāni; ʔiza mnīḥ,   here? – Yes, there is; see, there's
    mnākol fī [DA-46]   another one; if it's good, we'll eat
                                          there'

    Similarly, in attributive clauses, a resumptive pronoun in Arabic may correspond to 'where' in English:

28. *ɛanna biʔamērka fī maḥallāt*   'In America we have stores where you
    btəštəri mənha kəll šī lāzmak   can buy everything you need' (lit.
    [DA-129]   "...stores you buy from them...")

The Indefinite Demonstrative *hēk*

The word *hēk* (or *hēke*) 'so, such, thus, that' differs from the pronominal and locative demonstratives in that is substitutes only for indefinite terms [p.494], including non-verbal predicates, complemental clauses, and supplemental phrases.

Examples, predicative:

1. *šu mbayyen mašǧūlīn ʰktīr –*   'It looks as if you're (pl.) quite
   walla dāyman hēk [DA-294]   busy. – Well, it's always this way'

2. *hāda ktīr, mū hēk?*   'That's too much, isn't it?'

    mū hēk (məš hēk) is an important anaphoric substitution phrase, literally "not so?" (cf. Fr. n'est-ce pas, Ger. nicht wahr), whose English translation varies, depending on the antecedent clause: *ɛali bəl-bēt, mū hēk?* 'Ali's at

home, isn't he?', *btəži maƐna, mū hēk?* 'you're coming with
us, aren't you?', *rāḥ Ɛal-bēt, mū hēk?* 'He went home, didn't
he?', *byə⁹⁹dru yaƐ⁹mlū, mū hēk?* 'They can do it, can't they?'
See also ex. 27, below.

3. <u>hēk</u> *⁹d-dənye*

                                'That's the way things are' (lit.
                                "Such is the world")

4. <u>hēk</u> *taṣarrfo l-Ɛādi*

                                'That's his usual behavior'

        Examples 3 and 4 show predicate-subject inversion [p.419],
but unlike most inverted predicates, *hēk* does not usually
take the main sentence accent.

Examples, complemental:

5. *lamma šāf <u>hēk</u>, fāt Ɛal-balad*
   [AO-83]

                                'When he saw that, he entered the
                                town'

6. *bət⁹ammal <u>hēk</u>*

                                'I hope so'

7. *law šəftha bər-rabīƐ kənt*
   bət⁹ūl ǧēr <u>hēk</u> [DA-250]

                                'If you saw it in springtime, you
                                wouldn't say that' (lit. "you'd say
                                otherwise")

8. *w-ḍallu <u>hēk</u> ḥatta nāmu* [AO-107]

                                'And they stayed that way until they
                                went to sleep'

9. *w-⁹ttafa⁹u <u>hēk</u> w-rāḥet ⁹l-Ɛažūz*
   b-sāƐətha la-bēt ⁹l-bənt [AO-113]

                                'And they agreed on that, and then
                                the old woman went to the girl's
                                house'

10. *haṣ-ṣabbāṭ ⁹rxīṣ w-⁹mbayyen*
    Ɛalē <u>hēk</u>

                                  'These shoes are cheap, and they
                                look it!' (lit. "...and it appears
                                of them so")

Examples, after prepositions:

11. *⁹aqwāl mət⁹l <u>hēk</u> ṣaƐ⁹b ⁹əsbāta*

                                'Statements like that are hard to
                                prove'

12. *ya Ɛēb ⁹š-šūm šayyətkon ⁹aƐazz*
    mən <u>hēk</u> b-⁹ktīr

                                  'Oh really, your visit means much
                                more to us than that'

13. *mā fī tarkībe ⁹aktar mən <u>hēk</u>*

                                  'He's more fun than anything!'
                                ("There's no card more than so")

14. *w-⁹zyāde Ɛan <u>hēk</u> mā bsadd⁹o*

                                  'And what's more, I don't believe
                                him' ("And[in]addition to that...")

15. *mənšān <u>hēk</u> mā brūḥ ⁹abadan*
    Ɛas-sīnama

                                  'That's why I don't ever go to the
                                movies' (lit. "because of such...")

16. *w-la-hēk ʔəlt la-ḥāli mā ḥəlwe*   'And so I said to myself, it wouldn't be nice' (lit. "And for such...")

The classicism *li-zālek* 'therefore' is often used as a stylistic variant of *la-hēk*.

Examples, adverbial:

17. *fīk taɛmśla hēk ʔaw hēk*   'You can do it this way or that way'

18. *lēš mā byāxədhon maɛo lamma byərǧaɛ? — bẓənn-əllak hēk bəddo yaɛmel* [DA-75]   'Why doesn't he take them with him when he goes back? — I think that's what he intends to do' (or 'I think he intends to do so')

19. *w-hēk byəbnu, šwayy wara šwayy, kəll ᵊl-ḥīṭān mən taḥt la-fōʔ* [AO-75]   'And in this way they build, little by little, all the walls from the bottom up'

20. *mlīḥ hayk?* [SAL-41]   'Is that all right?' (lit. "Good so?") (*hayk* [Leb. for *hēk*, p. 14] supplements the one-word clause *mlīḥ*.)

In supplementation to adjectives (participles):

21. *b-ḥayāti mā šəfᵊt wāḥed ᵊmwaldan hēk*   'I've never in my life seen anyone so childish'

22. *ʔālət-lo lēš hēk zaɛlān?* [AO-114]   'She said to him, "Why are you so annoyed?"'

Examples, supplemental to nouns (*hēk* precedes the noun):

23. *hēk nās byəʔᵊtlu zalame bidūn ma trəff-əllon ɛēn*   'People like that could kill a person without batting an eye'

24. *mā fī ʔaṭyab mən hēk ṭabᵊx* [DA-199]   'I've never tasted such good food' (lit. "There is no tastier than such food")

25. *mā fīni ʔəṭṣawwar ʔənno hiyye btaɛmel hēk šī*   'I can't imagine her doing such a thing'

26. *b-hēk səɛᵊr kənt ᵊštarēt sayyāra ʔaḥsan*   'At that price I'd have bought a better car'

27. *mālak mənṭəẓərni sadde? hēk xuzaɛbalāt, mū hēk?*   'You don't expect me to believe such balderdash, do you?'

Note, in ex. 27, that *mū hēk* may be used in sequence to a negative statement as well as to an affirmative one.

Preceding a noun or adjective *hēk(e)* is sometimes used
to indicate vagueness or inexactness: 'sort of', 'something
like':

28. *š-šō⁹ byəži hēke mōžāt*   'The yearning comes in waves, sort
                                                 of'

29. *dzakkar-lak šī ḥādse hēke ṣg̱īre*   'Think up some anecdote, you know, a
                                                 short one, like'

The classicism *kaza*, or *kaza w-kaza*, is used in the sense
'such-and-such' or 'so much', etc.: *l-bāxra kaza w-kaza* 'such-
and such a ship', *kaza dōlār* 'so many dollars' (i.e. such-and-
such an amount). *hākaza* is used in somewhat formal style
similarly to English 'thus'.

The Presentational Particles[1]

The forms *hayy*, *lēk*, and *šaɛ-* are widely used in Greater Syria as "exclamatory" or "imperative" demonstratives, which serve to direct someone's
attention to what the following noun or pronoun refers to: *hayy ᵊktābak*
'Here's your book' or 'There's your book', *lēk maṣārīk* 'Here's your money',
šaɛo ⁹əža 'Here he comes' or 'There he comes' (or 'Here he is', 'There he
is', lit. "There he is, he has come".)

hayy as a presentational particle is not always clearly
distinct from the feminine demonstrative pronoun: *hayy*
wāḥde tānye 'Here's another one (f.)' or 'This is another
one (f.)'. As a presentational particle, however, its form
remains *hayy* regardless of the number/gender of what follows:
hayy ⁹aḥmad 'There's Ahmed', *hayy ᵊwlādi žāyīn* 'Here come my
children'.

šaɛ- is always – and *lēk* usually – followed by a pronoun
suffix, regardless whether a noun follows or not: *šaɛon*
maṣārīk 'There's your money', *lēkon maṣārīk* 'Here's your
money'. *hayy* is usually not used with a suffix, except in
Palestine: *hayyo hunāk* 'There it is over there'.
Unlike *hayy* and *lēk*, *šaɛ-* is not generally used while
handing something to someone, but is more of a "distal"
demonstrative; it usually directs attention to something
away from the speaker (though not necessarily away from the
person spoken to). *šaɛ-* is presumably a shortened form of
⁹šāɛ 'look, see' (imperative of the verb *⁹əšeɛ, byə⁹šaɛ* 'to
see, look at'), while *lēk* is associated with the preposition-
pronoun phrase *lēk* 'to you, toward you' [p.480].

---
[1] Though the presentational particles are deictic or demonstrative elements
par excellence, they are not actually "substitutes" in any straightforward
sense – there is no other kind of word or phrase which, in their place, woul[
result in the same construction. This construction produces a special kind [
sentence, which is neither statement, command, call, or exclamation [p.378].

Examples:

1. *hayy ṭayyāra žāye mən ʔamērka.*
   šaɛhon ʔr-rəkkāb nāzlīn mənha
   [DA-249]

   'There's (or That's) a plane that's come from America. Here come the passengers disembarking'

2. *fī xaṭṭ trāmwāy ɛal-marže kamān.*
   lēko ʔəža wāḥed [DA-44]

   'There's a streetcar line on the Marjé too. Here comes one now'

3. *ṣ-ṣābun wəl-līfe šaɛhon bəl-ʔxzāne* [DA-181]

   'The soap and sponge are there in the cabinet' (lit. "The soap and the sponge, there they are in the cabinet") (Extraposition [p.435])

4. *l-maġsale šaɛha hnīk* [DA-199]

   'There's the washstand over there'

5. *hayy ʔl-ʔotēl ʔəddāmak* [DA-16]

   'There's the hotel in front of you'

6. *hayy ʔawwal ḥarf*

   'Here's the first letter'

7. *hā, lēkak hōn*

   'Oh here you are!'

8. *šaɛni žāye*

   'Here I come!'

9. *lēkhon hayy banātak rāžɛīn mn ʔl-madrase* [DA-238]

   'Here are your daughters coming back from school' (lit. "Here they are, here are your daughters...")

Certain other presentational forms are heard in various parts of Greater Syria. Note the Damascene forms *šaɛōk* and *šaḥḥāke: wēn bərnēṭṭi? — šaḥḥāke* 'Where's my hat? – Here it is'. *šaɛ-* is also sometimes pronounced with *-ḥḥ-* rather than *-ɛḥ-* (or even rather than *-ɛ-*): *šaḥḥa* 'There it (f.) is', *šaḥḥon* 'There they are', *šaḥḥo, šaḥḥōk* 'There it(m.) is'.

INTERROGATIVE SUBSTITUTES

The main forms of the interrogative substitutes, or question words, are:

mīn .... 'who'

šū and *ʔēš* .... 'what'

ʔaddēš .... 'how much'

kamm .... 'how many'

ʔanu and *ʔayy* .... 'what, which, which one'

wēn and *fēn* .... 'where'

kīf and *šlōn* .... 'how'

ʔēmta .... 'when'

lēš .... 'why'

In a simple substitution-question [p. 379] the question word usually comes first in Syrian Arabic (as in English), regardless which part of the clause in represents: *šū Ɛməlt?* (object) 'What did you do?', *wēn ʔabūk?* (predicate) 'Where is your father?', *kīf sāwētha?* (supplement) 'How did you do it?'. Some of the question words commonly follow prepositions or nouns in construct, however, though the phrase itself ordinarily comes first: *Ɛala ʔanu wāḥde ḥa-təḥkī-lna?* 'Which one are you going to talk to us about?' (lit. "About which one...").

The question word generally carries the main accent of the sentence, and the highest pitch: *wēnak hal-ʔiyyām mā ḥada bišūfak?* 'Where have you been these days, that no one sees you?' See p. 379.

With a question-word complement, the subject of a verbal predication usually follows the verb: *ʔaddēš byāxod ᵊš-šofōr?* 'How much does the driver get?'.

Extraposition of the subject [p. 434] is common, however, with complemental and supplemental question words. (No resumptive pronoun is used [cf. p. 530].): *š-šofōr ʔaddēš byāxod?* "The driver — how much does he get?", *ʔaxūk lēš mā ʔəža?* 'Why hasn't your brother come?' (or *lēš mā ʔəža ʔaxūk?* or *lēš ʔaxūk mā ʔəža?*).

Besides their use in simple or direct substitution questions and in extraposition, the interrogative substitutes are used in complemental clauses: *ʔāl-lo šū sāwa* 'He told him what he had done', *mā baƐref lēš ʔaxi mā ʔəža* 'I don't know why my brother hasn't come'.

Some of the question words are used in supplemental clauses formed with *ma* '-ever': *šū ma* 'whatever...', *ʔēmta ma* 'whenever...', etc. See p. 338.

Unlike English 'who', 'which', and 'where', the Arabic words *mīn*, *šū*, *ʔēš*, *wēn* are not used to introduce attributive clauses [pp.498,561], nor does *ʔēmta* introduce supplemental clauses like English 'when' (cf. *lamma*, p.529). (In parts of Palestine, however, *lēš* is used in the sense 'because' as well as 'why'.)

šū (often unaccented, written *šu*), *kīf*, and *ʔaddēš* have special exclamatory uses (pp.570,572,576). *kamm* has a non-interrogative sense 'some, several' [p.470], and *ʔayy*, *ʔanu* have the sense 'any' [p.574].

A.) Examples, *mīn* 'who':

1. *ya nabīha **mīn** ʔəža?* [DA-217]   'Who's that, Nabiha?' (lit. "O Nabiha, who has come?")

2. ***mīn** yalli xarbaṭ-li wrāʔi?*   'Who (is it that) messed up my papers?'

3. ***mīn** mənkon katab waǧīft ə l-fīzya?*   'Which of you has done the physics assignment?'

4. ***mīn** haš-šabāb?*   'Who are these young men?'

The form *mən-* is used as an extraposed subject with the apocopated subject pronouns *-u*, *-i*, *-hən*: *mənu bəl-farīʔ?* 'Who's on the team?' See p.547.

5. ***mīn** bəddak?*   'Whom do you want?'

After prepositions and nouns in construct:

6. *mən ɛand **mīn** bədžīb əǧrāḍak?* [DA-128]   'Whom do you get your things from?' (lit. "From with whom..." [p.486])

7. *sāɛet **mīn** hayy?* (or *la-mīn has-sāɛa,* or *tabaɛ **mīn** has-sāɛa?*)   'Whose watch is this?' (or 'Whose is this watch?')

8. *dōr **mīn**?*   'Whose turn [is it]?'

9. *la-**mīn** ʔaɛazz mənkon bəddi ʔaɛṭi bənti?* [AO-55]   'To whom dearer than you would I give my daughter?

In complemental clauses:

10. *kənt ʔana ɛandak w-mədri **mīn** ʔəža la-ɛandak...*   'I was with you, and I don't know who [it was that] came to see you ...'

11. ...fa-ɛam-ṭəšfon hiyye ya   'and she's thinking, "I wonder who
     tara <u>mīn</u> fī ɛandak halla?   is with you now?"'

12. fīk ᵊtfīdni <u>mīn</u> lāzem ʔābel 'Could you tell me whom I should
     b-hal-ᵊxṣūṣ? [SAL-93]   see about this?'

       <u>mīn</u> is also sometimes used in a non-interrogative sense
     'someone', as object with an (objective) complemental clause:

13. yaɛni bəddak <u>mīn</u> iʔəl-lak   'You mean you need someone to tell
                                         you'

B.) Examples, <u>šū</u> 'what':

1. <u>šū</u> ṭəleɛ maɛi ya dəktōr?   'What have I got, Doctor?'
    [DA-204]   ("What's come up with me?")

2. <u>šū</u> ʔəsmo halli bisāwi   'What's the name of the one that
    <u>š</u>-šabābīk wəl-ᵊbwāb?   makes windows and doors?' (Comment-
    [DA-243]   topic Inversion, p.434.)

3. <u>šū</u> l-fawāki yalli bətrīdha?   'What fruit do you want?' (lit.
    [DA-107]   "What's the fruit that you want?")

4. <u>šū</u> ɛalē, <u>šū</u> byəṭlaɛ maɛak,   'What of it? What's come over you?
    <u>ḥkī</u>   Speak up!'

5. <u>šū</u> kənt ɛam-ᵊtsāwi?   'What were you doing?'

6. ṭayyeb <u>šū</u> bətlāʔi mnāseb   'All right, what do you think would
    ləṭ-ṭarafēn? [DA-291]   be suitable for both parties?'

       With extraposed subject or object:

7. tnēn w-ᵊtnēn <u>šū</u> byaɛᵊmlu?   'What do two and two make?'
    [DA-5]

8. sabānex <u>šū</u> biʔūlúwa   'What do they call 'sabānex' in
    bəl-ʔanglīzi?   English?'

9. r-rəǰǰāl halli bəddna nzūro   'The man we're going to see — what
    <u>šū</u> byəštáǵel? [DA-75]   work does he do?'

       In ex. 9 <u>šū</u> is a predicative complement [p.444]; cf.
     byəštáǵel mikanīki 'He works as a mechanic'.
       Sometimes <u>šū</u> as a predicative complement has to be trans-
     lated 'how' rather than 'what'. In ex. 8, for instance, if
     biʔūlúwa is given its more standard English rendering 'they
     say (it)', then <u>šū</u> biʔūlúwa is 'How do they say it?' Note
     also:

10. <u>šū</u> bətfasser haš-šī?   'How do you explain this?' (or 'What
                                         do you make of this?')

11. *šū byə°rabkon?* [SAL-64]　　　'How is he related to you(pl.)?'
　　　　　　　　　　　　　　　　　(or 'What kin is he to you?')

　　　šū is often followed by a quasi-verbal predicator [p.412]
plus a complement of specification [510]; the English translation of this construction is often 'what' plus a noun:

12. *šū bəddkon fawāki?* [DA-47]　　'What fruit do you want?' (cf. ex.
　　　　　　　　　　　　　　　　　3, above) or 'What do you want in
　　　　　　　　　　　　　　　　　the way of fruit?'

13. *šū maƐo šhādāt?*　　　　　　　'What diplomas has he?'

14. *šū fī °akə l, °ana žōƐān*　　'What is there to eat? I'm hungry'

　　　šū is sometimes used after a preposition or noun in construct, but *°ēš* is more common in these constructions (see
below):

15. *Ɛala šū Ɛtamadt?*　　　　　　'What did you decide upon?'

　　　In complemental clauses:

16. *waḷḷa mā baƐref šū bəddi*　　'I really don't know what to tell
　　　°ə l-lak　　　　　　　　　　you'

17. *taƐāl nəs°alo šū ṣār maƐo*　　'Come on, let's ask him what hap-
　　　bət-talavəzyōn　　　　　　　pened to him on television'

18. *°axīran laḥ-li šū kān*　　　　'It finally dawned on me what he
　　　Ɛam-yəƐni　　　　　　　　　meant'

19. *ya samīr šūf haš-šāy šū*　　　'Samir, see what's happened to the
　　　ṣār fī　　　　　　　　　　　tea'

　　　The complemental clause *haš-šāy šū ṣār fī* is an extraposition of *šū ṣār b-haš-šāy.* The extrapositional word
order makes it possible also to interpret *haš-šāy* as object of *šūf:* 'Look at the tea, what's happened to it'.

　　　A subject *šū* + prepositional predicate *bo, bāk,* 'with
him, with you, etc.' [p.415] is usually shortened to *šu* or
(most often) *šə,* and pronounced as a single unit: *šú-bak*
or *šə́-bak* (= *šū bāk*) 'What's [wrong] with you?':

20. *šə-bo hal-°add xāyre*　　　　'Why is he so down in the mouth?'
　　　Ɛazāymo?

21. *ya banāt tsallu, šə́-bakon*　　'Enjoy yourselves, girls! What's the
　　　bi-hal-bəzrāt yəllī　　　　matter with (you, with) those seeds
　　　°əddāmkon?　　　　　　　　[hors d'oeuvres] in front of you?'

Exclamatory *šū:*

22. *šū ḥaṭ-ṭaʔṣ yalli biʔammeṭ*   'What miserable weather!' (lit. "What
    ᵊl-ᵊalb!   is this weather, that opresses the
                                          heart!")

23. *ʔamma šū zalame nahfe mn*   'But what a card that fellow is!'
    ᵊn-nahfāt!

    šū is also used, unaccented (written *šu*), as a sentence
supplement [p. 526] and introducer; this expression is generally too mild to be translated as an interjection 'What?!',
but may be roughly rendered as 'well', 'oh', 'so', or left
untranslated:

24. *šu byəǧhar ḥālt ᵊl-balad*   '(Well), it looks as if conditions
    ᵊmnīḥa [DA-77]   in town are good'

25. *Ɛafwan, šu btəḥki Ɛarabi?*   '(So) you speak Arabic?'
    [DA-16]

26. *šu mā šāfak ᵊl-ḥakīm?*   '(Oh,) hasn't the doctor seen you?'

C.) *ʔēš* 'what' is commonly used instead of *šū* after a preposition or a
    noun in construct:

1. *la-ʔēš byəlzamo l-Ɛarabi?*   'What does he need Arabic for?'
    [DA-173]

2. *bi-ʔēš mənsāfer?* [DA-248]   'How will we go?' ("In what..." or
                                  "By what...")

3. *bḥəbb ʔaƐref Ɛala ʔēš*   'I'd like to know what they live on'
    Ɛāyšīn

4. *laḥ-sāfer la-*Michigan   'I'm going to Michigan to study engin-
    məšān ʔədros handase. –   eering. – What kind of engineering?
    handast ʔēš? – handase   (lit. "Engineering of what?") – Civil
    madaniyye   engineering'

5. *dzakkar-lak šī matal mən*   'Think of some proverb from Damascus.
    ᵊš-šām. – matᵊl ʔēš yaƐni?   – Like what, how do you mean?'

    In various parts of Greater Syria *ʔēš* (often shortened
to *ʔəš* or *ʔaš*) may be used in more or less the same ways as
šū: ʔēš bəddak? 'What do you want?', *ʔaš hāda?* 'What's
that?', etc.

D.)   ʔaddēš 'How much':

1. <u>ʔaddēš</u> ʔəžʔrto bəs-səne?   'How much is the rental of it for
   [DA-225]   a year?'

2. <u>ʔaddēš</u> ṭalabu ṣḥābo?   'How much did its owners ask?'
   [DA-291]

3. <u>ʔaddēš</u> bəddak ikūn   'How old do you want her to be?' (lit.
   ɛəmʔrha? [DA-80]   "How much do you want her age to be?")

   In reference to time and distance, ʔaddēš is commonly
translated into English as 'how long' and 'how far':

4. <u>ʔaddēš</u> ʔbtəbɛed ʔaʔrab   'How far is it to the nearest city?'
   madīne?

5. <u>ʔaddēṣ</u> ṣar-lak hōne   'How long have you been here in the
   b-ʔamērka?   States?' (ʔaddēš + ṣ- → ʔaddēṣ‿ṣ-)

   After prepositions and nouns in construct:

6. w-la-<u>ʔaddēš</u> bəddak ʔtkūn   'And for how long do you want the
   məddet ʔl-qarḍ? [DA-297]   loan to run?'

7. b-<u>ʔaddēš</u> ʔs-sīnama hōn?   '[For] how much is (the price of) the
   [DA-18]   cinema here?'

8. daxlak hal-lūbye b-<u>ʔaddēš</u>?   '[At] how much are these beans,
   [DA-129]   please?'

9. kəll <u>ʔaddēš</u> biwazzɛu   '[Every] how often do they deliver
   l-barīd hōn?   the mail here?'

   ʔaddēš is often followed by a verb plus a complement of
specification (cf. šū, p. 569); the English translation is
usually 'how much' + noun:

10. <u>ʔaddēš</u> byāxod maɛāš   'How much salary does he get a month?'
    bəš-šahʔr?

11. <u>ʔaddēš</u> ʔstaxražu faḥʔm?   'How much coal did they mine?'

12. <u>ʔaddēš</u> btədfaɛu fāyde?   'How much interest do you pay?'
    [DA-293]

   In complemental clauses:

13. bəddi ʔaɛref <u>ʔaddēš</u> ʔs-sāɛa   'I want to know what time it is'
    [AO-71]   (lit. "...how much the hour is")

14. *šəft ʔaddēš hōn ᵃl-hawa*   'Do you see how much cooler the air
    ʔabrad? [DA-172]   is here?'

15. *šāyef hal-ʔarāḍi ʔaddēš*   'See how green this country is?'
    xaḍra [DA-235]

      Note the extraposition of *hal-ʔarāḍi* in ex. 15. Cf. ex.
19, p. 569.

      Exclamatory use of *ʔaddēš*:

16. *ʔaddēš ᵃtɛallamtu!*   'How much you've learned!'

17. *ʔaddēš ᵃl-balad ḥəlwe!*   'How pretty the town is!'

18. *ʔaddēšak laṭīf!*   'How nice you are!'

      The exclamatory *ʔaddēš* may take pronoun suffixes as in
ex. 18. See p. 547. Note that with adjectival complements,
ʔaddēš is generally translated 'how' (without 'much').

E.) *kamm* 'how many' is usually followed by a noun in the singular.
    Examples:

1. *kamm nəžme fī bəs-sama?*   'How many stars are there in the sky?'
   [AO-83]

2. *kamm səne ṣar-lak hōne?*   'How many years have you been here?'

3. *kamm dars kān ɛandak...*   'How many classes did you have...'

4. *kamm nāyeb bimasslu*   'How many delegates represent these
   hal-muḥāfaẓāt? [SAL-152]   mohafazats?'

      Note, in ex. 4, that the *kamm* phrase with an animate
noun [p. 420] takes a plural verb despite its singular form.
In ex. 3, on the other hand, the linking verb *kān* remains
singular. The agreement is partly optional, depending on
how much one wishes to emphasize plurality.

      In complemental clauses:

5. *zən-li hal-baṭṭīxa la-šūfha*   'Weigh this watermelon for me, so I
   kamm kīlo bṭəṭlaɛ [DA-128]   can see how many kilos it comes to'

      With *fī* and other quasi-verbal predicators, *kamm* may
stand alone, with its noun as specificative complement following the predicator (cf. *šū*, p. 569):

6. *kamm fī mətr ʔmrabbaɛ
   fi had-dāʔire? (or
   kamm mətr ʔmrabbaɛ fī
   b-had-dāʔire?)*

'How many square meters are there in
this circle?'

F.) *ʔanu* 'which, what, which one' may be used either independently or in a
noun phrase. Examples (independent):

1. *ʔanu ʔaḥsan maxzan
   bəl-balad?*

'Which is the best store in town?'

2. *ʔanu l-ʔašya l-mafʔūde?*

'Which are the things [that are]
missing?'

3. *ʔanu bətšūf bikūn ʔaḥsan?*
   [DA-109]

'Which do you think would be better?'

Examples, in noun phrases:

4. *ʔanu sāɛa bəṭṭīr ᵊṭ-ṭayyāra?*
   [DA-249]

'What time does the plane take off?'

5. *ʔanu wāḥed bəddak?*

'Which one do you want?'

6. *ʔanu ʔāle bəddəʔʔ ɛalēha
   ʔaḥsan šī?*

'What instrument do you play best?'

After prepositions:

7. *la-ʔanu maṣyaf rəḥᵊt?*
   [DA-171]

'Which summer resort did you go to?'

8. *ḥaḍᵊrṭak mən ʔanu wilāye
   bi-ʔamērka? [DA-76]*

'Which state in the United States are
you from?'

With feminine (or inanimate plural) nouns, the form *ʔani*
is often used rather than *ʔanu:*

9. *ʔani šanta naʔʔēt?*

'Which bag did you choose?'

10. *ʔēmta bəddon yəžu, ʔani
    sāɛa?*

'When are they supposed to come — at
what time?'

In the independent use, the form *ʔanon* may be used for
the plural:

11. *ʔanon ᵊwlāda?*

'Which ones are her children?'

The form *ʔayy* is used in noun phrases in the same way as *ʔanu:*

12. *ʔayy sāɛa bəddon yəžu?*

'What time will they come?'

The forms *ʔayyi* and *ʔayya* are also used in some parts of Greater Syria.

ʔanu, ʔani, and *ʔayy* may be used with nouns in the non-interrogative sense 'any':

13. *fī ʕandak ʔayy suʔāl tāni?*   'Have you any other question(s)?'

14. *ʔani šaġle ʔaḥsan mən bala*   'Any job is better than none'

G.) *wēn, fēn* 'where', examples:

1. *wēn ʔaʔrab ʔotēl?*   'Where is the nearest hotel?'

2. *fēn ḅāba ḥatta ʕāyed ʕalē*
   w-ʔāxod ʕīdīti [DA-298]   'Where is Daddy? [I want to know] so I can give him holiday greetings and get my holiday gift'

3. *wēn ḥaṭṭ haž-žarāyed*
   ᵊl-ʕəta??   'Where shall I put those old newspapers?'

4. *w-ʔana fēn bəddi rūḥ*
   ᵊl-yōm? [DA-300]   'And where might I go today?'

5. *halla? wēn ᵊwṣalna*
   bəl-ʔakᵊl, ya xānom?   'Now, where have we gotten with the [preparation of the] food, madam?'

With translocative verbs [p.486] the form *la-wēn* 'where to, whither' is more usual than simply *wēn* or *fēn* as in ex. 4 and 5:

6. *la-wēn rāyeḥ halla??*
   [AO-47]   'Where are you going now?'

7. *hal-xaṭṭ la-wēn biwaddi?*   'Where does this line lead to?' (Extraposition of *la-wēn biwaddi hal-xaṭṭ?*)

With *mən* 'from', *wēn* takes the form *-ēn: mnēn* 'from where?':

8. *w-hal-ġēm mnēn ʔəža kəllo*
   ʕala ġafle [DA-153]   'And where have these clouds come from all of a sudden?' (Extraposition)

In many cases *mnēn* is translated simply 'where', and in some cases, 'how':

9. *mnēn štarēt hal-bərnēṭa?*   'Where did you buy that hat?'

10. *mnēn ᵊmnāxod ᵊl-baṣṣ?*   'Where do we get the bus?'

11. *mnēn marrūḥ?* 'How do we go?' or 'Which way do we go? (Cf. *man hōn* 'this way', *mn ᵊhnīk* 'that way')

12. *mnēn ᵊƐraft?* 'How do you know?' or 'Where did you find out?'

In complemental clauses:

13. *fa-šu ᵊana fakkart Ɛam-tasᵊalni mnēn ᵊante* 'And I thought she was asking me, "Where are you from?"'

14. *fī wāḥed xalaṣ w-wāḥed Ɛam-yadros mā baƐref wēn* 'There's one who's finished, and one studying I don't know·where'

Predicative *wēn* takes pronoun suffixes as subject [p.547]:

15. *ᵊammi wēnkon? šu mā fī ḥada bal-bēt?* 'Mother, where are you all? Isn't there anybody home?'

16. *wat-tnēn wēnhon?* [DA-75] 'And where are the two of them?'

17. *wēno ᵊabᵊn Ɛammi?* 'Where is my cousin?' (Comment-topic inversion [p.434])

H.) *kīf* 'how':

1. *kīf kān ᵊṭ-ṭaᵊṣ Ɛandkon baž-žbāl?* 'How was the weather where you were in the mountains?'

2. *kīf ᵊṣ-ṣaḥḥa samīr bāša?* 'How is your (lit. "the") health, Samir Pasha?'

3. *kīf baddi sāwīha?* 'How should I do it?'

4. *kīf laᵊēt ᵊalƐet ᵊbƐalbak?* [SAL-117] 'How did you like (lit. "find") the castle of Baalbek?'

5. *kīf ᵊƐreft waḷḷa ᵊannak ḥazzīr tamām* 'How did you know? You're certainly a good guesser!'

In complemental clauses:

6. *lāzem ᵊaᵊᵊtlak ᵊawām, ᵊal-li kīf baddak ᵊtmūt* [AO-116] 'I must kill you immediately; tell me how you want to die'

7. *btaƐref kīf ᵊn-naḥḥāt hēke biṣawwer ᵊl-marᵊa mn ᵊz-zawāya l-ǧamīᵊa yaƐni* 'You know how the sculptor sort of depicts the woman from the hidden recesses, so to speak'

Note also the common expressions *šāyef kīf?* 'See how it is?', (also *lāḥaẓt kīf*), *Ɛrəft kīf?* 'Know what I mean?', and the like.

kīf (like *šū* [p.570]) has two kinds of exclamatory use:

8. *šu mā fī Ɛandak samak?*   'Don't you have any fish? — Of course
   — *kīf mā fī!* [DA-17]   I do! ("How [could it be that] there
                                                     is none!")

The milder exclamatory *kīf* introduces questions, in much the same way as *šu:*

9. *kīf, Ɛaẓᵊbtak wašᵊnṭon?*   'Well, did you like Washington?'

The predicative *kīf* (ex. 1, 2) takes pronoun suffixes [p.547], especially in asking 'How are you?': *kīfak?, kīfkon?.*

I.) *šlōn* 'how' is not generally used in the coastal regions; in Damascus it is used in some of the same ways as *kīf*. Examples:

1. *daxlak šlōn ᵊl-ḥāle hallaʔ*   'Say, how are things now in San
   bi-sān fransīsko? [DA-77]   Francisco?'

2. *šlōn bəddak ᵊr-raʔbe?*   'How do you want the neck?' (barber
   [DA-179]   speaking)

3. *šlōn ᵊt-tannūra ž-ždīde,*   'How about the new skirt? Has it
   nšālḷa ḥāzet ʔəƐžāb   won the admiration of the multitudes?'
   ᵊž-žamāhīr?

4. *šlōn xallētī yəṭlaƐ*   'How could you let him go out in
   b-hal-bard? [DA-198]   this cold?'

5. *šlōn šəfto hal-məstašfa?*   'What do you think of this hospital?'
                                                     ("How do you see...", lit. "How have
                                                      you seen...") Comment-topic inversion
                                                      [p.434]

šlōn also takes pronoun suffixes in the role of subject: *šlōnak?* 'How are you?'.

6. *šlōnhon ʔənšālḷa mabṣūṭīn?*   'How are they? Well, I trust?'

7. *w-ᵊšlōnek b-šəġl ᵊl-bēt?*   'And how are you(f.) at housework?'
   [DA-99]

J.) *ʔēmta* 'when':

1. *ʔēmta žāyīn? — yaɛni ʔēmta*
   bəddon yəžu, sāɛa waḥde
   bəl-lēl? lā ykəl-lak fəkre

   'When are they coming? — Well when
   <u>would</u> they come? One o'clock in the
   morning? Not likely!'

2. *ʔabi ʔēmta ɛandak waʔt*
   ᵊmnənzel ɛas-sū??

   'Father, when will you have time [so
   that] we can go down to the market?'

3. *ʔēmta l-mūsem byəbda?*

   'When does the season begin?'

4. *mən ʔēmta kān hāda?*

   'How long ago was that?' (lit. "Since
   when...")

In complemental clauses:

5. *biʔūl ʔēmta byəži?* [PVA-2]

   'Does he say when he's coming?'

6. *šūf ʔaḥmad ʔēmta bəddo*
   yəži

   'See when Ahmed intends to come' (With
   extraposition of subject in comple-
   mental clause [cf. ex. 19, p.569])

K.) *lēš* 'why':

1. *lēš ṭləɛᵊṭ? kənt lāzem*
   təbʔa mərtāḥ bəl-bēt
   [DA-218]

   'Why did you go out? You should have
   stayed and rested at home'

2. *šū ʔəṣṣtak w-ᵊhkāytak w-lēš*
   kənt bəl-ʔəmʔom? [AO-116]

   'What's your story, and why were you
   in the bottle?'

3. *ʔē lakān lēš xāyef ʔiza*
   mā baɛrᵊfa?

   'All right then, why are you afraid
   if I don't know heŕ?'

4. *lēš hal-labake, lēš*
   labbaktu ḥālkon hal-ʔadd?

   'Why this bother? Why did you(pl.)
   go to so much trouble?'

5. *lēš ᵊt-trēn kəll hal-ʔadd*
   maɛžūʔ ᵊl-yōm?

   'Why is the train so crowded today?'

6. *lēš ya tara has-shūl*
   žarda? [DA-250]

   'I wonder why these plains are bare?'

In complemental clauses:

7. *haʔīʔatan mā baɛref lēš*
   mafruḍ fiyyi...

   'I really don't know why I've had
   to...'

The form *lē* (or *lēh*) is also heard in various parts of
Greater Syria. *lēš* is a reduced form of *la-ʔēš* 'what for'
(cf. *ʔaddēš ~ ʔadd + ʔēš* 'amount of what'). *ʔēš* is in its
turn a syncopated form of *ʔayy šī* 'what thing'.

INDEX

Arabic words, affixes, and grammatical terms are alpha-
betized in the order shown on page 1.

CPSIA information can be obtained
at www.ICGtesting.com
Printed in the USA
BVHW041954030919

557197BV00039B/138/P